Praise for *Rogues and Early Modern English Culture*:

". . . makes a deliberate attempt to bridge the gap between social history and literary study. Scholars will find the collection useful throughout, and undergraduates may particularly appreciate the essays touching on frequently taught works such as Henry V, *The Roaring Girl*, and *Moll Flanders*."
—*Choice*

"Those at the periphery of society often figure obsessively for those at its center, and never more so than with the rogues of early modern England. Whether as social fact or literary fiction—or both, simultaneously—the marginal rogue became ideologically central and has remained so for historians, cultural critics, and literary critics alike. In this collection, early modern rogues represent the range, diversity, and tensions within early modern scholarship, making this quite simply the best overview of their significance then and now."
—Jonathan Dollimore, York University

"*Rogues and Early Modern English Culture* is an up-to-date and suggestive collection on a subject that all scholars of the early modern period have encountered but few have studied in the range and depth represented here."
—Lawrence Manley, Yale University

"A model of cross-disciplinary exchange, *Rogues and Early Modern English Culture* foregrounds the figure of the rogue in a nexus of early modern cultural inscriptions that reveals the provocation a seemingly marginal figure offers to authorities and various forms of authoritative understanding, then and now. The new and recent work gathered here is an exciting contribution to early modern studies, for both scholars and students."
—Alexandra W. Halasz, Dartmouth College

Caravaggio, *The Cardsharps* (I Bari) ca. 1594
37-1/8 x 51-5/8 (94.2 x 130.9 cm.) Photographer: Michael Bodycomb
Copyright © Kimbell Art Museum

ROGUES

and Early Modern English Culture

CRAIG DIONNE AND STEVE MENTZ, EDITORS

THE UNIVERSITY OF MICHIGAN PRESS
Ann Arbor

For Shay and Brenan,
and for Alinor, Ian, and Olivia

For their love and support

First paperback edition 2006
Copyright © by the University of Michigan 2004
All rights reserved
Published in the United States of America by
The University of Michigan Press
Manufactured in the United States of America
⊗ Printed on acid-free paper

2009   2008   2007   2006   5   4   3   2

A CIP catalog record for this book is available from the British Library.

Library of Congress Cataloging-in-Publication Data

Rogues and early modern English culture / Craig Dionne and Steve
   Mentz, editors.
      p.   cm.
   Includes bibliographical references and index.
   ISBN 0-472-11374-7 (cloth : alk. paper)
      1. English literature—Early modern, 1500–1700—History and criticism.   2. Rogues
and vagabonds in literature.   3. Rogues and vagabonds—England—History—16th
century.   4. Rogues and vagabonds—England—History—17th century.   5. Literature
and society—England—History.   6. Peddlers and peddling—England—History.
7. Vagrancy—England—History.   8. Outlaws—England—History.   9. Vagrancy in
literature.   10. Outlaws in literature. I. Dionne, Craig.   II. Mentz, Steve.
PR428.R63R64   2004
809'.93352694—dc22   2003022740

ISBN 0-472-03177-5 (pbk. : alk. paper)
ISBN 978-0-472-03177-1 (pbk. : alk. paper)

Acknowledgments

This collection is the product of several years of collaboration among a wide variety of scholars, institutions, and other gatherings. We would like to thank several conferences for providing us with space to advance our discussions of the rogue: the 1998 Central New York Conference in Language and Literature in Cortland, New York; the 2000 Northeastern Modern Language Association in Buffalo; the 2001 MLA in New Orleans; and the 2002 Renaissance Society of America in Scottsdale, Arizona. We have also benefited from talking to numerous individual scholars who encouraged us to pursue this project, including Derek Alwes, A. L. Beier, Karen Helfand Bix, William Carroll, Arul Kumaran, Ted Leinwand, Martine van Elk, Lawrence Manley, Lori Newcomb, and Linda Woodbridge. Finally we would like to thank Ron Sheriff for his help indexing the collection.

Craig Dionne warmly acknowledges the many colleagues who assisted at various stages with his ongoing work on early modern rogues: Crystal Bartolovich, for organizing important Group for Early Modern Cultural Studies and MLA panels; Steve Zwicker and other faculty of the "Habits of Reading" National Endowment for the Humanities Institute at the Folger Library— Richard Helgerson, William Sherman, Kevin Sharpe, Anthony Grafton—and to all the participants of this group for their feedback, especially David Evans and Derek Alwes. Thanks to Gary Waller, who let his pocketbook copy of Salgãdo's *Cony-Catchers and Bawdy Baskets* be filched (I still have it, Gary) way back when. John Twyning helped with the urban contexts. Thanks to Kenneth Kidd for his ideas on tricksters. The staff of University of Michigan's Harlan Hatcher Graduate Library deserve mention. Thanks also to comrades Mark Douglas and Maria Magro for their support (and the Caravaggio reference). At Eastern Michigan University, Robert Holkeboer and the Office of Research and Development supported this project at important stages of its evolution; to all the members of the EMU Department of English who graciously helped, especially the Literature faculty writing group: Laura George, Jim Knapp, Annette Saddik, Andrea Kaston Tange, Joe Csiscila, Lori Burlingame, Annette Wannamaker, and Christina Milletti.

Steve Mentz would like to acknowledge the institutional support of St. John's University and his colleagues in the Department of English. Over the course of this project, he also received support from Iona College, and he would like to thank Alex Eodice, Helen Bauer, Tom Pendleton, John Mahon, Deborah Williams, Margo Collins, and Laura Shea. He would also like to thank Annabel Patterson, Lawrence Manley, John Rogers, and Ramie Targoff for continuing advice and resources. He owes a continuing debt to staff at the libraries of Yale University, Iona College, the Folger Shakespeare Library, and the British Library. A Folger Institute Seminar on Print Culture lead by Elizabeth Eisenstein was particularly helpful in laying the groundwork for this project, and he would like to thank the members of that seminar for their continuing support, advice, and encouragement.

Contents

Introduction: Rogues and Early Modern English Culture   1

PART I. THEORIES OF THE ROGUE

Fashioning Outlaws: The Early Modern Rogue and
Urban Culture   *Craig Dionne*   33

The Reckoning of Moll Cutpurse: A Transversal Enterprise
Bryan Reynolds and Janna Segal   62

New Historicism, Historical Context, and the Literature of
Roguery: The Case of Thomas Harman Reopened   *A. L. Beier*   98

APPENDIX: The Case of Nicholas Jennings Alias Blunt
Before London's Court of Aldermen 13 January, 9 Elizabeth I (1567) 114

The Counterfeit Vagrant: The Dynamic of Deviance in the
Bridewell Court Records and the Literature of Roguery
Martine van Elk   120

PART 2. MARKETPLACES AND ROGUE ECONOMICS

The Peddler and the Pawn: Why Did Tudor England Consider
Peddlers to Be Rogues?   *Linda Woodbridge*   143

"Masters of Their Occupation": Labor and Fellowship in the
Cony-Catching Pamphlets   *Karen Helfand Bix*   171

Making Vagrancy (In)visible: The Economics of Disguise in
Early Modern Rogue Pamphlets   *Patricia Fumerton*   193

PART 3. ROGUES AND THE EARLY MODERN CITY

·⊂⟶⟶⊃·

Sin City and the "Urban Condom": Rogues, Writing, and the
Early Modern Urban Environment *Adam Hansen* 213

Magic Books: Cony-Catching and the Romance of Early
Modern London *Steve Mentz* 240

PART 4. TYPOLOGIES OF THE ROGUE

·⊂⟶⟶⊃·

Vagabond Veterans: The Roguish Company of Martin Guerre
and *Henry V* *Linda Bradley Salamon* 261

Black Acts: Textual Labor and Commercial Deceit in Dekker's
Lantern and Candlelight *Laurie Ellinghausen* 294

Englishing the Rogue, "Translating" the Irish: Fantasies of
Incorporation and Early Modern English National Identity
Brooke A. Stafford 312

The Ambivalent Rogue: Moll Flanders as Modern *Pícara*
Tina Kuhlisch 337

Afterword: (Re)presenting the Early Modern Rogue
Arthur F. Kinney 361

Contributors 382

Index 387

CRAIG DIONNE AND STEVE MENTZ

Introduction

Rogues and Early Modern English Culture

He that cannot dissemble cannot live.
—CUTHBERT CONY-CATCHER

The shallow ploughman can distinguish now
'Twixt simple truth and a dissembling brow.
Your base mechanic fellow can spy out
A weakness in a lord, and learns to flout.
—MIDDLETON'S *A Mad World, My Masters* (1.1.139–42)

Under various names—rogues, molls, doxies, cony-catchers, masterless men, caterpillars of the commonwealth—an emerging class of displaced figures, poor men and women with no clear social place or identity, exploded onto the scene in sixteenth-century England. Early modern representations of the rogue and moll in pamphlets, plays, poems, ballads, historical records, and the infamous Tudor Poor Laws treated these figures as harbingers of emerging economic and social changes. Reflecting such historical developments, images of the early modern rogue created a cultural trope for mobility, change, and social adaptation. The underclass rogue in many ways inverted the familiar image of the self-fashioned gentleman who has traditionally been the literary focus and exemplar of the age, but the two characters have more in common than courtiers or humanists would have admitted. Both relied on linguistic prowess and social dexterity to manage their careers, whether by exploiting the politics of privilege at court or surviving by their wits on urban streets.

The word *rogue* was coined in the 1560s, possibly by Thomas Harman, to describe vagrants who used disguise, rhetorical play, and counterfeit gestures to insinuate themselves into lawful social and political contexts. As plays, pamphlets, court records, and other historical and literary documents described this figure, the term *rogue* took on a large range of connotations, including "scoundrel," "villain," "atheist," and "double-crosser." *Rogue* became a catchall term for a variety of social deviants and outcasts, from rural migrants to urban con artists. Images of the rogue took on varied associations, signifying the pervasive concern with self-invention as well as ideas of coterie culture or secret bonds. In a short time the term became popular and polysemous. Hamlet condemns himself as a "rogue and a peasant slave" because he cannot feign remorse for Hecuba, and Emilia unknowingly alludes to her own husband Iago as the "insinuating rogue . . . the cogging, cozening slave" who has slandered her mistress. Rogues were not uniformly unsympathetic; the word was also a term of endearment, as when Doll Tearsheet tells Falstaff: "Ah, rogue! i'faith, I love thee." This usage attests that *rogue* articulated a private camaraderie or intimacy that can be connected to its identification with covert fraternities. By taking on these contradictory cultural meanings, the word began to mediate the clashing social ideals of the age—economic individualism, social mobility, linguistic improvisation, and intimate fraternity.

The prototypical representations of these figures appear in the so-called rogue pamphlets, also called "cony-catching" pamphlets. These texts, which arrived on the literary scene after 1550, describe the criminal underworld as an autonomous social space with different classes or "degrees" of thieves, each with its own distinct language and traditions. The underworld anatomies, crime reports, gallows tales, and rogue ballads of the sixteenth and seventeenth centuries followed the examples of these pamphlets by including lexicons of cant, eyewitness accounts of foiled crimes, indoctrination ceremonies into underworld mysteries, detailed protocols of London's tricksters, and descriptions of particular con games, both successful and not. Through these accounts, the urban underworld became a semi-independent site of cultural meaning, an alternative to the court and stage, and a leading indicator of changes in English society. Texts such as *The Defence of Cony-Catching*, which purports to be an attack on Robert Greene's cony-catching exposés but seems to have been written by Greene himself, transform the discourse of rogues and molls into a broad and suggestive critique of early modern urban life. Cuthbert Cony-Catcher, fictional rogue and narrator quoted in the first epigraph, who both impersonates and attacks Greene, claims to expose a basic truth about the early modern city: "He that cannot dissemble cannot live." Pamphlets like this one, along with evidence from contemporary woodcuts, military records, and mercantile tracts, accent the pervasiveness of the rogue in early modern England.

The second epigraph to our introduction, from Middleton's *A Mad World, My Masters,* emphasizes the double-sided nature of underworld literacy. Middleton offers the commonplace: "The shallow ploughman can distinguish now / 'Twixt simple truth and a dissembling brow." Yet this description of social knowledge is part of a complaint made by a pandering mother, who makes her living by pimping her daughter, the lovely courtesan Frances Gullman. In this context the statement serves both as complaint about how consumers now recognize her rogue machinations and as a grievance over competition in the workplace:

> Your base mechanic fellow can spy out
> A weakness in a lord, and learns to flout.
> How does't behoove us then that live by sleight,
> To have our wits wound up to their stretched height!
>
> (1.1.141–44)

She suggests that knowledge of the rogue's craft is so generally dispersed, so much a part of the repertoire of the streetwise urban reader, that now any "base mechanic" can take advantage of the "weakness in a lord." The rogue pamphlets produce this mixture of complicity and strategy, in which knowledge of the deceitfulness of urban encounters leads to a more guarded consumer, but also a consumer whose strategies of self-display are taken out of the rogue's own playbook. Even though the rogue was a time-bound and local figure in early modern English culture, in many ways the myth of the rogue is as real today in the United States as it was in early modern England, as images of rogues and their legendary tricks are part of the unspoken background of contemporary urban culture, and may continue to be a metaphor for self-invention generally. To understand how the rogue recurs in contemporary contexts, we begin with a scene from a recent popular film that uses images of the underworld trickster to speak a ready-made language about the place of rogues in the everyday landscape.

It Takes One to Know One

In one of the opening sequences of the Renny Harlin film *The Long Kiss Goodnight,* starring Geena Davis and Samuel L. Jackson, a comical scene depicts a solicitous encounter between a gullible tourist and urban swindler. The scene follows a monologue by the protagonist of the movie, Samantha Kane—played by Davis—who has suffered from "focal retrograde amnesia" ever since she woke up on a beach eight years ago with no clue to her identity. Now living a middle-class lifestyle as wife, mom, and grade-school teacher, Samantha's life appears idyllic and secure. "The woman I was, what I used to be," we're told in voiceover during a Christmas party with friends, "I kissed goodnight long ago on that beach." The next shot introduces a new setting—police forcibly entering a shady hotel room—and is posed as a response to Samantha's quiet musings on her lost identity.

> *Tourist:* [Naked in bed with woman, throwing sheets over himself]: Hey, what the hell is this?
>
> *First Cop* (Samuel Jackson): Don't give me attitude, sir. You're assuming I won't shoot your sorry ass! And everyone knows when you make an assumption you make an ass out of yourself. Now, I'm Sergeant Madigan. Vice. You are under arrest for the crime of prostitution. [To other cop] Read him his rights.
>
> *Second Cop:* Rights? Uh . . . You have the roommate . . . Uh, the right to be silent.
>
> *Tourist:* Hey wait! I'm a married man!
>
> *First Cop:* [Looking at prostitute] I can see from your choice that you're not a wealthy man. . . . [Angry look on woman's face.]
>
> *Tourist:* You got to listen to me, man! This is the first time I ever done something like this!
>
> *First Cop:* In light of the damage this kind of arrest can do to you, I think we can make some kind of arrangement . . . [Second cop sits down and throws up.]
>
> [Cut to office. New scene. Woman playing prostitute is counting money.]
>
> *Woman:* Gotta stop using bums.
>
> *First Cop:* Forget that. They look like cops! We pulled it off didn't we?
>
> *Woman:* It was embarrassing.
>
> *First Cop:* You want me to hire actors, for christsakes? These guys are cheap. They work for food.
>
> *Woman:* So when they throw up on you, is that like a refund?

The con game depicted in this scene sets the tone for the following story, which centers on the mysterious "double identity" of Samantha, who slowly learns that before her rather curious case of amnesia she led a life as an underground assassin working for the CIA. The movie suggests in its cut to this dark world of scams and rip-off artists that Samantha's soft, blissful domestic space is the opposite of this world of shifting identities and duplicitous double-crosses. Jackson's character, Mitch Henessey, when not involved in confidence tricks at night as "Detective Madigan," is a private detective working to find Samantha's lost identity. Though marketed as an action film with recognizable hyperbolic elements of this genre (slow-motion gunfights, exploding buildings and bridges, harrowing escapes from captivity), *The Long Kiss Goodnight* is really a story about self-discovery. The movie works almost as an allegory of reawakening; the narrative focus is on the discovery of Samantha's authentic self—who am I? Or more appropriately, who was I? The story dramatizes the problem of fixing one's identity by depicting the choice Samantha must make to renounce her nefarious history and establish her "real" self. The film uses the scene of the false-prostitute con to speak in a condensed syntax about the overlapping worlds of middle-class identity and its underworld counterpart.

The film implicitly relies on a long history of association between bourgeois identity and the underworld. The underworld literatures of the early modern period that are the focus of this collection of essays make a similar point about the compatibility of in-law and outlaw worlds. This scene from *The Long Kiss Goodnight* serves as a useful starting point because of the connection it articulates between bourgeois culture and the underworld, between legitimate society and its fugitive other, a binary that pervades Western culture's fixation on antiheroes, outlaw identities, and the lauded, transient freedoms associated with outsider status. In this opening sequence, before Samantha's empowered self is released, her real identity is only suggested through juxtaposition: this establishing sequence implies Samantha really belongs to this gritty world even though she thinks she kissed it goodnight long ago. When Mitch scares the innocent tourist into coughing up money to stay out of jail, his duplicity is both a foil for Samantha's innocence and also a foreshadowing of her ultimate unmasking. Significantly, Mitch's con game borrows from a long history of underworld literature, especially in its deployment of stock images of cheats who threaten the security of naive city tourists, a scene that takes us directly to the earliest constructions of underworld culture in English, since it is an incident that the screenwriter of *The Long Kiss Goodnight*, Shane Black, could have taken nearly word for word from any number of English Renaissance rogue manuals printed during the late sixteenth century.

"Now, sir," Robert Greene begins one of the many tales of urban encounters that appear in his *Notable Discovery of Cosenage, Now Daily Practiced by Sundry Lewd Persons* (1592), there "comes by a country farmer, walking from his inn to perform some business and, seeing such a gorgeous damsel, he, wondering at such a brave wench, stands staring at her on the face." In what follows, Greene describes one of the most notorious con games of Elizabethan

London, the "crossbite," or the "crossbiting law." Greene dissects the scripted roles played by the team of rogues—"shifters and cozeners"—who descend on the innocent citizens of London's new market stalls, "merchants, prentices, serving-men, gentlemen, yeoman, farmers and all degrees." As in many rogue pamphlets of the period, there is a precise description of the language used by the rogues, suggesting to readers that the story is a kind of index to the language of the street:

> In Crossbiting Law
> The whore, the *traffic*
> The man that is brought in, the *simpler;*
> The villains that take them, the *crossbiters.*

> (135)

In his inimitable discourse Greene continues his narrative: when the "trull," who is really the wife of a "brave fellow[ ], but basely minded, who living in want, as [his] last refuge, fall[s] into the crossbiting law," confronts the "simplers"—"men fondly and wantonly given, whom for penalty of their lust [are] fleece[d] of all that ever they have"—the plot thickens . . .

> Beginning her exordium with a smile, she saith: "How now my friend! What want you? Would you speak with anybody here? . . . If the fellow have any bold spirit, perhaps he will offer the wine, and then he is caught. 'Tis enough. In he goes, and they are chambered. Then sends she for her husband, or her friend, and there either the farmer's pocket is stripped, or else the crossbiters fall upon him, and threaten him with Bridewell and the law. Then, for fear, he gives them all his purse, and makes them some bill to pay a sum of money at a certain day. (139)

Like the scene in *The Long Kiss Goodnight,* the confrontation is a candid moment of unmasking in which the citizen traveler is threatened with the harsh penalty of imprisonment for his indiscretion. It is a scene that recurs throughout the cony-catching manuals. The emphasis, oddly, is on the vulnerability of the "cony" (a term that means rabbit, which in early modern idiom was not associated with the idea of wily or crafty rodent, but signified "willing prey" or "naive quarry"). The encounter interrupts and threatens legitimate business transactions:

> If the poor farmer be bashful, and passeth by one of these shameless strumpets, then will she verse it with him, and claim acquaintance of him, and, by

some policy or other, fall aboard on him, and carry him in to some house or other. If he but enter in at the doors with her (though the poor farmer never kissed her), yet then the crossbiters, like vultures, will prey upon his purse, and rob him of every penny. . . . Ahh gentlemen, merchants, yeoman and farmers, let this to you all, and to every degree else, be a caveat to warn you from lust, that your inordinate desire be not a means to impoverish your purses, discredit your good names, condemn your souls, but also that your wealth got with the sweat of your brows, or left by your parents as a patrimony, shall be prey to those cozening crossbiters! (139)

A kind of crossbiting that is even more disturbing for Greene, more "pestilent," as he says, is when the crossbiters pose as constables; if they "learn[ ] some insight in the Civil Law, walk abroad like apparitors, summoners and informers, being none at all, either in office or credit, go spying." Greene reminds his readers, regardless of their class—"all degrees" of citizens—that these rogues pose a threat to the everyday affairs of commerce. Much of the indignation registered in passages like this hinges on the dissembling of the urban rogues, who barge in on the citizen and the prostitute not only to extort money but also to remind the gentlemen of their own fraudulent behavior. But who is wearing the mask? The crossbiter? Or the "innocent" simpler? These narratives echo the peculiar Renaissance anxiety over the difference between inward and outward shows, especially the way they signal the crisis of identity felt by the legitimate citizen now exposed as complicit with the rogue's culture of self-display. In this type of scene, the proper citizen is stripped of his façade—made a partner to underworld vice—and the brief comic moment begins to lose its humorous edge and comes to function as a nightmare of being unmasked by London's very own false-seemers.

Greene was drawing from—and in large part reinventing—an entire genre of criminal pamphlets in his *Notable Discovery*, sometimes playing the rogue himself by plagiarizing huge passages of the previous printings and marketing them as eyewitness accounts of his own day-to-day interaction with Londoners. Much of this literature—like Gilbert Walker's *A Manifest Detection of Dice-Play* (1552), Thomas Harman's *A Caveat or Warening for Common Cursetors Vulgarely Called Vagabones* (1566), and John Awdeley's *The Fraternity of Vagabonds* (1561)—manufactured an imaginary criminal underworld for London's growing metropolis, displacing dominant notions of social hierarchy and order onto the growing populations of homeless.[1] Published between 1550 to 1620, these pamphlets reshaped the image of the unfortunate vagabond into a willing and stealthy member of a vast criminal network of organized guilds, complete with their own internally coherent barter economy, master-apprentice relations, secret languages, and patrons. The texts were extremely popular; their vision of urban space shaped the repertoire of the urban reader. The various orders of rogues and vagabonds found in these pamphlets became familiar characters in the novels and plays of London's print industry throughout the modern period, with recurring images of a thriving underworld whose tradition runs from Iago to Defoe's Moll Flanders, from the Artful Dodger to Doyle's Moriarty and his minions.

Looking back, literary critics infer that rogues are, in a powerful sense, *us*, the prototypes of the citizens of modern urban capitalism, in part because they provide a potent image of the social adeptness required in a society premised on mobility and the endlessly changing conditions of exchange that constitute modern capitalism. As the social historian Burton Bledstein once surmised about the underlying conditions of modernity, "the person with a 'middling interest' live[s] suspended between the facts of his social condition and the promise of his individual future. Now he protect[s] his precious right to play the game of fortune seriously, to wear disguises and assume aliases in the gamble of life, to deceive and to be deceived in the race for success" (22). Similarly, the representation of the rogue mediated the "game" of fortune for those experiencing—from the sixteenth-century English context—the brute fact of economic "freedom" in early modern London; the rogue was born out of this complicated relationship between new middle-class readers and the economic and legal modes of social exchange that shaped their tentative position in the race for status and recognition.

The double bind of sympathy and disgust, admiration and fear, that the rogue creates remains powerfully relevant today. A Google search on the word *rogue* in January 2003 produced over 1.8 million hits. Like so much of the World Wide Web, these sites are dominated by brand-names, from Rogue Wave Software to Rogue Ales, and thriving Internet subcommunities, like the network associated with the Rogue Worlds online fantasy game and its numerous fansites. The word *rogue*, however, has a wide set of meanings, and several sites related to education even appear, including the Rogue Librarian and Rogue Community College. The wide currency of this word suggests a cultural fascination, and we believe early modern rogue studies provide insight into the roots of this fascination. Specifically, we want to make three suggestions about how three different contemporary meanings of this term resonate with its early modern history: in popular culture, in the discourses of capitalism, and in international politics.

In popular culture, roguelike figures have consistently been in the limelight since the days of Harman, Greene, and Dekker. As Bryan Reynolds shrewdly discusses in the opening pages of *Becoming Criminal,* the modern American fascination with representations of the Mafia speaks to the continuing relevance of outlaw reflections of in-law business practices and family networks (2–8). Figures of rogues or con men as heroes are common in Hollywood films, including Robert Redford and Paul Newman in *The Sting* (1973), George Clooney and Brad Pitt in *Ocean's Eleven* (2001, a remake of the 1960 version with Frank Sinatra and Dean Martin), Leonardo DiCaprio in *Catch Me If You Can* (2002), and Nicolas Cage and Alison Lohman in *Matchstick Men* (2003). In these movies, as in popular novels by the likes of Elmore Leonard and Mario Puzo, the fraternal ties of rogue figures engage the audience's sympathies because they appear as more dramatic versions of our own affectionate bonds: in *Ocean's Eleven*, for example, the social loyalties of thieves and con men seem more human and sympathetic than the ruthless, loveless lifestyle of the casino owner. The rogues steal the casino's money, but the audience sympathizes with them because it is the casino owner who seems driven by greed, while the criminals are motivated by love and the thrill of the game.

This sense of business owners as ur-rogues, with all of the criminals' greed but none of their humanity, leads to our second suggestion about the cultural relevance of the rogue, in what we might term "rogue capitalism." As the details have leaked out in the first years of the century, an image has been created of financial markets and international capitalism being run through a semisecret culture of cynicism and corruption. The pictures of CEOs and CFOs in handcuffs on the evening news—that is, the designating of particular individuals as rogues who must be incarcerated rather than as symptoms of a corrupt marketplace—have served less to purify the existing system than to emphasize the powerful continuity between the tactics that land rogues in prison and those that land CEOs in corner offices. While many of the factual details of recent shady financial practices remain as murky as the true history of the early modern rogue, several features of modern American capitalism in its current crisis resonate with the interrogations early modern writers made of Tudor-Stuart rogues, including the mystique of a private language, an opaque but demonstrable solidarity among coconspirators, and a way of doing business that relies on the credulity of a vast number of conies. If it's unclear who might serve as the Greene or Dekker of our modern underworld, we might consider that *Time* magazine's persons of the year for 2002 were three whistleblowers, Coleen Rowley of the FBI, Sherron Walkins of Enron, and Cynthia Cooper of WorldCom. These social purifiers might not be any more successful in changing pervasive rogue behavior than Greene or Dekker were, but *Time*'s desire to laud them implies that the narrative of the cony-catching exposé, in which an initiate into a corrupt system saves society by revealing the underworld's secrets at significant personal risk, retains its currency.

Finally, perhaps the most consequential deployment of the word *rogue* in contemporary political discourse is the increasing reliance on the phrase *rogue nation* as an anathematizing term. When states are grouped into this outlaw category, a range of political options usually held off-limits becomes not simply thinkable but urgent. Given the widespread use of this term, it may be worth recalling in this context another sense of the category "rogue" that our collection emphasizes: the way in which the underworld inversion of the social order parallels and critiques in-law culture. Is there a sense that non-rogue nations depend on the presence of rogues to define themselves and to designate the outer reaches of acceptable behavior in international relations, just as we have argued that the cony-catcher serves as a demon Other and tutor for early modern men and women negotiating the cultural changes of the city? Or does the purportedly univocal use of *rogue nation* bespeak a loss of nuance in public discourse, in which the sympathy with which filmmakers and novelists still treat rogues gets written out of politics entirely?

If extending the implications of cozening and sundry rogue practices seems a stretch when applied to contemporary international politics, consider that when translating Montaigne's description of the Spanish conquest of the New World, John Florio described the colonial legerdemain for his early modern English audience in familiar terms; the Spanish used "policies and stratagems . . . emploied to cozen, to cunny-catch, and to circumvent" the Native Americans ("Of Coaches" 3:6, 822). The scene of cultural exchange and international domination is transposed into one of rogues and conies; the conquistadors appear as the caterpillars of the New World and the natives as receptive conies, "unsuspecting poore people, surprised under colour of amity and well-meaning faith." This striking image reminds us that early modern Europeans used the idea of cony-catching to think about various cultural phenomena, including the colonial project.[2] By implication, Florio suggests that Montaigne's skeptical demystification of colonialism is its own rogue manual, through which readers can imagine the conies arming themselves against the stratagems of their oppressors by adopting the machinery of literacy. "I say, take this disparity from the conquerors," Montaigne muses, "and you deprive them of all the occasions and cause of so many unexpected victories." We believe the early modern rogue initiated a cultural logic of social betrayal and cohesion, of tactical deception and threatened honesty, that remains with us today in just such terms. With this long legacy in mind, we offer the following essays as attempts to decipher the cultural meanings of this still-powerful combination of myth and history.

Toward a Rogue Studies

Rogues and Early Modern English Culture presents a wide-ranging series of critical essays on the rogue, using the most productive scholarly trends currently being applied to this material. Taken together, these essays highlight a series of fundamental splits within early modern studies: they approach the rogue through debates about history and theory, fact and fiction, revealing and representing, the conservative and progressive impact of cultural fictions, and even the moral or immoral effects of the fascination with criminality. These essays suggest that emerging critical modes are renegotiating these fault lines. The basic fact-or-fiction split—between reading the rogue as a historical figure who "reveals" something about the real social conditions of early modern England, or analyzing this figure as a cultural construction who "represents" an imagined response to cultural stimuli—remains an active divide in studies of early modern roguery. This split underlies the ongoing controversy among Renaissance literary scholars and social historians about the size and shape of London's alleged criminal underworld and its importance to writers and readers at the time. It also emphasizes the staying power and continued relevance of empirical and rhetorical modes of literary studies in early modern studies. At stake in this ongoing critical conversation is not merely the prestige associated with rival methodologies, but also practical questions of critical capability: what ways of reading do justice to the available evidence? Which sort of critical reader—the literary scholar, the social historian, or the high-theoretical critic—best reveals what rogues were for early modern English culture?

These rival schools engage each other directly in this volume. What finally emerges is more complex than the polemical engagement of rival positions of traditional archivalism, Foucauldian new historicism, Althusserian dialectical materialism, or Deleuzian poststructuralism. The essays in this collection, like the rogue that is their subject, blur the boundaries between the historical and the literary, objective and subjective understandings, public paranoia and private experience. They reveal a complex back-and-forth relationship between historical rogues like Mary Frith and Nicholas Jennings and authors-constructed-as-rogues like Robert Greene and Thomas Dekker. The fact-or-fiction paradigm becomes finally a focalizing aporia: because the rogue is, inescapably, *both* fact and fiction, this figure occupies an important space in the ongoing negotiations between various forms of historicism and literary culture. The collection as a whole gestures toward a new interpenetration and cross-pollination between rival paradigms.

The rival schools demonstrated by these essays reveal important methodological differences in disciplinary practices as much as rival critical paradigms. These essays expose competing practices, from literary close reading to archival source-work to high-theoretical critique, working in competitive and complimentary fashion to uncover the cultural work of the rogue in English culture. In this way, the subfield of rogue studies serves as a case study in the mutual interpenetration of and dialogic relationship between literary ("representing") and historical ("revealing") modes of analysis. Though it is true that the current state of early modern studies has largely assimilated new historicism and cultural studies, this collection demonstrates that it is perhaps more accurate to see various poststructuralist theories of representation being assimilated *unevenly* in scholarship on early modern literature and culture. Early theorists of cultural representation like Althusser and Foucault influenced the first generation of American new historicists (Greenblatt, Montrose, Goldberg, and Orgel, among others) and British cultural materialists (especially Dollimore, Sinfield, and Holderness) whose major works began to appear in the 1980s. Together these trends codified the dominance of theories of cultural representation as ways to renew the investigation of canonical and noncanonical early modern literature. This collection suggests, however, that these theories of "representation" are currently being challenged and reevaluated by new (and renewed) methodologies.

Renaissance literary criticism since the 1980s has drawn the rogue into the expanding canon of early modern literature. The early decades of rogue studies used brief snapshots of the rogue literature rather than treating the rogue as a distinct cultural phenomenon. Scholars would relegate the figure's development to footnotes, asides, and brief "homologies" that flattened the rogue's complexity and rich history. As such, rogues were both ubiquitous and marginal in many influential studies in Renaissance criticism. The last twenty years have seen new historicists, for example, use the rogue texts to describe the dynamics of power and social exchange. Stephen Greenblatt, in the seminal essay "Invisible Bullets," treats Harman's confidence trickster as a Machiavellian antihero whose subversion of the fraudulent practices of the "legitimate" gentleman plays out the dynamic of absolute containment. Similarly, Katherine Eisaman Maus argues that the cony-catcher is paradigmatic of a science of outward shows, a "calculated tactics" of "self-display and self-withholding" that extend far outside "courtly circles" and "penetrate . . . down the social scale" (26). Like the traditional criticism it means to supplant, however, new historicism's references to the rogue risk rewriting the cultural phenomenon of this trickster as background to the privileged literary texts of the time. Moreover, the subversion-containment dialectic, however seductive in theory, cannot account for the range of subject-positions of the authors and texts of rogue literature. The status of these studies of the early modern rogue—influential and ripe for revision—emphasizes the critical relevance of the essays gathered in this volume, which may be read as a self-conscious attempt to bring "rogue studies" from the margins of several critical discourses to the center of its own.

Recently these dominant paradigms have begun to shift as a new generation of scholars has returned to empirical modes of scholarship, in such areas as the history of the book, economic history, and the histories of subaltern groups such as women and the vagrant poor. No longer content with basic new historicist questions of containment and state power, critics are asking if new modes of social organization, discrimination, or sympathy are visible in the rogue literature. For these changing discourses, rogue studies offers a tempting subject of study: the early modern rogue is powerfully sexualized (key texts include Harman's racy descriptions of morts and doxies and the sexual privileges of "upright men" as well as Greene's female cony-catchers); they serve as stand-ins for the vagrant poor; they prey on luckless farmers in a way that resembles early capitalist entrepreneurs; and the works about them were printed and sold in London's emerging market for printed books. For new economic critics, the confidence jests in the cony-catching manuals rehearse allegories of modern alienation and reveal the anonymity implicit in market capitalism. Jean-Christophe Agnew, for example, sees the cony-catching pamphlets uncovering fraud at the heart of exchange itself, laying bare "the multiple and shifting intentionalities concealed behind the outward face of all exchange" (68–69). History-of-the-book scholars like Alexandra Halasz argue that underworld writing thematizes the "constant circulation and anonymity" of print culture and the marketplace (72). Shakespeare scholars like William Carroll have used discourses of poverty and roguery to shed new light on such figures as Autolycus in *The Winter's Tale,* Christopher Sly in *The Taming of the Shrew,* and Edgar in *King Lear.* Though moving beyond the marginal position of the rogue in earlier criticism, these and other critical appropriations of the cony-catching pamphlets still fall short of a full examination of the discursive interplay of the underworld literature as a distinct cultural phenomenon.

Our essays attempt in differing ways to produce a more complete critical method that will bridge the palpable divide between the social history of the rogue and literary studies of the texts in which these figures appear. Motivated by a full archive of relatively unread material, scholars have returned to empirical methodologies to enrich and complicate the theoretical formulations of early modern scholarship on the rogue. Furthermore, the theories of textuality and representation to which literary scholars are now replying have played only a minor role in the social histories that inform much of the primary historical scholarship on early modern poverty and poor laws (Slack; Beier). Our collection explores how this critical disjuncture makes rogue studies a nodal point in Renaissance criticism where conflicting ideas and critical practices converge. Bridging several divides within the profession gives rogue studies a representative quality in today's culture of early modern studies.

Our collection builds on the previous studies of rogue pamphlets that have brought these texts into contact with mainstream literary studies of canonical Tudor and Stuart literature. The modern scholarship of these texts began with Edward Viles and Frederick J. Furnivall's *The Rogues and Vagabonds of Shakespere's Youth* (1880), Charles J. Ribton-Turner's classic historical survey, *A History of Vagrants and Vagrancy and Beggars and Begging* (1887), F. W. Chandler's two-volume *Literature of Roguery* (1907), and Frank Aydelotte's influential early critical account, *Elizabethan Rogues and Vagabonds* (1913). A. V. Judges's *The Elizabethan Underworld* (1930) became for many years the definitive edited collection of primary materials, foregrounding the genre of the cony-catching pamphlet against the arc of established economic and historical scholarship. Judges's selection emphasized how the pamphleteers borrowed from each other, and the chronology of his list traces a gradual shift from the country to the city. His genealogy starts with Robert Copland's *Highway to the Spital-house* (1535), whose imagery and language is that of a pastoral complaint, and then leads to the metropolitan *A Manifest Detection of Dice-Play* by Gilbert Walker (1552). After Walker, the city becomes the most common site for the early modern rogue: John Awdeley's *The Fraternity of Vagabonds* (1561), Thomas Harman's *A Caveat or Warening for Common Cursetors Vulgarely Called Vagabones* (1566), and the cony-catching pamphlets of Robert Greene (1591–92) and Thomas Dekker (1608–12), among others.

With some variations, this canon of cony-catching pamphlets—if one can call it that while still doing justice to its minority position as a street literature termed "ephemeral" by mainstream scholars—was established in Judges's collection and remains central. Judges's valorizing of this literature also defined the continuing political inflection of rogue studies. His lauding of these once-ignored texts reflects his reaction to the crisis of twentieth-century orthodoxies and his heightened sensitivity to the plight of the underclass suffering from a world war and the economic upheavals that challenged the supremacy of Western capitalism. The angry-Whig tenor of Judges's preface would not have been lost on academics after the crash of 1929: "But what of the dispossessed? Did not the greedy monarch take their fat lands and pleasant cloisters unto himself, and reap a large fortune from their disposal? He did, it is true. That is to say, he took the whole, and returned a part, in the form of an extension of secular endowments and a scheme of pensions for those expelled religious who were put on the waiting list for livings" (xxiii). Political currents have always undergirded critical attempts to read the rogue in relation to poverty and disenfranchisement. The new historicist fascination with the rogue and the subversion-containment paradigm seem to capture the frustration engendered by the rise of Reaganism and the culture of conservatism in which we still live (Gallagher and Greenblatt 11–13). More recently, Linda Woodbridge has used rogue literature to examine the ideological origins of the early modern English nation's lack of compassion for the nonworking poor, and by extension modern America's as well.

These critical accounts note that the rogue pamphlets describe the criminal underworld as an autonomous social space with different classes of thieves who voice an incredulous and at times cynical perspective about the conventional views of order and degree promulgated by England's church and court. As scholars returned to the rogue after the 1970s and 1980s, the sense of rogue culture as a dark mirror for Renaissance culture became central to rogue scholarship. The most commonly used collections for this generation of scholars are Arthur F. Kinney's *Rogues, Vagabonds, and Sturdy Beggars: A New Gallery of Tudor and Early Stuart Rogue Literature* and Gãmini Salgãdo's *Cony-Catchers and Bawdy Baskets*. Treating these texts as examples of "the vitality and exuberance of Elizabethan life" (11), Kinney situated the rogue pamphlets on a cultural continuum between literary rogues like Falstaff, Autolycus, Jonson's Subtle and Doll, and the clowns in *Dr. Faustus* on the one hand, and historical developments like "the enclosure movement, the dissolution of monasteries . . . the disbanding of professional soldiers and the arrival, from western Europe, of gypsies" (19) on the other. Salgãdo, especially in his influential study *The Elizabethan Underworld,* emphasizes the social space of lawful London and its criminal underworld as parallel images of early modern life. Kinney's further suggestion that the rogue pamphlets reveal "nothing less momentous than the birth of the novel in England" (55) announces the literary turn that continues to bear fruit in scholarship, although few contemporary scholars of early modern fiction would use Kinney's terms.

Since the late 1990s, there has been a suggestive convergence of revisionist-historicist and poststructuralist accounts of the underworld literature as a site of discursive and ideological *contest,* where the making of culturally inscribed social differences—class, race, gender, and nation—are written in and through this experimental hybrid form of faux journalism. The range of responses to the early modern rogue shows itself in the sharp contrast between two recent books: Bryan Reynolds's theoretical study *Becoming Criminal* and Linda Woodbridge's archivalist debunking of the myth of the

historical rogue, *Vagrancy, Homelessness, and English Renaissance Literature.*
What seems most striking about the emerging rogue studies, however, is less
its viability in either the theoretical or historicist modes than its portrait of
contemporary critical practice as a dynamic conversation along several axes,
including history-theory, canon-margins, city-country, and literary criticism-
cultural studies. In *Becoming Criminal: Transversal Performance and Cultural
Dissidence in Early Modern England,* Reynolds engages in a post-Deleuzian
reading of the criminal underworld as a vehicle through which early modern
subjects experienced a divergent mode of cognitive freedom: "transversal
identity," "where someone goes conceptually and emotionally when they venture . . . beyond the boundaries of their own subjective territory and experience alternative sensations." He associates this mode of identity with the
"*modi vivendi* of sociopaths, schizoids, criminals, philosophers, artists, and
various other social, cultural, political nonconformists" (18) and such six-
teenth- and seventeenth-century cultural phenomena as the rogue manuals,
gypsy personae, cant discourses, and the nomadic space of the suburban theater. Similarly in a post-Reformation context, Hal Gladfelder's *Criminality and
Narrative in Eighteenth-Century England* employs a Foucauldian theoretical
model to read the complex representational strategies of seventeenth- and
eighteenth-century "crime writing"—the superfluously detailed "circumstan-
tially dense narratives" of trial reports, gallows writing, and criminal biographies—as a precursor to the novels of Defoe and Fielding. Both Reynolds and
Gladfelder consider the image of the rogue as a powerful constitutive force in
the construction of early modern subjectivity. The bourgeois reader's sense of
liberty is constructed, ironically, through a complicated identification with the
outlaw heroes in these early pieces of crime reporting. For these critics the
emphasis is less on the actual criminals themselves (though both studies
account for the historical populations of criminals) than the force the representation of criminality assumes in the mediation of in-law consciousness. But
what about the actual homeless and itinerant populations, actually criminal or
not, that lived, one might say, on the "other side" of this discourse?

Linda Woodbridge's *Vagrancy, Homelessness, and English Renaissance Literature* directly challenges the idea that these pamphlets should be read as
social complaints about a genuine organized criminal underworld. Woodbridge argues that this entire subgenre of pamphlets—she calls it a "sub-
species"—should be interpreted as an outgrowth of the jestbook tradition, an
argument formerly contained in brief asides like Greenblatt's remark that
Harman's *Caveat,* "like other cony-catching pamphlets of the period, has the
air of the jest book: time honored tales of tricksters and rogues, dished out as
realistic observation" (50). Rather than being sociological documents, Wood-

bridge sees the pamphlets as texts written for rather sophisticated readers who remember that in the earlier jestbooks fictive tricksters asked us to partici-pate—laugh *with* rather than curse *at*—scandalous summoners, wily priests, and their rogue cousins. "The collection of funny stories" in these pamphlets, "was a familiar enough feature of the cultural landscape . . . to make it natural for readers to place [these] works against this generic backdrop" (47). Wood-bridge asks us to frame the stories about confidence tricks and scams in the context of the jestbook *collection*. The comic tales about the merry tricksters undoing vanity and presumption in all its assorted forms—the "staple of Tudor jesting"—emerge as the origin of the Elizabethan rogue pamphlet. The "jest book humor," we are told, "subverts serious intent, and [their] prurience undermines moralizing" (67, 91).

By making such a strong case for the comic side of these pamphlets, Wood-bridge potentially undermines interpretations of the broad subversive influence of these pamphlets on social and political reforms. "Knowing that some of [Harman's] anecdotes originate in a literary tradition," she continues, "can one believe anything that Harman says? What if he simply stole some of his information and made up the rest, rather than interviewing vagrants at all?" (61). Considering these pamphlets as part of the larger humanist project that used humor and wit to scorn the vagrant poor and other masterless men into accepting their place in the order of things—"trickery, comic table-turn-ings, whippings, and buffetings . . . [all] the very stuff of late medieval and early Renaissance jesting"—exposes the schizophrenic nature of Reformation compassion that bolstered much social reform of the Tudor period. (One is reminded of a similar insight into the radical topicality of humor in Northrop Frye's assessment that the Romans would have guffawed at the Passion.) "Out of context," Woodbridge adds, "it is hard to tell whether some passages come from the comic literary tradition or a Reformation polemic: their tone is indis-tinguishable" (89). But her emphasis is on the disarming potential of the comic component since this potentially neutralizes the power these texts would have had as protest literature. Ultimately, Woodbridge's sympathies are for the dispossessed—the real targets of the moral ambivalence of rogue pamphlets—the poor and transient classes (out-of-work apprentices, dis-charged veterans, and displaced day laborers) as the dislocated objects of Reformation England's reactionary anxiety over social decay and its contempt for the able-bodied unemployed.

Rogues and Early Modern English Culture extends the groundbreaking work of Reynolds, Gladfelder, and Woodbridge in asking questions about how rogue texts helped construct the social imaginary of their readers. Even the compelling insights of these and other recent critics of the rogue may finally scant the polyvalence of these cultural figures. It may be that the best way to think of the contrary positions in which these texts put their readers is by thinking of modes like the comic, the subversive, the progressive, and the moralistic as potentially disruptive *but not controlling* features of their cultural meanings, each of which is fraught with all the potential dangers of guffawing at the passion play that was early modern life. As an example of the complex subject positions that the cultural representations of the rogue create, consider Caravaggio's famous painting *The Cardsharps* (1595; cover art, front.). Though Caravaggio's object is the gambling houses and brothels of Rome, the painting reflects a central early modern preoccupation with defining identity in urban space: how could one determine whom to trust in anonymous alehouse encounters like card games? Late-sixteenth-century London, while somewhat more sheltered than Rome, created a comparable sense of social dislocation for its residents, due to factors like mass migration, foreign visitors, and English soldiers returning from the Low Countries.[3] Caravaggio's painting, in its depiction of the tenuous and sinister associations that lie just beneath the surface of "innocent" encounters, foregrounds in visual terms the divided positions forced on readers of the rogue pamphlets.

The painting lures its viewer into participating in, and even conniving with, the ruse behind the card game. Deception underlies the propriety of the game, as the title indicates, but we are given a particularly intimate view of that deception. The face of the "sharp" (lower right) simulates a mock excitement that links his own (feigned) pleasure at viewing the scene with the viewer's interest in Caravaggio's canvas. The sharp's false eagerness shadows our own acts of interpretation. The mark or cony (left side) by contrast only has eyes for his cards; the world of seeing and interpreting is parceled out between the criminals and the audience while excluding the victim. In shielding this figure's eyes from our view, Caravaggio minimizes the sympathy the viewer may have for a presumably innocent victim. The third figure (center top) is the sharp's accomplice—both wear the predatory colors of beer hall collaborators—and he signs to his partner the suit for his next hand. This third figure, whose tawdry dress may signify the stock features of Rome's vagabond soldier, serves as a foil to the viewer's thrill at being in on the cheat. We the viewers stand behind the painter's back, reading over his shoulder, transfixed by the scene—do we expose the fraud? Or are we caught by our complicity? Whose side are we on? Viewers are meant to question their critical distance, their own detachment, because they are drawn into the drama of the trick. Further qualifying the merriment of the jest is the dagger's hilt that protrudes into the foreground of the frame, hovering as a memento mori along the visual plane of the canvas. This painting alludes to all the modes of engagement we have seen in recent rogue criticism: Reynolds's fascination with acts of subversion, Woodbridge's emphasis on rough dehumanizing play, and Gladfelder's focus on the construction of the interpreting subject through a complex identification with the rogue.

Caravaggio's painting demonstrates in visual terms how representations of the early modern rogue situate readers in conflicted positions. It calls attention to how the reader's interest in the trickster's nefarious goals stems from a less-than innocent position, a fictionalized complicity that always dampens the moral condemnations that so often conclude tales of roguery. Like the rogue, the viewer is invited to feign ignorance, to fashion an interest in the scene—to *perform* amazement—as a mirror to the accomplice figure's wide-eyed awe (what does he see?). Though we do not intend to totalize the reader of the rogue pamphlets or other early modern texts, the analogy offered by Caravaggio's painting illustrates the way representations of criminality place the reader in dialogue with the rogue. The criminal pamphlets of early modern England also play with their readers' interests: they pique our curiosity in criminal activity just enough to make us apprentices to underworld mysteries. We are not just invited to use this information to guard against the wiles of urban doppelgängers, but to think of ways of integrating modes of deception into our own personal schematics. These pamphlets work in diverse and sometimes conflicting ways, mixing social complaint with humor, to speak to readers interested in the possibility of disguise and dissembling as a means of controlling uncertain forms of social exchange. For readers attuned to the precarious nature of anonymous urban encounters, the rogue pamphlets work as early modern urban conduct books, offering cues to their readers of how to negotiate the perfidy that underlies the random social transactions of urban London.

Reading the Rogue

The essays in this collection appear in four parts, starting with a series of broad theoretical overviews of the rogue and rogue studies, moving to parts focused on early modern economics and the discourses of urban culture, and concluding with a part on "typologies" that place the rogue in a wider ranger of analytical frames, from national identity to the long-term changes in literary culture that led to the modern novel. An afterword by Arthur F. Kinney places this volume in the historical context of early modern literature and cultural studies.

Part 1: Theories of the Rogue

In the first chapter in this part, "Fashioning Outlaws: The Early Modern Rogue and Urban Culture," Craig Dionne analyzes how the rogue pamphlets founded an ideological community of urban citizens. While these pamphlets present the figure of the rogue or cony-catcher as an image of predatory "otherness" that appeared to threaten the new group of merchants and shareholders, the rogue also moved forward the cultural project of shaping these readers into a more a coherent form of class solidarity. Criminals who organized themselves into guilds or confraternities served as a powerful fantasy community for early modern businessmen and merchants. Dionne charts this ambivalent relationship through underworld episodes that mirror middle-class social practices. The initiation ceremonies of pickpockets and thieves into the various "orders" of fraternal gangs parody the installation rituals of city guilds, and the taxonomies of underworld tricks and disguises caricature humanism's emphasis on advancement through histrionic self-display. The rogue pamphlets provide glimpses of the slow cultural transformation of the migratory poor and disembodied urban "middling sort" into the modern working and bourgeois classes.

The second chapter, Bryan Reynolds and Janna Segal's "The Reckoning of Moll Cutpurse: A Transversal Enterprise," takes up the salient case of Mary Frith (aka Moll Cutpurse). From the perspective of contemporary theoretical scholars, Frith has become one of the most representative figures of England's early modern period. This female rogue, cross-dresser, prostitute, gang leader, and violent criminal has become a protofeminist icon and an early avatar of gay, lesbian, and/or transvestite power. She has become a cultural exemplar of the blurring of sexual roles and a preferred subject for critical approaches informed by feminist and/or queer politics. Reynolds and Segal treat the case of Mary more particularly in terms of a sociohistorical phenomenon that is a defining historiographical dilemma for rogue studies: what to do when a real-life historical figure is multifariously reenvisioned and appropriated in various narrative modes, including biography, fiction, theatrical, and critical discourse? Frith's life inspired many retellings, from Middleton and Dekker's play *The Roaring Girl* (1611) to John Taylor's poem "The Water Cormorant," Nathan Fields's play *Amends for Ladies* (1618), and the anonymous pamphlet, *The Life and Death of Mrs. Mary Frith* (1612). This confluence of the historical and the literary exemplifies the "subjunctive space" of a character who is neither purely historical nor literary but a combination of both. In the hypothetical space of "what if" that exists between and across the divide between fiction and reality, Mary/Moll's hybrid fictional and historical existence becomes less a conundrum for scholarship than a characteristic of a certain kind of cultural phenomenon, which is disruptive and threatening precisely because it cannot be firmly fixed in one position.

The third chapter in this part critiques recent theoretical readings of the rogue, including Reynolds's. A. L. Beier's "New Historicism, Historical Context, and the Literature of Roguery: The Case of Thomas Harman Reopened" attacks the new historicist and poststructuralist methods of recent literary and cultural studies by returning to the social and political contexts of Harman's *Caveat* and examining how he has been misinterpreted and misread. Beier notes that literary-theoretical modes have rejuvenated rogue scholarship, but he argues that the models deployed to understand Harman's tract have reduced and oversimplified the man, his work, and his historical context. Foucauldian and post-Marxist scholars in particular have made an important error about Harman's social status; he was not mercantile or professional, but solidly of the upper Kentish gentry. The (false) middle-class association has posited middle-class values behind the policing of vagrants, when in reality Parliaments and privy councils dominated by the landed classes controlled the new "political technology of the body." Harman's pamphlet does confirm the presence of new penal technologies, but it also shows that older, medieval punishments were being deployed alongside the new ones. Beier claims that "the discipline of historical context" replaces these formulations with more complex and interesting readings of rogue culture. Harman was no ordinary country squire, and he was not, it seems, a member of Kent's commission of the peace. The highest office he held was as commissioner of sewers, which put him in close contact with the London authorities and means he was likely knowledgeable about the criminal worlds he described.

More particular examples of roguery appear in the concluding chapter of this part, Martine van Elk's "The Counterfeit Vagrant: The Dynamic of Deviance in the Bridewell Court Records and the Literature of Roguery." Van Elk juxtaposes the discourses of vagrancy with the minutes of the Court of Governors at Bridewell, where many vagrants were examined and punished. She asserts that rather than demonizing and isolating the crime of vagrancy, the Bridewell records reveal close connections between different types of social offenses, thus connecting offenders from a range of social backgrounds. In treating various crimes similarly, the records provide evidence of a dynamic of deviance that is not unique to a growing group of masterless men and women but instead frighteningly pervasive. This expansion of deviant culture is precisely what emerges from the rogue literature, which pinpoints the problem of identity and crime as a matter of exchange and negotiation rather than a set of marked differences between classes. Van Elk argues against recent critics, including Beier and Woodbridge, who have discounted the rogue pamphlets as sources of historical information about vagrants. By noting connections and interrelations between the "literary" pamphlets and the "historical" records at Bridewell, she finds that they both share a view of the social order as undermined by pervasive immorality and constituted through action and exchange rather than essence. Vagrancy and "lewdness" are found at the heart of English society, posited as a threat that cannot simply be isolated or removed through punishment.

Part 2: Marketplaces and Rogue Economics

The connection between masterless men and mercantile exchange was deeply rooted in early modern culture. In the first chapter of part 2, "The Peddler and the Pawn: Why Did Tudor England Consider Peddlers to be Rogues?" Linda Woodbridge focuses on how the building of London's Royal Exchange legitimated trade as a vested and official civic practice. Woodbridge demonstrates that peddlers during this period were demonized as vagabonds. In premodern cities, marketplaces, associated with the alien cultures of traveling merchants, marked boundaries between the legitimate and illegitimate forms of social exchange. As markets become governed by guilds and craftsmen, market stalls and scenes of trade became linked to civic locales: cathedrals (like St. Paul's), "exchanges," and official guildhalls. Woodbridge explores how London represented masterless men and women as sources of social disorder in order to police its own subsistence tradesmen. The newly built Royal Exchange, in particular, became an emblem of civic pride for London and economic prowess for England, but this public space defined itself by excluding peddlers and other mobile merchants. Reading a variety of texts including Thomas Heywood's *If You Know Not Me, You Know Nobody, Part 2*, Woodbridge exposes a history of exclusion and banishment, in which city guilds drove peddlers and other undesirables away from the steps of the Royal Exchange. As London experienced its first great burst of international trade (which was deplored by many sixteenth-century economic writers), the demonization of peddlers and shunning of local marketplaces like fairs functioned discursively as a project of civic and national image-making. The up-market shopkeeper in fixed premises was valorized, while mobile merchants such as peddlers or stallholders at fairs were roguified.

In the second chapter in this part, " 'Masters of Their Occupation': Labor and Fellowship in the Cony-Catching Pamphlets," Karen Helfand Bix analyzes more broadly how the rogue pamphlets reflect competing models of market exchange in early modern economic literature. Such works as Greene's *Notable Discovery* (1591), and Thomas Dekker's *The Bellman of London* (1604) and

Lantern and Candlelight (1608) juggle contentious attitudes about private initiative, the profit motive, marketplace competition, and the demise of traditional agrarian ethics. Helfand Bix demonstrates that the flexible idiom of the rogue pamphlets exposes the cultural disturbances caused by early capitalist development. She demonstrates that the pamphlets reflect growing concern about economic changes through strategies of moral equivocality and rhetorical indeterminacy. The cony-catchers' strategizing parallels the tactics of early modern entrepreneurs who needed to gamble in new and varied markets. The pamphlets therefore articulate a new form of labor—emphasizing mental acuity, adaptability, and risk management—applicable to flexible markets divorced from vocational regimes. Such narratives emphasize the lack of parity between large-scale acts of extortion and expropriation by "respectable" members of the commonwealth and the petty thefts of rogues. Helfand Bix situates the rogue pamphlets in the broader context of economic discourses that registered a proto-Hobbesian perspective on human behavior, leveling "in-law" and outlaw "cony-catchers" to a universal law of self-interest.

In the concluding chapter of this part, "Making Vagrancy (In)visible: The Economics of Disguise in Early Modern Rogue Pamphlets," Patricia Fumerton examines what she calls the "heretical disconnection" in early modern England between vagrant professions, popular print culture, and lower-order subject-positions. She begins by tracing the outlines of a newly emergent "vagrant" economy that was characterized by mobility, diversity, alienation, freedom, and tactical (as opposed to strategic or authorized) crafts. Such vagrant economics, and not roguery per se, she argues, are the real subject of the early modern rogue pamphlets. Representing crafty vagrants who deftly disguise themselves in changing occupational and social roles—epitomized by the Counterfeit Crank of Harman's *Caveat*—these works are themselves disguised voicings of fear of and investment in new market processes that required multiple jobs, frequent job-switching, and above all geographical mobility. Fumerton explains that Harman's deceitful rogues are only itinerant laborers thinly disguised. Subsequent rogue pamphleteers, such as Thomas Dekker and the most popular of all, Robert Greene, capitalize on such disguising to the point that the laborer himself or herself becomes visible only in trace. These later writers reinvent the vagrant subject through the tactics by which disguised rogues enact their deceit. For Greene and Dekker theatricality itself has become a part of the lived experience, and the idea of disguise becomes a metaphor for the varied ways of opportunity, low and high, speculated upon and seized. Fumerton argues that rogues in the end are not simply or clearly literary or historical. In the course of the fashion for rogue pamphlets and subsequent beggar/rogue drama, the history of vagrants and the representations of that history confusingly converge. Just as itinerant laborers were historically treated as one and the same with vagrants, the vagrant laborers of history and the disguised rogues of literature finally, in the minds of their contemporaries, came to occupy the same space.

Part 3: Rogues and the Early Modern City

This part opens with an overview of early modern urban discourses, Adam Hansen's "Sin City and the 'Urban Condom': Rogues, Writing, and the Early Modern Urban Environment." Hansen explores the ungovernable nature of London, the largest physical embodiment of the diverse community that was the English nation. Hansen contends that despite the best efforts of English authorities, the spatial segregation of social groups deemed "licit" and "illicit" was impossible in the complex cultural geography of early modern London. Metaphorically and materially, opposed and divergent groups mixed. The London that accommodated rogues and texts about them, and that was reproduced *in* such writing, attests in numerous ways to this intermingling. Even if contemporary fears about a vagabond "crisis" were exaggerated, the presence of such fears suggests that the rogue pamphlets served as "figurative acts of settlement." The city the rogues settled, however, was no simple cultural object. Urban rogue texts by Thomas Dekker, Robert Greene, and Thomas Nashe, among others, responded and contributed to a changing urban environment in which spatial, social, and linguistic proximities exacerbated and were underwritten by inversions—and hence relativizations—of moral polarities.

Making a narrowly focused contrast to Hansen's broad critique, the following chapter, Steve Mentz's "Magic Books: Cony-Catching and the Romance of Early Modern London," also sees rogue pamphlets as involved in the construction of the experiences of nonelite citizens, but in Mentz's reading the pamphlets educate (or purport to educate) readers who fear city life. London's growth from a late medieval town into an urban metropolis posed a problem of cultural legibility: how were newly arrived citizens to read changing urban institutions through outmoded social conventions? One way authors exploited this cultural moment was by creating texts new enough to speak to a changing city but also familiar enough to match well-known narrative forms. Whether the claim in Greene's cony-catching pamphlets to expose early modern rogues as "pestilent vipers of the commonwealth" is sincere, ironic, or (most likely) both, Mentz argues that the larger project of the pamphlets—creating a vocabulary to rewrite the experiences of urban citizens—encompasses both sympathy for the conies (as victims of a harsh new order) and admiration for the cony-catchers (as dexterous manipulators of the new order). The cony-catcher/cony relationship produced an early critique of market relations in human interaction. Rather than driving such a critique to an apocalyptic end, however, Greene's pamphlets reconfigure the city as a variation on romance, full of dangers and narrow escapes, but forgiving in the end. Greene's exposés serve as "magic books," initiating his readers into the new language of the urban world and making the city legible in the reader-friendly terms of romance.

Part 4: Typologies of the Rogue
The first chapter in the final part begins with figures who shift from the center of national ambition to the margins of English life: ex-soldiers. Linda Bradley Salamon's "Vagabond Veterans: The Roguish Company of Martin Guerre and *Henry V*" notes that among early modern rogues, veterans have a distinct place. The veteran as rogue emerged as military forces were being transformed from knights and feudal retainers to independent companies of trained recruits. The case of Martin Guerre provides a thick description of the fate of former soldiers, and it fleshes out briefer representations of these figures in More's *Utopia* (1515), Awdeley's *Fraternity of Vagabonds* (1561), Harman's *Caveat* (1566), and Greene's *Notable Discovery* (1591). In Guerre, Salamon argues, lie all the constitutive features of Awdeley's and Greene's rogues: attempted theft of property, imposture, a high level of risk or "gamble," folk ritual, and illicit sexuality. *Henry V* also presents a group of veterans, Falstaff's former company augmented by a recruit whose name means "thief," who follow the signature practices of vagabond rogues: gambling, drunkenness, theft, and sexual excess. Their primary incentive for the French campaign is financial gain, including profiteering, looting, and the theft of sacred objects. The leading entrepreneur among them plans a post demobilization career as pimp, thief, and faker of war wounds—the vagrant veteran of cony-catching pamphlets. These texts, like repeated Elizabethan statutes, attempt to police veteran rogues by naming and characterizing them as outlaws.

The next chapter in this part, Laurie Ellinghausen's "Black Acts: Textual Labor and Commercial Deceit in Dekker's *Lantern and Candlelight*," addresses the conflation of professional author and cony-catching rogue. Thomas Dekker's *Lantern and Candlelight* (1608) was the first to record a type of criminal that must have alarmed aspiring writers: the "falconer," who manipulates both patronage-based and market-based literary systems. The falconer commands a book to be printed at his own cost and sets off to the countryside in search of potential patrons. At each estate, he affixes a custom-made epistle dedicatory and thereby cozens a gentleman out of a sum of money. By the time the patron suspects, he cannot trace the source of the book among the city's myriad printers. The falconer thus shrewdly culls profit from old and new literary systems; he uses patronage to make his profit and print to cover his tracks. Dekker's outraged response attempts to demarcate an absolute distinction between falconers and legitimate "scholars," but the difference between falconers and professional authors like Dekker remains unclear. Like the rogue, the professional author is an expert creator of fictions that gain the attention of paying audiences. Dekker's text, consciously or not, undermines the legitimacy of professional writers by interrogating the marks of "learning" that might otherwise serve to identify the "true" writer. This skeptical construction of authorship further destabilizes print culture's presumed "fixity" by describing authors who are savvy about the print market's opportunities for crafty rogues.

The third chapter, Brooke Stafford's "Englishing the Rogue, 'Translating' the Irish: Fantasies of Incorporation and Early Modern English National Identity," examines the impact of not-quite-other populations on English national identity. She argues that textual representations of rogues and other "internal aliens," particularly the Irish, reveal cultural anxieties about the English imagining of the nation. She reads several rogue pamphlets in the context of the English colonization of Ireland, and explores how the processes of "Englishing" and translation, central to both canting dictionaries and the colonial project set out in Spenser's *A View of the Present State of Ireland* (1596), prove to be unstable metaphors for the creation of a unified national identity. As the texts she examines demonstrate, nation-making processes are seldom unidirectional. Investigating the centrality of language to national identity and to threats against that identity exposes fault lines in the connection between language and nation. Both canting dictionaries and Spenser's treatise, Stafford argues, reveal that the project of establishing a permanent national linguistic identity by attempting to "English" outsiders unwittingly undermines itself. There are no guarantees in the project of "Englishing" texts or people, as the enduring, dangerous appeal of the rogue culture and Irish culture demonstrates. Texts that set out to define end up blurring definitions, inadvertently exposing the "degeneration" that threatens English national identity and its rootedness in linguistic unity.

The final chapter in this part, Tina Kuhlisch's "The Ambivalent Rogue: Moll Flanders as Modern *Pícara*," takes up *Moll Flanders*, a novel written 130 years after the Tudor-Stuart cony-catching pamphlets. Daniel Defoe's manipulation of the picaresque genre harkens back to its roots in *siglo de oro* Spain and sixteenth-century English rogue texts. The flexibility of these models allows him to make a political critique that oscillates between approval and disapproval of the status quo. Defoe uses the double structure of the picaresque to capture his ambivalence about the role of unrelenting economic ambition in early capitalism. His picaresque narrator relates her life retrospectively and supposedly has been purified by experience. As in early modern rogue literature, however, the twofold structure makes the narrator's claim of moral purity appear hypocritical, since Moll's ethical admonitions pale before the indulgent description of her crimes. Moll's career remains morally ambiguous. She transgresses social conventions and is ruthless in the pursuit of wealth. Her ambition for wealth and ease reflect the maturation of capitalist desire in English society. In *Moll Flanders* Defoe returns to the material of the rogue pamphlets to express deep ambivalence about the moral consequences of emerging capitalism.

Afterword

Lastly, the afterword, "(Re)presenting the Early Modern Rogue," is written by Arthur F. Kinney, whose *Rogues, Vagabonds, and Sturdy Beggars* remains the definitive collection of the rogue pamphlets for scholars and critics. Kinney's afterword addresses what is probably the key conundrum facing scholars of these texts: are they, in the end, better read as factual histories or literary fictions? Considering both primary sources and historiographical theories, Kinney emphasizes that these texts contain both literary and historical materials, which finally cannot (and should not) be separated. This definitive statement of the ambiguous appeal of the rogue literature closes our collection by emphasizing the cultural hybridity and polyvalence of the early modern rogue.

NOTES

1. Harman's title is often modernized "Caveat for Common Cursitors." Its 1566 date is speculative; the first surviving edition is 1568. The text was entered into the Stationer's Register on 8 January 1566 (67). See Kinney's textual note, 296.

2. William Hamlin, author of *The Image of America in Montaigne, Spenser, and Shakespeare: Renaissance Ethnography and Literary Reflection*, assisted us with our reading of Florio's translation of Montaigne; in an email communiqué Hamlin explained that "Florio does here [in the cony-catching phrase] what he so often does in his translation—he takes a single verb in Montaigne and renders it with a number of different English verbs. So, in this case, Montaigne writes as follows: 'Car, pour ceux qui les ont subjuguez, qu'ils ostent

les ruses et batelages dequoy ils se sont servis a les piper. . . .'; 'piper,' which means to deceive, becomes 'to cozen, to cunny-catch, and to circumvent.' This is actually an excellent example of Florio-esque proliferation."

3. Our reading of Caravaggio is indebted to Helen Langdon's *Caravaggio: A Life*. Langdon identifies the clothing of the cheats in *The Cardsharps* as "predatory in gaudy blacks and yellows," marking them as *bravi*, "soldiers of fortune, a type thrown up by disastrous upheavals of the sixteenth century, without trade or home, hangers-on at the small courts of the nobility, fomenting civil strife . . . forced to live by their wits, and act as pandars, pimps, hangman's helpers; through gaming and cheating they struggle to keep their body and soul together" (91).

WORKS CITED

Agnew, Jean-Christophe. *Worlds Apart: The Market and the Theater in Anglo-American Thought, 1550–1750*. Cambridge: Cambridge: UP, 1986.

Awdeley, John. *The Fraternity of Vagabonds*. [1561; 1565; 1575]. In Judges.

Aydelotte, Frank. *Elizabethan Rogues and Vagabonds*. Oxford: Clarendon P, 1913.

Bledstein, Burton J. *The Culture of Professionalism: The Middle Class and the Development of Higher Education in America*. New York: Norton, 1978.

Carroll, William. *Fat King, Lean Beggar: Representations of Poverty in the Age of Shakespeare*. Ithaca: Cornell UP, 1996.

Chandler, F. W. *The Literature of Roguery*. New York: Houghton Mifflin, 1907.

Cockburn, J. S. "The Nature and Incidence of Crime in England, 1559–1625: A Preliminary Survey." *Crime in England, 1550–1800*. Ed. J. S. Cockburn. London: Methuen, 1977. 62–63.

Dekker, Thomas. *The Bellman of London*. 1608. In Judges.

Gallagher, Catherine and Stephen Greenblatt. *Practicing New Historicism*. Chicago: U Chicago P, 2000.

Gladfelder, Hal. *Criminality and Narrative in Eighteenth-Century England: Beyond the Law*. Baltimore: Johns Hopkins UP, 2001.

Greenblatt, Stephen. *Shakespearean Negotiations: The Circulation of Social Energy in Renaissance England*. Berkeley and Los Angeles: U of California P, 1988.

Greene, Robert. *A Notable Discovery of Cozenage*. 1591. In Judges.

Halasz, Alexandra. *The Marketplace of Print: Pamphlets and the Public Sphere in Early Modern England*. Cambridge: Cambridge UP, 1997.

Hamlin, William. *The Image of America in Montaigne, Spenser, and Shakespeare: Renaissance Ethnography and Literary Reflection*. New York: St. Martin's, 1995.

Hanson, Elizabeth. *Discovering the Subject in Renaissance England*. Cambridge: Cambridge UP, 1198.

Harman, Thomas. *A Caveat or Warening for Common Cursetors Vulgarely Called Vagabones*. 1566. In Judges.

Judges, A. V. *The Elizabethan Underworld*. London: Routledge, 1930.

Kinney, Arthur F., ed. *Rogues, Vagabonds, and Sturdy Beggars: A New Gallery of Tudor and Early Stuart Rogue Literature*. 2d ed. Amherst: U Massachusetts P, 1990.

Langdon, Helen. *Caravaggio: A Life*. New York: Farrar, Straus and Giroux, 1999.

The Long Kiss Goodnight. Dir. Renny Harlin. New Line Cinema, 1996.

Maus, Katherine Eisaman. *Inwardness and the Theater in the English Renaissance*. Chicago: U of Chicago P, 1993.

Middleton, Thomas. *A Mad World, My Masters*. 1606. Lincoln: U of Nebraska P, 1965.

Montaigne. *The Essayes of Montaigne: John Florio's Translation*. New York: Modern Library, 1933.

Reynolds, Bryan. *Becoming Criminal: Transversal Performance and Cultural Dissidence in Early Modern England*. Baltimore: Johns Hopkins UP, 2002.

Ribton-Turner, Charles James. *A History of Vagrants, Vagrancy, and Beggars and Begging*. London: Chapman and Hall, 1887.

Salgãdo, Gãmini. *The Elizabethan Underworld*. London: Rowman and Littlefield, 1977.

Slack, Paul. *The English Poor Law, 1531–1782*. Basingstoke: Macmillan Education, 1990.

Viles, Edward and Frederick J. Furnivall. *The Rogues and Vagabonds of Shakespere's Youth*. London: Trubner, 1880.

Walker, Gilbert. *A Manifest Detection of the most vile and detestable use of Dice-play, and other practices like the same*. 1552. Judges.

Woodbridge, Linda. *Vagrancy, Homelessness, and English Renaissance Literature*. Urbana: U of Illinois P, 2001.

Wright, Louis B. *Middle-Class Culture in Elizabethan England*. Chapel Hill: U of North Carolina P, 1935.

PART I

Theories of the Rogue

CRAIG DIONNE

Fashioning Outlaws

The Early Modern Rogue and Urban Culture

It is a curious paradox of sixteenth century social development that the towns, although the home of the more revolutionary changes of the age—in commerce, industry and political thought— . . . preserved in [their] organization a truer perception than did the countryside of the medieval ideal: a place for Everyman, and Everyman in his place.

—A. V. JUDGES, *The Elizabethan Underworld*

Against this description of the "social consciousness of the corporate town," given in the 1930 edition of Judges's *Elizabethan Underworld,* we can begin to picture the particular ideological function of the body of noncanonical literature commonly referred to as "rogue literature" or the "cony-catching manuals." These pamphlets were published between 1550 and 1620 and helped reshape the image of the hapless vagabond into the covert member of a vast criminal underground of organized guilds, complete with their own internally coherent barter economy, master-apprentice relations, secret languages, and patrons. Much of this literature—like Gilbert Walker's *A Manifest Detection of Dice-Play* (1552), Thomas Harman's *A Caveat or Warening for Common Curse-tors Vulgarely Called Vagabones* (1566), John Awdeley's *The Fraternity of Vagabones* (1561), and Robert Greene's *A Notable Discovery of Cosenage* (1591)—manufactured an imaginary subculture for London's growing metropolis, displacing dominant notions of social hierarchy and order onto the growing populations of homeless.[1] Harman's *Caveat* went through five printings; his inventive sketch of pickpockets and thieves (most of which, ironically, he lifted from Walker) was later codified in William Harrison's *Description of England* (1587), as a bona fide list of "degrees" or social classes. Harrison writes:

A gentleman . . . of late hath taken great pains to search out the secret practices of this ungracious rabble. And among other things he setteth down and describeth three-and-twenty sorts of them, whose names it shall not be amiss to remember, whereby each one may take occasion to read and know, as also by his industry, what wicked people they are and what villany remaineth in them.

THE SEVERAL DISORDERS AND DEGREES AMONGST
OUR IDLE VAGABONDS

1. Rufflers [thieving beggars, apprentice uprightmen]
2. Uprightmen [leaders of robber bands]
3. Hookers or anglers [thieves who steal through open windows with hooks]
4. Rogues [rank-and-file vagabonds]
5. Wild rogues [those born of rogues]
6. Priggers of prancers [horse thieves]
7. Palliards [male and female beggars, traveling in pairs]
8. Fraters [sham proctors, pretending to beg for hospitals, etc]
9. Abrams [feigned lunatics]
10. Fresh-water mariners or whipjacks [beggars pretending shipwreck]
11. Dummerers [sham deaf-mutes]
12. Drunken tinkers [thieves using the trade as a cover]
13. Swadders or peddlars [thieves pretending to be peddlers]
14. Jarkmen [forgers of licenses] or patricoes [hedge priests].

OF WOMENKIND

1. Demanders for glimmer or fire [female beggars pretending loss from fire]
2. Bawdy baskets [female peddlers]
3. Morts [prostitutes and thieves]
4. Autem [married] morts
5. Walking [unmarried] morts
6. Doxies [prostitutes who begin with uprightmen]
7. Dell [young girls, incipient doxies]
8. Kinchin morts [female beggar children]
9. Kinchin coes [male beggar children].

(184–85)

So hugely popular were these pamphlets that their vision of urban space would shape the symbolic repertoire of the literate urban reader. The various orders of rogues and vagabonds found in these earlier pamphlets will become familiar characters in the novels and plays of London's print industry throughout the modern period.[2] By the time Henry Peacham wrote his *Art of Living in London* (1642), readers were already quite familiar with the stereotypes of London's rogue classes. "All [their] tricks of late years," Peacham explains, "have been so plainly discovered and are so generally known almost to every child that their practice is out of date and now no great fear of them" (249).

Reading Rogues

In the following, I want to explore how the cony-catching texts constructed the image of the rogue in response to economic and legal changes in sixteenth-century England. The cony-catching pamphlets, I will argue, functioned as domestic handbooks that restructured a civic urban identity important for the materialization of an emergent bourgeois culture. Before analyzing the image of the rogue as an ideological reaction to the complex changes associated with modernity, I want to examine carefully how critics have responded to the validity and forcefulness of these pamphlets. When reviewing the vast amount of criticism that already exists on the cony-catching pamphlets, one finds that there are a few distinct ways to interpret these texts, interpretive strategies that are circumscribed by institutional and disciplinary boundaries.[3] One way to read them is as biographical testimonies, literary recordings of the invisible network of criminals that haunted Shakespeare's England. A. V. Judges's collection was the first to appropriate this loosely connected group of popular ballads and manuals as an important subcanon that offered a risqué if not scandalous look at Shakespeare's London. The best exploration of these texts, and perhaps the most often cited, is Gãmini Salgãdo's *The Elizabethan Underworld*, written as a critical reader into the cultural world revealed in the primary texts of Judges's anthology. The problem with this interpretive strategy is that it is working within a humanist literary ideology that values the colorful tales of London's tricksters and hucksters as aesthetic forms.[4] Not only do these accounts generally accept the stories told in these books as real events, the critic always seems to be reminding the reader of an unchanging social condition reflected in the narrative. "Anyone who has any experience of the seamy side of the 'entertainment' world in a large city," Salgãdo writes, "will recognize the shifts and stratagems of Elizabethan dice-cheats. Neither the practitioners nor the apparatus nor the victims have changed, except outwardly" (37). Throughout these critical accounts we are reminded that these pamphlets have an ancillary role as a window into the artistic representation provided for us in the theater. Thus we find Arthur Kinney, in the introduction to his edited anthology *Rogues, Vagabonds, and Sturdy Beggars*, relegating matters of historical concern to a fuller sense of authorial experience: "Disturbers of the peace, enemies of law and order, the terror of the simple farmer, the most pressing social problem of the Tudor years of England, these throngs of beggars and their wenches were never absent from city or shire. . . . Little do we wonder, then, at Falstaff's easy familiarity with the life of the petty criminal, whether at Mistress Quickly's tavern or on the highway at Gad's Hill" (11–12). So when Greene's con men assume the role of the gentleman, feign friendship and win over the innocent farmers and tourists in London, literary humanists hear the voices of the vice characters from the plays, and they delight at the textual interplay at work behind these documents. "The paraphernalia used in th[ese] form[s] of cheating," Salgãdo explains, "had all the imagination, energy, sense of timing and understanding of character that we find in the Elizabethan drama itself" (38).

The second way to read these texts is from an empirical perspective.[5] A. L. Beier's *Masterless Men* is a good example of a serious historical analysis of the problem of social displacement during this period, viewing the tales about London being overridden with cozeners and pickpockets as "incorrect" or "skewed" when examined next to the court justices' proceedings. The "interpretations" of a "highly organized" vagabond society—with "divisions of labor, demarcated areas of operation, systems of disposing of goods and for training recruits . . . are misleading," Beier argues. "Based largely upon literary sources, they exaggerate the underworld element among vagrants" (124). For Beier "the evidence adduced to show that vagabonds . . . organized in gangs is unconvincing" (124). What was an important literary text to the humanist becomes just another piece of evidence to aid in the overarching questions that concern the social historian most: how many masterless men were there in England during this time, and how organized were they? It is not surprising that these pamphlets lose their luster when held next to the actual judicial records and examinations. If the literary humanist acknowledges the fictional status of the rogue literature in order to aestheticize the underworld as an important element of the literary "background," the empirically minded social historian considers the fictional status of the genre a form of conscious misapprehension: "the extent of professionalism is overstated by the rogue writers," Beier adduces, "who were catering for a market in which a full-fledged criminal was more exciting than an amateur" (127). An interesting counter to Beier's study is John McMullan's *The Canting Crew*. No less empirical, McMullan's curious book was published in Rutgers's Crime, Law and

Deviance series, and provides a sociological accounting of the criminal associations and underworld networks by reading these cony-catching pamphlets
as ethnographic inscriptions of deviant behavior. *The Canting Crew* argues
against the idea that rogue literature expresses "the febrile imaginations of
contemporaries"; he believes rather it is "the gullibility of historians" that
"contributes to erroneous reconstructions" (2). McMullan's ambitious sociohistorical account is meant to settle the score, and find out the truth about these
criminal gangs, but his own discourse of criminology objectifies the cony-
catching manuals by reading them as an instance of an ahistorical entity called
"crime," a term whose social meaning is contingent upon changing historical
perspectives. Moreover, by bestowing authenticity on characters and incidents
in these texts as precursors to mob patterns found today, McMullan overlooks
the fact that the pamphleteers were consciously working within an emerging
genre, reproducing their stories by borrowing their lists of canting terms and
catalogs of thieves, not to mention their so-called eyewitness accounts, from
previous pamphlets.

Neither the humanist nor the empirical interpretive strategy pays much
attention to the social attitude or ideological perspective these pamphlets
helped alter or secure. Even the recent new historicism tends to ignore the
particulars of these pamphlets, relegating much of this material to footnotes.
The paradigmatic text of the new historicism that examines the representation of the rogue in relation to Elizabethan and Jacobean theater, Stephen
Greenblatt's infamous "Invisible Bullets," approaches such images in seemingly metaphoric terms, so that the idea of exposing a counterfeit appears to
lose its specific historical character as a legal practice peculiar to the dissolution of feudalism and becomes an instance of an abstract process of reconstituting an all-pervasive "order" or "power," whose most aesthetically rendered expression is found in the drama of the period. Greenblatt identifies the
moral aim of these pamphlets—to "despise and prosecute" the "deep dissembling" of the rogues—as an ambivalent, aesthetically pleasing process: "to
like reading about vagabonds is to hate them and to approve of their ruthless
betrayal" (52). It is a characteristic move of some historicist readings of the
Renaissance to conceptualize the text's hold on its reader as transhistorical, a
reading that inscribes the process of identifying with royalist power as an ideology that is coterminous with twentieth-century modes of social administration. In the same breath Greenblatt continues: "Shakespeare . . . takes the discursive mode that he could have found in [cony-catching pamphlets] and
intensifies it, *so that the founding of the modern state, like the self-fashioning of
the modern prince,* is shown to be based upon the acts of calculation, intimidation, and deceit. And these acts are performed in an entertainment for which

audiences, the subject of this very state, pay money and applaud" (52–53; emphasis added).

As literary historians we find it difficult to construct genealogies of early modern social practices without relating them to our own social world. Such a move honestly foregrounds the self-referential nature of interpretive praxis, giving space to reflect on how our positions as interpreters of the past are influenced by present-day ideologies. Yet the self-referential historicist strategy purchases rhetorically an awareness of the political implications of artistic appreciation at the expense, I would argue, of misrecognizing the historical differences between dice cheats then and dice cheats now, or the self-fashioning of a prince and (ambiguously enough) the modern state. Such a move, as much as it links literature to political practices—and indeed, our own aesthetic pleasures to a larger political history—can potentially negate the difference of the past by rendering early modern social activities a kind of allegory of the present. On a certain philosophical level, it will be impossible to escape such an account of sixteenth- and seventeenth-century vagabonds and rogues as instances of our own vexed interpretive imaginaries, no less haunted by hegemonic images of welfare cheats and counterfeit "legitimate" officials, CEOs, and politicians. On another level it is equally impossible to ignore (if materialist history is to mean anything) what makes rogues and vagabonds of the sixteenth and seventeenth centuries distinctly different, especially when we situate these texts in the context of a fractured, culturally diverse social space of early modern metropolitan London. Reading the cony-catching pamphlets as products of an ideological apparatus that attempted in its own limited terms to make rationally coherent this emergent space will allow us to approach them dialectically, as fact and fiction, both a literary genre that expressed an imaginary fear of an illusory criminal underworld and a discursive or ideologically constitutive set of beliefs that produced for their reader what Louis Althusser defined as a "lived relation" to the real.[6]

This middle position, reading the early modern rogue as both fact and fiction, as real, in the Elizabethan mind's eye as witches or cannibals, or alternatively, as unreal as well-poisoning Jews, defines a new interpretation of the discursive function of the rogue as a complex mediation of early modern social governance and domestic management. This interpretive position is still characterized by a range of critical methods that reflect the humanist and empirical practices mentioned above—which come to shape ends of a critical spectrum, really, as seen in this collection. Nonetheless, the new return signaled by recent publications to the social meaning of the criminal underworld seeks a more nuanced appreciation for the time-bound and contingent nature of poverty and crime and the role literary texts have played in the "authentic description of a social fiction and a fictive account of [the] cultural fact" of early modern organized crime (Twyning 123). Along these lines, Bryan Reynolds's highly theoretical *Becoming Criminal: Transversal Performance and Cultural Dissidence in Early Modern England* recognizes the criminal culture of sixteenth-century England constituting a "subnation that illegitimately occupied *material and conceptual* space within the English nation" (1; emphasis added).[7] Similarly, Linda Woodbridge's historicist *Vagrancy, Homelessness, and English Renaissance Literature* argues that the pamphlets on roguery functioned as fictional entertainment, as generic vestiges of joke books, whose tales of comic inversions, "trickery, comic table-turnings, whippings, and buffetings . . . [all] the very stuff of late medieval and early Renaissance jesting," rationalized the world of the poor and dispossessed in familiar terms (89).[8] Another recent literary analysis of the fictive status of the underworld is Hal Gladfelder's *Criminality and Narrative in Eighteenth-Century England: Beyond the Law*, which explores the indebtedness of early experiments in the novel to the narrative features of published legal documents, court proceedings, and crime trials. Though the focus is on representations of criminality in the late seventeenth and early eighteenth centuries, his argument about the ideological effects of crime writing could easily apply to the earlier generative moments in the Elizabethan cony-catching pamphlets: "Once readers are drawn into imaginative complicity with deviance, they may not recoil when called on. For not only does the criminal protagonist embody and act on the impulses encouraged by bourgeois individualism itself—that is, by the very ideology underlying the system of property and social relations the law exists to secure—but the audience for criminal writing might share, at least in part, the outlaw's alienation from the centers of economic and ideological power" (9).

Reynolds, Woodbridge, and Gladfelder argue forcefully that the crime literature of the early modern period worked to construct a readership whose fantasies of freedom and social being were shaped by images of the itinerant vagabond and his or her expressions of resistance, rivalry, and mutual comradeship. Their work clears a path for a more thorough analysis of how images of the rogue worked as factual fictions through which the various classes of the "middling sort" of Tudor and Stuart society could project their own anxieties and desires about social mobility and change. In the following, I want to explore how the cony-catching texts participated in the discursive construction of a distinctly urban culture whose new civic ideals of propriety and domestic order fixated on the dislocated figure of the rogue as urban counterfeit, a figure of radical alterity to the humanist consciousness that sought to promote its culture through the hyperstylization of social tropes. The cony-catching pamphlets, I will argue, can be read as domestic handbooks that offer not only clues to detect the subtle crafts of dissembling crews of able-bodied hoodlums, but also primers tendering modes of social interaction crucial for the early modern subject's negotiation of London's public spaces.

Popular Literacy and Corporate Hegemony

As a familiar figure in the city handbooks of early modern London, the rogue played a crucial role in the formation of corporate hegemony. Specifically, these pamphlets promoted an image of otherness that was on the surface inimical to the legal and economic practices of a new group of merchants and shareholders whose cultural affinities had yet to develop into a coherent form of class solidarity. At the same time, however, this image of outcast criminals who shared intense fraternal bonds with freedom from legal strictures provided a powerful fantasy for a group of businessmen and merchants whose own economic practices of investment and foreign trade maintained an ambivalent position in relation to the established medieval traditions of domestic production.

To this degree the representations of criminality reproduced in these pamphlets helped realign social relations from a feudal, domestic model of production to a corporate one by hailing a type of subject that would come to identify with emerging modes of civic conduct associated with legal and economic management new to urban capitalism. The rogue literature played upon the anxieties of this heterogeneous audience. The title page to Robert Greene's *A Notable Discovery,* which would have been used as an advertisement in book stalls, hails "Gentlemen, Citizens, Apprentices, Country Farmers and yeoman." Typical of the rogue pamphlets, such a list imagines a kind of popular literacy, one that searches for a language of address that will allow loosely aligned readers to share common cause; citizens with apprentices, landowning farmers with yeomen, and, interestingly, guildsmen with the emerging gentleman merchants, whose growing wealth and prestige throughout this period did not always sit well with the various craftsmen whose traditional sense of corporate affinity was strained by the emergent autonomy of mercantile trading companies.[9] The ideological function of the burgeoning print culture in urban London during this time was to ameliorate these economic and social divisions. It is in this specific context that we can understand Judges's initial observation that the cultural work of the cony-catching pamphlets was to provide a kind of looking glass through which these readers could imagine their relations in opposition to an underground (the "other" world of London's urban space) that is cast in specifically nostalgic terms, an image of a well-governed, underground guild system, "everyman in his place," each criminal trade and mode of pilfering and looting its own unique craft. The ideological function of such an image was to rationalize the changing economic shifts in early modern London in distinctly archaic terms.

The cony-catching pamphlets must be situated next to those other literatures that helped promote a distinctly mercantile cultural ideal. According to Laura Stevenson, the common idealization of prosperity found in many of the books like Thomas Deloney's novel *Jack of Newbury* (1597) played a predictable role in shaping an incipient ideology of commercial success. "By creating and perpetuating tales of London's most prestigious citizens, the popular authors could attract audiences by expressing in exaggerated fashion the small man's hopes of becoming so rich he would never have to face want again, or by assuring the moderately prosperous man that money, properly spent, was a symbol of patriotism, charity and civic pride, not just hard-earned personal success" (30–31). The "paradox" in such praise, of course, is that the phenomenal wealth gained by merchants during this time contradicted the craft system at its core: "men who did well in trade tended to take power in both the guilds and towns away from men who manufactured goods" (37). Such a contradiction found its ideological resolution in many of the civic practices involved in promoting a cohesive urban ideal. For the emerging modern metropolis, this crisis could be resolved through the objectification of a far greater enemy to social order: the vagrant, the sign of the able-bodied poor, whose transient lifestyle was more than a symbol of the breakdown of manorial production. The idea of an underworld rogue helped solidify a consensus among readers who were starting to feel what might be called the weight of historical transition. The idea of the rogue inspired images of a radically conspiratorial network of ne'er-do-wells who rebound from plight and prosper in the social margins through covert forms of organized labor. To this degree the rootless vagabond as represented in the cony-catching manuals appears as a semiotic antinomy central to the lived realities of modernity itself, for the urban bourgeoisie can only come to imagine itself in opposition to and in affinity with the displaced laborers who are to become its ticket to economic independence and its political nemesis.

The rogue pamphlets are just a small part of London's popular print industry that tailored its wares to "both the wealthier merchant and craft families of London and the gentry, nobility, and their retainers who frequented the court and capital" (Wiltenberg 30). When historicizing the early modern print culture we should not shy away from situating it in the broadest of terms, as an industry bound up with the complex global transformations that made London the center of trade, shifts in economic and national-political interests that, for Richard Halpern, mark a chronological "dislocation" in the development of capitalism: "the dispossession of the feudal petty producing class was in no sense a planned preparation for capitalist manufacture. On the contrary," he explains, "the lack of employment for the dispossessed classes in the sixteenth century and early seventeenth centuries was one of the factors that made primitive accumulation [of wealth for future investment] an explicit social crisis" (68). This crisis was to express itself in the laws and social policies that meant to secure order by fixing an imaginary place for the new class of jobless poor.

The image of a "sturdy beggar"—the migrant unemployed marked as able-bodied or *potentially productive*—takes on the full symbolic weight of this crisis for London's literate classes. "The masterless man represented mutability," Beier claims, "when those in power longed for stability" (8). The idea of order and stability promoted in church and court during this time is not merely a product of the dominant ideology that sought to legitimate feudal relations, as the new historicist readings of monarchical power have emphasized. As Max Weber reminds us, the obsession for "order" longed for by the merchants during this time belongs to a political project not entirely commensurate with feudal ideology. The push toward a juridical order is meant to anchor the ebb and flow of exchange into a predictable set of permanent laws and actually contradicts an absolutist legal system that divvies out privileges based on shifting alliances or contested lineages. Weber characterizes this idea of stability as a kind of early modern cyborg, a Talus of the Royal Exchange, or in his words, "an automatic statute-dispensing machine." Capitalism requires "a system of justice and . . . administration whose workings can be *rationally calculated* . . . according to general fixed laws" that are "on the whole predictable" (Lukács 96). Without such stability, investment would simply not be profitable. "Modern businesses with their fixed capital and their exact calculations are much too sensitive to legal and administrative irrationalities" (Lukács 96). The Talus of Tudor hegemony would fixate on the vagabond as the dislocated agent of social decay.

Stability found its binary opposite in those migrant vagabonds who were described by William Harrison in his *Description of England* as "the caterpillars in the commonwealth" who "lick the sweat from the true laborers brows" and "stray and wander about, as creatures abhorring all labor and every honest exercise" (183). The phrase "caterpillar of the commonwealth" has a long history as an excoriation used in the popular "complaint literature" of the time, where honest tenant farmers lament enclosure practices as a threat to their livelihood. Interestingly, for Harrison it is no longer the landlord or sheep farmer who is the enemy, but vagabonds, many of them the victims of such enclosures. The discursive shift points to an appropriation of the moral high ground of the antienclosure complaint literatures; but is also accurately marks the successful redefinition of property itself. As Andrew McRae has observed, the enclosure policies of this period "privilege[d] individual interests over communal relations, and thus facilitate[d] the gradual formulation of a modern conception of property, as a right 'to exclude others from some use or benefit of something'" (42). Now it is the vagabond who is the transgressor, not the farmers who use land for producing wool. A parasite on true labor, the vagabond is now a sloth whose rootless and unpredictable migrant lifestyle is anathema to this new notion of property, a manifestation of a morally corrupt or debauched corporal body, "the quintessential 'other' of English society," Halpern declares, "a precocious and nightmaringly exaggerated image of *modernity*. . . . For whereas late feudal ideology tended to bind the poor to a corporative social and religious body, early modern ideology worked to expel them as alien and threatening" (74). No longer the sacred symbol of mendicant iconography or the idealized reapers of a once-harmonic pastoral vision, the image of the vagabond—or worse, the skeptical rogue—ruptured the coherence of the nostalgic discourse of community and commonwealth that underscored the Tudor social contract.[10]

Able-Bodied Poor and Social Decay

The cony-catching pamphlets used stereotypes of sloth and indolence to incite anger in their readers about the transient poor. In so doing they worked to provide ideological reinforcement to the legal reforms that attempted to deal with the effects of severe social and economic shifts at root in the dislocation of manorial production: rapid industrial expansion, dispossession of tenant farms, debasement of currency, periods of uncontrolled inflation, a doubling of population, all this during a time of "heavy government expenditures for defense, exploration, and an expansionist economy" (Kinney 22). By 1620 London saw an average of fifteen hundred illegal vagrants a year, who resided in the alehouses and lodging houses of the nebulous space of London's suburbs. "There was something like a state of war between the City authorities and the suburban vagrant," Beier explains. The vagrant "came into the center [of the city] where a bevy of officials caught him, sent him to Bridewell hospital for chastisement, and then back outside the walls. Lacking any tight controls over these areas, however, they could not solve the problem, for what was to prevent the vagabond from returning again and again?" (43).

The Tudor Poor Laws attempted to deal with the problem of migration with a strange mixture of draconian coercion and medieval *caritas*. "To put it crudely," John Twyning explains, "unemployment became a crime because the authorities had no way to deal with . . . the 'dispossessed' other than by demarcating them from the rest of society through branding and whipping, eradicating them altogether by hanging, or by sending them back to where they had been evicted or disenfranchised" (121). All towns and counties were forced to adopt a poor tax and to construct "stocks of working materials and houses of correction . . . 'to the intent,' Elizabeth's 1572 Act reads, 'that such as be already grown up in idleness . . . may not have any excuse in saying they cannot get any service or work'" (Judges xxx). Queen Elizabeth's edict declares that upon conviction, rogues and vagabonds are "to bee grevouslye whipped, and burnte through the gristle of the right Eare with a hot iron of the compasse of an Inch" (Ribton-Turner 106). Second offenders were made to work as servants for two years; those caught a third time were punished as felons without benefit of clergy. These acts of state torture were designed to make the crime of idleness legible on the body, to mark a common or public flesh with the indelible signature of the monarch's will. The demarcation of the sturdy beggar's flesh was a small part of the ceremony of public punishment that the Tudor regime utilized to maintain an organized spectacle of punitive practices. "Whippes . . . shall be made, ordayned, or appoynted for the punishment of such idle persons," reads the mandate of a chief officer of a prison during this time:

> roags, vacabonds, or sturdie beggars, or such like people, as for theire idlenes, wantones, and lewde demenour, shal be sente thether, shal be made with two cordes without knotts; and the partiie that shall receyve this punishment shall have his or theire clothes turned of theire shoulders to the beare skin downe to the waste, and then have that correction by the whipp as before set downe and appointed for them. (Ribton-Turner 117)

Whipping, the stocks, clogs, shackles, public executions, all were meant to treat the crime of idleness as a corporeal transgression.[11] Whipping was thus more than a public show of judicial might: it symbolically linked in the cultural imaginary the idea of sloth to a carnal contagion. Sturdy beggars were meant to wear the social meaning of their transgression etched in their flesh, the scars a grisly livery of their indolence.

A long list of classes are punishable under this act of Parliament (14 Eliz. c. 5): "procurators . . . using subtyll craftye or unlawfull Games or Playes . . . [or] fayninge themselves to have knowledge in Pisnomye [physiognomy]

Palmestry or other abused sciences . . . all Fencer Bearewardes Common Players in Enterludes and Minstrels . . . all Jugglers Pedlars [and] Tynkers" (Kinney 13). This law is infamous because in the same stroke it equates the emerging professional theater with criminality, while licensing those players
"belonging to any Baron . . . or honorable Personage of Greater Degree"
(Kinney 13). The "aged and impotent poore people" were declared vagabonds
proper, and given a license to beg. It is precisely the motley group of people
that fall outside the "legal poor" that the cony-catching pamphlets attempt to
classify with an almost encyclopedic zeal.

Belonging to a long line of legal attempts by the Tudor state to deal with the
problem of mass unemployment, this law reveals the curious paranoid concern
for fraud that is fomented in the cony-catching pamphlets into a cultural obsession if not a national frenzy. In the works of Awdeley's *The Fraternity of
Vagabonds* and Harman's *A Caveat or Warening for Common Cursetors Vulgarely
Called Vagabones* the catalog is expanded so that the migrant unemployed belong
to hidden guilds that specialize in exotic forms of plundering—bawdy baskets,
cutpurses, foists, knaves, doxies, and morts—all organized into a clandestine
fraternity with its own covert canting called "Peddlars' French."[12] The cozeners
(or frauds), Robert Greene tells us in *A Notable Discovery*, practice the "black
arts"—"most loathsome and detestable sins"—and threaten to "overthrow [the]
honest and wealthy citizen" and grow to such "a dangerous enormity," that they
"discredit . . . the estate of England" (Judges 121). He calls for the court justices
to cure the corporal infection of idleness, to "weed . . . out such worms as eat
away the sap of the tree, and root [out] . . . this base degree of cozeners of so
peaceable and prosperous a country" (Judges 121). The nationalism that develops out of these descriptions does not attempt to mystify how its concern for
country is at one and the same time a concern for good husbandry.

Rogue Manual as Domestic Handbook

The early modern criminologist records the rogue's hidden practices by
inscribing their derelict and mischievous activities as a dangerous excess of
liberty. Like the domestic handbooks of the period, these pamphlets call for a
more austere form of civic management in response to what appears to be a
spontaneous generation of social decay that encroaches upon the public space
of the commonwealth.[13] Thomas Harman's *Caveat* can be read as a special
warning to London's property owners about the upcoming onslaught of
migrant homeless. Harman has been read for years as a magistrate for Kent,
though his actual biography is only now being reexamined (see Beier's essay

in this volume); it is commonly noted that Harman drew upon his own personal experiences with litigants to survey the moving populations of rogues that traveled these roads into London. His eye for detail is indeed exceptional, and his descriptions of the day-to-day affairs of this mobile underworld is notoriously extolled by Judges and others as having the "deftness of the trained sociologist" (495). At each turn in Harman's text there is the invasion of established boundaries: "hookers" are pilfering clothes off hedges, rogues mill about the roads, "priggers" steal horses from stables, "abrammen" feign madness in hospitals, "counter-feit cranks" stage their epileptic seizures in the Inns of Court, young "doxies" with "spoiled maidenhead . . . indifferent" to "any who will use" them stand at the gates of a "noblemen's place . . . lurking on the back-side about back-houses . . . in hedgerows, or some other thicket, expecting their prey, . . . the uncomely company of some corteous guest" (Judges 106). The victims of displacement are made its perpetrators.

The cony-catching pamphlets can be read as domestic handbooks enacted on a grander scale, defining the domestic "commonwealth" scene of good governance, where being "master of mine own" meant reading the subtle signs of deception that veil the true commotions of daily life: out-of-work spinsters begging in the street? Or homeless doxies preying on their noblemen's courtesies? The crisis of permeable social boundaries is evinced in those descriptions of sexual bonding that center around the "uprightman," a kind of able-bodied rogue whose youth and strength allow him to maintain the underworld pecking order, a man "of great authority. . . . For all sorts of beggars are obedient to his jests" (Judges 72). The uprightman is the equivalent of the paternal master whose rule over his subjects is recorded in ways that reproduce interestingly the paternal ideology that is central to the civic project of order. "These upright men," Harman explains, "stand so much upon their reputation, as they will in no case have their women walk with them, but separate themselves for a time, a month or more, and meet at fairs, or great markets, where they meet to pilfer and steal from stalls, shops, or booths . . . lie and linger in highways, by-lanes [where] company passeth still to and fro" (Judges 70). The spontaneity of these encounters is described in a way that titillates as much as it admonishes. Once received by those illegitimate alehouses that have special rooms for them, they

> shall be conveyed either into some lost out of the way, or other secret corner not common to any other. And thither repair at accustomed times their harlots, which they term morts and doxies. . . . At these foresaid pelting

peevish places and unmannerly meetings, oh, how the pots walk about! Their talking tongues talk at large. They boll and bouse one to another, and for the time bousing belly-cheer. And after their roisting recreation, if there be not room enough in the house, they have clean straw in some barn or backhouse near adjoining, where they couch comely together, and it were dog and bitch. And he that is hardest may have his choice, unless for a little good manner. Some will take their own they have made promise unto, until they be out of sight, and then, according to the old adage, out of mind. (70)

The organization of paternal authority is here defamiliarized as a mere show of strength with no particular fealty or honor to the spouse. Matches are arbitrary, fleeting, subject to chance encounters. The representation of the illicit bonding rituals of rogues is mediated in Harman's passage by the standard cultural tropes of moralism, whose most interesting poetic technique is to frame descriptions of lubricious and corrupt practices in a catalog of cumbersome alliterative clauses that have the effect of running away from the narrator and shrouding the actual immoral "referent" as an absence that exists in a kind of resplendent ambiguity.[14] The effect of this cadence of indignation— "pelting peevish places," "roisting recreation," "bousing belly-cheer"—is to structure the representation of sinful acts within a libidinal grammar that links the imaginary moment of covert sexual encounter in the underworld to the act of an unpardonable sin. The incendiary moral fervor renounces such abominable acts at the same time it conjures them as an absence of the text, allowing readers to delight at the sustained list of loathsome activities all tied together in syllabic bursts as a deferral of the witnessed act itself.

It is not surprising that Harman obsesses over the pairings that erupt between vagabonds in covert places. The paternal gaze in these instances encodes public space as a set of permeable moments of makeshift rendezvous too easily manipulated by the migrant rogue. Harman entices his readers by suggesting that one's own backyard is prone to the intrusion of carnal excess. A burial of one beggar, he notes, inspires the townsfolk of Kent to prepare a large barn for the inordinate numbers of "beggars, and poor householders dwelling thereabouts" that would otherwise "lie or stand about the house" (64). But the story of empathy soon turns to yet another recognizable parable of licentiousness:

The other wayfaring bold beggars remained all night in the barn; and the same barn being searched with light in the night by this old man . . . with the others, they told seven score persons of men, every of them having his woman, except it were two women that lay alone together for some especial cause. Thus having their makes to make merry withal, the burial turned to bousing and belly-cheer, mourning to mirth, fasting to feasting, prayer to pastime and pressing of paps, and lamenting to lechery. (Judges 64)

This encounter is interesting because it plays out the primal fear around which the paternal gaze of these texts is structured: not only in the sense that it seems to trip upon the idea that some of these women do not necessarily answer to their upward men, "for some especial cause" (this could just as easily denote the culturally accepted practice of same-sex sleeping partners), but also in the suspicion that the underworld rogue is incapable of remorse. The moment of sorrow is instantly changed into an unstable moment of carnival (a cloaked wake?), suggesting that these sturdy subjects are impervious to the ideological work of penitence and grace, and thus potentially impervious to interpellation by the church.[15]

When turning this paternal gaze to urban space, the idea of good husbandry takes on its other associative meanings: managing one's estate with thrift in that nebulous space of exchange and trade. If for Harman the social order is threatened by the possibility of sexual transgression in the henhouse, for the city merchant the underlying crisis is one of internal economic control: Whom do the dice cheats and cardsharps of London threaten, exactly? Greene is quite clear: "The poor 'prentice, whose honest mind aimeth only at his master's profits, by these pestilent vipers of the commonwealth is smoothily enticed . . . and robbed of his master's money" (Judges 121). Passages like this could be read to suggest that the early modern discourse of criminality helped configure a semiological infrastructure necessary for the historical emergence of a new corporate sensibility, whose own ascetic workaday world of trade and investment finds its opposite in a domestic national enemy whose licentious practices and wayward life, "fraternal" bonds and veiled intimacies, violate the legitimacy of property. This is the native other of London's corporate society: a loose coalition of merchants, craftsmen, and shareholders who may, between the lines of their "otherizing" gestures, recognize something of themselves in these images of a society of men that survives through unspoken covenants, coordinated systems of illicit trafficking, and a professional dialect. The narrator of Thomas Dekker's famous cony-catching rag, *The Bellman of London* (1608), spies on a fraternal ceremony where one young apprentice is "stalled" in the underground order of thieves. Dekker's description is ambiguous. Does he despise these rogues for their moral turpitude? Or does he identify with their communal spirit? As he watches the "the idle drones of a country, the caterpillars of the commonwealth, the Egyptian lice of a kingdom," the ethnocentric drive to otherize the migrant poor as "counterfeit gypsies" merges with a civic duty that cannot help but voice an unconscious affiliation with a group that luxuriates in a manor hall for a feast and whose members bathe in their own "hospitable familiarity"—"a people," Dekker tells us, "for whom the world cares not, neither care they for the world. They are all freemen. . . . They are neither old serving-men that have been courtiers . . . nor young gallants . . . nor hungry scholars, neither are they decayed poets, nor players. . . . No, no, this is a ging [*sic*] of good fellows in whom there is more brotherhood" (Judges 307).

Rogue Skepticism and Its Political Unconscious

Though it is true these representations of the underworld fraternities reveal a residual sense of order, particularly the master-apprentice nature of this underworld, they nonetheless depict a London that is beset by competitive social relations. The idea of tricking others out of money to support one's livelihood becomes a metaphor to rethink the authenticity of older forms of social status. One of the con men in Gilbert Walker's *A Manifest Detection of Dice-Play* defends his craft by telling his apprentice that everyday life of feudal decorum and propriety is a sham:

> Though your experience in the world be not so great as mine, yet am I sure we see that no man is able to live an honest man unless he have some privy way to help himself withal, more than the world is witness of. Think you the nobleman could do as they do, if in this hard world they should maintain so great a port only upon their rent? Think you the lawyers could be such purchasers if their pleas were short, and all their judgment, justice and conscience? Suppose ye that offices would be so dearly bought, and the buyers so enriched, if they counted not pillage an honest point of purchase? Could merchants, without lies, false making their wares, and selling them by a crooked light, to deceive the chapman in the thread or colour, grow so soon rich and to a baron's possessions, and make all their posterity gentlemen? (Judges 38)

Walker's con man is seditious, yet his skepticism about aristocratic status and the legal institutions that secure that status is empowered by a crass acknowledgment of the fact that wealth is the ballast of privilege. In passages like these, then, we get a glimpse of the political unconscious of the underworld narratives, an anxious expression about the dissolution of the social order.[16]

The ideology of such passages reveals the double logic of the discourse of criminality, in which an emerging dissident perspective is given free rein to demystify the legal apparatus that legitimates demesne production and mercantile exchange as a set of sinister practices, only to expose the devilish curse of such Machiavellian realism as the origin of social decay itself. Through the articulation of this curse a loose coalition of administrative and professional vocations is conjured into being: those tied to the gentrified trades of the labor-rent and mercantile systems can share community through the objectification of criminal "cheats" such as this one. The dissolution of social degree whereby merchants "grow so soon rich and to a baron's possessions" is displaced onto an incorrigible urban other: the criminal whose exiled society of canting cronies oddly resembles the insider discourse of the elite group of shareholders in the burgeoning trading practices central to the colonial enterprise. If the social order is under siege, it is because the very system of exchange that composes the "money relation" of modern capitalism is insinuating itself into the cultural psyche (aren't offices bought to pillage others? don't lawyers overcharge? don't merchants buy low and sell high?), a social arrangement that another London rogue would describe as "an objective system of production that sweeps away the train of ancient venerable prejudices" until "man is at last compelled to face with sober senses, his real conditions of life, and his relations with his kind" (Marx 83). One cannot avoid such a revelation, our underworld others tell us. To "help yourself," Walker's con man explains, by following the legitimate paths of work and toil, by "following your nose, as they say, always straight forward, [one] may well hold up the head for a year or two, but the third [one] must needs sink and gather the wind into beggars haven" (Judges 38). In these descriptions of a ruthless world of sturdy beggars and vagabond cheats Judges's Everyman is transformed into every man for himself.

Obsessed with all forms of villainy, the most heinous of crimes for the pamphleteer is not that of cheating the "cony"—the hapless victim—out of his money through some elaborate swindle, but the practice of duplicity itself, of counterfeiting friendship.[17] This, the very definition of "rogue," is a far more treacherous practice because the ingenuity lies in tailoring the mode of cheating to the specific whims and fancies of the intended gull. It is the "first travail" of the "taker-up" (the person who persuades us to join his company) "to seek by all means they can to understand [the cony's] nature, and whereunto he is inclined" (Judges 45). The real crime here is the manipulation of one's desires as objects of a purposeful and rational target of exploitation. The taker-up, Walker explains, is a skillful man in all things, who hath by long travail conned, without the book, a hundred reasons to insinuate himself into a man's acquaintance. Talk of matters of law: and he hath plenty of cases at his finger's ends that he hath seen tried and ruled in every King's courts. Speak of grazing and husbandry: no man knoweth more shires than he; no man knoweth better when to raise a gain, and how the abuses and overture of prices might be redressed. Finally, enter into what discourse of things they list . . . it shall escape him hard, but that ere your talk break off, he will be your country-man at least, and per adventure, either of kin, or ally, or some sole sib unto you. (Judges 47)

The taker-up is a broker in identity, dealing in the bastard trade of predicting human behavior through the subtle calculations of demographic and professional affiliation. In fact, the highly ritualized and orchestrated con games—elaborately described and categorized complete, from Harman's *Caveat* onward, with a dictionary of the secret canting language—rely on the idea that the targeted victim will be willing in some way to learn the art of the trick and play it on some other unsuspecting person.

In one of the more famous card tricks—called "the Barnard's law"—described again and again in these manuals, the "cony" is "caught" when he agrees to help swindle someone else. The unsuspecting citizen is first confronted by a spy—a person who merely seeks information about the town or region the cony is from. This information is then given to the taker-up or "verser," who as his name implies can parrot different regional accents and pretend to be from the same county. "See, Gentlemen," Robert Greene tells us in his *Notable Discovery of Cozenage*, "what great logicians these cony-catchers be, that have such rhetorical persuasions to induce the poor countryman to his confusion" (Judges 126). It is the rhetorical skill of the verser who gets the cony to come to a local tavern. "I pray you," he explains, " 'dwell you not in Derbeyshire [or] in [some]such a village? . . . I am going out of town and must send a letter to the parson of your parish. You shall not refuse to do a stranger such a favour as to carry it [to] him'. . . . 'Sir' (replies the cony) 'I'll do so much for you with all my heart.' " Once there, they are confronted by the "setter," who encourages both of them to play a friendly game of "cut the deck" to buy the next round of drinks. The verser teaches the cony a simple trick to cheat at the cut while the setter is away from the table, and what follows is a predictable story where the cony slowly becomes confident in the reliability of the trick, while the verser and cony slowly win more and more money from the setter—who himself is only pretending to be a victim—until eventually the cony is betting his entire purse. The success of the entire trick—like many of the exposed confidence games—depends on the culpability of the cony, on his "having [a] covetous mind," Greene explains. (In the "cross-biting law" trick—another story told often in these pamphlets—the cony is seduced by a prostitute, who either steals his money while he sleeps or is confronted by someone playing a corrupt constable who then exacts a bribe from a cony willing to do anything to keep out of the clink.) The entire scam relies on the interest of the cony in doing to others what is, ironically, being done to him, as it were.

It is easy to read the ideological impulse behind cony-catching stories like this one as an attempt to rationalize crime as an aberration of the more authentic ideals of reciprocity and fraternity—to seize upon the zeal of the readers' sense of community and realize for them an other who can be identified as a hidden cause of social discord: the fraudulent rogue who uses the guildlike skills of maintaining a clandestine craft through a secret language of artifice to take advantage of others (who wish, in turn, to *know more about taking advantage of others*). In this way, the cony-catching stories can be interpreted as simple morality tales, since they not only displace the cause of crime and social discord onto a reprobate Other, "mere atheists," as Greene calls them, "flat dissemblers," but write the story of legal transgression within the familiar narrative of avarice and cupidity, wherein the innocent cony who wishes to play with the devil "gets his due" and confirms for the reader a deeper sense of moral equity in the turns of the world.

Though it is true these pamphlets share in the general ideology produced in complaint literature, emphasizing this may be to miss the development of an ironic double-sidedness that emerges in the rogue literature as it moves away from the ethical dimension of Copland's *Highway to the Spital-house* (often written of in anthologies as a kind of origin to the genre) and into the early modern city, where it finds an audience alive to a different social register concerning the ambiguity over the performative nature of status. In the context of the city, the cony-catching pamphlet is doing a different kind of psychological work since it is not only healing the imaginary wounds caused by the disintegration of the old world ideals of degree and place, but hailing a reader who is already "caught," as it were, as someone interested in the activity of social pretension and self-fashioning. While commonplacing the stories of fraud from within a traditional interpretive context as stories of moral lapse, the reader is at the same time being pulled in the direction to see underworld knowledge as having a practical use-value of a different kind. In this sense, the cony-catching pamphlet can be read as a handbook for the urban pedestrian, a rhetorical primer into the ways of social miming at St. Paul's Church or in the alleys and market stalls, as offering not just clues to defend against the versers and setters, but perhaps a commodified guide to one-up the rogue at his own game.

It is this playful ambivalence that is foregrounded occasionally, less as a textual instability and more as a tongue-in-cheek incidental reference that enters the text to flag the reader's attention to the possible use-values inherent in the text. We hear behind the injunctions of the rogue in Gilbert Walker's *Manifest Detection of Dice-Play,* for example, a nervousness about the possible uses of the secrets he imparts to the urban reader:

> Alas! this is but a warning, and, as it were, the shaking of a rod to a young boy to scare him from places of peril. All that I have told you yet, or that I have minded to tell you, 'greeth not to the purpose to make you skillful in cheaters' occupation. For as soon would I teach you the next way to Tyburn as to learn you the practice of it! Only my meaning is to make you see as far into it as should a cobbler into a tanner's faculty; to know whether his leather be well liquored, and well and workmanly dressed or not. And, like as I would not wish a cobbler a currier, let two sundry occupations running together into one, might, perhaps, make a lewd London medley in our shoes, the one using falsehood in working, the other facing and lying in uttering; so seek I to avoid, that ye should not both be a courtier, in whom a little honest, moderate play is tolerable, and, withal, a cheater, that with all honesty hath made an undefensible dormant defiance. (Judges 42)

Walker's analogy runs away from him, here making the use-value of his cony-catching devices like the knowledge of tanning the cobbler must have in order to buy good leather for his shoes—a knowledge inherent in his work and trade. But Walker immediately sees the problem with his analogy, since the guilds work so closely and are so categorically similar that he eventually intuits that the knowledge he imparts could potentially lead to a "lewd London medley" where the tanners and the cobblers—with benefit of the knowledge of how to dress something up better than it appears, to make it look "well liquored, and well and workmanly dressed"—blur into one, the cheaters and cheated all mix into one assembly of deceivers. He rebounds by relying on the reader's ability to note the difference between the courtiers and cheaters of the world, but by now his readers have been made aware of the special knowledge the cony-catching pamphlets have to offer as documents to aid in the consuming and selling of wares. The market is figured here as the reason to maintain a sense of moral conduct but also the very reason authenticity and social distinction are so perfectly difficult to solidify.

"Honest, Moderate Play": Rogue as Parody of Humanism

The distress over false seeming reproduced here and throughout many of these pamphlets is a renunciation of counterfeit modes of behavior, but they are also expressing a displaced apprehension over the alienating effects of a science that commodifies identity in order to divine one's inner motivations. "Rhetorical wherewithal—the ability to manipulate with logic and eloquence," Reynolds observes, "was crucial to the perpetration of many cons; it was necessary to influence the victim's minds" (121). This science of "dissemblance," I would argue, is a ghoulish parody of humanism's rhetorical emphasis on the grammar of self-advancement, the instrumentalization of the linguistic codes needed to fashion a niche in the affairs of state by construing the "mind" of one's addressee. The taker-up can parrot any vocational or familial discourse—lawyer, farmer, neighbor—all are vulnerable to the mimetic pretensions of this urban doppelgänger who could have learned his black arts from any number of rhetorical primers. One finds in the popular courtesy literature of the day a similar push to predict the inner proclivities of one's audience in their vocations. Richard Halpern has argued that the sixteenth-century humanist project should be situated in the larger historical context of the emergent bourgeoisie's struggle for control of the economic and legal institutions necessary for the accumulation of political power. By modeling a "mimetic" form of learning, the humanist courtesy book "helped articulate a new class culture within nascent bounds of 'civil society.' This it did by imparting behavioral discipline, encouraging the stylistic assimilation of cultural authority, and distributing individual differences within a regularized system" (45).

One gets a sense of this "regularized system" in John Hoskyns's description in his famous *Directions for Speech and Style* (1599) of how to avoid language that is too "far-fetched" or "base" in the Inns of Court. One should, Hoskyns explains, "delight generally [by] tak[ing] those terms from ingenious and several professions; from ingenious arts to please the learned, and from several arts to please the learned of all sorts . . . from the better part of husbandry, from the politic government of cities, from navigation, from military profession, from physic; but not out of the depth of these mysteries" (McDonald 208). Or consider Count Annibale Romei's *The Couriers Academie* (translated in 1598):

> To be acceptable in companie, we must put of as it were our own fashions
> and manners, and cloathe our selves with conditions of others, and imitate

them so farre as reason will permit . . . touching the diversitie of the persons with whom wee shall be conversaunt, wee must alter our selves into an other. (Whigham 44)

Ironically, the otherness of underworld villainy gives voice to the anxieties of a social disruption brought about by the very practices that empowered London's new corporate class: self-advancement through histrionic manipulation of the social and linguistic registers of court and state. Frank Whigham examines in his *Ambition and Privilege: The Social Tropes of Elizabethan Courtesy Theory* how the courtesy books printed during this period radically reconfigured the epistemological grounds that defined the traditional meaning of social status, where any "real" or "true" notion of aristocratic behavior became subjected to a version of existential bracketing. "The gentleman," Whigham explains, "is presumed to act in certain ways; the limiting case would have it that only a gentleman *can* act in those ways" (33). This presumption required that one hide or mask one's ability to mime, since the "the symbolic referent here is ascriptive identity that by definition cannot be achieved by human effort." Whigham continues:

As a result there arose a basic governing principle of the display of *effortlessness*, Castiglione's *sprezzatura*, designed to imply the natural or given status of one's social identity and to deny any earned character, any labor or arrival from a social elsewhere. In this group we may discern . . . the rise to rhetorical consciousness of the reification of the subject, insofar as such behavior involved the "the effacement of the trace of production on the [subject]." The "natural" self is here recognized, perhaps for the first time, as a product, and soon, with the aid of courtesy books, becomes a commodity. (33)

In the cony-catching pamphlets the hidden mode of self-production is laid bare: the taker-up represents the alterity of a rhetorical consciousness that seeks to promote itself through the hyperstylization of social tropes. In the court, such linguistic theater was evidence of having possession of the natural accoutrements of an educated, self-fashioned gentleman; in the street it was evidence of being in league with the enemy. And we must not forget that on the stage of history (or on the scaffold depending on one's relative position in this story) the true crime of the vagabond was to remind everyone of the ephemeral nature of the social order, his presence an unpleasant symbol to those newly "stalled" men in the legitimate corridors of power that their own identity was also a sham.

The implicit message to the reader in many of these tales of cozenage is to guard one's self from the urban stranger. Only then is the taker-up powerless to fake friendship and the rogue shut out from citizenship. This, ultimately, is the moral of these stories. "Let not vain and by-occasions take you off," Henry Peacham advises us in his *Art of Living in London,* from "your chiefist care" when coming to the city, "as going to taverns, seeing plays, and now and then to worse places." He continues:

> [W]alking abroad, take heed with what company you sort withal. If you are a countryman and but newly come to town, you will be smelt out by some cheaters or other, who will salute, call you by name—which perhaps one of their company meeting you in another street hath learned by way of mis-taking you for another man, which is an old trick—carry you to a tavern, saying they are akin to someone dwelling near you, etc. (249)

The solution? "To avoid these, take a private chamber wherein you may pass your spare time in doing something or other . . . without going upon the score, especially in city alehouses, where in many places you shall be torn out of your skin" (248). It is a poignant image of a solitude predicated on moral rectitude, social defensiveness, a fear of the city mob. "You shall not do amiss if you send for your diet to your own chamber a hot joint of meat, of mutton, veal or the like," and in the same breath: "keep out of throngs and public places where multitudes of people are—for saving your purse" (249).

Peacham reveals the kind of identity that bourgeois culture conjures, whose "civic" duty to maintain order is at one and the same time a kind of dissociation from the very public it means to serve. Best take one's meals alone in private chambers. Detach oneself from others in public space—by hiding one's hometown, one's intentions, one's job, one's place of residence, ultimately, any form of past association or origin—so that the only clue to one's status is the material signifier of outward appearance. The contradiction that stirs at the heart of these texts that played such a crucial role in the discursive construction of modern urban space is that while they condemn the criminal underworld as a society of misbegotten vocations and outcast fraternities, they summon a world of anonymity, an austere vision of identity that is no less an act of masking one's real self and manipulating one's appearance. The self-retreat tacitly summoned in these oddly modern descriptions of urban space necessitated the objectification of the throng at St. Paul's Church and London's many market stalls and fueled the fires of far more satanic mills in London's ensuing years.

NOTES

Published in an earlier form with the title "Playing the 'Cony': Anonymity in Underworld Literature," *Genre* 30.1 (1997): 29–49, this essay appears here by permission of *Genre* and the University of Oklahoma.

1. Unless otherwise noted, my references to these pamphlets are to be found in Judges's edition.

2. For a description of the range and influence of the rogue character as literary trope, see Chandler's "The Type Defined" in *Literature of Roguery* 1–35.

3. Michel Foucault's ideas of disciplinary formations are given full elaboration in Messer-Davidow, Shumway, and Sylvan.

4. See Chandler, and Aydelotte 76–102.

5. See A. L. Beier's essay in this volume for an assessment of the empirical-historical work in this area. Also see Slack for a concise survey of recent research about welfare legislation in early modern England, including an appendix that lists relevant acts of Parliament during these years.

6. Althusser 164–65.

7. This essay provides a materialist examination of the dissident potential of these pamphlets, while Reynolds's book combines a thorough historiography with an aggressive use of poststructural theory. Using Félix Guattari and Gilles Deleuze's postulations about deviant personality structures, Reynolds investigates the social types and aberrant practices evident in the cony-catching pamphlets—the gypsy as antiestablishment figure, cant as dissident language, theater as nomadic space—with the aim of drawing larger theoretical claims about "transversal power." At times, Reynolds's own structurally diverse critical method (akin to the antiphilosophy espoused by its progenitors), which combines empirical historicism and psychologism with poststructuralist critique of discourse, reveals an affinity with the nomadic practices he charts. As a result, transversal power is described at times as a kind of self-generating process, the working of an inner psychological condition ("being" as potentially always already nomadic, as it were), while elsewhere Reynolds flatly refuses the ahistorical pretexts of such an equation. Is criminal culture internally motivated by its own "nomadism?" Or defined by institutions that give it explicit historical content? The answer can be as fluid as the cloaked characters Reynolds examines and applauds: "The fetishized criminal culture was not the antithesis of official culture and its Christianity," Reynolds explains. "On both personal and sociocultural levels, it is criminal culture's conceptual and material nomadism, best exemplified by its transient parasitism, promiscuity, and theatricality, that made it so transversal" (154).

8. Woodbridge argues: "I read these texts aiming mainly at entertainment, with a veneer of 'warning as a public service' either as a sop to respectability or as a part of the joke, since repressive seriousness can make a trickster tale even funnier" (91). But who, exactly, is being laughed at in these pamphlets? She argues that the poor are victimized through the jest, yet her own examples beg questions about who is the object of the shaming: "An old man's neighbors laugh heartily when he is held up by the highwayman. . . . After robbing a parson, two scoundrels force him to drink to their health" (49). Woodbridge's forceful argument sometimes calls into question the broader influence these pam-

phlets had as protest literature to effect social and political reforms. Importantly, in taking the risk of making these texts speak to our own histories she makes her textual politics serve the purpose of an unspoken humanism: Harman's "every syllable," she writes, "bespeaks an antivagrant agenda, unsettlingly prophetic of a modern American idiom of law and order, of getting tough with 'welfare bums'" (42). And: "rogue literature was a crucial intervention in society: the waning of the medieval ideal of the sanctity of poverty and the spiritual benefits of charity, while opening the door to more secular, government-oriented concepts of charity and poor relief, also spawned harsh attitudes toward the poor that were rampant during the early modern period *and are also widespread today*" (41; emphasis added).

9. For a more complete picture of this autonomy and its relation to the use of merchant monopolies see Unwin, *Gilds and Companies of London*. His *Industrial Organization in the Sixteenth and Seventeenth Centuries* examines how the various merchant guilds are brought together to share a loose association separate from the masters of London. The most succinct account of why the sixteenth century saw the disintegration of traditional guilds can be found in Stevenson. A more carefully detailed picture of the political consequences of the growing autonomy of the merchant companies that sought revenues from colonial enterprises can be found in Brenner. Brenner posits that in spite of the common cultural affinities shared among corporate classes during this time, the restless oppositions that grew between the "company merchants" and "City's domestic tradesman" became "an important underlying basis for the political and ideological struggles in London during the Civil War" (89).

10. See Koch.

11. Michel Foucault describes in *Discipline and Punish* the "juridico-political function" of public torture and execution during this period as a ceremony linked primarily to the spectacle of a threatened sovereign power, a practice "by which a momentarily injured sovereignty is reconstituted" (48). The "truth" of the king's power becomes manifest through the ritualistic display of absolute force, whose most potent "mechanism," Foucault explains, was making "the body of the condemned man the place where the vengeance of the sovereign was applied . . . [and] an opportunity of affirming the dyssymmetry of forces" (55). Not emphasized enough in Foucault's narrative, in my opinion, is the way such a ceremonial display actually invested the criminal's actions (in this case "idleness") with the power to threaten court and state. In other words, the public nature of such punishment did not merely extend and strengthen state power; it also constituted in and through the ceremony of torture the criminal's offense as a legitimate threat to sovereign rule.

12. See Reynolds 64–94.

13. Compare to Steve Mentz's "Magic Books: Cony-Catching and the Romance of Early Modern London" in this collection for another way to see these pamphlets as handbooks.

14. Harman's rhetoric is reproduced in Philip Stubbes's infamous *The Anatomie of Abuses* (1583). As in Harman, the stock list of roguish crimes—being idle, dissembling, lying, cheating, falsifying (even "flattering")—are associated with venery. Here Stubbes describes the "flocking and running" to playhouses

to see plays and interludes, where such wanton gestures, such bawdy speeches, such laughing and fleering, such kissing and bussing, such clipping and culling, such winking and glancing of wanton eyes, and the like is used, as is wonderful to behold. Then these goodly pageants being done, every mate sorts to his mate, every one brings another homeward of their way very friendly, and in their secret conclaves (covertly) they play the sodomites, or worse. And these be the fruits of plays and interludes, for the most part. And whereas, you say, there are good examples to be learned in them: truly there are, if you will learn falsehood; if you will learn cozenage; if you will learn to deceive; if you will learn to play the hypocrite, to cog, lie, and falsify; if you will learn to jest, laugh, and fleer, to grin, to nod and mow; if you will lean to play the Vice, to swear, tear, and blaspheme both heaven and earth; if you will learn to become a bawd, unclean, and to devirginate maids, to deflower honest wives; if you will learn to rebel against princes, to commit treasons, to consume treasures, to practice idleness, to sing and talk of bawdy love and venery; if you will learn to deride, scoff, mock and flout, to flatter and smooth . . . etc. (McDonald 340–41)

15. The idea of carnival, as examined in Mikhail Bakhtin's influential *Rabelais and His World*, is treated as a genuine model for interpreting "plebian" or "popular" culture in Bristol.

16. I am using Fredric Jameson's now famous formulation that literature can be seen to articulate unconsciously its role in the ongoing process of modernity; or, in his terms, "The task of cultural and social analysis . . . will be the rewriting of [literature's] materials in such a way that this perpetual cultural revolution can be apprehended and read as the deeper and more permanent constitutive structure in which the empirical textual objects know intelligibility" (97).

17. Martine van Elk's "The Counterfeit Vagrant: The Dynamic of Deviance in the Bridewell Court Records and the Literature of Roguery" in this collection makes the case for criminal category of dissembling—identified as a form of "social exchange . . . employed at every level as an open playing field"—as the target of Bridewell's many court hearings.

WORKS CITED

Althusser, Louis. *Lenin and Philosophy and Other Essays*. London: New Left Books, 1971.

Aydelotte, Frank. *Elizabethan Rogues and Vagabonds*. Oxford: Clarendon P, 1913.

Bakhtin, Mikhail. *Rabelais and His World*. Trans. Helene Iswolsky. Cambridge: MIT P, 1968.

Beier, A. L. *Masterless Men: The Vagrancy Problem in England, 1560–1640*. London: Methuen, 1985.

Brenner, Robert. *Merchants and Revolution: Commercial Change, Political Conflict, and London's Overseas Traders, 1550–1653*. Princeton: Princeton UP, 1993.

Bristol, Michael. *Carnival and Theater: Plebian Culture and the Structure of Authority in Renaissance England*. New York: Routledge, 1985.

Chandler, F. W. *Literature of Roguery*. Cambridge: Riverside P, 1907.

Foucault, Michel. *Discipline and Punish: The Birth of the Prison*. Trans. Alan Sheridan. New York: Pantheon, 1977.

Gladfelder, Hal. *Criminality and Narrative in Eighteenth-Century England: Beyond the Law*. Baltimore: Johns Hopkins UP, 2001.

Greenblatt, Stephen. *Shakespearian Negotiations: The Circulation of Social Energy in Renaissance England*. Berkeley: U of California P, 1992.

Halpern, Richard. *The Poetics of Primitive Accumulation: English Renaissance Culture and the Genealogy of Capital*. Ithaca: Cornell UP, 1991.

Harrison, William. *The Description of England*. 1587. Ed. Georges Edelen. New York: Dover, 1994.

Jameson, Fredric. *The Political Unconscious: Narrative as a Socially Symbolic Act*. Ithaca: Cornell UP, 1981.

Judges, A. V., ed. *The Elizabethan Underworld*. London: Routledge, 1930.

Koch, Mark. "The Desanctification of the Beggar in Rogue Pamphlets of the English Renaissance." *The Work of Dissimilitude: Essays from the Sixth Citadel Conference on Medieval and Renaissance Literature*. Ed. David Allen and Robert White. Newark: U of Delaware P, 1992.

Kelly, J. Thomas. *Thorns on the Tudor Rose: Monks, Rogues, Vagabonds, and Sturdy Beggars*. Jackson: UP of Mississippi, 1977.

Kinney, Arthur F. *Rogues, Vagabonds, and Sturdy Beggars*. Barre: Imprint Society, 1973.

Lukács, Georg. *History and Class Consciousness*. Trans. Rodney Livingstone. Cambridge: MIT P, 1971.

Marx, Karl. *The Communist Manifesto*. Trans. Samuel Moore. London: Penguin, 1985.

McDonald, Russ. *The Bedford Companion to Shakespeare: An Introduction to Documents*. Boston: St. Martin's, 1996.

McMullan, John L. *The Canting Crew: London's Criminal Underworld, 1550–1700*. New Brunswick: Rutgers UP, 1984.

McRae, Andrew. *God Speed the Plough: The Representation of Agrarian England, 1500–1600*. Cambridge: Cambridge UP, 1996.

Messer-Davidow, Ellen, David R. Shumway, and David J. Sylvan, eds. *Knowledges: Historical and Critical Studies in Disciplinarity*. Charlottesville: UP of Virginia, 1993.

Peacham, Henry. *The Complete Gentleman, The Truth of Our Times, and The Art of Living in London*. 1634; 1638; 1642. Ed. Virgil Heltzel. Ithaca: Cornell UP, 1962.

Reynolds, Byran. *Becoming Criminal: Transversal Performance and Cultural Dissidence in Early Modern England*. Baltimore: Johns Hopkins UP, 2002.

Ribton-Turner, Charles James. *A History of Vagrants, Vagrancy, and Beggars and Begging*. London: Chapman and Hall, 1887.

Rose, Lionel. *"Rogues and Vagabonds": Vagrant, Underworld in Britain, 1815–1985*. New York: Routledge, 1988.

Salgãdo, Gãmini. *The Elizabethan Underworld*. Totowa, N.J.: Rowman and Littlefield, 1977.

Slack, Paul. *The English Poor Law, 1531–1782*. Basingstoke: Macmillan Education, 1990.

Stevenson, Laura Caroline. *Praise and Paradox: Merchants and Craftsmen in Elizabethan Popular Literature*. Cambridge: Cambridge UP, 1984.

Twyning, John A. "The Literature of the Metropolis." *A Companion to English Literature and Culture*. Ed. Michael Hattaway. Oxford: Blackwell, 2000.

Unwin, George. *Industrial Organization in the Sixteenth and Seventeenth Centuries*. Oxford: Clarendon P, 1904.

———. *Guilds and Companies of London*. London: Frank Cass and Company, 1908.

Whigham, Frank. *Ambition and Privilege: The Social Tropes of Elizabethan Courtesy Theory*. Berkeley: U of California P, 1984.

Wiltenberg, Joy. *Disorderly Women and Female Power in the Street Literature of Early Modern England and Germany*. Charlottesville: UP of Virginia, 1992.

Woodbridge, Linda. *Vagrancy, Homelessness, and English Renaissance Literature*. Urbana: U of Illinois P, 2001.

BRYAN REYNOLDS AND JANNA SEGAL

The Reckoning of Moll Cutpurse

A Transversal Enterprise

Outside of Shakespeare's plays, Thomas Middleton and Thomas Dekker's *The Roaring Girl* has been among the most discussed of early modern English plays over the last twenty years. To those familiar with trends in both literary-cultural criticism and popular culture since 1980, the reason for this may seem fairly obvious. As a play about a powerful woman cross-dressed as a man, it was especially ripe for second-wave feminist literary-cultural criticism and as subject matter for the emergent field of gender studies. After the publicized advent of the AIDS epidemic in the early 1980s, attention to gay culture increased dramatically, quickly becoming commonplace discourse in all media, from the nightly news to cinema to academic research. However, the focus of this attention in scholarship was often, and increasingly so, not AIDS, but rather identity formation and the sociocultural politics and subject positioning that informed it. Phenomenological and formalist approaches waned in popularity as poststructuralism, particularly the move to simultaneously historicize, de-essentialize, and relativize cultural products (from literary texts to human subjectivities), became increasingly predominant. In effect, all meaning, in such forms as categorizations, determinations, and interpretations, was seen as ideologically constrained and specific to its social, cultural, and historical situation; the catchwords *discursive, network, representation, construction, appropriation, blurring, crossing, passing, mutability, undecidability,* and *indeterminacy* became common parlance in literary-cultural criticism.

The idea that social identity (sexual, gender, class, ethnic, racial) was not inherent and was imposed, composed, and/or had to be performed convincingly enough that one "passed" (that is, would be identified positively)

BRYAN REYNOLDS AND JANNA SEGAL

The Reckoning of Moll Cutpurse

A Transversal Enterprise

Outside of Shakespeare's plays, Thomas Middleton and Thomas Dekker's *The Roaring Girl* has been among the most discussed of early modern English plays over the last twenty years. To those familiar with trends in both literary-cultural criticism and popular culture since 1980, the reason for this may seem fairly obvious. As a play about a powerful woman cross-dressed as a man, it was especially ripe for second-wave feminist literary-cultural criticism and as subject matter for the emergent field of gender studies. After the publicized advent of the AIDS epidemic in the early 1980s, attention to gay culture increased dramatically, quickly becoming commonplace discourse in all media, from the nightly news to cinema to academic research. However, the focus of this attention in scholarship was often, and increasingly so, not AIDS, but rather identity formation and the sociocultural politics and subject positioning that informed it. Phenomenological and formalist approaches waned in popularity as poststructuralism, particularly the move to simultaneously historicize, de-essentialize, and relativize cultural products (from literary texts to human subjectivities), became increasingly predominant. In effect, all meaning, in such forms as categorizations, determinations, and interpretations, was seen as ideologically constrained and specific to its social, cultural, and historical situation; the catchwords *discursive, network, representation, construction, appropriation, blurring, crossing, passing, mutability, undecidability,* and *indeterminacy* became common parlance in literary-cultural criticism.

The idea that social identity (sexual, gender, class, ethnic, racial) was not inherent and was imposed, composed, and/or had to be performed convincingly enough that one "passed" (that is, would be identified positively)

62

became a common denominator to the leading critical methodologies (psychological, materialist, deconstructionist), even when applied to various areas of interest (from literary texts to theatrical characters to living cultural icons). The long-standing nature/nurture dichotomy changed nomenclature, transforming into essentialist/constructivist, eventually giving way to the rhetoric of the constructivist position. As a result, for many critical thinkers, social identity was, and continues to be, articulated processually, the temporal outcome of which remains socially, culturally, and historically contingent and negotiable. Insofar as sexuality and gender, and their links with ethnicity, class, and culture, are guiding principles behind most human relationships, the chief preoccupations of this movement in critical inquiry were sexual-gender potentiality and its effect on conventional class demarcations.

The main concern of this new focus for those either supporting or opposing the status quo and majoritarian cultural traditions was the fact that anything (conceptual, emotional, or material) that challenges dominant ideological perspectives on sexual, gender, ethnic, race, and class difference threatens a society's network of familial, educational, religious, and juridical structures. In the language of "transversal theory," the critical approach initiated by Bryan Reynolds that guides the present analysis,[1] these structures are referred to as "sociopolitical conductors," a term that he coined as a corrective to Louis Althusser's ahistorical concepts of "Ideological State Apparatuses" and "Repressive State Apparatuses" (127–88). Reynolds's term accounts for the historically specific sociopolitics and conditional states of both dominant and counterhegemonic machinations for prescribing ideologies, whereas Althusser reduces these conductors to a binary system of a monolithic state, and simultaneously does not acknowledge the similarly functioning, often multiple and contradictory, ideological machinations of non-state-promoting entities.[2] While sociopolitical conductors reinforcing a given society are mutually dependent on the dominant ideological perspectives, other sociopolitical conductors operating within or beyond the society, such as in forms of mass media and pedagogical practices, may oppose the dominant perspectives, either wholly or in part.[3] The amalgamation of a society's state-serving sociopolitical conductors must, in the interest of fostering a "rational" social system, support and generate "state power." State power refers to forces of coherence, whether acted consciously and/or not by or upon "individuals" (meaning humans individuated from other humans) or "groups" (a social clustering of otherwise individuated humans). In transversal terms, the amalgamation is referred to as "state machinery,"[4] a concept that accounts for the singular and/or plural, human and/or technological influences that work tirelessly but ultimately futilely to manufacture moral, ideational, and governmental coherence and symbiosis. According to transversal theory, hegemonic work is, in the end, futile if totalization is its goal because totalization is a social impossibility as long as physical movement and change are constant realities. Consequently, an absolute state for both individuals and/or the society they comprise is never a real prospect, but the quest for stable states and the fear of achieving them will nevertheless always stimulate solidarities and antagonisms among sociopolitical conductors with various views on what the ideal society and state should be.

Such a reality serves the noneconomistic, neo-Gramscian post-Marxists Ernesto Laclau and Chantal Mouffe,[5] who emerged influentially on the academic scene in the 1980s with the publication of their *Hegemony and Socialist Strategy* (1985), and continue to maintain their same views into the twenty-first century.[6] The world's constant flux is compatible with their poststructuralism insofar as they imagine an overarching hegemony ("a collective will") constituted through the "politico-ideological articulation of dispersed and fragmented historical forces" that can only and must be resisted through antagonism (67). The ceaseless production of antagonism is therefore at the "centre" of their mission to keep what they identify abstractly as the political "Left" and "Right" from meeting harmoniously, presumably on any issues, in the "Centre" of what they believe is a linearly manifest continuum of political thought and activism (xiv–xv). Strategically, Laclau and Mouffe's "new left-wing hegemonic project" stresses the need for antagonism as instigated through the "recognition" of value and "redistribution" of power as best suited to their greater purpose, the pursuit of a "radical and plural democracy" that cultivates endlessly the extension of long-established democratic struggles for representation, equality, and liberty to and within marginalized class, race, ethnic, gender, and sexual identities (xviii). Their insistence on an indefatigable "hegemonic struggle" (xix), combined with their resistance to classical Marxism's totalizing and deterministic sociohistorical schema, clashed with the precursory and more influential historical materialism of Fredric Jameson.

Jameson argues in his provocative Althusserian-Freudian-Marxist merger, *The Political Unconscious* (1981), that the mediation of differences in identity and subjectivity, among other sociohistorical phenomena, is, while often convincing, misleading, or confusing, finally unable to detract from the fact that "social life is in its fundamental reality one and indivisible, a seamless web, a single inconceivable and transindividual process, in which there is no need to invent ways of linking language events and social upheavals or economic contradictions because on that level they were never separate from one another" (40). Although he also argues (but "not [to be] understood as a wholesale endorsement of poststructuralism") that "only the dialectic provides a way of 'decentering' the subject concretely" (60), Jameson's insistence on "the reality of history" (82) suggests essential or preexisting, perhaps also unconscious, selves on which social identities are based regardless of the extent to which identities are obscured as constructed discursively by "transcoding," which Jameson defines as the strategic "invention of a set of terms" by which "levels of reality" are mediated, comprehended, and imbricated (40). As a result of this deep-seated structuralism, Jameson's new brand of Marxism made many second-wave feminists apprehensive and anxious about alliances between Marxism and psychoanalysis (see Schwab; Martindale; and McCallum), just as other feminists concerned with minoritarian struggles became skeptical and wary of Laclau and Mouffe's dismissal of classical Marxism's ontological privileging of class difference as vital to understanding historically, and producing in the here and now, socioeconomic, and thus social identity, transformations (see Smith, *Laclau and Mouffe;* Stabile; Ebert; and Wood).

The new sociopolitical, identitarian trends in critical theory, educational interest, and scholarship in general reflected as much as they produced a phenomenon that was encapsulated in another popular catchword, "cultural anxiety." The title to Marjorie Garber's *Vested Interests: Cross-Dressing and Cultural Anxiety* (1992), a book that characterizes the first decade of the first wave of "gender studies," what we call the "engendered years," brilliantly captures the tenor of the times. Garber's *Vested Interests* was published by Routledge, a trade press (rather than an academic press) that had quickly become the leader in the publication of books in the newfangled fields of cultural and gender studies. While Garber's book reflected the concerns of the era of its inception, the book that was to most influence the second decade of gender studies was Judith Butler's *Gender Trouble: Feminism and the Subversion of Identity* (1990), also published by Routledge (from the press's new series, Thinking Gender). In *Gender Trouble*, while implicitly dismissing the dialectic Jameson prescribes but remaining very much aware of the hegemony that is Laclau and Mouffe's focus, Butler argues that social identity is constituted only through performance (in speech, behavior, and style) and works to further a political agenda. Whether performed consciously or unconsciously (people are typically unaware of how and why they act and dress in certain socially coded ways), there is nothing essential or natural about sexual-gender identities. The categories "man" and "woman" are sociocultural constructs for which there is no original on which to base one's performance. These genderized, "performative" (Butler's adaptation of J. L. Austin's term) categories, affirmed or contested depending on the social actions repeated, are simply manifested ideas only inasmuch as people willfully or inadvertently subscribe to them.

The recent constructivist development in academic thought and research was paralleled in various popular media, perhaps most notably on film and television, a trajectory that began primarily with men cross-dressing as women (*Dressed to Kill* [1980], *Bosom Buddies* [television, 1980–82], *Tootsie* [1982], and *Mrs. Doubtfire* [1993]), then moved to include women cross-dressing or performing "male" (*Victor/Victoria* [1982], *Yentl* [1983], *Shakespeare in Love* [1998], and *Triumph of Love* [2001]), and ended up showing people not just cross-dressing as a means to an end (such as for a job), but actually psychologically at odds with their designated gender identity, that which was socially prescribed based on the sexual organs they possess (*Silence of the Lambs* [1991], *The Crying Game* [1992], *Boys Don't Cry* [1999], and *All about My Mother* [1999]). In turn, and consistent with concerns of the time, the different approaches to "gender trouble" represented on film coincide with work done by literary-cultural critics on transvestism and gender difference on both the stage and street in early modern England. While Shakespeare's plays, particularly *As You Like It* and *Twelfth Night,* have received much attention, the play most consistently discussed in regard to both stage and street cross-dressings is Middleton and Dekker's *The Roaring Girl.* Historiographically, it is unlike any other extant play from the period. Not only is *The Roaring Girl* rare in that it represents, by name, a living London personality as a character, the playwrights' choice of "personality" for performance was a notorious gender-blurring icon of her own time, the infamous Mary Frith, also known as Moll Cutpurse. As suggested by Middleton and Dekker's character Sebastian's comparison of her to a religious icon ("I must now, / As men for fear, to a strange idol bow" [1.1.117–18]) and his reference to her notoriety ("a creature / So strange in quality, a whole city takes / Note of her name and person" [1.1.100–102]), Mary Frith/Moll Cutpurse achieved "celebrity" status in the seventeenth century, and into the twenty-first, because she publicly defied conventional dress codes and sumptuary laws by donning man's apparel and was, allegedly, an activist for this practice. According to a January 27, 1612, entry in *The Consistory of London Correction Book,* Mary/Moll refused, even after being officially condemned for her behavior, to refrain from unconventional acts of self-fashioning:

And further [Mary Frith] confesseth *t*hat since she was punished for the misdemeanors afore mentioned in Bridewell she was since vpon Christmas day at night taken in Powles Church *w*ith her peticoate tucked vp about her in the fashion of a man *w*ith a mans cloake on her to the great scandall of diu*ers* pe*rs*ons who vnderstood the same & to the disgrace of all womanhood.[7]

Her public displays of transvestism, along with other "criminal" or transgressive practices, including cursing and thieving, cast her into the sociohistorical category, as Middleton and Dekker's character Laxton identifies her, of "Base rogue!" (2.1.271).

For many scholars today as well as for her contemporaries, Moll Cutpurse/Mary Frith's "celebrity" and/or "criminal" status make her an especially appealing historical figure of social deviance for a case study by which to proffer a theory of the early modern rogue, and of deviant identities and practices in general. In most of the early modernist scholarship discussed in the following pages, Moll/Mary exemplifies one or a combination of several recent postmodern formulations of subject positioning: (1) of what Laclau and Mouffe refer to as a "nodal point" (derived from Lacan's "*point de capiton*"—in English literally, "quilting point"),[8] which is an empty signifier capable of partially fixing and centering (like a Derridean "supplement") the substance of a range of floating signifiers (in this case, Mary Frith, Moll Cutpurse, rogue, roaring girl, transvestite, deviant, protofeminist, queer, celebrity, among others) by articulating them within a chain of equivalential identities among different elements that are seen as expressing a certain sameness (celebrity, queer, protofeminist, deviant, transvestite, roaring girl, rogue, Moll Cutpurse, Mary Frith, and so on);[9] (2) of what Foucault calls "points of resistance," which are sources of antagonism, in such forms as dissenting or faltering subjects, within a society's strategic field of power relations (95–96); (3) of what Jameson considers subjective products of "transcoding," the sociohistorical processes by which one can "make connections among the seemingly disparate phenomena of social life" (in the case at hand, late-twentieth-century feminism and early-seventeenth-century criminality, among others); and (4) of what neo-Marxist Paul Smith identifies as an outcome of "the cerning of the subject," whereby "the contemporary intellectual abstraction of the 'subject' [such as of the historical persona Mary Frith] from the real conditions of its existence continues—and is perfectly consonant with—a Western philosophical heritage in which the 'subject' is construed as the unified and coherent bearer of consciousness," and which in effect works "to encircle" or "to enclose" the subject theoretically and rhetorically as a way of limiting the definition of the human agent in order to be able to call him/her the "subject" (xxx).

Throughout the course of the present analysis, we tango with each of these perspectives as they are reflected in the materialist and constructivist accounts of Mary Frith/Moll Cutpurse as a means by which to chassé into our own alternative theoretical understanding of deviant identity formations, in varied historical forms and different social contexts, as potentially "transversal agents." Our primary aim is to analyze the vast amount of criticism published on *The Roaring Girl* and Mary/Moll as an avenue through which to examine the preoccupations of recent literary-cultural criticism and the ideologies and methodologies that have fueled it in order to assess the impact of both Middleton and Dekker's *The Roaring Girl* and Moll Cutpurse/Mary Frith on contemporary academic discourse. Specifically, we are interested in the transhistorical phenomenon of what we call "Mary/Mollspace," particularly in how this "space" achieved such high status within the past twenty years and how it might influence the critical future. We will begin by explaining Mary/Mollspace in the process of delineating key components to transversal theory. Then we will review the different approaches to *The Roaring Girl* and Moll Cutpurse/Mary Frith, distinguishing them by ideology, methodology, and interpretation, as a way of moving into our own assessment of Mary/Mollspace as subject matter for a literary-cultural-critical-historiographical project.

Transversal Initiatory, Subjunctive Space

From the perspective of scholars today, Mary Frith/Moll Cutpurse, competing with Christopher Marlowe, is possibly the most notorious cultural icon of England's early modern period. As with Marlowe, whose sexuality has also been a subject of debate since early modern times, the emphasis on gender differentiation in literary-cultural studies over the past twenty years has undoubtedly contributed hugely to Mary/Moll's current iconic status. Resurrected in the postmodern period as a prototypical feminist and an early avatar of gay, lesbian, and/or transvestite power, Mary/Moll has become a vehicle for discourses on the blurring of sexual-gender roles and for feminist and queer politics generally. Moreover, she is also emblematic of a criminal culture that has become increasingly important to scholars of England's early modern social history, especially as scholarship has become more aware of the period's complex sociocultural dynamics across class, religious, gender, and ethnic divisions.[10] Consequently, in our view, Mary/Moll provides a fertile landscape from which to harvest an understanding of the production and consumption of transhistorical "celebrityness," and in this case a celebrityness born out of social deviance. She testifies to the creation of a plurality of spaces that, like "Shakespace," moves discursively, and often transversally, conceptually, emotionally, and physically, across space-time dimensions.

Shakespeare-influenced spaces, however conventional, alternative, or sometimes both, are what Donald Hedrick and Bryan Reynolds call "Shakespace,"[11] a term that accounts for these particular spaces and the time or speed at which they move from generation to generation and from era to era. For a variety of reasons, Shakespace is an especially strong exemplar of "transversal power," which, as will be explained shortly, refers to any force that induces people to permeate the organized space of subjectivity.[12] Shakespace's unique functions as resistor, generator, and conductor of transversal power result from phenomena that within and passing through Shakespace are the epochal forces and transformations wrought by a multiplicity of social, cultural, and economic influences: by early capitalism; by the great experiment of the new public entertainment industry in early modern England; by the interrogation of socially prescribed gender roles; by aristocratic and legitimation crises; by the desacralization of absolutist sovereignty; by cross-cultural collisions and relativizations deriving from exploration and colonization; by the scientific revolution and its confounding of official knowledge; and—to follow this space into our own time—by the recursive force of the Western canonical tradition itself on Shakespeare's work.[13]

The kind of iconic status *The Roaring Girl* has achieved is comparable to that of Shakespeare's *Romeo and Juliet,* whose title characters have become emblematic of a socially prescribed ideal form, or perfect incarnation, of "true love"—heterosexual, monogamous, and worth dying for—that has been officialized through space-time in the image of its similarly iconicized author, William Shakespeare.[14] The use of Shakespeare's play to promote a heteronormative conception of desire is an example of his functioning as a sociopolitical conductor, an ideologically driven mechanism that works to create "subjective territory," an individual's combined conceptual and emotional scope, the "place" or vantage from which members of a given society relate to their surroundings. Defined succinctly, "Subjective territory is delineated by conceptual and emotional boundaries that are normally defined by the prevailing science, morality, and ideology. These boundaries bestow a spatiotemporal dimension, or common ground, on an aggregate of individuals or subjects, and work to ensure and monitor the cohesiveness of this social body" (Reynolds, "Devil's House" 146). In order to develop and sustain subjective territories, the state machinery of a society, an assembly of sociopolitical conductors (educational, familial, juridical, and religious structures), continually manufactures a dominant, "official culture."[15] As a result, "Official culture's sociopolitical conductors work to formulate and inculcate subjective territory with the appropriate culture-specific and identity-specific zones and localities, so that the subjectivity that substantiates the state machinery is shared, habitually experienced, and believed by each member of the populace to be natural and its very own" (Reynolds, "Devil's House" 147). Subjective territory, then, is a domain of intangible boundaries produced by state machinery and reinforced through the imposition of an official culture, with its laws and enforcements, in order to control, through subjectification, the public and private, emotional and physical behaviors and thought-processes of a given populace. Restated in quasi-Laclau-Mouffeian terms ("quasi" because of certain conceptual incompatibilities), subjective territory is informed by the differential relations of a sociopolitical environment's multiple subject positions and is itself comprised of multiple, spatiotemporally specific nodal points; these nodal points coordinate the subjective territory's multidimensional positionality relative to other subjective territories in the interest of promoting coalescence and fixity within both its own conceptual and emotional range and the greater sociopolitical field it occupies.

For Laclau and Mouffe, whose theory of subject formation comes predominantly from Lacanian psychoanalysis, the subject, like desire, is predicated on lack,[16] and it can only establish itself as a subjectivity through a common grounding and knotting together of equivalential identifications (subject positions with a recognizable and/or persuasive degree of sameness) into a singular nodal point that creates and endeavors to sustain a fully achieved social identity. The nodal point, as Slavoj Žižek explains Lacan's formulation, "*as a word*, on the level of the signifier itself, unifies a given field, constitutes its identity: it is, so to speak, the word to which 'things' themselves refer to recognize themselves in their unity" (95–96). By extension, through linked equivalential identifications, society is also pursued by hegemonic forces. However, according to Laclau and Mouffe, such "suturing" together of seeming equivalences can never produce ultimately either a subject, an individual, or a society because there are always antagonisms from without that work hermeneutically to "overdetermine" (a Laclau-Mouffeian borrowing from Freud) the presence of some of the sutured social identities and social positions vis-à-vis others, causing either their condensation or displacement, and thereby transferring the focus onto another set of equivalencies so as to fixate another nodal point, and so on. Laclau and Mouffe's sense of stepping-stone subject formation is much like Derrida's theory of *différance*, which accounts for the phenomenon that a signifier has significance given that it is a product of difference, but that its significance is simultaneously unstabilizable and always deferred because it can never achieve absolute meaning as a transcendental signified.[17]

Unlike Foucault, who sees antagonism as internal and "never in a position of exteriority" to power relations of a particular society (93–96), Laclau and Mouffe argue that "antagonisms are not *internal* but *external* to society; or rather, they constitute the limits of society, the latter's impossibility of fully constituting itself " (125). As Žižek eloquently summates:

> The thesis of Laclau and Mouffe that "Society doesn't exist," that the Social is always an inconsistent field structured around a constituted impossibility, traversed by a central "antagonism"—this thesis implies that every process of identification conferring on us a fixed socio-symbolic identity is ultimately doomed to fail. The function of ideological fantasy is to mask this inconsistency, the fact that "Society doesn't exist," and thus to compensate for us for the failed identification. (127)

But for Laclau and Mouffe it is not only society that is negated, but also the identifiable human agents who might have sociopolitical power should it be possible for them to be members of a society. Laclau expresses this concept succinctly:

> The question of *who* or *what* transform social relations is not pertinent. It's not a question of "someone" or "something" producing an effect of transformation or articulation, as if its identity was somehow previous to this effect. . . . It is because the lack is constitutive that the production of an effect constructs the identity of the agent generating it. (210–11)

Articulated in the space of "everyday life," should you want a mechanic to work on your car, you might as well solicit anyone to assist you, because it is impossible for you to know who is or is not a mechanic until a person demonstrates mechanical skills, and even then, we might ask: How skilled must he/she be to be a mechanic, and who is qualified to make this evaluation? Of course, we might respond to such queries with: Would seeking a state-certified mechanic at a state-licensed automobile repair shop increase the odds of her being skilled enough? Empirically, if what appeared to need fixing appears to have been fixed by the mechanic, then chances are it was. Within the relevant, local interpretive community, agency was identified and meaning was achieved, as predicted by the preestablished parameters of the quest for car repair. Transposing this example to one more in line with Laclau and Mouffe's political agenda, we might ask: Doesn't the revolutionary potential of individuals, perhaps measured by past expressions of dissidence, matter when pursuing alliances for the revolution?

Alternatively, transversal theory and methodology are all about potential. They work discursively to empower social identities and groups recognizably striving—conceptually, emotionally, and/or physically—to transcend their subjective territories. As stated, according to transversalism, the idea of totalized or absolute subjectivities, identities, societies, or states is an obvious impossibility insofar as movement and change are fundamental to the world's existence. Transversal theory's subjective territory, very different from the always already lacking and failed subject for Laclau and Mouffe, is not an ahistorical phenomenon continuously manifested, expanded, and discombobulated through just antagonism, but a space socially, culturally, and politically generated and maintained through antagonisms as well as other conceptualizations and experiences, including growth, evolution, curiosity, imagination, kindness, empathy, desire, passion, and love. As described above, subjective territory is a conceptually and emotionally constrained, multidimensional space through which humans with social identities and varying degrees and kinds of agency navigate their consciousness and presence within specific social, cultural, and historical parameters of space-time. Subjective territory is an unfixed, permeable, and processual space that thrives on its interactive relationship with "transversal territory."

In contrast, and opposing, state-orchestrated subjective territory, transversal territory is the nonsubjectified space of one's conceptuality and emotionality. According to transversal theory, "transversal movement," that is, the conscious and/or subconscious breach and transcendence of one's subjective territory into either the subjective territory of an other (or others) or a nondelineated alternative or alternatives, threatens the stability of the state machinery and its regulating, official culture.[18] Transversal movements are propelled by "transversal power," a fluid and discursive phenomenon defined as any force—physical or ideational, friendly or antagonistic—that inspires emotional and conceptual deviations from the established "norms" for an individual or group. Transversal movements indicate the emergence and inhabitance of transversal territory, a chaotic, boundless, challenging, and transformative space people traverse when they violate the conceptual and/or emotional boundaries of their prescribed subjective addresses. Transversal territory is a conceptual-emotional space people inhabit transitionally and temporally when subverting the hierarchicalizing and homogenizing assemblages of a governing organizational structure. To reside permanently in transversal territory, rather than pass through it, would be to subsist without any kind of cognitive stability or control. In effect, transversal territory threatens "official territory," the ruling ideology, propriety, and authority that provide the grounding and infrastructure of a society, by offering a space through which to transcend it.

Passing through Shakespace

Responding to Shakespeare's past, present, and future workings as sociopolitical conductors and conductors of transversal power, Hedrick and Reynolds explain that "the historical spaces through which Shakespeare has passed as an icon have been extraordinarily diverse and numerous. Shakespeare has stimulated, occupied, and affected countless commercial, political, social, and cultural spaces" ("Shakespace" 8). Thus, Shakespace is a helpful term for analyzing the various constructions—literary, cinematic, official, and unofficial—of Shakespeare since it accounts for the elongated history of the official, "subjunctive," and transversal uses of Shakespeare. As with other icons whose work and "affective presence"—a subject/object's "combined material, symbolic, and imaginary existence" that "influences the circulation of social power" (*Becoming Criminal* 6)—have spawned transversal spaces, such as controversial icons like Jesus of Nazareth, Marx, Freud, Mao Tse-tung, and Osama bin Laden (about which there has been abundant discourse and action),[19] the dissemination across space-time of Shakespeare and his plays, propagandized as icons of official culture, has "encourage[d] alternative opportunities for thought, expression, and development," just as it has, alternatively, "promote[d] various organizational social structures that are discriminatory, hierarchical, or repressive" (Hedrick and Reynolds, "Shakespace" 9). For instance, *Romeo and Juliet* has worked to popularize a notion of romantic love specific to heteronormative sociality as well as to subvert that determination and provoke transversal movements.[20]

As much as Shakespeare has been constructed and utilized to impose limitations on social behavior, his characters, like Middleton and Dekker's title character in *The Roaring Girl*, often engage in transversal movements, defying or surpassing the boundaries of their prescribed subjective addresses, opening themselves, as it were, to subjective awareness outside the self or selves. In Shakespeare's plays, ruptures in subjective territory frequently occur through the transversal, transformative process of desire, a productive process of "becoming-other" defined against the desire constructed and regulated by and for state power in the interest of maintaining official culture:

> Transversality, on the other hand, produces and expresses desire in the dynamic form of what Gilles Deleuze and Félix Guattari term "becoming." Becoming is a desiring process by which all things (energies, ideas, people, societies) change into something different from what they are; and if those things were, before their becoming, identified, standardized or normalized

by some dominant force (state law, Church credo, official language), which is almost inevitably the case, then any change whatsoever is, in fact, a becoming-other. The metamorphosis of becoming-other-social-identities trespasses, confuses, and moves beyond the concepts of negation, essentialism, normality, constancy, homogeneity, and eternality, that are fundamental to subjective territory. ("Devil's House" 150–51)

A quick survey of Shakespeare's plays would reveal desire as an indispensable and transformative process undertaken by many of the main characters to achieve a new social identity, becoming-an-other within, without, and/or against an official culture: Macbeth, conforming to the prevailing ideology of his subjective territory, follows his ambitious desire to become a king; Desdemona's passion for and ensuing marriage to Othello in spite of racial prejudices challenges the boundaries of a dominant discourse on desire; the exiled Prospero, in enacting his revenge upon King Alonso and Antonio, his brother, the current duke of Milan, seeks to disrupt state power from afar; and Iago, operating from within Venice's official culture, plans to destroy Othello, thereby overthrowing state power. From different angles of readership (and we cannot emphasize enough the flexibility with which the examples can be read, even contradictorily), these Shakespearean examples illustrate processes by which identities are transformed and thus revealed to be nonessential, socially constructed designations: Macbeth moves swiftly up, then down, the ranks of feudal power; Desdemona becomes "our great captain's captain" (2.1.74), a whore, a victim, and then a martyr; Prospero reclaims his lost dukehood and forgoes his magic power, and with it his reign over Sycorax's island; and Iago is transformed from the state-loved, seemingly "Honest Iago" (1.3.295) to tortured captive of the Venetian state.[21] Like these Shakespearean characters, Middleton and Dekker's Moll Cutpurse experiences ongoing processes of identity formation, performance, and transformation that extend far beyond the play into and through the various discourses in which Moll Cutpurse/Mary Frith journeys transhistorically.

The Roaring Girl and Moll/Mary emerged out of roughly the same historical context—early modern England, specifically London, Southwark, and the theater community—and traveled both diachronically and synchronically in a similar, although lower-profile, scholarly discourse as Shakespeare-as-literary-cultural-icon has in the last twenty years. For this reason, we imagine Mary Frith/Moll Cutpurse, a dual historical persona, occupying a comparable discursive space, the aforementioned Mary/Mollspace, that embodies and meta-morphs a variety of identity formulations, from heterosexually married woman to rogue to drag king to a representation of the Madonna-whore dichotomy. We see the case of Mary/Moll as being exemplary of a sociohistorical phenomenon that is also a historiographical dilemma: What to do when a real-life historical figure is multifariously reenvisioned and appropriated transhistorically in diverse narrative modes, including biography, fiction, theatrical, and critical discourse? Using the case of Mary Frith/Moll Cutpurse, we will demonstrate the value of transversal poetics' critical methodology, known as the "investigative-expansive mode of analysis" (the "i.e. mode"), a critical approach that first breaks the subject matter under investigation into variables and then partitions and examines them in relation to other influences, both abstract and empirical, beyond the immediate vicinity.[22] A chief objective of this expansive methodology is to contextualize historically, ideologically, and critically both the subject matter and the analysis itself within local and greater milieu. A mobile approach, the i.e. mode continually reparameterizes in response to the unexpected emergence of glitches and new information, and resists anything resembling predetermination or circumscription. The employment of the i.e. mode allows us to explore the ways in which the case of Mary/Moll exemplifies what we call "subjunctive space," the hypothetical space of both "as if" and "what if," which is our overarching purpose in the upcoming analysis.[23]

According to transversal theory, subjunctive space, because of its openness and uncertainty, is like "transversal territory," whose indeterminate mappings can occupy, transgress, and expand—to borrow Raymond Williams's terminology—the "residual," "dominant," and "emergent" aspects of a culture. In this respect, subjunctive space is a subset of transversal territory or, more accurately, it is an in-between space operative between subjective and transversal territories in which the subject necessarily retains agency and can self-consciously hypothesize scenarios and experiences, thereby self-activating her/his own transversal movements. Yet because of its telegraphed parameters of potentiality, predicated on or manifested by the "suggestive information" identified within the subject matter under investigation (whether it be philosophies of time management, schisms in religious teachings, or a theatrical text, to name some), subjunctive space can also spur resistance to transversal territory insofar as subjunctive space allows for and includes all potentialities. Put differently, the anticipated, contingent, and/or possible "ifs" that can work to empower the subject through transversal movement can also stabilize, empower, and/or disempower the subject by further subjectifying her/him within her/his prescribed subjective territory.

Supporting Derrida's answer of *différance* and supplementarity to the problem of logocentrism and hermeneutics focused on ontology, subjunctive space also provides a way out of both the circumscribing Husserlian focus on intentions and their objects (of both readers and authors, for instance) and the Geneva School's, and later reader-response critics', enhanced focus on the consciousness of individuals (of both readers and authors) that has characterized phenomenological literary-cultural criticism and has been informed much by neoconservative humanist criticism of the last twenty years, such as, in English Renaissance studies, that of Richard Levin and Brian Vickers. Subjunctive space accepts all decentering, ungrounding, disseminating deconstructive machinations as a means by which, in Paul Smith's terms, the "subject/individual" ("the human entity to whom qualities of being a 'subject' or an 'individual' are commonly assigned") can become discerned or discern his/herself (xxxv). In our view, subjunctivity allows the subject to become at least provisionally uncontained and unconstrained so as to point in certain directions and to certain places, to elsewheres, past, present, and future, indicated and imagined by the projections of "as if" and "what if." Moreover, and contrary to the Derridean perspective, whereas the subject may be vulnerable to deconstructionist procedures because the subject is already a negotiated construct within a fluctuating and often struggling subjective territory, according to transversal theory, the individual always negotiating—consciously and/or not—his/her subjectification and social identity in relation to transversal power cannot be completely deconstructed and/or contained, regardless of whether the power is willfully generated by the individual and/or manufactured through engagement with the social factory of which he/she is a product. When the deconstructionists' rhetorical dust settles discursively or continues discursively to cloud the air, no less than a phenomenon remains: a human being experiencing idiosyncratically a field of consciousness and possessing degrees of agency and potential peers on.

In subjunctive space, then, the individual is neither necessarily forever pulling the rug out from under her/his fugitive feet as she/he tries to escape the logocentrism infrastructurally reinforcing her/his subjective territory, the sociopolitical conductors inscribing and maintaining that territory, and the state machinery in which those conductors operate; nor is she/he ineluctably and desperately striving to concretize her/his consciousness in cahoots with the intentions of an author, group of authors, and ruling authorities or the state, thereby, in theory, achieving self-value through the actualization of an aesthetic object in the living world. Instead, subjunctive space opens up opportunities for coordinating one's own subjective territory vis-à-vis competing ideologies and objects/subjects to the extent that one can imagine alternative conceptual, emotional, and physical coordinates. In the case at hand, the discourse and those exposed to the discourse of Mary Frith/Moll Cutpurse, including the writers and readers of this essay, are the subjects and subject matter under investigation. Venturing now into a subjunctive space while moving backward and forward investigative-expansively, we journey to and through historiographical coordinates and discourses on *The Roaring Girl,* associated celebrity spheres—from the Virgin Mary to Christopher Marlowe to the modern Madonna—and the interrelated subfluxation of Mary/Mollspace.

Still Roaring after All These Years

Mary/Moll has occupied various spaces since the emergence of her publicized criminal persona in the seventeenth century,[24] when her notoriety as a cross-dressing cutpurse manifested itself in her appearance as the subject of popular literary and theatrical fare. During her own lifetime, she appeared in multifarious textual guises, from criminal in court documents, to subversive recalcitrant at a public penance immortalized in John Chamberlain's 1612 letter, to onstage performer in the afterpiece advertised in the epilogue to Middleton and Dekker's play.[25] Her social deviance and appealing personality made her a newsworthy subject for mythmaking discourse. Shortly after her death in 1659, she was reborn as a royalist cross-dressing Robin-hooder who eventually seeks redemption in *The Life and Death of Mrs. Mary Frith, Commonly Called Mal Cutpurse* (1662), a three-part self-declared biography that includes the "real" Mary Frith's supposed diary.[26] After her rebirth during the Restoration, Mary/Moll remained relatively quiet on bookshelf coffins until the twentieth century, when she was revived, first in an effort initiated in 1927 by T. S. Eliot to rescue and/or redeem Middleton's playwrighting skills from critical dismissal by focusing on the "realness" of *The Roaring Girl's* title character: "Middleton's comedy deserves to be remembered chiefly by its real—perpetually real—and human figure of Moll" (99). While Eliot's essentialist mission to salvage Middleton and Dekker's Moll Cutpurse—for no other reason than because she is a "real and unique human being" (89) who "remains a type of the sort of woman who has renounced all happiness for herself and who lives only for a principle" (96)—is often cited today in critical discussions of the play, *The Roaring Girl* went dormant for another forty years until the emergence of the "sexual revolution" and first-wave feminism in the West.

Beginning in the 1970s, Mary/Moll began to be mobilized via productions of Middleton and Dekker's play to address feminist issues.[27] Academics followed suit beginning in 1984 with the publication of Mary Beth Rose's "Women in Men's Clothing: Apparel and Social Stability in *The Roaring Girl*."[28] From 1984 to 2002, rescuing and/or redeeming Mary/Moll, either from literary and/or historical obscurity, from her representation in *The Roaring Girl*, or from mythologized readings of her based on "fact" or fiction, has become the modus operandi of critical considerations of her deviance and dissident potential in both the public sector of early modern England and the institutionalized realm of postmodern scholarship. In recent years, Moll/Mary has been salvaged and revitalized in numerous shapes and sizes, ranging from protofeminist heroine, dissident disrupter of dominant gender and sexual codes, and less-than-transgressive transvestite, becoming a contested site/sight for feminist, queer, new historicist, and/or materialist discourses.[29] As our brief examination of the more recent critical constructions of Mary/Moll will show, redeeming the "real" Mary and/or the theatricalized Moll has generated multiple, and sometimes overlapping, Mary/Mollspaces in which she is reconfigured, redisplayed, and re-remembered as an academic icon of dominant critical discourses and as a spearhead for various (mostly liberal/leftist) political agendas.

As T. S. Eliot predicted, Middleton and Dekker's *The Roaring Girl* has been "remembered chiefly" for its re-creation of the "real" (99). The majority of critical discussions of Mary Frith/Moll Cutpurse's potential for disruption of the dominant order offstage has focused on Moll as represented on the stage of the Fortune Theatre in the original 1611 production of the play.[30] With scant "hard" evidence of the historical Moll's life, critics have turned their attention to the seemingly more "stable" theatrical text. The play itself is atypical of the seventeenth-century stage, not only because of its dual authorship and unconventional city comedy conclusion,[31] but in its real-life, then still-living subject. As Katherine Eisaman Maus notes, the Moll of *The Roaring Girl* is "the first positively identifiable living person to be translated into a quasi-fictional dramatic realm" (1371). Maus considers Mary Frith's social status as the cause for the exception to early modern England's censorship rules, which "prohibited theatrical depiction of politically powerful, socially prominent people" (1371). While Mary's nonprominent social status may have granted the playwrights latitude when breaching contemporary censorship laws, Mary Frith the icon nonetheless functioned as a space through which Middleton and Dekker could produce the previously unpresentable. Recasting the "real" in the representational, Middleton and Dekker generated the perhaps first in a plurality of Mary/Mollspaces that have continued to emerge and expand into the twenty-first century. Their version of Moll, while debatedly transgressive in relation to their official culture's gender and/or sexual codes, subverted state-imposed dramatic conventions. By exposing the ban on blurring the fictional with the living-real to be blurable itself, Middleton and Dekker, with a transversal thrust, later domino-effected by Eliot's campaign, opened doorways not only for future theatrical rule-breaking, but for modernist and postmodernist challenges to both social identities and to sociopolitical conductors informing and performing identity formations.

Crossing thresholds into subjunctive space, whether championing the theatrical or "real" Moll, modern critics have mobilized Mary/Moll to investigate structuralist and poststructuralist configurations of, in transversal terms, the sociopolitical conductors that inscribe subjective territories and prescribe social identities. The majority of recent criticism on Mary/Moll can be succinctly categorized—taking into consideration variances and overlappings—according to four major "camps," three of which have revived Mary/Moll as an exemplar of the performability of gender and/or sexual subject-positions: (1) feminist/queer critics who, focusing on *The Roaring Girl*, identify the theatricalized Moll as a progressive transgressor of gender, sexual, and/or class systems (Rose; Comensoli; Miller; Dollimore; Howard; Orgel; Mikalachki; Kermode; Rustici; Heller; and Reynolds); (2) feminist/queer critics who, seeking to demystify the Moll Cutpurse of Middleton and Dekker's re-creation, position the "real" Moll, in contrast to the play's representation of her, as radically oppositional to dominant views of sexual, gender, and class differentiations both in early modern England and today (Krantz; Baston); (3) feminist/queer/materialist/(new) historicist critics who, focusing on *The Roaring Girl*, present the scripted Moll as a performed affirmation of a patriarchal order who has been misread as radically progressive (Mulholland; Garber; Jacobs; Krantz; Baston; Forman; West); and (4) historiographers who focus on the 1662 biography to contest or support previous politicized readings of the "real" and theatricalized Moll Cutpurse (Nakayama; Todd and Spearing; and Ungerer).[32] In the course of these diverse readings, multiple Molls have been constructed and deconstructed, suggesting the very subjectivity of "reading" identity, the potential for re-forming identities, and the mutability of the seemingly static page.

Within the four camps, since her 1984 "rescue" by Rose, Mary/Moll has been discursively reconfigured, sometimes simultaneously, as (1) an early modern exemplar of women's lib (Rose; Comensoli; Miller; Baston; and Kermode); (2) a conduit for destabilizing dichotomous gender and/or sexual structures (Dollimore; Howard; Orgel; Nakayama; Todd and Spearing; Mikalachki; and Krantz); (3) a cant-talking, class structure breacher in breeches (Orgel; Mikalachki; and Reynolds); (4) a homoerotic spectacle for mass male consumption (Garber; and Orgel); (5) a celebration of homoerotic desire (Howard; Herbert); (6) an emblem for the theater itself (Heller); (7) a conflated figure of the cant pamphlet-producing Dekker (Mikalachki); (8) a "compensatory fiction" for the commodification of identity via capitalism

(Forman); (9) a commodified product of the then-emerging market culture (Ungerer and Forman); (10) a celebratory figure of the subversive potential in smoking the herb of the "real" and representational roaring girl's choice (Rustici); and (11) a mystified, misread, "transvestiting," nontransgressing affirmation of a patriarchal, dominant order (Mulholland; Garber; Jacobs; Ungerer; Maus; and West).

In all of these formulations, manipulations, and interpretations, Mary/Moll, "real," theatrical, and/or/as represented by critics, has occupied discursive, cross-pollinated spaces that, moving transhistorically from the seventeenth to the twentieth and into the twenty-first century, have sought to redefine, reclaim, and redeem what Moll Cutpurse has been and is becoming over 325 years after Mary Frith was. Apparently deeply invested in early modern England as a foundation for the postmodern present,[33] these critics have generated contradictory and sometimes self-competing Mary/Mollspaces that map out subjective territories from the "then" and project them onto the "now"—possibly hoping to construct a space through which they can strut with, against, and/or/as "Proud Mary."[34]

While Moll/Mary has been jolted forward, backward, and across spacetime in her projected (or not) political radicalness, she has retained her image, archivally emplotted, as a public persona in the criminal celebrity sphere of England's early modern period. Despite Eliot's insistence that the roaring girl "deserves" to be remembered as a "human figure" (99), Middleton and Dekker's version of Moll is generally read less as "human" than as a sociohistoricalizing, contextualizable, still-living museum piece of dissidence and/or subservience. She has become a sign-object—the biunivocal (two-into-one) conceptual and emotional expression of the different signifiers and signifieds associated with her—who has been fetishized, like the Virgin Mary and the modern pop star Madonna, as both commodity and political cathexis. Through fetishization, the sign-object Moll/Mary has achieved affective presence; its amalgamated material, ideational, symbolic, and wish-fulfilled subsistence and becomings have produced, reproduced, and delineated Mary/Mollspace. Inasmuch as Mary/Mollspace operates like a transversal whirlwind of its own, having been unleashed and nourished by the critical energies of performers, academicians, educators, and intelligentsia who have so assiduously invested themselves into Mary/Mollspace, Mary/Mollspace has blown the gates off subjective territories.

Whether spun as a protofeminist icon, as a reformed version of the "real" transgressor (Moll's offstage, historical counterpart), or as a mythologized commodity born of a market culture manufacturing commodified criminality, Middleton and Dekker's Moll and/or Mary Frith's self-fashioned Moll Cutpurse have been fetishized and reactualized to exemplify the period's shifting sociopolitical systems and their capacity for disruption or affirmation, either on and/or off the stage. Reconceived in the majority of modern scholarship—characterized by its own investment in the marketability of Moll/Mary as an icon for furthering certain political agendas and academic careers—as a product of the early modern era, Moll Cutpurse, theatrical and "real," criminal and corrective, appropriated and/or not, has been rendered into a symbolic figure of a then still emergent capitalist system, a figure of either exploitation by, from within, or of systems we would define as organized clusters of sociopolitical conductors. Under, against, and/or in support of the maintenance of the conductors' corresponding official and subjective territories, Moll/Mary was generated and generates alternative selves, thereby initiating and perpetuating a becomings-Mary/Mollspace with an enduring affective presence whose substances, traces, and phantasmagoria effectuate transversal movements into both navigatable and unchartable territories across space-time.

Subjunctive Mappings, Critical Coordinates

Moll/Mary has become a space-time-traveling iconicized celebrity who reveals an inclination, despite the onslaught of Derridean decenteredness, to find a precedent for contemporary methods of dissent. This is the case especially in interpretations that position Mary/Moll as a "progressive" subverter of a dominant order. Employed by feminist, queer, new historicist, and materialist critics, as we have seen, Mary/Moll, like Shakespeare, has been mapped across spatial, temporal, emotional, conceptual, and sociocultural boundaries; thus, she has been imagined by some English Renaissance scholars of the postmodern age (including Rose; Garber; Orgel; Howard; Todd and Spearing; Kermode; and so on) as a transhistorical transgressor and/or affirmer of official culture. By projecting Mary/Moll into simultaneous pasts, presents, and futures, these critics have rejected conventionalized spatiotemporal demarcations. However unproblematic or not, the projections of Mary/Moll we could or could not be "proud" of today have led some down the critically disavowed path of universalization plaguing, in Margreta de Grazia's estimation, New Historicist literary-cultural criticism (an assessment echoed in Craig Dionne's essay in this volume).

In reference to the "early modern" labeling of protocapitalist England, de Grazia has noted the predilection among new historicists to analyze the present by its relation to a period of history conceived of as a precursor to the now. De Grazia rejects the label *early modern* as a universalizing technique counter to the new historicist project: "There is a way in which seeing the Renaissance as the Early-Now commits itself to the very universalizing tendency that historicizing set out to avoid in the first place. As if *the* relevant history were a prior version of what we already are and live" ("Ideology of Superfluous Things" 21). Dionne reverberates de Grazia's criticism, noting that "the self-referential historicist strategy" he identifies as characteristic of new historicism "can potentially negate the difference of the past by rendering early modern social activities a kind of allegory of the present" (38). Deborah Jacobs makes a similar claim in reference to what we would term "feminist early modernist" readings of Middleton and Dekker's re-creation of Moll Cutpurse. Arguing against "novelized" reading that "renders its own motives and politics invisible and remakes in the reader's own image" (75), Jacobs critiques new historicists' "willing[ness] to historicize context but not an individual subject's consciousness" and materialist "feminist discourse that is willing to rigorously historicize the material conditions of women's existence but still retains a transhistorical resistant 'woman' and is, furthermore, determined to find 'her' in other cultures" (79–80). Like the precursural "early modern" in de Grazia's analysis, and the renderings of past social practices into an allegorical present noted by Dionne, the transhistoricalized, protofeminist Moll Jacobs critiques runs the risk of universalizing and thereby erasing social, cultural, and historical differences by identifying potentially resistant women then as prototypical of "Early-Now."

While Jacobs focuses her critique on interpretations of Moll as protofeminist, citing Rose and Howard as prototypical of the "novelized" reading she dismisses, her assessment of this transhistoricalizing approach can also be applied to critical disavowals of Mary/Moll's transgressive potential. By judging the early modern "real" criminal/English theatrical character according to contemporary evaluations of what constitutes dissidence, Mary/Moll has emerged in some circles as not transgressive enough, as incapable of transcending the official territory that, in her own time, inscribed Mary Frith as a criminal element in a hegemonic order. Through processes that historicize the present in their historicism of the past, Mary/Moll has been transcribed into, as Eliot remarked seventy-five years ago, a figure capable of being "perpetually real" (99), and, as we have shown, an icon capable of being subjunctively affective.

The transhistoricalizing processes through which Mary/Moll has been revamped disclose more than the subjectiveness of the interpretative act. As Jacobs argues, Mary/Moll has been reconfigured through a series of "novelized" readings that "renders its own motives and politics invisible and remakes in the reader's own image" (75). Visibly written from the position of politicized author motivated by what she assesses is critical misrepresentation, Jacobs's devaluation of the "novelizing" formations of Mary/Moll suggests that objective interpretation is an achievable goal, a goal that her own article throws into doubt. Selecting and dissecting evidence in support of any argument is a process of manipulating the material to support "the reader's own image" as the authorial figure on the given material. Assessing the subjective vacuum of the interpretative act is not the issue here; rather, our focus is on the critical spaces Mary/Moll has occupied and transgressed in response to discourses developed to address subjective awareness and the positionality of the subject within its subjective territory. Space-time traveled, transfigured, and in some instances transversalized, Mary/Moll—at least the fetishized sign-object of Mary/Moll—has crossed the disciplinary map, and Mary/Moll-space has evolved into a terrain on which to critically evaluate investments in sociocultural, historical, and theoretical models. Like the Virgin Mary, Mary Frith/Moll Cutpurse has been appropriated and mobilized by forces in- and de-scribing residual (from early modern English to the present), dominant (contemporary official cultures), and emergent (critical future) landscapes, and it is her very decenteredness, her lack of fixity and a consistent referent in the historiographical record, that allows for continuous reformations of her as both a formative and performative figure of sociopolitical structures. Immortalized in her own time primarily in fictional modes (theatrical and "biographical") and in second-person narrative accounts of her public behavior, Moll/Mary is mostly known today as a mythologized figure of the imagination, and is thus open to reinscriptive imaginings of her social deviance and transversal agency and power.

Revived in the now for her behavior and/or representation in the then, Mary/Moll has been rendered into the ambiguous present-space of here and the past-, future-present, and/or present-absent-space of there, a multipolar sphere of potentiality. She is a paradoxical figure incapable of containment by a single discourse or narrative mode, as is evident by the multiple textual forms and discursive formations in which she has appeared. Mary/Moll, fetishized or otherwise, presently occupies what we call the subjunctive space of "as if/what if." In the roughly twenty-year debate over her potential dissidence, as we have seen, scholars have projected her into a realm of possibilities by considering her "as if " she were a protofeminist, a homoerotic spectacle, a conservative commodity, and so on, inscribing her within the framework of "what ifs." Functioning in the subjunctive realm of possibilities of future-, present-, past-, and absent-space, Mary/Moll has become and invigorates multifarious hypotheticals that allow for imaginings of her potential as a disruptive force both diachronically and synchronically.

Novelized Moll: Venturing Further into "Iffyness"

Continuing to move investigative-expansively into subjunctive space, we want to consider yet another rendering of Mary/Moll, something less in the recent tradition of academic discourse, but rather in the mode of biography. As has been shown, the "as if/what if" processing of Mary/Moll has primarily operated in the realm of academic configurations of Mary/Mollspace. However, Ellen Galford's novel *Moll Cutpurse: Her True History* (1985), self-consciously framed as a "novelized" reading of Mary/Moll, projects Moll into the realm of "subjunctivity" by asking "what if" Moll Cutpurse were a lesbian, Robin-hooding protofeminist, and then by telling her "real" story "as if" Moll "really" were. The title of Galford's novel advertises the work as "True History" ("as if" History needs to be qualified), but the "Historical Note" at the conclusion of the text describes the piece as a fictional improvement upon the factual sources on which the book is based: "Some of the episodes in this story are derived from these sources: the others may be as close—or closer—to the truth" (221). The novel positions this Moll as a version "close—or closer—to the truth," and the novel functions as a "rescue" of the "real" Moll from fallacious textual renderings. As evident from the multivariate Molls redemptively constructed in the discourses previously discussed, "the truth" imagined by Galford is, despite the author's claim of a less distant relation to authenticity, only one of multiple potential truths or "what ifs."

In the Moll narrative as told by Galford, the "if" of Moll's sexual-gender-social identity is projected onto Bridget, the former lover of Galford's Moll. Bridget, an apothecary Moll went to see to inquire about a sex change— "'Turn me into a man,' was all she said" (14)—reremembers and narrates the now-deceased Moll's life for the reader. As established in the narrative, Moll was closeted about their relationship at Bridget's request, but now that Moll has passed away, Bridget is coming out to "rescue" Moll from male-authored renderings of Moll Cutpurse: "Now, so many years later, I feel the time has come to yield up that secret. Or all that will be left to keep alive Moll's memory will be the fabrications of *men*" (12). Those fabrications include *The Roaring Girl*, a play that did not displease Moll, since "those who wrote it were her old-boozing companions in any case" (12), and the *The Life and Death of Mrs.*

Mary Frith, Commonly Called Mal Cutpurse, written by a "dull scribbler who never knew her [but] has taken it upon himself to tell her story" (12). The impetus for the story is Bridget's coming out, and Moll's life history is conflated with the autobiography of Bridget, the novel's narrator with whom the reader is led to identify with: "So it falls to me, because I knew her best and loved her most, to tell Roaring Moll's true story, and my own with it" (12).

In Galford's appropriation of the romance novella form, Mary/Moll functions as a space not only through which lesbian relationships are normalized for a nonheterosexualized target audience, but through which autobiography—a process in which one can construct a self or selves for a reading public—can be scripted. Through the retelling of Moll's "True History," Bridget can author her own sociosexual identity; however, Bridget's personal inscription is not self-fashioned, bur rather conditioned by her sociosexual referent, the symbolic figure of Mary/Moll. Bridget's self-formulation is dependent upon her reclaiming of "Moll's memory" (12), and, as such, she is defining her self in relation to a fetishized other. Furthermore, the primary motivation for Bridget's identity-construction is not a desire to produce a self unrestrained by her own subjective territory, but to recuperate Moll from male-orchestrated commodifying processes that have challenged Moll's value as a sign-object for non-normative sexual practices and breaches of gender-power structures: as Bridget states, if Moll is not reauthored by Bridget, Moll will remain inscribed by "the fabrications of *men*" (12). Bridget's transcription of Moll Cutpurse's "True History" produces a Mary/Mollspace consciously seeking to counter a dominant patriarchal structure by appropriating and fetishizing an icon misrepresented by members of that order ("men"). The framework of the novel demonstrates its own investment in and mobilization of Mary/Moll as a phenomenon of the then with affective power in the now. Projecting Bridget and Moll into the subjunctive space of possibilities is framed as a personal enterprise against sociopolitical conductors of present-space subjective territory, for if Moll is not retranscribed, Bridget (the reader/the author) cannot tell her "own story" (12). In this subjunctive journey into Mary/Mollspace, Bridget's (and the reader's/the author's) identity-formation is dependent upon the hypothetical of Moll Cutpurse's "iffy" sociosexual identity.

Rematerialized Moll/Mary: Becomings-Marlovian

Rather than wrapping up this essay with the expected clever conclusion, a finale that subtly reenacts the gist of the arguments as it directs the readers intriguingly to grander implications off the stage of the page, we considered returning to *The Roaring Girl* by offering our own close reading of the representation of Middleton and Dekker's Moll Cutpurse. Having debated whether or not to throw our two cents into the already overflowing critical cup, we opted for another, uncharted strategy more in keeping with our own transversal enterprise. Before embarking on this voyage, let us clarify our reasoning for our readers, whom we imagine are wondering why we have not also chosen to "redeem," denounce, heroize, and/or fetishize Mary/Moll. Having mapped out previous literary-cultural-historical criticism of *The Roaring Girl*, we agreed that we have little new to offer in terms of readings of Moll's representation in the play. Instead, by manufacturing our own Mary/Mollspace out of various "historicalities" (material, theoretical, symbolic, and spectral vestiges), we prefer to propel the Mary/Moll of fact and/or fiction into the comparably subjunctified realm of Marlowespace. By merging these emotional, conceptual, and historical spaces, we hope to further illustrate the mechanics and potentialities of subjunctive ventures, and to briefly explore and point toward further expansions of Mary/Mollspace that move beyond the constraints and tautology of the established critical discourse on Mary/Moll and *The Roaring Girl* so that new critical, pedagogical, and performance frontiers can be discovered. In our now-embryonic "Mary/Marlowespace," we ask "what if" Mary/Moll was Christopher Marlowe and/or imagine *The Roaring Girl* "as if" it were penned by Marlowe. By thrusting Mary/Moll and Marlowe into a joint subjunctive sphere, we posit one of the plethora of possibilities on the horizon of critical considerations and mobilizations of Mary/Moll, Marlowe, and the continually reassessed and expanding early modern English canon.

In our fabrication to follow, Mary/Moll is meta-morphed with Marlowe, the "roaring" Moll's possibly leading rival historical figure of potential dissidence in early modern English studies. Endowing Marlowe with the symbolic value of Mary/Moll, and Mary/Moll with the literary-historical value of Marlowe, we produce "Mollowe," a cross-dressing, playwrighting, caped crusader who, operating much like the malcontented heroes of Marlowe's drama,[35] is capable of transgression accompanied by disruption that we characterize as transversal movement. Appropriating act 3, scene 1 of *The Roaring Girl*, the scene most frequently cited in scholarship on the representation of Moll Cutpurse in the play,[36] we welcome our readers to join us in this brief, concluding excursion into Mary/Marlowespace.

Scene: Night, Gray's Inn Fields. Enter Saxton.
Saxton: Who's there?

Enter Mollowe, dressed like a man.

Saxton: Nay, answer me. Stand and unfold yourself.

Mollowe: [*Aside.*] Oh, here's my frizzied gentleman. Like Faustus in prestige, but with Wagner's boyish looks. Little does he know he is to be
robbed in the Inn. How his eye is like a Robin's, but he lacks his clown-
ish Dick. [*To Saxton.*] Come sir, the readiness is all?

Saxton: Ho, sir, ready for what?

Mollowe: Ingrammercy, do you ask that now, sir? You, who have conjured me?

Saxton: [*Aside.*] "Conjured me"? Egads, is it you, Kit? [*To Mollowe.*] You
seem some familiar. Have we known each other?

Mollowe: Thou art too ugly to attend on me. [*Mollowe starts to go.*]

Saxton: Who's this? Kit? Not Kit, but Honest Moll? Stay, I charge thee.

Mollowe: Not since Deptford have I been thus hailed.

Saxton: Hark, what word from yonder cloak doth break? "Deptford"?
Are thee not Kit, schooled in night to divide the day? [*Reaching to touch
Mollowe.*] A phantom from fashion of himself? I did love you once!

Mollowe: Nay, I said "Stepford!"

Saxton: Faites excuse! I mistook you for a university wit I once well knew.
Alas, Moll, of most excellent fancy.

Mollowe: Purblind? You're an old wanton in your eyes, I see that. [*Removing cloak.*]

Saxton: No, not here. We shall be espied.

Mollowe: [*Drawing sword.*] Aye, there's the rub. [*Showing money.*] Here's
the gold with which you hired your hackney. Racking hard, your bones
will feel this. Ten angels of mine own I've put to thine. You lay the
odds on the weaker side.

Saxton: Hold, Moll! Mistress Mary. Strike a woman? I'm afeard you make
a wanton of me.

Mollowe: [*Stabbing at Saxton.*] A rat! Dead for a ducat, dead.

Saxton: [*Backing away.*] Call me not "rat"? My rodent name from Witten-
berg. [*Draws sword.*] By heaven, figured like the poet that's dead! Haste
me to know it, that I with wings as swift as thoughts of love may resist
your revenge. [*They fight. Mollowe wounds Saxton.*] A hit, a very palatable hit.

A cage descends from above.

Mollowe: You're fat, and scant of breath.

Saxton: [*Wounded, crawling as Mollowe approaches.*] Kit, forgive me my
transgressions, I knew not what I did when I stabbed you over the right
eye with a depth of two inches and the width of one.

Mollowe: Kit? Nay, it's Kitty now. What, is great Saxton so cowardly he fears the rage of Mollowe. [*During the following speech, Mollowe backs Saxton into the cage.*] Is great Saxton so passionate for being deprived of the joys of Mollowe's flesh? Learn thou of Kitty's manly fortitude, and scorn those joys thou never shalt possess. [*Throwing the money at Saxton.*] Go bear these triflings to your whoreson. Seeing Saxton hath already incurred eternal death by desperate acts against Kitty. I'll teach thee to behave thyself. [*Kicking Saxton into the cage. Mollowe follows.*] Letting you live in all voluptuousness, having thee ever to attend on me, to give whatsoever I shall ask, to do whatsoever I demand, and to always be obedient to my will. [*Saxton rises, teary-eyed.*] Too much of water hast thou?

Saxton: Tears seven times salt burn out the sense and virtue of mine eye! I forbid my tears; but yet it is our trick; nature her custom holds, let shame say what it will.

Mollowe: Poor Saxton. Flowering tears thou shed. [*Removing Saxton's clothes.*] When these are gone, the woman will be out that pierced the fearful hollow of thine eye. My life, for you was just one night in jail.

Saxton: Believe me, love, it was not just one night in jail. But in my bosom, to be to thee that night since a constant torchbearer to our love.

Mollowe: It so, I have more care to stay and let our deaths be one.

Saxton: [*Removing Mollowe's clothes.*] Art thou back so? Love, lord, poet, ay husband, friend, spy, I must love thee in every hour.

The cage begins to ascend as they embrace.

Mollowe: I again behold my rat. Ay, so conjured.

Saxton: Ay, a cutpurse of the empire and the rule.

NOTES

We are grateful to Steve Mentz and Craig Dionne for their helpful comments in the writing of this essay, and especially Craig for his tireless correspondence with us over a great many particulars.

1. Transversal theory was introduced by Reynolds in "The Devil's House." For more on transversal theory, see Reynolds's *Becoming Criminal* and *Performing Transversally*.

2. From a classical Marxist standpoint of theorists like Nicos Poulantzas, Althusser's division of the state is problematic not only because of its ahistorical qualities, but also because it "diminishes the specificity of the *economic state apparatus* by dissolving it into the various repressive and ideological apparatuses; it thus prevents us from locating the state network in which the power of the hegemonic fraction of the bourgeoisie is essentially centered" (*State, Power, and Socialism* 33).

3. For a critical consideration of "state machinery" and "sociopolitical conductors," see the following works by Reynolds: *Becoming Criminal*, "The Devil's House," and *Performing Transversally*.

4. Reynolds's conception of "state power" as any force from any source that works to consolidate social entities (toward the creation of a society) differs from that of classical Marxists like Nicos Poulantzas: "When we speak for example of *state power*, we cannot mean by it the mode of the state's articulation and intervention at the other levels of the structure; *we can only mean the power of a determinate class* to whose interests (rather than to those of other classes) the state corresponds" (*Political Power* 100).

5. Laclau and Mouffe self-identify as "post-Marxist" (4), as in their case the term is typically applied to any antiessentialist and/or antideterminist reformulation of Marxism.

6. In their preface to the second edition of *Hegemony and Socialist Strategy*, Laclau and Mouffe maintain that "Given the magnitude of these epochal changes ["the end of the Cold War and the disintegration of the Soviet system"], we were surprised, in going through the pages of this not-so-recent book again, at how little we have to put into the question the intellectual and political perspective developed therein. Most of what has happened since then has closely followed the pattern suggested in our book, and those issues which were central to our concerns at that moment have become ever more prominent in contemporary discussions" (vii). Since, in their estimation, there is no need for them to update their theories so that they may better account for and engage with either sociopolitical changes or developments in scholarship over the last twenty years, they conclude their preface with the declaration: "So our motto is: 'Back to the hegemonic struggle'" (xix).

7. The 1612 entry in *The Consistory of London Correction Book* cited here appears as appendix E in Paul Mulholland's edition of Middleton and Dekker's *The Roaring Girl* 262–63. The entry is also reprinted in Todd and Spearing's introduction to *Counterfeit Ladies* vii–viii; xiv–xv.

8. For Lacan, *points de caption* operate within a system of discourse, and a certain number of these quilting points are "necessary for a human being to be called normal, and which, when they are not established, or when they give way, make a psychotic" (268–69).

9. See Laclau and Mouffe 112. For Laclau and Mouffe, the "nodal point," which they also refer to as a "master-signifier" (xi), can also function like Derrida's conception of the "transcendental signified": "'Man' is a fundamental nodal point from which it has been possible to proceed, since the eighteenth century, to the 'humanization' of a number of social practices" (117). See Derrida for a similar, but more complexly theorized, concept of "supplementarity."

10. Among the more recent critical works on criminal culture in early modern England are Bryan Reynolds's *Becoming Criminal* and Linda Woodbridge's *Vagrancy, Homelessness, and English Renaissance Literature*.

11. "Shakespace" was first introduced in Donald Hedrick and Bryan Reynolds's "Shakespace and Transversal Power."

12. For more on transversal power, see the following works by Reynolds: *Becoming Criminal*, "The Devil's House," and *Performing Transversally*.

13. For further considerations of the "spaces" Shakespeare has occupied and critical

mobilizations and mutations of Shakespeare's work, see Reynolds, *Performing Transversally*, and Hedrick and Reynolds, *Shakespeare without Class*.

14. In "The Ideology of Romantic Love: The Case of *Romeo and Juliet*," Dympna Callaghan argues that the play, reflective of its historical moment, presents an ideology of love that "consolidates a certain formation of desiring subjectivity attendant upon Protestant and especially Puritan ideologies of marriage and the family required by, or least very conducive to the emergent economic formation of, capitalism" (59). Callaghan also identifies the "oppressive effects" of the construction and perpetuation of this ideology: "the dominant ideology of (heterosexual, monogamous) romantic love relegates homosexuality to the sphere of deviance, secures women's submission to the asymmetrical distribution of power between men and women, and bolsters individualism by positing sexual love as the expression of authentic identity" (60). While Callaghan cites Shakespeare as supportive of this "official" and "oppressive" Renaissance conception of love, she recognizes that the play offers "multiple and contradictory discourses of the desire" (72). Furthermore, she acknowledges that "Shakespeare's text has been used to perpetuate the dominant ideology of romantic love," and argues that "its initial ideological function has intensified since its first performance" (60–61). In "'Death-Marked Love': Desire and Presence in *Romeo and Juliet*," Lloyd Davis argues that the play offers an unromantic depiction of desire as inescapable from social forces: "comparable effects occur throughout *Romeo and Juliet*, where moments of romantic union are disrupted by ongoing events that undercut their idealism. The mixed genres in these tales represent desire as a hybrid of the comic, tragic and ironic" (63). In "*Romeo and Juliet*'s Open Rs," Jonathan Goldberg also argues that "love, from the start of the play, is implicated in the social, not separate from it," and discredits the "ideological function" of the romanticized "idealization of the lovers" as heterosexual icons by arguing that the play revolves around the lovers' threat to the homosocial order (223). In agreement with Davis's and Goldberg's assessment of the nonprivatized, social implications of desire in the play, but without denying the historicity of Shakespeare's text as discussed by Callaghan, we see *Romeo and Juliet* as an exemplar of the tragedy of their "subjective territory," the "conceptual and emotional boundaries" drawn and perpetuated by the state power in Verona (Reynolds, "Devil's House" 146), boundaries that confine the title characters within a dominant culture that prevents them, despite their romantic idealism or the power of their forbidden love, from transcending their socialization and achieving self-authored identities. Coming soon to a journal near you is our transversal reading of *Romeo and Juliet*, "Names, Planes, and Transversal Terrains in *Romeo and Juliet*: 'Some Other Where' beyond Verona's Walls."

15. While the conductors of state power function to create a hegemonic culture and "image of the totalized state," as Reynolds specifies, the "use of the term 'state machinery' should make explicit the multifarious and discursive nature of state power, and thus prevent the misperception of this dynamic as resultant from a conspiracy led by a monolithic state" ("Devil's House" 145).

16. We do not share this belief that desire is predicated on lack. For a detailed account of Reynolds's perspective on desire as both the subject and object of desire, see "Becoming a Body without Organs: The Masochistic Quest of Jean-Jacques Rousseau," *Deleuze and Guattari: New Mappings in Politics, Philosophy, and Culture*, 191–208.

17. Making an argument for Laclau and Mouffe's essentialism, Jacob Torfing sums up

the apparently self-defeating ("double-edged sword") logic to their conceptualization of antagonism: "Hence, if antagonism is constitutive of all social identity, if there is always a constitutive outside that is both the condition of possibility and the condition of impossibility of any identity, there is an essential accidentalness that is constitutive of identity. However, if this accidentalness threatens an identity, that identity will be experienced as incomplete, as the vain aspiration to a fullness that will always escape it" (51–53).

18. For more on transversal movement and territory, see Reynolds's *Becoming Criminal*.

19. For further discussion of "affective presence" in reference to major cultural icons, see Reynolds's *Becoming Criminal* and *Performing Transversally*.

20. In "No Holes Bard: Homonormativity and the Gay and Lesbian Romance with *Romeo and Juliet*," Richard Burt examines the history of "queer" adaptations of *Romeo and Juliet* that have challenged heteronormative readings of the play, including "homonormative" versions that counter authorized sexuality "either by seeking to be unlegible as gay or by designifying gender difference" (157).

21. For related transversal readings of *Macbeth*, *Othello*, and *The Tempest*, see Bryan Reynolds's "Untimely Ripped," Fitzpatrick and Reynolds; and Bryan Reynolds and Ayanna Thompson's "Inspriteful Ariels: Transversal Tempests," all of which appear in Reynolds's *Performing Transversally*.

22. Bryan Reynolds and James Intriligator introduced the investigative-expansive mode of analysis in a paper entitled "Transversal Power," given at the Manifesto Conference at Harvard University on May 9, 1998. For more on the "i.e. mode," see also Fitzpatrick and Reynolds; Hopkins and Reynolds; and Hedrick and Reynolds, "Shakespace."

23. For another discussion of "subjunctive space," see Bryan Reynolds's "Transversal Performance: Shakespace, the September 11th Attacks, and the Critical Future" in *Performing Transversally*.

24. For a chronology of Mary Frith's (1585–1659) criminal career, see Ungerer. According to Gustav Ungerer, Mary Frith (1585–1659) was first indicted on purse-snatching charges, along with two other women (Jane Hill and Jane Styles), in 1600 (62), and her "deviant behavior as a transvestite dates from about 1608" (55).

25. The January 27, 1612, entry in *The Consistory of London Correction Book* has been used by many critics and historiographers to establish that Mary Frith at least once appeared on stage, as advertised in the epilogue to *The Roaring Girl*, at the Fortune Theatre following the performance of the play. In an oft-cited letter to Sir Dudley Carleton dated February 12, 1612, John Chamberlain recounts Mary Frith's drunken, disorderly public penance at St. Paul's Cross the previous Sunday (334). In addition to her theatrical representation as a character in *The Roaring Girl*, Moll Cutpurse was also a character who briefly appeared in Nathaniel Field's *Amends for Ladies* (1618). Moll Cutpurse's notoriety is also evident by the number of literary works published during her lifetime that made reference to her, including Thomas Dekker's *If It Be Not Good, the Devil Is in It* (1611/12), William Rowley, Thomas Dekker, and John Ford's *The Witch of Edmonton* (1621), and Richard Brome's *The Court Beggar* (1640). As Mulholland notes, the now lost *Madde Pranckes of Mery Mall of the Banckside, with Her Walks in Mans Apparel, and to What Purpose* by John Day, entered on August 7, 1610, in the *Stationer's Register*, may be the earliest literary representation of Mary Frith (*Roaring Girl* 13). "Biographical" accounts of

Mary/Moll include *The Life and Death of Mrs. Mary Frith, Commonly Called Mal Cutpurse* (1662) and Alexander Smith's *A Complete History of the Lives and Robberies of the Most Notorious Highwaymen, Shoplifts, and Cheats of Both Sexes* (1719). For a record of the various documentary sources, theatrical representations, and literary references to Mary Frith/Moll Cutpurse dating from the seventeenth to the eighteenth centuries, see Mulholland's introduction to *The Roaring Girl* 1–65; Nakayama vii–xxix; Todd and Spearing; and Ungerer.

26. For a debate over the authenticity of *The Life and Death of Mrs. Mary Frith, Commonly Called Mal Cutpurse*, see Ungerer. Critical of Todd and Spearing's assessment of the biography as "the only [text] that gives anything like an account of the actual woman rather than a mythical figure, or that could derive from information given by the original 'Moll,' Mary Frith herself" (x), Ungerer argues that the "fragmentary" biography is "male-orientated," and that the work offers only a fictionalized account intended for public consumption: "The biographers were committed to adjusting their subject in conformance to the stereotypical criminal of fictional biography" (42).

27. For a survey of the seven revivals of *The Roaring Girl* produced between 1951 and 1983, see Mulholland's "Let Her Roar Again" and his introduction to his edition of *The Roaring Girl*. Among the seven productions Mulholland discusses, two date from the 1970s, including Sue-Ellen Case's 1979 production at the University of California at Berkeley, and three from the early 1980s, among which is the 1983 Royal Shakespeare Company production starring Helen Mirren as Moll. It is Mulholland's contention that while the most recent productions he considers have used the source text as a platform to address feminist issues, the play itself does not support a feminist reading, and must be altered (and adulterated, in his opinion) to produce a more contemporary message concerning gender politics ("Let Her Roar Again" 25; *Roaring Girl* 53).

28. Articles on *The Roaring Girl* appearing shortly before the publication of Mary Beth Rose's piece include two works by Paul A. Mulholland, "The Date of *The Roaring Girl*" and "Some Textual Notes on *The Roaring Girl*," both of which focus on intertextual evidence that can be used to historicize the play. Other pre-Rose works that offer a more critical analysis of the play include Patrick Cheney's "Moll Cutpurse as Hermaphrodite in Dekker and Middleton's *The Roaring Girl*," in which Cheney identifies Moll's "paradoxical" portrayal as stemming from her roots in the hermaphroditic Platonic and Neoplatonic tradition popularized by Spenser. Comparing *The Roaring Girl* to Spenser and others, Cheney argues that Moll is a hermaphroditic ideal synthesis of male and female traits, a unity of "opposites" that, functioning as a "symbol" for combinations of genre, authorial, and sexual identity formations, has transgressive social, personal, and artistic potential (132). His reading of Moll as a unity of "opposites" whose opposing forces negate sexual desire (130) could be read as an affirmation of a binary gender system that disallows desire to those who cross its constructed paths. Nonetheless, while Cheney's article is generally unacknowledged by post-Rose critics rereading *The Roaring Girl*, his piece appears to be the first published scholarly article to consider sexuality and gender formation in Middleton and Dekker's play. For a brief consideration of *The Roaring Girl* published prior to the publication of Rose's piece, also see Linda Woodbridge's *Women and the English Renaissance*, in which Woodbridge labels the playwrights' re-creation of the "real" as a "favourable treatment to a man-clothed virago" (250).

29. In 2001 the Shenandoah Shakespeare Company produced *The Roaring Girl*, contextualizing it topically with current politics and popular trends. For instance, the canting was done like a rap song. In the words of Craig Dionne, who saw the production, "The point was to show Moll as a transhistorical object of vexed desire via pop culture" (email correspondence, December 8, 2002).

30. Of the thirty recently published works on Mary Frith/Moll Cutpurse considered here, only three focus primarily on a Mary Frith of biographical and/or historical record rather than on the Moll Cutpurse of theatrical fare: Nakayama's introduction to *The Life and Death of Mrs. Mary Frith;* Todd and Spearing's introduction to *Counterfeit Ladies;* and Ungerer's "Mary Frith, Alias Moll Cutpurse." While some recent scholarship, such as Ungerer's, has sought to retrieve Mary from the Moll of the theatrical stage and/or the Moll of the biographical page by focusing on the Mary Frith of historiographical "fact," most critics, rather than contending with archival-based conjectures, focus on Middleton and Dekker's projection of the public persona, referencing the 1612 record of Mary Frith's arrest for her onstage appearance at the Fortune Theatre and/or Chamberlain's 1612 letter recounting Mary Frith's public penance to legitimate the transgressive potential of the "real" Moll Cutpurse. Jane Baston, for instance, contrasts archival accounts of Frith with her theatricalized counterpart to construct her argument that while Mary Frith was a transgressive figure who subverted the patriarchal order through her cross-dressing and public penance, Middleton and Dekker's "sanitized Moll" is orchestrated to "subtly undercut her political potency" ("Rehabilitating Moll's Subversion in *The Roaring Girl*," 323). Jean Howard, on the other hand, references the 1612 entry documenting Mary Frith's arrest for lute-playing cross-dressed at the Fortune Theatre to argue that the theatrical Moll is more transgressive then the real. Howard argues that while "[t]he original Moll . . . was transgressive for playing her lute on the public stage," Middleton and Dekker's Moll "is even more transgressive in that her instrument is not the lute, able to be tucked decorously beneath the breast, but the viol, played with legs akimbo. Moreover, she seems to appropriate this instrument not so much to make herself an erotic object, as to express her own erotic subjectivity" (184).

31. For considerations of *The Roaring Girl* as an unconventional text in its breaching of genre and authorship conventions, see, among other works, Cheney; Rose; Comensoli; and Forman.

32. For feminist/queer readings of Middleton and Dekker's version of Moll Cutpurse as a progressive transgressor of patriarchal gender, class, and sexual structures, see, among others, Rose; Comensoli; Miller; Dollimore, *Sexual Dissidence* 293–99; Howard; Orgel; Mikalachki; Kermode; Rustici; Heller 151–70; and Reynolds, *Becoming Criminal* 64–94. Feminist/queer/materialist/new historicist critics who read the theatrical Moll as an affirmation of the dominant order and position the "real" Moll Cutpurse as the "truly" dissident figure include, among others, Krantz; and Baston. For feminist/queer/materialist and/or (New) historicist readings of Middleton and Dekker's Moll as a critically misread figure, see, among others, Mulholland's "Let Her Roar Again," and Mulholland's introduction to his edition of *The Roaring Girl;* Garber; Jacobs; Krantz; Baston; and Forman. For a reading of Dekker and Middleton's Moll as a figure affirming a hierarchical class structure, see West. For historiographical accounts of Mary Frith that, focusing on the 1662 biography, cast the "real" Moll Cutpurse as a dissident figure, see Nakayama; and

Todd and Spearing. For a historiographical critique of mystifications of the "real" Mary Frith based on assumptive readings of the 1662 biography as "fact," see Ungerer.

33. For a critique of postmodern investment in the English Renaissance as "Early Modern," see de Grazia, Quilligan, and Stallybrass.

34. At this point, while simultaneously writing this essay and listening for the umpteenth time to Tina Turner's rendition of Creedence Clearwater Revival's 1969 smash-hit "Proud Mary," Bryan starts rambling (and shimmying) senselessly in cant, claiming to be the rock-star reincarnation of Moll Cutpurse, while Janna, puffing nervously away on the butt of her thirty-sixth cigarette of the wee hours while wearing a false mustache, strategically projects herself into a lute-playing Mary Frith in order to lull Bryan/Moll/Tina into calmness.

35. For a reading of Faustus's malcontention and transgressive power, see Dollimore, *Radical Tragedy*.

36. Those critics that cite 3.1 from *The Roaring Girl* in support of their arguments include Cheney (1983); Rose (1984); Comensoli (1987); Miller (1990); Dollimore (1991); Garber (1991); Jacobs (1991); Howard (1992); Orgel (1992); Mikalachki (1994); Krantz (1995); Baston (1997); Kermode (1997); Rustici (1999); and Heller (2000).

WORKS CITED

Althusser, Louis. *Lenin and Philosophy and Other Essays*. Trans. Ben Brewster. New York: Monthly Review P, 1971.

Baston, Jane. "Rehabilitating Moll's Subversion in *The Roaring Girl*." *Studies in English Literature 1500–1900* 37.2 (1997): 317–35.

Burt, Richard. "No Holes Bard: Homonormativity and the Gay and Lesbian Romance with *Romeo and Juliet*." *Shakespeare without Class: Misappropriations of Cultural Capital*. Ed. Donald Hedrick and Bryan Reynolds. New York: Palgrave/St. Martin's, 2000. 153–86.

Callaghan, Dympna. "The Ideology of Romantic Love: The Case of *Romeo and Juliet*." *The Weyward Sisters: Shakespeare and Feminist Politics*. Ed. Dympna Callaghan, Lorraine Helms, and Jyotsna Singh. Oxford: Blackwell, 1994. 59–101.

Chamberlain, John. *The Letters of John Chamberlain*. Ed. Norman Egbert McClure. Vol. 1. Philadelphia: American Philosophical Society, 1939.

Cheney, Patrick. "Moll Cutpurse as Hermaphrodite in Dekker and Middleton's *The Roaring Girl*." *Renaissance and Reformation* 7.2 (1983): 120–34.

Comensoli, Viviana. "Play-making, Domestic Conduct, and the Multiple Plot in *The Roaring Girl*." *Studies in English Literature 1500–1900* 27.2 (1987): 249–66.

Davis, Lloyd. "'Death-Marked Love': Desire and Presence in *Romeo and Juliet*." *Shakespeare Survey 49: Romeo and Juliet and Its Afterlife*. Ed. Stanley Wells. Cambridge: Cambridge UP, 1996. 57–67.

de Grazia, Margreta. "The Ideology of Superfluous Things: *King Lear* as Period Piece." *Subject and Object in Renaissance Culture*. Ed. Margreta de Grazia, Maureen Quilligan, and Peter Stallybrass. Cambridge: Cambridge UP, 1996. 17–42.

de Grazia, Margreta, Maureen Quilligan, and Peter Stallybrass, eds. *Subject and Object in Renaissance Culture*. Cambridge: Cambridge UP, 1996.

Derrida, Jacques. "Structure, Sign, and Play in the Discourse of the Human Sciences." *Writing and Difference*. Trans. Alan Bass. Chicago: U of Chicago P, 1978. 278–94.

Dollimore, Jonathon. *Radical Tragedy: Religion, Ideology, and Power in the Drama of Shakespeare and His Contemporaries*. Sussex: Harvester P, 1984.

———. *Sexual Dissidence: Augustine to Wilde, Freud to Foucault*. Oxford: Clarendon P, 1991.

Ebert, Teresa. *Ludic Feminism and After: Postmodernism, Desire, and Labor in Late Capitalism*. Ann Arbor: U of Michigan P, 1996.

Eliot, T. S. "Thomas Middleton." *Elizabethan Dramatists*. New York: Haskell House, 1964. 87–100.

Fitzpatrick, Joseph, and Bryan Reynolds. "Venetian Ideology or Transversal Power? Iago's Motives and the Means by Which Iago Falls." *Othello: New Critical Essays*. Ed. Philip C. Kolin. New York: Routledge, 2002. 203–19.

Forman, Valerie. "Marked Angels: Counterfeits, Commodities, and *The Roaring Girl*." *Renaissance Quarterly* 54.4 (2002): 1531–60.

Foucault, Michel. *The History of Sexuality*. Vol. 1, *An Introduction*. Trans. Robert Hurley. New York: Random House, 1990.

Galford, Ellen. *Moll Cutpurse: Her True History*. Ithaca: Firebrand, 1985.

Garber, Marjorie. "The Logic of the Transvestite: *The Roaring Girl* (1608)." *Staging the Renaissance: Reinterpretations of Elizabethan and Jacobean Drama*. Ed. David Scott Kasdan and Peter Stallybrass. New York: Routledge, 1991. 221–34.

Goldberg, Jonathan. "*Romeo and Juliet's* Open Rs." *Queering the Renaissance*. Ed. Jonathan Goldberg. Durham: Duke UP, 1994. 218–35.

Hedrick, Donald, and Bryan Reynolds. "Shakespace and Transversal Power." Hedrick and Reynolds, *Shakespeare without Class* 3–47.

———, eds. *Shakespeare without Class: Misappropriations of Cultural Capital*. New York: Palgrave/St. Martin's, 2000.

Heller, Herbert Jack. *Penitent Brothellers: Grace, Sexuality, and the Genre in Thomas Middleton's City Comedies*. Newark: U of Delaware P, 2000.

Hopkins, D. J., and Bryan Reynolds. "The Making of Authorships: Transversal Navigation in the Wake of *Hamlet*, Robert Wilson, Wolfgang Wiens, and Shakespace." *Shakespeare after Mass Media*. Ed. Richard Burt. New York: St. Martin's, 2002. 265–86.

Howard, Jean E. "Sex and Social Conflict: The Erotics of *The Roaring Girl*." *Erotic Politics: Desire on the Renaissance Stage*. Ed. Susan Zimmerman. New York: Routledge, 1992. 170–90.

Jacobs, Deborah. "Critical Imperialism and Renaissance Drama: The Case of *The Roaring Girl*." *Feminism, Bakhtin, and the Dialogic*. Ed. Dale M. Bauer and Susan Jaret McKinstry. Albany: SUNY P, 1991. 73–84.

Jameson, Fredric. *The Political Unconscious: Narrative as a Socially Symbolic Act*. Ithaca: Cornell UP, 1981.

Kermode, Lloyd Edward. "Destination Doomsday: Desire for Change and Changeable Desires in *The Roaring Girl*." *English Literary Renaissance* 27.3 (1997): 421–42.

Krantz, Susan E. "The Sexual Identity of Moll Cutpurse in Dekker and Middleton's *The Roaring Girl* and in London." *Renaissance and Reformation* 19.1 (1995): 5–20.

Lacan, Jacques. *The Psychoses*. Trans. Russell Grigg. New York: W. W. Norton, 1993.

Laclau, Ernesto. *New Reflections on the Revolution of Our Time*. London: Verso, 1990.

Laclau, Ernesto, and Chantal Mouffe. *Hegemony and Socialistic Strategy: Towards a Radical Democratic Politics*. London: Verso, 1985.

Levin, Richard. "The Poetics and Politics of Bardicide." *PMLA* 105.3 (1990): 491–504.

Martindale, Kathleen. "Fredric Jameson's Critique of Ethical Criticism: A Deconstructed Marxist Feminist Response." *Feminist Critical Negotiations*. Ed. Alice Parker and Elizabeth Meese Amsterdam: John Benjamins, 1992. 33–43.

Maus, Katherine Eisaman. Introduction to *The Roaring Girl*. *English Renaissance Drama: A Norton Anthology*. Ed. Katherine Eisaman Maus and David Bevington. New York: Norton, 2002. 1371–76.

McCallum, Pamela. "Question of Ethics: Reading Kathleen Martindale Reading Fredric Jameson." *Resources for Feminist Research* 25.3–4 (1997): 64–69.

Middleton, Thomas, and Thomas Dekker. *The Roaring Girl*, in *English Renaissance Drama: A Norton Anthology*. Eds. David Bevington et. al. New York: Norton, 2002. 1377–1451.

Mikalachki, Jodi. "Gender, Cant, and Cross-Talking in *The Roaring Girl*." *Renaissance Drama* 25 (1994): 119–43.

Miller, Jo E. "Women and the Market in *The Roaring Girl*." *Renaissance and Reformation* 19.1 (1990): 11–23.

Mulholland, Paul A. "The Date of *The Roaring Girl*." *Review of English Studies* 28 (1977): 18–31.

———. "Let Her Roar Again: *The Roaring Girl* Revived." *Research Opportunities in Renaissance Drama* 28 (1985): 15–27.

———. "Some Textual Notes on *The Roaring Girl*." *The Library* 32 (1977): 333–43.

———, ed. *The Roaring Girl*. Thomas Middleton and Thomas Dekker. Manchester: Manchester UP, 1987. 1–65.

Nakayama, Randall S., ed. *The Life and Death of Mrs. Mary Frith, Commonly Called Moll Cutpurse*. New York: Garland P, 1993.

Orgel, Stephen. "The Subtexts of *The Roaring Girl*." *Erotic Politics: Desire on the Renaissance Stage*. Ed. Susan Zimmerman. New York: Routledge, 1992. 12–26.

Poulantzas, Nicos. *Political Power and Social Classes*. London: NLB and S and W, 1973.

———. *State, Power, Socialism*. London: Verso, 2000.

Reynolds, Bryan. "Becoming a Body without Organs: The Masochistic Quest of Jean-Jacques Rousseau." *Deleuze and Guattari: New Mappings in Politics, Philosophy, and Culture*. Ed. Eleanor Kaufman and Kevin Jon Heller. Minneapolis: U of Minnesota P, 1998. 191–208.

———. *Becoming Criminal: Transversal Performance and Cultural Dissidence in Early Modern England*. Baltimore: John Hopkins UP, 2002.

———. "The Devil's House, 'or Worse': Transversal Power and Antitheatrical Discourse in Early Modern England." *Theatre Journal* 49.2 (1997): 143–67.

———. *Performing Transversally: Reimagining Shakespeare and the Critical Future*. New York: Palgrave/Macmillan, 2003.

Rose, Mary Beth. "Women in Men's Clothing: Apparel and Social Stability in *The Roaring Girl*." *English Literary Renaissance* 14.3 (1984): 367–91.

Rustici, Craig. "The Smoking Girl: Tobacco and the Representation of Mary Frith." *Studies in Philology* 96.2 (1999): 159–79.

Schwab, Gabrielle. "The Subject of the Political Unconscious." *Politics, Theory, and Contemporary Culture*. Ed. Mark Poster. New York: Columbia UP, 1993. 131–58.

Smith, Anna Marie. *Laclau and Mouffe: The Radical Democratic Imaginary*. London: Routledge, 1998.

Smith, Paul. *Discerning the Subject*. Minneapolis: U of Minnesota P, 1988.

Stabile, Carol. "Feminism and the Ends of Postmodernism." *Materialist Feminism: A Reader in Class, Difference, and Women's Lives*. Ed. Rosemary Hennessy and Chrys Ingraham. New York and London: Routledge 1997. 395–458.

Todd, Janet, and Elizabeth Spearing, eds. *Counterfeit Ladies: The Life and Death of Mal Cutpurse, The Case of Mary Carleton*. London: William Pickering, 1994.

Ungerer, Gustav. "Mary Frith, Alias Moll Cutpurse, in Life and Literature." *Shakespeare Studies* 28 (2000): 42–84.

Vickers, Brian. *Appropriating Shakespeare: Contemporary Critical Quarrels*. New Haven: Yale UP, 1993.

West, William, "How to Talk the Talk; or, The Work of Cant on the Jacobean Stage." *English Literary Renaissance* 33.2 (2003). 228–51.

Wood, Ellen Meiksins. *The Retreat from Class: A New "True" Socialism*. London: Verso, 1986.

Woodbridge, Linda. *Vagrancy, Homelessness, and English Renaissance Literature*. Urbana: U of Illinois P, 2001.

———. *Women and the English Renaissance: Literature and the Nature of Womankind, 1540–1620*. Urbana: U of Illinois P, 1984.

Žižek, Slavoj. *The Sublime Object of Ideology*. London: Verso, 1989.

A. L. BEIER

New Historicism, Historical Context, and the Literature of Roguery

The Case of Thomas Harman Reopened

Renaissance England's literature of roguery has received considerable attention in recent literary criticism, especially in its new historicist variants.[1] Critics have given particular attention to Thomas Harman's *Caveat for Common Cursitors Vulgarly Called Vagabonds,* long regarded as the most original and credible exemplar of the genre. Certainly, prima facie, the *Caveat* has some credentials that suggest we should take it seriously. It was written by a member of the Kentish gentry who is thought to have served in the office of justice of the peace, which was a key position in the enforcement of the Tudor vagrancy laws. The pamphlet's publishing history is impressive. It appeared in four Elizabethan editions (one in 1566, two in 1568, and one in 1573); its taxonomy of rogues was adopted in William Harrison's *Description of England,* which appeared in Holinshed's *Chronicles* (1577, 1587); and, it was plagiarized by, among others, Thomas Dekker in *Lantern and Candlelight* (1608) and Richard Head in *The English Rogue* (1665).[2] Critics continue, moreover, to consider the *Caveat* a seminal source, one authority describing it as "the most complete of the many rogue books" published in Renaissance England and a second praising Harman's "groundbreaking account of criminal culture."[3]

The new historicist interest in Harman's tract has a number of components. First, despite its preeminent position in the rogue literature, the pamphlet is still a noncanonical piece of writing that enables critics to go beyond mainstream texts to configure various modes of representation.[4] Thus the parallels found between the discourses of vagabondage in Harman and in characters in some of Shakespeare's plays (Greenblatt 37–39; Carroll, pt. 2; Woodbridge

204). Second, Harman's tract represents social worlds that are of marginal significance in most canonical texts, engaging critics in social history, particularly questions of identity, women, the poor, and criminals. This engagement with the world of the nonelite in turn assists critics in delineating dominant cultures (e.g., Dolan; Hall). Third, many scholars are interested in the roguery texts as evidence of discourse. Harman's pamphlet, for all its rhetoric and attempts at humor, is considered a powerful statement of the mid-Tudor view of vagabondage that may represent a new technology for control of the lower classes. Even his jokes about beggars can be reinterpreted to reveal an ideological topos, one scholar arguing that his funny stories were intended to belittle and marginalize the able-bodied poor (Woodbridge 102, 128).

In contrast to new historicist critics, social historians have become skeptical about the value of the literature of roguery. While in the 1930s A. V. Judges believed that Harman's was "the best sixteenth-century account of vagabondage and roguery" and that its author had "all the deftness of the trained sociologist," a later generation has been less impressed.[5] Paul Slack observed that the gangs of vagrants with hierarchies of leaders and followers and a canting vocabulary "were by no means as common as Harman and particularly his later plagiarists suggested" ("Vagrants" 377). Still more forcefully, James Sharpe found that "the literary image of the Elizabethan vagrant evaporates as soon as court records are examined" (143). Only recently has Harman's reputation improved among historians, Paul Fideler observing that, despite its limitations, the pamphlet presents a "unique history of the undeserving poor" and a "series of anti-vagrancy 'moments' or preoccupations, each shaped by its migratory, able-bodied poor."[6] My own research indicated that, although legal records were more reliable guides to who vagrants actually were, the literature was still a valuable source because, however distorted its images, it crystallized and reflected the discourses of official and learned opinion (*Masterless Men* 7–8). Moreover, new historicists were seriously engaged with theory, including the work of Freud, Marx, and Foucault, which has long been a preoccupation of my own scholarship, whereas historians were rejecting "grand theory" in favor of the descriptive "microhistory."[7]

The object of this essay is to determine where we stand with the theorizing and historicizing of Harman. First, the essay explores how critics have reinterpreted the text using the theories of Freud. This section examines their interpretations of Harman's views on sexuality and gender and how that body of criticism relates to current historical writing. Can we verify that he interviewed female vagabonds for the purpose, whether consciously or not, of hearing them "talk dirty"? (Carroll 91–92). Where does his representation of women stand in relation to early modern patriarchalist discourse, which feared them as threats to the social order? What role did conventional religious values play in Harman's view of sex?

Second, the paper seeks to determine whether the theories of Marx and Foucault are relevant in historicizing Harman, as some critics have held, and whether traditional historical methods have anything new to tell us about Harman and his pamphlet. What was Harman's social and political position? Was he bourgeois and, as is widely assumed, a member of the commission of the peace in Kent? The essay also asks whether, as some critics maintain, the *Caveat* should be considered a serious contribution to the literature on state control of society (Greenblatt 37). Finally, the paper attempts to establish what the ideological and social context of Harman's work actually was and, thus, to locate it in relation to the boundaries of the disciplines of history and literature.

Harman and Freud

Recent interpretations have represented Harman's tract in Freudian terms. One authority finds Harman's pamphlet full of sexual innuendo and "titillation" in its representation of sex and gender relations. It is a "telling articulation of juridical prurience"; Harman interviewed female rogues in order to "grope" their minds and possibly even their bodies, which was consistent with his fantasies (Mikalachki 130–31). Carroll's study cites Harman's obsession with female sexuality in his interviews of vagrant women, which were "voyeuristic" and in which he engaged in "aural sex" (83, 91). More generally, Reynolds states that the *Caveat* "could easily be generically categorized as early modern erotica or fantasy" (62).

The question of sexuality in Harman's tract is chiefly important because of its wider implications for historical methodology. In sum, it provides an opportunity to confront new historicist theoretical borrowings with old historicist empiricism. To employ post-Freudian labels such as "obsessive" and "prurient" to describe Harman's interviews with female vagrants might be accurate. They may even demonstrate the man's hypocrisy; that is, that he interviewed vagrants because he secretly fancied them and envied their liberated sex-lives (Carroll 91–92).

There are several difficulties, however, with invoking the Freudian paradigm in the analysis of Harman. One is that new historicist critics seem to call up the paradigm in their critical discourse without consciously theorizing it. As a result, other psychoanalytical theories, whether Jungian or post-Freudian, are not considered. Why not, following Jung, put into play a mythic underworld as a feature of Harman's mental furniture? Or an Eriksonian identity-crisis as an explanation of the youth of the vagrants he interviewed? Or, move beyond personality theory to grapple with the rich body of social psychological models of significant others, role theory, projection, and cognitive dissonance?[8] Another difficulty with using the language of Freud is that it tends to endorse the values of Victorian prudery. What do we mean by saying that Harman, or any other text, caused titillation? Are we then not in the seemingly otiose position of making value judgments about texts from another time and culture? Do we then launch attacks against Chaucer for the Wife of Bath's salty character; upon Shakespeare for Cressida's infidelity, for Kate's rebellion, for Cloten's notions of bliss? Clearly, there are dangers in transposing our value judgments upon societies whose mores are different from our own and, more specifically, in interpreting texts like Harman's with modern concepts rather than as artifacts of Tudor morality.[9] We also run the risk of trivializing Harman's statements about sex by treating them as individual psychoses rather as cultural artifacts with broader meanings.

Beyond the theoretical and epistemological issues, there are other difficulties with a Freudian perspective. The first concerns evidence, which makes documenting Harman's psychopathology extremely difficult. Because his emotional life is poorly documented compared to a Luther or a Gandhi, the model will not take us very far: we cannot invite Harman to our couch and psychoanalyze him! A second drawback is that the value of psychoanalysis, as suggested, lies chiefly in its diagnosis of individuals. Generalizing its findings to groups of people is far more problematical, because we know so little about the inner lives of groups, even elite ones. Yet for Harman's fantasies to have larger significance would require that his "case" be typical of Tudor upper classes; that we have indications that their policymaking was wrapped up in their psychopathology. A third difficulty is that by focusing solely on Harman's psychoses we risk creating a one-dimensional man and ignoring other discourses about sexuality in the pamphlet (Stannard; Gay).

Certainly some readings are more persuasive when they state that Harman represented female sexuality as "aggressive, disorderly, and a social threat," which opens up another line of country and some well-known aspects of patriarchal attitudes of the period (Carroll 90; cf. Davis 124–27). More generally, I would argue that the most obvious moral topos of the *Caveat* is its conventional Christian view of sex and marriage. This position does not necessarily conflict with seeing Harman as voyeuristic or prurient; rather it simply opens a further and—I believe—more significant dimension. In fact, although little noticed by scholars, the tract contains a wealth of references to morality and to its key role in the Tudor commonwealth. For example, Harman described "indecent" and "lewd" behavior by vagrants, including their "lechery" and "harlots," which were standard terms of moral condemnation in sixteenth-century Christianity (110–12, 123, 129, 135, 137, 139).

Although most analyses of Harman's moralistic rhetoric focus on his views of females, his preoccupation with sex was not confined to them. He recounted that male rogues were "beastly begotten in barn or bushes" and that they lived "wallowing in lewd lechery, but that is counted amongst them no sin" (123). He discussed in detail the sexual exploits of the "upright men" who he said engaged in "lewd, lecherous loitering." They partied at night and after their "roisting recreation" retired to outbuildings with female partners, "where they couch comely together, and [as?] it were dog and bitch, and he that is hardiest may have his choice." The upright men also deflowered the "doxies"; the walking morts, or single females, were "ready always for the upright men" (117–18, 137, 143–45). While we are obviously listening here to Harman's fantasies—the uprightness of the males being a fairly blatant tip-off—the author's language still maintained the tone of moral condemnation found elsewhere in the pamphlet.

The most striking example of Harman's negative representation of *male* sexuality occurs in his story of a charivari against a Kentish farmer who tried to cheat on his wife. The incident involved a vagrant woman or "walking mort" and allegedly took place in east Kent in the summer of 1566. Pregnant and craving oysters and mussels, she was gathering them along the shore when she fell into a hole up to her waist. Unable to extricate herself and fearing the rising tide, she called out to a man who came and helped her out of the mire. Her savior, a local husbandman, demanded a promise of sex before he would effect the rescue, to which she not surprisingly assented. She postponed the tryst, however, on the grounds that she needed to clean herself up and departed offering to rendezvous with him later in his barn.

But the walking mort was friendly with the farmer's wife and proceeded to his house and reported the matter to the woman, who laid a trap for her husband. She had the vagrant woman go to the barn to await him and contacted five local "gossips," neighbors and friends, to plot a reception for him. To make a long story short, they lay in wait for him, disguised or "muffled for knowing." As he prepared to have sex with her, the vagrant woman invited him to lower his stockings to his ankles, whereupon the gossips attacked, trussing him up with his own hosiery, after which the six women beat him bloody with birch sticks. The upshot, the walking mort told Harman, was that she had heard "a very good report of him now, that he loveth his wife well and useth himself very honestly" (139–42).

This anecdote, which is one of the lengthiest in the pamphlet, raises questions about Harman's views on gender and sexuality. To recount his condemnation of the walking mort's immorality, while ignoring her part in reporting the farmer's advances and participating in the charivari against him, does not do justice to the complexity of Harman's views (Carroll 91). Nor does the statement that "the concluding spectacle of a naked man duped and beaten by women offers its own titillation" add very much to the discussion (Mikalachki 131–32). On closer examination, we find that Harman described the errant male in the same moralistic terms he used for female vagrants—as "a naughty, lewd, lecherous husband," guilty of "insatiable carnality." Harman's rhetoric took the same tack against the man as against the mort: his wife hoped by his punishment that "'he may save his soul that God so dearly bought.'" As further evidence of the man's perfidy, one of the gossips reported that the "faithless husband" had tried to seduce and rape her (140–41).

This evidence does not square with an interpretation that Harman treated vagrant women purely as sexual objects. Even when he discussed their sexuality, it was not always in terms of sex per se or titillation. Rather his discourse was mainly moralistic and wholly consistent with prevailing views about marriage and fidelity. The charivari, moreover, raises questions about his views of women more generally. We are discovering new evidence of early modern women's resistance to male authority, of which Harman's story can be considered an example. Female insubordination is well documented when it triggered the picturesque "ridings" that mocked males who did not control their wives. While ridiculing husbands, such events of course had as their chief purposes the controlling of unruly wives.[10] Similarly, women might appear briefly as transgressors against patriarchy by murdering their husbands, but they were soon subdued through the judicial system (Dolan 48).

Recent research has unearthed new realms in which women actively pursued independent roles without inspiring the sensationalism of the public riding or the horrific homicide and without always being co-opted. From the medieval period onward English women are found turning the world upside down (Hanawalt 100, 109). In the early modern period cases of outright resistance to male authority have been found to include women claiming to possess supernatural powers through magic and witchcraft and veterans' widows who went to court to secure pensions during the civil wars and Interregnum (Kermode and Walker 5–6, 10, 48–49). Sexual defamation was another vehicle for female assertiveness, because it provided a means to complain about men and to impugn their character (Gowing 29–30, 35, 38–40, 43). Still more assertive were scolds, who were accused of verbal abuse but also of disrupting neighborhoods through their contentiousness, which might include public slander and demonstrations against community leaders (Ingram, "'Scolding Women'" 51, 65).

Where does Harman's tract fit? "Gossips" of the kind that he cited were another source of female independence, as a recent study of women and authority has shown (Capp 117–45). Technically the term derived from "god-sips" or relatives through baptism, who in theory might be of either gender, but who were usually women. In practice the term had a number of meanings. It could have a negative connotation when males referred to women spreading rumors, but it was also employed simply to mean a group of female friends, who were especially prominent in supporting one another in the experience of childbirth (Capp 129).

But there was more to gossiping than births, church rituals, and sociability because, as represented in Harman's tract, it gave women a focus for loyalty and collective action. Gossips spread rumors and hurled insults, especially of a sexual nature, engaged in the shunning of alleged offenders, and even attacked their homes. As in Harman's tale, they defended wives wronged by husbands, but unlike Harman usually by publicly denouncing and sometimes inflicting beatings on the women with whom the men were consorting. By picking on the offending female parties, of course, the gossips did not directly threaten patriarchal authority, and in this respect Harman's story of a man being beaten may stretch the bounds of credibility. But there are sufficient instances of similar attacks upon men in both judicial and literary sources to suggest they were not wholly exceptional (Capp 117, 132, 134–37). Harman's story of husband-beating may be overstated, even invented, but that he included it in his pamphlet, condemned the husband's plans to cheat on his wife, and described his humiliation by the women in a positive light, shows that he did not represent women simply as titillating sex-objects or victims. After all, the *Caveat* was dedicated to Elizabeth, countess of Shrewsbury, aka Bess of Hardwick, one of the most formidable women of the age.[11]

The foregoing suggests that discussions of women's positions have too narrowly focused on binary distinctions between submission and resistance and that in reality there was a wide spectrum of reactions to male dominance, many of which involved give-and-take and, ultimately, compromise. Likewise the neat division between private and public spheres. Women had no formal role in public life, but they frequently participated in it, acting independently to pursue their interests as they perceived them—as gossips, defamers, witches, rioters (Capp 125, 137–40). More generally, Harman's *Caveat* suggests that the application of Freud's theories is as likely to distort as to inform. Freudian notions that postulate voyeurism and titillation are misleading when applied to Harman. Sex *was* a focus of his pamphlet, but not only in the senses that some have concluded. He was also concerned to safeguard standards of sexual morality and to condemn deviations by vagrants and nonvagrants, women and men alike. Further, like many of his contemporaries, he believed that immorality was a threat to society's spiritual and material well-being.

Marx and Foucault

If a Freudian shoe does not fit Harman very well, what about Marxist and Foucauldian ones? In his famous essay "Invisible Bullets: Renaissance Authority and Its Subversion," Greenblatt took a Marxist line with an Althusserian or Foucauldian twist, arguing that Harman was a "middle class Prince Hal" engaged in the politics of control; that is, a respectable person who thwarted the underworld's subversion of authority by practicing hypocrisy—feigned sympathy, as in the Prince of Wales's criminal high jinks with Falstaff and company. According to Greenblatt, Harman, like Prince Hal, deserves a place in "the founding of the modern State." They both discovered worlds of disorder, which threatened to subvert the status quo, but by uncovering these underworlds they checked the subversions, ratifying the old order, and generating positive moral values.[12] It can be more broadly argued that Harman, like many Elizabethans, believed in an ideal moral universe in which good—or the good—balanced evil and the wicked. He was therefore prepared to condone the gossips' charivari against the farmer and to accept a wide range of judicial violence against vagrants, because it held in check an underworld of malefactors.

Recent criticism has developed theoretical perspectives similar to Greenblatt's. Carroll presents a Marxist/Foucauldian interpretation in describing Harman as a "bourgeois" author and an "expert practitioner" in what Foucault termed the "political technology of the body" (83, 86). For his part, Reynolds adapts the philosophy of Althusser and his concept of a "(Repressive) State apparatus" in alliance with dependent "Ideological State apparatuses," which, taken together, combined to "advance the image and development toward the totalized state." Lacking a standing army, however, governments in Renaissance England were insufficiently developed to fit the Althusserian model of repression.[13] Because of this incomplete development, the upshot was that, contrary to many new historicist critics, criminal subversion of established order was not contained. Rather a "distinct criminal culture" emerged in the sixteenth century, a "subnation" with its "own laws and customs" and "united by its own aesthetic, ideology, language, and lifestyle"

(Reynolds 1, 16). The path for the emergence of the underworld was "transversal power," a social force created by an "affective presence" and self-identification, which enabled the criminal culture to confront the social and political orders both as real and perceived threats.[14] Further questioning new historicist criticism, Reynolds assigns less prominence to Harman, who he says actually took pleasure in writing about the sex lives of criminals, arguing that his observations contained "a mixture of contempt and enthusiasm" (61–62).

What *were* Harman's social and political positions? Does the *Caveat* articulate the convergence of bourgeois ideology, class, and the state that some critics observe? Does it represent a new technology of punishment for the poor? Since Harman was himself supposedly a justice of the peace, a key officer of law enforcement, was the pamphlet itself possibly an instrument of this technology of state power?

From the outset serious misconceptions about Harman's social status must be corrected. He was most definitely *not* "middle class" *or* "bourgeois" in rank, nor even of the "middling sort." The latter is a label somewhat more acceptable to early modern historians to describe people in trade or manufacturing, but it does not fit Harman, so that we can rule out a vulgar Marxist interpretation equating new institutions of state power with that old chestnut "the rise of the middle classes." Although, as will shortly be seen, Harman had links with London's mercantile elites and knew about metropolitan crime and criminal justice, he was solidly of the upper gentry and therefore of requisite rank to hold high local office. He was described as "esquire" in a patent roll entry of 1557 concerning land in St. Mary Magdalene parish in Bermondsey, Surrey, and his coat of arms was listed in the heralds' visitation of Kent in 1574, confirming his assertion in the pamphlet that he was an esquire whose pewter dishes were "well marked and stamped with the cognizance of my arms."[15] Harman's family was prominent and well connected. His grandfather was described as a clerk of the Crown under Henry VII and held land at Elham and Maystreet in Kent from 1480. His father added to the family holdings the manor of Maxton or Mayton in the county, and Thomas inherited the whole of the estate and resided at Crayford near Dartford from 1547. He married the daughter of Sir Edward Rogers, who was listed as holding the office of "controller," and he was of sufficient wealth and standing to purchase the wardship of a member of the Boughton family in 1559.[16]

The author's official position has also been misunderstood. Although he held important public office, he was not apparently a member of the commission of the peace for Kent when his pamphlet was published, even though he reported that he was and numerous scholars have accepted the claim.[17] If Harman held no official position in which he might have prosecuted the vagrants he claimed to have interviewed, can we really charge him with "duplicity" and entrapment as Greenblatt claimed? I have searched the Pipe Rolls from Michaelmas 1545 to Michaelmas 1567, which recorded the service of justices eligible for a per diem from the crown, and the entries for Kent, which included dozens of JPs, did not list Harman. It is possible that he did not apply for the four-shilling-a-day allowance, but persons of his rank were eligible and many put in claims; those who did not were usually of knightly status or higher.[18] There is further evidence that Harman did not serve on the commission in Kent in the period of the *Caveat*. He was not listed in commissions of 1559 or 1562, and he was absent from returns of JPs sent to the privy council by bishops in 1564. At any rate, by his own account he mainly gathered information from vagrants when he was housebound due to illness rather than while serving as a JP.[19] The conclusion seems inescapable that if Harman did serve as a justice, it was possibly in an earlier time, before 1545, in another county, or that if he did hold the office in Kent, he was unrecorded or did not claim his per diem.

While probably not on the commission of the peace, Harman did hold important local offices that, even if they did not put him directly in contact with vagrants, show that he was a person of standing. In 1550 he was named to a commission in Kent to collect a "relief" or tax granted in Parliament in November, which is a sign of rank in the community.[20] Harman also served in another important local office in the reign of Mary I, that of commissioner of sewers, which placed him in contact with London officials and with social conditions in the capital. In 1554 and again in 1555 he was appointed to the commission for Kent, which was responsible for the river Thames and its tributaries from Ravensbourne near Southwark down river to Gravesend bridge.[21]

While it is amusing that Harman the student of society's lower depths might be responsible, literally, for the flotsam and jetsam of the Thames, this should not detract from the office's weightiness. In reality, it would be difficult to find a stretch of water more central to the country's economy and security. The commissioners were appointed by the highest officers of state next to the sovereign—the lord chancellor, the lord treasurer, and two chief justices (Kirkus xxii). This region of the Thames was vital to the nation's shipping, its defense, and its trade. It was particularly important for the country's export trade, over which London was developing a virtual monopoly, and for the provisioning of the capital, particularly in Mary I's reign, when England was in the throes of a trade depression and a number of dreadful harvests (Gould 125–29; Hoskins 28, 36).

Harman's metropolitan connection was apparent in the commission of

1554, which included Sir Martin Bowes, a Lord Mayor of London in the mid-Tudor period, a prime mover in hospital reforms under Edward VI, and a founder of Bridewell, the City's innovative new institution for policing vagrancy and prostitution that was founded in 1553. Sir Martin had a house and lands southeast of the City on the Thames at Woolwich and just a few miles from Harman's residence at Crayford. Both places are no more than about a half mile in distance from the river (Slack, "Social Policy" 109–11, 115; *DNB*).

Harman Recontextualized

Although Harman was not of the quorum in the commission of 1554, his presence on it and his association with Sir Martin Bowes, placed alongside his social position of esquire, suggest he was a man of substance with significant contacts among major players in City government. Greenblatt has proposed that Harman's purpose was "to understand and control the lower classes," and that he "literalizes the power of the book to hunt down vagabonds and bring them to justice" (49, 51). These assertions have until now lacked substance, because so little was known about Harman's social and political roles. This gap in new historicism's scholarship is symptomatic of a more general issue which, as Gabrielle Spiegel has observed, is fundamental to its practice; that is, that new historicism will lack credibility until it "is able to explain the supposed links between literary and social praxis in concrete and persuasive terms that can be generalized" (71 n. 43). Beyond the immediate text, was Harman really linked to any new "political technology" for the policing he described? Beyond generalized formulations about "political man," what can we discover about Harman's involvement?

There is no doubt that the author's concerns focused on London, the main seat of political power but also the site of the revolutionary new institution of Bridewell, which was designed to rehabilitate the vagrant poor through incarceration.[22] The *Caveat*, combined with independent judicial documentation, allows one to delineate Harman's connections with London's criminal justice system, his own theories about punishment, and how they related to thinking of the time. Purely at a descriptive level, the pamphlet's geography shows the author's extensive links with the metropolis. While there are occasional references to some western shires, the geographical grid was mostly London and the Home Counties. Kent itself figured prominently, but most of the action actually took place in the capital or its immediate environs (111, 115–17, 119, 121, 124, 128, 130–32, 134, 138–39, 145, 148).

The prime piece of evidence showing that Harman was in contact with the London authorities concerns a centerpiece of the tract, the case of the false epileptic beggar or "counterfeit crank" Nicholas Jennings alias Blunt, which played out in the City and Southwark in 1566 and 1567. We do not know whether the first edition of the *Caveat*, of which no copies survive, contained the Blunt story, but Harman's references in subsequent editions to the Court of Aldermen's action against the offender show that Harman was *au fait* with events in the capital. This would not be surprising. His fellow commissioner of sewers and neighbor Sir Martin Bowes had been an alderman since 1536 and had committed offenders to Bridewell during the first years of its existence after 1553. Even though Sir Martin died in the summer of 1566, since Harman knew this leading figure in London government, it would be reasonable to think he was acquainted with others who could have informed him of the Blunt case.[23]

Blunt is important because he provides a rare glimpse of a real live rogue who appears in official court records as well as in the literature. Harman actually claimed to have participated in the Blunt episode, beginning in November 1566 when the man approached him in his London lodgings in Whitefriars and before he came to official notice. Harman reported that he interviewed Blunt, even checking his story that he had previously received succor in Bethlehem hospital, which Harman found was false, and then had the man followed into Southwark where he escaped after his fraud was exposed.[24] In January 1567 Blunt was arrested and brought before the Court of Aldermen, because he "counterfeited himself to be a diseased person with the grevious [*sic*] disease of the falling sickness." He was ordered whipped at a cart's tail through the City's markets with a picture of his fraudulent deformed body carried before him on a pole. Then he was recommitted to Bridewell and put to hard labor.[25] Even if Harman heard about Blunt's arrest after the fact and included it in later editions, the example still demonstrates a "true crime" element that is lacking in most of the literature.

The 1573 and third edition of the *Caveat* expanded the Blunt story and elaborated on his arrest and his punishment in Bridewell, where he was made—literally—a poster child of street crime. He was arrested in Whitefriars while begging in a new disguise—his third, having dressed up as a shipwrecked sailor after playing a false epileptic. Although he attempted to escape, Harman's printer, who previously had pursued Blunt the epileptic, called a constable and then a deputy alderman to make the arrest. Blunt admitted his frauds and was treated to an impressive array of punishments. After several days in a compter (a temporary jail) he was sent to Bridewell, where he was stripped naked, dressed in his "ugly attire" to the astonishment of the governors, and dispatched to "the mill" there for hard labor, during which time his picture was drawn. Then he was made to stand in the pillory in Cheapside dressed both in his handsome and begging clothing and was afterward whipped at a cart's tail through the City. During this progress, as the Court of Aldermen document stated, his portrait was displayed before him and then, finally, in front of his own house. The grand finale was his return to Bridewell, where he was eventually released on the promise of honest work, and where his picture was kept "for a monument" of his deceitful life (298–99).

Blunt's story in the 1573 edition of the *Caveat* is an emblem of the old and new punishments for vagrancy. Incarceration in a compter, humiliation in the pillory, and whipping behind a cart were traditional punishments, but being stripped naked, dressed up, and put to hard labor in Bridewell were recent in origin and represent the cutting edge of the new penal technology. Having one's portrait drawn and publicly shown was similarly novel, rather like FBI mug shots in the post office, but the pièce de résistance was the placing of Blunt's portrait in a prominent position in Bridewell as a warning to others. The pamphlets included illustrations of most of these events, including pictures of Blunt naked, in his real clothing, in his disguise as a false epileptic, being whipped at the cart's tail, and even the whips and manacles used. A more complete recitation of the penal process would be hard to find in early modern literature.

The *Caveat* had another connection with legal processes of the period. One of Harman's claims to credibility—which recurs in the literature of roguery, from Harman to Henry Mayhew's reports of London's poor in the mid-nineteenth century and to Hunter S. Thompson's rides with the Hell's Angels in the twentieth—is that he had firsthand evidence of their lives because he interviewed them. Whatever the veracity of the claims, there was an actual parallel to Harman's interviews in the legal process, which resulted in a rich documentary source, the deposition or "examination." Provoked, it seems, by a fear of conspiracies and riots, these documents become increasingly abundant in Tudor quarter sessions records, reflecting their wider use by justices of the peace under a statute of 1555. They provide a wealth of detail about the lives of the vagrant poor, including their occupations and migrations, as well as their sex lives. Even if Harman did not sit on the bench in Kent, it seems plausible to think that he knew enough about the new legal procedures to have employed a similar technique in his encounters with vagrants.[26] Once again, he appears to be on the cutting edge of the Tudor system of criminal justice.

Harman was not, however, solely concerned with reconstituting power through institutional means such as punishments and the examination process. A further, little-noticed feature of Harman's tract is that, more than other pieces of the rogue literature, its author engaged in Renaissance discourses about crime and poverty. For example, he was aware of the extensive legislation attacking vagrancy under the Tudors, for he cited "the most wholesome statutes and necessary laws made" for the purpose. His reasoning contained a principle dear to Tudor social commentators and legislators since the 1530s, that is, that giving alms to the able-bodied poor had deleterious consequences. It deprived the really destitute of succor. It fostered crime by failing to prosecute people who were allowed to run free, to steal horses, pigs, and poultry, to rob people on the highway, to lift linen and clothing from hedges and open windows, and to burgle homes and shops (110). In this manner Harman's tract reached farther than simply recuperating power relations by paralleling examination procedures and referencing legislation. As has been argued regarding crime in eighteenth-century novels, the *Caveat* actually defined mid-Tudor norms of social relations, particularly with the poor and the criminal, by its recording of deviance.[27]

What lay behind Harman's prescriptive discourse on crime and the poor were two themes that pervaded Tudor social thinking—the glorification of God and advancement of the commonwealth. By punishing the wicked and relieving the worthy, he said, "then shall not sin and wickedness so much abound among us; then will God's wrath be much the more pacified towards us." The pamphlet employed the Christocentric language of the Protestant reformers and magistrates like Sir Martin Bowes, who reformed London's hospitals and founded Bridewell in the late 1540s and early 1550s. It promised that the wicked might through "true labor and good life, in the world to come . . . save their souls, that Christ, the second Person in Trinity, hath so dearly bought with His most precious blood." Then would ensue "the amendment of the commonwealth" so that "then shall this famous empire be in more wealth and better flourish." Plagues would be dispelled, the queen and nobles would enjoy prosperous and felicitous rule, and the common people would experience peace in mind and body.[28]

Harman's ideas were also closely attuned to early Elizabethan policies on the policing of the able-bodied poor. The period from 1547 to 1563 saw five changes of monarch, serious rebellions in 1549 and 1554, three alterations in the official religion, a major depression in the country's main export trade of woolen cloth, and large-scale conflicts with Scotland and France that resulted in the loss of England's last outpost on French soil.[29] Whether or not these events constituted a systemic crisis, they upset people in authority, who set about reassessing Tudor social policies, including those affecting the able-bodied poor. Harman's tract should be seen as belonging to that phase of reassessment, which evinced feelings of fear and frustration and which prompted government activism.

Not surprisingly, the authorities considered desperate measures to deal with the able-bodied poor. In 1559 an anonymous list of "Considerations delivered to the Parliament," which was probably the work of a privy council committee, contained a proposal that an act of 1547 be revived that included slavery as a punishment for vagrancy. As for unemployed cloth-workers, Sir William Cecil, the queen's principal secretary, proposed that they be gathered up and sent to Ireland, presumably not on a voluntary basis.[30] These particular proposals were not put into effect, but they do capture the mood of the times. No wonder that Harman frequently referred to hanging as a solution for vagrancy and cited with approval the torture of a false dumb man to make him speak (110, 112, 115, 117, 133 [dumb man], 143).

There was, in reality, serious, widespread action taken to police the able-bodied poor. Special searches for vagrants were conducted locally in the early 1560s as Parliament considered its options. The Poor Law passed in 1563 contained few new provisions governing the unemployed, but the Statute of Artificers of 1563, which sought to "banish idleness," provided that laborers without letters from previous employers would be liable to punishment as vagrants. In an undated memorandum that may date from 1566, Cecil took the trouble to write in his own hand a definition of vagrants and what looks like a schedule for arresting them. Then between 1569 and 1572 the Privy Council ordered a nationwide campaign of roundups.[31] Harman's animosity toward the able-bodied poor was of a piece with the 1560s and should be read in that context.

Harman Reconsidered

Literary critics have done scholars a great service in reexamining Harman's *Caveat*. Historians had become skeptical about the literature of roguery almost to the point of denying it any value whatsoever. Where historians feared to tread, critics stepped in to attempt to historicize Harman's text by connecting it to other modes of representation, both canonical (the theater) and noncanonical (jestbooks). In the process, students of literature have made significant strides across the traditional boundaries between the disciplines. They have also brought theoretical perspectives to the text and its author by applying the challenging models of Freud, Marx, Althusser, and Foucault.

But neither the historians' rejection of the texts nor the new literary approaches is entirely persuasive. This paper has attempted to show that, contrary to some historians' skepticism, the *Caveat* is a rich and complex text which, while open to a variety of readings, can still be productively studied with traditional historical methods. The paper has undertaken this task in ways that would be familiar to the founder of modern historical research, Leopold von Ranke: first, by a close rereading of the *Caveat* in the light of new scholarship; second, by going beyond Harman's text to find documentation that might confirm, refute, or at least flesh out his statements; third, by seeking new evidence that previous scholars had not unearthed; and, fourth, by attempting to re-create the historical context to which the author and his pamphlet belonged.

How productive has the exercise been? On the question of Harman's representation of sex more than one reading seems feasible and a purely Freudian perspective appears rather limiting. As regards new and collaborative evidence, we now seem better placed to locate the author in relation to the social and political structures of Kent and London. It seems Harman was actually far more than a sickly and retired JP who interviewed vagrants at his front gate. His official position was an important one that put him in contact with the elites of London; his knowledge of the judicial system is apparent by the Blunt affair. As regards context, Harman's pamphlet, despite its seemingly "marginal" subject matter, should be considered part of the mainstream of social and religious discourse in the 1560s, because his positions on sex, morality, and the poor were closely attuned to the discourses of his times.

In the manner of old historical methods, to historicize Harman has led this paper to critical assessments of theory. Given the richness of the material in his text, the Freudian perspective might seem a fruitful one, but evidence cannot be produced to prove it correct or incorrect. Harman was interested in representing sex, but was this the product of personal pathology or of a wider culture that, judging by Renaissance poetry, chapbooks, and church court cases, was similarly preoccupied with the subject? Was he captivated by sex qua sex or by the moral issues that sexual violations posed? Did he perhaps use sex rhetorically to score points against those he considered dangerous rather in the manner of Richard III's propaganda against his enemies?[32] It is extremely difficult to disentangle the personal and ideological in Harman's sexual discourse, but the multilayered ways in which he discussed the issues strongly suggests that his interest was more than personal.

As regards a Marxist interpretation, a better understanding of Harman's position in the landed upper classes permits a swift rejection of the assumption that he was of the middling sort. It is true that he was in contact with the London elites and that he shared their ideas about policing the able-bodied, for we know that Sir Martin Bowes and his fellow magistrates created Bridewell and its new police measures in this period. But we should also remember that Par-

liaments filled with men of Harman's social ilk had been passing similar legislation and new measures such as examination-process since the reign of
Henry VIII. We should attempt to rid ourselves of the notion that new ideologies and institutions are always co-equivalent with the middle classes in the
Renaissance.

Foucault's theory of the potency of power and ideology is possibly the
most relevant to the Harman text, which does incorporate many of the new
early modern concerns about policing the vagrant poor—the fear and hatred
of the able-bodied malingerer; the conviction that political disorder, moral
decay, and eternal damnation will result from ignoring idleness; and, a willingness to deploy a great variety of institutional strategies to police offenders.
Foucault's theory, however, tells us both too much and too little. It is too
sweeping in its breadth, including almost all institutions in a society, and runs
the risk of erecting a straw man whose sole identity in life is to engage in social
control. Yet the history of the 1560s shows that factors besides the political
impinged upon the production of the *Caveat,* including economic, religious,
and military ones. Foucault's theory, moreover, pays too little attention to
specific policies, institutions, and the conditions that produced them. It is true
that Bridewell represented a new technology of punishment based, as it was,
on new principles of disciplining and molding the souls of offenders. But
while Blunt's painful experience of the judicial system in London contained
elements of the new penal technology, it also included remnants of the old. In
sum, recent theoretical perspectives on Harman, while fruitful sources of fertile error, are no substitute for the discipline of historical context.

APPENDIX

The Case of Nicholas Jennings Alias Blunt before London's Court of Aldermen, 13 January, 9 Elizabeth I (1567)

At this Court it was ordered and agreed that Blunt being a sturdy vagabond
who is lawfully convicted and attainted as well by good and sufficient witness
as by how own pp [*sic*] confession of that that he has diverse and sundry times
heretofore used and counterfeited himself to be a diseased person with the
grievous disease of the falling sickness and has also of a set purpose disfigur-
ing his body with diverse loathsome spots and other filthiness in his face and
other parts of his body to the only intent to be thereby the rather permitted to
beg and still to delude (as he hath already of a long time done[ )] the good and
charitable people before whom he hath or might come, shall upon Wednesday
now next coming being tied naked to the girdlestead at a cart's tail be whipped

throughout all the common market places of this city having a picture of his own personage deformed in the manner and form aforesaid as he was wont to use, the same carried before him upon a long pole and then to be re-committed to Bridewell there to be set to labour by the governors of the said house in such wise as they shall think mete and convenient, etc.

Source: Repertory of the Court of Aldermen, vol. 16, fol. 149a, Corporation of London Records Office. Spelling and dates modernized.

NOTES

Reprinted from *English Literary Renaissance* 33.2 (2003): 181–200 with permission of the editors. I wish to record my gratitude to my friend and former colleague, William C. Woodson, a true Shakespearean scholar, for his advice and support.

1. The classic text is Chandler. For recent scholarship see Kinney in Harman, "Acknowledgements"; Carroll; Reynolds; Greenblatt; Woodbridge.

2. For two reprints, see Judges 61–118, 515 (n. 13 on Dekker's plagiarism); Salgãdo 79–153. The edition by Kinney is preferred here because it returned to the earliest extant version of 1568: see Kinney in Harman, "Acknowledgements," n.p. For a useful discussion of the first four editions and information on plagiarists, see Carroll 70–71. For Harrison, see 184–85.

3. Carroll 70; Reynolds 29. I wish to thank Drs. Craig Dionne and Steve Mentz for bringing the latter to my attention.

4. For overviews of new historicist literary studies, see Kinney; Montrose 6–7 (italics in original); Howard.

5. Judges 495. Cf. Pound 29. In reality, Judges was poorly placed to assess the *Caveat*, because as his footnotes show he had done no original research on the subject apart from literary sources and possibly statutes.

6. Fideler 65. I am grateful to Prof. Fideler for sending me a copy of his paper.

7. E.g., Beier, "Poor Relief"; for more recent developments in the discipline, see Burke.

8. For the underworld myth, Taylor; identity-crises, Erikson, esp. part 4; for social psychology, Beringer 69ff.

9. I owe this point to Craig Dionne.

10. Ingram, "Reform" 90; Ingram, "Mocking Rhymes" 169, 172, 173 (although husband-beating was not illegal).

11. Durant, but it is even more informative to follow the references in the index of Stone.

12. Greenblatt 50, 52. Greenblatt's views might be considered either Althusserian or Foucauldian because both authors focused attention upon the role of government in social formations, although the latter emphasized the role of class rather less than the former.

13. Reynolds 9, 158 n. 9. For trenchant critiques of Althusser's version of Marxism and its application to English history, see Thompson, *Poverty* 193–406; Thompson, *Whigs* 258–69.

14. Reynolds 6, 8, 17–18. Whether the author makes a convincing case for the existence of an underworld cannot be addressed here, but will be in a review to appear in *Modern Philology* (forthcoming).

15. *Patent Rolls: Philip and Mary* 3:437; Bannerman 61; Harman 119; cf. Greenblatt 37; Carroll 86.

16. *The Visitation of Kent, 1530–1 and 1574* 61; *Patent Rolls: Elizabeth (I)* 27; see also *DNB* and Glover. The *DNB* is the source of the confusion concerning Mayton or Maxton. The latter was the one possessed by the Harmans: Ireland, *The County of Kent: from the Earliest Records to the Present Time* 141 (Maxton and the Harmans). For Thomas Harman as a Crayford landowner, see Hasted p. 279, IX, pp. 459–60.

17. Kinney 134; cf. Beier, *Masterless Men,* 160; Archer 204; Cockburn, 224; Carroll 73; Reynolds 62.

18. Public Record Office, E. 372/391–412. For a thoughtful discussion of these records see Hurstfield 90.

19. Gleason 122–23; Bateson 57–58 (forty-six justices listed but no Harman); Harman 109–10.

20. *Calendar of the Patent Rolls, preserved in the Public Record Office: Edward VI* 355.

21. *Calendar of the Patent Rolls, preserved in the Public Record Office: Philip and Mary* 1:36; 2:110.

22. For a fuller discussion, see Beier, "Foucault *Redux?*"; also Spierenburg.

23. Beaven 1:11; Bridewell Hospital Court Books, 1560, fol. 92a.

24. Harman 129–32; Carroll 70, usefully disentangles the editions.

25. Repertory, Court of Aldermen, 16/149a, Corporation of London Records Office. See the appendix for a transcript.

26. See the discussion in my book, *Masterless Men* 157–58.

27. Cf. Gladfelder. I owe this reference to Dr. Craig Dionne.

28. Harman 110–11. For how these ideas were developed in London in the period preceding the "Caveat," see Beier, "Foucault *Redux?*" Harman's confessional views are otherwise unknown. There were Harmans in both Catholic and Protestant camps in the county, although whether they were related to Thomas is unclear: Clark 31, 66. See also Koch.

29. Jones; and for a more anodyne description, Loach and Tittler.

30. Power and Tawney, eds., 1:325 ("Considerations"), 2:47 (Cecil plan); on the committee, see Bindoff.

31. Cunnington 1:43; Essex Record Office Q/SR 11A; *Tudor Economic Documents, Tudor Economic Documents* 1:339, 342; Public Record Office SP 12/41/76; Beier, *Masterless Men* 155–56.

32. I owe the point about Richard III to my friend and former colleague Dr. Alexander Grant.

WORKS CITED

Archer, Ian W. *The Pursuit of Stability: Social Relations in Elizabethan London.* Cambridge: Cambridge UP, 1991.

Bannerman, W. Bruce. *The Visitation of Kent, 1530–1 and 1574*. London: Harleian Society, vol. 74, 1923.

Bateson, Mary, ed. "A Collection of Original Letters from the Bishops to the Privy Council, 1564, with Returns of the Justices of the Peace." *The Camden Miscellany*. Camden Society, n.s. 9. London, 1895.

Beaven, Alfred B. *The Aldermen of the City of London*. 2 vols. London: Eden Fisher, 1908.

Beier, A. L. "Foucault *Redux?* The Roles of Humanism, Protestantism, and an Urban Elite in Creating the London Bridewell, 1500–1560." *Criminal Justice History* 17 (2002): 33–60.

———. *Masterless Men: The Vagrancy Problem in England, 1560–1640*. London: Methuen, 1985.

———. "Poor Relief in Warwickshire, 1630–1660." *Past and Present* 33 (1966): 77–100.

Beringer, Richard E. *Historical Analysis: Contemporary Approaches to Clio's Craft*. New York: Krieger, 1986.

Bindoff, S. T. "The Making of the Statute of Artificers." *Elizabethan Government and Society: Essays Presented to Sir John Neale*. Ed. S. T. Bindoff, J. Hurstfield, and C. H. Williams. London: Athlone P, 1961. 56–94.

Burke, Peter, ed. *New Perspectives on Historical Writing*. University Park: Pennsylvania State UP, 1991.

Capp, Bernard. "Separate Domains? Women and Authority in Early Modern England." *The Experience of Authority in Early Modern England*. Ed. Paul Griffiths, Adam Fox, and Steve Hindle. London: Macmillan, 1996. 117–45.

Carroll, William C. *Fat King, Lean Beggar: Representations of Poverty in the Age of Shakespeare*. Ithaca: Cornell UP, 1996.

Chandler, Frank Wadleigh. *The Literature of Roguery*. 2 vols. Boston: Houghton Mifflin, 1907.

Clark, Peter. *English Provincial Society from the Reformation to the Revolution: Religion, Politics, and Society in Kent, 1500–1640*. Hassocks, Sussex: Harvester, 1977.

Cockburn, J. S. "Early-Modern Assize Records as Historical Evidence." *Journal of the Society of Archivists* 5.4 (1975): 215–31.

Cunnington, B. H., ed. *Some Annals of the Borough of Devizes, 1555–1791*. 2 vols. Devizes: G. Simpson, 1925.

Davis, Natalie Z. "Women on Top." *Culture and Society in Early Modern France*. Stanford: Stanford UP, 1975.

Dolan, Frances E. *Dangerous Familiars: Representations of Domestic Crime in England, 1550–1700*. Ithaca: Cornell UP, 1994.

Durant, David N. *Bess of Hardwick: Portrait of an Elizabethan Dynast*. London: Weidenfeld and Nicholson, 1977.

Erikson, Erik H. *Childhood and Society*. 2d ed. New York: Norton, 1963.

Fideler, Paul A. "*Societas, Civitas,* and Early Elizabethan Poverty Relief." *State, Sovereigns, and Society: Essays in Honour of A. J. Slavin*. Ed. Charles Carlton with Robert L. Woods, Mary L. Robertson, and Joseph S. Block. New York: St. Martin's P, 1998. 59–69.

Gay, Peter. *Freud for Historians*. New York: Oxford UP, 1985.

Gladfelder, Hal. *Criminality and Narrative in Eighteenth-Century England*. Baltimore: Johns Hopkins UP, 2001.

Gleason, J. H. *The Justices of the Peace in England, 1558–1640: A Later Eirenarcha.* Oxford: Oxford UP, 1968.

Glover, Judith. *The Place Names of Kent.* London: B. T. Batsford, 1976.

Gould, J. D. *The Great Debasement: Currency and the Economy in Mid-Tudor England.* Oxford: Clarendon P, 1970.

Gowing, Laura. "Language, Power, and the Law: Women's Slander Litigation in Early Modern London." *Women, Crime and the Courts in Early Modern England.* Ed. Garthine Walker and Jenny Kermode. Chapel Hill: U of North Carolina P, 1994. 26–47.

Greenblatt, Stephen. "Invisible Bullets." Berkeley: University of California P, 1988. 21–65. In *Shakespearean Negotiations: the Circulation of Social Energy in Renaissance England.* Berkeley, 1988; orig. pub. *Glyph* 8 (1981).

Hall, Kim F. *Things of Darkness: Economies of Race and Gender in Early Modern England.* Ithaca: Cornell UP, 1995.

Hanawalt, Barbara A. *"Of Good and Ill Repute": Gender and Social Control in Medieval England.* New York: Oxford UP, 1998.

Harman, Thomas. *Caveat for Common Cursitors Vulgarly Called Vagabonds.* In *Rogues, Vagabonds, and Sturdy Beggars.* Ed. Arthur F. Kinney. Amherst: U of Massachusetts P, 1990.

Harrison, William. *The Description of England.* Ed. Georges Edelen. Washington, D.C.: Folger Shakespeare Library, 1968. Reprint, New York: Dover, 1994.

Hasted, Edward. *The History and Topographical Survey of the County of Kent.* 4 vols. Canterbury.

Hoskins, W. G. "Harvest Fluctuations and English Economic History, 1480–1619." *Agricultural History Review* 12 (1964): 28–46.

Howard, Jean E. "The New Historicism in Renaissance Studies." *English Literary Renaissance* 16.1 (1986): 13–43.

Hurstfield, Joel. "County Government, 1530–1660." *Victoria County History of Wiltshire.* Vol. 5. Published for the University of London, Institute of Historical Research by Oxford UP, 1957. 80–110.

Ingram, Martin. "Ridings, Rough Music, and Mocking Rhymes in Early Modern England." *Popular Culture in Seventeenth-Century England.* Ed. Barry Reay. London: Routledge, 1988. 166–97.

———. "Ridings, Rough Music, and the 'Reform of Popular Culture' in Early Modern England." *Past and Present* 105 (November 1984): 79–113.

———. "'Scolding Women Cucked or Washed': A Crisis in Gender Relations in Early Modern England?" *Women, Crime and the Courts in Early Modern England.* Ed. Jenny Kermode and Garthine Walker. Chapel Hill: U of North Carolina P, 1994. 48–80.

Ireland, W. H. *England's Topographer, or A New and Complete History of the County of Kent; From the Earliest Records to the Present Time, Including Every Modern Improvement.* 4 vols. London: G. Virtue, 1828–30.

Jones, W. R. D. *The Mid-Tudor Crisis, 1539–1563.* London: Macmillan, 1973.

Judges, A. V., ed. *The Elizabethan Underworld.* London: Routledge and Kegan Paul, 1930.

Kermode, Jenny, and Garthine Walker, eds. *Women, Crime, and the Courts in Early Modern England.* Chapel Hill: U of North Carolina P, 1994.

Kinney, Arthur F., ed. *Rogues, Vagabonds and Sturdy Beggars*. Amherst: U of Massachusetts P, 1990.

———. "Preface: Studies in Renaissance Historicism." *English Literary Renaissance* 16.1 (1986): 3–4.

Kirkus, A. Mary, ed. *The Records of the Commissioners of Sewers in the Parts of Holland, 1547–1603*. Lincoln Record Society, vol. 54. Lincoln, 1959.

Koch, Mark. "The De-sanctification of the Beggar in Rogue Pamphlets of the English Renaissance." *Dissimilitude: Essays from the Sixth Citadel Conference on Medieval and Renaissance Literature*. Ed. David Allen and Robert White. Newark: U of Delaware P, 1992. 91–104.

Loach, Jennifer, and Robert Tittler, eds. *The Mid-Tudor Polity, c. 1540–1560*. London: Macmillan, 1980.

Mikalachki, Jodi. "Gender, Cant, and Cross-Talking in *The Roaring Girl*." *Renaissance Drama*, n.s. 25 (1994): 120–43.

Montrose, Louis. "Renaissance Literary Studies and the Subject of History." *English Literary Renaissance* 16.1 (1986): 5–12.

Pound, J. F. *Poverty and Vagrancy in Tudor England*. London: Longman, 1971.

Power, Eileen E., R. H. Tawney, eds. *Tudor Economic Documents*. 3 vols. London: Longman, 1924.

Reynolds, Bryan. *Becoming Criminal: Transversal Performance and Cultural Dissidence in Early Modern England*. Baltimore: Johns Hopkins UP, 2002.

Salgãdo, Gãmini, ed. *Cony-Catchers and Bawdy Baskets: An Anthology of Elizabethan Low Life*. Harmondsworth: Penguin, 1972.

Sharpe, J. A. *Crime in Early Modern England, 1550–1750* 2nd ed. London: Longman, 1999.

Slack, Paul A. "Social Policy and the Constraints of Government, 1547–1558." *The Mid-Tudor Polity, c. 1540–1560*. Ed. Jennifer Loach and Robert Tittler. London: Macmillan, 1980. 94–115.

———. "Vagrants and Vagrancy in England, 1598–1664." *Economic History Review*, 2d ser., 27.3 (1974): 360–79.

Spiegel, Gabrielle M. "History, Historicism, and the Social Logic of the Text in the Middle Ages." *Speculum* 65.1 (1990): 59–86.

Spierenburg, Pieter. *The Prison Experience: Disciplinary Institutions, and Their Inmates in Early Modern Europe*. New Brunswick: Rutgers UP, 1991.

Stannard, David E. *Shrinking History: On Freud and the Failure of Psychohistory*. New York: Oxford UP, 1980.

Stone, Lawrence. *The Crisis of the Aristocracy, 1558–1641*. Oxford: Clarendon P, 1965.

Taylor, Rogan. *The Death and Resurrection Show: From Shaman to Superstar*. London: Anthony Blond, 1985.

Thompson, E. P. *The Poverty of Theory and Other Essays*. London: Merlin, 1978.

———. *Whigs and Hunters: The Origin of the Black Act*. New York: Pantheon, 1975.

Woodbridge, Linda. *Vagrancy, Homelessness, and English Renaissance Literature*. Urbana: U of Illinois P, 2001.

MARTINE VAN ELK

The Counterfeit Vagrant

The Dynamic of Deviance in the Bridewell Court Records and the Literature of Roguery

Rogue literature of the early modern period is notoriously ambiguous in its presentation, characterized by a curious combination of jest and morality that has been the subject of much critical discussion. Early twentieth-century historians and readers of rogue literature tended to treat these works as serious anthropological descriptions of the Elizabethan underworld, but more recently, with the exploration of key archival sources, the consensus has become that much of what is "uncovered" in the rogue literature bears little relationship to the historical record of the period, especially because of the absence of any evidence for the guildlike organization of rogues and for canting, both of which figure so prominently in rogue literature.[1] This essay does not make a case for a return to an older notion of the rogue literature as a reflection of real underworld practice. Instead, it puts forward a different model for reading both the rogue literature and the legal records as equally mediated representations and for understanding the deep ambivalence that characterizes both these types of sources. The minutes of the meetings of the Court of Governors at Bridewell Hospital show a surprising parallel with the most popular rogue literature. Both attempt to end the rogue's subversion of social order through disclosure and exposure of the "truth" about his or her trickery, yet they simultaneously present their readers with a disturbing representation of deviance as a pervasive dynamic. In spite of the explicitly stated purpose of doing away with deviance, these texts end up producing a representation of a society in which identities of self and other are malleable through performance and manipulation of conventionally assumed codes of behavior.

While in recent years it has become customary to treat rogue literature as distinct from other, "real" representations of vagrants as separate types of discourse, the relationship between the literature and the legal record has yet to be explored more fully.[2] In *Vagrancy, Homelessness, and English Renaissance Literature*, Linda Woodbridge places the literature of roguery firmly in the tradition of the jestbook genre. Although she takes these works very seriously as cultural representations of the demonized vagrant and although her work does much to situate them in the context of the discourses of reformation, emerging civility, nationhood, and humanism, she writes, "I read these texts as aiming mainly at entertainment, with a veneer of 'warning as a public service' either as a sop to respectability or as part of the joke, since repressive seriousness can make a trickster tale even funnier. . . . I suspect that few sixteenth-century readers took these works seriously as public service announcements" (91). Historians like A. L. Beier have made arguments similar to Woodbridge's in the recent past. Although Beier claims that early modern rogue literature "was believed," he emphasizes in his *Masterless Men* that "legal records present a different picture from the literary one." J. A. Sharpe concludes in *Crime in Early Modern England, 1550–1750* that the "vagrant emerges as a much tamer phenomenon" from the court records than from the rogue literature.[3]

The virtual absence of underworld hierarchies and canting in the legal record has perhaps blinded us to what a reevaluation of the relationship between such records and the literature of roguery can clarify.[4] Most examinations of early modern representations of rogues have emphasized the specificity with which they were demonized, isolated, and scapegoated, although in very different ways. In 1996, William Carroll's *Fat King, Lean Beggar* began a detailed exploration of the contradictory nature of the discourse on poverty. Recently, Bryan Reynolds and Craig Dionne have pointed in similar directions by examining the ideological ambivalence of literary texts on the subject of vagrancy.[5] The Bridewell court records help us explore further the notion of a complicated discourse on vagrancy and of its implications for the social order at large. An important feature of the Bridewell Court Books is that they present us not merely with a set of records about vagrants, but with a *spectrum* of socially condemned behavior, linking the crime of vagrancy to crimes of sexuality and insubordination more generally—the various crimes are reported in the same way and generally punished in the same way. This treatment would have enhanced the impact of stories of vagrants such as those found in the rogue literature, which must have resonated in a much wider way with deviant behavior at all levels of society. Ostensibly, the legal texts serve the purpose of harnessing social stability by imposing fixed identities on offenders. However, the similarity between different types of offenders, of different social backgrounds and certainly not all labeled "vagrant," shows that the Bridewell governors present us with a world in which at every level individuals construct their own, unauthorized identities, whether we are dealing with a sturdy beggar who pretends to be lame or with a woman who falsely claims that her husband was executed during the realm of Queen Mary. While order depends on subjects' acceptance of their proper place as it is assigned to them by the powers that be, the records suggest that in practice it is all too easy to counterfeit identity and ignore the strictures of early modern society to acquire a measure of upward mobility.

The sheer pervasiveness of such behavior in the records suggests that the social order is permeable and permeated by deviance. The rogue literature of the late sixteenth and early seventeenth centuries also presents trickery as allowed and even produced by the rules that govern social exchange. Offering attractive or familiar social positions to their victims, the cony-catchers are able to solidify their own forged identity, eliminating the belief that essential differences between class and gender matter to actual engagement between citizen and rogue.[6] As we shall see, deviance turns out to be not simply the attribute of a particular type of individual, but a more fleeting product of exchange between two people, a *dynamic* rather than a fixed essence. While there is an obvious danger to using the premise of a unified "early modern reader," I want to suggest that this model of crime must have constituted a powerful source of anxiety for early moderns, which may be deflected through laughter, but which nonetheless haunts the literature as much as the records.

In December 1602, the governors at London's Bridewell Hospital uncovered a plot hatched by Mall Newberry (or Newborowe) and Nell Badford to escape, "first by breakinge upp the lockes and so to have gone out of the windowes in the Roome nexte to Charitie hall and to gett downe by hanginge sheetes out of the said windowe." The plot was foiled by a snitch. Being brought before the governors, the two women refused to confess but were nonetheless punished and assigned to hard labor. On January 10, 1603, Newberry appeared again before the governors. This time she had been converted by a preacher, who had been asked to do so by one of the governors. Newberry's conversion turned out to have been a success, unlike in the case of her accomplice, the record notes, because "Newborowe in outward shewe seemed to have the more repentinge and meltinge hart as partlie by her teares appeared." Soon thereafter, she was released.[7] The record, which is a bit of a rarity in its involvement of a priest and its account of a conversion, shows Bridewell capable of performing its idealist function. While the hospital was founded in 1553 as a penal institution, historians have noted that it operated on the relatively new principle that incarceration and forced labor would lead to the reform, and not simply the punishment, of individuals.[8] But the language of the record describing Mall's rehabilitation suggests a degree of unease: the use of "outward show," "seemed," and even "partly" tells us that the governors are aware of the possibility of histrionic manipulation. Mall could be simply adopting a role that is most profitable to her. Can real reform take place if identity can be manipulated through such compliant performativity? The ultimate acceptance of the performance by the governors suggests a real problem in imposing identities on the slippery individuals who are confronted with authority: from their perspective, the governors cannot assess the veracity of Mall's performance, but instead have to base their judgment on her "outward show," which is all that can be known for certain. In rogue literature, we would expect a similar cynicism about such a conversion, as easily adopted as any of the many roles the cony-catchers and crossbiters put on. If disclosure of identity can only be a matter of the outward and a product of social exchange, here between prisoner and governors, a troubling mystery about the essence of individuals will always undermine the law's attempt to maintain social stability.

In spite of the impossibility of the institution's goals, the governors of Bridewell were assigned the task of eliminating the problem of the sturdy beggars who haunted the city, as well as of the unemployed who might be more willing to work, but were unable to find a position with a master.[9] Although Bridewell Hospital had been founded specifically with an eye to controlling vagrancy, the court books show that a large percentage of those examined and judged by the governors were not vagrants. Expanding its original mission to include the correction of all types of offenders, the Court of Governors dealt with a range of crimes. All sorts of sexual transgressions were punished (from simple adultery and prostitution to sex with a "black-amoor" and "buggery" with a child), as were insubordination and immoral behavior of any kind.[10] The number of vagrants presented at Bridewell increased over the course of the sixteenth and into the seventeenth century, but other types of behavior perceived as criminal continued to have a substantial presence in the records through the beginning of the seventeenth century.[11] Narratives of sexual transgression tend to take up most space in the early volumes of the court books, but a second prominent category is constituted by servant-master conflict. Ian Archer and Joanna Innes have both emphasized this aspect of Bridewell jurisdiction. While Innes argues that Bridewell served specifically "to correct the faults of a servant class," Archer focuses more on the apprehension and punishment of apprentices, even though he acknowledges the difficulty of establishing the exact degree to which crime in early modern London was dominated by juveniles and servants (Innes 47; Archer 206–10). Even before we examine any records in detail, then, we can see that vagrancy and the deviant behavior associated with it is by no means as isolated or specified as a crime as many recent works on the discourse of poverty would suggest.

The examinations in the Bridewell Court Books usually supply us with basic information about when the individual was brought in, the nature of the offense, and the response to the accusations (most frequently a confession), to conclude with an indication of the punishment, followed by either incarceration or discharge. Such punishment ranges from having the offender "well-whipped," carted, or committed to Newgate prison (for serious offenses such as murder) to release, in which case the individual might be "discharged upon hope of amendment" or pardoned due to a lack of evidence, because there was no confession, or due to illness. It is important to realize that the records themselves are constructed narratives about vagrants and others, rather than uncomplicated recorded experience. Without any means to verify the facts behind the examinations or even the means by which the confessions have come about, we should treat them with a great deal of caution.[12] Even if we could be certain that examinations are transparent recordings of truthful confessions, we should note that in ordering and selecting the information given in the record, the governors nonetheless do not give us unproblematic access to vagrant lives. Instead, they tell stories with a clear beginning, middle, and end: the individuals are brought forward, their offense is recounted and explained, and the case is resolved through correction and punishment. For this reason, the examinations can be read as attempts on the part of the institution to impose identities on the offenders and thus regulate moral behavior. The "genre" of the examination, then, is not unlike the genre of the rogue tale in that both disclose the mechanics of trickery and crime, with the purpose to contain or end it.

The degree to which vagrancy is treated similarly to other crimes is clear in the limited vocabulary used to impose identities on offenders. Idleness, a central attribute of the sturdy beggar for which Bridewell was intended, is a characteristic of the disorderly servant and apprentice as well. For the governors, one of the favorite terms to describe criminal deviance is the adjective *lewd*, which points not only to evil in general, but also suggests lower-classness ("common," "base," and "ignorant," according to the *OED*) as well as lasciviousness. This lewdness is presented as a socially pervasive ill, in that the adjective is attached to people of different social backgrounds and professions, who have committed a range of crimes. It consists in a refusal to follow the rules that make up an orderly society, including dissimulation and deception of all kinds, practiced by members of different social groups and professions. In addition, the words *cozen* and especially *counterfeit* are applied to a range of different offenses to show that the problem with the sturdy beggar is one that besets the social order more generally. The counterfeiter refuses to accept the identity that has been socially prescribed for him or her, but constructs an alternative identity instead.

It has become a critical commonplace that the vagrant in the early modern period was a figure for a frightening mobility, both geographic and social, pointing to the larger historical, economic, and cultural shifts that made such mobility possible on all levels of society. While the mobility embodied by the vagrant is of course downward mobility, the idea of the rogue came to point to its opposite, upward mobility. The rogues in rogue literature cannot always be recognized as such, since they parade the streets of London in gentlemanly dress, assuming with virtuoso skill a linguistic and rhetorical mobility that allows them to use the material signifiers of class as evidence of their membership of any social group that is convenient and profitable to them.

"Counterfeiting" is central to the rogue's mobility in the rogue literature, and the declared purpose of authors such as Thomas Harman and Robert Greene is to put a stop to it, or, as Greene would have it, to "decipher" the "qualities" of the vagabonds, giving the readers the tools with which to place the rogue in his proper position as social outcast (*Notable Discovery* 157). Theoretically, the possibility of counterfeiting assumes a subversive model of social exchange that allows for individual agency in the construction of identity, a process that does not take place prior to but in the course of a conversation between two individuals. Keith Wrightson has argued that the "politics of subordination" in the early modern period depended on "the need to invest social relationships with meanings supportive of the legitimacy of structures of hierarchy and subordination—to supplement economic and political with cultural authority" (32). Faced with "corrosive processes of social change," the ability of Bridewell governors effectively to impose identities on offenders was central to the maintenance of order. These processes of social change have been related to the emergence of a new concept of the market, as traced by Jean-Christophe Agnew. With the definition of the market itself becoming increasingly tied to process rather than place, he argues, the older boundaries around self and other and, as a consequence, the idea of exchange itself were modified. The nostalgic, idealistic view of social exchange as establishing a clear-cut relationship that reflects and confirms social position is under siege in this period, as it becomes increasingly obvious that individuals can use exchange to contest authoritative impositions and negotiate a new identity, "insinuating" themselves into social circles at will and creating and destroying the relationships that are supposed to confirm order with a simple act of counterfeiting.

The central aim, then, with regard to vagrants who have been apprehended and presented in front of the Court of Governors, is to put a stop to counterfeiting and facilitate future identification. The records achieve this first and foremost through naming vagrants and thus labeling them as such in the record, an attempt to inscribe the vagrant permanently in a text.[13] The obsession with naming vagrants takes the shape of lists, in the absence of a more detailed record of the examination. In October 1602, the minutes offer a list of "Vagrants in the house," which includes name, place of birth, whether the vagrant had been incarcerated in Bridewell before, and, in light of the young age of many of the vagrants, whether they have family to support them, as in this example: "William Collet borne at the 3. Cranes a notable theif aged 12. yeeres or thereaboutes his father one Cooke a Costers monger hard by vintners hall."[14] This is clearly an attempt to reassert the possibility of an unproblematic type of social exchange given a textual, imaginary form, in which the governors name the prisoners, who submit silently (within the confines of the text at least) to such fixing of their identities. The same desire can be seen in the rogue literature too, especially in the work of Thomas Harman, who gives a list of names at the end of his *Caveat for Common Cursitors* (1566) that purports to have the same function as the court records (141–46). Harman seems to want to bolster the law here from his self-declared position as retired Justice of the Peace, a position now questioned by A. L. Beier, who also points out that the interviews with vagrants in the *Caveat* are an interesting parallel to the legal examination.[15] While Harman simply categorizes the vagrants in accordance with their perceived internal hierarchies (classifying them as "upright man" or "palliard"), the records add to the disclosure of the identity of the rogue, the place of origin (important in determining where he will be punished), criminal history, and the potential for rehabilitation. Such interest in simple, straightforward identification in the court records is of course a reflection of a larger obsession on the part of the authorities in general, as laws on carrying passports, badging, branding, and boring holes through ears of vagrants testify.

At times, one vagrant or cutpurse will use this desire on the part of the authorities to ingratiate himself with the governors. This is done by naming a group of other vagrants, as does John Banckes, himself "a coson," who has, appropriately for a cony-catcher, confessed to "cosen a boye of certen coniskynnes." He makes up for his offense by naming nine "common cosoners and cutpurses and comforters of them," one of whom "goes like a gent" and all of whom resort at the Two Footstools (presumably an alehouse or an inn) at St. Katherine's, reminding us of the stories of groups of vagrants gathering at inns, barns, in St. Paul's, and at other places in Harman's *Caveat*.[16] A baker named Thomas Getley, who has "confetered with alle these cutpurses," claims he has seen them do their work at markets and fairs. He offers their names, which include both men and women and some who have dwelling places and are therefore not strictly speaking vagrants. One of those named, brought into Bridewell five days earlier, is led to admit that he is indeed "one of the Faculty of Cutpursyng."[17] The term *faculty*, which is used for power or ability, may also mean, as I believe it does here, "That in which anyone is skilled; an art, trade, occupation, profession" (*OED* 2:8), a usage hinting at the rogue literature and its treatment of cony-catching as a perverse transformation of a respectable trade. In naming vagrants, then, the Bridewell records, like the rogue literature, promise to isolate the vagrant and attribute a firm identity to him or her. Indeed, the association of vagrancy with the notion of counterfeiting is so pervasive that it gains the form of vague accusations of being a "counterfeit loose varlet" or a "counterfet vagraunt," suggesting a pseudoreality to the category of vagrant in early modern London.[18]

Yet the frequency with which the governors of Bridewell punished those in possession of counterfeit licenses problematizes the attempt to use legal records to tie a person to a particular identity or, indeed, to limit the wandering of the rogue (cf. Carroll 45–48; Reynolds 96–101). The counterfeiting of licenses does not involve upward mobility, but simply allows the beggar to present himself as a beggar, using the authority of legal writing to back him or her up. It is also an abiding interest of the authors of rogue literature. John Awdeley's *The Fraternity of Vagabonds* (1561) lists types of vagrants, including three that counterfeit licenses or carry counterfeit licenses. Harman too emphasizes it in his description of the rogue. Though he points out that "you may easily perceive by their colour that they carry both health and hypocrisy about them whereby they get gain," identification turns out to be no easy feat after all:

> they will carry a certificate or passport about them from some Justice of the Peace, with his hand and seal unto the same, how he hath been whipped and punished for a vagabond according to the laws of this realm, and that he must return to T—, where he was born or last dwelt by a certain day limited in the same, which shall be a good long day. And all this feigned,

because without fear they would wickedly wander, and will renew the same where or when it pleaseth them; for they have of their affinity that can write or read. (97)

Harman offers his readers a detailed picture of the futility of everything that goes on in Bridewell, where vagrants are whipped and then given a passport to return to their parish. The very documents that are supposed to limit their future movements have become subject to a counterfeiting that frees the vagrant from legal control as soon as he is physically outside of Bridewell.

While most carriers of counterfeit licenses brought in to Bridewell are simply whipped, occasionally a more public punishment is required. One maker of counterfeit passports, Giles Stile, is ordered "whipped at a cartes arse."[19] Another case involves multiple forms of dissimulation:

> John Steele a prisoner of this house sent in by Master deputie Hickman for Counterfettinge a false licence to begge wthin the cittie of london under coullor that hee had his house burnt in lincolne and fayninge himselfe to be named Richard Codde cleane contrarie, and therebye hathe collected in severall parissshes the benevolence and charitie of diverse well disposed people, and so contrarie to the State hathe forged the pasport and cozened her majesties subjectes. Wich hee could not denye, but saithe that in dede hee bought that licence of a fellowe in Shordiche wich cost him ij s vj d and that in dede hee begde with that licence by the name of Richard Codde.[20]

Taking the simple counterfeiting of a legal document one step further, Steele adopts a false identity along with a story that explains his current situation, a complex assault on the unsuspecting citizen that combines the material evidence of identity with rhetorical evidence of selfhood—the forged document allows Steele to become another, more respectable beggar, whose story arouses pity and charity in a number of parishes. The marginal noting of his name reveals his duality: he has to be recorded as both Steele and Codde for future reference, as is true for numerous others in the records. In some sense, legally, then, Steele has become both, even if the purpose of the examination is to deny him his false identity.

What Steele has done, in effect, is to add a performance to the forged legal text, which is what troubles the governors in other instances of counterfeiting identity too. We see early modern rogue literature rehearse over and over again that many vagrants who beg pretend to be ill, impotent, lame, dumb, or in another form unable to take on regular employment, thus attempting, falsely, to place themselves in the category of the deserving poor. Awdeley and Harman describe the Abraham Man, who "feigns himself mad"; Harman devotes much attention to the "Counterfeit Crank" and the Dummerer (who pretends to be unable to speak); and many other texts feature examples of similarly devious actors. The Bridewell Court Books include numerous cases in the category of the counterfeit crank: soldiers who pretend to have been wounded in the wars, a beggar who "counterfeated the fallyng sycknes," others like Thomas Todman, who simply "counterfeateth him selfe to be syck," or Richard Flodd, who "counterfeyteth him selfe to be madd and trobleth the cittye and will not worke for his livenge."[21]

In two cases, the governors ordered a more elaborate punishment that involved, as in the case of Stiles, "publication" of the dissimulation for the sake of informing the inhabitants of London. William Worall was apprehended in December 1561 for pretending to be dumb, like Harman's dummerer, and therefore, "he the said William Worall shulled on Sondaye then nexte ensuenge stande at powles crosse before the precher with a paper on his breste written on this wise A Deceitfull beggar counterfetinge him selfe to be borne Dome and coulde alwayes speke and also that he shulld open unto the people his said practize."[22] A worse case of deception involved "Jane phelips also pole," who was found to have persuaded a thirteen-year-old boy named Edward Pewter "to feyne him selfe to be bothe deff and domb and caused a supplicacion to be framed by a skrevener to be exhibited to the Quenes highnes in his favour to have a lycence under the great seale to have gonn a beggyng, and hathe receaved soche mony of him as he daily gate with soche dissimulacion." For this crime, she "was adiudged to stand on a pillory and to have her lewd doynges to be in open maner publysshed to the people, and the sayd Boye to stand ther also and to speke to the peopl and to shewe his tonngue out and how he dissembled."[23] More intricate than the usual feigning of sickness, this examination strikes at the heart of Elizabethan attempts to exclude sturdy beggars from poor relief. Jane Phelips combines the deceit of the dummerer with the devious instruction of a young boy, and the employment of a scrivener to acquire not a counterfeit license, but a real one. Histrionic talent, here presented as passed on from woman to boy, allows Jane Phelips to acquire the highest authority, in the form of the queen's great seal, to back up her deception.

In order to assign the proper identity to these individuals, which in this case involves their status as healthy and therefore undeserving poor, the governors have both Worall and Phelips "publish" their deception through their own recounting of it, controlling the performance in which the truth about the self is revealed. In Worall's case this is accompanied by the exhibition of a piece of writing that marks him as a counterfeit and reinstitutes the legal text as authentic evidence of selfhood. Disclosure of the mechanics of deceit is for Edward Pewter supplemented by display of the body part that anchors the boy in his proper position, since, as Harman warns us, dummerers will "gape and with a marvellous force will hold down their tongues doubled" (118). In each case, then, the governors are only capable of preventing future counterfeit performances by using public staging. Rather than reinforcing a different model of social exchange as revealing the essence of these counterfeit vagrants, the means are entirely the same as those used by the vagrants. Much like the authors of rogue literature, then, the Court of Governors employs a public forum for the purpose of social education, which will ensure that gullible citizens will approach any beggar with a healthy dose of suspicion in future. But the way in which the disclosure proceeds undermines the notion that misidentification will be put to an end.

In the display of the tongue, the governors make clear that what is at stake in the deceit of the dummerer is merely a silent version of the deceitful rhetorical negotiation of identity that counterfeits take up to their advantage. Such trickery involves a false presentation of self, but is so persuasive because it simultaneously offers the victim a particular, familiar social position. Thus, the counterfeit crank pretends to be sick in order to place others in the position of the charitable, responsible members of the commonwealth they would like to be. Alternatively, elaborate tricks such as the famous Barnard Law tender the cony the position of friend and fellow cardplayer, while unsuspecting maids may be treated as beloved courtly ladies in order to gain access to their masters' linen, as happens in a story by Robert Greene.[24] In other words, social exchange involves a temporary transformation of self *and* other, a subversive construction of subject positions, which is what renders it potentially dangerous. In *The Second Part of Cony-Catching* (1592), Greene describes the tricksters as sirens, "who sitting with their watching eyes upon the rocks to allure sea-passengers, to their extreme prejudice, sound out most heavenly melody in such pleasing chords, that whoso listens to their harmony, lends his ear unto his own bane and ruin." For this reason, cony-catchers are compared to orators: "as they use rhetorical tropes and figures, the better to draw their hearers with the delight of variety, so these moths of the commonwealth apply their wits to wrap in wealthy farmers with strange and uncouth conceits" (207–8). The siren simile works to show the transformative power of social exchange—the only way to avoid it is by stopping your ears or refusing to engage in exchange at all, as Craig Dionne points out at the conclusion of his essay in this volume. The simile also highlights the similarity between prostitution and cony-catching: it is the seductive quality of trickery that gives the victim an attractive new position that enables deceit on all levels, which eventually results in profit for the trickster-prostitute and a loss of status for the victim.

Like the literature of roguery, the records uncover a large degree of fluidity in self-presentation with its counterpart in the temporary change in position for both trickster and tricked—seemingly effortlessly, vagrants present themselves as something they are not, whether it is with the help of a counterfeit license or without. But cases of counterfeiting, cozenage, and other forms of "lewd" trickery are by no means limited to beggars and vagrants. They involve apprentices and servants, wives and husbands, and seemingly respectable individuals with a profession and a dwelling place, and many sound as if they are taken straight out of cony-catching books. A woman named Wilmot Courtney confesses to having had a scrivener's boy draw up a counterfeit bond to make John Traubridge of Bramford, a gentleman, pay her forty pounds.[25] Sybbell Steyre goes around falsely claiming her husband has been "borned for religion at Canterbury in Quene Marys tyme & that she had viij children & loste by the death of her husbond a howse & ij acres of lande."[26] A tapster, Roger Colyns, gets a young boy to bring him his master's clothes.[27] A wife of a clerk, Elizabeth Wheatley, has falsely pretended to have delivered a baby, for which she is sentenced to public humiliation as the curate "shall make knowen her filthy dissimulacion unto the people" in church on Sunday, at which occasion she has to ask publicly for forgiveness.[28] In each of these cases, rhetorical manipulation of another, be it a scrivener's boy or an entire community, is based on a self-presentation that is invented. The effects of linguistic improvisation on social realities turn out to be pervasive, and so the records, in spite of their attempts at disclosing each of these crimes and returning individuals to their proper places, in fact end up producing a representation of a society in which its subjects are capable of using exchange to construct the identities of themselves and others at will by performing and thus capitalizing on the very conventions that govern exchange.

While those who are already marginal to the social order may pose a threat to it by working their way into respectability, insubordination by those who are viewed as respectable points to a hollowing out of authority at every level. Service is of course central to order. Hence servants and apprentices are presented as on a par with vagrants in the sense that a simple act, the refusal to obey orders, can lead in an instance to a shift into the social identity of vagrant or masterless man. The fact that Awdeley's *The Fraternity of Vagabonds* includes a catalog of trickster-servants points to the same potential conflation of servant and vagrant, in spite of the fact that he lists the two groups separately. At Bridewell, servants are punished for not bringing back money to their masters, forging keys in order to give others access to the house, stealing goods from their masters, and generally squandering their masters' money in dice and card games. Thus, their behavior directly affects their masters' status. Their acts are from time to time motivated, it appears, by a desire to switch places with their masters. Edward Worley confesses to having lifted the door to his master's bedroom off its hinges and having spent the night in the bed of his master and mistress, jesting with the maids, though (he claims) not sleeping with them.[29] Nicholas Hawkesworthe, apprentice to a silkweaver, is brought in for having threatened to run his master through with a knife and that "when he had so done hee would marrie his mistris," an incident that might not be as serious as it seems since the master asked to be able to take him back into his service on the same day he brought him in.[30]

One of these stories, which deserves to be reproduced in full, takes on the tone of a merry tale by Greene and offers the same representation of a social order undermined through disobedience:

Roger Wood the servant & apprentice of Alexandr Best haberdassher brought into this house by ye commaundment of Sr Rowland hill knight, for that the same Roger together with Thomas hopkyn his felow wer taken playeng at dyce all night in the house of John Alyn taylor &c, and beyng her examyned it hathe apered to fall out in this maner. The same night they wer apprehended, the master of the sayd Roger and Thomas went to bed at ix of the clock thinkyng his sayd servantes folowed him, but they came not to bed but took their masters keyes and locked the strete dore after them, went to the next house called Alyns house the taylor, and there playd at cardes. And about one of the clock it chaunced the sayd Alexander to ryse to the prevy, and missed his servantes, and therwith made him ready and went down to the strete dore to have gon foorth, but the dore was locked, and therfor he was compelled to open one of the shop wyndowz and went out that waye, and the sayd Roger and Thomas with ij other cam out of the sayd Alyns house and sodeynly set upon the same Alexander Best their master cryeng theves theves, and the sayd Best also cryed theves and they layd upon the said Best and put him in great fear of his life, for the whiche after examynacion the sayd Roger was her well ponysshed and so discharged.[31]

The story has all the elements of the rogue tale: playing at dice, the humiliation of the haberdasher, whose nocturnal visit to the privy is disturbed, the detail and tone of a jestbook story, and the finish with the collective attack on the respectable householder by the disorderly servants. The ending of the story resembles a number of Greene's tales, in which the cony-catchers, in order to cut a purse, orchestrate a fight in which the victim is involved. In *A*

Disputation between a He Cony-Catcher and a She Cony-Catcher (1592), a trickster starts a lawsuit against the farmer he wants to rob. Trying to have him arrested in St. Paul's, the cony-catchers by agreement violently defend the cony. The officer shouts "Clubs!" so that the apprentices become embroiled in the fight and it is easy to take the purse of the cony (275–78). The court record is, as might be expected, more complicated than the cony-catcher tale: the servants show a bewildering mixture of obedience and disobedience and lack the simple motivation of purse-cutting of the cony-catcher. In spite of their unauthorized dice-playing, they do take care to lock the house on their way out, preventing actual thieves from entering the master's household, but also preventing their master from following them too easily. Yet the disorder is created in both cases through a simple speech act. While the cony-catchers cleverly enlist the unwitting help of the officer, the servants too abuse the law's authority afforded by a simple act of crying "thieves." The poor haberdasher, whose single voice is drowned out by those of his servants, has no means to control a situation in which his identification is manipulated through collective "misnaming," which leads to the imposition of a criminal identity on him. The result is in each case a frightening chaos marked by close physical proximity, a condition in which physical force rather than social authority prevails.

In reproducing the story as an examination, with its beginning indicating the apprehension of the individual servant and its ending culminating in punishment, the Court of Governors seems to present us with the comforting notion that such offenses must come to a fall, but the servants too easily construct an alternative reality in which the master cannot keep his position of authority, suggestive of the effortlessness with which the cony-catchers deprive their victims of their position. While these servants manage to turn matters upside down by temporarily making their master a thief, other offenders are brought in for more straightforward impersonation. Richard Kelley, a smith living in Bridewell, confesses to having been involved in an elaborate setup to cheat on a merchant by posing as John Cockes, a skinner, who entered into a bond to borrow one hundred pounds. Posing as John Cockes, Kelley had dressed up in clothing that is appropriate and along with the two others, who each assumed names and professions other than their own, presented himself to the broker to collect the money. The examination repeatedly makes the point that the broker testifies "it was not this Cockes that knowledged the recognisance."[32] The attempt at identity theft is reminiscent of an examination in which a young woman confesses to having dressed up as a boy in order to visit her lover—while it enables her to come to his workplace safely, she is instantly recognized as herself and as female.[33] Such cases may prove to us that identity theft and impersonation were not always very effective, but the attempts themselves do show that such relatively ordinary individuals treat the social order and their identities as subject to negotiation.

The presence of these narratives of counterfeiting in the Bridewell Court Books allows us to contemplate the connection between all of the crimes committed by those who were turned in to this institution. Adultery and prostitution, vagrancy and disobedience, trickery and impersonation all involve violations of a social order ideally perceived as transparent and fixed, but which turns out to be open to contestation. Not only do violations of social order and attempts at acquiring some measure of mobility (in a wider, more abstract sense rather than the strictly social one) occur among seemingly respectable citizens and vagrants alike, but the records also show a general perception of social exchange as a means to change one's position in the social order. In *The Defence of Cony-Catching* (1592), Cuthbert Cony-Catcher (presumably Robert Greene) develops an idea proposed in one of the earliest works of rogue literature in English, Gilbert Walker's *Manifest Detection of Dice-Play* (1552). One of Walker's rogues famously suggests that cheating and trickery is by no means confined to rogues, but that it characterizes everyone, at every social level.[34] Cuthbert Cony-Catcher makes this point numerous times and backs it up with tales that involve not cutpurses and vagrants but housewives and householders. The moral condemnation attached to the offenders in the Bridewell Court Books cannot do away with the impression one gets that Cuthbert Cony-Catcher is right and that disorder is ingrained in the risk taken in social exchange in general.

The strongest assault upon the counterfeiting of this spectrum of offenders in the court records is through the record itself, which serves to define these slippery individuals. Presenting themselves much like Robert Greene in his proud claim to decipher the rogues, Bridewell governors force those brought into the house of correction to submit to their deciphering of them. Predictably perhaps, a case involving the sexual transgressions of a gentlewoman shows us the double standards of the governors, who discharge her because Sir William Howard, "brother to the Right honorable ye Lord Admirall," asks for her release. But they will not let her go before she has agreed to authenticate her confession through her signature, leaving a permanent record of her transgressions:

> I Elizabeth Evans do acknowledge that I am the daughter of Robert Evans who dwelte sometime on Stratford on haven A cutler in Warkeshire I have called my name sometime Dudley and sometime Carewe but I can shewe no reason that I tooke those names uppon me and further I do confesse I have

bin about London three or foure yeares and I do acknowledge that I have lived with losse of my bodye with divers persons diverse and sundrye times for which I am hartelye sorrye and do aske god and her majestie and all her majesties subiectes whome I have offended therebye forgivenes for the same and do promise by god his grace never heereafter to offend in the like fault againe. And in testimonye of the true repentaunce and sorrowfullnes of my hart and purpose of amendement of my life I have heere of my hand this first daye of Aprill 1598 And in the 40 yeere of her majesties Raigne that nowe is. Elis evens[35]

Even a clear-cut confession cannot secure her identity or dispel the impression of the changeability of this woman, whose accusation requires multiple testimonies and many pages of lengthy description of her "lewd" acts. Where does the confession originate? The language of the narrative points to the possibility that it has been constructed for her by the governors. If Evans herself came up with the confession, it shows her rhetorical ability to adopt a legal discourse that is acceptable to the governors and leaves deliberate gaps in motivation ("I can shewe no reason that I tooke those names upon me"). Whether the role is imposed or "voluntarily" adopted by Evans, the confession links her to Mall Newberry's performative compliance, proven by her tears of contrition. Both women remain impossible to interpret with any degree of certainty by the governors. In punishing Evans, the governors rely on a basic respect for the law and its forms of writing that their subjects have already rejected in their past actions. The literature of roguery and the Bridewell court records show that social exchange is employed at every level as an open playing field, an opportunity for shifting and using the easy assumptions and desires of others for profit. It is a market-based model of exchange that will continue to hollow out the social order from within.

NOTES

1. See Linda Woodbridge for a useful survey of the different positions in her introduction to *Vagrancy, Homelessness, and English Renaissance Literature*.

2. A recent exception to this disconnection between legal and literary sources can be found in Bryan Reynolds's *Becoming Criminal*, a work that investigates the theoretical ramifications of the popularity and "fetishization" of the rogue in helpful and refreshing ways. Yet Reynolds does not set out to explore the relationship between the historical record and the literary source as such. Instead, he treats both as essentially the same and as proof of a "real" criminal culture. We should also note that some of the more positive references to criminals, taken as evidence of a general "fetishization" in Reynolds's chapter

on gypsies, are usefully placed in a separate literary tradition of idealized treatments of beggars and vagrants by William Carroll in *Fat King, Lean Beggar* (see especially chapter 7).

3. Cf. Beier, *Masterless Men* 8; and Sharpe, *Crime in Early Modern England* 143. However, Paul Slack (96–97) argues that there were some examples of organized crime and vagrants who fit in with the categories listed in Thomas Harman's *Caveat for Common Cursitors* (1566).

4. There is some evidence, though very little, of canting in legal records. Rather than claiming that the rogue literature is showing real-life practice, Woodbridge makes the opposite case. She goes so far as to suggest that the six references to canting found by Beier may be the product of "literary influence on the judicial testimony" (41–43 and 10), though Beier's essay does not entertain this possibility. Cf. Beier's "Anti-language or Jargon?" For the opposite approach, see Reynolds, chap. 3.

5. Carroll finds the ambivalence mainly in literary texts. Where Reynolds emphasizes the "transversal power" of the rogue, whose movement between different subject positions questions everything state ideology attempts to impose on individuals, Dionne offers a reading that highlights the rogue texts as crucial elements in official culture's attempts to allow individual subjects to make the transition from a feudal to a protocapitalist society. Cf. Dionne's essay in this volume and "Playing the 'Cony.'"

6. In two ways, I am building here on the arguments offered by Reynolds and Dionne. Reynolds builds on Félix Guattari's notion of transversality, to show that the "transversal power" of the rogue allows him to move beyond the subject position assigned to him by the state and experience alternative "subjective territories" (18). Through performance, Reynolds argues, the rogue shows how "[t]he metamorphosis of becoming-other-social-identities confounds such concepts as the essential, the normal, the unified, and the universal" (21), making his presence a real threat to official state culture. Although he attaches less importance to these texts' ambivalence than Reynolds might, Dionne makes a more specifically historical connection between the rogue books and the domestic as well as courtly manuals, showing "an ironic double-sidedness that emerges in the rogue literature" located in the self-recognition of the upwardly mobile in the posturing and performing of the rogue (see both his essay in this volume and "Playing the 'Cony'"). Yet I argue that the threat identified by both is a product not only of the mere possibility of the performances of status by the members of a particular criminal culture, but also of the ways in which individuals engage with each other more generally. Put simply, we might say that the legal texts and the literature show that transversality is everywhere and performance involves everyone, not only the newly made gentlemen of the period.

7. Bridewell Court Books (hereafter "BCB"), vol. 4, December 8 and 11, 1602, and January 10 and 17, 1603.

8. For short histories of Bridewell, cf. Beier, *Masterless Men* 164–69; Carroll 108–24; and Innes.

9. The Court of Governors did not incarcerate those who were born outside of their London jurisdiction. In such a case, vagrants would be whipped, given a passport, and returned to their parish of origin.

10. For examples of references to these transgressions, see BCB, vol. 4, January 5, 1603, and vol. 1, October 11, 1560.

11. Although the number of vagrants examined and punished went up over the course of this period, as stated before, in the early 1560s 84 percent of those examined were not vagrants. The number of nonvagrants examined was 38 percent in 1600–1601 (Beier, "Social Problems" 204; Slack 93). Archer lists the exact numbers for each type of offense for three of the Bridewell Court Books (239).

12. That we should not treat the records as unproblematic evidence about the real lives of vagrants becomes clear when taking into account William Carroll's argument that Bridewell was specifically known for its cruel treatment of prisoners and as a place of torture where other prisons lacked the equipment (111–20). Although I have found no evidence of torture in the Bridewell court records, at times we can observe a curious shift in the behavior of the accused, from adamant denial to sudden confession. In one case, a constable named Leonard Sharpe is charged with persuading a servant to help arrest his master. Denying the accusation, Sharpe accuses the Bridewell governors of having used force to extract the confession from the servant: "the saide sharpe riported that the saide Pawle was whipped here to make him accuse him which is contrarie. And he saieth & denieth that ever he saide so directlie but saieth he did thinke he had bene whipped & forced to saie so" (BCB, vol. 2, June 1, 1575).

13. Slack argues, "The very process of labelling a man a vagrant helped to make him one. The first punishment was the decisive stage in the downward social spiral which produced a dangerous and incorrigible rogue" (99). Cf. also Carroll 42–45, on the marking of the rogue for future identification.

14. BCB, vol. 4, October 9, 1602.

15. See Beier's essay in this collection.

16. BCB, vol. 3, January 11, 1578.

17. BCB, vol. 1, July 10, 1560.

18. BCB, vol. 4, March 5, 1603, and April 18, 1603. The close proximity of this double use of the term may suggest an individual preference on the part of a governor or clerk. Reynolds explores a fascination connection between gypsies and rogues that highlights the ways in which texts encouraged a suspicion of the gypsy as a counterfeit, a dressed-up English rogue. He writes that "gypsy identity is depicted as a performative identity, available to anyone willing and capable of playing the part" (47). We might say that the many instances in which he finds the phrase "counterfeit Egyptian" in early modern texts are taken one step further in these references to the "counterfeit vagrant."

19. BCB, vol. 3, June 14, 1578.

20. BCB, vol. 4, February 12, 1602.

21. BCB, vol. 1, October 18, 1559, December 2, 1560, and vol. 3, December 29, 1577. Many other examples can be found.

22. BCB, vol. 1, January 5, 1562.

23. BCB, vol. 1, June 28, 1560.

24. See "Of the Subtlety of a Curber in Cozening a Maid," in Greene, *Second Part* 224–25.

25. BCB, vol. 4, May 24, 1598.

26. BCB, vol. 1, March 3, 1559.

27. BCB, vol. 1, January 7, 1561.

28. BCB, vol. 1, March 24, 1561.

29. BCB, vol. 4, July 8, 1598.

30. BCB, vol. 4, January 8, 1603.

31. BCB, vol. 1, February 14, 1560.

32. BCB, vol. 3, December 11, 12, and 16, 1577.

33. BCB, vol. 4, February 13, 1599.

34. Walker 43. Walker's trickster famously says, "Whoso hath not some anchorward way to help himself, but followeth his nose, as they say, always straight forward, may well hold up the head for a year or two, but the third he must needs sink and gather the wind into beggars' haven." See also Greene, *Notable Discovery* 174.

35. BCB, vol. 4, April 1, 1598.

WORKS CITED

Agnew, Jean-Christophe. *Worlds Apart: The Market and the Theater in Anglo-American Thought, 1550–1750.* Cambridge: Cambridge UP, 1986.

Archer, Ian W. *The Pursuit of Stability: Social Relations in Elizabethan London.* Cambridge Studies in Early Modern British History. Cambridge: Cambridge UP, 1991.

Awdeley, John. *The Fraternity of Vagabonds.* 1561. Salgãdo 59–77.

Beier, A. L. "Anti-language or Jargon? Canting in the English Underworld in the Sixteenth and Seventeenth Centuries." *The Social History of Language: Language and Jargon.* Ed. Peter Burke and Roy S. Porter. 3 vols. London: Polity P, 1995. 3:64–101.

———. *Masterless Men: The Vagrancy Problem in England, 1560–1640.* London: Methuen, 1985.

———. "Social Problems in Elizabethan London." *Journal of Interdisciplinary History* 9 (1978): 203–21.

Carroll, William C. *Fat King, Lean Beggar: Representations of Poverty in the Age of Shakespeare.* Ithaca: Cornell UP, 1996.

Dionne, Craig. "Playing the 'Cony': Anonymity in Underworld Literature." *Genre* 30 (1997): 29–50.

Greene, Robert. *A Disputation.* 1592. Salgãdo 265–315.

———. *A Notable Discovery of Cozenage.* 1591. Salgãdo 155–92.

———. *The Second Part of Cony-Catching.* 1592. Salgãdo 193–229.

Harman, Thomas. *Caveat for Common Cursitors.* 1566. Salgãdo 79–153.

Innes, Joanna. "Prisons for the Poor: English Bridewells, 1555–1800." *Labour, Law, and Crime: An Historical Perspective.* Ed. Francis Snyder and Douglas Hay. Tavistock: London, 1987. 42–122.

Reynolds, Bryan. *Becoming Criminal: Transversal Performance and Cultural Dissidence in Early Modern England.* Baltimore: Johns Hopkins UP, 2002.

Salgãdo, Gãmini, ed. *Cony-Catchers and Bawdy Baskets: An Anthology of Elizabethan Low Life.* Middlesex: Penguin, 1972.

Sharpe, J. A. *Crime in Early Modern England, 1550–1750.* 2d ed. London: Longman, 1999.

Slack, Paul. *Poverty and Policy in Tudor and Stuart England.* London: Longman, 1988.

Walker, Gilbert. *A Manifest Detection of Dice-Play.* 1552. Salgãdo 27–58.

Woodbridge, Linda. *Vagrancy, Homelessness, and English Renaissance Literature*. Urbana: U of Illinois P, 2001.

Wrightson, Keith. "The Politics of the Parish in Early Modern England." *The Experience of Authority in Early Modern England*. Ed. Paul Griffiths, Adam Fox, and Steve Hindle. Houndsmills, Basingstoke: Macmillan, 1996. 10–46.

PART 2

Marketplaces and Rogue Economics

The Peddler and the Pawn

Why Did Tudor England Consider Peddlers to Be Rogues?

Jacobean city comedy abounds in scenes of shopping, and no wonder: these were heady times for consumers. A northern people accustomed to buying local cabbages on market day when cabbage was in season could now buy Mediterranean oranges. Women who had spun their own yarn for generations could now visit Thomas Deane's haberdashery and buy thread from Pisa, silk thread from Bruges, ribbons from Spain, silk fringes from Genoa (Staniland 62). To one of England's importing tycoons, the ability to fetch grapes in midwinter, as Marlowe's Dr. Faustus does, might just have been worth selling one's soul for.

Thomas Heywood's *If You Know Not Me, You Know Nobody, Part 2* presents a spectrum of London commerce: a lowly peddler, a haberdasher so prosperous that the queen borrows money from him, and that apogee of commercial glamour, the 120 shops of the Pawn[1] at the Royal Exchange, "England's first shopping mall" (Saunders, "Organisation" 85). At first blush, the play looks like patriotic, consumerist propaganda,[2] as Thomas Gresham, a veritable merchant Tamburlaine of world-straddling trade, donates to the City of London a magnificent money exchange cum shopping mall, about which he rhapsodizes:

> It shall be the pleasure of my life
> To come and meet our merchants at their hour. . . .
> . . . .

'Twill do me good to see shops, with fair wives
Sit to attend the profit of their husbands.

(1127–36)

There is more ware there [in the shops of the Pawn] than in all the rest,
Here like a parish for good Citizens
And their fair wives to dwell in, I'll have shops
Where every day they shall become themselves
In neat attire.

(1211–15)[3]

At the other end of the commercial spectrum, "John Tawnycoat" at first seems
to fulfill the popular image of peddler as swindler—when he leaves Hobson's
haberdashery without paying for his goods, Hobson instructs his apprentices
to look sharp when chapmen come in to stock their packs: "'Mongst many
Chap-men there are few that buys," he bitterly observes (359). Elizabethan
legislation stigmatized peddlers and itinerant tradesmen as inveterate rogues.
But Hobson is wrong about Tawnycoat, who (it turns out) *accidentally* walked
out without paying and later goes to great lengths to return the money. Con-
versely, the play undermines Gresham and calls into question the luxury ethos
of England's first shopping mall. This apparently "palpable gross play" with
its noncatchy title actually accords nuanced treatment to a complex array of
commercial practices, and suggests why peddlers were stigmatized as rogues.

Before turning to the play, I will sketch the emerging commercial scene,
from the peddler to the Pawn.

Peddlers and the Growth of Retail Trade

The development of English shopping in the fifteenth and sixteenth centuries
is a tale of mobility yielding to settled trade, of outdoor vending modulating
into indoor selling, of produce in season replaced by produce brought long
distances out of season, of local and regional products supplemented and
often supplanted by imports. It is also a story of artisans who sell their own
product edged out by retailers selling what they have bought from others—
direct sales replaced by middlemen. One can track these changes from peddlers to fairs to markets to permanent retail shops and permanent quarters for
wholesale export and import traders.

I place peddlers at one end of this spectrum not because they chronologi-
cally came first—peddling developed around the fifteenth century, contempo-

rary with the heyday of the great fairs—but because on the spectrum I have just sketched, they represent the extreme of occasionality, mobility, and out-door selling, though they *are* middlemen. Their visits were irregular rather than upon regulated dates, they had no fixed premises but were entirely mobile, and they operated outdoors. Britain's great peddlers, the Scots, had trading networks across Britain and across Europe, especially Scandinavia and Poland. Peddlers got their merchandise from artisans in a home village, or as produce from farmers with whom they traded in kind (Fontaine 8–34).

More regular were fairs, a prominent feature of English life throughout the late Middle Ages. Fairs were arranged "so that merchants could move from one to another in a regular sequence"; in a highly regulated annual calendar, the year's first fair was at King's Lynn on Valentine's Day (Addison 29–30, 161). In days when most people traveled little in a lifetime, fairs were the year's one great orgy of mobility. Wholesale trade was prominent—at fairs, provisions were bought for princely, noble, and monastic households (Addison 59). But smaller-scale peddlers also frequented fairs, calling forth a unique legal institution, the court of piepowder, a term drawn from a French term for peddler—*pied pouldre,* "dusty-footed." Such courts were necessary since "wandering chapmen who frequented fairs . . . required an immediate settlement of their disputes at each before moving on to the next" (Addison 11–12). When in 1550 the new London borough of Southwark was chartered for a September fair, a "court of pye powders" was authorized (Stow, *Survey* 382). St. Bartholomew's was the greatest London fair; prominent nationally was the huge Sturbridge Fair outside Cambridge. Fairs with access to the sea, such as those in Winchester and Boston, already did considerable international trade in the Middle Ages, attracting inland merchants as well (Addison 32).

A further step in the direction of permanence was the weekly market, where local farmers and tradesmen direct-sold their produce and wares, joined by peddlers from afar. Fairs gradually declined as regular weekly markets took hold. Like peddlers and fairs, markets operated outdoors in this era, with temporary stalls erected weekly. They were highly regulated; for example, a baker who sold from his own premises during the week was obliged by law to sell only at the market on market days. Stall rental fees were collected at a toll booth; the importance of markets to towns is reflected in the fact that the Town Hall was called the Tolbooth in many market towns (Addison 69). A market was the raison d'être for many towns, including London: "From its very beginnings London seems to have developed along the lines of a market, increasing rapidly in size and importance from the bridge-head market that it must originally have been" (Holmes 30). Five great London markets, Billingsgate, Smithfield, Leadenhall, Spitalfields, and Covent Garden, operated much like markets in inland market towns, but were somewhat more specialized: Smithfield, for example, was a market for livestock, especially horses, while Newgate Market specialized in corn, meal, and other victuals.

Retail shops entered municipal records in the late Middle Ages, originally temporary buildings, some simple booths, some "more durable single-room sheds or huts, of which the upper half of the front would let down to form an open-air counter and display board" (Addison 71). They were commonest in larger market towns: "The now familiar village shop was an unheard of convenience in most parts of the country at the beginning of the nineteenth century. Packmen and pedlars still supplied most of the needs not met by farm or garden between the weekly market or the annual fair" (Addison 71). In London, outdoor stalls still abounded: a 1560 map shows stall posts and awnings folded together in the middle of Cheapside's broad street/market, ready to be set up for market (Holmes 35–36). Even shops in permanent buildings seemed to compromise between temporary and permanent, between indoor and outdoor: goods were set out on boards in front of shops, sometimes under a soler or sunshade—or had large shutters that let down to close the shop, like a fair booth. In the anonymous play *Arden of Feversham*, a murder is accidentally prevented when an apprentice drops the shutter at the end of the trading day, braining the thug who is waiting for his mark beneath it.

The architecture of London shops underwent a gradual evolution toward permanence. John Stow, in his *Survey of London*, 1598, recalls that in Cheap Ward, from the great conduit west, are now

> many fair and large houses, for the most part possessed of mercers, . . . [which were once] sheds or shops, with solers over them, as of late one of them remained at Sopar's Lane end, wherein a woman sold seeds, roots, and herbs; but those sheds or shops, by encroachments on the high street, are now largely built on both sides outward, and also upward, some three, four, or five stories high (263).

Houses of Billingsgate fishmongers "were at first but moveable boards or stalls, set out on market-days, to strew their fish there to be sold; but, procuring license to set up sheds, they grew to shops, and little by little to tall houses, of three or four storeys in height" (83). In one street, "stall boards were of old time set up by the butchers to show and sell their flesh meat upon, over the which stall boards they first built sheds to keep off the weather; but since [then]. . . they have made their stall boards and sheds fair houses" (322).

Many new retailers were supplied by international wholesalers. Two of the most powerful of London's twelve great livery companies, the Grocers and

Mercers, were international traders. A "grocer" was "one who buys and sells in the gross, . . . a wholesale dealer or merchant" *(OED)*; the Grocers company, originally the Pepperers, were wholesale dealers in spices and foreign produce. Mercers dealt in textile fabrics, especially "silks, velvets, and other costly materials" *(OED)*—the sort of merchandise featured at Thomas Deane's haberdashery in the Pawn.[4] These international importers had impressive permanent headquarters in the city—the Grocers' Hall, the Mercers' Chapel and Hall. The Royal Exchange was heavily sponsored by England's leading export consortium, the Merchant Adventurers. The permanence of a stone building like the Royal Exchange, like the English patriotism trumpeted by these merchants, masked a fundamental commitment to mobility on the high seas and on the Continent, and regular intercourse with the very foreigners London often greeted with xenophobic hostility.

London's first planned experiment with purpose-built retail shops was probably Goldsmith's Row, a setting for Middleton's *Chaste Maid in Cheapside*. This row of shops, built from an integrated plan, was the pride of London, at least until displaced in civic affections by the Pawn, a new shopping mall in the Royal Exchange built in the late 1560s, financed by the wealthy exporter Sir Thomas Gresham, on land purchased by the City by subscription from the twelve great livery companies and the powerful export companies, the Merchant Adventurers and Staplers (Saunders, "Organisation" 86; Imray 31). The Pawn had a definite air of permanence: shop leases were typically for twelve years. But the shops themselves resembled fair stalls, and indeed were called shops and stalls interchangeably (Saunders, "Organisation" 90). Shops were tiny,

> only 2.28 metres by 1.52 metres, much the size of small platform kiosks on the London Underground. The inventory of Deane's stock, the only one for any of the Exchange shops, is long and consequently gives the impression of a very packed space. . . . The inclusion of a "stall cloth" in the inventory suggests that Deane was able to lay out his wares on the stallboard of his shop when open for trading. The lock . . . may well have been used to secure the board over the shop aperture at night, a construction typical of medieval and Tudor shops. Clearly the form of the new Exchange's shops was traditional, any novelty lying in the bringing together of such a large and varied assemblage of retailing outlets under a single roof in a building dedicated to trading. (Staniland 60–61).

But then, the idea of a room permanently dedicated to *any* single purpose was novel in this period. When night fell in the late Middle Ages, beds had been rolled out into all-purpose rooms; but now rooms were becoming specialized as bedchambers. The old trestle table, dismantled after meals, was yielding to an immobile table with boards permanently joined. Similarly, what had been a temporary space in a street or even a field, now became a permanent shop. And just as premises were more permanent than ever before, so shops became almost permanently open—unlike a weekly market, shops in the Pawn were open every day.

Londoners fell in love with the Pawn the moment it opened, swelling with civic and national pride to behold "the great courtyard with the arcade around it and the shops above. The Flemish-inspired structure had a cosmopolitan air, it spoke of a sophisticated Europe beyond the experience of the less traveled London citizens" (Saunders, "Building" 43). In Jacobean city comedy, where paeans to shopping abound, the Pawn is a favorite destination: "You must to the Pawn to buy lawn; to Saint Martin's for lace" (Dekker and Webster 2.1.214–18). The Royal Exchange's governing committee included the highest dignitaries of the land, and small disagreements about leases or squabbles between shopkeepers were arbitrated at the highest levels. One such argument was taken to the lord mayor, the comptroller of the royal household (also a privy councillor), the chancellor of the exchequer, the lord chancellor, and the secretary of state. "What is amazing about this incident is . . . that such appeals should be made to the highest dignitaries in the land, and that they should respond immediately. Clearly, the smooth and honorable running of the Exchange was seen as a matter of national importance" (Saunders, "Organisation" 90–91).

The Exchange acquired central importance to civic and national image-making. Sir William Chester, a draper, as spokesman for the City in negotiations to purchase a site for the Exchange, reminded everyone that "Sir Thomas Gresham, knight, for the great good will and love he hath to this City, . . . promised unto the said Lord Mayor and Aldermen to build and plant within this City a burse to be more fair and costly builded in all points than is the burse of Antwerp" (Imray 27). London was self-consciously entering into international competition as an impressive city, whose bourse outshone any in Europe, even the two most impressive, Antwerp's bourse and the Rialto in Venice. The Exchange was proudly called "fair" and "comely." Minutes of the Court of Aldermen report that a "gentle and very friendly offer" was made by Gresham, "for the erecting and building at his only costs and charges of a comely bourse for merchants" (Imray 26). Robert Greene, in a dedicatory epistle to the citizens of London prefixed to his collection *The Royal Exchange*, proudly boasts that "your Exchange in London, every way duly weighed, excelleth all the Burse Reals [i.e., royal exchanges] in the world" (sig. [iii]);

another epistle, to the mayor and sheriffs of London, takes aim specifically at that premier commercial city, Venice: "Our City of London, . . . plotted and erected by Brute, . . . is more ancient far than their City of Venice" (sig. ii^v). England was becoming a player in international commercial circles. She had come a long way from the days of Scottish peddlers and local fairs.

And yet—horrors!—peddlers haunted the very courtyard of the Exchange. Wenceslaus Hollar's engraving of the Exchange does show "two Dutch merchants in fur hats," a satisfyingly sophisticated international note. But the engraving also shows, near the Dutch merchants, "a woman selling news-sheets or ballads" (Saunders, "Organisation" 87). The Exchange committee received complaints about "diverse abuses daily committed in the Royal Exchange by idle boys, beggars, cheaters and other people of base quality" (Saunders, "Organisation" 88). City fathers were horrified; and looking back, one can see that the peddler, far from disappearing as more settled forms of commerce took shape, became the nemesis of each settled form in turn: first fairs, then weekly markets, then retail shops, and finally the Pawn itself.

In the city fathers' wish for an impressive commercial building, in its outrage at incursions by scruffier, itinerant merchants, we can read the nervous inferiority complex of an up-and-coming city terribly eager to look impressive and sophisticated to the rest of Europe. Civic disdain for itinerant merchants, and for nondescript outdoor markets such as that in Leather Lane near Smithfield Market, finds instructive echoes in a more recent struggle. Kathryn Chase Merrett traces the history of the city market in Edmonton, Alberta, a semipermanent building with adjoining outdoor booths. It is a tale of continual conflict, over the market's one-hundred-year history, between the scruffy, popular weekly market and civic forces striving to oust it from the city center and replace it with impressive civic buildings, befitting an up-and-coming, prosperous city that didn't want to appear hokey to the rest of North America. After sixty-four years of struggle, the city fathers succeeded in building an imposing civic complex (federal building, library, theater) on the spot, displacing the old market into the red-light district, where it stubbornly persists to this day. Here, reborn, are Renaissance London's poles of peddler and Pawn. Intimating that nonpermanent vendors belong in a league with prostitutes, Edmonton's authorities would have understood the Elizabethan belief that a peddler was a rogue.

Why was a peddler so threatening? Every mode of commerce—fairs, markets, retail shops, even the Pawn—presented opportunities for shady dealings. The committee governing the Pawn was once obliged to decree that shopkeepers who "darken their lights with canvas, blinds or anything" were "to pull down the same" (Saunders, "Organisation" 93). Donald Lupton wryly observed in 1632 that the patriotic aura imparted by the Exchange's statues of English kings was insufficient to impede crooked dealing by merchants on the main floor: "They will dissemble with and cozen one another, though all the kings that ever were since the Conquest overlooked them." Why, then, did Elizabethan legislation single out peddlers? The 1572 Act for the Punishment of Vagabonds classified itinerant merchants (peddlers, chapmen, ballad-sellers) and itinerant tradesmen (tinkers, cobblers) as rogues and vagabonds. Thomas Harman warned against peddlers and tinkers in his 1567 taxonomy of "rogues," *A Caveat or Warening for Common Cursetors Vulgarely Called Vagabones,* though he couldn't put his finger on what was so roguish about them. Tinkers might be deceitful, making extra holes in pots to create a need for their services, but peddlers, he admitted, "be not all evil, but of an indifferent behavior" (93). But he still classified them as rogues.[5] A common slang term for thieves' cant was "Pedlars' French." Peddlers were stigmatized in other parts of Europe, too. France enacted repressive legislation against the *porteballe* (packman) and the *marcelot* (wandering trader), considered tricksters and cheats. Laurence Fontaine documents constant friction between traveling and sedentary merchants in Germany, France, and Italy, the latter accusing the former of smuggling, tax evasion, and general bad citizenship (1, 32). Admittedly, some peddlers were dishonest; but why, out of the whole commercial spectrum, were peddlers singled out?

The fact is that criminalizing peddlers served several economic interests. As direct-sales vendors and tradesmen with low overhead, they undercut the prices of shopkeepers, of town guilds whose monopolistic practices kept prices high, and even of stallholders in fairs. Across Europe, as Fontaine shows, "shopkeepers demanded their expulsion from the towns and markets," squeezing them out by "put[ting] up obstacles to their having political rights and only grant[ing] them reduced citizenship"; smaller towns copied the legislation of larger towns, to keep peddlers out (23). Trade guilds, too, opposed peddlers and pressured governments to outlaw peddling networks such as the Savoyards: in Zurich in 1539, "the guilds of the cutlers, locksmiths, clockmakers, makers of spurs, armourers and papermakers, as well as the burgomaster and the town council, enjoined the law-enforcing agents to rid the countryside of all Savoyard haberdashers" (Fontaine 25). Fairs too demanded protection against peddlers. In Poland, Scottish peddlers were charged with undermining the whole system of fairs: "as soon as the autumn fairs were over, the itinerant merchants and their servants then traveled from village to village with their clothes and pottery and, in the countryside, bartered and sold so effectively that the peasants no longer found it necessary to take their own wares to the fair" (Fontaine 29). Peddlers were called vagabonds, and at English fairs, town fathers tried to rid fairs of vagabonds with something of the air of banishing evil spirits. The proclamation opening the Ely fair commanded optimistically that "all vagabonds, idle and misbehaving persons, all cheaters, cozeners, rogues, sturdy beggars and shifters do depart out of this fair immediately after this proclamation" (Addison 22).

It is not surprising that legislation classified peddlers among rogues and vagabonds. If Thomas Harman was puzzled about why peddlers were considered rogues, at our historical remove the answer seems clear: these all-too-successful merchants were objects of pressure from competing commercial interests: fairs, weekly markets, trade guilds, shops, and ultimately Goldsmith's Row and the Pawn. The historical shift we have been tracking, toward indoor shops and fixed premises, would ultimately leave earlier commercial forms behind: markets displaced fairs, fixed shops displaced markets, and—a process maturing in our own time but begun with the Pawn—shopping malls displaced individual shops. One would think that the quaint peddler with his pack would also have been left behind—certainly those in charge of fairs, markets, shops, and shopping malls did their best to leave him behind. However, the peddler stubbornly flourished well into modern times. I suggest that the distinction between the peddler and the Pawn was to some degree illusory.

International Peddling

When we see Heywood's John Tawnycoat stocking his peddler's pack at a fashionable London haberdashery, the wheel might seem to have come full circle, the primitive foot slogger absorbed into the fabric of more modern and completely sedentary commerce. But in fact peddling had been part of an integrated system of commerce almost from its medieval beginnings. Contrary to popular stereotype, peddlers were not solitary wanderers but part of mercantile networks. As Fontaine shows, the peddler on foot with his pack was usually, across Europe, the low man on a totem pole whose higher reaches included town-based merchants and bankers. The network was often related by consanguinity and marriage, and ultimately connected with the same village, although more prosperous and settled network members often tried to keep secret their connection with outright peddlers. It was often out of such peddling networks that large-scale import and export firms grew. Fontaine gives one example of "the road to success" beginning with "peddling on a small scale in Scotland": Matthew Cuming, a seventeenth-century Scottish peddler,

> profiting both from his income and from the credit to which he then had access, . . . loaded up his ass with bundles of material, which he then took to London to sell in order to finance the importation of dyes from Holland, and to get a share in a boat bringing sugar and tobacco from Virginia. He thus broke into the world of "big business" and prepared to venture onto the Continent. (14)

On the continent, he would have had contacts: Scottish peddling networks existed in western France, Scandinavia, and Poland. In 1621 "the Scottish emigrant population in Poland was estimated at 30,000 people." Locals lodged complaints against Scottish peddlers, who "did business on credit terms or in exchange for farm produce or raw materials" and often cornered a local market in butter, tallow, or leather (Fontaine 10, 29). The more sedentary branches of such networks often intermarried with local merchant families and strove to blend in. As Fontaine reports of an Italian network in Germany, "It is not always easy to highlight the link between the merchant businesses and peddling since the Italian merchants who had succeeded in getting themselves accepted as citizens of the town where they had their shop made every effort to conceal it" (18).

Peddlers, then, seemingly local foot-soldiers of commerce, were actually cogs in the wheels of international trade. As Fontaine shows, European peddling developed in mountainous areas (including Scotland) where agriculture was migratory: shepherding peoples moved up and down mountains seasonally, and vendors followed them. In Europe, mountain passes became essential parts of overland trade routes—essentially extensions of peddling territories. "A division of trade was established: heavy foodstuffs, such as cereals, were transported by sea; luxury goods by land, along routes such as the Alpine ones. Mule trains, weighed down by silks, precious dyes, indigo, and gold and silver thread, took the mountain paths and every mountain pass had its share of traffic" (9). Many items inventoried in Thomas Deane's shop in the Pawn must have crossed Europe in such mule trains: several dozen yards of silk and golden lace, French parchment, seven different kinds of silk (see Staniland). The goal of Merchant Adventurers was basically the same as that of pack peddlers: to transport goods for sale over long distances. Merchant Adventuring was peddling writ large. And peddling, seemingly at the opposite pole from the elegant Pawn, we actually find installed at its heart.

Tradin' in the Rain

The Pawn was only half of the scene at the Royal Exchange: the initial impetus for building the Exchange had come not from retailing but from international wholesalers and currency traders, who cut international deals in goods and currencies in an open courtyard in the center of the Exchange. The building could be conceptualized as an area of wholesale trading surrounded by a shell of retail trading, as if English shopkeepers masked from the London public view the wholesalers within who trafficked with foreigners.

The money merchants—large-scale lenders, borrowers, and currency speculators—had traditionally operated in Lombard Street, so called for the Italian merchants and money traders from Lombardy who had operated there since the twelfth century. As if in a patriotic move to reclaim this ground symbolically for England, those favoring an Exchange initially tried to build it in Lombard Street itself, in 1538, but couldn't get hold of the property (Imray 23). Heywood's *If You Know Not Me* stresses weather as a prime impetus for building a new exchange: Thomas Gresham is outdoors in Lombard Street, negotiating with a fellow merchant about a long-standing dispute over some real estate, when a storm blows in. Gresham grows angry:

> And [i.e., if] we stay long we shall be wet to the skin.
> I do not lik't, nay and it angers me
> That such a famous city as this is,
> Wherein so many gallant merchants are,
> Have not a place to meet in, but in this,
> Where every shower of rain must trouble them.
> I cannot tell, but if I live—let's step into the Pope's head,
> We shall be dropping dry if stay here—
> I'll have a roof built, and such a roof,
> That merchants and their wives, friend and their friends
> Shall walk underneath it as now in Paul's.

> (536–46)

Other contemporaries also mentioned the rain: "merchants and tradesmen, as well English as strangers, for their general making of bargains, contracts and commerce . . . did usually meet twice every day . . . but their meetings were unpleasant and troublesome, by reason of walking and talking in an open narrow street, . . . constrained either to endure all extremities of weather, viz. heat and cold, snow and rain" (Stow, *Annales* 668). But I suspect that merchants dreaded rain not for its dampness so much as for what associations went with conducting financial business outdoors: doing business outside aligned one with stallholders in fairs, or (worse) with peddlers. In a 1561 letter, Richard Clough, Gresham's agent in Antwerp, declares it a scandal, "considering what a City London is, . . . that in so many years they have not found the means to make a burse, but must walk in the rain when it raineth, *more like pedalers than merchants*" (Imray 26; emphasis added).

But oddly, when the Exchange was finally built, the money merchants and international wholesalers were still pretty much out in the rain. The wholesale trading and exchange area was roofless, open to the elements. The arcade afforded shelter, and Heywood suggests that merchants might have dived into the "cellerage" when "heaven gives comfortable rain unto the earth" (1194–96). In Heywood's play, Gresham had originally been moved to donate funds for an Exchange by the inconvenience of seeking shelter during "every shower of rain"; it seems odd that he now shrugs off rain as "comfortable." The outdoor trading floor now signals for him openness and honesty in commercial dealing: "This space . . . hides not heaven from us" (1199)—or "us" from heaven, presumably. Why the about-face? Why did this culture, fully capable of engineering large roofed buildings, choose to build its showcase international trading arena without a roof, especially seeing that the need for a roof was a persistent reason for building an exchange in the first place?

The honesty ensured by Heaven's direct lighting is certainly one answer—contemporaries suspected that shoddy merchandise was passed off in dark shops. We have already seen evidence of such shady practices in the Pawn itself. As an example of a cultural association between open air and open dealings more generally, in Shakespeare plays deceit and hypocrisy often flourish indoors (the court of Claudius in *Hamlet* or of Frederick in *As You Like It*), while characters confront truth in outdoor scenes (*Hamlet's* sentried battlements, Lear's heath, the forest whose wintry storms Duke Senior in *As You Like It* recognizes as "no flattery" but "counselors / That feelingly persuade me what I am" [2.1.7–11].) But more specifically, the Exchange's open-air architecture, open to the heavens yet with shelter at hand, enclosed by a building yet open to the world on one side, was an emblem of the liminal zone occupied by England's international traders. Rejoicing in the splendor and impressiveness of a substantial, imposing building, the equal of any bourse in Europe, the Exchange also retained the outdoor, temporary air of traditional commerce. Those minutes of the Court of Aldermen called the projected Royal Exchange a "comely burse for merchants to assemble upon" (Imray 26)—not "to assemble *in*": London city fathers seemed to think of trading as something that went on outdoors. After all the donations and subscriptions, the traders were still outside. At some level the high-flying international wheelers and dealers must have recognized that they were peddlers at heart.

The Peddler Meets the Pawn

International merchants negotiated hefty loans to national governments, and their loan guarantees kept afloat every English government since Henry VIII. Douglas Bisson shows that England's great export consortium, the Merchant Adventurers (prime mover behind construction of the Royal Exchange) "fulfilled the indispensable role of surety for the Crown's foreign borrowing" (1–2). The Merchant Adventurers were employed by Gresham "to restore and then maintain the credit of the Crown by propping up the rate of exchange in both Antwerp and London" (Bisson 25). They "proved astonishingly successful in establishing a symbiotic relationship with the Tudor dynasty, convincing its financially embarrassed monarchs that all would be well if the City elite were left to pursue their advantage" (Bisson 102).[6]

The Merchant Adventurers often smeared their enemies as peddlers, stigmatizing their greatest English rivals, the Staplers, as behaving in a peddlerlike manner, engaging in a "straggling trade," itinerant selling outside the jurisdiction of foreign trade regulators (Bisson 7–8). John Wheeler, secretary of the Merchant Adventurers, reported in a 1601 defense of his company that cloth merchants at one point seceded from the Adventurers, hawking merchandise "peddler-like" from town to town in Europe, which lowered the price of English goods, until Parliament legislated against this (293).

Like the Merchant Adventurers, peddlers traditionally acted as moneylenders. Fontaine describes the way "sedentary merchants denounced the credit arrangement which bound the peasant clientele to the itinerant merchants" (31). Tudor England was becoming a culture of credit, as Craig Muldrew shows, and despite persistent outcries against usury, lending was increasingly acceptable. The anonymous *The Execution of Neschech and the Confining of His Kinsman Tarbith, or a Short Discourse Showing the Difference Betwixt Damned Usury and That Which is Lawful* distinguished between acceptable and unacceptable degrees of usury, warning that "forbidding of all usury, is the very maintaining of damned usury" (32). Just as condemning fiendishly excessive "damned usury" helped legitimate other forms, so criminalizing small-time moneylenders such as peddlers helped legitimate big-time moneylenders such as the Merchant Adventurers.[7]

But the two groups were disarmingly alike, not least in that neither group grew or manufactured things: both merely sold things. Since the late fourteenth century, both had been pure sellers in a world where most selling was done by producers. In the late Middle Ages, selling, as opposed to growing or fabricating, was mostly a seasonal activity, for which one traveled to a seasonal fair. Although this traditional view of the cyclical nature of selling gradually came into tension with a new view of commerce as a full-time job requiring permanent quarters—retail shops—it had since the Middle Ages been in tension with two groups who sold year-round and were exclusively sellers: peddlers and international traders like the Merchant Adventurers.

To an age attuned to traditional producer/seller patterns, those who exclusively sold, and sold year-round, seemed unnatural, perverting the original purpose of exchange. They valued things only for salability, reducing objects to what Marx calls their exchange value, indifferent to their use value. Suspicion of sellers, of middlemen, was endemic during the sixteenth century's various economic crises. Buying vegetables at a fair, one handed over money to the very gnarled hands that had hoed the vegetable patch. But a pure seller, a middleman, seemed not to work in the sweat of his brow, but to usurp the sweat of others. Sweat-usurpation was often a charge leveled against vagrants—"rogues," as they were called. The preacher John Downame, for example, describes "sturdy beggars, and vagrant rogues, the blemish of our government" as men who "like idle drones, . . . live by the sweat of other men's brows" (38–39).[8] No wonder peddlers, as middlemen, were classified as rogues: they too seemed to usurp others' sweat. Merchant Adventurers could be seen as drones of commerce, too: they not only lived by selling the products of others' sweat, but also by manipulating money, one step farther from Nature. Thomas Milles, in a 1604 rant against the Merchant Adventurers, declares that money should be only a means to the end of obtaining wares; but now merchants are "making a ware and merchandise of money" (4). To Clement Armstrong, when merchants forsake dealing in clothes "to occupy their money by exchange," it is "plain usury" (107).

But if importers, exporters, and peddlers had for centuries engaged in selling rather than producing/selling, commerce in general moved increasingly in that direction during the sixteenth century. Retail shops sprang up, devoted simply to selling, unlike earlier shops such as bakeries that had sold goods produced on the premises. Before Thomas Deane opened his up-market haberdashery in the Pawn specializing in imported luxury items, he had been a fletcher, producing feathered arrows; at the time his goods were inventoried, he possessed not only the contents of his leased shop in the Pawn but a large house containing a shop, perhaps once an outlet for products of his trade. But the inventory lists no merchandise in this shop, except a few dusty arrows (Staniland 59). Deane had gone over, from production into sales.

The popularity of retail shops didn't wholly efface public distrust of modern departures from the seasonality of direct-sales fairs and markets, of retail shops run by middlemen maintaining no contact with the natural rhythms of crops and livestock. Clement Armstrong inveighs passionately against London's "adventurers and . . . buyers and sellers of all artificiality [artificers' goods], whereby all poor handicraft [men] are brought into need and necessity" (111). He believed that middlemen—haberdashers, hardware men—lapped up the profits of poor artificers who used to sell directly. A person couldn't make a living by handicraft now, he charged; many had turned to alehouse-keeping (112)—a situation resembling the recent U.S. shift to service industries while manufacturing is done abroad.

The shops in the Pawn leaned heavily toward sales rather than crafts: fifty-five haberdashers, twenty-five mercers, seventeen merchant tailors, twelve grocers, ten leathersellers, ten stationers, seven drapers, two milliners (sellers of goods from Milan), a bookseller, a salter. Some craftsmen did have shops—portrait painters, embroiderers, saddlers, upholsterers—but the tiny size of each shop militated against much exercise of a craft: these were mainly showrooms for sales rather than workshops for painting or saddlery.

When middlemen such as retailers came under suspicion as drones living off the sweat of others, a handy scapegoat was to hand: resentments were easily displaced onto peddlers, whom shopkeepers already resented for undercutting their prices. Peddlers also made handy scapegoats because they seemed foreign. In England, many peddlers were Scottish; and even those who were English were not local people, but had traveled from afar. At the other end of the commercial spectrum, the Royal Exchange with its Pawn was heavily promoted as truly English, the nation's pride and joy and its entry in the international commercial prestige stakes. Not everyone, however, bought this patriotic line. The Pawn brimmed with imported goods; and to build the Exchange, Thomas Gresham, who had spent much of his commercial life in Antwerp, got a special license to employ "strangers," or foreigners, and brought in Flemish builders. This provoked an industrial dispute with London bricklayers, who went on strike and created a public disturbance. Their ringleader was haled before the lord mayor of London and charged with "very lewd demeanor towards Henrick the said Sir Thomas Gresham's chief workman" (Saunders, "Building" 39). The hyperpatriotism of these wool exporters could not pull their primary commodity over everyone's eyes. I will argue that Heywood's *If You Know Not Me* is among the texts that cast a skeptical eye on the new commercial practices of the age.

Heywood Dramatizes Peddler and Pawn

At first glance, *If You Know Not Me, You Know Nobody, Part 2* seems heavily invested in the Royal Exchange as a sign of England's arrival as an European commercial power. The grand opening of the Exchange gets a bigger play than the defeat of the Armada: the sea battle occupies 147 lines, as against 216 for the opening of the Exchange, which signals England's triumph in the pan-European best-bourse competition:

> *1st lord:* You have traveled, sir; how do you like this building?
>   Trust me it is the goodliest thing that I have seen,
>   England affords none such.
> *2nd lord:* Nor Christendom;
>   I might say all the world has not his fellow.
>   I have been in Turkey's great Constantinople,
>   The merchants there meet in a goodly temple,
>   But have no common Burse in Rome, but Rome's
>   Built after the manner of Frankfort, and Emden;
>   There where the greatest marts and meeting places
>   Of merchants are have streets and pent-houses,
>   And as I might compare them to themselves,
>   Like Lumber-street [i.e., Lombard Street] before this Burse was built.

Clinching England's stature as a cosmopolitan world-player, the Exchange is the architectural equivalent of Queen Elizabeth's ability, dramatized in the play, to speak to each visiting ambassador in his own language.

The hero of the Exchange is its builder Thomas Gresham, historically a moving spirit behind the Merchant Adventurers and, as a special financial advisor to the queen, a kind of Elizabethan Alan Greenspan. As the play opens, Gresham is negotiating with a Barbary merchant for a monopoly of sugar trade to his country in exchange for "threescore thousand pound." Such enormous sums create for Gresham heroic stature of a new sort. He casually dispatches agents over huge geographic areas—"Go, fit you for the sea, / I mean to send you into Barbary, / You unto Venice, you to Portingale" (79–81)—he becomes a veritable Tamburlaine of commerce, glorying in vast commercial horizons to be conquered, a hero for a new age.[9] Like a hero, he delivers soliloquies: reflecting on the pending Barbary deal, he exhorts himself, "Let not the hope of gain / Draw thee to loss. I am to have a patent / For all the Barbary sugars at a rate, / The gain clears half in half, but then the hazard. . . . / It stands in this as in all ventures else / Doubtful" (45–54).

Gresham's risk-taking is integral to his heroic stature, and when risks result in breathtaking losses (the king of Barbary's successor disowns the sixty-thousand-pound debt, and Gresham's ships are lost at sea), he shrugs off the reversals with a dashing nonchalance that earlier ages associated with legendary romantic aristocrats. Lesser mortals can only kneel down and wonder: "How will he take this news, loss upon loss?" one lord worries, as the lord mayor confides, "These losses would have killed me" (1495, 1511). Awestruck at Gresham's heroic shrug, another lord places him even beyond romantic aristocrat: "This Gresham is a royal Citizen" (1375), "as royal in his virtues as his buildings" (1510). Gresham inspires the whole merchant class to plan deeds of philanthropy, a largesse once the hallmark of the nobility. It seems quite over-the-top, and Brian Gibbons dismisses the play's representation of Gresham as "a piece of banal mercantile hagiography" (118).

And yet there is something nonheroic about money, especially when brutally called Cash. Gresham, greeting his factor "How thrives our Cash? what, is it well increased?" (58), sounds disconcertingly like Jonson's Volpone bidding "Good morning to the day; and next, my gold!" (1.1.1). A factor's fulsome praise of Gresham is tinged with uneasiness: "'Tis held your credit, and your country's honor," he begins patriotically, "that being but a merchant of the city, / And taken in a manner unprovided / You should upon a mere presumption / And naked promise, part with so much Cash, / Which the best merchants both in Spain and France, / Denied to venture on" (68–74). Except for the clankingly unheroic phrase "to part with so much cash," this *sounds* like praise, but also conveys the information that the Barbary deal was previously turned down by leading Spanish and French merchants, and that Gresham has parted with the sixty thousand pounds without so much as a written contract. This is the money Gresham will soon have to shrug off. Heroic, or foolhardy? It may be both—a devil-may-care attitude and thrilling risk-taking may be part of Gresham's appeal. But his heroic indifference to mere money comes and goes: when news comes of the battle of Alcazar, it is Hobson who expresses shock at the death of the English hero Stewkeley; Gresham attends only to the death of the king of Barbary, who owes him sixty thousand pounds (1265–80). And Sir Thomas is undercut in other ways as well.

Stubborn and inflexible, Gresham won't give in, in a long-standing real estate dispute with Thomas Ramsey, although legal fees threaten to exceed the value of the property: "Ere Gresham / Will give away a tittle of his right, / The law shall beggar me" (344–46). He finally compromises only when an arbitrator denounces both men for spending their money "in a brabbling controversy, / Even like two fools," like scolding fishwives (403–4, 425). Gresham is also unabashedly vainglorious: speaking of himself in the third person as if imagining posterity's accolades, he resolves "to erect this worthy building to his name, / May make the city speak of him forever," jauntily crowing, "up goes my work, a credit to the land" (1115–16, 1124).

The worst shortcoming, especially in a merchant, is that Gresham is a poor judge of character. He taxes his nephew John with "bad husbandry, / Careless respect, and prodigal expense" (87–88), but naively takes seriously as a sentiment "virtuous and religious" John's cheeky rationale for buying a prostitute a dress: "the poor whore went naked, and you know the text commands us to clothe the naked . . . God help the elect" (120–22). John then asks for a new outfit for himself— "better than seven years' 'prentiship, / for [good clothes will] make a man free of any, nay of all companies without indenture" (137–39), a view cynical and idle enough to make a merchant's flesh creep. Readily agreeing, Gresham suits out John in fancy clothes, to present him as a prospective apprentice to Hobson the haberdasher. Hobson's flesh indeed creeps: he finds John's outfit and "curled pate" absurd, informing both Greshams that "Hobson's men are known / By their frieze coats; and [i.e., if] you will dwell with me, / You must be plain, and leave off bravery" (280–83). As a supposedly canny merchant and long associate of Hobson's, why didn't Gresham know this? Even a clown finds Gresham a fool for trusting John (892–93).[10] Gresham's indulgence toward the feckless John is given a puckish twist: he forgives John for absconding with one hundred pounds of his money, with a "boys will be boys" attitude. John is a chip off the avuncular block: "When I was young I do remember well / I was as very a knave as he is now" (949–50). This may be meant as endearing, but gradually grows more alarming than charming as John emerges as a really nasty piece of work: he sets up Hobson to blackmail him, and later nearly succeeds in getting a fellow apprentice hanged. A callous streak seems to run in the family: when John plays a very expensive prank on his master Hobson, Gresham laughs it off on Hobson's behalf. But Hobson isn't laughing.

Although ultimately an admirable figure, haberdasher Hobson can be a poor judge of character too, mistaking a courtesan for a commodity dealer. And his forthright devotion to cash resembles Gresham's: in a startling entrepreneurial reminiscence, Hobson fondly recalls having cornered the market in rosaries: "In [King] Edward's days, / When popery went down, I did engross / Most of the beads that were within the kingdom, / That when Queen Mary had renewed that church, / They that would pray on beads were forced to me: / I made them stretch their purse-strings, grew rich thereby, / Beads were to me a good commodity" (451–57).

Apprentices in London's posh shops aren't an edifying spectacle either. When we first meet Hobson's apprentices, they are arguing over which one has to mind the shop while the other goes to the tavern. When the peddler comes to return the ten pounds he forgot to pay Hobson, they are rude to him since they can't find him in the account book—they had never thought to ask his name and had simply nicknamed him Tawnycoat. Although Hobson had made a fuss about the ten pounds at the time, neither he nor the apprentices now recalls the incident, or recognizes the peddler. When after great prompting the incident does come to mind, they explain not recognizing him: he is now wearing a gray coat. Hardly a display of respect for him as a person.

The play's one wholly admirable figure is in fact "Tawnycoat" the peddler. Vindicating his honesty against Hobson's antipeddler prejudice by returning the ten pounds—"There 'tis to a doit I warrant it, you need not tell [i.e., count] it"—Tawnycoat also defends fellow peddlers: "I'll assure you we are honest all the generation of us" (1084–85). The peddler's honesty is juxtaposed with dishonesty in the mercantile elite: just after Tawnycoat is suspected of walking out owing ten pounds, John Gresham absconds with one hundred pounds. The peddler returns the money; John does not. The idleness of Hobson's apprentices is also juxtaposed with the peddler's account of industrious country salesmanship. But the most telling juxtaposition is of Tawnycoat's actions with Gresham's.

Having lost his ships and his sixty thousand pounds, Gresham makes a grand gesture. Like a bombed-out modern Londoner laughing defiantly at the Blitz, he grinds up a pearl worth fifteen hundred pounds, and drinks it in wine, explaining, "I do not this as prodigal of my wealth, / Rather to show how I esteem that loss / Which cannot be regained." The mayor applauds this heroic, magnanimous gesture: "You are an honor to all English merchants / As bountiful as rich" (1526–31). Rich, yes, but "bountiful"? Drinking a pearl seems less an act of bounty than of conspicuous consumption in the most literal sense. If it is meant to elevate him as nonmercenary, indifferent to mere money, rejoicing in aristocratic nonchalance, why is the pearl-swilling scene juxtaposed with a scene of abject poverty? In the next scene, Hobson by chance meets a broken Tawnycoat, who cannot repay the twenty pounds Hobson has advanced him on credit: "The goods you trusted me withal, I have not wasted / In riot and excess, but my kind heart, / Seeing my helpless neighbors in distress, / By reason of the long and extreme dearth, / Some I relieved, some trusted with my goods, / Whose poverty's not able to repay" (1616–21). Suddenly the word "bountiful" takes on new meaning. We have just witnessed Sir Thomas Gresham ingesting a pearl worth fifteen hundred pounds, while the nation of which he is allegedly the ornament is suffering a "long and extreme dearth." A humble peddler displays bounty by extending credit to the poor, which ruins him; Gresham grows "bountiful" by drinking crushed pearl.

To put in perspective the magnitude of Gresham's guzzle, the former peddler (now a stone-digger) earns three pence per day, and still hopes to save enough eventually to repay the twenty pounds. Hobson marvels, "Dost thou think to pay me twenty pound, / And keep thy charge [i.e., support your family], earning a groat a day?" To make up the value of the pearl Gresham crushed, even without supporting his family, Tawnycoat would have to work for 329 years.

Hobson elects to aid the ruined Tawnycoat. To read this as a complacent celebration of mercantile charitability (Jankowski 316) is to miss Hobson's transformation. In a modest version of King Lear's closely contemporary meeting with Poor Tom, Hobson sees in Tawnycoat a microcosm of England's working poor: "Poor soul I pity them, / And in thy words as in a looking-glass, / I see the toil and travail of the country, / And quiet gain of city's blessedness" (1646–49). It is possible to read these lines as complacently "locat[ing] such 'toil and travail' in the country, preserving for the city a life of 'quiet gain'" (Bonahue 80), but given the starkness of Hobson's epiphany about the poor, I think the lines more likely mean, "I see how the rest of the country (England) is toiling just to make ends meet, while London quietly gets rich." Even so, Hobson is momentarily tempted to take the pittance the peddler offers; but then he recoils: "No, God forbid, old Hobson ne'er will eat, / Rather than surfeit upon poor men's sweat" (1661–62)—a stunning reversal of the standard sweat-usurpation trope. Preachers, one recalls, inveighed against "sturdy beggars, and vagrant rogues," who "like idle drones . . . live by the sweat of other men's brows" (Downame 38–39). Hobson's blinding insight is that it is the rich who live off the sweat of the poor.[11]

When we last see the former peddler, he is thriving and successful. Hobson has taken seriously the new philanthropic responsibilities of his class, but crucially, rather than giving alms[12] to the desperately poor Tawnycoat (who now finally gains a name, John Rowland), he enables him to use his professional expertise in becoming a businessman again: "Sort thee out forty pounds worth of such wares / As thou shalt think most beneficial: / Thou art a free-man, up with thy trade again" (1705–7). Hobson does not meddle, like some officious Overseer of the Poor, with the choice of wares: he trusts to Rowland's professional knowledge. The play seems ultimately to recognize that a peddler *is* a businessman, and that his business, far from being classifiable with the business of pickpockets, thieves, and other rogues, exists on a continuum with the commercial practices of London and the country at large.

Indeed, he is a liaison between London and the country. Hobson relies on peddlers like Rowland for information on country markets and fairs: "what's the news / At . . . Sturbridge Fair? . . . / What news i' the country? what commodities / Are most respected with your country girls?"[13] Rowland reports, "our country girls are akin to your London courtiers, every month sick of a new fashion" (210–25). He finds consumerism rampant in the countryside: "your mask, silk-lace, wash't gloves, carnation girdles, and busk-point suitable, as common as coals from Newcastle, you shall not have a kitchen-maid scrape trenchers without her washed gloves, a dairy wench will not ride to market to sell her buttermilk, without her mask and her busk" (242–46). Hobson is glad to hear it: "Feed their humors, and do not spare, / Bring country money for our London ware" (250–51). The scene bears out Fontaine's view of peddlers as an integral part of trading networks.

Refuting the stereotype of peddlers as solitary, antisocial rogues, *If You Know Not Me* also provokes questions about whose interests are served by criminalizing small-time itinerant merchants. The historical record suggests that the interests of the entire commercial spectrum were served: those involved in fairs, weekly markets, shopkeeping, the Pawn—all whose bottom line was threatened by the better prices and sometimes wider selection a peddler could offer. The play also confirms the peddler's function as a scapegoat whose criminalization drew public scrutiny away from his high-caste double, the high-flying international trader.

Though we see Gresham dispatching agents to foreign lands, the only scene set outside England involves nephew John, supposedly a factor, disporting himself a French brothel. John calls a courtesan his "commodity" and then a "jewel"—an image following close upon his uncle's pearl consumption (1750, 1755). Later he calls her "chapman's ware" (1827). When his master Hobson barges in, John passes off the courtesan as a commodities dealer, delighting in his own double entendres equating sex with commercial dealing:

> *Hobson:* Is not this gentlewoman a dealer?
>   And hath she not a good commodity?
> *John:* Yes by my faith sir, I confess both.
> *Hobson:* Hath she not ware?
> *John:* She hath, and at a reasonable reckoning.
> *Hobson:* And may not then a chapman deal with her?
> *John:* Marry, may ye, sir.
>
>   (1924–30)

Hobson here includes himself as a "chapman," a word that had, over the last two centuries, modulated from its more general meaning, "a man whose business is buying and selling; a merchant, trader, dealer" (and sometimes "peo-

ple engaged in buying and selling; market people") to its more specific meaning from the late 1590s on: "an itinerant dealer who travels about from place
to place selling or buying; . . . a hawker, pedlar" *(OED)*. Hobson situates
himself among peddlers, market people, and general retailers; but John imagines himself among those swashbuckling exporters, the Merchant Adventurers. The luxury commodity he trades in will be commercial sex. "Who would
not be a merchant venturer, and lay out for such a fair return?" John playfully
inquires (1748–49), playing on the sexual sense of the term "lay out," otherwise meaning to invest or speculate, particularly in global sea voyages. By
this time it is clear that whoever has any dealings with John Gresham is likely
to get—well—laid out, as poor Hobson learns when Jack begins blackmail-
ing him.

And this is the wealthy commercial class that has stigmatized peddlers as
rogues, thieves, and vagabonds, clearly a projection of its own dark side. Peddlers were othered as foreigners rather than local people, as peripatetic in an
age when retailing was moving toward sedentary immobility; this drew attention away from those equally mobile English merchants who dealt regularly
with foreigners and often lived abroad themselves, the international traders.
Heywood's play seems to unmask such scapegoating. A peddler is his most
honorable character—honest, hardworking, thrifty, charitable—while those
representing international exporting, Gresham and his unspeakable nephew,
swill crushed pearls and buy sex in a retail brothel.

The Merchant Adventurers had reason to protect themselves by pointing
the finger at others.[14] They had been vigorously attacked in such treatises as
Thomas Milles's *The Customers Reply . . . an answer to a confused treatise of
public commerce, . . . in favor of the private society of Merchants Adventurers,*
1604, which accused exporters of "setting thousands on work beyond seas,
when God knows the wants and hears the cries at home" (sig. [A4]). As Douglas Bisson shows, Tudor public policy was in the pocket of the Merchant
Adventurers, even when this worked to the detriment of English tradesmen
and artificers:

Opportunities for fostering the development of the cloth industry were usually sacrificed to the needs of the Merchant Adventurers Company. The
King-in-Parliament might pass the great Statue of Artificers in distress over
the ever-growing number of former husbandmen and clothiers tramping
through the counties of the realm, but concern for the trade of the Merchant
Adventurers Company and the revenue it supplied outweighed even these
pressing domestic problems. The unquestioned utility of the company in
the fields of foreign borrowing and the "chaunge and rechaunge" of money

rendered the Crown more amenable to the requirements of the trading colossus than to the needs of the lowly handicraftsmen. (47)

The perceived sacrifice of domestic manufacturers, tradesmen, and merchants on the altar of international trade was widely resented, as was the perceived contribution of international trade to runaway inflation. In Sir Thomas Smith's dialogue *Discourse of the Commonweal of this Realm of England*, circa 1549, a husbandman, a merchant, a knight, an artificer, and a scholar discuss the nation's economic woes, especially high prices. The husbandman accuses the knight of raising rents on land; the knight accuses the husbandman of raising the price of commodities the knight buys from him (butter, corn, etc.); each agrees to lower prices if the other will, but the husbandman can do this only if supplies he depends on are held steady or reduced in price, and some come from abroad (38–40). How can such suppliers be forced to sell at lower prices? the husbandman demands: "They be strangers [i.e., foreigners], and not within obedience of our sovereign lord, that do sell such wares, as iron, tar, flax" (40). Speakers consider reducing English dependency on foreign commodities, but admit that some luxury goods have become virtual necessities, without which the English "would live grossly and barbarously, as without wines, spices, and silks: these must be brought from beyond the seas" (42). Luxury imports have become essential to national pride. But finally, for Smith, there is no getting around it: England should avoid excessive exports and "spare many . . . things that we have now from beyond the seas" (63). Local manufacturing of commodities now imported would create jobs (63). In other words, a glamorous shopping mall like the Pawn, heavily oriented toward luxury imports, is fomenting inflation that renders laborers like Tawnycoat unable to buy necessities on their fixed salaries.

Thomas Heywood, it is to be feared, was less sophisticated about economics than Sir Thomas Smith, and *If You Know Not Me, You Know Nobody, Part 2* is finally ambivalent about Gresham. However much the play undercuts him, there *is* something heroic about Heywood's Gresham; he *is* in some sense a "royal Citizen." And Heywood does soften the historical facts, for example staging happy construction workers erecting the Exchange with no hint of the bitter labor dispute protesting Gresham's importation of foreign workers. Heywood never overtly suggests that despite public demonization of peddlers, it is their upper-crust cousins, international traders like Gresham, who are most to blame for economic hard times. But if Heywood is not consciously undermining Gresham, international traders, and London's affluent classes, then the play's political unconscious has emerged with a vengeance, in a notable return of the repressed. This is apparent in the ending: first, the queen narrowly escapes assassination by a foreign agent acting on behalf of the Catholicism of Rome; and second, the Spanish Armada is defeated. The play begins with England proudly engaging in international trade, and ends with England proudly repulsing foreign invasion. The political and military situations seem to project the economic situation, in embodying the danger of foreign invasion.

The play stages an episode so famous it was retold by every early modern student of London: the renaming of the Royal Exchange by Queen Elizabeth. But as Julia Gasper writes,

> There was something very odd about Queen Elizabeth visiting Gresham's Burse, as it was first called, and honoring it with the title of the Royal Exchange. The Burse had been modeled on the one at Antwerp, where Gresham had spent so much of his career as the financial agent of the Crown. In Antwerp, the trade in bills of exchange was unregulated by the government, but in England the Crown had long claimed a prerogative of controlling currency exchange and regulating the rates. This control, like any arbitrary control, could be highly unwelcome to those trying to operate in an open, international market. The title of "Royal Exchange" or "Cambium Regis" was given by Tudor monarchs to the minister whose job it was to exercise this control. Yet Elizabeth did, in 1571, bestow the very same title on Gresham's Exchange, where merchants from all over Europe were doing free-trade business. But what could Elizabeth do to stop them? (104)

The renaming of the Royal Exchange was an admission that England's economic policy was dictated by international traders and money speculators, not by the Crown. In another return of the repressed, the play acknowledges this in its very rhyme scheme. The queen makes this proclamation:

> Proclaim through every high street of this city,
> This place to be no longer called a burse,
> But since the building's stately, fair and strange,
> Be it forever called the Royal Exchange.
>
> (2052–55)

How appropriate that "Exchange" is rhymed with "strange," whose primary meaning was "foreign." And how fitting that the one character on whom to play bestows unalloyed praise is clothed not in silk fringes from Genoa sewn with black thread from Pisa, but in a tawny coat, no doubt of British manufacture.

NOTES

1. A *pawn* was a "colonnade, a covered walk or passage, especially one in a bazaar, exchange, or arcade, alongside of which wares are exposed for sale" *(OED)*. Its etymology is different from the "pawn" involved in pawnbroking, but the two meanings were historically contemporary (see, for example, Shakespeare's *Richard II* 2.1.293). Hearing about the elegant shopping mall the Pawn, contemporaries might sometimes have heard connotations of desperate indebtedness and pawning one's goods.

2. Indeed, this is how the play has traditionally been read. Barbara Baines, noting that "Gresham embodies the wealth, power, and growth of the middle class through prudent use of capital in trade and industry," concludes that "clearly Heywood's play is a celebration of this social and economic change" (35). Theodora Jankowski argues that the play "develops the notion of merchants as true 'conquerors,' valorizes those merchant adventurers who expand trade and capital beyond England's boundaries, and shows how the rise of capitalist society eliminates social ills at home and supports the government economically while providing financial reward to the adventurous capitalists themselves" (308). Edward Bonahue calls the play "a palatable lozenge for citizen consumption" (90).

3. Citations of the play are to the line numbers provided in the online database English Drama (1280–1915). Spelling and punctuation have been modernized.

4. The second half of the sixteenth century and early years of the seventeenth century also witnessed an explosion of new chartered companies dealing in international trade: the Muscovy Company, Eastland Company, Levant Company, Barbary Company, East India Company, and Virginia Company.

5. Patricia Fumerton's essay in this volume also comments on Harman's view of peddlers.

6. Royal Exchange merchants also engaged in other commercial activities, including insurance underwriting, as had Lombard Street merchants before them. "After the opening of the Exchange in 1569, long before Lloyd's existed, the underwriters did their deals in the courtyard of the building" (Sibbett 77).

7. On the gradual legitimation of usury, see the work of Lorna Hutson, William Ingram, Norman Jones, Benjamin Nelson, and Teresa Nugent.

8. On tropes of labor and sweat employed to legitimate commerce, see Leinwand 111–38 and Karen Helfand Bix's essay in this volume.

9. Jankowski argues that in contrast to the monarch who is the "protagonist of the traditional history play," Heywood makes a radical move in his *Edward IV* plays and his two *If You Know Not Me* plays: "an attempt to create a new 'aristocracy' based solely on capital or trading ability" (311).

10. Jankowski's view of John as an endearingly blundering scoundrel "designed to take the heat off" the powerful merchant class by imparting to it an air of harmlessness (325) is plausible, but neglects the impact of John's behavior on how we see Gresham. "No one in his/her right mind would take John Gresham seriously as a factor," Jankowski rightly notes (325)—but both Hobson and Gresham do so, to their cost.

11. Heywood also recognizes that this insight is no news to the poor: the impoverished

"Tawnycoat" notices in bitter soliloquy that in modern times, "the mightier / Tear living out of us" (1555–56).

12. Most critics of the play consider Hobson's action to be a kind of alms, simple old-fashioned "Christian charity" (see, for example, Bonahue 80).

13. Later we see Hobson arranging a shipment of merchandise to Bristol Fair (1304–5).

14. Merchant Adventurers deflected resentment of import/export trade not only onto peddlers but also onto foreign traders, especially the Hanse, a powerful Germanic trading league whose extensive trading privileges in London had been "extracted from Edward IV by the league in return for services rendered during his campaign to reclaim the English throne in 1471" (Bisson 48). During Elizabeth's reign, the trading privileges of the Hanse were finally extinguished, largely owing to the efforts of Thomas Gresham. But it continued useful for the Merchant Adventurers to emphasize their own patriotic Englishness and deflect resentment of their foreign dealings by scapegoating such "real" foreigners as the Hanseatic League.

WORKS CITED

Addison, William. *English Fairs and Markets*. London: Batsford, 1953.

An Act for the Punishment of Vagabonds, and for the Relief of the Poor and Impotent. London: Richard Jugge, 1572. STC 9478.

Armstrong, Clement. "A Treatise Concerning the Staple, and the Commodities of this Realm." Ca. 1519–35. *Tudor Economic Documents*. Ed. R. H. Tawney and Eileen Power. 3 vols. London: Longmans, 1924. 3:20–114.

Baines, Barbara J. *Thomas Heywood*. Boston: Twayne, 1984.

Bisson, Douglas R. *The Merchant Adventurers of England: The Company and the Crown, 1474–1564*. Newark: U of Delaware P, 1993.

Bonahue, Edward T., Jr. "Social Control, the City, and the Market: Heywood's *2 If You Know Not Me, You Know Nobody*." *Renaissance Papers* 1993:75–90.

Dekker, Thomas, and Webster, John. *Westward Ho*. In *The Dramatic Works of Thomas Dekker*. Ed. Fredson Bowers. 4 vols. Cambridge: Cambridge UP, 1953–61. 2:313–403.

Downame, John. *The Plea of the Poor, Or A Treatise of Beneficence and Alms-Deeds*. London: E. Griffin, 1616.

The Execution of Neschech and the Confining of His Kinsman Tarbith, or a Short Discourse Showing the Difference betwixt Damned Usury and That Which Is Lawful. London, 1616.

Fontaine, Laurence. *A History of Pedlars in Europe*. Trans. Vicki Whittaker. Durham, N.C.: Duke UP, 1996.

Gasper, Julia. "The Literary Legend of Sir Thomas Gresham." Saunders, *The Royal Exchange* 99–107.

Gibbons, Brian. *Jacobean City Comedy*. 2d ed. London: Methuen, 1980.

Greene, Robert. *The Royal Exchange*. London: J. Charlewood, 1590.

Harman, Thomas. *A Caveat or Warening for Common Cursetors Vulgarely Called Vagabones*. 1566. 2d ed., London: W. Griffith, 1567, STC 12787. London: H. Middleton, 1573, STC 12788. *The Elizabethan Underworld*. Ed. A. V. Judges. 2d ed. New York: Octagon, 1964. 61–118.

Heywood, Thomas. *If You Know Not Me, You Know Nobody, Part 2*. London: N. Butter, 1606.

Holmes, Martin. *Elizabethan London*. New York: Praeger, 1969.

Hutson, Lorna. *The Usurer's Daughter: Male Friendship and Fictions of Women in Sixteenth-Century England*. New York: Routledge, 1994.

Imray, Jean. "The Origins of the Royal Exchange." Saunders, *The Royal Exchange* 20–35.

Ingram, William. "The Economics of Playing." *A New History of Early English Drama*. Ed. John D. Cox and David Scott Kasten. New York: Columbia UP, 1997.

Jankowski, Theodora. "Historicizing and Legitimating Capitalism: Thomas Heywood's *Edward IV* and *If You Know Not Me, You Know Nobody*." *Medieval and Renaissance Drama in England* 7 (1995): 305–37.

Jones, Norman. *God and the Moneylenders: Usury and Law in Early Modern England*. Cambridge, Mass.: Basil Blackwell, 1989.

Jonson, Ben. *Volpone*. In *Ben Jonson*. Ed. C. H. Herford, Percy Simpson, and Evelyn Simpson. 11 vols. Oxford: Clarendon P, 1925–52. 5:15–136.

Leinwand, Theodore B. *Theatre, Finance, and Society in Early Modern England*. Cambridge: Cambridge UP, 1999.

Lupton, Donald. *London and the Country Carbonadoed and Quartered into Several Characters*. London: Nicholas Okes, 1632.

Merrett, Kathryn Chase. *A History of the Edmonton City Market, 1900–2000: Urban Values and Urban Culture*. U of Calgary P, 2001.

Milles, Thomas. *The Customers Reply. . . . an answer to a confused treatise of public commerce, . . . in favor of the private society of Merchants Adventurers*. London: James Roberts, 1604. STC 17932.

Muldrew, Craig. *The Economy of Obligation: The Culture of Credit and Social Relations in Early Modern England*. London: Macmillan, 1998.

Nelson, Benjamin. *The Idea of Usury: From Tribal Brotherhood to Universal Otherhood*. Chicago: U of Chicago P, 1969.

Nugent, Teresa Lanpher. "Usury and Counterfeiting in Wilson's *The Three Ladies of London and The Three Lords and Three Ladies of London*, and in Shakespeare's *Measure for Measure*." *Money and the Age of Shakespeare: Essays in New Economic Criticism*. Ed. Linda Woodbridge. New York: Palgrave, 2003. 201–17.

Saunders, Ann. "The Building of the Exchange." Saunders, *The Royal Exchange* 36–47.

———. "The Organisation of the Exchange." Saunders, *The Royal Exchange* 85–98.

———, ed. *The Royal Exchange*. London: London Topographical Society, 1997.

Shakespeare, William. *As You Like It*. In *Complete Works*. Ed. David Bevington. 4th ed. Glenview, Ill.: Scott, Foresman, 1992. 292–325.

Sibbett, Trevor. "Early Insurance and the Royal Exchange." Saunders, *The Royal Exchange* 76–84.

Smith, Sir Thomas (probable author). *A Discourse of the Commonweal of This Realm of England*. Ca. 1549. Ed. Elizabeth Lamond. Cambridge: Cambridge UP, 1929.

Staniland, Kay. "Thomas Deane's Shop in the Royal Exchange." Saunders, *The Royal Exchange* 59–67.

Stow, John. *A Survey of London.* 1598. Ed. Henry Morley. London: Routledge, 1890.

———. *Annales, or, a Generall Chronicle of England.* Revised Edmund Howes. London: John Beale et al., 1631.

Wheeler, John. *A Treatise of Commerce, wherein are shewed the commodities arising by a well-ordered and ruled trade, such as that of the Society of Merchants Adventurers is proved to be; written principally for the better information of those who doubt of the necessariness of the said society in the state of the realm of England.* London: John Harrison, 1601. In *Tudor Economic Documents.* Ed. R. H. Tawney and Eileen Power. 3 vols. London: Longmans, 1924. 3:280–304.

"Masters of Their Occupation"

Labor and Fellowship in the
Cony-Catching Pamphlets

What scholars have called the "double tone" of the cony-catching pamphlets is nowhere more evident than in the pamphlets' treatment of urban commercial developments and their social effects. The dual perspective evinced in such works as Robert Greene's *Notable Discovery* (1597) and its sequels and Thomas Dekker's *The Bellman of London* (1604) and *Lantern and Candlelight* (1608) lends itself to the expression of a wide range of contemporary models of economic change, as well as a composite portraiture of an emerging commercial scene, which is truly remarkable for its subtlety and breadth. The pamphlets distinctively express psychic and cognitive disturbances provoked by only partially understood socioeconomic phenomena, along with the kind of compound sentiments generated by the multiple collapses and evolutions that were occurring in urban spaces—for instance, the mixture of cynicism and exhilaration—with which many Londoners responded to the transformation of their city and its markets. They brilliantly reproduce the moral equivocation and rhetorical indeterminacy that characterize transitional economic discourses and draw out elusive patterns, correspondences, and contradictions between and among noncomplimentary or even contradictory social ideologies.

This chapter focuses on the ways in which the pamphlets interrogate and juxtapose competing economic perspectives in order to yield new and imaginative responses to the social and normative questions that the expanding market posed. In a very broad sense, the cony-catching narratives alternate between two overarching visions of economic change. Drawing upon conservative commonwealth rhetoric, the pamphlets project a conception of the marketplace as a solvent of Christian and communal principles and a catalyst for unwholesome appetites and compromised ethics. This critique of market culture deviates substantially from the kind of doctrinal complaint that pervades the earlier "vagabond" literature of Thomas Harmon and Frank Awdeley, generally omitting, for instance, appeals to older, customary practices associated with a bounded, rural, authoritarian order. (Where the later pamphlets do invoke Harman-like apocalyptic laments over the "spoil and ruin" of "the realm" perpetrated by amoral rogue predators, the sermonizing is at best perfunctory and more often meretricious [Judges 151].) Rather, the conycatching texts appear less concerned with the values of order and stability than with the demise of social decency and honesty, and the replacement of such ethics with new exploitational structures and ideologies.

At other times, the pamphlets emphasize the liberating potential of open exchange, even the progressive notion that an unfettered market rewards individual talents that are democratically dispersed. On occasion, they enlist contemporary arguments that naturalize trade as a social practice in order to revalue morally questionable commercial behaviors. Such an anticipatory "natural law" form of argument underpins the numerous analogies drawn between outlaw and respectable "cony-catchers"; the texts thus disperse the drive for profit as well as dubious marketplace activities across the social order ("to all conditions and estates of man") (Salgãdo 346). Although these analogies are voiced ambivalently, they establish a schema by which the pamphlets rework such negative associations with the exchange economy as competitiveness, opportunism, and ambition—in such a way that they appear as not only normative, but admirable and attractive. It is against this schema that the pamphleteers slyly celebrate the cony-catchers' cunning, resourcefulness, and aggressive individuality, demonstrated within the fray of urban life.

What emerges from the confluence of these interpretive models is an assessment of the limitations and potentials of economic developments that is at once pragmatic and morally driven. Although the pamphlets' overall critique of commercial structures and practices is in many respects progressive, it is not subversive in the sense of endorsing systemic alteration or any substantial departure from existing arrangements. Rather, the pamphlets enact a kind of reckoning, balancing the excesses of the exchange economy against its promises and possibilities, while occasionally indicating measures to mitigate its more disturbing social consequences. While they insistently dramatize the propensity for exploitation in exchange, the potential for social disintegration brought about by open competition and individualist ethics, and the continuity between residual and emergent modes of social differentiation, the pamphlets invoke such issues to appeal for a greater measure of social honesty, equality, and toleration in a system that they perceive as pliant and susceptible to intervention. In the following pages, I examine the ways in which the pamphlets read current vocational literature and study the effects of market forces upon community, ultimately to coax a vision of inclusive and democratic social relations adaptable to the structures of commerce and exigencies of urban life.

Underworld Profanity and Moral Exemption

The cony-catching literature's ideological multivalence, its ability to draw out subtle patterns and contradictions within and among synchronous economic perspectives, may be attributed in part to the "flexible idiom" of the pamphlet form and its ability to encompass the disruptive social developments that provided their subject matter (Manley 355, 367–69). But it also has something to do with the malleability of the rogue figures themselves. As Linda Woodbridge has recently observed, because the vagrant figures whom the pamphlets purported to represent were for the most part "voiceless," their interpellation went largely uncontested, such that "rogues and vagabonds" were continually reshaped as the genre developed to serve varying interests (160).[1] Although in the later pamphlets the cony-catcher becomes more individualized and less emblematic, he never possesses anything like a consistent, unitary identity, so that he is able to register opposing psychological and ideological impulses unconstrained by precepts of rationality or coherence.

Perhaps the sole consistent feature of the rogue throughout the genre's evolution is that he is unreformable, dismissed from any possibility of salvation or rehabilitation. The authors of the earlier, mid-sixteenth-century pamphlets insisted on the rogue's incorrigibility, such that they were free to describe him without adhering to the reformist ethics (or principles of charity) that characterized official discourse about the "deserving poor" to whom he was opposed. While in the rogue's later permutation as cony-catcher, he becomes more of an embodiment of urban-generated vice than specifically a reprobate figure, he remains "incurable" and permanently excommunicated from both nostalgic and novel ideals of social organization.

For pamphleteers like Greene and Dekker, who were interested in conveying the complex social and moral effects of economic change, the rogue's outsider, unassimilable condition afforded a crucial measure of license from some of the ideological and discursive constraints that plagued literatures that either excoriated market culture or praised it. The moral instruction resisting socioeconomic transformation emphasized the incompatibility of self-interested and profit-driven behaviors with customary theological standards, but its arguments tended to be grounded in an outmoded social vision. To a large degree, such literature remained trapped in binaries of covetousness and altruism, ruthless self-advancement and benevolence, and rivalry and brotherhood, while hedging or denying the tangible social and material developments that the expanding market was generating (the growing dependence of Crown and aristocracy on the capital of London merchants and their bankers, mass participation across classes in credit networks, and the visible growth of trade and industry) (Appleby 67). Sixteenth-century pamphlets and treatises by merchants and government officials designed to dignify commercial activities sought ideally to reconcile trade practices and principles with traditional moral and social assumptions. Yet they were hindered by the problem that the valorization of commerce and the attitudes supporting it were most often "figured in the person of the merchant," who had inherited such an extensive backlog of complaints that his sixteenth-century defenders drastically overdrew his sanitization, tending to suppress even the merest hint of moral compromise (Solomon 78). Attempting to lend substance to commercial activities by celebrating the achievements of successful merchants, while protecting them from historical charges of covetousness and exploitation, led market advocates to "ignore the merchant's financial dealings entirely" or to omit any representation of trade itself (Stevenson 38, 106).

As several scholars have indicated, the projection of objectionable commercial practices and values onto rogues served both "to relieve the public of the promptings either of pity or of responsibility" for the poor, and to deflect social resentments away from merchants (Woodbridge 19). Regardless of the crucial social consequences this scapegoating eventuated for vagrants and other figures identified as rogues, the removal of economic practices and principles to the "profane" context of the underworld enables the pamphleteers to examine subtle questions about commerce free from many of the ideological complications that cluttered its representation in alternative literatures. Insofar as the rogues are excluded from the prospect of redemption (and thus exempted from theological and moral imperatives), the pamphleteers can "anatomize" their motives and "abuses" (which shadow those of legitimate economic actors) in a unconstrained, "secular" mode. The rogue "subculture," in this sense, serves as an ideal conceptual space for a candid examination of a market-oriented society, "a harmless outlet for criticism of ('the right') order and for the open presentation of alternatives" (Slack 25).[2]

Roguery and Vocational Discourse

Among the economic phenomena about which the pamphlets are especially fractured is the changing constitution of labor in the new, more flexible, unregulated economy. The most persistent accusation against the rogue in the earlier "vagabond" literature of Awdeley and Harman is, of course, his deliberate shirking of work. As William Carroll remarks, the rogue (in his previous persona as "sturdy beggar") is objected to not only insofar as he personifies the venal sin of sloth, but because "he subverts or even invalidates the prevailing ideology of work: his able body resists participation in economic production, choosing instead the role of the parasite" (85).[3] Yet Elizabeth Hanson has recently observed that Harman's *Caveat for Common Cursitors* (1566) evinces a disjunction between the text's claims about the rogues' essential idleness and the considerable energy they exude (96).[4]

The "rift" between idleness and exertion is perhaps even more conspicuous in the later pamphlets. Although the sturdy beggar occupies a less central position in this literature, Greene and Dekker continue to invoke the cultural (and statutory) formulation of willful idleness, but with a considerable measure of slippage. Within a single pamphlet, for instance, Greene asserts, and then reverses, a central trope for idleness, complaining first that rogues "like drones eat away what others labor for," and a short while later that the cony-catchers who scope Westminster for gulls, "work like bees," likening them as well to "provident husbandmen" for "the term time is their harvest" (Judges 151, 164). Dekker's rogues are "idle Drones of a Countrie, the Caterpillars of a Commonwealth," yet he draws an even more explicit analogy between the "sweat" and "strain" that the nips and foists who "ply Weftmifter hall" expend and the exacting toil of agricultural workers (long the literary synecdoche for strenuous labor): "Michaelmas terme is their haruest and they fweat in it harder than reapers or hay-makers doe at their workes in the heate of fommer" (*Lantern* 3:82, 157).

While the pamphleteers complain about the "cursed crews" who "set, with the epicures, gain and ease, their *summum bonum*," and sometimes include scenes of underworld "tavern cheer" (and other forms of "recreation"), they almost never portray cony-catchers in a sedentary or slothful condition (Judges 152). Rather, the cony-catchers consistently demonstrate energy, rigor, and a kind of physical exuberance. The rogues who attend the famous quarter-dinner in Dekker's *Bellman of London* live "the life of a solder," suffering "hunger and cold in the winter," and "heat and thirst in the summer" while traversing their assigned territories (Judges 309–10). The legers or "crafty colliers" who vend bags of coal stuffed with "shruff dust . . . riseth very early in the morning" to trudge to markets in "Croydon, Whetstone, Greenwich or Romaford," while other rogues "labor all night for their living" (Judges 143, 146, 152). The collaborators of the Barnard's law "trauell vp and downe the whole land," the prigger "vp and down the whole kingdome vpon his geldings" (Dekker, *Lantern* 3:125, 143). The narrator of Luke Hutton's *The Black Dog of Newgate* (1596) states outright that "cony-catchers are never idle" (Judges 282).

The extent to which "cony-catching" is characterized as an active, dynamic, and effort-laden endeavor not only disrupts the cony-catchers' identification as "loiterers" and "dai-sleepers," but situates cony-catching as a tenable if deviant form of labor. Such framing (while farcical) yields significant implications when cony-catching is positioned against contemporary formulations of labor in merchant pamphlets and other vocational literatures. Unlike the muscular exploits of Awdeley's and Harman's "mighty beggars" and highway robbers, the cony-catchers' labor is, of course, more ingenious than physical, and it is for their mental agility and cunning that the pamphleteers most frequently betray their admiration. Departing from the "fraternity" and "ragged regiment" narratives that relocate to rogue society the authoritarian, hierarchical structures of trade guilds, cony-catching shadows the behavior of the kind of independent operators who were transgressing the closed orders of freemen. The cony-catchers' acumen in scoping and sizing up a cony, their capacity for strategic dissimulation and rhetorical versatility in insinuating themselves into his confidence, their spontaneity and adaptability to changing circumstances, and their ability to innovate novel opportunities for exploiting their "devices" parallel financial talents that were being widely recognized as instrumental in the urban marketplace.

According to the business historian Richard Grassby, rather than specific skills, acquired through apprenticeship or formal education, the early modern "ad hoc" marketplace set a premium on "innate" proclivities like intuition and spontaneity, creativity and resourcefulness (196). Competent marketing "depended fundamentally not on logic or intellect, but on instinct, experience and flair, keenness and vigor." Merchants, particularly those involved in long-distance trade, "needed common sense rather than rational, cognitive skills, insight rather than calculation . . . and discriminating judgment rather than formal knowledge," while in retail trade, "the volume of sales" was partly determined "by the flamboyant talents of the hustler" (Grassby 196, 175). A London shopkeeper had to possess a genius for intuiting the varied motives and desires of a diverse clientele, and for "fitting . . . himself to a diversity of forms" in order to respond to individual fancies, biases and vulnerabilities

(Solomon 109; Daniel Tuvill, quoted in Solomon 119). For entrepreneurs, the crucial determinant of success was an instinct for appreciating new possibilities for profit (Sullivan 36).

The pamphleteers' acknowledgment of faculties in the cony-catchers that were elsewhere being promoted as fiscally advantageous responds to several strains in contemporary economic thought. Like previous rogue literature, the cony-catching pamphlets gesture (somewhat more subtly) to the economic potential of the lower orders. As Carroll has noted, the view of the "masterless man" as an untapped productive resource informed even the earliest rogue pamphlets, reflecting the reformist trend in Tudor debate and legislation concerning the poor that inaugurated the plethora of (largely dubious) schemes for setting vagrants to work (85, 127). Such pamphlets were produced at a time when the preoccupation with "making the poor industrious" ran up against the realities of an economic scene in which unskilled labor was only "conditionally and occasionally needed" (Appleby 153). But cony-catching literature looks forward to a period in which the expansion of domestic trade, the diversification of commercial life, and new agricultural developments and intensification begins to make the systematic, "serial" mobilization of lower-class labor both feasible and financially advantageous (as did demands for the widening of domestic consumer markets, and the cultivation of "national prosperity"). In such a climate, the reformist ethics of the earlier era were channeled into a germinating doctrine of economic freedom. Corollaries to this ideology were the postulates that economic potentials are individualized and that the flexible market would reward the hard work and natural talents of even the average, propertyless man (Appleby 112ff.; McRae 162, 167).

In celebrating the cony-catchers' mastery of marketplace skills and contingencies, the pamphlets seem to endorse the egalitarian notion that economic talents are randomly dispersed. At other times, they more subversively suggest that the *superior* endowments of cony-catchers somehow level the playing field.[5] Such radical implications are challenged, however, by the reduction of the cony-catchers' capacities to the product of their immoral disposition, such that even those of their abilities that reflect legitimate vocational skills are degraded to forms of "deviousness," "shifting," and "subtlety." I do not mean to collapse the rogues' illicit activities into the legal-if-suspect commercial practices that they only shadow, nor to ignore how seriously were taken the violations of property and of the (precontractual) imperatives of trust and accountability that the rogues enact. Yet the pamphlets' vacillation between praise and deprecation specifically of the cony-catchers' "profitable facult[ies]" calls attention both to the conflicting attitudes of Jacobeans toward the characterological properties and economic capacities of the lower orders, as well as to arbitrary distinctions drawn by mercantile writers between "unjuste" and "tolerable . . . ways of deceit" (Salgãdo 341; Scott 35). By framing cony-catching as a "trade," the pamphlets in one sense gesture to the emancipatory potential of new conceptions of labor. Simultaneously, they point to the exclusionary machinery of commercial vocational discourse—its mechanisms for reinforcing social divisions even as it advances alternative modes of valuation designed to cut across traditional notions of status and individual worth.

In another respect, the shifting valuations of cony-catching labor expose the pathological tendency toward social differentiation that "economic leveling among merchants, landed gentry, and nobility produced" (Leinwand, *City Staged* 36). Insofar as the tactical skills entailed in cony-catching were being nurtured as modes of self-empowerment in texts ranging from courtesy literature to humanist rhetorical primers to Francis Bacon's scientific essays, they persistently aroused a defensive preoccupation with their selective distribution. The rhetorical gymnastics by which merchant pamphleteers distinguished their strategies from "politicke" manipulations and Machiavellian forms of misrepresentation were reproduced with remarkable consistency at all levels. As Julie Solomon has observed, tracts by public officials and royal counselors that cultivated tactics modeled on the practices of merchants ("secrecy, dissembling, self-effacement, world-attentiveness, adaptability, and manipulation of others' desires") elevated such faculties to forms of high-minded "prudence" when directed to civic-minded professionals, while inevitably depreciating them as "craft," "deceit," or "guile" in "profit-seeking individuals" (118–19).

The pamphlets' ambivalent formulations of the cony-catchers' economic capacities are also registered in the dual identifications of cony-catching as a "Trade" and as an "Art" (Agnew 67–68). When presented as a form of native artistry, and aligned with theatricality, the cony-catchers' abilities are coded as imaginative and spontaneous, rather than practiced and disciplined. Such an appraisal indirectly reassociates cony-catchers with the charge of idleness, such that they appear as ingenious but effortless "procurers of great gain," while downplaying their intellectual abilities (Judges 390).

Yet the cony-catchers are seen actively, meticulously to tax and tune their natural abilities to acquire "mastery" in their "vocations," to exploit, as it were, whatever resources they possess to their maximum value. Greene's Ned Browne takes "pains" (as well as pride) in developing "expertise" in his "profession": "The most expert and skilful Alchemist never took more pains in experience of his metals, the physician in his simples, the mechanical man in the mysteries of his occupation, than I have done in plotting precepts, rules, axiomes, and principles" (Judges 256). Other rogues express a competitive pursuit of proficiency. "What art is more excellent," asks Lawrence, the "hee-conny-catcher" in Greene's *A Disputation,* "to try the ripeness of the wit, or the agility of the hand, than that for him will be master of his trade must pass the proudest juggler alive the points of legerdemain" (Judges 211). Veteran rogues and "elders" inculcate their "stalls" or apprentices with the values of hard work, exaction, and tenacity. "If thou wilt only do common work," one seasoned "nip" scolds a stall who shies away from a challenging foist, "and not make experience of some hard matters to attempt, thou wilt never be master of thine occupation" (Judges 166). Along these lines, it seems significant that the pamphlets increasingly depict cony-catchers deliberately rejecting the easiest or most labor-saving course of action—less demanding or more conventional "sleights" and cozenages—in favor of more exerting and challenging ones. In *The Third Part of Cony-catching,* for example, a cutpurse teases his fellows about the predictability of their prosaic foists, boasting that he can come up with a ruse "of more value than forty of yours":

> In faith, masters, these things are prettily done—common sleights, express-ing no deep reach of wit. And I wonder men are so simple to be so beguiled would fain see some rare artificial feat indeed, that some admiration and fame might ensue the doing thereof. I promise ye, I disdain these base and petty paltries. . . . ye shall hear, my boys, within a day or two, that I will accomplish a rare strategem indeed. (Judges 182)

Such narratives are travestying the rogues' pretensions of legitimacy in call-ing their chicanery occupations or vocations. But the satiric valence is under-cut by the unmistakable image of industry that the cony-catchers' commit-ment to mastery, their ceaseless trafficking and indefatigable plotting call up. The extent to which "the art of cony-catching" is underscored as the product of diligent effort, meticulous calculation, and workmanship not only disrupts the rogues' characterization as "idle predators" but in some sense seems to jus-tify their profits (Judges 157).

In emphasizing the "strain" and "pains," "the "sweat" and "travail" the cony-catchers undergo in executing their cozenages, the pamphlets invoke a contemporary ideological equation that justified private profit through the merchant's strenuous labor, the "toile" that he underwent in accruing his wealth.[6] Assimilating the Christian ethic of "redeeming" labor to occupations divorced from traditional vocational regimes and material production, six-teenth- and early-seventeenth-century merchants drew upon "travail" to bol-ster their moral authority and sanction their profits (McRae 202; Agnew 143; Leinwand, *Theatre* 116). A businessman's claims of hardship and effort worked to counter the historical castigation of merchants as the indolent recipients of returns on loans, or at least to distinguish him from the mass of "idle benchpresses" arraigned in moral complaint (Sullivan 56; Solomon 75). As Jean-Christophe Agnew points out, labor sanitized commerce, absolving it of its "predatory and illicit connotations" (142–43). The value of "toil" was similarly upheld in Puritan codifications of economic virtues, and in hus-bandry and later improvement literature. Yet to greater degree, its function for merchants was tactical and rhetorical, especially when applied to large-scale speculators or "armchair" entrepreneurs, who profited primarily from passive investments and by directing the labor of others (McRae 202). "Travail" fortified a merchant's reputation for honesty, which determined his access to credit. For entrepreneurs trying to attract investors for high-risk schemes, it provided "an affective ballast (an implicitly ethical security deposit)" (Lein-wand, *Theatre* 12).

The increasing appearance of travail in mercantile texts coincided with an equally widespread tendency to deflect the charge of idleness onto peddlers and other roguish figures, which Woodbridge traces in this volume. Against this background, the pamphlets' elaboration of cony-catching as "toilsome" seems to mock the commercial elite's self-aggrandizing appropriation of "travail." But while unmasking the rhetorical promiscuity of toil, the pamphlets appear to endorse authentic labor as a legitimate standard of value, especially in those tales where they contrast the rogues' exertions with the extravagant ambitions of city conies who hope to make an easy profit without breaking a sweat.

It has been noted that the cony-catchers increasingly single out corrupt or corruptible victims, tailoring their ruses to exploit the cony's particular vices and vanities.[7] While a cony's greed or arrogance, or his willingness to violate ethics of neighborliness, may make him especially vulnerable to the cony-catchers' scams, his moral culpabilities are inevitably augmented by his assumption that profit, along with other rewards, can be generated effortlessly, without the need for labor (Judges 260). Such wild aspirations, "a golden age desire of getting something for nothing," drives even the wariest of conies—those well-tutored in cony-catching chicanery (thanks to the pamphleteers' earlier "discoveries")—to let down their defenses, and "be wrought . . . like wax" (Brunning 10; Dekker, *Lantern* 3:232). The cony-catchers who go to St. Paul's or to the Exchange dressed as prosperous merchants to sell counterfeit bonds capitalize most decisively on the conies' hopes of making an elaborate killing, "thinking, perhaps, by one clause or other to defeat [the disguised cony-catcher] of all he hath" (Judges 261). Other conies eager for an extravagant windfall buy into the rather fantastic eventuality that a solvent international merchant might stroll into an ordinary and foolishly barter away his bond for "two or three ships of coal new come from Newcastle" for "forty shillings" (Judges 261).

By emphasizing the conies' latent ambitions for labor-free rewards, the pamphlets cleverly redirect the stain of idleness to the respectable. But what is really being discredited in such narratives are the exaggerated promises of the "free market," the vast overestimations of its liquid capacities promulgated as much in mercantile propaganda as in the "rags to riches" legends of bourgeois fiction. Whatever moral failings a cony may possess, his credulity in the possibility of a transforming one-stroke bargain ultimately rests on a misplaced conviction that the prospects of the market economy are inexhaustible and undiscriminating.

It is similarly the conies' pathetic expectations of instant, pain-free advantage that makes them susceptible to the cony-catchers' ludicrous claims of alchemy and magic. Ned Browne, confessing the "villainies" of his "companions," comments that when one spies a cony who is "covetously bent . . . they will tell you wonders of the philosopher's stone, and make you believe they can make gold of goose-grease" (Judges 258). Other cony-catchers vend "love powders" and aphrodisiacal rings "that if a wench put it on her finger, she shall not choose but follow you up and down the street" (Judges 260). Of course, it is precisely the cony-catchers' alchemical capacities—their seeming ability to generate wealth out of nothing but "the fee simple of their wits," to triumph inexplicably over their material limitations—that accounts for their allure, just as the pamphlets' promise to disclose "the mysteries of [their] occupation," and by association the "opaque" workings of the market, which partly explains their popularity (Dekker, *Lantern* 3:163). What we see instead is that cony-catching magic almost always requires hard work, whether creative or physical.[8] "So the juggler's conveyance seemeth to exceed the compass of reason till ye know the feat," says Gilbert Walker's "M." "But what is it that labour overcometh not?" (Judges 39). The pamphleteers, in fact, go out of their way to demystify the rogues' occult associations (Manley 349). Dekker, for instance, reveals "the mistical meaning" of the "Blacke Art, by which men conjure up Spriits, and raise Divels in Circles" as the "English Picking of Lockes," and debunks rogue alchemy altogether in the tale of the "Jack-in-the-Box" who changes "gold into silver" (by pawning a box of gold to a goldsmith, switching the original box with one full of shillings, then disappearing with the gold-smith's loan of silver as well as his own gold) (Judges 356–58).

What is emphasized in such exposures is that the cony-catchers are active, rational, self-reliant agents in the transformation of their own resources, how-ever restricted or strictly "immaterial," into assets. Like the wealth generated from the expanding market, their profits are neither inexplicable nor unnat-ural. Nor are they unlimited or accrued without expense. Against the popular, hyperbolic fictions of self-made men, the pamphlets express a profoundly pragmatic view of the limitations and possibilities of the new economic arrangements. They embrace the potential for upward mobility but under-stand that mobility can take place in both directions. They suggest that the unfettered market offers increased maneuverability and varied opportunities for the street-smart, enterprising individual to profit, but emphasize the effect of privilege on bargaining and insist that commerce disproportionately rewards those who possess "advantage" in the first place.

To the extent that the pamphlets traffic with contemporary labor discourse, their intervention is ambivalent. They appear to endorse alternative assess-ments of labor that assimilate new methods of creating wealth, and to support the principle of reward for industry, even as they interrogate the multiple mystifications of self-interest in fashionable vocational rhetoric. Whether the latter impulse constitutes any kind of serious-minded *political* critique is a question of ongoing scholarly debate, but the pamphlets' authentication of the cony-catchers' fiscal talents, nerve, and intelligence coincides with their increasingly pronounced indictments of the hypocrisy of respectable culture, and their concurrent resistance to facile, self-serving interpellations of the criminal underclass. Without devaluing the meritocratic arguments that undergird the new vocational literature, the pamphlets express impatience with the use of such arguments by the mercantile establishment to mask exploitation and to exclude the less entitled from the privileges and opportuni-ties that the expanding market afforded. By establishing a parity between the skills entailed in cony-catching and mercantile practices, and inflecting cony-catching as labor-intensive, the pamphlets question official culture's denigra-tion of rogues (and the underemployed laborers and vagrants who stand behind them) as characterologically and constitutionally deficient, unfit to participate in legitimate trade and undeserving of its rewards. While exempli-fying "the exclusionary conventions developing within the class and market structures of English capitalism," the pamphlets' treatment of labor neverthe-less holds out the possibility of reform insofar as it identifies the impediments to equitable competition and social inclusion as cultural rather than systematic (Agnew 68–69).

Cony-Catching Fellowship and the *"Sociability of Commerce"*

That the pamphlets are interested in the problem of human sociability against the taxing effects of economic transition is a critical commonplace. Recent work has more fruitfully examined the changing position of rogue culture vis-à-vis the decline of customary social ethics through progressive stages of the genre. As has been widely observed, the earlier literature relentlessly displaces the disruption of "neighborly ethics" onto rogues and vagabonds, such that they appear as the catalysts of social deterioration in an otherwise "harmonious" and "flourishing realm" (Hanson 101; Knapp 67; Judges 61, 121). The removal of rogue culture to an urban landscape in the later literature elicits an alternative to the view that the rogues benefit primarily by encroaching upon stable social mores and communal relations. Recent scholarship of the pamphlets has suggested that, rather than expectations of trust and neighborliness, a preexistent erosion of cultural integration and social conventions in the marketplace most enable the cony-catchers. From this perspective, the cony-catchers capitalize most crucially on the variables of population mobility, the necessity of bargaining with unknown partners in the shifting communities of commodity exchange, and commercial culture's subsequent habituation to immediate impressions and uncertain criteria for assessing individual moral and economic worth. Such conditions allow the cony-catchers repeatedly to alter their public personas and to infiltrate trade and credit networks by simulating respectability and solvency.

While the cony-catchers may nurture anonymity for strategic purposes, they are otherwise described as outstandingly social creatures (and preoccupied with advancing their "reputations"). The cultural criticism that argues that the pamphlets convey the "growing obscurity of new commercial relationships," or the depersonalizing effects of a "placeless" market, has tended to neglect or downplay the positive forms of sociability evoked in the narratives of cony-catching fellowship (Agnew 67–69). As Linda Woodbridge points out, portrayals of rogue geniality are part and parcel of the larger "glamourization of [the] urban underworld which masks the lower order's suffering" (22). Despite the mystification of poverty that they enact, the scenes of cony-catching convocation are significant insofar as they infuse a sense of localism and cohesiveness into a transient, fragmented population, abridged from all manners of institutional and kinship ties. By conceiving forms of positive social relations among the most marginal and dislocated members of the commonwealth, the pamphlets suggest the potential for sociability and communal identification even in the ephemeral marketplace.

Against studies that privilege the impeding effects of self-interest and open competition on urban social relations, I set my examination of cony-catching fellowship beside the new revisionist histories of early modern commerce that underscore "the localized character" of trade and the persistence of traditional social moralities in nascent capitalist structures (Sullivan 19). Craig Muldrew, a central architect of this alternate model, argues that "Christian notions of neighborliness," "charity," and communal obligation were sustained in late-sixteenth- and seventeenth-century commercial relationships by virtue of expanded credit structures that "bound everyone together in chains of mutual responsibility" (199, 136). The economic necessity of maintaining trust and cooperation to keep networks of mutual investment from breaking down coincided with a "tremendous desire to maintain harmonious relations within local communities"—to avoid unneighborly disputes and to preserve "peace and good order" (199, 200). While complaint moralists continued to stress the destructive role of private profit-seeking on human relations, a wide range of contemporary writings emphasized commerce as a force for strengthening social bonds and facilitating conversation and productive communication (138). Muldrew additionally calls attention to the productive role of credit in traversing fixed social hierarchies and promoting a "potential moral equality" across class lines, predicated upon mutual consent and on "the equality of bargaining and contract" (97, 133).[9]

By and large, rogue literature is skeptical about the social effects of credit, tending to disregard its enabling potential and associating it most often with rural impoverishment and disappropriation. Robert Copland identifies among the beggars in *Highway to the Spital-house* men from "all manner" of "estates" who have lost their homes and fallen into vagabondage as the result of default. In *The Counter's Commonwealth*, William Fennor contemplates the pervasiveness of bad faith and coercive practices among creditors and condemns the injustice of a system that levels "heedless . . . young gentlemen" and prodigal "elder brothers," with "forsaken serving men . . . broken citizens, and [the] country clients" of usurers, consigning each alike to the horrors of debtors' prison (Judges 425).[10] Where they are not portrayed as the victims of usurious lenders, the rogues appear as master manipulators of credit culture, infiltrating its complicated networks of promises and reckonings and abusing its instruments always somehow to extract their profits in hard cash.

Yet even as the cony-catchers model the potential for exploitation in a system dependent on the contingent values of trust and obligation, they simultaneously rehearse the ethics and forms of sociability that historians like Muldrew associate with early modern commerce. Infra-fraternally, they stress the principles of mutuality and consensual cooperation. Cony-catching fellowship encompasses impulses for financial advantage and affective bonds and provides a form of communal identification premised on mutual interests and shared sociopolitical values. Unlike the vagabond confederacies, cony-catching collaborations eliminate hierarchical divisions and project a standard of equality founded upon a reciprocity of rights. They dispense as well with the confederacies' oaths and bonds of loyalty and disciplinary regimes to advance a fluid conception of trust, which is voluntary and unregulated. Collusion provides the cony-catchers with an opportunity for energetic social intercourse, the exchange of banter and boasting, canting terms and wit. In a broader sense, the fellowships suggest the potential of commercial interaction to foster tolerance and inclusion and to readjust social relations along more equitable lines.

Critically, cony-catching alliances deviate dramatically from the fanciful conceptions of fellowship in earlier and later rogue literature. Against the covert and pernicious "subnations" of vagabond confederacies, or the benign kingdoms of the later "merry beggar" plays, cony-catching fellowship is integrated into the nexus of urban life. Rather than recycle models of community that are either anachronistic or in decline, or appeal to utopian formulations, the pamphleteers experiment with modes of collective association assimilated to the exigencies and prerogatives of the marketplace. The positive forms of sociability they explore work in tension with a pragmatic acknowledgment of the corrosive effects of open competition and individual ambition to suggest the ways in which commerce can generate both estrangement and alliance, trust and betrayal.

The fellowships are informed, but not monopolized, by what Agnew calls a "logic of instrumentality" (69). The cony-catchers are in the first place bound together by economic dependency since many of their operations necessitate the pooling of mental resources, capital outlay, and the distribution of risk. While their collective ruses require meticulous organization and a division of labor, they reject the regimentation and status-based assignments of the earlier confederacies. Instead, the codified ranks of the fraternities give way to informal networks that favor innovation, improvisation, and the appreciation of individual talents, and that allow for chance encounters and instant collaboration. The absence of stratification fosters more relaxed, spontaneous social intercourse, but it is also instrumental in that it creates a climate of tolerance and maneuverability that facilitates more effective collective brainstorming. If one or another cony-catcher takes the lead in these exchanges, it is no longer rank or seniority that distinguishes him but his initiation of a particularly "subtle" or "ingenious" strategy.

As noted earlier, one of the idiosyncrasies of cony-catching alliances is their inclination for more challenging or "rare strategems" over more prosaic, if equally effective, schemes. Scholars have sometimes construed this tendency as a dissident impulse—a collective desire to overwhelm a society that demeans them by flaunting their superior mental prowess (Reynolds 62, 154–55). Although the subversive, even retributive, capacity of cony-catching is discernable throughout the genre, the relish that the cony-catchers take both in planning and executing their cozenages seems to be grounded in something more than their resistance to interpellation. If they sometimes tailor a scheme to give a cony his comeuppance, the cony-catchers seem as much interested in winning the admiration of their fellows, or in amplifying their "fame" (Judges 413). In another respect, the cony-catchers' increasing attraction to shrewder, more wary conies, and to ever more daunting contingencies, indicates the sheer pleasure that they take in the game. Greene's later pamphlets tend to devote more space to the rogues' breathless collusions than to the thefts themselves, and, as Arthur Kinney comments, the cony-catchers frequently appear more involved in devising a scheme than in performing it (Kinney 35).

Although the pamphlets laugh at the rogues' swaggering claims of "genius" in cozenage, the broader valorization of cunning that emerges in the fellowship narratives complicates, even if it does not transform, "the adversarial, competitive nature of urban life" (Manley 451). The formulation of the fellowships as meritocracies of wit bears a formal resemblance to the structures of city comedies, in which gulling, because it is "predicated on a hierarchy of sophistication or cleverness," allows "disparate status groups" to compete at a remove from class and rank distinctions (Leinwand, *City Staged* 53). Yet here such a model serves less to realign power relations than to diffuse the tensions of urban commercial life, by providing a regenerative outlet for interpersonal contest and alternative grounds for individual prestige. Rather than producing a "utopian resolution of social conflict" (which ultimately reinstates "the logic of exploitation"), the elevation of wit as the prime standard of merit in the fellowships enables a fluid, egalitarian space and a medium for social intercourse that is at once productive and pleasurable (Manley 451).

Greene's narratives of cony-catching collusion are infused with a spirit of team sports and gaming. "A kind conceit of a foist performed in Paul's," for instance, features a group of foists vigorously taxing their wits to outsmart a particularly "wary" and "subtle churl, that either had been forewarned of Paul's, or else had aforetime smoked some of that faculty" (and thus "keeps his hand close in his pocket and his purse fast").

> The foists, spying this, strained their wits to the highest string how to compass this bung, yet could not all their politic conceits fetch the farmer

over, for jostle him, chat with him, offer to shake him by the hand, all would
not serve to get his hand out of his pocket. At last one of the crew, that for
his skill might have been doctorate in his mystery, amongst them all chose
out a good foist, one of a nimble hand and great agility, and said to the rest
thus: "Masters, it shall not be said such a base peasant shall slip away from
such a crew of gentlemen-foists as we are, and not have his purse drawn,
and there for this time, I'll play the stall myself, and if I hit him not home,
count me for a bungler forever." (Judges 168)

Like the kind of alehouse camaraderie Patricia Fumerton has investigated,
sociability here is discursively and culturally gendered. The scene combines
the drive for "scrappage" with mental-muscle-flexing and excitement at the
prospect of a good fight. Despite the intervention of the "doctorate in his
mystery," the plan is generated through give and take and consolidated by
mutual consent. While the backslapping, the esprit de corps, and the doctorate's gross bravado inflect the scene with a degree of farce and buffoonery, it
nevertheless evokes a confirmation of identification with other men and a
modified form of obligation—something along the lines of not letting down
one's chums—that modulates the aggressive pursuit of profit. Like many narratives of cony-catching convocation, the tale is set in St. Paul's Cathedral, a
site "consistently mentioned as one of criminal culture's principal haunts"
both in popular and state literature, and thus, a scene of increased surveillance
(Reynolds 111). Liberated from the fierce authority of upright men and the
confederacies' mandatory fines for "faintheartedness" or desertion, the cony-
catchers are staking not merely the success of their scam, but their freedom
and bodily welfare, on the voluntary cooperation of their fellows. Yet despite
the numerous opportunities for absconding (since only one rogue puts his
hands on a cony's purse) and considerable rewards offered by the "officers of
Newgate" for informing, the incidence of betrayal in cony-catching fellowships is extremely rare. Rather than a fanciful elaboration of "honor among
thieves," the fellowship narratives suggest the ways in which equitable and
inclusive relations can foster trust and cooperation.

Greene never resolves the problem that the fraternal spirit and social com-
munion the cony-catchers enjoy are ultimately grounded on acts of aggression against the respectable. But while cony-catching fellowship does not provide a panacea for class strife or the mercenary nature of commercial rivalry,
it evokes the potential for social cohesion, tolerance, and intimacy even in a
world "composed of lyes, fraud, and countefet dealings," and significantly
disrupts the "'natural' premise that acquisitiveness governs all forms of contemporary life," by which the "speaking rogues" elsewhere vindicate their

practices (Scott 35; Manley 351). The pamphlets do not go so far as to suggest that "goodfellowship" and the infusion of mental sport into commercial competition can transcend strict lines of social demarcation. Yet it is worth noting that the cony-catchers' valorization of wit extends to their occasional appreciation of the "subtlety" of a cony who challenges or outdoes them, and that they sometimes lend their wits to the task of humiliating conies who betray or offend members of their own caste. In Greene's "A pleasant tale of a country farmer," for instance, a crew of rogues "apply [their] wits" to punish a farmer for ridiculing a neighbor who has had his purse cut (Judges 213–14). "Some lamented [the neighbor's] loss, and others exclaimed against the cutpurses, but this farmer he laughed loudly at the matter, and said such fools as could not keep their purses no surer were well served" (Judges 214). By subjecting the farmer to an elaborate ruse, involving among other indignities, his arrest by (real) sergeants of the Counter (but taking pains to prevent his prosecution), the foists provide the neighbor with the pleasure of seeing the farmer receive his deserts—"Well," says his neighbor, "who shall smile at you now?"— although, of course, the rogues keep the cony's purse.

Elsewhere, cony-catching fellowship is predicated on the shared values and aspirations of the disenfranchised. The cony-catching episodes that take place between veteran cozeners and their stalls debunk the glorification of formalized subjection in apprentice literature and merchant pamphlets where "young scholars" were tutored in lessons of respect, "lowliness," and "sufferance" (Burnett 117). In Greene's pamphlets, master cony-catchers inculcate their stalls with the values of emancipation and rebellion, encouraging them to follow their own intuition and to disrespect all structures of authority, including their own "indentureship," that stand between them and their due. In Greene's "A Tale of a Nip," a "grand cutpurse" takes his "'prentice" to the burial of a wealthy gentlewoman in order "to teach him the order of striking and foisting,"

and coming thither very devout to hear the sermon, thrust with his apprentice amidst the throng, [and] lighted upon a rich parson in Essex. . . . The priest was faced afore with velvet, and had a good bung, which the nip espying, began to jostle the priest very hard at the entrance of the door, and his apprentice struck the strings, and took his bung clear. Well, it so fell out that when the bung came to sharing, the 'prentice and his master fell out, and the master controlled him and said, "Art not my 'prentice and hast not bound thyself to me for three years? Is not thy gettings my gains? Then why dost thou stand upon the snap?" "Why," says the prentice, "brag you so of my years! Shall I be made a slave because I am bound to you? No, no! I can quittance my indenture when I list." His master in a great rage asked how. "Marry!" says the prentice: "I will nip a bung, or draw a pocket, openly, and so be taken, arraigned and condemned; and then Bull shall cancel my indentures at Tyburn, and so I will not serve you a day after." At this, his master laughed and was glad for further advantage to yield the bucklers to his 'prentice, and to become friends. (Judges 153–54)

Despite his initial reaction, by the end of the tale, the elder nip is both amused and impressed by his student's feisty self-assertion and his paradoxical formula for liberation. His ultimate affection for the stall and desire "to become friends" is founded in part upon the stall's potential for yielding "further advantage," but also on an affinity for his resistance to social pressure and subordination. While the camaraderie that the tale figures is classed-biased and oppositional, the narrative subtly suggests how the recognition of mutual benefit can provide a basis for negotiation among parties of unequal power.

The provision for reform and reconciliation evinced in these narratives tends to disappear in Greene's later pamphlet, *The Defence of Cony-Catching* (1592), where cony-catching fellowship evolves into a solidarity against the abuses of the wealthy and socially stronger. The pamphlet is an extended confrontation between a speaking rogue and the absent author in which the former haughtily chastises Greene for his moral blindness in focusing so exclusively on the cony-catchers' relatively "harmless" pilferings, while overlooking the "palpable enormities" of "mightie cony-catchers" (Salgãdo 346). Although Greene is far more vociferous in criticizing the greed and hypocrisy of in-law figures here, the pamphlet's most cogent critique can be located in its extensive demystification of the underworld. In a dramatic departure from the earlier literature, Greene lets his ventriloquized Cuthbert Cony-Catcher allude to the socioeconomic sources of poverty and vagrancy, and lay bare the correspondence between roguery—or property crime—and subsistence scrupulously censured throughout the genre. By situating cony-catching as a struggle against scarcity and exposing the rogues' "desperate laws" as the necessary instruments of survival ("sith he that cannot dissemble cannot live"), the pamphlet underscores the disproportionate pressure that socioeconomic developments impose upon the lower strata (Salgãdo 343). Nevertheless the transgressive implications of the pamphlet are muted by Greene's ultimate recourse to forms of cultural nostalgia, and the Harman-like strategy of simply displacing the forces of social dissolution onto singular infiltrators of stable, agrarian communities.

The Defence's flirtation with, but ultimate retreat from, radicalism is symptomatic of the ways in which the cony-catching pamphlets, even when they foreground the insidious dialectics of poverty, or the fraught moralities of the marketplace, fall short of endorsing any departure from existing political or economic arrangements. Despite the rampant abuses and hypocrisies that the cony-catchers either enact or expose, the pamphlets refuse any simple opposition between the values and practices of commerce and moral decency. The subtle pleas for equality and tolerance buried in these texts testify to the degree to which the pamphleteers understand the economic only in social and moral terms, answerable to cultural traditions and the moral sensibilities of individual actors. The truly subversive power of the pamphlets resides instead in their unprecedented use of rogues to model not only the "grosse faults" of the marketplace or the "villainies" of the respectable, but the ways in which society could and should reconfigure itself.

NOTES

1. "The image became distorted because rather than being based on observation it was often constituted by projection. . . . This image-making went all in one direction, the vagrants having left no writings" (Woodbridge 160). The "voiceless class" is Annabel Patterson's useful term to indicate the absence of any substantial self-representation by the early modern poor (33).

2. Of course, the rogue is just one among a wide range of marginalized figures onto which conflicts about socioeconomic developments were projected. See Jean-Christophe Agnew's incisive discussion of the ways in which the "felt contradictions" provoked by the expanding market were projected onto a range of "figures already identified as foreign" (76).

3. "Idleness became both a venial and an economic sin, a rebuke to those who worked, a dereliction of various written and unwritten social duties, and an unacceptable choice of sloth" (Carroll 4). Gradually, it came to be "inflected in terms of economic transgression so that the sign was more important than the spiritual state it pointed to" (Carroll 6).

4. Hanson aligns the literary labor of the pamphleteers with the "busyness" of rogues to argue that "claims about labor and claims about truth in these pamphlets signify disruptively in relation to one another" (96).

5. See Brian Reynolds's *Becoming Criminal* for indications in the pamphlets that the "mental abilities" of the rogues surpass those of the "average person" (122).

6. I am heavily indebted for this discussion to Theodore Leinwand's examination of the affect of "laboriousness" in historical examples and early modern market-related texts. I draw particularly from Leinwand's treatment of *The Alchemist*, in which he argues that the "strain" exerted by Jonson's cozening "venture tripartite" discredits "passive investment" (*Theatre* 106). "Those who are convinced that they can get ahead not by exertion but by purchase are ranked first among the plays' dupes" (*Theatre* 132).

7. Lawrence Manley notes that Greene's pamphlets progressively feature gulls "who

stand on and exploit their status" (350). Examining Greene's version of "the Barnard's law," Craig Dionne points out that "readers are consistently reminded of the culpability of the cony himself . . . who seems perfectly willing to deceive and 'cog' others" ("Suspecting Readers").

8. "Just as magic provided a convenient metaphor for the abstract powers of a nascent commercial capitalism, so it promised a method for the demystification of commerce" (Agnew 72). Interestingly, in William Fennor's *The Counter's Commonwealth* (1617), occult practices become the exclusive province of "cruel creditors" as they "spell charms" over potential debtors (Judges 443).

9. "Although society was divided by hierarchical gradations of status, wealth and patriarchy, it was still bound together by contractually negotiated credit relationships made all over the social scale and this introduced some limited degree of equality to social exchanges" (Muldrew 97) More recently, Nina Levine has argued that credit "provide[ed] a structure for negotiating equality in political as well as economic exchanges" (406). My discussion of cony-catching sociability is informed by Levine's superb study of the ways in which credit fosters community in Shakespeare's *Henry IV* plays.

10. The motif of the "fall" into roguery frequently invoked in earlier pamphlets implicitly figures a disablement from participation in honest labor or trade, reasonably associated with default, disappropriation, and the ruination of one's "good name" or credit standing. In *A Manifest Detection*, for instance, the "great league" of rogues is comprised of "all kind of people that from a good order of civility are fallen" (Judges 35).

WORKS CITED

Agnew, Jean-Christophe. *Worlds Apart: The Market and the Theater in Anglo-American Thought, 1550–1750.* Cambridge: Cambridge UP, 1986.

Appleby, Joyce. *Economic Thought and Ideology in Seventeenth-Century England.* Princeton: Princeton UP, 1978.

Brunning, Alizon. "'In His Gold I Shine'; Jacobean Comedy and the Art of the Mediating Trickster." *Early Modern Language Studies* 8.2 (2002): 1–25.

Burnett, Mark Thornton. "Apprentice Literature and the 'Crisis' of the 1590s." *Yearbook of English Studies* 21 (1991): 27–38.

Carroll, William. *Fat King, Lean Beggar: Representations of Poverty in the Age of Shakespeare.* Ithaca: Cornell UP, 1996.

Dekker, Thomas. *The Bellman of London.* 1604. *The Elizabethan Underworld.* Ed. A. V Judges. New York: E. P. Dutton, 1930.

———. *Lantern and Candlelight.* 1608. *The Non-dramatic Works of Thomas Dekker.* Ed. Alexander B. Grosart. London: Hassell, Watson, and Viney, 1885.

Dionne, Craig. "Suspecting Readers and Gullible Consumers." Paper presented at the Annual Meeting of the Modern Language Association, 2001.

———. "Playing the 'Cony': Anonymity in Underworld Literature." *Genre* 30.1 (1997): 29–50.

Fumerton, Patricia. "Not Home: Alehouses, Ballads, and the Vagrant Husband in Early Modern England." *Journal of Medieval and Early Modern Studies* 32.2 (2002): 493–518.

Grassby, Richard. *The Business Community of Seventeenth Century England*. Cambridge: Cambridge UP, 1995.

Greene, Robert. *A Notable Discovery of Coȝenage*. 1591. Judges 119–48.

———. *The Second Part of Cony-catching*. 1591. Judges 149–78.

———. *The Third Part of Cony-catching*. 1592. Judges 179–205.

———. *A Disputation between a He-cony-catcher and a She-cony catcher*. 1592. Judges 206–47.

———. *The Black Book's Messenger*. 1592. Judges 248–64.

———. *The Defence of Cony-Catching*. 1592. Salgãdo 339–78.

Hanson, Elizabeth. *Discovering the Subject in Renaissance England*. Cambridge: Cambridge UP, 1998.

Judges, A. V., ed. The *Eliȝabethan Underworld*. New York: E. P. Dutton, 1930.

Kinney, Arthur F. *Rogues, Vagabonds, and Sturdy Beggars*. Barre: Imprint Society, 1973.

Knapp, Jeffrey. *Shakespeare's Tribe: Church, Nation, and Theatre in Renaissance England*. Chicago: U of Chicago P, 2002.

Leinwand, Theodore B. *The City Staged*. Madison: U of Wisconsin P, 1986.

———. *Theatre, Finance, and Society in Early Modern England*, Cambridge: Cambridge UP, 1999.

Levine, Nina. "Extending Credit in the *Henry IV* Plays." *Shakespeare Quarterly* 51.4 (2000): 403–31.

Manley, Lawrence. *Literature and Culture in Early Modern London*. Cambridge: Cambridge UP, 1995.

McRae, Andrew. *God Speed the Plough: The Representation of Agrarian England, 1500–1660*. Cambridge: Cambridge UP. 1996.

Muldrew, Craig. *The Economy of Obligation*. New York: St. Martin's, 1998.

Patterson, Annabel. *Shakespeare and the Popular Voice*. Cambridge: Basil Blackwell, 1989.

Reynolds, Bryan. *Becoming Criminal: Transversal Performance and Cultural Dissidence in Early Modern England*. Baltimore: Johns Hopkins UP, 2002.

Salgãdo, Gãmini, ed. *Cony-Catchers and Bawdy Baskets: An Anthology of Eliȝabethan Low Life*. London: J. M. Dent, 1977.

Scott, William. *An Essay of Drapery*. Ed. Sylvia L. Thrupp. Cambridge: Harvard U Printing Office, 1953.

Slack, Paul. *Poverty and Policy in Tudor and Stuart England*. New York: Longman, 1988.

Solomon, Julie Robin. *Francis Bacon and the Politics of Inquiry*. Baltimore: Johns Hopkins UP, 1998.

Stevenson, Laura. *Praise and Paradox*. Cambridge: Cambridge UP, 1984.

Sullivan, Ceri. *The Rhetoric of Credit: Merchants in Early Modern Writing*. Teaneck: Fairleigh Dickinson UP, 2002.

Woodbridge, Linda. *Vagrancy, Homelessness, and England Renaissance Literature*. Urbana: U of Illinois P, 2001.

PATRICIA FUMERTON

Making Vagrancy (In)visible

The Economics of Disguise in Early Modern Rogue Pamphlets

Assessing the stories of Nicholas Blount alias Nicholas Jennings, introduced in Thomas Harman's *A Caveat or Warening for Common Cursetors Vulgarely Called Vagabones* (1566; 1568, two editions; and 1573), William C. Carroll remarks, "In the various accounts, Genings plays many roles; foremost is the Counterfeit Crank [one who feigns epilepsy] . . . but he is also an Upright Man [high in Harman's hierarchy of vagabonds], a Mariner or Whipjack, a hat-maker, a serving man, a rogue, an artificer, a parody of himself [in picture], and finally 'a moniment' in Bridewell" (81–82). This vagrant with multiple roles captured the imaginations of Harman's audience (leading to textual and visual embellishments of his story in subsequent editions) as well as of mod-ern cultural critics of Harman's work, including Stephen Greenblatt, Eliza-beth Hanson, and (most fully) Carroll. All of these critics, together with scholars of rogue pamphlets in general, focus on the roles vagrants such as Jennings are said to play and inevitably turn to a discussion of some theatrical work, the favorite being *King Lear* (in Greenblatt; Carroll; and Linda Wood-bridge's recent book).

This is not a naive move. Although the unquestioning conflation of the his-tory of vagrants with the literature of roguery characterized early writers about rogue pamphlets, later critics have attempted to separate out fact from fiction. Nevertheless, they characteristically adopt a sequential pattern of analysis that itself suggests convergence: that is, they typically trace a narra-tive line that leads, as if necessarily, from historical vagrants to rogue pam-phlets to drama or theatricality.[1] Such would seem the logical direction to take, given the rogue pamphleteers' own obsession with the role-playing of rogues, which was bolstered by the government's 1572 inclusion of itinerant players into its list of the legally vagrant. Nevertheless, I propose that we resist the push to theatricality, for so many of the "roles" Harman says Jennings and other vagrants played—mariner, hatmaker, servingman, artificer—could be "played" by a vagrant laborer in earnest. They typify a new economic network, a "vagrant" economy, constituted out of multiple, serial, and itinerant employment that may well have unmoored class, gender, and even historical identities. But if the displaced workers of such a vagrant economy necessarily *speculated* in different roles, they were not, nor could they afford to be, role-*playing*. A brief survey of the new mobile labor market of late-sixteenth- and early-seventeenth-century England will allow us more fully to understand its *mis*-representation as manifold disguising in the rogue pamphlet of Thomas Harman, whose influence reached beyond the "fictions" of literature to the "facts" of history.[2]

First, two "caveats" of my own. First, when I use the word *new*, I do not mean to imply *original*. Change is rarely sudden, and what might appear new at any one moment in time might in fact be an old bird in new dressing. A sense of newness, for instance, may be a response not so much to actually new phenomena as to an intensifying of already existing institutions and events. Certainly, as David Harris Sacks has noted, mobility, by-employments, and vagrants were not entirely new in the sixteenth century, any more than were alehouses, which housed and fed the itinerant. It was the burgeoning of such phenomena, among others, at the end of the sixteenth century—fueled by rapid expansion of manufacturing centers, preeminently London, and by growing dependence on credit—that created the impression of an emergent, destabilizing "new" economy.[3] Second, although my focus is decidedly "low" in this essay, I do not mean to deny that a certain degree of instability and displacement characterized all classes of early modern society who were involved in the new money market, as Lawrence Stone has shown. For example, the upper sorts, specifically wealthy merchants, yeomen, and gentry, engaged extensively in the mobility of "improvement." But in speaking of a vagrant economy, I am far more focused on the radical mobility of actual vagrants and the itinerant laborers who were often arrested as vagrants. Included in the latter body of unsettled working poor were huge numbers of servants and apprentices who, willingly or not, frequently changed positions. We know, for instance, that 60 percent of apprentices in London around 1600 (and an even higher percentage of apprentices in other major cities, such as Norwich, Bristol, and Salisbury) never completed their terms. Many such apprentices were arrested for vagrancy, and many as well would have joined the nomadic labor pool on the fringe of vagrancy (im)proper.[4] Thomas Spick-ernell, for example, was listed by the town clerk of Maldon in 1595 as "som-tyme apprentice to a bookebynder; after, a vagrant pedler; then, a ballet singer and seller; and now, a minister and alehouse-keeper in Maldon." Ilana Ben-Amos cites a host of other such mendicant laborers among early modern youths. One such youth worked at various times as an errand boy, a domestic servant, a gunmaker's apprentice, a pitman, a coachman, a driver, an agricul-tural laborer, a beggar, and a gardener.[5]

It is but a sidestep from such diversely employed youths, dispersed spatially as well as economically over the English landscape, to the peddlers and chap-men of all ages discussed by Linda Woodbridge, who linked town and coun-try in a growing network of exchange. As Woodbridge points out in this vol-ume, the mobile economics such traders embodied uncomfortably touched upon respectable big business, newly sited in the Exchange: "Merchant Adventuring was peddling writ large." Indeed, so necessary were peddlers to the dissemination of consumer goods that the new vagrancy law of 1604 omit-ted them from the list of the legally vagrant (although they continued to be persecuted well into the late seventeenth century).[6] Peddlers and petty chap-men specialized in trading in the diverse cheap luxury goods of a burgeoning new domestic economy discussed at length by Joan Thirsk. The late sixteenth and early seventeenth centuries, Thirsk notes, saw the rise of new goods that capitalized on surplus labor. Lacework, stocking knitting, the making of pins and buttons, and distilling aqua vitae were all new domestic trades (see Thirsk 6). That they were conceived of not only as requiring few start-up costs but also as occupying a space outside the traditional labor force is suggested by the setting up of vagrants to work in such trades in institutions, called "bridewells," designed during this period for employing the poor.[7]

Even outside the workhouse, much of the lower spectrum of society was engaged in by-employments of these kinds in addition to their "established" trade. Holding down more than one job was becoming the norm. As Thirsk points out, "poorer men had two and three occupations at once. Licensed ale-house keepers in Staffordshire, for example, were also tailors or weavers, shearmen or wheelwrights, husbandmen, shoe makers, dyers, or joiners" (172). Such multitasking was the geographically placed equivalent to the other common practice of shifting from job to job (into which simultaneous multi-ple employment easily converted) that especially characterized the wage-earner and other laboring poor. As Jeremy Boulton observes in his study of Southwark, "One Henry Ducklyn was . . . described as labourer, servingman and chamberlain; Richard Beldam as a servingman, labourer, horsekeeper, husbandman and victualler" (72–73).[8] North Norfolk laborers, A. Hassel

Smith finds, developed such a "multi-faceted fringe economy" of job switching that they sometimes could and would not make themselves available for seasonal hire in local husbandry. "Hence," Smith concludes, "the comments by seventeenth century authors—writing from the viewpoint of would-be-employers—about the shiftlessness of the labouring poor and their disinclination to work. 'Work' meant something quite different for each of the parties concerned" (380–81).

Confusion over the diffusion of labor can be seen in the conceptual problem authorities faced when listing the "occupation" of those arrested for vagrancy. Typically, as with the occasionally and serially employed Wiltshire man arrested in 1605—identified as "sometimes a weaver, sometimes a surgeon, sometimes a minstrel, sometimes a dyer, and now a bullard"—the vagrant laborer would be accused of having "no trade to live by" (Beier, *Masterless Men* 88). Behind this conceptual block lay yet another: resistance to the notion that work and need could go hand in hand. The idea of a new category of poor, neither deserving impotent nor undeserving sturdy rogue, but deserving, sturdy indigent who sought but could not find enough work, did slowly seep into the official consciousness. The 1572 vagrancy law, for instance, although severe against offenders, also included for the first time a proviso for itinerant harvest workers and for servants who had been turned away or whose masters had died. And later statutes attempted to employ resident "able" poor by providing for parish apprenticeships and workhouses, as we have seen (although both projects ultimately failed). For all its well-meaning efforts, however, authorities continued to have difficulty distinguishing the unemployed, the underemployed, and the multitasked or in-transit laboring poor from the incorrigibly idle or "sturdy beggar." Such a crisis of categories could fuel fears and hostilities on the part of authorities.[9]

The common man, however, most likely experienced a conflicting mixture of fear, antagonism, and sympathy in thinking of the vagrant. Such conflicted feelings would have been inflected by the extent to which contemporaries actually saw themselves in such impoverished itinerants. A large percentage of householders did not pay poor rates but were not on poor relief (44 percent in Warwick in 1583, for instance; 43 percent in Boroughside, Southwark, in 1618; 50 percent in Aldenham, Hertfordshire, in the early seventeenth century) (see Boulton 115; Hindle 131). These unrelieved householders were able—but just able—to maintain their families in "normal" years. They generally came from the poorer trades (petty craftsmen, manual laborers, minor retailers, and the like). Whether we call these people "the poorest of the middling sorts," "the low," or just "the poor," we can recognize that they constituted the group just above those on parish relief and the vagrant, householders who were most prone to unemployment, multiple employment, desperate indigence, and mobility. Destabilizing poverty could unpredictably strike their families at any point in the "life cycle," as Hindle shows. In the parish of Aldenham, Hertfordshire, Hindle finds, "the correlation of family constitution and poor law records suggests that of the sedentary families, thirty-five percent were recorded as poor at some period during their marriage. Only fifty percent of families were wealthy enough to be assessed for contributions to the parish poor rate. More significantly, different families appear to have been relieved or assessed in different phases of the life-cycle rather than one group of families always rich and another relatively poor" (131).[10] Given the unexpected and intermittent nature of poverty's embrace, one would expect that especially for this lowest sector of housed society, uneasy identification with the "vagrant" migrant/laboring poor could have been very strong.

This is where Thomas Harman, and the other pamphleteers who followed suit, stepped in. They capitalized on and assuaged such ambivalence by transforming the *fact* of a vagrant economy grounded on a shifting mass of itinerant labor into the *fiction* of role-playing rogues. Although the vagrant, laboring poor are everywhere evident in his tract, that is, Harman works hard to suppress their "fact." The itinerant laborer at the hands of Harman becomes thinly disguised as a deceitful rogue. Instead of changing jobs or holding multiple jobs, such vagrants are imaged as donning disguises. But the itinerant laborer, and the unstable or "vagrant" economics he serves, continually peaks out from behind Harman's role-playing masks.[11]

Harman repeatedly points to vagrant economics, for instance, in what he clearly sees as a disturbing insistence on the part of the various rogues he catalogs to *sell* the food they acquire through begging, stealing, or selling wares. If the Upright Man "be offered any meat or drink," Harman says, "he utterly refuseth scornfully, *and will naught but money*" (117; emphasis added). Others, such as palliards and their morts, will travel separately and beg food as well as alms but "what they get, as bread, cheese, malt, and wool, *they sell the same for ready money*" (125; emphasis). The Abraham man is of like mind: "*These beg money;* either when they come at Farmers' houses they will demand Bacon, either cheese or wool, *or anything that is worth money*" (125; emphasis added). Indeed, the Demander for Glimmer—one who feigns having been made destitute by fire—sounds very much like a peddler with her pack of mostly foodstuffs that she trades for money (although peddlers did not as a rule carry perishables). She travels, Harman informs us, "walking with a wallet on her shoulders wherein she put the devotion of such as had no money to give her: that is to say, Malt, wool, bacon, bread, and cheese. And always, as the same was full, so was it ready money to her when she emptied the same, wheresoever she travelled" (134). In Harman's view the fact that these vagrants beg for money or sell wares, especially food, for money proves them to be undeserving. The truly deserving poor would exist on a subsistence level and thus be forced to eat any food they acquired. They would not have the luxury to sell it. But the very fact of acquiring and selling food suggests that these vagrants are products of and participants in the new money market where money freely circulates along with goods and where value is transferable. Such a system of acquiring an income included in its ranks not only rogues but the laboring, vagrant poor who begged as well as worked and did accumulate some cash, if only in small amounts.

Indications that the laboring, vagrant poor lurk behind Harman's rogues is everywhere evident in his tract. We see them in the formerly employed life some rogues are said to have led before they became idle wanderers: one Abraham Man, for instance, was Lord Stourton's man until the lord was executed (128); and dells (virgin young women) "go abroad young," often because of "some sharp mistress that they serve"—so they "do run away out of service" (144). Most significantly, for all Harman's determination to show such ex-workers as now turned roguishly idle, we also see them as laborers in the here and now.

Priggers, for instance, "will also repair to gentlemen's houses and ask their charity, and will offer their service. And, if you ask them what they can do, they will say that they can keep two or three Geldings, and wait upon a Gentleman" (124). Interestingly, this claim is neither denied by Harman nor turned into an act of roguery. So too, Raffe Kyteley, although listed under "Rogues" in the appendix to Harman's tract, is described thus: "A lusty and strong man, he runneth about the country to seek work, with a big boy his son carrying his tools as a dauber and plasterer, but little work serveth him" (148). Does "little work serveth" Kyteley because he cannot work or because he will not work? Harman would appear to mean the latter, but the former meaning is most prominent given the rest of his description. Even drunken tinkers are grudgingly granted work by Harman: "Thus with picking and stealing, mingled with a little work for a color, they pass the time" (133).

Peddlers are most problematic: "These Swadders and peddlers be not all evil, but of an indifferent behavior. These stand in great awe of the upright men, for they have often both wares and money of them. But forasmuch as they seek gain unlawfully against the laws and statutes of this noble realm, they are well worthy to be registered among the number of vagabonds, and undoubtedly I have had some of them brought before me when I was a Commission of the Peace as malefactors for bribing and stealing. And now of late it is a great practice of the upright man, when he hath gotten a booty, to bestow the same upon a pack full of wares, and so goeth a time for his pleasure because he would live without suspicion" (133–34). In Harman's mind, the problem with peddlers is that they are legally vagrant and therefore they must be in cahoots with rogues. But at the same time Harman recognizes their "indifferent behavior"—indeed, that they "be not all evil"—so much so that their occupation could cast an aura of respectability on the Upright Man. Working for a time as a peddler, the Upright Man could "live without suspicion."

Women are also vagrant laborers. The walking mort defensively affirms to Harman, "how should I live? None will take me into service. But I labor in harvest-time honestly" (139). Most industriously, Bawdy-Baskets work in many of the new domestic trades. These latter women "go with baskets and Capcases on their arms, wherein they have laces, pins, needles, white inkle, and round silke girdles of colors. These will buy conyskins and steal linen clothes off of hedges. And for their trifles they will procure of maiden-servants, when their mistress or dame is out of the way, either some good piece of beef, bacon, or cheese that shall be worth twelvepence for twopence of their toys" (137). Harman goes on to note that these women also casually "trade" themselves, as was common among women vagrants: "as they walk by the way, they often gain some money with their instrument, by such as they suddenly meet withal." So the trade in wares becomes, by the end of his commentary, a "trade" of "their lives in lewd, loathsome lechery" (137). Moral condemnation translates into roguery all the multifarious ways these women are invested in the new domestic economy. But the women are clearly foremost transient workers, not rogues.

The case of the Upright Man is one of the most telling. For a nasty rogue, he is quite a worker. Not only does he often "goeth a time" as a peddler, as noted above, with "a pack full of wares . . . because he would live without suspicion" (133–34). He also takes on many other jobs, if only through a slip of the tongue or a printing error. Harman declares, "Of these ranging rabblement of rascals, some *be* serving-men, artificers, and laboring men, traded up in husbandry" (116; emphasis added). That is, they *are*, not were, practicers of these trades. Furthermore, Harman later again notes at length that some of these so-called rogues work honestly as wage-laborers: "And some of them useth this policy, that although they travel into all these shires abovesaid, yet will they have good credit, especially in one shire, where they work a month in a place or more, and will for that time behave themselves very honestly and painfully and may at any time for their good usage have work of them. And to these at a dead lift, or last refuge, they may safely repare unto and be welcome when, in other places, for a knack of knavery that they have played, they dare not tarry" (118). "Rogue" in some places, "honest wage-laborer" in others. Does not this shift approximate the situation of the itinerant laborer who between jobs is legally vagrant—a rogue—but respectable when locally employed?

We might now return to our Counterfeit Crank, Jennings. When we first meet Jennings in the second edition of Harman's work, he appears solely in the guise of one who has "the falling sickness" (128), which Harman, with the help of his printer and his apprentices, determinedly exposes as counterfeit. In the fourth edition, the same story ends and starts up again on a new note of respectability: we are told Jennings "had both house and wife in the same parish" where he begged and thus profited from the money that Harman previously seized from him, which was distributed to the poor (298). Harman proudly declares that his printer at length searched out Jennings's habitation, "dwelling in Master Hill's rents, having a pretty house, well stuffed, with a fair joint-table, and a fair cupboard garnished with pewter, having an old ancient woman to his wife" (299). The implication, of course, is that Jennings was in fact undeserving of poor relief; but then why would he have received it from the parish in which he lived? Indeed, pewter, as Woodbridge points out, was by no means a sign of affluence in the period, but was increasingly owned by the lower orders (see Woodbridge 78 n. 17).

That Jennings might be "like" a poor householder worthy of relief is underscored by the other "disguises" he adopts: he appears "in mariner's apparel" and as an unemployed hatmaker. The latter is very realistically portrayed: "I came from Leicester to seek work," Jennings tells the printer when confronted by him, "and I am a hat maker by my occupation, and all my money is spent; and if I could get money to pay for my lodging this night, I would seek work tomorrow amongst the hatters" (298). This story is more than plausible, given the huge number of vagrants (on the order of some ten thousand a year) flooding London at the time in search of work and relief (Beier and Finlay 9). And though Harman takes pains to describe Jennings as exceedingly well-dressed in "a fair black frieze coat, a new pair of white hose, a fine felt hat on his head, [and] a shirt of Flanders work esteemed to be worth sixteen shillings," it seems odd that Jennings would attire himself so lavishly if his goal on that occasion was, as Harman's sentence concludes, "to beg" (298). Harman is "embellishing" somewhere here.

My point is not to discount all of Harman's claims of roguery on the part of Jennings as pure invention. As Carroll notes, there is historical evidence that a person going by the name of Jennings's alias, "Blunt," was convicted of being in fact a Counterfeit Crank (and punished in like manner to that described by Harman). Carroll further finds that a "Nicholas Jennings" was also arrested and set free on bond in Harman's home county, Kent (82–83). But even after acknowledging these "facts," it would nevertheless seem that the lines between role-playing rogue and vagrant laborer continually blur in Harman's story. And the more Harman adds to the tale, the more confusing it all gets.

Consider the woodcut (fig. 1) that Harman placed in the chapter related to Jennings in the third and fourth editions of his book.

This illustration was accompanied by the following verse:

These two pictures lively set out
One body and soul, God send him more grace:
This monstrous dissembler, a Crank all about.
Uncomely coveting of each to embrace,
Money or wares, as he made his race.
And sometime a Mariner, and a serving man:
Or else an artificer, as he would feign then.
Such shifts he used, being well tried,
Abandoning labor till he was espied.
Condign punishment for his dissimulation
He surely received with much exclamation.[12]

"As the verse makes clear," Jean-Christophe Agnew remarks, "only the faintest of lines separated the multiple by-employments of the rural out-worker from the multiple impostures of the professional rogue" (66). But, as we have seen, it was more than the rural outworker who was employed in such job diversity. It was the lower orders generally, including householders.

Harman's spelling of what has been modernized as "feign" in line 7 of his poem about Jennings underscores this mingling of pretend and for real. He spells it "faine" in the 1568 edition and "fayne" in the 1573 edition, both of which renderings might mean "take to gladly" *(OED)*, not "feign." That is, one might be inclined to read the serial occupations of mariner, serving man, and artificer as jobs Jennings would be glad to have, not only as jobs he feigns. Agnew goes on to argue, "To the jaundiced Elizabethan eye, the casual laborer and the wandering rogue were virtually indistinguishable from the itinerant actor, so that few would have been entirely surprised when, in 1572, players themselves were placed under the force of the Vagabond Act" (66). But I wonder whether the reader/viewer might read not the professional actor but himself or herself in Jennings's variously assumed work roles.

The accompanying picture reinforces this possible reading of the verse. As Carroll observes, Jennings here appears "as two people, standing side by side

Thomas Harman, *A Caveat or Warening for Common Cursetors
Vulgarely Called Vagabones*, 1573. The image also appeared in the
1567/68 edition of Harman's work. (Reproduced by permission of
the the Huntington Library, San Marino, California.)

as mirrored images": "A upright man Nicolas Blunt," whom Carroll describes
as "extremely well-dressed" and "prosperous," and "The counterfeit Crank,
Nicolas Genings," who, Carroll notes, is "dressed in rags, the mud/blood visible on his face, almost precisely according to Harman's description of him in
the text." "The two figures merge," Carroll points out, "in the middle where
the walking stick of 'Blunt' seems to pass through the hand, but behind the
hat, of 'Genings'" (79–80). I'm not sure I see the figure on the left as
"extremely well-dressed," though he does look like someone from the middling ranks of society, such as the hatmaker Jennings claimed himself to be.
He appears quite literally an "upright," as in "respectable," man—someone
with whom the viewer might well identify. What then might such a viewer
make of the merging of the two figures at the center of the picture? I would

argue that such merging suggests not how Jennings can "play" two roles, and thus (in Agnew's reading) is equivalent to an actor; but rather, it illustrates how any respectable, hardworking citizen, and especially those of the lower and lower-middling ranks, can unexpectedly turn vagrant.

Such a social and economic "declination," which is the last word of the 1567/68 verse accompanying the picture (translated in 1573 into the cry of "exclamation" in its stead), is undoubtedly presented by Harman as deceitful role-playing because, as many critics have noted, Harman wants to picture the sturdy beggar as willfully idle, and hence morally depraved and punishable. This vision of rogues disguising themselves seized the imagination of Harman's pamphleteering followers and also of the authorities. Kathleen Pories, Jodi Mikalachki, and Linda Woodbridge have shown that rogue pamphlets influenced the language of legislation against vagrants, such as the use of *rogue* in the 1572 statute.[13] I would take such influence even further and question whether some of the historical documents frequently cited for "evidence" and "facts" of vagrancy are not, in fact, Harmanesque fiction in historical guise.

I have in mind the "facts" repeatedly cited by authorities of the period about respectable persons willfully "going over" to the "sweet" "liberty" of vagrancy, or of vagabonds pretending to be glassmen or servants of nobles, or of shoemakers or yeomen pretending to be gypsies, and gypsies pretending to be tinkers, peddlers, or jugglers, and so on.[14] These "facts" so resemble the role-playing fictions of rogue pamphlets that the two become at times indistinguishable. We might take as an example the oft-quoted letter of 1596 by Edward Hext, a Somerset justice, to Lord Burghley. Lamenting the inability to effect justice against the "Infynytt numbers of the wicked wandrynge Idle people of the land," who "multyplye daylye to the vtter impoverysshinge of the poore husbondman that beareth the greatest burthern of all services," Hext cites as one instance the problem that such "stout roages . . . wilbe present at every assise, Sessions, and assembly of Iustices and will so clothe them selves for that tyme as anye shold deame him to be an honest husbondman, So as nothinge ys spoken, donne, or intended to be donne but they knowe it" (quoted in Aydelotte 168–73). According to Hext, poor honest husbandmen are done in by vagrants in disguise as poor honest husbandmen. But as with such disguising in Harman's tract, and at the risk of sounding paranoiac—or rather of accusing the early modern authorities of cultural paranoia—might not the "guise" of honest husbandman be "real"? Given what we know of the workings of the period's vagrant economy, might not an honest husbandman become, or even at one and the same time be, a transient wage-earner, and thus *appear* vagrant? What might seem a guise might *in fact* be a change or shift in occupation. This conjecture is further supported in Hext's letter by his complaint that, unlike gypsies, stout vagrants are hard to detect because they do not travel "visibly in on[e] company" (172). Rogues have a certain invisibility to them (as did the laboring poor). Ironically, such invisibility is made visible when it is reimaged as a disguise. One cannot but wonder how much Hext was influenced by Harman's similar rendering of the vagrant, laboring poor. Certainly his text ends with the familiar claim of Robert Greene, Thomas Dekker, and other rogue pamphleteers that he is writing to expose these ills although his life is thus endangered: "I will not leave yt unadvertysed thowghe I shold hazard my lyef by yt" (173). By 1596, when Hext writes, such a heroic stance was a worn convention in rogue pamphlets.

What is unnerving in Hext's letter, for contemporaries as well as cultural historians, is the inability to distinguish between the invisible rogue and the invisible itinerant poor. Followers of Harman imitate his double-edged reaction to this problem in extreme forms: in their works vagrants are always adopting some kind of disguise or role and at the same time they imitate the hierarchical structures of society, especially of middle-class guilds. They have apprentices, laws, even their own hall where the craft members meet. In the process the "real" vagrant, laboring poor are reduced in these works to but a trace.

But there is a medium where the vagrant and the culture of mobility gain a truer representation, and it is not, for the most part, in the drama of the period. For the theater, by virtue of its theatricality, reinforces the illusion promoted by rogue pamphlets that vagrants were rogues in disguise. If we are truly to see the mobile lower orders, we must instead look to more lowly street literature. I am here thinking of broadsides, such as *The Town Crier* (1590s) and especially ballads, such as *Turner's Dish of Lentten Stuffe, or a Galymaufery* (1612), which embraced the diverse labors of itinerant workers. Indeed, broadside ballads offer not only "realistic" representations of the vagrant, laboring poor but also undisguised voicings of their multiple role speculations (not role-playing) necessitated by shifting from job to job and place to place. Ballads allowed for a "no cost" multifarious role speculation in the singing of the various parts, which was vicariously experienced by their audience in the very process of listening and, especially, singing along. Through these popular songs that were also ownable texts—the only works of the period that could really be afforded, and thus made their own, by the lower orders so prone to actual vagrancy—the voice of the vagrant subject becomes truly spacious. And if not always seen, it could be heard, *undisguised*. To such lowly street literature, not to rogue pamphlets or drama, we must turn if we are fully to inhabit the aesthetic space of the itinerant working poor.

NOTES

Reprinted from *English Literary Renaissance* 33.2 (2003): 211–27 with permission of the editors.

1. Early studies that tend to read rogue pamphlets as if they were historical documents, despite occasional qualifications, include Aydelotte, Judges, and McPeek. Later believers include McMullen and Salgãdo. Though highly sophisticated in approach, I would also place Reynolds in this camp. More recent studies that are more careful to separate out the "history" from the "fiction" of vagrants, but which follow a narrative line from vagrancy to drama/theatricality (usually through rogue pamphlets) include Woodbridge; Dubrow; Hanson; Sullivan; Carroll; Knapp; Jankowski; McDonald; Gaby; Greenblatt; and, an early instance of this methodology, Berlin.

2. For a fuller discussion of the background "vagrant" economy discussed here, see my "London's Vagrant Economy" and my forthcoming *Vagrant Subjects*.

3. See Sacks. I would like to thank Professor Sacks for generously providing me with a copy of his response.

4. See Beier, "Social Problems" 215. Griffiths provides statistics on the high dropout rates: *Youth and Authority* 330, n 172. See also his "Masterless Young People" 146–86. In Beier's accounting, three-quarters of the arrested vagrants of London whose occupations were listed between 1597 and 1608 were from the ranks of servants and apprentices (214). Certainly some apprentices profited from early termination, as Steve Rappaport argues, breaking their indentures in order to return to their homes with their newly acquired skills ("Reconsidering Apprenticeship" 239–61; see also his *Worlds within Worlds* 311–15). But given the large numbers of apprentices among those arrested for vagrancy, a less rosy picture of broken terms colors the urban scene. Archer (15) also takes objection to Rappaport's overly optimistic vision of the apprenticeship system.

5. Maldon Borough records, D/B 3/3/397/18, cited by Clark 6–7; Ben-Amos 82; see also 82–83. Ben-Amos has a habit of ending the youth's story with placement as an apprentice, but, given the large drop-out rate of apprentices, in many cases such placement would be but a stage in a continuous process of displacement.

6. Spufford provides the best account of such itinerant sellers.

7. Among the twenty-six "Artes, Occupations, Labors, and Works, to be set up in Bridewell" in London, for instance, were included such new domestic labors as the making of "nayles," "gloues," "Combes," "Inkle and Tape," "silke Lace," "Pinnes," "Pointes," "bayes," and "feltes," as well as the "knitting of hose," "spinning of Linnen yarne," and "Drawing of wier"; *Orders Appointed to be executed in the Cittie of London, for setting roges and idle persons to worke, and for releefe of the poore* (London, n.d.). The *Orders* were probably printed in 1582 or 1586. See also Thirsk 65–66.

8. See also Thirsk 3, 7–8, 110–11, 148, and esp., 155–57. See also Wrightson and Levine 22–23. As Thirsk adds in her study, a "flexible, even casual, attitude to the choice of an occupation" characterized even more well-to-do entrepreneurs in the new domestic trades, who might shift from job to job (171, 172). Archer similarly observes an increasing tendency toward the end of the sixteenth century for freemen of particular companies in London to take on other trades. For example: "During the first decade of the seventeenth century the Blacksmiths admitted at least three tailors, two hatmakers, two goldsmiths, a

coachmaker, a pointmaker, an embroiderer, a carman, and a wheelwright, and it is unlikely that all cases were recorded" (115). Such job-shifting by the "middling sorts" suggests that vagrant economics was truly spacious, extending beyond the itinerant and multitasked laboring poor.

9. *The Statutes of the Realm*, IV.i.592. Slack notes that the concept of the laboring poor can be found as early as a survey of the poor in London in 1552 and monastic visitation injunctions in 1535–36. But frequent references to this shadowy category of poor only become prevalent in the late sixteenth century; for instance, the matter of who was to be counted as a vagrant was "a topic much disputed in the Commons in 1571 and 1572" (*English Poor Law* 12, 20). Norwich in 1570 and Ipswich in 1597 were among the first towns to recognize that the resident needy could include the employed and underemployed, not just the disabled, old, and orphaned. Nevertheless, although both towns increased their rates to supplement more workers, the resistance to this notion was strong, and many indigent but "able" workers continued to be deprived of regular relief. Furthermore, transient workers from outside the community were ruthlessly turned away. See Pound, *Norwich Census*, and "Elizabethan Census" 135–61, where he more clearly delimits the "success story" of Norwich; and Webb. Slack sums up the general situation nationwide: "in the 17th century, as it became increasingly difficult to find masters to take on poor apprentices, as the number of the unemployed outgrew the facilities of the small workhouse, and as many in employment also came to require public alms to support their families, the burden on the poor-rate became unmanageable" (*Poverty* 4). Many houses of correction soon lapsed from workhouses into "penal colonies," Beier adds (*Masterless Men* 146–70).

Official attacks (proclamations, statutes, roundups) against "vagrancy" thus proliferated. And although the vagrancy laws might appear to have softened as the sixteenth century progressed—as punishments shifted from ear-borings and death to (more typically) whippings—such "leniency" was in fact aimed at widening the punishing reach of the law (Archer 244–45).

10. See also Wales 351–404. I would like to thank Deborah Harkness for helping me think through the knotty problems of categorizing the poor and mobile.

11. Craig Dionne, in his "Fashioning Outlaws" in this volume, offers a different and more solidly middle-class perspective on how rogue literature mirrored the boundary-breaking features of early modern economics. Specifically, he sees rogue pamphlets as playing out an ambivalent fantasy of unlicensed urban economics for a newly emerging corporate hegemony: "These pamphlets promoted an image of otherness that was on the surface inimical to the legal and economic practices of a new group of merchants and shareholders whose cultural affinities had yet to develop into a coherent form of class solidarity. At the same time, however, this image of outcast criminals who shared intense fraternal bonds with freedom from legal strictures provided a powerful fantasy for a group of businessmen and merchants whose own economic practices of investment and foreign trade maintained an ambivalent position in relation to the established medieval traditions of domestic production." While I recognize the merits of Dionne's approach and findings, I am less interested in the urban corporations who profited from the new economics than in the more mobile lowly workers who formed its unstable ground. Linda Woodbridge, it should be observed, in her essay in this volume, "The Peddler and the Pawn," sees a

closer connection between respectable merchants and the lowly peddler; both, she argues were engaged in an economics dependent upon an unsettling mobility, hence the scape-goating of peddlers in the service of respectable merchants. Finally, Karen Helfand Bix sees a marked difference between earlier pamphleteers, such as Harman, and the later "cony-catching" pamphleteers, such as Greene and Dekker. In the later, she finds embrace along with criticism of "the new, more flexible, unregulated economy" and of "occupations divorced from traditional vocational regimes and material production."

12. I have here taken and modernized the poem from Harman's 1573 edition to the illustration in D2r (Kinney's modernized edition, which I cite throughout my essay, does not reproduce either the woodcut or verse). My rendering mostly follows that of Judges's edition of Harman's pamphlet facing 90, where readers can find a modernization close to the one I make. Both picture and poem, it should also be noted, were cribbed by the author of *The Groundworke of Conny-catching* (1592). In the 1567/68 edition of Harman's pamphlet, the illustration and verse are essentially the same as those in his 1573 edition. The one significant difference in the verse—the last word—is noted elsewhere in this chapter.

13. Woodbridge 4; and Pories 38, specifically note the adoption of the term *rogue* in official legislation *after* Harman's influential pamphlet. Mikalachki looks at the legal case of a female vagrant in the 1620s, in which the participants seem influenced by, or at least in dialogue with, Harman's text.

14. Quote from Edward Hext, in a letter of 1596 (discussed in more detail below), cited in Aydelotte 171. Among those given to vagrant wandering, complains Hext, is the son of a gentleman, with inheritance (171). Reported as pretending to be gypsies were gentlemen (Judges xxiv), a shoemaker (Salgádo 154), and yeomen (McPeek 252ff.). Officially responding to the perceived problem is An Act for Punishment of Rogues, Vagabonds and Sturdy Beggars, which expands the definition of rogues to include "all such persons not being Felons wandering and pretending to be Egyptians, or wandering in the Habit, Form or Attire of counterfeit Egyptians" (*Statutes of the Realm*, 39 Elizabeth c. 4). The latter wording leaves open the possibility that such rogues are pretending to be pretend gypsies! For more on this phenomenon, see Reynolds 23–63. Vagrants pretending to be legally sanctioned glassmen became such a problem that a statute under James I responded by making glassmen legally vagrant (*Statutes of the Realm*, 1 James c. 7). For vagrants pretending to be servants of nobles, see McPeek 10, and for gypsies pretending to be tinkers, etc., see Samuel Rid, *The Art of Juggling or Legerdemain* (1612), in Kinney 266.

WORKS CITED

Agnew, Jean-Christophe. *Worlds Apart: The Market and the Theater in Anglo-American Thought, 1550–1750*. Cambridge: Cambridge UP, 1986.

Archer, Ian W. *The Pursuit of Stability: Social Relations in Elizabethan London*. Cambridge: Cambridge UP, 1991.

Aydelotte, Frank. *Elizabethan Rogues and Vagabonds*. Oxford: Clarendon, 1913.

Beier, A. L. "Social Problems in Elizabethan London." *Journal of Interdisciplinary History* 9.2 (1978): 203–21.

————. *Masterless Men: The Vagrancy Problem in England, 1560–1640*. London: Methuen, 1986.

Beier, A. L., and Roger Finlay, eds. *The Making of the Metropolis, London, 1500–1700*. London: Longman, 1986.

Ben-Amos, Ilana Krausman. *Adolescence and Youth in Early Modern England*. New Haven: Yale UP, 1994.

Berlin, Normand. *The Base String: The Underworld in Elizabethan Drama*. Rutherford, N.J.: Fairleigh Dickinson UP, 1968.

Boulton, Jeremy. *Neighbourhood and Society: A London Suburb in the Seventeenth Century*. Cambridge: Cambridge UP, 1987.

Carroll, William C. *Fat King, Lean Beggar: Representations of Poverty in the Age of Shakespeare*. Ithaca: Cornell UP, 1996.

Clark, Andrew, ed. *The Shirburne Ballads, 1585–1616*. Oxford, 1907.

Dubrow, Heather. *Shakespeare and Domestic Loss*. Cambridge: Cambridge UP, 1999.

Fumerton, Patricia. "London's Vagrant Economy: Making Space for 'Low' Subjectivity." *Material London ca. 1600*. Ed. Lena Cowen Orlin. Philadelphia: U of Pennsylvania P, 2000. 206–25.

————. *Vagrant Subjects: The Culture of Mobility in Early Modern England*. Chicago: U of Chicago P, forthcoming.

Gaby, Rosemary. "Of Vagabonds and Commonwealths: *Beggar's Bush, A Jovial Crew*, and *The Sisters*." *Studies in English Literature* 34 (1994): 401–24.

Greenblatt, Stephen. "Invisible Bullets." *Shakespearean Negotiations: The Circulation of Social Energy in Renaissance England*. Berkeley and Los Angeles: U of California P, 1988. 49–65.

Griffiths, Paul. "Masterless Young People in Norwich, 1560–1645." *The Experience of Authority in Early Modern England*. Ed. Paul Griffiths, Adam Fox, and Steve Hindle. New York: St. Martin's, 1996. 146–86.

————. *Youth and Authority: Formative Experiences in England, 1560–1640*. Oxford: Clarendon P, 1996.

Hanson, Elizabeth. *Discovering the Subject in Renaissance England*. Cambridge: Cambridge UP, 1998.

Harman, Thomas. *A Caveat or Warening for Common Cursetors Vulgarely Called Vagabones*. In *Rogues, Vagabonds and Sturdy Beggars: A New Gallery of Tudor and Early Stuart Rogue Literature*. Ed. Arthur F. Kinney. Amherst: U of Massachusetts P, 1990.

Hindle, Steve. "Exclusion Crises: Poverty, Migration, and Parochial Responsibility in English Rural Communities, c. 1560–1660." *Rural History* 2 (October 1996): 125–49.

Jankowski, Theodora A. "Historicizing and Legitimating Capitalism: Thomas Heywood's *Edward IV* and *If You Know Not Me, You Know Nobody*." *Medieval and Renaissance Drama in England*. Ed. Leeds Barroll. New York: AMS P, 1995. 7:305–37.

Judges, A. V. *The Elizabethan Underworld: A Collection of Tudor and Early Stuart Tracts and Ballads Telling of the Lives and Misdoings of Vagabonds, Thieves, Rogues and Cozeners, and Giving Some Account of the Operation of the Criminal Law*. New York: E. P. Dutton, 1930.

Kinney, Arthur, ed. *Rogues, Vagabonds & Sturdy Beggars: A New Gallery of Tudor and Early Stuart Rogue Literature*. Amherst: U of Massachusetts P, 1990.

Knapp, Jeffrey. "Rogue Nationalism." *Centuries' Ends, Narrative Means.* Ed. Robert Newman, Stanford: Stanford UP, 1996. 138–50.

McDonald, Marcia A. "The Elizabethan Poor Laws and the Stage in the Late 1590s." *Medieval and Renaissance Drama in England.* Ed. Leeds Barroll. New York: AMS P, 1995. 7:121–44.

McPeek, James A. S. *The Black Book of Knaves and Unthrifts in Shakespeare and Other Renaissance Authors.* Storrs: U of Connecticut P, 1969.

McMullen, John L. *The Canting Crew: London's Criminal Underworld, 1550–1700.* New Brunswick, N.J.: Rutgers UP, 1984.

Mikalachki, Jodi. "Women's Networks and the Female Vagrant: A Hard Case." *Maids and Mistresses, Cousins and Queens: Women's Alliances in Early Modern England.* Ed. Susan Frye and Karen Robertson. New York: Oxford UP, 1999. 52–69.

Pories, Kathleen. "The Intersection of Poor Laws and Literature in the Sixteenth Century: Fictional and Factual Categories." *Framing Elizabethan Fictions: Contemporary Approaches to Early Modern Narrative Prose.* Ed. Constance C. Relihan. Kent, Ohio: Kent State UP, 1996. 17–40.

Pound, John F. "An Elizabethan Census of the Poor: The Treatment of Vagrancy in Norwich, 1570–1580." *U of Birmingham Historical Journal* 8 (1962): 135–61.

———, ed. *Norwich Census of the Poor, 1570.* Norfolk Record Society, vol. 40. 1971.

Rappaport, Steve. "Reconsidering Apprenticeship in Sixteenth-Century London." *Renaissance Society and Culture: Essays in Honor of Eugene F. Rice, Jr.* Ed. John Monfassani and Ronald S. Musto. New York: Italica, 1991. 239–61.

———. *Worlds within Worlds: Structures of Life in Sixteenth-Century London.* Cambridge: Cambridge UP, 1989.

Reynolds, Bryan. *Becoming Criminal: Transversal Performance and Cultural Dissidence in Early Modern England.* Baltimore: Johns Hopkins UP, 2002.

Sacks, David Harris. "The Nature of Reality: Historical Facts and Fictions." Response to a panel for the North American Conference on British Studies, "History, the New Historicism, and the Renaissance Literature of Roguery: New Perspectives." October 13, 2000.

Salgãdo, Gãmini. *The Elizabethan Underworld.* New York: St. Martin's P, 1992.

Slack, Paul. *The English Poor Law, 1531–1782.* London: Macmillan, 1990.

———, ed. *Poverty in Early-Stuart Salisbury.* Devizes: Wiltshire Record Society, 1975.

Smith, A. Hassel. "Labourers in Late Sixteenth-Century England: A Case Study from North Norfolk [Part II]." *Continuity and Change* 4 (1989): 380–81.

Spufford, Margaret. *The Great Reclothing of Rural England.* London: Hambledon P, 1984.

Stone, Lawrence. "Social Mobility in England, 1500–1700." *Past and Present* 33 (1966): 16–55.

Sullivan, Garrett A., Jr. "Knowing One's Place: The Highway, the Estate, and *A Jovial Crew.*" *The Drama of Landscape: Land, Property, and Social Relations on the Early Modern Stage.* Stanford: Stanford UP, 1998. 159–93.

Thirsk, Joan. *Economic Policy and Projects: The Development of a Consumer Society in Early Modern England.* Oxford: Clarendon P, 1978.

Wales, Tim. "Poverty, Poor Relief, and the Life-Cycle: Some Evidence from Seventeenth-Century Norfolk." *Land, Kinship and Life-Cycle*. Ed. R. H. Smith. Cambridge: Cambridge UP, 1984. 351–404.

Webb, John, ed. *Poor Relief in Elizabethan Ipswich*. Suffolk Records Society, vol. 9. 1966.

Woodbridge, Linda. *Vagrancy, Homelessness, and English Renaissance Literature*. Urbana: U of Illinois P, 2001.

Wrightson, Keith, and David Levine. *Poverty and Piety in an English Village: Terling, 1525–1700*. New York: Academic P, 1979.

PART 3

Rogues and the Early Modern City

Sin City and the "Urban Condom"

*Rogues, Writing, and the
Early Modern Urban Environment*

The Prophylactic and the Proximate

Richard Sennet's brilliant interrogation of Western urban experiences, *Flesh and Stone*, describes the process by which the "unclean" Jewish social body was divided from the rest of Venetian Renaissance society in a "prophylactic space," founded on spiritual, moral, and material edifices:

> In Venice, the physical character of the city made it possible finally to realize the rule prescribed by the Lateran Council—Venice a city built on water, water the city's roads which separated clusters of buildings into a vast archipelago of islands. In the making of the Jewish Ghetto, the city fathers put the water to use to create segregation: the Ghetto was a group of islands around which the canals became like a moat. (215, 228, 216)

The "spatial solution" to deal with "impure" Jewish bodies employed "an ancient Venetian urban form, the *sottoportegho*" (227, 232). Locked doors, water-gates, and surveillance prevented inappropriate proximities. Jews did not endure this alone of course; Germans, Greeks, and Turks suffered similar regulation. Such groups were granted contact with the rest of Venice only as economic necessity dictated. In some senses, ghettoization, despite the heinous privations it enforced, was beneficial to the Jews: during Lent, 1534, Christian mobs could not attack when the windows were closed and the bridges drawn up. Equally and crucially, though densely overcrowded and uncomfortable, the space was not burdened with the transformative responsibilities of the Roman ghetto. Rome needed to convert its landlocked, close-living inhabitants. In Venice, a city of islands, *insulae*, it was much more practical to enact isolating measures. Yet such insulation was completely impossible in what would soon become the greatest city of the age: London.

The Italian Renaissance spawned a Christian-humanist drive to organize the urban world, intent on shaping motley early modern cities in a manner "closer to the rational order of the cosmos" (Paster 26–27). But as Brian R. Goodey comments, Thomas More's paradigmatically humanist *Utopia*, of course, "cannot be mapped" (21). More also imposed the "traditional rivalries of the English gardeners" onto the urban context of his seemingly pleasant paradise, wryly recognizing the potential for contention in any state, however contrived (26). An insightful Londoner could truly do little else.[1]

For the capital, and images of it, evinced the coalescence of seemingly contrary elements and forces, presenting a topography of ambiguity, incontinence, and proximities, proximities that confounded crude binary oppositions, whether spatial, cultural, social, or literary. Thomas Dekker addressed London as such in his *Seven Deadly Sinnes* (1606):

> Thou art the goodlieft of thy neighbors, but the prowdeft; the welthieft, but the moft wanton. Thou haft all things in thee to make thee faireft, and all things in thee to make thee fouleft: for thou art attir'd like a Bride, drawing all that looke vpon thee to be in loue with thee, but there is much harlot in thine eyes. (10–11)

The metropolitan urban environment was perpetually prone to ambivalent apprehensions. From Augustine onward two models emerged of "the city as a visionary embodiment of ideal community" and "creativity," a heavenly place, as against "the city as a predatory trap, founded in fratricide and shadowed by conflict" (Paster 2–3). Thus Dekker exalted London as "Empresse of Cities, *Troynovant*," "*Europs* Jewell; *Englands* Jem: / Sister to great Jerusalem" (*Plague Pamphlets* 89–90). *Looke on Me London* (1613) consolidated this view, figuring the capital as "the paragon of Christendom" (162–63). It could likewise seem, in William Fennor's words, "a heaven on earth . . . Elysium" (450). But, simultaneously, in the "good city" are "many alectives to unthriftiness" (Johnson 162–63). It might offer even more rivers than the netherworld, "in which a soul may sail to damnation" (Dekker, *Lantern* 356).

Conceptually, London had "many guises" and "multiple identities" (Orlin,

Material London 3). But in its material realities the city was no less plural. It offered "the best and the worst of urban worlds": "a fabulously wealthy elite living cheek by jowl with a thoroughly destitute majority" (Rappaport 3). Though rural modes were still pervasive, the "juxtaposition of divergent personalities and modes of life" was remarkable (Wirth 15; see de Vries 255).

The experience of living in zones "contiguous," while "widely separated," was perhaps a "process of segregation" of sorts, creating "a mosaic of little worlds," islands that touched but did not "interpenetrate" (Park 126). True, there were some "topographical concentrations of marginal groups"; but this urban society was "too turbulent," too agitated by ideas, people and goods, to be divided without compromise "along social lines" (Jütte 165).

Figures cited by Roger Finlay suggest that the number of aliens in the capital (the Scots or French, for example, not simply those of English birth from outside London) rose as a percentage of total population through the late 1500s—4.7 percent in 1567, 4.9 percent in 1571—to reach a peak in 1573 of 5.3 percent (67–68, table 38).[2] Londoners lived in a "multitude of worlds within worlds" (Rappaport 215). The foreign, and displaced, were native: "the vast majority of those who made London were in some way dispossessed from their livelihood and/or their family, but always from the society and culture which provided them with their identity" (Twyning 1–2). In *The Counter's Commonwealth* (1617), Fennor's narrator is baffled by the argot of his local guide, understanding "the Hebrew, the Syriac or Chaldean language as well as his speech" (431). Of course, linguistic and demographic variety need not necessarily lead to harmonious social hybridity. As David Harris Sacks notes, London was viewed "as a proverbial site of dissension, where not even the tolling bells could agree on the hour" (21).

Attempted specializations of spatial function, and the selected or coerced habitation of certain places by certain groups, each with a "distinctive demography," differentiated urban areas (Finlay 16). But differentiation, as Jütte notes, though "fervently imagined," could not deny proximity, being only ever "ineffectually maintained" (165). The geography of small parishes and "a continued pattern of medieval infilling" ensured "social intermixing" (Pearl 7–8). And homes, whether of the poorest, or artisans, were "multifunctional," with "bipermeable" rooms (Gowing 134–36). Complete privacy was a near impossibility, and the boundaries of some households, separated by what residents complained was a "comen doore," were provisional (Griffiths 121–22).[3] In the liberties, relatively unregulated outskirts and suburbs, where dwellings were partitioned to exploit the need for accommodation resulting in a dense, often illicitly employed, socially and spatially marginal and transient population, all kinds of associations developed, within and beyond these areas.[4] Thus, as Joseph P. Ward asserts, as much as freemen and merchants felt "threatened" by economic developments in, and were mindful of the "licentiousness" of, these areas, they often considered such spaces "integral parts" of the metropolitan environment, not to mention "sources of opportunity" (144, 8).

M. J. Power notes that new gentrifying developments in Ratcliff and Limehouse attracted "great numbers of poor people and 'loose' immigrants" ("East London Housing" 246).[5] The varied modes and needs of consumption of such people, and those higher than them in the social order, animated the commingling of diverse types. Peter Burke suggests that "learned" and "popular" cultures "were not hermetically sealed off from one another" ("Popular Culture" 143). In the City itself, commercial enterprises were conducted in the "shadows of a great religious edifice": St. Paul's was a thoroughfare, marketplace, social meeting point, and criminal haunt (Miller 4; see Awdeley 68). Less lofty interstices were inns and taverns, "amphibious sites" by whose fires even gentlemen "might on occasion be found," among the young, the drunk, the itinerant, apprentices, prostitutes, or actors, despite "the risk of being set upon" (Griffiths 121; Clark, *English Alehouse* 123).

Crucially, all such circulations, interactions, and fabrications, in a city where "boundary-hopping was a day-by-day routine," disallowed the isolation of the licit from the illicit, the normative decent from the roguish deviant: this was a place of "perpetual transgressions" (Griffiths 128). Few were untouched by the implications of this. Patricia Fumerton has argued that contemporary vagrancy actuated an "open identity," consolidated by, among other things, economic insecurity (anyone might have to become socially or geographically mobile), and institutional confusions surrounding the taxonomizing of the poor. And in the capital, this identity was *particularly* open. Fumerton notes that "to be a Londoner in the sixteenth and seventeenth centuries was to experience a degree of alienation and anonymity cognate with the vagrant experience . . . many of the lower orders within London and beyond experienced its workings physically and topographically, that is, in the form of formless or spacious wandering" ("London's Vagrant" 215).

This hybrid sociogeography ensured that crime was only ever "quasi-segregated" from the proper pursuits of the populace; the activities of intermediaries, such as fences, promoted "relations between the underworld and the wider social order" (McMullan 77). Indeed, the calumnies constantly heaped on bawdy houses, dicing dens, and prostitutes ironically attest to their social centrality: "the pox" of venereal disease is "so surely now rooted in England" says Nan in Robert Greene's *A Disputation* (1592), that "it may better be called a *morbus Anglicus* than *Gallicus*!" (224).

The capital offered a sizable concentration of competitive and conspicuous consumers, with portable and accessible material wealth, just waiting to be preyed upon. As provincial incomes were spent in London, joining rural and city worlds, so, according to Greene in *The Second Part of Cony-Catching* (1592), rogues were conjugated to urban socioeconomic rhythms: "the term time is their harvest" (212). The transient could ambulate in markets, fairs, and inns, with an anonymity impossible in provincial spheres. *Looke on Me London* declaims that hunting "petty brokers or cherish-thieves" (*cherish* was an adjectival form of *chare*, or "back lane": that was where they hid and resided) "was mere vanity" (172). Criminals simply stepped into "some blind ale-house" to safely divide up spoils (Greene, *Notable Discovery* 172).

Slipping in and out of "decent" communities was not difficult for the mobile: nothing, ultimately, marked them out as different.[6] To Greene, ingenious criminals could "undo the hardest lock," often aided by members of the household they were robbing (*Second Part* 226).[7] The lowest "bash not to insinuate themselves into the company of the highest" (Walker 38). Ultimately, wrote John Awdeley, the illicit were omnipresent: "For nowhere shall ye walk, I trow, / But ye shall see their kind" (61).

Hence the valence of the idea of the "urban condom" (Sennet 228). Yet hence too the fact that the inhabitants of the fabulous, "goodly, fair and most rich city" of "Gazophylacium," as envisioned in *Martin Markall* (1610), are still perpetually "troubled and pestered" by nefarious "Thievingers":

> This city is very strongly defenced, for it is environed about with a wall of silver beaten out with the hammer; and yet, for all this, the inhabitants are very covetous and fearful to lose that which they have got together. (397)

It is important not to subscribe too completely to the anxieties of contemporaries, and eminently possible to question the validity of the outcry over the vagabond crisis in the early modern period, if crisis indeed it was.[8]

Nonetheless, the London that contained rogues and writing about them, and that was reproduced, however archly or inaccurately, in such writing, attests to the defiance of projects intent on reducing its heterogeneous thrill and noise, and the extent to which the city was constituted of "administratively debatable suburban areas," in which the illicit could bustle and thrive alongside the licit, in aggregations irreducible by schemes of social and geographical taxonomy (Spraggs 50).

Writing the Incontinent City

In a country whose capital was a Jerusalem and simultaneously a Babylon, the opposition between the licit and the illicit was a false and futile one, an untenable contrivance given sociogeographical realities. Rogues, in some writings about them, display an awareness of the limits of the authorities, and those authorities are as degenerate as the criminally wicked.[9] Legislation, rather than exposing misdemeanors, actually renders them invisible: apprehended vagrants, wrote Samuel Rid, "dare no otherwise than say they are Englishmen, and of such a shire" (*Art of Juggling* 266). Moreover, as A. L. Beier has observed, issuing licenses to mendicants encouraged forgery (*Masterless Men* 121–22). Luke Hutton's *Lamentation* depicts a rogue who was once a jailer (293).[10] Comparably, in *The Counter's Commonwealth*, a "paradox" is recognized, in terms that appropriate the language more commonly used to describe rogues: "The most ravening and cruel monsters in *our* land are the shoulder-clapping purse-biting mace-bearers; a necessary evil and plague-sore in the body of an infected City, and a disease that the most of the gentry is sick of" (Fennor 455). Clearly, certain writings about the illicit forcefully identify, explore, and represent this interorientation of roles, spaces, and people, and the attendant moral relativizations.

In *Christ's Tears over Jerusalem* (1593), for example, Thomas Nashe cross-examines the secret workings of the capital:

London, what are thy suburbs but licensed stews? Can it be so many brothel-houses of salary sensuality and six-penny whoredom (the next door to the magistrates) should be set up and maintained, if bribes did not bestir them? (483)[11]

Parentheses demarcate syntactically and ironically where no spatial distinction is possible. Nearness compromises moral definition: "I accuse none, but certainly justice somewhere is corrupted" (483). This process of perversion infects language and what it signifies. In the context of the Reformation's disruptions, with once holy orders now deemed vagrants devoid of calling, terms and sites with suggestions of edification are restructured to describe irresolute dilapidation: "Whole hospitals of ten-times-a-day dishonested strumpets have we cloistered together" (483). Words themselves betray the occupation of the same verbal space by heterodox and conflicting elements, echoing plural voices, sites, and significances. When the text refers to "legerdemain," it means a light-handed con, yet intimates *demesne*, a domain, estate, or province (484). This is a zone of chicanery where possession (sexual and material) is appropriated and reassigned in fleeting, almost invisible or indecipherable moments, to be registered verbally only by the sudden suggestive concatenations of half-words in pun. Here, in a place designated criminal by those within and without it (but more importantly by the interactions between the two), other binaries fervidly intercourse. Blasphemy defines piety, and vice versa:

> Not in all their whole life would they hear of GOD, if it were not for their huge swearing and foreswearing by Him. (483)

In what Nashe terms "a shop of incontinency" dissimulations, sex, and money come together (484). As John Twyning observes, Nashe "disclosed the uncontained flow of extra-mural commercial activity which the cash nexus brought to human relations" (58). This facility whereby permeable thresholds are easily crossed, differences are potently transgressed, and repentance involves a close connection to crime, is everywhere:

> They [clients] forecast for backdoors, to come in and out by, undiscovered. Sliding windows also and trapdoors in floors to hide whores behind and under, with false counterfeit panes in walls, to be opened and shut like a wicket. (484)

From this deviant locus reputable society is penetrated, as it in turn chooses to penetrate the illicit world itself, the distinction between—and due to—the vigorous activities of both becoming difficult to make, as pronouns confuse who is "them" and who is "us":

> Prentices and poor servants they encourage to rob their masters. Gentlemen's purses and pockets they will dive into and pick, even whiles they are dallying with them. (483)

Perversely, the whorehouse and its inhabitants divine a truth of sorts, insofar as they allow the reality of social appearance to be perceived: "Great cunning do they ascribe to their art, as the discerning, by the very countenance, a man that hath crowns in his purse" (483). This perspicacity is notably lacking in the blind eyes and sleepy wits of "grave authorized law-distributors" (484). This, again, must be evidence of corruption, an absence of moral integrity and intent on the part of such figures to permit their own extrication from intimate affiliation with the criminal elements of "this city-sodoming trade," a phrase that evokes the deep, perverse penetration by ostensibly marginal types into the supposed center of the socioeconomic fabric (484).[12]

Given the power and proximity of temptation, the extent of venality, and the ease with which the bad elides into the good, roguish writing about London consistently suggests that it is a brief and slippery sloping back-alley from propriety to turpitude. Thus "the man that is enticed to be a dicer, of his own accord will become a whoremaster" (Johnson 164). It becomes hard to separate the righteous from the wicked. As prisons are full of all sorts of people, Hell, it seems, is replete with not only "swaggerers," "drunkards and epicures" but also *reputable* characters: courtiers, soldiers, scholars, citizens, and farmers (Fennor 466; Dekker, *Lantern* 319). So too the terms describing the acts of legitimate entrepreneurs can be seen as homologous with the antics of less decent souls. Lawyers employ tricks to "worm" money from the accused (Fennor 435). Those unscrupulous businessmen termed "merchant venturers" are positively piratical, sailing "from ordinary to ordinary" (*Lantern* 327). Evidently, differentiating definition proves problematic once more:

> I pray you what say to Mounser the miller with the gilden thumb, whether think you him a cony-catcher or no? (Greene, *Defence* 353)

Any candid appraisal of contemporary urban socioeconomics accepts that "few men can live uprightly"; "all conditions and estates . . . seek to live by their wits," as "every thing now that is found profitable is counted honest and lawful" (Greene, *Notable Discovery* 174). If mercantile modes were practiced by all, so too was an underhandedness deemed to be integral to, not deviant from, those values:

> A number of tailors would be damned for keeping a hell under their shopboard; all the brokers would make their Wills at *Tyburn*, if the searching for stolen goods which they have received should like a plague but once come amongst them; yea, if all were served in their right kind, two parts of the land should be whipped at Bridewell for lechery, and three parts, at least, be set i'th stocks for drunkenness. (Dekker, *Bellman* 311)

In such a context, after such eloquent legitimations of their creed—notably invariably *by* criminal spokesmen, however—roguish cultures can but be afforded priority: "there is no estate, trade, occupation, nor mystery, but lives by cony-catching"; those who "cannot dissemble," Cuthbert Cony-Catcher says, in Greene's *Defence* of 1592, "cannot live" (376, 346). Even emperors perform dirty political tricks, as the sly reference to underhand events in Boulogne in Gilbert Walker's *A Manifest Detection* of 1552 implies (34).

This perhaps constitutes a critique of the established, licit order, betraying the contiguities its murky dealings have with a "world" barely "under" in reality. The critique, enacted by those criminal articulators, extends to lambaste those who would hypocritically presume to condemn, and whose persecution of poor vagrants, and seeming indulgence of the degeneracy of the reputable, "would strain a gnat, and let pass an elephant" (Greene, *Defence* 343, 346).

These attacks call into question the ability of *anyone* to bring cony-catchers to account, because *everyone* is implicated, on the take, on the make, in a country and city designed for, and resigned to, the fact.

Producing the Criminal

The significance of such critiques, haphazard and conditional as they are, cannot be underestimated. Vagabonds may be a "people for whom the world cares not, neither care they for the world" (Dekker, *Bellman* 306). Nevertheless, they are defined *by* that world, as their "unlawful" acts define the margins, limits, and failings of the lawful: rogues are rogues "by Act of Parliament" (Harman 82; Dekker, *Bellman* 307). These bestial, devilish aliens are not so unambiguously dissimilar to, or disconnected from, those around them (Manley 84).

As they are described in Robert Copland's *Highway to the Spital-house* (1535–36), vagrants wear the colors of the monarch, in "soldiers' clothing"; so do they claim to be "poor scholars," attaching to themselves intellectual prestige; their "rogations" punningly mimic formerly solemn supplications for alms (7, 9, 10). In Greene's *The Black Book's Messenger* (1592) Ned Browne tells of how expedient his disguise as a constable proves to be (324). Such trickery can only ever be "mimetic," utilizing and enhancing the unstable possibilities of normative systems (Taylor 4). Rapacious criminals, observes Christopher Hill, take "to an extreme" the "logic" of their contexts (17).

Tropes of contamination or disease (rogues cast as "pestiferous carbuncles" and the "wounds of a Commonwealth") might suggest the facility of a textual mechanics of discovery and deciphering, a dissecting scrutiny, with illicit practices "lively anatomized."[13] Yet such tropes also imply some fundamental incorporation of putatively malignant entities within the body politic. Equally, to employ images describing rogues, or indeed anyone (including sergeants) as "an excremental reversion of sin," "base excrements of dishonesty," or "the excrement that proceeds from the body of a commonwealth," is to do more than offer a simply denigrating reference to their status as the useless, superfluous dregs of society: it is to recognize that they are a growth, however hybrid or excrescent, from that society.[14]

Nevertheless, efforts were desperately undertaken by those compelled to refute this knowledge, guiltily recognizing that roguery was not some isolated, aberrant force in the land but a terrifying manifestation of the values of a society they upheld, "now based" notes Beier, "upon self-interest, not paternalism" ("Vagrants" 28). As Jonathan Dollimore puts it: "The other may be feared because structured within an economy of the same" (229).

Exculpation and the Pleasures of Narrative

However, as if to audaciously, irresponsibly exacerbate the moral confusions described, some writing about rogues tends—in supremely sophisticated fashion—to exculpate those portrayed.[15] The failings and proclivities of conies are mercilessly shown as being instrumental in their downfall. The "sweetness of gain" makes them "frolic" (Greene, *Notable Discovery* 169). They are "lasciviously addicted" and "covetously bent," "lewdly" longing for intimacy with those who will ultimately con them (Greene, *Black Book's Messenger* 330; Harman 122). Voicing a stern morality, Greene, in his *Notable Discovery* (1591), issues a "caveat" to warn "gentlemen, merchants, yeomen and farmers" against their own "inordinate desire," lest they "impoverish" their "purses" and reputations (181). Gulls, indeed, blind with greed or lust, are themselves opportunistic and eager to cozen:

> At last, with entreaty on both parts, he giveth the ring-faller the money and so departeth, thinking he hath gotten a very great jewel. (Awdeley 71)

They are willing, if losing, participants, baffled by the ingenious conceits of the rogues. In Greene's *Notable Discovery*, a cony who "asketh as though he were not made privy to the game" in the hope of conning another, is in reality *not* privy to the true scam (166). One even presumptuously announces he will employ what (little) he has learned of the trick on his unsuspecting friends (168). Yet no matter how cunning the con, the fact remains that most gulls are represented as extremely "foolish" and "ignorant," and their idiocy is portrayed without pity (Harman 98; Greene, *Notable Discovery* 162). A citizen, by "not knowing his own trunk," realizes he has "beguiled himself" in Greene's *The Third and Last Part of Cony-Catching* of 1592 (258). As popular phrasings have it, emphasizing the shift in legitimacy and culpability (everyone knows them—if you choose not to heed the proverbial message, the fault is all your own), "the prey makes the thief" (Greene, *Second Part* 215).

Thus, as appearance can only be expediently disguised in a culture that privileges it, so crime is not possible without the chances that conies offer. The demand for prostitutes is simply met by supply. Cross-biting tricks require the enthusiastic involvement of a *senex fornicator;* any subsequent "loss" is "voluntary" (Greene, *Notable Discovery* 172). Even when prospective gulls state they will not be conned, in loud and proud terms, it is demonstrable that they invite the attentions of equally proud rogues, eager to apprehend difficult prizes (Greene, *Second Part* 217).

When shown confessing and repenting, paying lip-service to moral standards that will invariably ensure their redemption, roguish characters themselves are not slow to offer mitigating or justifying explanations for degenerate lives. Thus a rogue in Greene's *Disputation* laments:

> For the extreme love of my parents was the very efficient cause of my follies, resembling herein the nature of an ape, that ever killeth that young one which he loveth most, with embracing it too fervently. So my father and mother, but she most of all, although he too much, so cockered me up in my wantonness, that my wit grew to the worst, and I waxed upward with the ill weeds. (227)

It is notable that the pamphlets generally avoid too obvious attributions of criminal activity to factors such as poverty. Yet such connections are nevertheless implied, if only by the success of rogues' appeals for charity (Harman 129).

Crucially, some rogue pamphleteers are "like a kind mother that, having seen her child do some witty unhappy trick, stands in doubt whether she shall laugh at him and let him escape, or frown at him and correct him" (Fennor 456). For laughter, to be sure, does often ensue. In the irresponsible hands of certain of these commentators crime is full of fun and vigor. Numerous narratives are introduced as being "pleasant" or "merry" (Greene, *Second Part* 199, 215). The humor is barely disguised: "Laugh as you like" (Greene, *Black Book's Messenger* 448). Those gulled are communally ridiculed, some even mocking their own daftness (Harman 91; Greene, *Second Part* 218; Greene, *Third Part* 244). Incredibly, there is pleasure for all, even those who suffer:

> The delights of these tabling houses are so pleasant and tempting, that a man when he hath there lost all his money, will be most willing, even in the place of his undoing, to stand moneyless, and be an idle looker on, of other men's unthriftiness. (Johnson 165)

For readers, much gratification comes in seeing smug, boastful conies (erroneously thinking themselves distinct from and superior to others, in particular the cozened and cozening mass constituting the audience) establish the tension of a challenge to would-be rogues, and then endure the same fleecing by some ingenious ruse as everyone else (Greene, *Disputation* 214).

Vagabonds are shown to be deeply gratified by what they do. The "teeth" of one rogue "watered" at a cony's "goodly chain": full of sensual desire, they are motivated by more than mere banal need (Greene, *Third Part* 253). When they can so often joyously indulge themselves "at their pleasures uncontrolled," how could it be otherwise? (Rid, *Art of Juggling* 266). Luke Hutton may be lamenting, but he takes time to point out, "All men in Yorkshire talk of me; / A stronger thief there could not be" (*Black Dog* 293).

Conventional repentant blubberings continually fade into tales of criminal thrills:

> But what should I stand here preaching? I lived wantonly, and therefore let me end merrily, and tell you two or three of my mad pranks and so bid you farewell. (Greene, *Black Book's Messenger* 328)

Consequently, the charge that rogues, villains, and vagabonds are layabout do-nothings is hard to uphold. For all their—largely false—modesty ("this was one of my ordinary shifts"), to dismiss a trick, though undoubtedly performative, as merely "a game," is a mistake: "These cony-catchers are never idle" (Greene, *Black Book's Messenger* 328; Greene, *Third Part* 242; Hutton, *Black Dog* 282). They invest their projects with great industry, in Greene's words "diligently" scrutinizing potential prizes (*Third Part* 236). To Dekker, in *Lantern and Candlelight* (1608), they "dig silver out of men's purses all the day"; all their "fish" come "to net" (243). With their expertise, virtuosity, and inventiveness, thieves are seductively skilled. Their hands have a "fine and nimble agility"; their tricks possess "a subtle shift to blind the world," and their minds "a thousand inventions" (Greene, *Second Part* 220, 221; Greene, *Black Book's Messenger* 328). It is unsurprising that verbs proliferate in descriptions of rogue acts: "by their close villainies they cheat, cozen, prig, lift, nip," writes Greene (*Third Part* 233). The gory, lurid threat that rogues will be "lively anatomized" encodes a destructive violence toward them, that, paradoxically, at the same time suggests an eminently engaging, marketable *vivification* of the deviant (Fennor 426).

Such verbal vitality infuses rogue narratives with sensational immediacy and verve. Thus, in one tale in Greene's *Third Part of Cony-Catching*, the tense of description slips into the present: "to bed are they gone," "None are now up" (240). Compounding the assimilation, the aforementioned notions of tension and challenge inherent to tricks likewise inform the workings of the pamphlets themselves, as we are defied not to enjoy the revelation of their processes.[16] Greene subtitles *The Second Part of Cony-Catching* with the words

> Discourfing strange cunning in Coosnage, which if you reade without laughing, Ile give you my cap for a Noble. (193)

It would seem that wanting to use narrative to scrupulously control, parenthesize, moralize, and segregate, in taxonomies and objective observation, is not only impossible, but undesirable.

Translations and Transgressions

These cultivated ambiguities are only amplified and underwritten by the high degree of linguistic assimilation enacted between standardized English and "cant" in writing about rogues.[17] Capitalizing on the interorientations of the urban scene, vagrants and criminals are represented as insinuating themselves superbly into pockets, beds, and homes, to go about their "pilfering, picking, and spoiling" (Harman 85). But such *material* arrogations and insinuations are often predicated upon rogues adeptly and expediently parodying, occupying, and performing various expressive modes, adopting diverse linguistic and intellectual personae, pilfering and picking out from decent discourses useful words, phrases, and forms to adapt to their nefarious purposes, and thence, perhaps spoiling those discourses by qualifying their authority and integrity.[18] In writing about rogues, this is represented textually as a polygraphic, polyphonic babble, itself completely concordant with the conceptual and actual sociogeographical hybridity that was London, as described by John Earle: "a heap of stones and men, with a vast confusion of languages, and were the steeple not sanctified, nothing liker Babel" (Salgãdo, *Elizabethan Underworld* 9).

If cant lexicons are inefficacious in objectively demarcating dialects, it is hardly surprising. Such problems afflicted all taxonomical and regulatory procedures in writing about rogues. The mental and textual resources of the writer inadequately comprehend the depths of vagabond cunning. The Latin tag suffixing Greene's list of miscreant practices in *A Notable Discovery* (1591) makes this clear: "Cum multis aliis quae nunc praescribere longum est" [With much else too long to set down here] (177). At times, as Greene shows, apprehension is baffled:

> If I should spend many sheets in deciphering their shifts, it were frivolous, in that they be many and full of variety, for every day they invent new tricks

and such quaint devices as are secret, yet passing dangerous, that if a man had Argus' eyes, he could scant pry into the bottom of their practices. (174)

The extensive appliance of alliteration in writing about rogues was, in one sense, a vital instrument in textually and acoustically punctuating the illegible mass, crafting readable patterns of consonance among forces of dissonance, while definitely and evocatively associating them with negative characteristics.[19] With insistent repetitions of damning phrases and confounding sounds that can but imprint themselves on a consumer's consciousness, Thomas Harman's *Caveat* (1566), for example, abundantly configures the "detestable behaviour of all these rowsey, ragged rabblement of rakehells," these "wily wanderers" with their "deep dissimulation and detestable dealing," "undecent, doleful dealing and execrable exercises" and "scelerous secrets" (81–83).

Yet as much as the burgeoning mechanics of print offered the potential for standardized clarity, so did they engender unprecedented, unclassifiable modes: "Pornography as well as piety assumed new forms" (Eisenstein 130). And thus alphabetization, the lexicographical compilation of roguish words and practices, was not as objective as it might seem, becoming a site of conflict between authors (*Martin Markall* 410–11). Similarly, alliteration can be seen to descend into parody, evidence of ludicrously spluttering hyperbole (Greene, *Notable Discovery* 178). Thus, in *A Disputation*, Greene enjoys a cheeky reference to Harman's work and workings:

> Wishing therefore my labours may be a caveat to my countrymen to avoid the company of such cozening courtesans. (208)

And all these issues also apply to treatments of cant. Admittedly, glossaries explicitly clarify, telling readers who, among a bewildering gallery of names and roles, is what.[20] Yet translation operates in more subtle ways, with explanations of words and phrases contained in parentheses that do not necessarily impede the flow of the narrative, and alien terms being quickly put "all in English" (Dekker, *O Per Se O* 367–69). No simply passive process, this represents the active arresting and exposition of a seditiously alternative exclusive "unknown tongue"; hence Dekker's supposed retaining in his "service" of a vagabond youth from whom he can acquire an awareness of cant, and the dynamic use of "Englished" as a verb (Harman 146; Dekker, *O Per Se O* 367–69; Greene, *Disputation* 208).

Plainly, the internal-foreign is sought out in a "linguistic mission" (Greenblatt, *Learning* 16). Translation can thus be seen to be a powerful "reassertion of mastery by the users of the dominant language," indicative of "an ideology of univocal discourse," exemplifying "that quest for cultural and national identity which lies at the heart of Elizabethan literary activity."[21] This was a high ideal, preserving English from "barbarism," and making "the vulgar sort here in London, which is the fountain whose rivers flow round about England, to aspire to a richer purity of speech than is communicated with the commonalty of any nation under heaven" (Nashe, *Pierce* 91). Translation was, however, an ambiguously successful program of aggrandizement, as Stephen Greenblatt observes:

> To learn another language is to acknowledge the existence of another people and to acquire the ability to function, however crudely, in another social world. (*Shakespearean* 49)[22]

To translate is to communicate; to communicate is to place oneself in propinquity with the other, simultaneously disclosing connection and difference. Thus even as the supposed rogue's vernacular is estranged, by being conferred with precedent it is normalized and shown to have a pedigree, however bastardized: "this their language they spun out of three other tongues, viz. Latin, English and Dutch . . . notwithstanding some few words they borrowed of the Spanish and French" (*Martin Markall* 421). And while "Pedlars' French" is not explicitly legitimized, it *is* recognized as another tongue in a polyglot nation already resounding to a multiplicity of dialects, registers, and tongues, licit and otherwise:

> If you marvel at these mysteries and quaint words, consider, as the carpenter hath many terms familiar enough to his prentices, that others understand not at all, so have the cony-catchers. (Harman 85)[23]

Therefore, as Harman goes on to describe cant as the "lewd, lousy language of . . . loitering lusks and lazy lorels, wherewith they buy and sell the common people as they pass through the country," he admits that its alterity is not absolute: the terms of this "unknown tongue" were, in this national circulation of people, words and things, "half mingled with English when it is familiarly talked."[24] That the translation of cant necessarily employs and activates a mechanics of conjugation and comprehension however partial, reproducing linguistic, semantic, syntactic, and grammatical logic and proximity—as much as distinction—is realized in *Caveat:*

> A prigger of prancers be horse-stealers; for to prig signifieth in their language to steal, and a prancer is a horse. *So being put together, the matter is plain.* (103; emphasis added)

In cant glossaries a similar process of accretion is at work. Certain seemingly impenetrable entries rely on an attentive reader's retention of previous meanings:

A KITCHIN MORTS

A Kitchin morts is a girl; she is brought at her full age to the upright man to be broken, and so she is called a doxy, until she come to the honour of an altham. (Awdeley 66)

This applies to descriptions of tricking methodology too. In Samuel Rid's *Art of Juggling* (1612) after several references to one part of the act of an illusion, one is simply told to "use words etc." in the manner of previous sleights (271).

As proximities are realized, however, languages, genres, meanings, and moralities jostle in the words of lines on a page. Hence, as Patricia Fumerton puts it: "The very act of translating a minor into a major language . . . could cause the latter to degenerate" ("Subdiscourse" 77). In the period, the process of attaining and reifying linguistic purity and security all too often actuates linguistic hybridity and mutability, "entropy and disintegration" (Helgerson 297).[25] With this in mind, it ultimately matters little whether cant was a prevalent sociolinguistic phenomenon or a gross exaggeration. Representations of rogues' usage of cant convey a sense of how norms of communication might not simply be rejected but also subversively inhabited, "half mingled," by parody, by changing meanings, or by "formal techniques" such as "substitutions, affixing or reversal of consonants, vowels and syllables" (Jütte 183). Significantly, such techniques are comparable with those alliterative tics and alphabetical tricks so beloved by rogue pamphleteers themselves.

Where things come together in this roguish world, the contiguities are not merely graphical or verbal, but ideational and epistemological also. Authority resides neither in the common standards of English, nor the defiant otherness of cant: "Me non speak English, by my fait" (Copland 10). Attentive readings of glossaries identify crossings-over and slips of empathy and voice. Harman translates the term *queer cuffin* as "a hoggish and churlish man." Yet he glosses it elsewhere as "the Justice of Peace." As Gãmini Salgãdo importantly notes, the two are synonymous "from the speaker's point of view" (Harman 149, 147, 384–85). In Greene's *A Notable Discovery*, King Solomon's words are used to rail against trulls; yet the same register and terms of biblical ire are directed in pseudosermon form at those who irresponsibly frequent them (180–81).

Thus in a paradigmatic moment in Dekker's *Lantern and Candlelight*, brilliantly concatenating all the material, linguistic, and stylistic factors, and forces of ambivalence examined here, a reader ends up at once alienated from useless, senseless authority (even as that authority is petitioned), *and* estranged from the rogues that that authority should be ranged against (even as the passage offers a veritable script or handbook for any prospective cony-catchers wishing to evade interrogation and avoid apprehension).

As Dekker's narrator has it, a "punk" stops a constable's mouth "with sugar-plums, that's to say, . . . she poisons him with sweet words" (350). Caught up in delectation of the scam, the narrator checks himself—by *translating* his register from delight to disgust—voicing the requisite distaste. Yet the pleasure of the trick has been savored, a limit has been transgressed, and the whore's words thus remain both "sweet" and "poison" long after she, and her words, have, to paraphrase the Virgil quoted in the text, faded—escaped, that is—into the insubstantial air. After lamenting and insulting the ridiculous dysfunction of the "dull," defeated "Lantern and Candlelight" ("how art thou made a blind ass"), the narrative proceeds—with not a little italicized exasperation, as much at the realization of the ground still to be covered by the hapless agent as at the fact that he does not and cannot do so—to tell him what to do, where to go, who to follow, "that's to say, *commit, commit.*" The narrator states:

> You are the pruning knives that should lop off such idle, such unprofitable, and such destroying branches from the vine. The beams of your authority should purge the air of such infection. (350)

One is left with a sense of disparity, of things not done that should be, and of things that should not be done being simultaneously enjoyed. In the reveling in the play and only partial condemnation of the confusingly, excitingly, intercoursing "witty unhappy" state, absolute morality and essential truth are lost (Fennor 456). One sentence both condemns poison and gasps at delicious "sugar-plums," and as each is shown in proximity; neither is afforded priority.

The subsequent concluding "night-piece" of the work is likewise "drawn in sundry colours." "Pluto's beadle" walks streets seeing "midwives running" to attend to "young maids, being big with child by unlawful fathers"; in other alleys he meets "servants in whose breast, albeit the arrows of the plague stuck half way, yet by cruel masters were they driven out of doors at midnight and conveyed to garden-houses" to die; he spies others "purloining fardels of their masters' goods," to deliver them up to "common strumpets." As it is perceptively put, in a poignant, stunning realization of the infinitely multiple experiences of the early modern city and the dramatic inefficacy of material separations that might hinder penetrative speculation, "A thousand of these comedies were acted in dumb show, and only in the private houses" (*Lantern* 364–65).

Dekker's *O Per Se O*, published four years later (1612), consciously continues what was only seemingly finished, and it is evident that, again, this is a cataloging that is coincidentally no reduction, the drifting, dark wanderings being responsive to the "psychogeography" of the city, adumbrating "*new emotional maps* of existing areas" (Gray 8–9). All the horror, revenge, amorality, pathos, desperation, and morbidity of life is here, with attendant vitality. "Lust" still kisses "Prodigality," and while the Devil's "messenger" may laugh to see his master's work so readily undertaken, there is a powerful sense that due to the sequential descriptions and interlocking narratives, the moral ambiguities and proximities evoked ensure that though good and bad exist, the triumph of one over the other is never confirmed or resolved (*Lantern* 364). By consistently embracing and enacting this irresolution, rogue pamphlets and texts sharing their concerns convey a sense of the ceaselessly renegotiated, and sometimes ignored, conflicts and congruences between disparate cultural, social, and political spheres taking place in London.

Conclusion

Critical attestations of the innate conservatism of rogue pamphlets and their authors abound, emphasizing their drive to render legible and contain the illicit, and not without justification.[26] Even the infamously licentious Greene offered a moment of insightful and honest repentance:

> But I thanke God that hee put it in my head, to lay open the moft horrible coofenages of the common Conny-catchers, Coofeners, and Croffebiters, which I haue indifferently handled in thofe my severall discourses already imprinted. And my truft is that thofe difcourfes will doe great good, and bee very beneficiall to the Commonwealth of England. (*Repentance* 178)

Such seemingly transparent admissions inform some present-day perspectives on the qualities of "containment" that may be found in some writing about rogues. As Jean-Christophe Agnew asserts:

> Like the estates literature that preceded it, rogue literature served as a figurative act of settlement: exposing, dissecting, and classifying all that threatened to confuse the social relations of Elizabethan England, tying the loose ends of commerce and crime back to the frayed fabric of society. (65)

But in early modern London, fabricating visions of social reality teased other matters out. Thus, despite any overt didacticism it is possible to discern in the work of individuals even as well-connected as Thomas Harman—a man of some rank, and cognizant of the practical workings of social and criminal administration—exaggerated and stylized gestures toward irresponsibility, an ambivalence concerning the efficacy and intent of measures that would repress the frequently animating and exciting activities of rogues, villains, and vagabonds, with whom even the most righteous, one realizes, share traits. Dekker himself spent considerable amounts of time in prison for debt, and while there wrote and published substantial sections of the pamphlets discussed here. Arguably, his experiences of a "fraught authorial position" and institutional iniquities actuated his "deep ambivalence about the function of the penal system and the value of imprisonment" (Twyning 98).[27]

David Margolies convincingly argues that such inconsistent strains are actually present in all of Greene's earlier pamphlets, merely becoming more "explicit" in *The Defence*, "to the extent of saying, more or less, that conny-catching redresses social injustice or effects class justice" (134). This latter claim is less tenable. Nevertheless, all things becoming relative, even as reformative lessons are often presented in short sections resolving texts, such segregation nevertheless subtly compromises the power of the moral imperative. Truth is not plainly apparent or inherent: it must be worked free, extracted, imposed, painstakingly constructed graphically and textually. As such it is contingent upon, and prey to, prior disturbances and contraventions of its clarity, a phenomenon complicated by the fact that, as Sandra Clark argues in *The Elizabethan Pamphleteers*, the reading public was "plainly interested" in those transgressive disturbances; in other words, "the sheer mechanics of cozenage" (49).[28]

As clear moral strategies are deliberately disintegrated, it is evident that certain of our guides through this design of a chaotic urban world—watchmen, constables, narrators, and pamphleteers alike—themselves participate in, and sometimes succumb to, the seductions, deceits, and confusions of that world.[29] In so doing they offer vivid representations responsive to what Burke has termed the risings, sinkings, and "fuzzy" definitions of and between popular and high cultures, spaces, places, people, authorities, and roguish deviants (*Popular Culture* xvi, 59–62). Crucially, rogue writings, at their best and most ambivalent, no more purely delineate and insist on their own revelatory and corrective qualities than they crudely evoke parodic inversions of the hierarchies of "ordinary" society.

In ways of immense consequence for future literatures, writings about rogues respond and contribute to the intricate coalescences of the city, emphatically concatenating, relativizing, and hybridizing the subversive and reputable, licit and illicit, conservative and irresponsible, flesh and stone, at one and the same time, in the same space, line, and breath.[30] Such concatenations were both cause and effect of the intricate relations of the early modern urban environment, wherein facts, fictions, and extremes are not simply engaged in mutual definition (conflicting, consensual, or otherwise), but endure and enjoy the most incredible negotiations, juxtapositions, and intimate proximities.

NOTES

1. Comparably, Wells offers a stimulating account of the complexity of contradictions within hegemonic ideology governing the City of London, with reference to cultural products seeking to explore and negotiate these contradictions, specifically the drama of Jonson, Marston, and Middleton.

2. For a superb account of the differences between "aliens," "foreigners," and "native" Londoners in the city's uniquely permeable places, how these differences were sometimes obscured, and the tensions that developed precisely because they *were* obscured, see Howard.

3. For a detailed appraisal of the intricacies, and intricate wrangles, of housing arrangements, see Orlin, "Boundary Disputes" 363, 365–67.

4. See Clark, "Migrant" 142. On the sociocultural constitution of London's liberties, and their status as places of both freedom and restraint, see Wells 41–42.

5. See also Braudel's comments on suburbs throughout Europe, 59–61.

6. This was the rogue's great threat: see Woodbridge, "Impostors" 1–11. Sharon Gmelch's studies of Irish traveling people sustain the idea of historically permeable boundaries, even if temporary, between sedentary and mobile communities, a perspective confirmed by the brilliant analyses offered by Leo Lucassen, Wim Willems, and Annemarie Cottaar. On the indeterminacy surrounding the status of vagrants and itinerants see also Hufton and Fontaine.

7. See Beier, *Masterless Men* 131. As Florike Egmond notes of the efforts of authorities in Amsterdam, in locking gates every night and lowering iron barriers into the canals to control illicit urban mobility, "quite a few thieves had developed their own methods of circumventing such barriers" (32).

8. On the exaggeration of the vagrant threat, see Manley 309; Archer 204; Slack, "Vagrants" 365, 377, *Poverty* 102; and Beier, "Vagrants" 8, 18. For perspectives on the stability of London in the period, see Rappaport 4–5, 27; and Power, "London and Control." Despite the anxieties of the authorities, rogues were no more intentionally disruptive in the provinces. See, for example, Thomas, "Rogues" 22, "Elizabethan Privy Council" 15–24. Historians are similarly skeptical about the extent of the organization of vagrants and rogues. See Sharpe 141–54; Slack, *Poverty* 101; and Archer 206. In the research of court records undertaken for "Overlapping circles," Paul Griffiths finds "no solid evidence of an underworld," but notes, in recidivism rates, "a degree of collectivity and

longevity in relations between criminals" (120–21). Title of work notwithstanding, Egmond is unconvinced that any coherent underworld existed in Holland (16–17, 40–44, 181).

9. In Greene's *A Disputation*, a cutpurse argues with an officer who has infringed upon sanctuary rights in a "place of privilege" (214–15). See McMullan 7.

10. Hutton, *The Black Dog of Newgate* (1596?) 293. See also Fennor 426–29, 444–45. For examples of the recruitment of the practical enforcers of justice from the ranks of criminals, see Robin 235–36.

11. For an account of the ownership of brothels by "legitimate" interests, see Ashton 13–14; McMullan 138–39; and Burford 147–84.

12. Gowing posits a usefully complementary account of the eroticization of urban space, and the specifics of the multiple interrelations between places and illicit pursuits (146–47).

13. Rid, *Art of Juggling* 265; Johnson 169; Fennor 426.

14. Greene, *Notable Discovery* 178; Greene, *Second Part* 210; Fennor 456. On the ambivalence of symbolic formulations of "images of faeces and urine" see Bakhtin, *Rabelais* 151; also see the account of the excrementalizing of the Other in Woodbridge, *Vagrancy* 185–87. Significantly, some of the terms used to describe groups of Dutch criminals, such as "bende" (band) and "troep" (troop), have a similar valence. Such terms also meant "rubbish, mess, dirt," and though they may have been used to disparage the bands, and their lack of organization, they imply a fundamental connection between decent society, and those marginalized, cast-off "persons out of place"; see Egmond 7–8.

15. For more on the ambivalence of sympathy represented in these writings about rogues, see Steve Mentz's "Magic Books" in this volume.

16. For a stimulating depiction of the strange congruences between pamphlet production and pamphlet content, focusing on the "vagrancy" of both, see Halasz 72–77, 116, 181–82.

17. Whether or not cant existed, and if it did, how widespread or exclusive it was, are not of concern here. What *is* significant are the ambiguities inherent to *treatments* of cant, actual or imagined, and the ways in which cant is shown to inhabit, pervert, distort, and upset communicative norms. For superlative discussions of the extent, credibility, politicality, and subversiveness (or otherwise) of cant see Beier, "Anti-language" 64–101; Beier, *Masterless Men* 125–26. Also see Slack, *Poverty* 104. In *Becoming Criminal*, Bryan Reynolds suggests that cant is the "prevalent factor unifying criminal culture" in "literary representation" (29). Reynolds argues that, even as it was fetishized in such representations, cant was a private and secure antilanguage that allowed, in its sophisticated usage, "difference and resistance" within licit terrains (64; see 64–94). On the historiography of cant and its existence elsewhere in Europe at the time, see Burke's introduction to Burke and Porter; and Burke, "Languages" 24–32.

18. On the materiality of language in the period, see Sinfield 76.

19. See Manley 85; Copland 13; and Rid, *Martin Markall* 407–9.

20. See Dekker's *Lantern and Candlelight* 340, 359; Greene's *Notable Discovery* 176–77.

21. Taylor 11, 18; Ebel 595. On the centrality of linguistic imperialism to Tudor statecraft, see Leith, *Social History* 161.

22. Taylor also offers a superb reading of this ambiguity in Harman's *Caveat* (15–18).

23. See also Greene, *Notable Discovery* 173. For a polemical and invigorating account of the importance of recognizing linguistic diversity in the period, especially in London, see Leith, "Tudor London."

24. On the lexical, lexicographical, and social "boundary crossing" involved in the uses and explications of cant, see Beier, "Anti-language" 92–93.

25. See also Fumerton, "Subdiscourse" 79.

26. See Sharpe 235–36; Baumgartner 70–71; Curtis and Hale; also Berlin 264; Price 132–39; and Brand 18–20. Stephen Greenblatt offers a compelling reading of rogue pamphlets that asserts their status as only superficially seditious texts, arguing that for all the force of their equivocations, vacillations, and inconsistencies, rogue pamphlets are instruments of the assault on, and containment of, the subversive (*Shakespearean* 50–53). Yet one might argue that this containment is imperfect, given that the application of monolithic inflexible moralities to any reading of rogue pamphlets and those texts sharing their sensibilities and concerns discredits them. Greenblatt's contention that liking "reading about vagabonds" is "to hate them" can be qualified, for, truly, even to write about rogues all too often manifests an animation and engagement that contends with (while not necessarily defeating) any strident moralizing (52). In *London Dispossessed*, Twyning argues that Dekker and Greene were deeply implicated in the formulation of perspectives to identify and diminish the threat of urban disorder. One might counter that while they do do this, this is not all they do. As Twyning admits, though Dekker, for example, promised "to make his readers feel more secure," he also "often upset their looked-for sense of security" (65–67, 76). Thus, in "Magic Books" in this collection, Mentz employs a thoroughly literary analysis to usefully think beyond the containment/subversion model to convey the marketable instrumentality of cony-catching pamphlets, how they endowed purchasers and readers with a desirable, inoculating, privileged knowledge to read the perilously illegible novelty of the urban scene, and how this knowledge was transmitted via older generic forms (namely romance). Yet Mentz also signals that a rehearsal of the threat posed by the ingenious rogue was fundamental to the successful functioning of the texts in this way.

27. See also Shaw 372–74.

28. Peter Lake presents a characteristically well-argued case for the capacity of popular pamphlets to "engage the voyeuristic attention of the reader, but also to stimulate and exploit his or her anxieties, impulses and (surreptitious) pleasures" (240).

29. See Relihan's fine article.

30. On this, see Bakhtin's comments in "Prehistory" 50.

WORKS CITED

Agnew, Jean-Christophe. *Worlds Apart: The Market and the Theater in Anglo-American Thought, 1550–1750*. Cambridge: Cambridge UP, 1986.

Archer, Ian W. *The Pursuit of Stability: Social Relations in Elizabethan London*. Cambridge: Cambridge UP, 1991.

Ashton, Robert. "Popular Entertainment and Social Control in Late Elizabethan and Early Stuart London." *London Journal* 9 (1983): 3–19.

Awdeley, John. *The Fraternity of Vagabonds.* 1561. Salgādo 59–78.

Bakhtin, Mikhail. "From the Prehistory of Novelistic Discourse." *The Dialogic Imagination: Four Essays by M. M. Bakhtin.* Ed. Michael Holquist. Trans. Michael Holquist and Caryl Emerson. Austin: U of Texas P, 1981. 41–83.

————. *Rabelais and His World.* Trans. Hélène Iswolsky. Bloomington: Indiana UP, 1984.

Baumgartner, Paul R. "From Medieval Fool to Renaissance Rogue: *Cocke Lorelles Bote* and the Literary Tradition." *Annuale Medievale* 4 (1963): 57–91.

Beier, A. L. "Anti-language or Jargon? Canting in the English Underworld in the Sixteenth and Seventeenth Centuries." Burke and Porter 1–21.

————. *Masterless Men: The Vagrancy Problem in England, 1560–1640.* London: Methuen, 1985.

————. "Social Problems in Elizabethan London." *The Tudor and Stuart Town: A Reader in English Urban History, 1530–1688.* Ed. Jonathan Barry. London: Longman, 1990. 121–38.

————. "Vagrants and the Social Order in Elizabethan England." *Past and Present* 64 (1974): 3–29.

Berlin, Normand. "Thomas Dekker: A Partial Reappraisal." *Studies in English Literature* 6 (1966): 263–77.

Brand, Dana. *The Spectator and the City in Nineteenth-Century American Literature.* Cambridge: Cambridge UP, 1991.

Braudel, Fernand. "Pre-modern Towns." Clark, *Early Modern Town* 53–90.

Burford, E. J. *Bawds and Lodgings: A History of the London Bankside Brothels, c. 100–1675.* London: Peter Owen, 1976.

Burke, Peter. Introduction. Burke and Porter 1–21.

————. "Languages and Anti-languages in Early Modern Italy." *History Workshop Journal* 11 (1981): 24–32.

————. *Popular Culture in Early Modern Europe.* Aldershot: Scolar P, 1978. Reprint, 1994.

————. "Popular Culture in Seventeenth-Century London." *London Journal* 3 (1977): 143–62.

Burke, Peter, and Roy Porter, eds. *Languages and Jargons: Contributions to a Social History of Language.* Cambridge: Polity P, 1995.

Clark, Peter. *The English Alehouse: A Social History, 1200–1830.* New York: Longman, 1983.

————. "The Migrant in Kentish Towns, 1580–1640." Clark and Slack 117–63.

————, ed. *The Early Modern Town.* London: Longman, Oxford UP, 1976.

Clark, Peter, and Paul Slack, eds. *Crisis and Order in English Towns 1500–1700: Essays in Urban History.* London: Routledge, 1972.

Clark, Sandra. *The Elizabethan Pamphleteers: Popular Moralistic Pamphlets, 1580–1640.* London: Athlone P, 1983.

Copland, Robert. *The Highway to the Spital-House* 1535–36. Judges 1–25.

Curtis, T. C., and F. M. Hale. "English Thinking about Crime, 1530–1620." *Crime and Criminal Justice in Europe and Canada*. Ed. Louis A. Knafla. Ontario: Wilfrid Laurier UP, 1981. 111–26.

Dekker, Thomas. *The Bellman of London*. 1608. Judges 303–11.

———. *Lantern and Candlelight*. 1608. Judges 312–65.

———. *O Per Se O*. 1612. Judges 366–82.

———. *The Plague Pamphlets*. Ed. F. P. Wilson. Oxford: Clarendon P, 1925.

———. *The Seven Deadly Sinnes of London*. 1606. *The Non-dramatic Works*. Vol. 2. Ed. Alexander B. Grosart. New York: Russell and Russell, 1963.

de Vries, Jan. *European Urbanization, 1500–1800*. London: Methuen, 1984.

Dollimore, Jonathan. *Sexual Dissidence: Augustine to Wilde, Freud to Foucault*. Oxford: Clarendon P, 1991. Reprint, 1996.

Ebel, Julia G. "Translation and Cultural Nationalism in the Reign of Elizabeth." *Journal of the History of Ideas* 30 (1969): 593–602.

Egmond, Florike. *Underworlds: Organized Crime in the Netherlands, 1650–1800*. Cambridge: Polity P, 1993.

Eisenstein, Elizabeth L. *The Printing Press as an Agent of Change: Communication and Cultural Transformations in Early Modern Europe*. Vol. 2. Cambridge: Cambridge UP, 1979.

Fennor, William. *The Counter's Commonwealth*. 1617. Judges 423–87.

Finlay, Roger. *Population and Metropolis: The Demography of London, 1580–1650*. Cambridge: Cambridge UP, 1981.

Fontaine, Laurence. *History of Pedlars in Europe*. Trans. Vicki Whittaker. Cambridge: Polity P, 1996.

Fumerton, Patricia. "London's Vagrant Economy: Making Space for 'Low' Subjectivity." Orlin, *Material London* 206–25.

———. "Subdiscourse: Jonson Speaking Low." *English Literary Renaissance* 25 (1995): 76–96.

Gmelch, Sharon. *Tinkers and Travellers*. Dublin: O'Brien P, 1975.

Goodey, Brian R. "Mapping 'Utopia': A Comment on the Geography of Sir Thomas More." *Geographical Review* 60 (1970): 15–30.

Gowing, Laura. "'The Freedom of the Streets': Women and Social Space, 1560–1640." *Londinopolis: Essays in the Cultural and Social History of Early Modern London*. Ed. Paul Griffiths and Mark S. R. Jenner. Manchester: Manchester UP, 2000. 130–51.

Gray, Christopher. "Essays from Leaving the Twentieth Century." *What Is Situationism? A Reader*. Ed. Stewart Home. Edinburgh: AK P, 1996. 3–23.

Greenblatt, Stephen J. *Learning to Curse: Essays in Early Modern Culture*. London: Routledge, 1990.

———. *Shakespearean Negotiations: The Circulation of Social Energy in Renaissance England*. Oxford: Clarendon P, 1988.

Greene, Robert. *The Black Book's Messenger*. 1592. Salgãdo 317–38.

———. *The Defence of Cony-Catching*. 1592. Salgãdo 339–78.

———. *A Disputation*. 1592. Judges 206–47.

———. *A Notable Discovery of Cozenage*. 1591. Salgãdo 155–92.

———. *The Repentance of Robert Greene Maifter of Artes*. 1592. *The Life and Complete*

Works in Prose and Verse of Robert Greene. Vol. 12. Ed. Alexander B. Grosart. New York: Russell and Russell, 1964.

———. *The Second Part of Cony-Catching.* 1592. Salgādo 293–30.

———. *The Third and Last Part of Cony-Catching.* 1592. Salgādo 231–64.

Griffiths, Paul. "Overlapping Circles: Imagining Criminal Communities in London, 1545–1645." *Communities in Early Modern England: Networks, Place, Rhetoric.* Ed. Alexandra Shepard and Phil Withington. Manchester: Manchester UP, 2000. 115–33.

Halasz, Alexandra. *The Marketplace of Print: Pamphlets and the Public Sphere in Early Modern England.* Cambridge: Cambridge UP, 1997.

Harman, Thomas. *Caveat for Common Cursitors.* 1566. Salgādo 79–154.

Helgerson, Richard. "Language Lessons: Linguistic Colonialism, Linguistic Postcolonialism, and the Early Modern English Nation." *Yale Journal of Criticism* 11.1 (1998): 289–99.

Hill, Christopher. *Liberty against the Law: Some Seventeenth Century Controversies.* Harmondsworth: Penguin, 1996. Reprint, 1997.

Howard, Jean E. "Women, Foreigners, and the Regulation of Urban Space in Westward Ho." Orlin, *Material London* 150–67.

Hufton, Olwen. "Begging, Vagrancy, Vagabondage, and the Law: An Aspect of the Problem of Poverty in Eighteenth-Century France." *European Studies Review* 2.2 (1972): 97–123.

Hutton, Luke. *The Black Dog of Newgate.* 1596. Judges 265–91.

Johnson, Richard. *Looke on Me London.* 1613. Marshburn and Velie. 161–75.

Judges, A. V., ed. *The Elizabethan Underworld.* London: George Routledge and Sons, 1930.

Jütte, Robert. *Poverty and Deviance in Early Modern Europe.* Cambridge: Cambridge UP, 1994.

Lake, Peter. "From Troynouvant to Heliogabulus's Rome and Back: 'Order' and Its Others in the London of John Stow." *Imagining Early Modern London: Perceptions and Portrayals of the City from Stow to Strype, 1598–1720.* Ed. J. F. Merritt. Cambridge: Cambridge UP, 2001. 217–49.

Leith, Dick. *A Social History of English.* London: Routledge, 1983. Reprint, 1997.

———. "Tudor London: Sociolinguistic Stratification and Linguistic Change." *Anglo-American Studies* 4 (1984): 59–72.

Lucassen, Leo, Wim Willems, and Annemarie Cottaar, eds. *Gypsies and Other Itinerant Groups: A Socio-Historical Approach.* Basingstoke: Macmillan, 1998.

Manley, Lawrence. *Literature and Culture in Early Modern London.* Cambridge: Cambridge UP, 1995.

Margolies, David. *Novel and Society in Elizabethan England.* London: Croom Helm, 1985.

Marshburn, Joseph H., and Alan R. Velie, eds. *Blood and Knavery: A Collection of English Renaissance Pamphlets and Ballads of Crime and Sin.* Cranbury, N.J.: Associated UP, 1973.

McMullan, John L. *The Canting Crew: London's Criminal Underworld, 1550–1700.* New Brunswick, N.J.: Rutgers UP, 1984.

Miller, Edwin Haviland. *The Professional Writer in Elizabethan England: A Study of Nondramatic Literature.* Cambridge: Harvard UP, 1959.

Nashe, Thomas. *Christ's Tears over Jerusalem*. 1593. Nashe, *Unfortunate Traveller*.

———. *Pierce Penniless*. 1592. Nashe, *Unfortunate Traveller*.

———. *The Unfortunate Traveller and Other Works*. Ed. J. B. Steane. Harmondsworth: Penguin, 1971. Reprint, 1972.

Orlin, Lena Cowen. "Boundary Disputes in Early Modern London." Orlin, *Material London* 344–76.

———, ed. *Material London, ca. 1600*. Philadelphia: U of Pennsylvania P, 2000.

Park, Robert. "The City: Suggestions for the Investigation of Human Behaviour in the Urban Environment." *Classic Essays on the Culture of Cities*. Ed. Richard Sennet. New York: Meredith Corporation, 1969. 91–130.

Paster, Gail Kern. *The Idea of the City in the Age of Shakespeare*. Athens: U of Georgia P, 1985.

Pearl, Valerie. "Change and Stability in Seventeenth-Century London." *London Journal* 5 (1979): 3–34.

Power, M. J. "East London Housing in the Seventeenth Century." Clark and Slack 237–62.

———. "London and the Control of the 'Crisis' of the 1590s." *History* 70 (1985): 371–85.

Price, George R. *Thomas Dekker*. New York: Twayne, 1969.

Rappaport, Steve. *Worlds within Worlds: Structures of Life in Sixteenth Century London*. Cambridge: Cambridge UP, 1989.

Relihan, Constance L. "The Narrative Strategies of Greene's Cony-Catching Pamphlets." *Cahiers Elisabethains: Late Medieval and Renaissance Studies* 37 (1990): 9–15.

Reynolds, Bryan. *Becoming Criminal: Transversal Performance and Cultural Dissidence in Early Modern England*. Baltimore: Johns Hopkins UP, 2002.

Rid, Samuel. *The Art of Juggling or Legerdemain*. 1612. *Rogues, Vagabonds, and Sturdy Beggars*. Ed. Arthur F. Kinney. Amherst: U of Massachusetts P, 1990. 265–91.

———. *Martin Markall*. 1610. Judges 383–422.

Robin, Gerald D. "The Executioner: His Place in English Society." *British Journal of Sociology* 15.3 (1964): 243–53.

Sacks, David Harris. "London's Dominion: The Metropolis, the Market Economy, and the State." Orlin, *Material London* 20–54.

Salgãdo, Gãmini. *The Elizabethan Underworld*. Stroud: Sutton, 1977. Reprint, 1992.

———, ed. *Cony-Catchers and Bawdy Baskets: An Anthology of Elizabethan Low Life*. Harmondsworth: Penguin, 1972.

Sennet, Richard. *Flesh and Stone: The Body and the City in Western Civilization*. London: Faber and Faber, 1994.

Sharpe, J. A. *Crime in Early Modern England, 1550–1750*. Harlow: Longman, 1984. Reprint, 1999.

Shaw, Phillip. "The Position of Thomas Dekker in Jacobean Prison Literature." *PMLA* 62 (1947): 366–91.

Sinfield, Alan. "*Poetaster*, the Author, and the Perils of Cultural Production." Orlin, *Material London* 75–89.

Slack, Paul. *Poverty and Policy in Tudor and Stuart England*. London: Longman, 1988. Reprint, 1993.

————. "Vagrants and Vagrancy in England, 1598–1664." *Economic History Review* 27 (1974): 360–79.

Spraggs, Gillian Mary. "Rogues and Vagabonds in English Literature, 1552–1642." Ph.D. diss., Cambridge University, 1980.

Taylor, Barry. *Vagrant Writing: Social and Semiotic Disorders in the English Renaissance.* Hemel Hempstead: Harvester Wheatsheaf, 1991.

Thomas, Phillip V. "The Elizabethan Privy Council and Soldiers at York in a Time of War: Deserters, Vagrants, and Crippled Ex-Servicemen." *York Historian* 13 (1996): 15–24.

————. "Rogues and Vagabonds in Elizabethan York." *York Historian* 16 (1999): 16–31.

Twyning, John. *London Dispossessed: Literature and Social Space in the Early Modern City.* Basingstoke: Macmillan, 1998.

Walker, Gilbert. *A Manifest Detection of Dice-Play.* 1552. Salgãdo 27–58.

Ward, Joseph P. *Metropolitan Communities: Trade Guilds, Identity, and Change in Early Modern London.* Stanford: Stanford UP, 1997.

Wells, Susan. "Jacobean City Comedy and the Ideology of the City." *English Literary History* 48 (1981): 37–60.

Wirth, Louis. "Urbanism as a Way of Life." *American Journal of Sociology* 44 (1938): 1–24.

Woodbridge, Linda. "Impostors, Monsters, and Spies: What Rogue Literature Can Tell Us about Early Modern Subjectivity." *Interactive Early Modern Literary Studies Dialogues* 4 (1999): 1–11. http://purl.oclc .org/emls/iemls/dialogues/01/woodbridge .html. Accessed October 10, 2000.

————. *Vagrancy, Homelessness, and English Renaissance Literature.* Urbana: U of Illinois P, 2001.

Magic Books

Cony-Catching and the Romance
of Early Modern London

Hee that cannot dissemble cannot liue.

—*The Defence of Cony-Catching*

Thus we sat both amorous of other: I lasiuously, & he honestly.

—*Conversion of an English Courtesan*

The transformation of London from late medieval town to early modern metropolis gave rise to a crisis in cultural legibility, as citizens tried to read changing urban institutions through existing social conventions. In the cultural sphere, this crisis animated the literary forms that Lawrence Manley has called "techniques of settlement," including city comedy, verse satire, and urban pamphlets (297–99).[1] The tradition of rogue pamphlets, as it evolved from the pastoral complaint of Robert Copland's *Highway to the Spital-House* (1535) to the urban exposés that followed Gilbert Walker's *Manifest Detection of Dice-Play* (1552), was an important part of this settlement literature. A large part of Robert Greene's contribution to this tradition in his six cony-catching pamphlets (1591–92) was to complete the urbanization and localization of the rogue: Greene's cony-catchers live, learn, and work in London.[2] What is most surprising about Greene's rogue pamphlets, however, is not their basically traditional use of materials from Walker and Harman, but the literary form into which Greene assimilated this material: prose romance.[3] Greene's pamphlets address the threats represented by "these pestilent vipers of the commonwealth" (10:9) who cheat poor apprentices at cards, but they also contain these vipers within a forgiving plot structure. Greene's stories of cony-catchers serve as "magic books" for London's citizen-readers, initiating them into the new languages of urban culture and making the city seem manageable if viewed through the lens of romance.

When I call Greene's cony-catching texts romances, this generic term refers broadly to the immense category of loss-wandering-recovery tales from Homer's *Odyssey* forward, and also to the Elizabethan fictions of Lodge, Greene, Sidney, and others. The first epigraph of this essay, "Hee that cannot dissemble cannot liue" (Greene 11:51) captures the central feature of romance that Greene's texts exploit: romance makes deceptive practices morally safe. As Greene inherited the genre from Greek romance, medieval hagiography, the Boccaccian *novella,* and the *Odyssey,* among other sources, romance rehabilitates deceptive tactics and purges them of malice.[4] The shrewdness with which Penelope keeps the suitors at bay, the clever delaying tactics of the wandering heroine of Heliodorus's *Aethiopian History,* the witty manipulations that characterize *The Decameron* from the story of the false saint Ciappelletto (1.1) to that of Patient Griselda (10.10): these literary mainstays of the tradition of romance stand behind the tricks played by and on Greene's cony-catchers. Cony-catchers are predatory heroes, and thus more like Odysseus (and his grandfather Autolycus) than Penelope, but their tendency to deceive those around them does not depart from but exaggerates one of romance's core tropes. Like traditional romances, Greene's cony-catching tales contain tactical dissembling within a moral superstructure: the greediest characters often end up most injured, whether those figures are conies whose desire to win at cards makes them fall for the Barnard's Law or overly aggressive cony-catchers who are fleeced by rivals or clever citizens.[5] This ethical overlay aligns these tales with a genre that by the Elizabethan era had become very sophisticated, as readers of the romances of Sidney, Spenser, and Shakespeare know.[6] Greene's cony-catching pamphlets use the structure of romance to give readers access to urban indirection while shielding them from its moral stain.

For Greene's readers, London's dangers thus become part of the predictable wandering phase of literary romance, which is always followed by recovery. In other words, the city's dangers become formulaic and part of a new stable order. Investigating the reading of the cony-catching pamphlets means uncovering the possible of strategic uses of behaviors presented as criminal. Roger Chartier has observed that early modern popular texts worked through the "recurrence of extremely coded forms" (14), and I believe this to be so true in Greene's case that his tales of thief-filled London could be recognized by his readers as following the wandering-recovery pattern of Elizabethan romance. In this generic frame, danger must be followed by rescue, even if the rescue seems long in arriving or merely fortuitous when it comes.

This deep generic coding allows threatening events and hostile characters to both expose and reconfigure social anxiety. These pamphlets teach individuals that the city is a dangerous place and also that it is possible to live there if one reads the right books.[7]

Rereading the Rogue

Greene's pamphlets self-consciously address many of the diverse groups who swelled the ranks of literate Londoners at the end of the sixteenth century; the title page of his first cony-catching volume, *A Notable Discouery of Coosnage* (1591), claims to be written for "all Gentlemen, Citizens, Aprentises, Countrey Farmers, and yeomen" (10:3). Greene further claims that writing these books represents his own personal transformation; wanton romances like *Pandosto* (1588) and *Menaphon* (1589) now give way to works that honor his civic duty. Greene's title page Latin tag registers his purported change of heart: he no longer advertises his work with the pleasure-seeking "Omne tulit punctum qui miscuit utile dulce" [He who mixes pleasure and usefulness wins every prize] but rather the patriotic slogan, "Nascimur pro patria" [We are born for our country].[8] Despite Greene's claims of moral and literary transformation, however, his rogue pamphlets rewrite the thief-filled city in literary terms familiar to readers of his previous works. His own professional dissembling, which insists that the cony-catching pamphlets are new and different, parallels his broader repackaging of tactics of deception in fiction and urban life. In Greene's cony-catching pamphlets, informed strategic deception makes the frightening city a somewhat more hospitable place.

Linking the rogue pamphlets to the discourses surrounding early modern urbanization has proved a popular and productive critical gambit, as essays by Adam Hansen and Karen Helfand Bix in this volume demonstrate.[9] By adding to this mix an examination of Greene's manipulation of the popular genre of prose romance, I intend to show that while the rogue and the city may have tended to erode existing social structures, the emergence of popular literary culture provided authors and readers with ways of processing this anxiety-producing material. Romance, which Fredric Jameson has influentially called "an imaginary solution to . . . [a] real contradiction," serves as a device to reduce this anxiety (118). New material that seemed to threaten social stability is presented as part of the wandering phase of romance, so that, to the extent that early modern readers brought their generic expectations with them when reading, they could rest assured that their anxieties would be soothed in the end.

Craig Dionne and I argue in our introduction to this volume that the early modern rogue serves as a catchall symbol of deviant and acceptable forms of social mobility. The city of London, as numerous critics have emphasized, provided a capacious symbolic home for this new mobility and social instability. This essay's particular contribution to the investigation of the urban rogue is the suggestion that, in part because of its roots in traditional culture, the genre of romance brought these two phenomena together. Romance, especially in the hands of a practiced master like Greene, thrives on defusing social and personal anxieties, since it treats even the most radical forms of mobility as alternative routes home.[10] Greene's texts, however, should not be thought of as merely rewriting a nostalgic vision of stable culture; rather, they treat the instability and mobility of city life as a means to discover (or invent) a new kind of stability. The narrative format that popular romance provides for urban culture contains danger and anxiety within a reassuring frame. Through the lens of fiction masquerading as fact (these distinctions were only emerging in late-sixteenth-century culture, but Greene emphasizes the status of his work as factual), a romance narrative about the world of cony-catching, with its competitive "laws" and cozening tricks, can serve as a primer in ways of surviving in the city.[11] With Greene's books in hand, London citizens could counteract the threat of the cony-catchers with an urban self-education.

The fictional nature of the self-help message in Greene's books places his cony-catching pamphlets in slightly unfamiliar company, alongside the embryonic culture of literary fiction typified by the works of Lyly, Gascoigne, Barnabe Rich, Lodge, and above all the "King of the Paper Stage," Greene himself. Placing Greene's texts in the context of popular literature and the history of published fiction departs from one popular critical method within rogue studies, which uses these texts as cultural documents to investigate large-scale historical and social conditions. The subtitle of Adam Hansen's essay in this volume, "Rogues, Writing, and the Early Modern Urban Environment," describes a major critical project in this cultural-studies-inflected mode, the reconstruction of the early modern city as what Lawrence Manley has called "the largest and most widely experienced human creation in Britain" (1). By contrast, my subject is less the city as a whole entity than the (necessarily conjectural) local experiences of early modern citizens reading the rogue pamphlets. Like most critics interested of the "history of reading," I am aware that most acts of reading leave no historical traces, and my assumptions about the "imagined reader" of Greene's pamphlets may be open to question. I recognize that my claims for the consequences of reading a given set of texts risk flattening out heterogeneous individual acts of reading, but Greene, perhaps more than any other author of Elizabethan prose fiction, actively shaped his audience's reception of his books. This shaping process, which presupposes the reader's awareness of generic norms, provides valuable evidence for how Greene's texts seem designed to have been read.[12]

My basic claims for the impact of Greene's books on his readers—that they are romances, and that that they can be read as tactical instruction manuals for urban life—modify two standard approaches to the rogue pamphlets. Responses to these texts have generally followed one of two main lines: either the rogue pamphlets are genuinely subversive, dangerous revelations from a threatening underworld, or their potentially subversive force gets contained according to the familiar model espoused by Stephen Greenblatt in the 1980s.[13] The moral ambiguity of the cony-catcher, whose ethics are demonized but whose social acumen is celebrated, however, remains problematic for both these critical approaches: if the texts are subversive, then the cony-catcher appears too conventional in his social tactics, and if they are morally doctrinaire, then he seems too sympathetic. I propose a different model of the effect of reading these pamphlets, in which the social anxiety produced by London's voracious underworld gets balanced not by Greenblatt's global "affirmation of order" (52), but by the education of individual readers through the accommodation of urban experience to fictional form. In an important sense, Greene's pamphlets make mini-Don Quixotes out of his readers, who will be guided in their urban adventures by what they have read. This transformation makes them practical city dwellers, not insane knights-errant. They do not tilt at windmills in a world full of giants and enchanters, but rather expose cardsharps in a city filled with thieves and con men. Unlike Don Quixote, Greene's readers lived in an environment that they rightly (not madly) believed was threatening, and reimagining their experiences through the lens of fiction may have helped them learn to live in an unfamiliar place. The result is that cony-catchers are still threatening, but Greene's readers (and only Greene's readers) have a countercharm.

This focus on individual readers of the cony-catching pamphlets contrasts explicitly with one influential vision of the global effect of the rogue pamphlets in early modern England, that described in Greenblatt's "Invisible Bullets." As an early recognition of the cultural importance of the rogue texts, in particular Harman's *Caveat*, this essay and its subversion-containment paradigm define the early New Historicist engagement with rogue literature. Without discussing the many critical rejoinders to subversion-containment since the 1980s,[14] I return briefly to Greenblatt's essay to see how his critical formulation subtly distorts the rogue pamphlets and their likely audience by switching attention from individual readers to an imagined social totality. While Greenblatt observes that Harman's tales have "the air of a jest book"

(50), he also emphasizes that Harman's book caused society as a whole to hate rogues. In positing this hatred as the primary effect of the book on its readers, he slides uncomfortably close to the category error made by the generation of historians that preceded him, mistaking the sentiments in Harman's text for sociological facts, when the book seems better understood as to some degree fictional with a complex web of sympathies.[15] Greenblatt appears to accept that Harman's own claims of facticity, which parallel similar claims by Greene, were taken at face value by his readers. Uncritically accepting these texts as history or sociology, however, overlooks the formalized and conventional nature of Harman's and Greene's works. It is in part the generic nature of these tales, in fact, which has led more recent social historians—like A. L. Beier in this volume—to discount their value as factual histories. My analysis begins by accepting the nonhistoricity of most of the material in Greene's books, but I then argue that it is precisely their conventional nature that makes them serve a social function for nonelite readers. Greene wrote in a form his readers could recognize, and that form placed the complexities of city life in a manageable framework.

Greenblatt's key formulation claims that "printing is represented in [Harman's text] . . . as a force for social order and the detection of criminal fraud" (50–51). While I believe that there is social value produced by reading these texts, I depart from Greenblatt's notion of rogue texts as attempts to police or control deviance by demonizing the rogue.[16] These texts do not simply make their readers "hate [rogues] and approve of their ruthless betrayal" (52), but rather they offer readers habits of behavior and tactics of display that will enable them to survive in turbulent London.[17] In revising Greenblatt's formulation, the first and the third terms—"printing" and "detection of criminal fraud"—need to be modified to produce a clearer sense of how rogue texts appear designed to serve as a "force for social order." The first term, "printing," while in this case perhaps simply a metaphor for Harman's book, seems overly abstract and disembodied. Especially when dealing with self-conscious authors like Robert Greene, the source of a text's social power seems less the simple fact of print and more its appearance in a community of literary forms under the sign of an author's name.[18] In Greene's case, this socioliterary impact seems clearly related to the name on the title page. Greene was one of the stars of the Elizabethan fiction market, his books were widely read, and his titles—including *Greenes Never Too Late* and *Greenes Groatsworth of Wit*— often called attention to himself.

Greenblatt's third term, "detection of criminal fraud," underestimates what Harman's texts, and more directly Greene's, provide for their readers. These texts actively model the skills of cony-catching, and they thus make possible not just the expelling of antisocial figures, but the addition of new tactics—including deception, disguise, and secret languages—to urban life. (In fact, if carefully read, these texts would make it harder to detect fraudulent practices because these tactics would become generally available to citizens at large.) Rogue texts in the hands of a literary author like Greene are "forces for social order," but not in the top-down policing way that Greenblatt's article suggests.[19] Rather, Greene's portrait of himself as author, cony-catcher, and urban citizen helps create an alternative social order in which the criminal serves as both threat and teacher.

My insistence that the cony-catching pamphlets be read as literary productions growing out of the emerging sphere of popular print culture has notable affinities with Linda Woodbridge's recent reconsideration of the rogue pamphlets. Woodbridge follows social historians like Beier and others in rejecting the historiographical validity of the pamphlets, and she instead treats them as "mythmaking engines" (2) whose affinities lie with the tradition of jestbooks. Woodbridge argues persuasively that the cony-catcher as he appears in early modern texts throughout the sixteenth and early seventeenth centuries is more a literary than a historical character, organized by a generic rather than empirical logic. Her focus on jestbooks contrasts with my emphasis on the more self-conscious literary genre of romance, but the jestbook tradition has long-standing cultural affinities with romance.[20] Woodbridge's further claim that rogue literature, which she terms "the tabloids of the day" (3), may have "influenced statutes" (4) and helped bring about the brutal regime of the Elizabethan Poor Laws provides a thorough historicist extension of Greenblatt's notion of the rogue texts as policing agents. Turning away from these texts' possible effects on the state apparatus, however, I offer an analysis of their particular value for London readers, who were patently not destitute if they could afford to buy books. Unlike Woodbridge, I suggest that the fictional frames of many rogue tales, particularly Greene's, serve not only to dehumanize the poor (though I agree they may have done that), but also to empower potential victims and provide them with ways to reconceptualize the competitive nature of urban life.

To flesh out my notion of the cony-catching pamphlets as "magic books" that used a familiar fictional frame to acclimate early modern readers to urban life, I shall investigate two episodes within Greene's pamphlets that at first seem to oppose each other. The first, the prefatory epistle to the *Defence of Cony-Catching* (1592), takes up the notion of cony-catchers as predators who are also models who provide strategic instructions for early modern citizens. An episode in the life of Cuthbert Cony-Catcher demonstrates the surprising outcome of a series of battles between cony-catchers and citizens, when these citizens have read the appropriate sections of Greene's books. After examining this active and threatening cony-catcher, I turn to "The Conversion of an English Courtesan," which appears in Greene's fourth cony-catching volume, *A Disputation between a He Cony-Catcher and a She Cony-Catcher* (1592). This tale, which rehearses the plot of *Moll Flanders* 130 years before Defoe's novel, chronicles the transformation of an underworld prostitute into a happy citizen and wife. These two episodes provide my essay's two epigraphs: the *Defence* accents the necessity of dissembling to living in the city, and the "Conversion" reveals the fine, nearly imperceptible line between "honest" and "dishonest" behavior.

Defending Cony-Catchers

The prefatory material to Greene's *Defence* narrates one of many episodes within Greene's pamphlets in which his books protect their readers. The prefatory epistle "To All My Good Frends" (sic) is among the clearest examples of this motif, and it is also unusual because the *Defence* is alone among the six cony-catching pamphlets in being published pseudonomously, under the name "Cuthbert Cony-Catcher." The author claims to be a frustrated member of the criminal underworld who offers this volume as "Confutation of those two iniurious Pamphlets published by R. G." (11:41). (Like most modern critics, I believe that Greene wrote the *Defence* and that Cuthbert is an invention, perhaps loosely modeled on Cuthbert Burbie, who had just published Greene's *Third Part of Cony-Catching.*) The prefatory epistle indicates that Cuthbert and his cony-catching brethren believe Greene's previous pamphlets have injured them materially. The story Cuthbert relates of his search for R. G., however, reads less like an indictment than a tale of discovery, a romance in which two wanderers—Cuthbert and the reader—delve into a maw of social disruption that has two things at its center: R. G., and the city of London.

The story begins with Cuthbert, a graduate of "Whittington Colledge" (11:43), leaving London to wander in the country and practice his urban art of fleecing conies. He first meets his match in Exeter when he attempts to rob "a pesant [who could] cant the wordes of art belo[n]ging to our trade" (11:45). The peasant (actually a tanner) exposes Cuthbert because he has learned from Greene's books a pair of technical terms: "conny-catcher" and "setter." The terms preempt Cuthbert's ruse and serve as unanswerable accusations; when the peasant uses these words against him, Cuthbert becomes fixed as a criminal and exchanges his social mobility for a brief stay in jail. In case the moral is not sufficiently clear, the peasant relates that he owes his newfound power to having purchased and read Greene's books: "I haue for 3. Pence bought a little Pamphlet, that hath taught me to smoke such a couple of knaves as you be" (11:45). As Cuthbert complains, the peasant's new power and his new vocabulary ("smoke" is also a cant term) arise from "this cursed book of Conycatching" (11:45).

Cuthbert's wanderings next bring him to a Cornwall alehouse, where he encounters another set of likely conies—"halfe a doozen countrie farmars at cardes" (11:46)—and again he loses to Greene's books. By this time, the social force of reading these books has become clear. In order to defeat cony-catchers, common people need three things: Greene's books, money to buy them (the peasant's three pence), and enough basic literacy to read them. These things make ordinary readers resistant to criminal tricks. Cuthbert, watching the farmers play and looking for an opening, hears them rebuke one of their own number in the language of the underworld: "What neighbor wil you play the cony-catcher with us? no no, we have read the booke as wel as you" (11:46). Greene's books empower these farmers, and in fact they seem to have become potential cony-catchers themselves. (One wonders at the fate of any poor simpleton who has not read Greene's books who sits down at this card table.) The books appear to stand for a debased but practical extension of humanist education.

When Cuthbert finally returns to London, he discovers not a set of conies to be fleeced, but the arch-cozener himself, the author, R. G.: "At last I learned that hee was a scholler, and a Maister of Artes, and a Conny-catcher in his kinde, though not at cards" (11:47). R. G. replaces Cuthbert's intended victims and Cuthbert himself in this final scene; he is both a model of deception and a cure for deceptive practice. The three-stage journey narrated here, from an Exeter peasant's haunts to a Cornwall tavern to a London filled with both Greene and the cony-catching "crue," suggests that the city contains the heart of the problem. Dissembling is the way of life in the city, and R. G.'s books—themselves deceptive—serve as talismans against master deceivers and primers in properly deceptive conduct. Each time a reader foils a cony-catcher, the narrative draws closer to the source of the criminals' power for social disruption (the urban underworld) and the totemic figure who counteracts it (R. G.). In this way, Greene treats himself and London as complementary forces; the city fosters crime, and Greene inoculates his readers against it. The main text of Cuthbert's pamphlet links many urban figures, including lawyers, courtiers, and pamphlet-writers, to cony-catching tactics, but R. G. has already rescued the reader.

Courtesan or Citizen?

The "Conversion of an English Courtesan," by contrast, rescues a cony-catcher, or at least a protagonist who has fallen from a prosperous life into their world. This inset tale, which Greene splices into a volume that contains a competitive dialogue between a male and a female criminal arguing over who causes more damage to the commonwealth (the woman, Nan, wins the argument), presents itself as a factual addendum to this dialogue.[21] Greene notes in his epistle, "I have set downe at the end of the disputation, the wonderful life of a Curtezin, not a fiction, but a truth of one that yet liues, not now in an other forme repentant" (10:201).[22] The emphasis on the courtesan's penitence, however, gets undercut by the remaining sentences of Greene's epistle, which portray her as a cony-catcher and threat to honest citizens: "In the discourse of the whole life, you shall see how dangerous such trulls be to all estates . . . [and] therefore my labors may be a caueat to my country-men, to auoyde the companie of such cousoning Courtezins" (10:201). The doubled portrait— the courtesan is both cozener and penitent, both threatening and reformed— echoes the two faces of the rogue in the *Defence*. The courtesan resembles both Cuthbert (as a threat to the countrymen) and R. G. (as a model of repentance). Even more thoroughly than the *Defence*, the "Conversion" explores the story of a rogue's life; the "whole life" of the courtesan takes her from a prosperous home to a life of sin in London to a final redemptive marriage. This biography, with its clear roots in medieval parables and penitence tales as well as the story of the Prodigal Son, becomes in Greene's hands a masterplot for personal success.[23] The nameless courtesan, more explicitly perhaps than any other figure in the rogue pamphlets, demonstrates the close connection between rogues on the streets and citizens in their houses.

The courtesan's early life makes a familiar tale: the only daughter of prosperous country parents, she is beautiful, witty, and wanton: "I was the fairest of all, and yet not more beautifull then I was witty, insomuch that beeing a pretty Parrat, I had such quaint conceipts, and witty words in my mouth, that the neighbours said, I was too soone wise, to be long olde" (10:238). By this moment in the tale, the reader perceives that Greene is not just retelling the medieval parable of the penitent prostitute, he is also rewriting the prodigal son tales that typify the 1580s fictions produced by himself, Lyly, Gascoigne, and others. In this model, the narrator-courtesan's misuse of her good education, and her unwillingness to listen to the sage advice of her uncle, parallel a generation of prodigal writers like Greene who reject political service for fiction writing, but whose guilty conscience eventually caused them to return to moralistic writing (see Helgerson). The distinction in this case is that the courtesan's wayward life, while criticized, becomes the means by which she exchanges her country home for a new life in the city.

The courtesan in her youth displays a complex understanding of herself that helps explain the attraction of penitent figures for writers like Greene and his urban readers. After she has run away from her parents with a guitar player, then exchanged him for his friend the sonneteer, she defines a paradox at the center of her character through a pair of Euphuistic "unnatural natural history" similes: "as the Tygre though for a while shee hide her clawes, yet at last shee will reueale her crueltie, and as the Agnus Castus leafe when it lookes most drye, is then most full of moysture, so womens wantonesse is not quallified by their warinesse, not doe their charinesse for a moneth, warrant their chastitie for euer" (10:252). On the one hand these statements about female duplicity recall Greene's familiar faux-classical misogyny, but examined more closely, the tropes reveal a logic of personal concealment and transformation that enables the courtesan to reinvent herself later in the tale. To extend the implied narrative of these similes, all women must be in the process of becoming their opposites, just as all tigers will eventually reveal their cruelty and all dry cactus leaves their moisture. To the extent that she is the tiger, the courtesan's present calm (she is living in false marriage with the sonneteer in Bath) will reveal a later storm, and the apparent dryness and stability of her situation also covers her present inner turmoil. These tropes extend Greene's long-running fascination with images of female characters and also demonstrate the continuity between cony-catcher and citizen: whenever she seems most solidly on one side of this equation, she is about to shift to the other.

As the courtesan's tale grows more intricate, a series of cony-catching tricks assume prominence in the plot. Notably, the most complex and successful trick is played not by the narrator, who at this point is still more courtesan than citizen, but by her second lover, the sonneteer who stole her away from his guitar-playing friend but who then seems content to live as her "supposed husband" (10:254) in Bath. The sonneteer straddles the cony-catcher/citizen divide; he stole the courtesan away from his friend and lives with her without marriage, but also he tries to make a stable and socially acceptable life for the pair. When he notices the awakening love between the courtesan and one of his gentlemen friends, he attempts to smother it with a story. The tale, which reprises an inset tale in Gascoigne's influential fiction *The Adventures of Master F.J.* (1573), describes the reformation of an adulterous wife by her wise husband.[24] In the key moment in the inset tale, the husband "cures" his wife by treating her as a prostitute: after he discovers that she is the lover of his friend, he continues to sleep with her but gives her "certaine slips, which are counterfeyt peeces of money being brasse, & couered ouer with silver" (10:260).

When the wife realizes that the slips accuse her of being a prostitute, she is struck by contrition, rejects her adulterous behavior, and even convinces her lover to change his ways and return to his former friendship with her husband. Two things seems noteworthy about this inset tale: first, it is through the cony-catching trick of privately identifying his wife as a prostitute that the husband preserves his family's public honor and gets a loving wife back. In this way, cony-catching duplicity serves moral and civic ends. Second, and more importantly, the honest citizen apparently has access to counterfeit "slips." Given the seriousness of the crime of counterfeiting, his access implies a radical continuity between the underworld and the respectable world. This husband's trick works because of the perceived closeness between the two social worlds: prostitutes resemble counterfeit wives (as the courtesan's larger narrative will eventually show), and good husbands make good cony-catchers.

This trick converts the courtesan's current lover to a virtuous life, but it does not work on the courtesan herself. She soon finds another man, who takes her away from the Bath sonneteer and abandons her where Greene's readers must have anticipated she would eventually arrive: London. Unlike the naive citizens whom Greene describes falling victim to urban tricks in his other pamphlets, the courtesan is immediately at home in the big city: "now being brought to *London,* and left here at random, [I] was not such a housedoue while any friend staied with me, but that I had visite[d] some houses in *London,* that could harbour as honest a woman as my selfe" (10:268). The courtesan now finds her ideal place, "the hell of voluptuousnes" (10:269), and she even compares herself to Messalyna in Rome (10:269). At this point, her story parallels that of Cuthbert Cony-Catcher: both have been drawn to London as the source of sin and corruption. Unlike Cuthbert, however, she finds there not the devilish author R. G., but a "propper yoong man" (10:270) who will accomplish her final conversion.

The second epigraph of my essay comes from the description of her first encounter with this man, and it presents a peculiar version of love at first sight: "thus we sat both amorous of other, I lasciuously, & he honestly" (10:271). The mirror structure of this description points to a crucial fact about in-law and outlaw desire: they must be opposites (or else social prohibitions have no meaning), but they cannot be distinguished from each other. At this point, the virtuous husband looks with as much amorous desire as the courtesan he will redeem; there is no empirical way to distinguish honest love from lasciviousness. (Or, more threateningly, perhaps honest love *is* lascivious.) This passage presents the opposite notion to Cuthbert's "Hee that cannot dissemble cannot live": while Cuthbert suggests that the tactics of the cony-catcher are essential to early modern life, the courtesan and her future husband emphasize that social organization requires that a distinction be maintained between the out-laws and in-laws, even when that distinction seems impossible to verify.[25] Courtesans and proper young men feel the same way about each other, just as they frequent the same urban spaces. They cannot be the same, but they are.

The tactics through which this young man (a "Cloathier," and thus part of the mercantile class that often falls victim to cony-catchers in Greene's pamphlets)[26] converts his courtesan make a moral contrast with the cony-catching methods of the sonneteer's tale. He instead uses another literary genre, one to which Greene would turn increasingly during the final year of his life in 1592, the sermon.[27] The young man's sermon seems doctrinaire enough, and it recapitulates the courtesan's story in biblical terms: "oh thou art made bewtifull, faire, and well fourmed, and wilt thou then by thy filthie lust make thy bodie, which if thou bee honest, is the Temple of God, the habitation of the diuel? Consider this, and call to God for mercy, and amend thy life" (10:275). The plea for repentance departs from popular sermons like those by Arthur Dent and Henry Smith, however, by offering a tangible reward for virtuous actions: "leaue this house," the young man continues, "and I will become thy faithfull friend in all honestie, and vse thee as mine owne sister" (10:275). The proposal of sisterly affection, like the courtesan's reply that after leaving the brothel she would "hold him dear as the father that gaue me life" (10:275), serves as a smokescreen to conceal (and eventually gratify) their mutual amorous desire. As the reader expects, they are soon married, and the courtesan, like Moll Flanders, assumes a conventionally happy life.[28] Her rescue from her own depravity, however, cannot finally conceal the basic continuity between her life with cony-catchers and her life apart from them. The image of the virtuous man lusting after an immodest woman lingers to emphasize the shared space of courtesans and citizens. The courtesan's narrative may not be a perfect "how-to" story, but following Greene's admonition on the title page to "read, laugh, and learne" (10:195), it lays bare the overlap between two opposed social worlds. Greene's readers gain access to both worlds at once.

Rogues and Romance

These episodes conform to the basic plot structure of end-determined romances: the conies have been wandering, but they are saved by the magic of Greene's books. It is important at this point to recall Greene's intended audience: "all Gentlemen, Citizens, Aprentises, Countrey Farmers and yeomen," as the *Notable Discovery* has it, or "Gentlemen, Marchants, Apprentises, and Countrey Farmers" (10:197), according to the *Disputation*. We may doubt that all these readers could appreciate Greene's Latin tags and allusions to Cicero and Plato, but the inclusive gesture marks Greene's attempt to define his own readership. Greene's cony-catching pamphlets use their accessible literary structure to establish an intimate relationship with his audience: he figures himself as a man who knows the secrets of the city, and his readers as urban neophytes whom he must instruct. Repentance and personal transformation, which were recurring tropes in Greene's career, are better seen as directed performances than sincere transformations (see Barker).

The romance frame shared by the *Defence* and the "Conversion" reveals a common structure undergirding Greene's cony-catching tales. The vision of urban life that these pamphlets produce is both forgiving (because even the courtesan gets saved) and demanding (because you have to read the right books to know your way around the city). Greene had already made clear, in his first volume of cony-catching, that the cony-catcher's code of ethics was grasping, competitive, and a virtual mirror of changes in urban life. In that volume, a cony-catcher who anticipates Cuthbert defends his occupation by emphasizing the value of his particular skills: "the two ends I aime at, are gaine and ease, but by what honest gaine I may get, neuer comes within ye compasse of my thoughts. Thogh your experience in trauaile be great, yet in home matters mine be more, yea, I am sure you are not so ignorant, but you know that fewe men can liue uprightly, vnlesse hee haue some prety way, more than the world is witnes to, to helpe him withal" (10:34). The "prety ways" and "home matters" of the cony-catcher define the tactics these volumes make available to the general reader. Greene soon expands these private notions to a general mercantilized ethic of urban life, as the cony-catcher continues: "my resolution is to beat my wits, and spare not to busie my braines to saue and help me by what meanes soeuer I care not, so I may auoide the danger of the lawe" (10:35). The "wits" and "braines" of the cony-catcher model the means by which any frightened citizen may survive the "danger" of the city, and while these tactics threaten the uninitiated, they serve as models for Greene's readers.

Reading Greene's pamphlets as self-consciously literary fictions has consequences for emerging trends in rogue studies, not least of which being returning literary genre to a position of importance in a field that has productively engaged with historicist and theoretical concerns. This practice suggests the value of extending Rosalie Colie's famous dictum that "literary invention . . . in the Renaissance was largely generic" (17) from literary creation to literary consumption (i.e., from writing to reading). In this sense, all forms of early modern reading must be examined through the interplay of generic structure, which may have greater importance for exploring texts' possible impact on contemporary readers than formerly assumed. In the case of Robert Greene, treating reading practices as generically determined reveals a strategic consistency in his varied career. Foundational studies of Greene's career in prose fiction have emphasized his repeated changes of direction, from Euphuistic texts to pastoral romances to cony-catching tales to his deathbed repentance tracts.[29] My suggestion that even the cony-catching pamphlets—self-consciously announced as rejections of Greene's former "uncertaine thoughts" for a turn to "repentant deedes" (10:5)—owe their basic structure to narrative romance helps reshape the biographical conundrums that have dominated scholarship on Greene. In writing semifictional explorations of the tactics of urban living, Greene extends, rather than departs from, his work as romance writer. Connecting Greene the cony-catcher to Greene the romancer advances the project of reintegrating the rogue texts into ongoing investigations into early modern reading practices and literary culture.

In addition, connecting the cony-catching pamphlets to Greene's lifelong experiment with the form of romance helps bring the literary itself back in touch with historicist critical modes. To the extent that the rogue pamphlets seem to provide an exemplary case study in the mutual interpenetration of literary and historical discursive modes, the reading practices inscribed by Greene's pamphlets can connect these two cultural spheres. The consequences of this mutual interpenetration, in Greene's case, can be seen by placing these texts in critical juxtaposition with Fredric Jameson's already-cited definition of romance as an "imaginary solution to . . . [a] real contradiction." Reading Greene's cony-catching pamphlets as explorations of the far boundaries of early modern romance provides an alternative reading of Jameson's (ultimately Lacanian) understanding of literary form as "imaginary." In Greene's case, the perceived "solution" to an existing set of social problems comes not from urban reality but from literary history. Rather than being the space of Althusser's revolution "that never comes," the imaginary solution in Greene's work is, quite literally, fictional form.[30] But if the solution Greene's readers arrive at is practical—if these texts serve to translate the frightening chaos of city life into a more palatable form—then the theoretical pessimism implicit in the term *imaginary* may need modification.[31] The problem of the early modern city was a problem of cultural legibility, and educating readers in techniques of reading may have provided "real" solutions in local, individual cases. The two stories I have examined—R. G. and Cuthbert jousting across St. Paul's, and the transformation of a courtesan into a happy wife—benefited early modern readers by identifying a series of urban crises and proposing literary solutions. The practical question for the critical reader is less whether such solutions are "real" or "imaginary," than how they may have operated at a given cultural moment. It may not be true that readers of Greene really were less likely to fall victim to petty crimes (though that does not seem impossible), but rather they seem to have been encouraged to believe that they were, thus gaining a self-conscious understanding of urban life.

NOTES

1. Manley juxtaposes these "techniques of settlement" with another group of forms, including Tudor epic and civic ceremony, which he calls "fictions of settlement" (125–27).

2. Macdonald ("Innovative Contributions" 129) notes that Greene urbanizes the tradition of the country rogue.

3. Prose romance is, as I discuss below, Greene's favorite form, and he had been writing romances since his first published work in 1580.

4. For an exemplary and influential reading of the role of deception in Greek romance, see Winkler.

5. Below I consider two episodes from Greene's later cony-catching pamphlets as his most elaborate engagements with the form of romance, but even the first three pamphlets, which do not contain as many continuous narratives, follow a basic moral pattern in which greed gets punished. These volumes trace an evolving pattern of cony-catching activity: the first volume (*A Notable Discovery*, 1591) shows cony-catchers caught by the laws of London; the *Second Part* (1591) presents more successful thieves, some of which are caught by readers of Greene's first book; and the *Third Part* (1592) presents cony-catchers beguiling (and hence punishing) each other. Into this urban world, which is both moral and chaotic, the narrative consistency I outline below adds a reliable sense of order.

6. For an elaboration of early modern romance as a skeptical and sophisticated genre, see Mentz, "Heroine." It seems likely that Nashe's courtesan, although her name comes from Heliodorus, was modeled on the figure in Greene's *Disputation* whom I discuss below. Nashe, however, is much more cynical and ambivalent about the courtesan's repentance.

7. For a comparable example of counterintuitively empowering reading practices, in this case of modern women who find in tales of rape and male domination a fictive "escape" from their own lives, see Radway, esp. 86–118. Renaissance readers, however, read not for escape but for plans for action, as several critics have noted. See Grafton and Jardine; Hutson.

8. For a reading of Greene's career organized through his changing title page Latin tags, see Jordan.

9. In addition to Manley, on urban culture and the rogue, see Twyning; Halpern 61–102; and Orlin.

10. On the trope of mobility in urban culture and the rogue pamphlets, see Hansen in this volume, and also Manley, who sees the alternative moralities endorsed by pamphlet culture as including "an endorsement of mobility, a cultivation of bohemianism and aggressive individuality, a new sense of 'crisis' and temporality geared to the rhythms of economic exchange, and a tendency to naturalize the frightening sense of change associated with London" (20). As will become clear, my analysis of Greene's pamphlets empha-

sizes the last of Manley's alternative moralities, the "naturalizing" of London as a cultural space.

11. For a useful comparison, see Dionne's claim in this volume that the rogue pamphlets serve as "domestic handbooks" for urban life. This reading, which was made in an earlier form in an article in 1998, has been influential on my understanding of rogue literature, but my emphasis on the importance of generic form departs from Dionne's methodology somewhat.

12. The reading practices outlined below of course describe only one mainstream way of reading Greene. Such important and idiosyncratic readers as Thomas Nashe, Thomas Dekker, and William Shakespeare demonstrate other ways of using of these pamphlets.

13. These two modes are made more sophisticated and flexible by several essays in this volume, notably Dionne, Woodbridge, Fumerton, and van Elk, but the fundamental divide still exists.

14. See, for example, the essays collected in Howard and O'Connor.

15. Greenblatt reserves his investigation of complex sympathies for the portrait of Hal in Shakespeare's Henriad; in part I wish to countersuggest that Greene, and even Harman to some extent, invokes the need for "acts of calculation, intimidation, and deceit" (52–53) not in the founding of the state but the survival of the individual.

16. This notion of the rogue texts as policing objects remains powerful, and is made more sophisticated in this volume in essays by Salamon, van Elk, and Hansen, among others. The opposite (or perhaps complementary) notion that these texts serve as "handbooks" for city life can also be found in Dionne's essay in this volume.

17. Not all recent readers agree about the recuperative social force of these pamphlets. For a major recent consideration of the rogue as a leading figure for genuine social revolution, see Reynolds.

18. The tendency to treat "printing" as an abstract and independent category and social agent derives ultimately from Eisenstein's magisterial summary. For a recent reply to Eisenstein that argues that the social meanings of "print" were culturally constructed during the early modern period, see Johns.

19. Valuable distinctions must be made between a literary author like Greene and a more public and political figure like Harman, but for an argument that Greenblatt misreads Harman's social status and positions, see Beier in this volume.

20. Early modern English jestbooks and romances share common ancestors, including the Boccaccian novella, Latin story compilations, and collections like Aesop's fables.

21. Nan, in a moment that anticipates the soon-to-be published *Defence*, threatens Greene himself at the end of her disputation: "mistresse Nan this good Oratresse, hath sworne to weare a long Hamborough knife to stabbe mee" (10:236).

22. Greene does not address and may not have noticed the implication that the dialogue itself, and by extension much of the material in Greene's cony-catching books, is by contrast fictional.

23. On Greene's updating of the medieval tale, see Macdonald, "Courtesan."

24. On this story in Gascoigne, and the relationship between the Italian novella and Elizabethan romance, see Mentz, "Escaping Italy."

25. Manley has suggested that Greene's cony-catching pamphlets describe his own "movement from an in-law to an outlaw point of view" (343). As I discuss above, I see

Greene problematizing the difference between these points of view in the cony-catching texts.

26. On the relationship between cony-catchers and merchants, see Karen Helfand Bix in this volume.

27. Greene's obsession with repentance, which is notable in his career since the mid-1580s, seems consciously modeled on such best-selling repentance sermons as Arthur Dent's *Sermon of Repentance,* which went through thirty-eight separate published editions between 1582 and 1638. See McClure.

28. On the "ambivalence" of Defoe's portrait of Moll Flanders, see Tina Kuhlisch's essay in this volume.

29. For standard readings of Greene's shifting career narrative, see Jordan, and Pruvost. More recent critics like Helgerson also treat his career as a series of mutually exclusive stages.

30. On the complex question of the use of the Lacanian "imaginary" in Althusser and other historical materialist criticism, see Sprinker.

31. Jameson's suggestion that romance as a form attempts to work out the problem of how the enemy can be both "evil" and also similar to the hero (118) has further applicability for the case of cony-catchers and citizens, in which an apparent dissimilarity masks a deep continuity of experience.

WORKS CITED

Barker, W. W. "Rhetorical Romance: The 'Frivolous Toyes' of Robert Greene." *Unfolded Tales: Essays on Renaissance Romance.* Ed. George M. Logan and Gordon Tesky. Ithaca: Cornell UP, 1989. 74–97.

Chartier, Roger. *The Order of Books: Readers, Authors, and Libraries in Europe between the Fourteenth and Eighteenth Centuries.* Trans. Linda G. Cochrane. Stanford: Stanford UP, 1992.

Colie, Rosalie. *The Resources of Kind: Genre-Theory in the Renaissance.* Ed. Barbara K. Lewalski. Berkeley and Los Angeles: U of California P, 1973.

Eisenstein, Elizabeth. *The Printing Press as an Agent of Change: Communications and Cultural Transformations in Early-Modern Europe.* 2 vols. Cambridge: Cambridge UP, 1979.

Grafton, Anthony, and Lisa Jardine. "'Studied for Action': How Gabriel Harvey Read His Livy." *Past and Present* 129 (1990): 30–78.

Greenblatt, Stephen. "Invisible Bullets." *Shakespearean Negotiations: The Circulation of Social Energy in Renaissance England.* Berkeley and Los Angeles: U of California P, 1988. 21–65.

Greene, Robert. *The Complete Works in Prose and Verse of Robert Greene, MA.* Ed. Alexander B. Grosart. 14 vols. London: Huth Library, 1881–86.

Halpern, Richard. *The Poetics of Primitive Accumulation: English Renaissance Culture and the Genealogy of Capital.* Ithaca: Cornell UP, 1991.

Helgerson, Richard. *The Elizabethan Prodigal.* Berkeley and Los Angeles: U of California P, 1976.

Howard, Jean, and Marion F. O'Connor, eds. *Shakespeare Reproduced: The Text in History and Ideology*. New York: Methuen, 1987.

Hutson, Lorna. "Fortunate Travelers: Reading for the Plot in Elizabethan England." *Representations* 41 (1993): 83–103.

Jameson, Fredric. *The Political Unconscious: Narrative as a Socially Symbolic Act*. Ithaca: Cornell UP, 1981.

Johns, Adrian. *The Nature of the Book: Print and Knowledge in the Making*. Chicago: U of Chicago P, 1998.

Jordan, John Clark. *Robert Greene*. Oxford: Oxford UP, 1925.

Macdonald, Virginia. "Robert Greene's Innovative Contributions to Prose Fiction in *A Notable Discovery*." *Shakespeare Jahrbuch (Weimar)* 117 (1981): 127–37.

———. "Robert Greene's Courtesan: A Renaissance Perception of a Medieval Tale." *Zeitschrift für Anglistik und Amerikanistik* 32 (1984): 210–19.

Manley, Lawrence. *Literature and Culture in Early Modern London*. Cambridge: Cambridge UP, 1995.

McClure, Millar. *Register of Sermons Preached at Paul's Cross, 1534–1642*. Ottawa: Dovehouse Editions, 1989.

Mentz, Steven R. "The Heroine as Courtesan: Dishonesty, Romance, and the Sense of an Ending in Nashe's *The Unfortunate Traveler*." *Studies in Philology* 98 (2001): 339–58.

———. "Escaping Italy: From Novella to Romance in Lyly and Gascoigne." *Studies in Philology* 101 (spring 2004), forthcoming.

Orlin, Lena Cowen, ed., *Material London, ca. 1600*. Philadelphia: Pennsylvania UP, 2000.

Pruvost, René. *Robert Greene et ses romans: Contributions à l'histoire de la Renaissance en Angleterre*. Paris: Société d'Editions "Les Belles Lettres," 1938.

Radway, Janice. *Reading the Romance: Women, Patriarchy, and Popular Literature*. Chapel Hill: U of North Carolina P, 1984.

Reynolds, Bryan. *Becoming Criminal: Transversal Performance and Cultural Dissidence in Early Modern England*. Baltimore: Johns Hopkins UP, 2002.

Sprinker, Michael. *Imaginary Relations: Aesthetics and Ideology in the Theory of Historical Materialism*. London: Verso, 1987.

Twyning, John. *London Dispossessed*. New York: St. Martin's, 1998.

Winkler, John J. "The Mendacity of Kalasiris and the Narrative Strategy of Heliodoros's *Aithiopika*." *Yale Classical Studies* 27 (1982): 93–158.

Woodbridge, Linda. *Vagrancy, Homelessness, and English Renaissance Literary Culture*. Urbana: U of Illinois P, 2001.

PART 4

Typologies of the Rogue

Vagabond Veterans

The Roguish Company of
Martin Guerre and Henry V

From my Foggy Bottom office on the edge of federal Washington, it is a ten-minute walk—past the headquarters of the U.S. Department of State and the National Academy of Sciences—to the now twenty-year-old Vietnam Memorial, where fifty-eight thousand names of war dead are incised with riveting clarity on a charcoal gray granite wall that deepens, then narrows toward its horizon as the stream of visitors passes. Forty paces away stands the realist image of heroism requested by Vietnam veterans themselves: a larger-than-life bronze of three slowly striding frontline infantrymen, bearing the heavy accoutrements of combat. Another half hour brings the resolute walker through heavy traffic to the monumental entrance of Arlington National Cemetery, resting place for veterans of every American military campaign since the Civil War. On behalf of the nation, Washington honors in high visual rhetoric those who have put their lives at risk for the safety and freedom of their countrymen.[1]

But when I walk past the Vietnam wall, sixty yards to the southwest facing the Lincoln Memorial I also encounter two no-longer-makeshift sheds that proffer military badges, pins, and wings for sale, along with bracelets that name MIAs/POWs. Weathered men in their sixties man the booths beside a plastic-covered page reporting "1905 still missing and unaccounted for" and a handmade sign insisting "as long as one person wears his bracelet, he cannot be forgotten." And each year in Washington, on the Sunday of Memorial Day weekend when the sacral and the patriotic virtually merge, the roar of thirty thousand motorcycles parading along the Mall creates "Rolling Thunder," a living—to some, menacing—memorial of the Vietnam era. A photojournalist is sure to capture a bulky, tattooed rider in leathers straddling a Harley-Davidson, beard considerably grayed, reflective sunglasses refusing the camera's gaze. My walk, and the bikers' ride, traverse contested sites in American cultural mythology. The noble representation of former soldiers whose military service entailed great sacrifice is central to conceiving the obligations of citizenship. Since 1968 or 1970, however, that overdetermined imagery has been complicated, troubled, or subverted—depending on the observer—by the presence within the culture of the "Other" Vietnam veterans, the men who returned psychically if not physically wounded to confront allegations (and sometimes memories) of "war crimes" beyond the scope of a naturalized combat.

In the early modern culture of the sixteenth century, however, the representation of ex-soldiers and their social position was not at all ambivalent. Except for noble knights like Philip Sidney, heroic in death, who could be seen through the very different lens of a dying chivalry, former soldiers who returned from battles foreign or civil were construed as a transgressive presence on the margins of public life: tramping the roadways, sleeping rough, foraging for their daily needs by any available means, indulging in petty vice. In English the social role of the veteran was not, in fact, formally constituted. The noun *veteran* first appeared in the knightly context of long military service in Stephen Hawes's *Pastime of Pleasure* (1505) and only began to signify a shrewd, experienced person more generally in Hooker's *Laws of Ecclesiastical Polity* (1597); the adjectival sense of *veteran* as greatly experienced in military life emerged in Speed's 1611 *History of Great Britain* (*OED* 19:583). The rise of a category for long-term soldiers, that is to say, developed in the course of the century; no parallel category for veterans as former soldiers arose in early modernity. Of course the men themselves existed, performing violent tasks deemed necessary by their society, and many of them were subsequently abandoned to poverty, hunger, and disability. The noble dead were idealized: Sidney received verbal laurels equivalent to a modern mausoleum in Arlington Cemetery. But there were no monuments for the ordinary dead. Common soldiers who lacked the grace to die, moreover, existed on the periphery of society, as guilty a reminder to their fellow citizens as the MIA advocates, a source of anxiety at least as frequent as the bikers of Rolling Thunder.

An early example of the troubling cultural presence of veterans is Thomas More's *Utopia* (1515), a putative inquiry into the "correct and prudent provisions" of societies newly discovered by Amerigo Vespucci and other globe-girdlers "as patterns to correct the errors of our own cities, nations, peoples, and kingdoms" (14). *Utopia* is most often recalled for Raphael Hythlodaye's long monologue on the eponymous island civilization, but the faux ethnography is contextualized by the later-written book 1, which, in dialogic form, both presents and craftily criticizes current European social and cultural practices. The first topic of discussion problematized by Cardinal John Morton and his dinner companions is men who roam the roads living by their wits and by their sticky fingers; simultaneously, the discussants argue about the best public policies to deal with such vagrants. And the first source of destitute potential robbers that Hythlodaye cites is military veterans, particularly disabled veterans, "the many soldiers who come home crippled from foreign or domestic wars. . . . They have sacrificed their limbs for the commonwealth or the king; their disability does not allow them to practice their former trades and they are too old to learn a new one" (19). Despite the apparent sympathy of this comment, More, ventriloquizing Hythlodaye, soon grows sententious on the subject of military plunder. "Robbers are no slouches as soldiers and soldiers are not the most lethargic of thieves—so finely matched are the two callings" (20–21). Hythlodaye evinces a thorough knowledge of how vagabond rogues with no social base spend their modest money: "The brothels, the bawdy houses . . . the wine bars and alehouses, and then so many crooked games of chance, dice, cards, backgammon, don't all these quickly empty pockets and send their votaries off to rob someone?" (25). Vice, vagrancy, and petty crime, closely connected with unemployed veterans—such is one English subculture that Utopian economic policies and practices might counter. Thus ex-soldiers slip into the cautious cultural criticism of a high-minded but ambitious young undersheriff of London. The image is only a minor part of More's disquisition on economic inequality, and its shady attributes are largely accrued by association with other displaced vagabonds.[2] More's brief reference, however, adumbrates a trope of soldiers and ex-soldiers as thieves and vice-ridden social parasites that develops through the century in England and on the continent.

In this chapter I want to explore that trope as it intersects with the pamphlets on roguery published in England around midcentury and with the later rise of cony-catching pamphlets. Assuming, with Louis Montrose, "the historicity of texts and the textuality of history,"[3] I unpack the presence of ex-soldiers in some exemplary rogue texts, and I sketch the transformation of military forces and tactics that, through the course of the century, put increasing numbers of former soldiers on the road at the criminalized margins of society. In Linda Woodbridge's summary, "scholars of early modern poverty recognize demobilized . . . and often disabled . . . soldiers as a persistent, significant element of the destitute homeless" (52). Like my colleagues in the other chapters of this part, then, I am defining a particular "kind" of rogue figure based upon binary distinction from the not-rogue (or the near-rogue). Laurie Ellinghausen assesses the (narrow) gap between the false authority of "falconers"—Dekker's "thieves of Wit"—and learned writers and lawyers; Brooke Stafford reviews the easy elision of the Irish to rogues on grounds of vagabond habits and distinctive, un-English language; Tina Kuhlisch depicts the shocking description, in Moll Flanders's own voice, of a fallen woman's attempt to clamber to financial success by a criminal ladder—a not-quite-picaro, a *femina oeconomica*. Thus we follow Woodbridge's insight into the emergence of rogue literature as a form of "Othering" by the entrepreneurial and law-abiding. Ex-soldiers, fake writers, Irish tinkers, and ambitious women all surely existed and raised bourgeois anxieties in early modern England; to varying degrees, however, my colleagues contest—with Beier, Fumerton, and Dionne—the existence of a recognizable, structured rogue subculture outside the texts that scapegoat vagrants. In 1704, after all, Defoe was, although not transparently, writing fiction.

In these chapters exploring the processes and inscriptions through which threatening cultural and economic figures are "rogued," in Ellinghausen's words we "point to the similarities in their situations and activities more than their differences" (295). For my part, after a look at the official treatment of men in the military, I turn to the mid-sixteenth-century narrative of Martin Guerre and to the late-century dramatization of the French campaign of Henry V, in order to tease out the representation of vagabond veterans within cultural texts that imply larger meanings about the place of warfare in early modern life. Veterans-as-rogues, after their wars are over, are key to understanding the apparently marvelous imposture of Martin Guerre; rogues-as-veteran-soldiers, set against the relics of medieval militarism, are central to Shakespeare's figuration of the British army in *Henry V*. Because the nexus between veterans and vagabonds has been little noticed, my inquiry employs basic elements of new historical analysis.[4]

Early modern soldiers, I suggest, are depicted as quintessentially male bodies: their physical aggression in combat—or at minimum, the threat of such aggression—defines them. Prominent among likely outcomes of their violent way of life is the mutilation in combat that leads to disabled bodies, which challenge social structures in additional ways. As powerful male bodies trained for aggression, soldiers bear a latent sexuality that can be unleashed as a weapon or channeled into acceptable expression; other carnal excesses, such as drunkenness and gluttony, seem naturally to follow. And early modern soldiers are, specifically, commodified bodies, coined as the means of exchange in geopolitical conflicts in which they have little or no influence or interest. What becomes of these dragon's teeth once the battles are over and their violent bodies are no longer useful: that social problem is the site—on the road—where veterans meet rogues, whether thieves or confidence men. They share the status of "masterless men" owing obedience to no lord or officer, moving through ungoverned space, free of any social control but a court system based on locality of residence, whether parish, hamlet, shire, wapentake, city, or town corporate.[5] To reach back to anthropologist Victor Turner's term, vagrants and ex-soldiers are alike liminal figures, who are

> neither here nor there; they are betwixt and between the positions assigned and arrayed by law, custom, convention, and ceremonial. . . . Their ambiguous and indeterminate attributes are expressed by a rich variety of symbols. . . . Thus liminality is frequently likened to death, . . . to invisibility, to darkness, . . . to the wilderness. As liminal beings they have no status, property, insignia, secular clothing indicating rank or role, position in a kinship system.[6]

Early modern soldiers specifically, once released from siege or battlefield with no further orders, were located between the ordered worlds of military camp and home place, between violent action and uncertain reintegration. In an era before consistent military uniforms, they could be identified largely by their recent association with killing and death.

The primary challenge of all the vagabonds in this unbounded space—challenging to them and to the structured cultures they passed through—was of course economic; their propertyless, masterless, and tradeless condition made their subsistence a daily problem and threatened a society already under transformative pressures like inflation. Together, they made up "reserve armies of the unemployed"—the soldiers, literally so. As More's Hythlodaye demonstrates early in the century, cultural representation of these men turns on their financial desire, coupled with ordered society's fear of their lawless demands: rogues will steal laundry from hedges, cozeners beguile bumpkins of their market takings, demobilized soldiers renege on their debts, limbless veterans rob with menaces. Some soldiers, with a worldly experience that transcends the body, may even steal the bourgeois skill of literacy and exploit its near-magical properties to forge social credentials for use in economic transactions. As ex-soldiers are assimilated to rogues, moreover, the capacity to falsify bodily identity—to fake wounds, to impersonate soldiers—enters the repertoire of minor crimes and misdemeanors. In the trope of soldiers as rogues, from More onward these transgressors of bourgeois financial security are also ascribed with less venal, more personal disorders: gambling, sexual irregularity, self-indulgence of every sort. As Greenblatt says of a parallel context, their reputation offers "an almost embarrassingly clinical delineation of the Freudian id" (*Learning* 232). Vice is added to crime; social deviance amplifies economic marginality.

Such a construction animates the presence of military veterans in the popular pamphlets first collected in 1973 by Arthur Kinney in *Rogues, Vagabonds, and Sturdy Beggars*. Kinney's title is paraphrased from the numerous parliamentary statutes, promulgated from at least 1578 to 1598, that aimed at comprehensive regulation of the poor; the repetition, and the enormous scope, of these statutes justifies Kinney's claim for vagabondage as "the most pressing social problem of the Tudor years of England" (11). As a group the cony-catching pamphlets take multiple forms (from catalog to brief narrative to protodrama), describe multiple shrewd means of stealing resources from the weak or naive, and speak in multiple, sometimes ambiguous tones ranging between scandalized (but often unconvincing) moralism and salacious glee over a clever caper. A sneaking admiration seems sometimes to be extended to the risks that rogues take and to the free play of impulse that their liminality allows. Although the texts' ostensible purpose is usually to warn the law-abiding and the law-enforcing, their variousness—and their great commercial success—testifies to the complexity of the "social problem" and its reception.

Veterans of war and their war wounds play a consistent, though elusive role in the community of rogues and cony-catchers that these texts imagine; I want now to unpack the qualities of vagrant soldiers, from impersonation to lechery. One subgenre of pamphlets, begun by John Awdeley's *The Fraternity of Vagabonds* (1561) and vastly amplified in Thomas Harman's *Caveat for Common Cursitors* (1566), provides a taxonomy of the rogues and beggars divided into categories of roles and modi operandi, each with a linguistically intriguing name. (The classification, with its insistence on naming, is itself an attempt to exert intellectual control over these unruly bodies.)[7] This carnivalesque social order has a rough-and-ready hierarchy of its own. With the authority of a 1531 statute of Henry VIII, the "Ruffler" is "placed as the worthiest of this unruly rabblement" (Kinney 115). Awdeley starkly states:

> A Ruffler goeth with a weapon to seek service, saying he hath been a Servitor in the wars, and beggeth for his relief. But his chiefest trade is to rob poor wayfaring men and market women. (Kinney 92)

The transformation from armed common soldier to highwayman robbing with menace seems straightforward. Harman, however, builds upon that slippery "saying" and complicates the figure: "Either he hath served in the wars, or else he hath been a serving-man" who, tired of upright labor, "doth choose him this idle life." With the smooth tongue that marks the confidence man, the Ruffler asks for charity so

> ruefully and lamentably, that it would make a flinty heart to relent and pity his miserable estate, how he hath been maimed and bruised in the wars, and peradventure some will show you some outward wound, which he [actually] got at some drunken fray. (Kinney 92)[8]

Begging based on false claims of military service—selected, no doubt, because they are effective with an audience, whether fearful or sympathetic—arouses Harman's rather ambivalent indignation:

> For be well assured that the [genuine] hardiest soldiers be either slain or maimed, . . . [or] they escape all hazards, and return home again. If they be without relief of their friends, they will surely desperately rob and steal, and either shortly be hanged or miserably die in prison. For they be so much ashamed and disdain to beg or ask charity, that rather they will as desperately fight for to live and maintain themselves as manfully, and valiantly, [as] they ventured themselves in the Prince's quarrel. (Kinney 115)

Good soldiers apparently succeed or die trying. No genuine unlucky veteran would stoop to begging (or accepting welfare); he would rather die or, by stealing, enter a higher rank of vagabond than mere beggars. Rufflers are thus one of the many forms of fakers in the company of rogues whose word cannot be trusted.[9] Harman suggests that true soldiers thrust into desperate straits, whom a harsh law will surely punish, are more to be pitied than censured. Less true-hearted soldiers become vagrant Rufflers.

The potential for leadership of veterans is greater, however, than mere priority of place in a text that simply echoes the categories of Henry's royal statute. As Harman concludes his description, "These rufflers, after a year or two at the farthest, become upright men, unless they be prevented by twined hemp." Far from being reformed to virtue as an alternative to hanging, "an Upright Man," in Awdeley's stern warning,

> is one that goeth with the truncheon of a staff. . . . This man is of so much authority that meeting with any of his profession he may call them to account, and command a share or "snap" unto himself of all that they have gained by their trade in one month. And if he do them wrong, they have no

remedy against him, no, though he beat them, as he useth commonly to do. He may also command any of their women, which they call "Doxies," to serve his turn. He hath the chief place at any market walk and other assemblies, and is not of any to be controlled. (Kinney 92)

This godfather among rogues, with his skimming of profits and claiming of women, *may* claim his authority from military experience, thus carnivalizing by imitation the captaincy of a typical sixteenth-century military company. His "great authority" extends, Harman adds, to licensing other men "to the Rogue, and . . . to cant; that is to ask or to beg for thy living in all places" (Kinney 119). If rogues were indeed forming companies with bivouac-like hideaways—an unlikely organization that Harman dates to 1521 (Kinney 111)—veteran sergeants accustomed to giving orders might be natural leaders.

The role of leader among vagrant beggars and armed highwaymen is not quite the only site of veterans in the taxonomic pamphlets. When Awdeley turns from vagabond rogues to urban "cozeners and shifters" who live by their wits, the first figure who "walketh about the back lanes in London in the daytime . . . and maketh humble salutations and low curtsey" to well-dressed, honest citizens is the "Courtesy Man," readily recognizable as the confidence man of modernity; his capers elicit a similar ambiguous amusement in the sternest of the sixteenth-century observers. This hustler attempts to make common cause with his prey as "wealthily brought up" and held "in good estimation," but the core of his patter is the now-familiar claim to be "lately come from the wars, . . . have nothing to take to, . . . and [know] no way whereby to earn one penny" (Kinney 94). When refusing a proffer of small change, he reproaches the donor on behalf of "such a company of Servitors as we have been" who can reasonably expect more.[10] (Again, a good soldier has a justified pride.) No other element in Awdeley's sketch of the Courtesy Man—the most detailed in his crisp catalog—suggests any truth in the claim of veteran status. The clever cozener simply fakes identity as a soldier in order to win credence and a larger reward. From Awdeley's summary description of these performers, which presents them as "without any weapon," "bear[ing merely] the port of right good gentlemen," and sneaking out of hostelries with unpaid bills and stolen sheets, it seems clear that their military bearing is just a clever imposture.[11] Such cozeners parody the image of a George Gascoigne, a Fulke Greville, a Philip Sidney: gentlemen veterans of campaigns in the Low Countries.

Those few instances—three rogue figures among the twenty-five male types cataloged in the two pamphlets—comprise the total explicit presence of veterans in Kinney's varied collection; as I have noted, moreover, truth-claims about that presence in Awdeley's and Harman's texts are rather insecure. But several other elements of the scandalous behavior ascribed to vagrant beggars are connected, however marginally, to old soldiers. Gambling is the primary deceitful practice of the cony-catchers in the pamphlets, and in his *Notable Discovery of Coʒenage* (1591) Robert Greene (misappropriating Herodotus) locates the origins of card and dice playing in the practices of the Lacedaemonians at the ancient siege of Thebes, when the defenders "beguil[ed] hunger with the new sports, . . . eating but every third day and *playing* two," until the siege was lifted and the city saved from sack (Kinney 164). Last among these liminal connections between vagrant and veteran, the pamphlets that focus on rural vagabonds take a prurient interest in their constant sexuality, a license made possible by the uncontrolled women (generically "doxies") loosed on the highways. Harman assimilates lechery to the ex-military in "Walking Morts," unmarried women who present themselves as widows whose "husbands died either at Newhaven [Le Havre], Ireland, or in some service of the Prince"; although lying, such women at least try to earn a legitimate income. His example of a Mort—that fake military widow—is the key figure in a lengthy anecdote from 1566 that meanders into a classic "bed trick" that ostensibly rebukes, yet abundantly displays, a knowing carnality all around. The desires of male military bodies, then, are expressed in the uncontrolled female bodies that dead soldiers leave behind (Kinney 138).[12] (By contrast, that later wandering woman Moll Flanders, ever on the economic make [see Kuhlisch 349], only seeks upward alliances with "gentlemen," whether ship captains, Virginia planters, customs-house officers—or her prize cony, a baronet. An army officer appears in Defoe's text only as the seducer who cuckolds Moll's banker.)

The fugitive attribution to veterans of theft, menace, lying, and vice in the rogue pamphlets, I will now suggest, both mirrors and interprets much cultural experience in the sixteenth century; that sense of recognition does much to explain their popularity. In an era of near-constant warfare somewhere in Italy, the Hapsburg lands, France, the Low Countries, or England, every spring and summer some men would inevitably be "gone for soldiers." And any ordinary citizen might encounter men leaving battlefields behind, alone or in small groups without military discipline, in a thousand straggling journeys of the defeated or in victorious returns to native places or *pays,* foraging from the land and local inhabitants. Civilians could reasonably assume that veteran soldiers had the capacity and quite probably the experience not only to rob but, if challenged or angered, to kill without compunction, drawing upon recent legitimized empowerment.[13] Ordinary people had no means to regulate their passage or confine their energies, and the hardened veterans themselves had little reason to regulate their energies or confine their desires. Moreover, the challenge inherent in military and ex-military bodies was growing. It is not only the emerging printing industry in the 1550s and 1560s that nurtured the rogue pamphlets, with their edgy images of veteran leaders: England's continental allies and opponents had been drawn into long wars driven by territorial ambition and religious difference, and soldiers were recruited everywhere. And the new surge of cony-catching pamphlets in the 1590s, with their bold claimants to war experience, followed the demobilization of the militias raised to defend against the Spanish Armada or to support the Dutch revolt, many of them—like masses of ex-soldiers across Europe—loathe to return to farm or workshop.[14]

Military practices of the early modern era help to explain why writers could so readily constitute veterans as vagrant thieves; in fact and in theory, slender attention was given to the future of disbanded soldiers. Across western Europe in the sixteenth century, the nature of warfare and of military forces was transformed, a change in which the adoption of gunpowder (from cannon to harquebus to musket) played, at least initially, a relatively small part.[15] In 1955, Michael Roberts first conceptualized a "military revolution"; ever since, historians have conducted a lively debate about its causes, its character, and its timing. But the outlines of change—thanks to J. P. Hale, Geoffrey Parker, and Jeremy Black, among others—are clear.[16] By 1510 the medieval military organization founded on heavily armored, mounted knights with a feudal obligation to respond to their sovereign's periodic summons, accompanied by foot soldiers/retainers similarly obligated to them, was in its twilight. Following the success of the Swiss mercenary force in Burgundy in the fifteenth century, which was widely publicized in Machiavelli's *Art of War*, such heavy cavalry gave way to dominance by infantry forces. These foot companies were composed of massed pikemen, initially still accompanied by bowmen (whose proportions, especially in England, declined only slowly), but over time increasingly surrounded by musketeers.[17] At approximately the same time, the new bastion—a squat platform projecting from a town's walls with cannon focused in multiple directions—dramatically improved defensive fortifications. As a result, the typical military action went from intense pitched battle to long-sustained siege, with slow mining—and starvation—as principal tactics. In Parker's words, "innovations in European military organization and military practice made victory on land increasingly difficult to achieve. Above all, it became almost impossible to win a land war *quickly*" (*Army* 5).

The broad trend to long campaigns and defensive tactics called for more men under arms over longer periods of time, and armies almost certainly grew much larger between 1520 and 1620. Henry VIII's entire standing force in 1513, for instance, consisted of a three-hundred- to six-hundred-yeoman personal bodyguard, a cadre of gentlemen-at-arms and their supporters of about two hundred, and the garrisons of some one hundred castles and fortresses, totaling less than 3,000.[18] Until the 1530s it is unlikely that any European army could muster 30,000 effectives; within fifty years, the Hapsburg forces, admittedly the largest, numbered 100,000 to 150,000 (Parker *Army* 6). The changed tactics of sixteenth-century warfare required more men, but men with no particular social standing and very little training: *cannon fodder* is an accurate contemporary term.

The powers that sought to wage war (not yet, at the beginning of the period, nation-states) faced a set of interrelated problems: how to recruit large numbers of soldiers in the absence of feudal compulsion, how to provision and pay them, how to keep them in service. The eventual solution to these problems would be standing armies of long-term professional soldiers funded by centralized fiscal powers, but such forces were not regularly achieved in the sixteenth century. Thus each new campaign could require the enlistment of new soldiers, almost all of them expendable infantrymen. The core military unit was a company, random-sized at the beginning of the century, led by a captain. Commonly, captains independently recruited men, under a commission from a prince determined on war, or on an entrepreneurial contract with such a prince. The latter version constituted the mercenary companies (less desirable because less centrally controllable) that were denigrated by theorists of every sort, but steadily employed.[19] The empowered captain and his drummers appeared at public sites and offered the able-bodied (who had to be masterless, not suborned peasants or retainers of a local lord) the chance to enlist in a foreign war for such enticements as shoes and a suit of clothes, or a modest but immediate sum of money—or, in bad economic times, for no signing bonus. Since the temporary company was formed for a particular campaign, soldiers were enlisted for its duration, whether three months or three years. While companies of gentlemen—some aspiring to command or to political careers—were also recruited, it is obvious that the poor and the desperate were the most likely candidates to sign on.

Given the relentless need for manpower in Italy, in the Low Countries, and—for England—in Ireland after the middle of the century, incentives to volunteer sometimes failed. Increasingly, sovereigns in England and in Spain mustered local militias both urban and rural, their regiments nominally led by a local gentleman-colonel, for service far beyond the civil defense of their regions.[20] While the goal was to find trainable volunteers of good character as well as physical strength and agility, eventually outright impressments occurred; in times of need, apparently, rogues might be turned into soldiers. In 1574, captain and military theorist Barnabe Rich despaired, when occasion is offered of service: then for the most part order is given either to the officers of every Parish, to take up roges, or masterless men, or inhabitants of prisons, such as if they had their deserts, they were to be sent rather to ye gallowes . . . or if a greater number must be taken; to the officers in the Countrey, . . . then to disburthen ye Parish of rogues, loiterers, pikars, & drunkards, and such as no other way can live. (Breight 186)

The enforced enlistment of vagrants and convicts (or simply those charged with misdemeanors) was officially ordered in England in 1559 and 1585 (Kinney 23). Sir John Smythe, author of the controversial *Certain Discourses Military* (1590) denied that it happened often. Only officers who need to explain massive losses, he asserted, unashamedly claimed that "the very scum, thieves, and rogues of England . . . have been very well lost; and the realm, being too full of people, is well rid of them, and that if they had not been consumed in those ward they would have died under a hedge" (25). In fact, he assured his readers (probably protesting too much),

Saving such as were levied in the city of London by commission, and some few rogues in one year in other shires, . . . they were in a very great part young gentlemen, and in a far greater part of yeomen and yeomen's sons, and the rest of the bravest sort of artificers and other lusty young men, desirous . . . to adventure themselves. (26)

Given the many opportunities for the well-to-do and the well connected to evade enlistment, no doubt impressments of criminals, as well as the destitute, sometimes occurred.

Once at the front, soldiers could expect the harsh privations and dangers of military life, in Cervantes's terms "the cold of the sentry-go, the danger of the assaults, the horror of the battles, the hunger of the sieges, the destruction of the mines" (Parker *Army* 185).[21] And crowded encampments made epidemic infection a constant possibility; Brooke Stafford's notion of the linguistic "translation" of the Irish to roguery is evidenced by soldiers' disdainful nomination of dysentery, that excremental malady, as "the Irish disease" (Gruber von Arni 6). Conditions of military service almost inevitably turned some soldiers into scroungers. Commanders at the end of a long logistical tail were often unable to provide basic needs: in 1588 Lord Admiral Howard decried that, even within England, "I am driven my self of force to come aland to see [the troops] bestowed in some logeinge and the beste I can get is barnes and suche oute houses and the releefe is small that I can provide for them here" (Breight 177). Little surprise, then, that garrisons between action, "bored, impoverished but well-armed young men inevitably formed a pool of lawlessness, of gambling and vice, crime and cruelty, lechery and licence in the centre of every community" (Parker *Army* 180). In 1548 the great commander and author of the age's most-quoted text on the arts of war, Raymond de Beccarie de Pavie, baron de Fourquevaux, indignantly ascribed all such bad behavior to bad captains who do not instill and maintain necessary discipline (*Warres* 53); the length and elaboration of his discussion of military justice, in the field and in camp, subverts his fervor.

Moreover, soldiers could not expect regular paydays; while their daily wages were calculated, except for mercenaries normally no payments were made until the war ended. In the interim soldiers maintained accounts with the army's sutlers (entrepreneurial provisioners) or coerced credit from local merchants in order to supply food beyond the army's minimal dole and other ordinary needs. When commanders finally settled with surviving soldiers at a war's conclusion, accumulated wages might occasionally enrich them, but the funds for full payment were often unavailable; while 75 percent payment was probably typical, as little as 30 percent might be granted, and costs for maintenance (whether or not food had been provided) might be deducted.[22] If a soldier had not already deserted from the miseries of maintaining a siege and the dangers of occasional fighting, he had every reason to decamp without settling his debts and every temptation to forage, scavenge, and outright pillage as he went. The construction of vagabond veterans in the rogue pamphlets is based on such experiences.

Given the circumstances of military service, it is not surprising that discussion of "veterans" in the term's modern senses is rare, whether in sixteenth-century texts or in recent historical analyses of the military transformation. The potential value of retaining ex-soldiers who had been through the wars was slow to catch on.[23] Of course mercenary captains and the skeleton forces they maintained between engagements were experienced; by the mid-1560s, in the Low Countries on both sides "contractors who provided troops in a war were often rewarded with a state pension after demobilization which was taken, at least by the government, to mean that the contractor would raise troops again whenever need arose" (Parker *Army* 38). In Spain's endless campaigns, even foot soldiers became veterans, for mercenary contractors' most fertile recruiting ground was a disbanding army, whose discharged laborers— if returning home was unappealing or uneconomic—simply signed on with new leaders (Hall 227–28). From the rising average age of soldiers by the 1590s, historians have deduced that military life had gradually become a career option for a small but growing group (Parker *Army* 36–37; Hale *War* 229). In France, Fourquevaux, farsighted in most military matters, urged at midcentury the advantage of maintaining a regional "national guard" that practiced monthly, rather than dismissing French forces after every campaign or (his bête noire) depending on mercenaries. In England, during Elizabeth's reign experienced men were increasingly retained by local militia colonels—although not without controversy—to train raw recruits (Boynton 98–100, 105–7). As late as 1593, the first serious English military theorist, Matthew Sutcliffe, championing the place of manual laborers and shopkeepers in an army, still had to argue that "of al others the old souldier, if such may be had, of what trade soever he is, deserveth the first place" (Breight 188). Almost all such elusive comments—written, of course, by officers—are concerned with the objective advantage of veterans to a commander; few consider the practiced soldier as subject or agent with his own perspectives on fighting. In general, the ordinary foot soldier is presented as little more than the vehicle to transport a weapon to the front line, direct it at the enemy, and utilize it; he is a body like a cavalry horse, albeit a less valuable commodity. Early modern soldiers, most illiterate, wrote no letters home, kept no battlefield diaries; unlike the American Vietnam veterans who contested an official memorial, they had no voice in the representation of their own experience.

A few contemporary texts show humanitarian concern for common soldiers, perhaps the last vestige of the noblesse oblige of previous centuries; the "normal duty of an officer to his troops" was low except in the locally raised militias, where officers commanded their tenants and neighbors paternalistically (Boynton 104). Smythe, for example, assured his readers that all good commanders "win the love of their soldiers by taking great care of their healths and safeties, . . . accounting of them in sickness and health or wounds received as of their own children" (19). But he admitted that some Low Countries commanders, "upon any accidents of sickness or wounds received . . . disesteemed [the soldiers] as base and vile, never coming amongst them neither in sickness nor health but only upon occasion of service" (19). Still more uncommon is any attention to the fate of the demobilized soldier, once given his wages and dismissed—the long-term, often disabled "vet."[24] At the end of a three-hundred-page treatise, Fourquevaux gives a few paragraphs to "recompense" along Roman lines, including distinctive garments, jewelry, the ."freedoms" of the realm, grants of property in conquered towns, even partial exemption from taxes; he notes particularly that "those that have been maymed of their limmes in the king his servicce, should be put into garrisons & be kept there," maintained like other inactive troops (*Warres* 301). Like Fourquevaux, the occasional English exception—such as a minor provision in a 1537 draft act of Parliament that the larger of the remaining monasteries might be used as old soldiers' homes (Cruikshank 193)—seems primarily intended to serve policy considerations. Thus military hospitals, initiated for English campaigns in 1600 after disastrous experiences of typhus and dysentery in France and Ireland, were proposed as cheaper alternatives to continuous replacement with new recruits (Gruber von Arni 1–7).[25] In the early modern era, the notion that a commander or a state might have any long-term responsibility for former soldiers, able-bodied or disabled, was anachronistic. As discharged employees they were simply turned loose on the road home, under statutory constraint not to linger. If not petty criminals when recruited, after the experiences of privation and lawlessness, underpayment and abandonment in foreign places, many "other ranks" became the rogues of the cony-catching pamphlets.

The confluence of veterans and vagrants, both in pamphlets and in historical accounts, also comes to light in sixteenth-century high-canonical representations. In the remainder of this chapter I want to explore the impact of the rogue-soldier trope on the popular sensation of Martin Guerre and on Shakespeare's bellicose *Henry V*. Both texts focus on male bodies, driven by financial gain and experienced in combat that can result in mutilation or death.[26] The hard conditions of their violent occupation are joined to roguish characteristics that enhance a soldier's liminality: high-risk behavior and petty gambling, criminal impersonation and confidence tricks, theft of property from innocent civilians, and sexual manipulation. The unsettled, unsettling bodies of veterans darken each text; their similarities may be greater than their differences.

As a thick description of the experience of one individual ex-soldier, I interrogate first the "real life" case of Martin Guerre. The story was initially published by the local magistrate, Jean de Coras, who passed judgment on the confidence trickster, and later canonically memorialized by Michel de Montaigne. In "Of Cripples" (*Des boyteux*, also translated as "Of the Lame," in 1585–88), Montaigne provides a sidelong glance at one peasant recruit, returned to southwestern France following a shadowy period of vagabondage living by his wits or by his luck at gambling. The mysterious veteran, a hole in Montaigne's text, has been elegantly explicated by Natalie Zemon Davis's *The Return of Martin Guerre* (1983) and Daniel Vigne's film (1982) of the same name. The ex-soldiers in the case are permanently home from their war: Spain's defense of its Flemish territory against French attack in the 1550s. As the story has been brought to full light by Davis, the apparent protagonist of the story settles down successfully; profiting from the skills and cunning learned on the road, he uses his cozening abilities and the credulity of simple villagers for sexual conquest and further enrichment. An air of transgression, of unspoken experiences, clings to his roaming life and to his end. The details of his status as veteran are something to be hidden: from the peasants within the narrative who might penetrate his story and, apparently, from superficial readers of Montaigne. Although the narrative is as grounded in fact as legal testimony can guarantee, it is nevertheless cast by Montaigne as ambiguous:

> In my youth, I read about the trial of a strange case, which Corras, a counselor of Toulouse, had printed, about two men who impersonate one another. I remember (and I remember nothing else) that he seemed to me, in describing the imposture of the man he judged guilty, to make it so marvelous and so far surpassing our knowledge and his own, who was judge, that I found much rashness in the sentence that had condemned a man to be hanged. (788)

The successful performer as husband and economic worker was, most evidence suggests, false and deeply thieving. But to Montaigne the executed man may or may not have been who he claimed, may or may not have been guilty, may or may not have had marvelous powers of memory or impersonation. The entire affair, "so far surpassing our knowledge," creates in Montaigne an epistemological uneasiness.

The representation of ex-soldiers as rogues inflects every important moment in the case. As Davis reports the facts, in 1548 the young peasant Martin Guerre—thanks to his Basque origins, already a semioutsider in Languedoc—suddenly abandoned his wife and his father's farm in the hamlet of Artigat. Eight and twelve years later, two successive claimants to Guerre's identity returned to Artigat from campaigns in Flanders and Picardy; early in the film Vigne represents the first of these veterans happily in his cups, full of tales about his adventures on the byways and his encounters with strange, hybrid figures.[27] Despite the discursive and sexual charm of the first/false Martin, he is engaged in a confidence trick aimed at predation: acquiring a family's property, and a woman's trust. His imposture is first potentiated by the exchange of personal information—data that seem uncanny, almost magical to the villagers—that he presumably acquired among soldiers encamped in small groups, forming the bonds of camaraderie that should cement them as a fighting force (Parker *Army* 177–78). The false "Martin" (in reality Arnaud duTilh, called "Pansette") betrays that bond, donning another identity as he dons his hose; the experience of one soldier, it appears, is much like another's so long as he can tell a convincing story and work hard on the land. Individual personality is as slippery as names. A major part of the betrayal, moreover, is Pansette's roguish willingness to bed another veteran's wife illicitly, to their mutual pleasure in Vigne's representation. *Pansette*—from "belly"—suggests sensual appetites, and duTilh was known from his early days for his generally dissolute behavior (Davis *Return* 37). In fact, he exemplifies the military recruit who was already a thoroughgoing rogue, hastily leaving his bad conduct behind when he enlists.

The talk of veterans also brings about the exposure of the confidence trick (at least as efficient cause, for the final cause is Pansette's own greed and sloth.) Another vagrant group of war-returnees, passing through the hamlet, recognizes Pansette—marked in Vigne's version by his passion for gambling and dicing—as clearly as Eurykleia recognizes Ulysses. Finally, the genuine Martin who dramatically arrives on the scene is not only a veteran but an embittered amputee on wooden leg and crutches, the consequence of war wounds.[28] In the orthogonal way that Montaigne uses his titles, Martin's military disability provides a material signifier for the place of this incident in an essay on the lame; nameless in Montaigne's text, he is effectively defined by his prosthesis. In Vigne's film, the wooden leg also offers an ironic visual coda to the only physical evidence against Pansette-as-Martin: the wooden foot-mould of the real Martin, retained by Artigat's shoemaker, is too large to serve for the imposter's new shoes. And the wounded veteran, although almost certainly the genuine husband and citizen, receives the colder welcome.

Within the narrative of two contesting ex-soldiers, the striking questions about the case (as Davis reads magistrate Coras reading the evidence) are less means than motive: why Martin Guerre left his home as a fugitive, stealing a modest amount of his father's resources, and why his wife Bertrande accepted an imposter to his identity. Davis suggests that Martin felt constrained in Artigat and that the soldierly life was a natural lure for the restless of the time and place: "There were the bands and legions of Francois I, being raised in Languedoc as elsewhere, . . . 'adventurers' among whom the Gascons loomed so large" (*Return* 22, 37). As deeper motivations emerge in historical texts and on film, the true Martin is exposed as a "false" husband who is mocked by the rural culture, in a carnivalesque charivari that borders on violence, as impotent and perhaps not even attracted to women.[29] On this account, Martin had good reason to abandon the surveillance of a suffocating community for life on the road—and Bertrande might well accept as her "true" lover and partner the clever, cheerful Pansette, a man's man and returned prodigal, apparently reformed. Vigne dramatizes as Arnaud duTilh's best defense, when accused of impersonation and thus theft, the testimony of Bertrande that confirms the identity of "Martin" through details of sexual intimacy both verbal and physical. The dangers and pleasures of sexuality, for a veteran who seizes his chances and a woman whose moral sense is questioned, become a powerful subtext in the tale of crime and punishment. At duTilh's appellate trial, despite audaciously calling the real Martin a "newcomer, evildoer, rascal" who has been bribed, the rascal was again convicted of "imposture and false supposition of name and person," in the category of crimes including fraud, perjury, and counterfeiting (Davis, *Return* 84, 86, 146n). Pansette's status as veteran made his confidence trick plausible; his intertwined status as rogue ultimately defeated him. Like hundreds of vagrants across Europe (perhaps in greatest numbers in England), he was hanged and his body burned, his extinction healing the social rupture he had caused.

One further element embedded in Vigne's film connects veterans with the discourse of roguery: the power of literacy. The 1561 account by Jean de Coras styles the Guerre story *prodigieuse* in part for the amazing success of Pansette's ability to "remember" copious details of village life supposedly more than eight years old—the skill of an oral culture. There was no schoolmaster in Artigat; its inhabitants employed notaries, they rarely signed contracts with their names, and few could write—or even read—French (Davis *Return* 15, 71, 137n). But the filmic Pansette, on the road in France and the *pays bas*, has learned to write. He transmits to Bertrande the marvelous gift of signature, and her demonstration that she can use it, rather than a forge-able *X*, is a triumphant moment in his defense. Unlike honest men, with their cosmopolitan talents rogues can write their own passes through the world.[30] At the peasant level, Pansette prefigures Dekker's "falconer" with his "mystification of writing," and he illustrates the reciprocal of Ellinghausen's deduction that "criminality assists in legitimating the social status of the 'deserving pen'" (see 296 in this collection). The power of the pen can legitimate a petty criminal.

The imposture of a vagabond veteran and the criminal judgment of his case lead Montaigne into larger, epistemological questions. When one steps back from the historical case of Martin Guerre to "Of Cripples" as a whole, one sees ironies on the surface of the text linked to aspects of the Guerre case that Montaigne has left suppressed. Immediately after alluding to it, for instance, he takes a turn toward witchcraft, noting how gullible people are about claims of magical phenomena, and musing skeptically on their probability; in the Guerre story, meanwhile, bewitchment or possession is the explanation given for the young husband's impotence, which a sadomasochistic exorcism briefly "cures." And near the essay's end, Montaigne turns even more sharply to analysis of a so-called ancient proverb that intercourse with a crippled person is especially pleasurable.[31] Sardonically, he provides two physiologically graphic reasons why this effect—like the erotic charms of women weavers—might be true; the two explanations appear to contradict each other. The invisible intertext of the Guerre story as Coras tells it, however, illustrates the falsity of the proverb: intercourse with the lame veteran is what

Bertrande least desires. In the complete essay, all these elements are woven into a meditation on the strong drive of the human mind to explain and hence to subdue the world, indeed on the social construction not so much of knowledge as of persuasive disinformation.

Why does Montaigne choose ex-soldiers as a subtle example of socially driven credulousness? As every reader of the *Essays* knows, the religious wars that he witnessed in midcentury France sickened him about the moral choices of "civilized men."

> There is nothing on which men are commonly more intent than on making a way for their own opinions. Where the ordinary means fail us, we add command, force, fire, and the sword. . . . To kill men, we should have sharp and luminous evidence; and our life is too real and essential to vouch for these supernatural and fantastic accidents [attributed to witchcraft]. (786, 789)

Obsessive, stubborn belief in one's convictions is the principal cause of violent disagreement. It is soldiers who are the agents of terrible wars over mere opinion, and—as "Of Cripples," like "Of Cannibals," slyly illustrates—society suffers from their experience in unplanned as well as predictable ways. Men go to war over ludicrous notions, when only compelling facts should allow legalized murder. For death is permanent, and, Montaigne quietly concludes, no man should be killed juridically while doubt persists. The confidence trickster and ex-soldier Arnaud duTilh, who had hypnotized the Languedoc hamlet into his vision of reality, was uneasily executed. But in the end of this harsh story, both Martin Guerres are thoroughly marginalized, both "disabled" from their cultural norms.

Finally, Shakespeare's *Henry V* is, despite its claims to historicity, an imagined text in which the trope of vagabond veterans fully enters literary culture.[32] Whereas "Martin Guerre" emerges from the road into a settled community, for the most part Shakespeare represents the company of men on the move: in the period prior to a campaign, during the ups and downs of its course, and immediately after its successful conclusion. The community at issue in *Henry V* is the entire realm of England; in the course of the play many of its economic practices, from acquiring land by conquest through war profiteering to small-scale theft, are called into question. Shakespeare depicts an array of the social classes and character types who go to war: lords loyal and traitorous; grizzled captains drawn from England's Celtic margins; common soldiers, some of them honest men and some rogue-entrepreneurs. As Breight has noticed, in the course of the Henriad Shakespeare gradually increases focus on lower-class characters (206–7). In *Henry V*, the most fully realized soldiers are the petty criminals, but they are a liminal presence even in this heterogeneous army. Within the play's text they are active practitioners of the military arts of eluding battle while plundering private property; they are not loosed on the civilian world until the play's end. But as veterans of past campaigns, they floridly display the familiar traits of rogues: ready anger, gambling, tavern- and brothel-haunting. Many of the military themes sounded in the play—the stresses of marching through hostile territory and Harry's nighttime encouragement of his troops, among others—can be found in sixteenth-century military manuals or the fifteenth-century chronicle *Gesta Henrici Quinti,* putatively written by King Henry's chaplain, who was present in the rear at Agincourt (Prestwich 1); the rogues are Shakespeare's originals.

Reprised from the *Henry IV* plays but now without Falstaff, Bardolph and Pistol sorely miss fat Jack's intelligence and insouciance; lacking the comic rogue who has rationalized their (mis)behavior, they are reduced to the signature traits of minor vice and petty crime. As the play opens Ensign Pistol is at daggers drawn with Nim over his brothel-keeper wife, and his irascible temper explodes; sack remains red-nosed Bardolph's reward of choice; the three gamble and renege on their debts (2.3.24, 34–37, 2.1.85–86, 95–96, 103–4). They form a band of brothers only through a truce to their arguments, and only for financial ends—the key to their representation. "For I shall sutler be / Unto the camp," proclaims Pistol, "and profits will accrue. . . . Let us to France, like horseleeches, my boys, / To suck, to suck, the very blood to suck" (2.2.100–102; 2.3.46–47).[33] He admonishes his wife to mind the home front in similar petty bourgeois terms that are far from patriotic: "Look to my chattels and my movables. / . . . The word is 'Pitch and pay' / Trust none, for oaths are straws, men's faiths are wafer-cakes" (2.3.40–42). Cynicism, greed, and self-protection form Pistol's entire outlook on life.

The level of military zeal of the unholy trio is exhibited at their first appearance by Nim, a new member of the gang, whose name is sixteenth-century slang for "thief" (Maus 1465). "I dare not fight," he says, "but I will wink and hold out mine iron [pike]" (2.1.4–5). Once they arrive in France, despite King Henry's urging into the breach at Harfleur and Bardolph's briefly excited echo, all courage or ambition fails them. Nim remonstrates that "the knocks are too hot, and for mine own part I have not a case of lives" (3.2.2–3), Pistol wishes himself back in a London alehouse (3.2.12–15), and all lay down their arms. No doubt they would willingly fulfill the king's threat to the governor of Harfleur that "the fleshed soldier, rough and hard of heart / . . . shall range / With conscience wide as hell, mowing like grass / Your fresh fair virgins" (3.3.88–91), but that is the only aspect of a soldier's vocation they seem ready to perform. The nameless page who once served Falstaff, now reduced to accompanying his recruits, understands these men exactly:

> Three such antics do not amount to a man. For Bardolph, he is white livered and red-faced—by the means whereof a f'aces it out, but fights not. For Pistol, he hath a killing tongue and a quiet sword—by the means whereof a breaks words, and keeps whole weapons. For Nim, he hath heard that men of few words are the best men, and therefore he scorns to say his prayers, lest a should be thought a coward. But his few words are matched with as few good deeds—for a never broke a man's head but his own, and that was against a post, when he was drunk. (3.2.29–39)

Each is duplicitous, falsely seeming to be one thing when he is in fact another. The false front is a soldier of minimal competence who can fight, break heads, and kill with swords as well as tongues; the reality is a drunken coward, either dumb or overvoluble, whose principal activity is theft. "They will steal anything, and call it 'purchase.' Bardolph stole a lute case, bore it twelve leagues, and sold it for three halfpence. Nim and Bardolph are sworn brothers in filching, and in Calais they stole a fire shovel" (3.2.39–42). Techniques of theft, moreover, include suggestively intimate robbing of the body. The page worries, "They would have me as familiar with men's pockets as their gloves or their handkerchiefs—which makes much against my manhood, if I should take from another's pocket to put into mine" (3.2.39–47). The Scots captain Gower even has a shrewd grasp of Pistol's long-term motives: "'tis . . . a rogue, that now and then goes to the wars, to grace himself at his return into London under the form of a soldier"—an Upright Man-to-be (3.6.63–65).

The lack of true manly courage in Pistol, Bardolph, and Nim contrasts with Henry's ambitious image for the character of his troops. He might as well be addressing the little band and their incentives when on St. Crispin's Day he scornfully suggests the ejection from "we happy few" of such mercenary weaklings.

> Proclaim it presently through my host
> That he which hath no stomach to this fight,
> Let him depart. His passport shall be made
> And crowns for convoy put into his purse.
> We would not die in that man's company
> That fears his fellowship to die with us.

> (3.3.34–39)

(Such sponsored passage home was statutorily defined as public policy for veterans in Tudor England, but not always supplied; here Henry shows more generosity—at least in verbal performance—than many soldiers actually experienced.) The king certainly is speaking about Bardolph, who has looted a sacred object from a church, when he issues a policy statement about looting and plunder that, without a second thought, condemns the drunken thief to hang:

> We would have all such offenders so cut off, and we here give express charge that in our marches through the country there be nothing compelled from the villages, nothing taken but paid for. . . . For when lenity and cruelty play for a kingdom, the gentler gamester is the soonest winner.
> (3.6.98–103)

His recognition of the havoc caused by invading armies is somewhat undercut by the metaphor of a great gamble.[34]

The post-Falstaffian rogues around Pistol, however, are far from the only veteran soldiers in *Henry V.* England's army retains some of the medieval character of a band of independent knights or *gens d'armes,* surrounded by foot soldiers. The distinction between aristocratic officers and common soldiers is clear in Henry's motivational speech before Harfleur in which true nobles carry the blood of warrior-ancestors and act as role models while yeomen, many of them "mean and base," are merely bodies bred like horses or greyhounds for the fight. But the image of chivalry has already been scarred by the willingness of some nobles—the silken traitors Grey, Cambridge, and Scrope, the last Harry's trusted confidant—to take bribes to betray him. Their mercenary motives incense him into entrapping them:

> Thou that . . . knew'st the very bottom of my soul,
> That almost mightst ha' coined me into gold,
> Wouldst thou ha' practised on me for thy use:
> . . . And from [the enemy's] coffers
> Received the golden earnest of our death,
> Wherein you would have sold your king to slaughter, . . .
> And his whole kingdom into desolation.
>
> (2.2.93–96, 162–69)

What they have attempted, as Harry sees it, is precisely the exchange of gold for his "coined" body, both commercial trafficking in human life and a confidence trick at the highest level. Counterfeiting as well, these three "English monsters" (2.2.82) (not freaks from beyond the borders) have presented themselves as "dutiful," "grave and learned," "spare in diet, / Free from gross passion, or of mirth or anger, / Constant in spirit, not swerving in the blood" (2.2.128–32)—qualities exactly opposite to those enacted by Bardolph, Nim, and Pistol. But, as much imposters as the rogue trio, they are not the dedicated soldiers that they seem. The parallel is emphasized when this potent scene of confrontation is framed by two scenes in the tavern where the common soldiers plan their war-profiteering; it will recur when Henry resolutely deals to Bardolph the same sentence of death without mercy as he accords the three knights. Any soldier, of any class, can betray calling or country for financial benefits.

In the course of the play Shakespeare offers another, quite different image of financial gain through warfare: the medieval practice of ransom. In chivalric ideology, ransom permits aristocrats who are taken prisoner to purchase their liberty from their counterparts/cousins on the other side, ostensibly because they have fought honorably in a cause they deem just. To pay ransom, of course, noble landowners must use the resources they have gained in large part from the sweat of their vassals; meanwhile, common soldiers in similar situations must die or, if they survive and escape, limp home alone. In *Henry V*, French king Charles VI broaches the concept in the play's second taunting of Henry, before Agincourt.

> Bid him therefore consider of his ransom, which must proportion the losses we have borne, the subjects we have lost, the disgrace we have digested. . . . For our losses, his exchequer is too poor; . . . and for our disgrace, his own person kneeling at our feet but a weak and worthless satisfaction. (3.6.113–19)

To the condescension in this assumption of French victory, Henry responds to Charles's herald with a personal commitment to combat. "Go, therefore, tell thy master here I am; / My ransom is this frail and worthless trunk" (3.6.139–40)—and he tosses the herald an insulting *pourboire* "for thy labour." Harry's defiance relies solely on the worth of his own body. His stark answer, glancing at the retrograde character of ransom as institutionalized practice, suggests that the highwayman's cry of "Your money or your life" is simply a criminalized version of that practice. At the highest levels, warfare can pay off.

The critique of class-bound ransom continues in the traditional nocturne in which the king doffs crown and sword to perform a benign imposture as a regular officer, scattering "a little touch of Harry in the night." As Taunton notes, there are both "doublenesses" and the power of surveillance behind his attempt "to be both affable and secret, to inform only as much as it takes to lull his men's apprehensions whilst giving nothing away of his own projects" (66). In his morale-building exercise Harry strikes up conversation with three more soldiers—Court, Bates, Williams—who are, evidently, the honest counterparts of the thieving triumvirate. Stoic and loyal men, they nonetheless aver that, had the king come to France alone on his quarrel, "[he] should . . . be sure to be ransomed, and a many poor men's lives saved" (4.1.116–17). Nobles save their skins or fill their coffers; poor men die. After a discussion of the high costs of battle for ordinary men, Harry truthfully volunteers, "I myself heard the king say he would not be ransomed" (4.1.177–78). The skeptical Williams sees his verbal gesture as mere rhetoric that cannot, after all, be monitored by dead men. When Williams later responds to the king's revelation of his true identity with an aggrieved, "You appeared to me but as a common man," he is paid off with a handful of crowns and the captain's shilling (4.3.57–58). Although Harry's noble ransom remains imaginary, he pays for bruising the Welshman's dignity.

The commodification of bodies through ransom turns to parody when Pistol, mistaken by a defeated French soldier for a gentleman, opportunistically accepts the imposture and claims a valuable prisoner: "thou diest, on point of fox, / Except, O Seigneur, thou do give to me / Egregious ransom" (4.4.9–11). To the threat of immediate throat-cutting the gravely courteous Frenchman—translated by the perceptive page—offers two hundred ecus; Pistol, in return to his original, mercenary purpose for coming to France, agrees: "As I suck blood, I will some mercy show" (4.4.57). But he may, in the next scene, betray his prisoner's bargain by cutting his throat; this atrocity represents probably the only French soldier that he kills. While Henry gives Williams a handful of crowns on the final battlefield, Pistol must accept a measly groat—and eat a leek. And the end of the play, for Pistol, is bad news from the home front: "News have I that my Nell is dead / I'th'spital of a malady of France / And there my rendezvous is quite cut off" (5.1.72–74). The resultant change in plans for his demobilization has, to anyone who knows the trope of rogue soldiers, an air of inevitability.

> Well, bawd I'll turn,
> And something lean to cutpurse of quick hand.
> To England will I steal, and there I'll steal.
> And patches will I get unto these cudgeled scar
> And swear I got them in the Gallia wars.
>
> (5.1.76–80)

His wife lost to venereal disease, he has become a vagrant veteran, ready as any palliard to pimp and to con all comers with his "war wounds."

In a play driven by desire for acquisition of property, power, and long-term inheritance—"crowns imperial, crowns, and coronets" (2.0.10)—Pistol's liminal gang represents only the most visible rapacity of this army.[35] The economic incentives of noble warriors, not different in spirit from pillage and plunder, run deeper than the bribery and ransom offered to English lords by the wily French. Henry's entire campaign, after all, is a high-risk venture to seize the French king's lands based on a sophistical justification that he attains by holding church property up for a form of ransom (1.1.76–90). Before the campaign actually begins, moreover, "th'ambassador from the French comes back, / Tells Harry that the King [of France] doth offer him / Catherine his daughter, and with her, to dowry, / Some petty and unprofitable dukedoms" (3.0.28–31). While the negotiation reflects the wisdom of Charles VI and his constable in respecting Henry's capacities (as the callow Dauphin does not), the offer is transparently a bribe, indeed almost tribute or "protection" to persuade Henry to take some profits and run. And the offer includes another commodified body, an available woman (like Bertrande de Rols) for a shrewd ex-soldier to take—this one, a princess who is only tangentially connected to the casus belli. Although the deal originally proposed falls through, the French are not dissuaded from their calculating approach. Observing the debilitation caused by the long English march across Picardy with no replenishment, the French, as complacent over their fine cavalry as their rich vineyards (3.5, 3.7), make a fatal misjudgment. As the prologue tells the audience, "The confident and overlusty French / Do the low-rated English play at dice" (4.0.18–22). The stakes in this gamble are not just a woman's body but a whole realm. Henry, who might as easily have lost, wins it all—including the traditional spoils. The fertile garden that is France has been laid waste. When Henry insists that Charles now "must buy that peace / With full accord to all our just demands," the "capital demand" is Catherine: a fertile woman expected to produce the heir that will secure title to France as well as England into the future. Harry's language shows that he also expects sexual pleasure from his "soldier-breeder"; he steals the kiss that she, as *indigne serviteur* (cognate to a contemporary English term for soldier), cannot prevent (5.2.70–71, 96, 171–72, 186–87, 193).

At play's end, the soldier-king has won a victory, a queen, and (at least for a time) a country, while the veteran rogues, exemplified by his outgrown boon companion Pistol, have returned to theft and vice. The future for his campaign's loyal veterans has concerned Henry only in his exhortation on the eve of Agincourt; what he imagines for them is annual admiration, an image of heroic glory in the minds of generations yet unborn—in effect, a living memorial. Their bodies, wounded, dead, or alive, are dismissed.[36] I have been suggesting that early modern culture found ex-soldiers, in fact or in uneasy consciousness, more difficult to dismiss. Absorbing them into the "pressing social problem" of beggars and other economically dislocated people condemned them to liminality: "to invisibility, to darkness, to the wilderness." Objectified as mere bodies, hardly able to speak for themselves, at the hands of pamphlet-writers they could accrue all the undisciplined impulses of greed and opportunism, gluttony and unfettered sexuality that defined rogues and cony-catchers. Once marginalized among the vagabonds, they too could be accused of imposture and lying about their wounds—thus, for the honest men among them, losing their identity as maimed military men. Loss is sometimes complete: like hundreds of actual vagabonds, Bardolph and Pansette are executed, ostensibly for unregulated theft but also for transgressive eruptions from a violent site into a civil society that would prefer to forget them.

The texts that I have interrogated constitute larger meanings for the trope, and they point to an expanded purview for rogue studies. Montaigne implicitly asks for suspension of judgment about the conduct of rogues with blurred identities, rather than conclusions warped by credulity, fear, hegemonic ideology, or economic influences. *Henry V* explores the motives for war-making as potentially corrupt and self-aggrandizing, and the conduct of war as summoning, at every rank, both integrity and venality. Important for those who are interested in the careers of rogues and cozeners, *Henry V* suggests that after the war, all bets are off. Some names are carved in stone that will last for centuries; others remain only in personal memory, or disappear in smoke. Among veteran bodies, rogues can be found wherever the cultural critic looks.

NOTES

1. My opening move is indebted to Certeau's chapter "Walking in the City" from *The Practice of Everyday Life* (91–110), which eerily begins at the World Trade Center. For recent commentary on the Vietnam Memorial controversy, see Menand; for a black poet's evocation of the walk past the wall, see Komunyakaa 159. Though citing American monuments and experiences, I do not privilege them in any way over the memorial practices of such other nations as England, France, and (perhaps especially) Australia.

2. More's irony—culminating in the "man-eating sheep" of enclosure—uncovers callousness toward economic inequity that has created many late-medieval vagabonds. When Hythlodaye remarks, "It would be better to make some provision for their livelihood, so that no one should labor under the cruel necessity first of stealing and then of dying for it," a lawyer happy to proffer brioche to the breadless counters, "We have made provision for that. There are trades; there is farming. From them they can make a living,

as long as they do not willingly prefer to be criminals" (19–20). Through another louche speaker, More also glances at mendicant friars as a form of lazy vagabond (33–34).

3. Montrose is quoted in Greenblatt, *Learning* 15.

4. The only significant attention to soldiers among the vagrants since Kinney's initial introduction is Linda Woodbridge's wonderfully suggestive discussion of *King Lear*'s hundred knights, falsely denounced by Goneril and Regan as "riotous" and "disordered" armed retainers who threaten sedition, rather than trusted household servant/companions who know their duty. Drawing on Kelly, Woodbridge attributes such fears to events like the threat Drake's disbanded soldiers posed to London in 1589, leading to the imposition of martial law (210–12). Lear's knights support my claim for the elusive nature of veterans and ex-soldiers: they appear only once, and only one briefly speaks (1.4); other "gentlemen" sympathetic to Lear appear in 2.4 and 3.2, but almost wholly for purposes of exposition.

5. Local jurisdictions adapted from the key statute 22 Henry VIII c. 12 (1531), extensively quoted by Kinney 43–44.

6. Turner, *Ritual Process* 95. Moving away from structuralist analysis to a more processual view of society, Turner expands on a notion he draws from Arnold van Gennep, positing liminality—based on Lat. *limen,* "threshold"—as an element in the fluid development of *communitas.* In *Dramas, Fields, and Metaphors* he situates the concept in mid-twentieth-century social theory more generally (23–57). My appropriation of liminality here excludes the element of religious ritual in Turner's initial examples from the field; his extended concept, however, includes hoboes and gypsies (*Dramas* 233).

7. In the context I am using, see Turner: "By verbal and nonverbal means of classification we impose upon ourselves innumerable constraints and boundaries to keep chaos at bay, but often at the cost of failing to make discoveries and inventions: that is to say, not all instances of subversion of the normative are deviant or criminous" (*Ritual Process* vii). Compare Certeau 97–105.

8. Another category of vagabond beggar, the palliard—to Harman, "the worst and wickedest of all this beastly generation" (Kinney 125)—exhibits false sores and injuries of all sorts, including war wounds that putatively disable them from working.

9. Kinney devotes a paragraph to the role of cozeners swept into military service and to the resultant problems at demobilization. He points to "'fresh-water soldiers' . . . who had never been in service but pretended that they had; . . . the charitable found they could not tell the real veteran from the counterfeit" (23).

10. Harman (who mines Awdeley for much of his material) attributes similar disdainful refusals of small gifts to the Upright Man (Kinney 117)—another con man masquerading as a veteran.

11. The imputation of leaving unpaid bills is not without foundation in fact, albeit officers were not usually charged. Soldiers at the end of a campaign were regularly underpaid, sometimes drastically so. See 273 of this chapter.

12. See also Harman's salacious special section on "their usage in the night," as well as his description of the "Glimmerer" (Kinney 144–45; 36); and Greene's presentation of "Crossbiters" who pimp their wives (177–79).

13. It is necessary to recall that, in Jeremy Black's words "violence was endemic in early modern Europe"—the normative means of settling disputes between individuals,

groups, and countries (*Origins* 1). Black quotes Michael Howard's mordant remark that, in this period, war was "a seasonal form of hunting" (*Origins* 5).

14. See, inter alia, Fourquevaux. "When as the warres do fayle, there are few souldiers that will labour or worke againe at the occupation that they did learne in their youth: and then, if they have nothing to maintain them to live idlely, they do become robbers & skouters upon ways"—and he names names (*Warres* 302).

15. Until at least the 1590s, the noise, flashing light, and explosion of early handguns and artillery—with a shock effect that replaced the cavalry charge of late-medieval warfare—were probably more effective than the accuracy of the projectiles; Fourquevaux is clear on the relative value of harquebusiers and pikemen. See Hall; the first exception he notes is the wheel-lock pistol.

16. This major historiographical question, with ramifications as large—in the case of Parker—as state formation and the origins of empire, cannot be presented briefly. Hale provides the classic view, Parker the broadest revisionist statement; Arnold offers an especially strong summary of the debate (155–57, 235–45). A measured comparison with other, mostly earlier military transformations is provided by Prestwich (334ff.). The most successful objections to Parker's thesis, based almost wholly on technology, have been raised by Hall. Black leads a newer, more contextualized approach to military history that is helpful in cultural studies; see also Dunn.

17. Boynton notes the slow pace of change in England, as affirmed by Henry VII's and Henry VIII's "strenuous efforts to encourage archery, and the supply of warhorses, by statutory duties which the government . . . enforced with growing success" (8). Roger Ascham's advocacy for the famed English archer in the midcentury *Toxophilus* (1545) is well known; as late as 1590, Sir John Smythe offered an impassioned critique of the abolition of longbow practice in his *Certain Discourses Military*, a text that was banned as subversive—although probably for other reasons—within days of its publication. See also Fissell 41–42, in a work that provides a wealth of thoroughly documented detail.

18. Cruikshank 188–89. Shakespeare cites castle garrisons of this size in *Richard II* 2.3.53–54; the depiction of Falstaff's recruiting "food for powder" in *I Henry IV*, act 4, seems historically right, and *II Henry VI* accurately alludes to many issues in sixteenth-century warfare, including costs. The tough military justice of *Henry V* follows Machiavelli and Fourquevaux; see Taunton.

19. More, for instance, weighs in firmly on what Hale has called "the unceasing arguments over the employment of mercenaries" (*War* 69), whom Hythlodaye claims may fight no more effectively than draftees but are far more destructive (21). More's views are surprisingly consonant with Machiavelli, who names mercenaries "disunited, ambitious, without discipline, disloyal; valiant among friends, among enemies cowardly" (Di Scipio 12). For a thorough recent analysis of Erasmus's writings about war, predictably negative, see Housley, esp. 269–72. The experienced commander Fourquevaux makes convincing charges against the value of mercenaries from his opening chapter onward. A helpful modern overview is Prestwich's chapter on mercenaries.

20. Cruikshank 193–94. See Boynton's seminal study of militias in Elizabethan England.

21. Cervantes was a soldier long before he was a writer; for his representation of Don

Quixote's encounter on the road with an honest youth who has been repeatedly driven by poverty to enlist and has not profited by it, see pt. 2, chap. 24.

22. Parker *Army* 181–84, 222–23; Hall 232–33. However destitute at the beginning of a campaign, on the other hand, some soldiers substantially enriched themselves. Fourque-vaux argues for decent pay precisely to motivate soldiers to fight, rather than pillage. Some officers enriched themselves corruptly, as well: charging for soldiers' maintenance but not supplying it, keeping dead men on their rolls and retaining their pay, etc. (*Warres* 300–301).

23. In England in 1518 Sir Henry Willoughby proposed that, in simple prudence, a few effective captains and their companies be kept in readiness in periods of peace (though paid the king's wages only when called up); the scheme, like others proposed in 1537 and 1551, was not implemented (Cruikshank 191). English resistance to standing armies was particularly long-lasting; see Cruikshank 188–89 and Schwoerer's study of late-seventeenth-century antiarmy ideology.

24. Cruikshank records an early case of compassion upon the unexpected dismissal of the long-term English garrison at Tournai in 1514, when the men and their families were provided with free passage back to Dover and a year's protection from their creditors (183).

25. Military medicine on any serious scale apparently began in the civil wars, following 1642; Parliament's New Model Army responded in part to the dictates of Christian charity propounded in Matt. 25:35–36 (Gruber von Arni 3).

26. Unfortunately Patricia Cahill's promising Columbia dissertation, "'Tales of Iron War': Martial Bodies and Manly Economies in Elizabethan Culture," is not yet in print. Her second chapter concerns impressments and "drama's role in the production of a discourse of expendable men and commodified labor"; her fourth reviews three plays on lame soldiers, *A Larum for London, The History of the Trial of Chivalry*, and *Shoemakers Holiday*—the last thematically related to the case of Martin Guerre.

27. The screenplay's tales, which enchant the Artigat auditors, are drawn in part from Montaigne's "Of Cannibals." As a foot soldier, "Martin Guerre" seems to have gained no plunder but experience. Davis reports that captains in the 1557 war in Picardy, on the other hand, had managed to seize opportunities for material success: "'We collected much booty, weapons, horses, golden chains, silver, and other things,' a Spanish officer crowed in his journal" (*Return* 26).

28. Coras reports (Davis, *Return* 46) that Guerre was shot by a French harquebus. Hale notes that, despite early inaccuracy, firearms did greater damage than bows, bills, or pikes, "for they broke bones and led to the loss of limbs by gangrene" (*War* 46); survival of such a wound was a stroke of good fortune.

29. On charivari, see Davis, *Society and Culture* 97–123. After his medical demobilization, Martin Guerre was granted "a position for life as a lay brother in one of the houses of the military order of St. John of Jerusalem," an all-male world where he remained for two years before returning to Artigat (Davis *Return* 82). In "Psychoanalysis and Renaissance Culture," Greenblatt offers a psychoanalytic interpretation of Guerre's "difficulty establishing himself in his masculine self-identity" and subsequent attempt to displace his father; Greenblatt further observes that the subjective individuation of Martin Guerre— the "object" in the legal case—was inconceivable in the sixteenth century.

30. The learned Coras, citing duTilh's near-supernatural abilities, compares him positively to "the great rememberers of antiquity, such as Seneca's friend Portius Latro" (Davis 112). The more effective magic is the capacity of literate rogues to assume or parody authority; Harman cites with wonder the "Jarkman" who can "write so good and fair a hand" and "set seals for licenses and passports," counterfeiting the papers that give official right to beg and that certify the bearer legitimately homeward bound (Kinney 134).

31. Recent disability studies confirm the phenomenon of sexual fixation on disabled bodies, particularly amputees, by persons diagnosed as "devotees"; see Stoller; Dixon. For a broader discussion of Montaigne's representation of disability, see Mitchell and Snyder.

32. The only previous discussion on this subject that I have found is a brief comment (32–34) in Lane's article, which focuses on lower-class characters as the king's interlocutors in broader terms.

33. See Parker on the opportunities for profit open to sutlers, or vivandiers (*Army* 176–77); Pistol is not, however, dramatized performing the function. All quotations from Shakespeare are drawn from *The Norton Shakespeare*, ed. Greenblatt et al.

34. The remainder of my discussion joins a line of radical reassessments of Henry-as-triumphal-warrior-hero that begins at least with Ornstein. I find particularly sympathetic the concluding section of Greenblatt's "Invisible Bullets," Dollimore and Sinfield's "History and Ideology," and Patterson. Many issues in the large critical literature on *Henry V*—the alleged atrocity in the king's order to "kill the prisoners," the echoes of *Tamburlaine* (see Hawkins), the insight into Harry's aggression offered by queer theory (see Corum), the treatment of women (see Howard and Rackin; Spencer)—lie just outside the optic I have taken. A study focused on aspects of *Henry V*, among other plays, in relation to sixteenth-century military theory and practice is Taunton's *1590s Drama and Militarism;* see also Webb.

35. As an obiter dicta in her strong "Princes, Pirates, and Pigs: Criminalizing Wars of Conquest in *Henry V*," Spencer notes that, as Pistol steals away to England to steal, so has Henry stolen France and will soon steal a kiss (176–77). The theme of money and property in the play—including the "heavy reckoning" that Williams claims the king owes those who will lose legs, arms, and heads at Agincourt—is raised in Kezar's discussion (445–47) of guilt and shame over the pleasures of performing war.

36. See Baldo's assessment of the political function of collective memory in Elizabethan state-formation and of *Henry V* as illustration of "the uses of forgetting for the consolidation of national memory." Citing Gary Taylor, Baldo notes that the word *memorable* appears four times in *Henry V* and in no other play.

WORKS CITED

Arnold, Thomas. "War in Sixteenth-Century Europe." Black, *European Warfare*. 23–44.

Ascham, Roger. *Toxophilus*. In *The Whole Works*. Ed. J. A. Giles. Vol. 2. London: John Russell Smith, 1864.

Baldo, Jonathan. "Wars of Memory in Henry V." *Shakespeare Quarterly* 47 (1996): 132–59.

Beier, A. L. *Masterless Men: The Vagrancy Problem in England, 1560–1640*. London: Methuen, 1985.

Black, Jeremy. *A Military Revolution? Military Change and European Society, 1550–1800*. Basingstoke: Macmillan, 1991.

———, ed. *European Warfare, 1453–1815*. New York: St. Martin's, 1999.

———, ed. *The Origins of War in Early Modern Europe*. Edinburgh: J. Donald, 1987.

Boynton, Lindsay. *The Elizabethan Militia, 1558–1638*. London: Routledge and Kegan Paul, 1967.

Breight, Curtis. *Surveillance, Militarism, and Drama in the Elizabethan Era*. New York: St. Martin's, 1996.

Cahill, Patricia Ann. "'Tales of Terror and Iron War': Martial Bodies and Manly Economies in Elizabethan Culture." Ph.D. diss., Columbia University, 2000.

Certeau, Michel de. *The Practice of Everyday Life*. Trans. Steven Randall. Berkeley and Los Angeles: U of California P, 1984.

Corum, Richard. "Henry's Desires." *Premodern Sexualities*. Ed. Louis Fradenburg and Carla Freccero. London: Routledge, 1996. 71–97.

Cruikshank, C. G. *The Army Royal: Henry VIII's Invasion of France, 1513*. Oxford: Clarendon, 1969.

Davis, Natalie Zemon. *The Return of Martin Guerre*. Cambridge: Harvard UP, 1983.

———. *Society and Culture in Early Modern France*. Stanford: Stanford UP, 1975.

Dionne, Craig. "Playing the Cony: Anonymity in Underworld Literature." *Genre* 30 (1997): 29–50.

Di Scipio, Giuseppe C. "*De Re Militari* in Machiavelli's *Prince* and More's *Utopia*." *Moreana* 20 (1983): 11–22.

Dixon, Deborah. "An Erotic Attraction to Amputees." *Sexuality and Disability* 6 (1983): 3–19.

Dollimore, Jonathan, and Alan Sinfield, eds. *Political Shakespeare: New Essays in Cultural Materialism*. Manchester: Manchester UP, 1985.

———. "History and Ideology: The Instance of *Henry V*." *Alternative Shakespeares*. Ed. John Drakakis. London: Methuen, 1985. 206–27.

Dunn, Diana E. S., ed. *War and Society in Medieval and Early Modern Britain*. Liverpool: Liverpool UP, 2001.

Fissell, Mark. *English Warfare, 1511–1642*. London: Routledge, 2001.

Fourquevaux, Raimond de Beccarie de Pavie, Baron de. *The Instructions sur le faict de la guerre*. Ed. G. Dickinson. London: Athlone, 1954.

———. *Instructions for the Warres . . . Discoursing the Method of Militarie Discipline*. Trans. Paul Ive (attributed to Guillaume DuBellay). London, 1589. STC 7264.

Fumerton, Patricia. "London's Vagrant Economy: Making Space for 'Low' Subjectivity." *Material London, ca. 1600*. Ed. Lena Cowen Orlin. Philadelphia: U of Pennsylvania P, 2000. 206–25.

Gesta Henrici Quinti: The Deeds of Henry V. Trans. Frank Taylor and John S. Roskell. Oxford: Clarendon, 1975.

Greenblatt, Stephen J. "Invisible Bullets." Dollimore and Sinfield, *Political Shakespeare* 42–47.

———. *Learning to Curse: Essays in Early Modern Culture*. London: Routledge, 1990.

———. "Psychoanalysis and Renaissance Culture." *Literary Theory/Renaissance Texts*. Ed. Patricia Parker and David Quint. Baltimore: Johns Hopkins UP, 1986. 210–24.

Gruber von Arni, Eric. *Justice to the Maimed Soldier: Nursing, Medical Care, and Welfare for Sick and Wounded Soldiers, 1642–1660*. Aldershot: Ashgate, 2001.

Hale, J. R. *On a Tudor Parade Ground: "The Captain's Handbook" of Henry Barrett, 1562*. London: Society of Renaissance Studies, 1978.

———. *War and Society, 1450–1620*. New York: St. Martin's, 1965.

Hall, Bert S. *Weapons and Warfare in Renaissance Europe*. Baltimore: Johns Hopkins UP, 1997.

Hawkins, Sherman. "Aggression and the Project of the Histories." *Shakespeare's Personality*. Ed. Norman N. Holland, Sidney Homan, and Bernard J. Paris. Berkeley and Los Angeles: U of California P, 1989. 41–65.

Housley, Norman. *Crusading and Warfare in Medieval and Renaissance Europe*. Aldershot: Ashgate, 2001.

Howard, Jean E., and Phyllis Rackin, eds. *Engendering a Nation: A Feminist Account of Shakespeare's English Histories*. London: Routledge, 1997.

Kelly, J. Thomas. *Thorns on the Tudor Rose: Monks, Rogues, Vagabonds, and Sturdy Beggars*. Jackson: U of Mississippi P, 1977.

Kezar, Dennis. "Shakespeare's Guilt Trip in *Henry V*." *Modern Language Quarterly* 61 (2000): 431–61.

Kinney, Arthur. *Rogues, Vagabonds, and Sturdy Beggars*. Barre, Mass.: Imprint Society, 1973.

Komunyakaa, Yusef. "Facing It." *Dien Cai Dau. Neon Vernacular: New and Selected Poems*. Hanover, N.H.: UP of New England, 1994.

Lane, Robert. "'When Blood Is Their Argument': Class, Character, and History Making in Shakespeare's and Branagh's *Henry V*." *ELH* 61 (1994): 27–52.

Maus, Katharine Eisaman. Introduction. *Henry V. The Norton Shakespeare*. Ed. Stephen J. Greenblatt et al. New York: Norton, 1997. 1445–52.

Menand, Louis. "The Reluctant Memorialist." *New Yorker*, July 8, 2002, 55–65.

Mitchell, David T., and Sharon L. Snyder. *Narrative Prosthesis: Disability and the Dependencies of Discourse*. Ann Arbor: U of Michigan P, 2000.

Montaigne, Michel de. *The Complete Works*. Trans. Donald M. Frame. Stanford: Stanford UP, 1957.

Montrose, Louis. "Professing the Renaissance." *The New Historicism*. Ed. H. Aram Veeser, London: Routledge, 1989. 15–36.

More, Thomas. *Utopia*. Trans. Clarence H. Miller. New Haven: Yale UP, 2001.

Ornstein, Robert. *A Kingdom for a Stage: The Achievement of Shakespeare's History Plays*. Cambridge: Harvard UP, 1972.

Parker, Geoffrey. *The Army of Flanders and the Spanish Road, 1567–1659*. Cambridge: Cambridge UP, 1972.

———. *The Military Revolution: Military Innovation and the Rise of the West, 1500–1800*. Cambridge: Cambridge UP, 1988.

————. "Afterword: In Defence of the Military Revolution." *The Military Revolution*. 2d ed. Cambridge: Cambridge UP, 1996. 155–77.

Patterson, Annabel. *Shakespeare and the Popular Voice*. Cambridge: Basil Blackwell, 1989.

Prestwich, Michael. *Armies and Warfare in the Middle Ages: The English Experience*. New Haven: Yale UP, 1996.

Roberts, Michael. *The Military Revolution, 1560–1660: An Inaugural Lecture Delivered before the Queen's University of Belfast*. Belfast: M. Boyd, 1956.

Schwoerer, Lois G. "No Standing Armies!" *The Antiarmy Ideology in Seventeenth-Century England*. Baltimore: Johns Hopkins UP, 1974.

Shakespeare, William. *The Life of Henry the Fifth*. In *The Norton Shakespeare*. Ed. Stephen Greenblatt et al. New York: Norton, 1997.

Smythe, Sir John. *Certain Discourses Military*. Ed. J. R. Hale. Ithaca: Cornell UP, 1964.

Spencer, Janet M. "Princes, Pirates, and Pigs: Criminalizing Wars of Conquest in Henry V." *Shakespeare Quarterly* 47 (1996): 160–77.

Stoller, Robert J. *Observing the Erotic Imagination*. New Haven: Yale UP, 1985.

Taunton, Nina. *1590s Drama and Militarism: Portrayals of War in Marlowe, Chapman, and Shakespeare's "Henry V."* Aldershot: Ashgate, 2001.

Turner, Victor. *Dramas, Fields, and Metaphors: Symbolic Action in Human Society*. Ithaca: Cornell UP, 1974.

————. *The Ritual Process: Structure and Anti-structure*. Ithaca: Cornell UP, 1977.

Webb, Henry J. *Elizabethan Military Science: The Books and the Practice*. Madison: U of Wisconsin P, 1965.

Woodbridge, Linda. *Vagrancy, Homelessness, and English Renaissance Literature*. Urbana: U of Illinois P, 2001.

Black Acts

Textual Labor and Commercial Deceit in Dekker's Lantern and Candlelight

When Thomas Dekker published his cony-catching pamphlets *The Belman of London* in 1607 and *Lantern and Candlelight* in 1608, he was contributing to an established genre in early modern English print culture. This point was ridiculed by one "S.R.," who accused Dekker of plagiarizing from Thomas Harman's *A Caveat or Warening for Common Cursetors Vulgarely Called Vagabones* (1566). While Dekker indeed borrowed much of his material from authors like Harman, John Awdeley (*The Fraternity of Vagabonds*, 1561), and Robert Greene (*A Notable Discovery of Cozenage*, 1591; *The Black Book's Messenger*, 1592), *Lantern and Candlelight* is the first to record a type of criminal that must have alarmed aspiring writers: the "falconer," a rogue who manipulates both patronage-based and market-based literary systems. The falconer commands a book to be printed at his own cost and sets off to the countryside in search of potential "patrons." Before he approaches each gentleman, he affixes an epistle dedicatory to the particular patron and thus successfully cozens him out of a sum of money. By the time the patron suspects something, he cannot locate the source of the book in London's myriad printing houses. The falconer's cleverness resides in his ability to cull the greatest possible gain from both old and new authorial modes by using the former to make his profit and the latter to cover his tracks. Dekker responds with outrage:

O sacred Learning! Why dost thou suffer thy seven-leaved Tree to be plucked by barbarous and most Unhallowed hands? Why is thy beautiful Maiden body polluted like strumpets and prostituted to beastly and slavish

Ignorance? O, you base brood, that make the *Muses* harlots, yet say they are your mothers! You thieves of Wit, cheaters of Art! traitors of schools of Learning, murderers of scholars! . . . You rob scholars of their Fame, which is dearer than life. You are not worth an Invective, not worthy to have your names drop out of a deserving pen. (238)

Despite Dekker's insistence on the superior education and character of "scholars" who make their livings by writing, the difference rings hollow when we remember that he himself is attempting success through print. Dekker's objection to the falconers is that they make writing purely instrumental, yet one wonders what could be more instrumental than writing to secure one's own maintenance.

I raise this issue in light of two recent observations concerning rogue literature in early modern England. First, literary critics and social historians have questioned the existence of a criminal "subculture" akin to the one imagined by rogue text authors. A. L. Beier writes that "the literature's taxonomy is superficial and its amusing stories trivial. Vagrant crime was protean rather than specialized, ranging from illegal begging to burglary. . . . those very qualities made it more difficult to suppress" (144). Later scholars have inferred from the research of Beier and others that the allocation of poverty and placelessness to a deviant "Elizabethan underworld" is a false one, for, as Patricia Fumerton tells us, "vagrancy" closely approximated the everyday lives of lower- to middle-class English people who experienced psychological estrangement from "continuing and displaced labor" in a "vagrant market" (206–25, 211, 215). Dekker's presumed distinction between scholars who write and falconers, then, may point to the similarities in their situations and activities more than their differences. Second, critics have noticed an affinity between rogue and nonrogue that is more specific to authorship: the degree to which the rogues' strategies resemble the strategies of cony-catching writers themselves. For example, Elizabeth Hanson finds in Harman's *Caveat* a "discoverer's" pretense to taxonomic objectivity that founders on the author's necessarily subjective point of view. Furthermore, the author who strives to paint a colorful picture of urban vice is a maker of *fiction* that he hopes will capture the imagination of readers (96). On the whole, rogue text authors' attempts to demarcate a "subculture" fail to draw workable distinctions between criminals and other participants in socioeconomic life; moreover, these authors' portrayals of rogues' expert dissembling best succeed when the authors themselves are expert tellers of tales. The author's reliability as discoverer continually runs the risk of getting lost in his fictions.

My aim in this chapter is to situate Dekker's falconer scenario within these critical strains while offering a more detailed account of the specific terms that Dekker applies to the experience of the professional author. If, as Michel Foucault proposes, the author is the "principle of thrift in the proliferation of meaning," then it would seem that Dekker's construction of the scholar as pure in character and motive helps define a kind of writer who is somehow above the market calculus (101–20, 18). That is to say, criminality assists in legitimating the social status of the "deserving pen" and its holder's claim to his own literary property. But, given the resemblance between author and rogue, this attempt to rein in the vagaries of the literary market ultimately fails.[1] Whether or not Dekker consciously sought to elevate his own position, he undermines his legitimacy and that of other professional writers by interrogating the very marks of "learning" that might otherwise identify the "deserving pen." He does this by having his rogues successfully perform learned languages, learned professions, and literary market strategies in ways that cast doubt on the very distinctions that he erects by way of the falconer scenario. The result is a text that leaves the true identity of the "discoverer" ambiguous, just as the professional's status somewhere between criminal and pure scholar is difficult to define in terms free of marketplace deception. In the end, Dekker's games with fiction making and narrative voice suggest an audience that is not naive, but well schooled in the tricks of the literary market.

Citizen Scholar and Latinate Rogue

Lantern and Candlelight begins with a conventional enough purpose: to help readers identify various criminal types that might otherwise pass undetected. Dekker frames the rogue problem as a threat to the health of the English nation, yet nationhood itself figures as a symptom of humankind's downfall. The first chapter ("Of Canting") opens with a rendering of the Tower of Babel story, which Dekker employs to show the deleterious cultural effects of the loss of a common language. This version of the biblical tale is tinted with nostalgia, looking back at a time of unfragmented corporate thinking and seamless communication:

> When all the *World* was but *one Kingdom*, all the *People* in that Kingdom spake but one language. A man couldel trav [*sic*] in those days neither by Sea nor land, but he met his Countrymen and none others. Two could not then stand gabbing with strange tongues, and conspire together (to his own face) how to cut a third man's throat, but he might understand them. There

was no *Spaniard* (in that Age) to *Brave* his enemy in the Rich and Lofty *Castilian*, no *Roman* Orator to plead in the *Rhetorical* and *Fluent Latin*, no *Italian* to court his Mistress in the sweet and Amorous *Tuscan*, no *Frenchman* to parle in the full and stately phrase of *Orleans*, no *German* to thunder out the high and rattling *Dutch*, the unfruitful crabbed *Irish* and the Voluble significant *Welch*, were not then so much as spoken of. The quick *Scottish* Dialect, sister to the *English*, had not then a tongue. Neither were the strings of the *English* speech, in those times, untied. When the first learned to speak, it was but a broken language: the singlest and the simplest *Words* flowed from her utterance, for she dealt in nothing but in *Monosyllables*, as if to have spoken words of greater length would have cracked her Voice. (214)

The fantasy of a lost "one Kingdom" suggests profound apprehension about inscrutability between and within cultures. Linda Woodbridge sees this passage as describing a fall into nationhood and vernacular languages. "Fall" is an apt term, since "strange tongues" are what enable two men to "conspire together (to his own face) how to cut a third man's throat." Criminality begins with the loss of shared legibility, and, according to Woodbridge, the thieves' language of "cant" represents anxieties about vernacular English replacing the universally understood Latin (259). Dekker's attention to the consequences of nationhood is framed by a dedicatory epistle "To my own Nation," where he warns his fellow English about the "Wild and Barbarous *Rebels*" who are now "up in open arms against the Tranquility of the *Weal public*" (213). He proclaims that the enemy is inside the country, assisted by a language of its own, and national duty compels him to provide a glossary of common rogues' terms.[2] The strangeness of the rogues' dialect marks out a foreign element within the nation, and yet, as we shall see, the rogues also become a repository for lost social meanings that have become foreign by virtue of their obscurity.

In *Lantern*, Latin represents a tie to a more virtuous, more artless past. But, as we know from Ben Jonson's famous taunt that Shakespeare knew "small *Latine* and less *Greeke*," knowledge of Latin also handily distinguishes the learned man. Indeed, Jonson's ability to translate a passage from the Latin Bible exonerated him from full punishment for manslaughter (Riggs 52). By implication, a learned man cannot be so irredeemable as one without learning or at least does not deserve prison or execution. Dekker himself claims "learning" as the mark of the noncriminal author, and in the dedicatory epistle, he links his role as a writer to his duty as a citizen. This ideal is erected in *The Sec-*

ond Part of the Honest Whore, where transparency distinguishes the scholar as a proper citizen of the realm. In a taxonomy of civic types, the character Candido describes the scholar according to his square cap:

> The city cap is round, the scholar's square,
> To show that government and learning are
> The perfect'st limbs i'th body of a state:
> For without them, all's disproportionate.
> If the cap had no honour, this might rear it,
> The reverend fathers of the law do wear it.
> It's light for summer, and in cold it sits
> Close to the skull, a warm house for the wits.
> It shows the whole face boldly, 'tis not made
> As if a man to look on't were afraid;
> Nor like a draper's shop, with broad dark shed,
> For he's no citizen that hides his head.
>
> (Scene 3)

This passage draws a separation between those who work with their minds and those who work in markets. "The reverend fathers of the law" wear the square cap, cueing readers and spectators to associate members of the learned professions with honor, forthrightness, and a sense of duty. Meanwhile, mercantile types who do business in "a draper's shop" shroud their own character for a reason.[3] Scholarship and learning are free of the market and its deceptions, while market participation contains infinite potential for deceit. Rogues, as perhaps the ultimate manifestation of marketplace corruption, erode the fabric of the "Weal public" while scholars, the falconers' diametrical opposites, enhance the health of the state.

Professional authors, who make their living by writing for the market, blur this boundary between scholarly purity and marketplace craftiness. Despite Dekker's protestations to the contrary, professional authors problematize clear distinctions between criminal and scholar. Correspondingly, the rogues are also difficult to separate from the trappings of the learned man. The discoverer's study of rogues' cant yields an observation that troubles the status of Latin as a conventional sign of difference between the learned and the unlearned:

> Now, as touching the Dialect, or phrase itself, I see not that it is grounded upon any certain rules. And no marvel if it have none, for sithence both the *Father* of this new kind of Learning and the *Children* that study to speak it

after him have been from the beginning, and still are, the *Breeders* and *Nour-ishers* of all base disorder in their living and in their *Manners,* how is it pos-sible they should observe any *Method* in their speech, and especially in such a Language, as serves but only to utter discourses of villainies?

And yet, even out of all that *Irregularity,* unhandsomeness, and Fountain of *Barbarism,* do they draw a kind of form: and in some words, as well sim-ple as compounds, retain a certain salt, tasting of some wit, and some Learn-ing. As, for example, they call a *Cloak,* in the *Canting* tongue, a *Togeman,* and in Latin *Toga* signifies a gown or an upper garment. *Pannam* is bread, and *Panis* in Latin is likewise bread. *Cassan* is Cheese, and is a word bar-barously coined out of the substantive *Caseus* which also signifies Cheese. And so of others. (Dekker, *Lantern* 217)

This passage, which follows closely on the Tower of Babel story, locates the rogues within a paradox. On the one hand, the rogues are the progenitors of disorder itself, and have been so "since the beginning." Yet their language contains traces of a Latinate past that is under threat of complete abandon-ment. Did the rogues themselves, with their thieves' cant, hasten the fall into the vernacular, or are the rogues relics of a Latinate age, whose language is now so rare as to be dubbed a mark of "learning"? There is another paradox as well: although their language has no apparent regularity or "method," they study it and, in doing so, "draw a kind of form." Like scholars, they operate according to a pedagogical system that enables them to become masters of rhetoric and style. Furthermore, the language they learn has a distinct tie to Latin and thus, if only by accident, "tast[es] of some wit, and some Learning." If nothing else, their expertise in the use of words aids their dissembling, and this expertise is not far from that of the rhetorician, the orator, the scholar, or the learned writer.[4]

The literary record in the decade surrounding *Lantern and Candlelight*'s publication reveals other instances of skepticism over Latin's reliability as a mark of scholarly character. An outstanding example is the *Parnassus* plays (Leishman), a trilogy of dramatic comedies staged at Cambridge University between 1599 and 1601. The last two plays brutally satirize the supposed promise of a university education to secure a young man's maintenance. A character named Ingenioso (based on another educated but embittered literary professional, Thomas Nashe) rails at his penurious lot and is accompanied by one "Furor Poeticus" who randomly tosses about Latin tags that bear no apparent significance to the play's events. Here, Latin functions as a sign empty of any real social currency. Dekker himself openly questions Latin's cultural capital in his pageant *The Magnificent Entertainment: Given to King*

James (1604). In contradistinction to Jonson, the pageant's collaborator, Dekker ridicules "the borrowed weapons of all the old Masters of the noble science of Poesy," particularly Latin poetry (Hunt 89). Although we do not know precisely how and where Dekker was educated, he demonstrates a clear readiness to hold knowledge of Latin up to scrutiny as a means of defining the learned poet, even though several of his own works utilize Latin quotes (Hunt 14). If the rogues' dialect contains traces of a learned language, then it is no wonder that the falconers convincingly can "carry about them some badge of a Scholar" (Hunt 234). Whether or not they understand Latin at all, they inadvertently command enough of it to tie them to a lost social status as well as a lost virtuous past.

Shape-Shifting Footman and "Treble-Voiced" Bellman

The rogues' accidental command of Latin raises the question of how *any* marks of status could be reliable, but particularly those that distinguish members of the learned professions from the rest of society. Dekker imagines the battle within the state to have special relevance to the print market and the potential abuses therein: the epistle to the nation indicates that the "day of Encounter" between the bellman and the rebels will take place in *"Paul's Churchyard, Fleet Street,* and other parts of the City" (20). The market for print becomes a space in which the forces of good and evil struggle for sovereignty. "Scholars"—that is to say, 'honest' authors—are citizens worth saving. The square cap that Dekker describes in *The Second Part of the Honest Whore* is also worn by "the reverend fathers of the law," linking scholars to lawyers as men whose command of learning designates them as upright contributors to the state. Yet *Lantern and Candlelight* fails to define the cultural capital of learning in a way that would compensate for the specter of the Latinate rogue. It is perhaps this very indeterminacy that prompts Dekker to erect the "scholar" as a control, in the Foucauldian sense, on the potential abuses of print. Dekker's assessment of the falconers indicates that learned men's professional viability and integrity are at stake:

> There be Fellows,
> Of coarse and common blood; Mechanic knaves,
> Whose wits lie deeper buried than in graves.
> And indeed smell more earth, whose creation
> Was but to give a Boot, or Shoe, good fashion.
> Yet these (thriving by the Apron and the Awl),

Being drunk with their own wit, cast up their gall
Only of ink; and in patched, beggarly Rhymes,
(As full of foul corruption as the Times)
From town to town they stroll, in soul as poor,
As th'are in clothes. Yet these at every door,
Their labors Dedicate. But (as at Fairs)
Like Peddlers, they shew still one sort of wares
Unto all comers (with some fil'd oration).
And thus to give books, now's an occupation.

(238)

Dekker's verse reveals several things. The concern over "Mechanic knaves" entering the print market implies the transgression of class-based hierarchies of work. In addition, the true poverty of these knaves is figured in an impoverished soul—"as poor, / As th'are in clothes"—that suggests continuity between an interior and an exterior self. The "soul" of the "scholar," by contrast, is virtuous, but it is only defined *negatively*. Clifford Siskin identifies the construction of a "deep self" as crucial to authorship's codification as professional identity (106). According to Siskin, a sense of writing as a special vocation involves a mixture of two elements: technicality (a systematic body of knowledge justifying expertise) and indetermination (the mystification of this body of knowledge) (116). Dekker's definition of the scholar as both learned and virtuous depends upon the mystification of, and continuity between, the scholar's craft and the scholar's "deep self." His response to the falconer scenario could thus be understood as an early attempt to construct writing as a "mystery."

The mystification of writing appears in other parts of the narrative where Dekker no longer addresses rogues in specific, but abusers of writing in general. Toward the pamphlet's conclusion, we learn of "certain straggling Scribbling Writers" who deserve hanging for counterfeiting the "Noble Science of Writing" by which scholars make an honest living (257). These writers can complete the same tasks as the scholar in at least half the time, while underselling the scholar's own textual products. They have "no quality in them so much as of swiftness," for both their approach to profit and their hollow character renders them unfit for the "noble science" (257). In Siskin's terms, they lack both the "deep self" and the understanding of craft necessary to be "true" writers, and Dekker's construction of writing as a "noble science" clearly assists in this portrayal. An instrumental approach to earning off of the literary market is indicative of a soul without depth.

But the rogues' language shows that the writer pure in motive does not have the market cornered on "wit." The Latinate rogue leads to a consideration of the extent to which *all* writers are prone to the temptation of exercising "craft" for personal profit in the literary marketplace. Dekker gives the question of temptation a moral edge by locating the crafty command of language and writing among the devil's party from which comes Pamersiel, a messenger who competes with the bellman as the pamphlet's main discoverer. This footman is "very nimble of his heels, for no wild Irishman could outrun him" and is easily recognized by dishonest merchant types such as "Pride, dressed like a merchant's wife," who instantly "tak[es] acquaintance of him" when he enters the city (226). Pamersiel, who has been sent to gather intelligence on criminal practices, brings "experience" to his survey of London's mercantile practices and finds himself welcome among "every Tailor [who] hath his Hell to himself under his shopboard where he dams new Satin" (226). Once again, the tailor's shop signifies suspect transactions made under the cloak of darkness; the shop is one permutation of the images of darkness that shroud all of the rogues' practices. Pamersiel's functioning as objective taxonomer is compromised by the fact that his viewpoint is not an objective one at all, but one defined by "experience" and, for this reason, deceitful mercantile types are drawn to him immediately. Likewise, honest merchants recognize the footman as one who could easily tempt them and thus bring about a loss of "conscience," such as one tailor who "spying the devil, suffered him to go, never praying that he would know the shop another time. But looking round about his warehouse, if nothing were missing, at length he found that he had lost his conscience; yet remembering himself, that they who deal with the devil can hardly keep it, he stood upon it the less" (227). In this first stage of his journey, Pamersiel causes market participants of a certain character to discover *themselves.* Only when he dons the appearance of an "accomplished gallant" and enters an ordinary does he recede into London's cultural landscape (227).

The devil's intelligencer emerges from a hell that operates according to abuses of language and, more specifically, writing and print. The setting— "Term-time in hell"—permits a lengthy look at how the denizens of hell function as lawyers. They conduct business in an environment that recalls the post-Babel confusion described in the previous chapter: "Nothing could be heard but noise, and nothing of that noise be understood, but that it was a sound of men in a kingdom when on a sudden in an uproar" (221). During this "Term-time," judgment is quickly dispatched, although very little is understood concerning these judgments. The term in hell functions only according to noise, not to a shared language among clients and administrators. It is an atmosphere in which legal pronouncements are devoid of any real meaning; yet at the same time, these judgments have dire consequences for the souls involved. As a complement to the confusion, Dekker describes the writing practices of the clerks:

> The Ink wherewith they write is the blood of Conjurers. They have no Paper, but all things are engrossed in Parchment and that Parchment is made of Scriveners' Skins flayed off after they have been punished for Forgery. Their Standishes are the Skulls of Usurers; their Pens, the bones of unconscionable Brokers and hard-hearted Creditors that have made Dice of other men's bones, or else of perjured Executors and blind Overseers that have eaten up widows and Orphans to the bare bones. And those Pens are made of purpose without Nibs, because they may cast Ink but slowly, in mockery of those who in their lifetime were slow in yielding drops of pity. (222)

This colorful passage complicates the moral imperative underlying the discoverer's project. On the one hand, it implies punishment of the world's abusers of administrative language and writing: scriveners who forge, brokers and creditors, "blind" administrators, and conjurers who manipulate the relationship between appearance and reality all become writing material for hellish legal clerks. On the other hand, the clerks in hell continue the activities of the abusers by making similar uses of their body parts. Unconscionable scriveners, creditors, and the like have their counterparts in hell, even as those counterparts supposedly mete out due punishment.

The relocation of Babel to an administrative legal environment troubles vocational indices of "character" by showing that, not only do many who write for a living do so in a way that merits damnation, but devils themselves can carry out the professions of the learned. Furthermore, the devils thrive off of print culture and particularly controversies surrounding print. The business of hell is described as "Black Acts," punning on the blackness of sin and the blackness of ink. In addition, the focus on "acts" of writing helps define abusive writing practices as those that sublimate the writer's content and character to the instrumental purposes of writing itself—as profit, as self-advancement, or as the instrument of punishment.

At this early stage in the narrative, the morally upright bellman threatens the corrupt writing practices that the devils and the falconers share. He maintains the pure objectivity of the ideal discoverer. The Devil is outraged at the bellman's proximity to "Black Acts" in which he never actually engages: "if such a conjurer at midnight should dance in their circles and not be driven out of them, Hell in a few years would not be worth the dwelling in" (224). The critical distance of the bellman contrasts with the "experience" that Pamersiel brings to his own discovery work. While the bellman merely skirts and witnesses "Black Acts," the world of the devils is saturated with pleasure taken in print culture and controversy. At the "Satanical Synagogue" where the devils plan their pursuit of the bellman, one proposes that "the Black dog of Newgate should again be let loose, and afar off follow the Bawling *Bel-man,* to watch into what places he went, and what deeds of darkness (every night) he did" (225). The famous contemporary ballad "The Black Dog of Newgate" figures as a weapon in the battle for souls. In addition to its easily recognizable status as a pamphlet, the "dog" would have been recognized as both a legendary spirit who wandered the streets during the reign of Henry III and the conscience of criminals in Newgate prison.[5] The devils are intimately familiar with ballads and their meanings. Likewise, the damned souls of thieves whom the bellman discovered spend their time in "those Fields of Horror where every night they walk, disputing with Doctor *Story* [a persecutor of reformers who was kidnapped by an English skipper while searching a ship for banned books] who keeps them company there in his corner cap" (225). Another devil proposes that these spirits be let loose to pursue the bellman as well. At this council, all plans to give the bellman his comeuppance through the weapons of print culture get rejected when they conclude that these weapons are too easily recognizable.

The weapon upon which the council finally agrees is a protean figure who comfortably blends into marketplace settings. Pamersiel is selected for the mission due to his ability to "thrust himself into such companies as, in a warrant to be signed for that purpose, should be nominated" (225). Pamersiel's task is to insert himself into groups that the bellman might target and win these groups back to the Devil's side. Thus, hell's most effective weapon is Pamersiel's ability to shape-shift and take advantage of the lack of cultural legibility that the bellman purportedly sets aright; the Devil orders this "Journey-man to Hell" to "[b]ind thyself prentice to the best trades," but also warns him, "if thou canst grow extreme rich in a very short time (honestly), I banish thee my kingdom, come no more into hell" (225–26). The terms by which Pamersiel enters London's socioeconomic life are vocational. If the bellman's main concern is to root out illicit commercial practices, Pamersiel shows how easily members of the Devil's party can insert themselves into seemingly licit forms of market engagement. He is at once "Journey-man to Hell" and "prentice to the best trades."[6] His ability to blend into the socioeconomic landscape undermines the cony-catching pamphlet's project of identifying criminal types. Even toward the end of the pamphlet, the narrator acknowledges that the ease of concealment makes commercial abuses innumerable and is prompted to ask, "How many *Trees* of *Evil* are growing in this *Country*?"

(253). Commercial practice itself allows deceivers to "engender with *Dark-ness*," while "*Candle-light* eye-sight grow[s] dimmer and dimmer" (258). The futility of compiling any reliable record of all criminals is underscored at the end of the pamphlet, where the devil's messenger is "driven into wonder why the night would fall in labor, and bring forth so many Villainies whose births she practiced to cover (as she had reason) because so many watchmen were continually called and charged to have an eye to her doings, at length he perceived that Bats, more ugly and more in number than these, might fly up and down in darkness." The bats "should strike the very bills out of those Watchman's hands" in a continual disruption of the discoverer's attempt to pin them down through writing (260). That which cannot be enumerated cannot be fully identified. This fact suggests other ways of viewing Dekker's aim as discoverer particularly since, as a writer for the print market, he too engages in the marketplace while still protesting that there is such a thing as a "deserving pen."

If, as Hanson and others have noted, cony-catching pamphlets leave the moral imperative of the author as discoverer open to question, *Lantern* adds new terms to this confusion not only by making writing itself a subject for investigation, but by introducing a competing character who is himself skilled at taxonomy. Pamersiel is both rogue and discoverer, and he blends into the criminal world so well that we lose surety of how and where to locate him. Once he enters the narrative as the bellman's competitor, he disappears from the sight of readers and appears again only toward the end of the pamphlet. The bellman too remains unseen throughout most of Dekker's survey of criminal activity. The discoverer becomes lost in his tales, as does his reliability, for the uncoverer of vice could be the author, the bellman, Pamersiel, or none of these. Indeed, Dekker's bellman is a "treble-voiced" reporter of literary crime (224). Thus one is led to wonder who has been delivering the verse that probes the "soul" of the falconer—does it come from the bellman's objectivity, from Pamersiel's "experience," or from the professional author's knowledge of authorship in all of its morally suspect forms? Who writes these entertaining tales of horse-coursers, jacks-of-the-clock-house, doxies, and moon-men, and describes his own glossary of cant as a "dish twice set before you . . . for our intent is to feast you with variety"? (219). It appears that the professional author, if not the bellman, derives his knowledge from his own loose affiliation with the devil's party, and his success depends on tempting readers to consume his tales with relish.

The pamphlet's final passage combines the "experience" of the devil's footman with the bellman's taxonomic imperative, leaving the author's true identity open to speculation. The authorial voice blends with those of these two characters in a way that highlights the pamphlet's status as a work of fiction on the print market. Pamersiel meets the bellman on his way home and mistakes the bellman for "some churlish *Hobgoblin* (seeing a long staff on his neck) and therefore to be one of his own fellows" (260). Like Pamersiel and the rogues themselves, the bellman is indistinguishable, according to outward signs, from those he pretends to expose. Pamersiel and the bellman converse, and Pamersiel emerges as the supplier of the bellman's data:

> The *Bel-ringer* Smelling what strong scent he had in his nose, soothed him up, and questioning with him how he had spent his time in the city and what discovery of *Land villainies* he had made in this *Island voyage*, the *Mariner* of *Hell* opened his char[t], which he had lined with all abuses lying either *East*, *West*, *North*, or *South*. He shewed how had had pricked it, upon what points he had sailed, where he put in, under what height he kept himself, where he went ashore, what strange people he met, what land he had discovered, and what commodities he was laden with from thence. Of all which the *Bel-man* drawing forth a perfect Map, they parted. (260)

The taxonomic pose of the bellman is subverted by the fact that he receives his information from Pamersiel's chart; Pamersiel himself has done the discovery work from which the bellman ultimately benefits. The bellman's "map" is thus informed by "experience," rather than by unfiltered observation, and the bellman is affiliated with hell itself in a collaborative discovery project. In turn, the bellman's map becomes the pamphlet: "Which Map he hath set out in such colors as you see, though not with such cunning as he could wish" (260). "Cunning" calls attention to the *presentation* of the discoverer's findings, which, according to the professional writer's need to capture the imaginations of readers, must yield "pleasure" more than alarm: "The pains are his own, the pleasure, if this can yield any pleasure, only yours, on whom he bestows it" (260). In order to maintain anything like the purity of the "scholar" who writes, the author must disassociate himself from any "pleasure" that readers derive. The bellman cum author "cares not to entertain them," but since the devil's footman is his source, the purity stance gives way to the pamphlet's value as entertainment.

Moreover, the author/discoverer's indication of "pleasure" as a potential reaction to his tale places readers in a moral dilemma. To refuse "entertainment" is to share in the author's strained insistence on remaining outside of the market calculus. However, the pamphlet as a whole raises the issue of how *any* engagement with the print market—as author or as reader—can avoid the deceit inherent in the market. To read *Lantern and Candlelight* is to be entertained by the stories that unfold, particularly since the pamphlet fails to outline specific ways to know criminals and their activities and also admits that criminals "engender" themselves indefinitely. Author and reader thus participate in a *shared* project of fiction-making—respectively, one creates and the other consumes. If the author of the rogue text undermines his own claims to learned purity, so must he interrupt readers' own pretenses to read the pamphlet only for information. The information therein reveals itself to be unreliable as objective record, because author, bellman, and devil's messenger are one voice. Likewise, readers who seek objective information must buy into authorial self-constructions that, over and over again, prove impossible within a literary market setting.

Conclusion: Criminal Literacy

In recent years, much scholarship has been devoted to interrogating Elizabeth Eisenstein's characterization of print as a medium that offered "fixity" and universality by anchoring language and culture in single, reliable textual artifacts that readers could trust to remain consistent across geographical and cultural borders (1:113, 43–159). Eisenstein contrasts "scribal culture" to "print culture" by defining the latter as free of the former's corruptions (1:71–88, 113–26). Perhaps the most useful intervention in the notion of "fixity" is that of Roger Chartier, who challenges us to view reading as "rebellious and vagabond" in contradistinction to writing, which he characterizes as "always aim[ing] at installing an order"—a contrast that reflects "the paradox underlying any history of reading, which is that it must postulate the liberty of a practice that it can only grasp, massively, in its determinations" (viii, 23). Print, in Chartier's view, pretends to impose a single order of meaning from which reading, by its very definition, continually strays. Nonetheless, Chartier maintains a view of the text adhering to a fixed order prior to readers' alterations. The transgressive potential of meaning itself lies entirely within the reader.

Cony-catching pamphlets, with their tendency to confuse categories and lay the author/discoverer's own motives open to question, suggest an author-reader relationship of a different kind. As a text that calls the distinction between "scribal" and "print" culture into question, *Lantern* mixes scribes and print authors together as abusers of writing by calling attention to writers' "characters" as preconditions of the text's creation. Readers are thus invited not only to seek the author behind the text, but to entertain suspicion of his motives. To complicate the reader's task further, *Lantern* subverts the conditions of its very existence as a product of the print market, as well as its author's reliability as a self-appointed citizen scholar. *Lantern* in no way seems to impose a clear "order" or meaning; rather, it involves readers in its own game by beginning with a clear moral purpose and ending by displaying the confusion wrought by its own games. Foucault raises Samuel Beckett's question, "What does it matter who is speaking?" as a framework for his analysis of the author function (101). Indeed, the reader of *Lantern* cannot tell who is speaking either, but I would argue that this ambiguity presents a challenge to the reader to *find* the author in discourse rather than an early modern dismissal of "authorship" writ large. Dekker engages the members of his buying public in a way that supposes that, if they are not already skilled readers of literary systems, they might at least be open to investigating traditional signs of learning within these systems. Dekker's readers become—if they are not already— skeptical about the social bases of the very pamphlets they buy and read. They become consumers who are well aware of abuses of "learning" and, by extension, savvy readers of markets. The picture of early modern readership becomes less like the one imagined Eisenstein or even Chartier, and more like one suggested by Adrian Johns, who characterizes early modern readers as engaging in "a critical appraisal of [the] identity and credit" of printed works. "Fixity," writes Johns, is not inherent to the medium but had to be "forged" (31, 5). Forging is what Dekker's falconer scenario allows him to do for the "scholar," but as we have seen, this strategy founders on Dekker's own interruption of the presumed continuity between outward shows of learning and the inner character. Dekker presumes that readers of rogue texts were not naive, but in fact literate about print culture and its participants' complex motivations.

Finally, I wish to suggest that Dekker's falconer scenario be considered as a precopyright attempt to define literary property, with criminality as a foil. While much recent scholarship on the history of the book locates the first notions of literary property within copyright debates, I want to call attention to how, prior to these legal developments, other cultural discourses have contributed to the history of the professional author.[7] The pretense to detective work that we find in rogue literature during the period suggests that overdetermined notions of criminal "subcultures" helped artificially separate the denizens of England into "honest" and "dishonest" socioeconomic agents. *Lantern* applies this configuration in particular to authorship by marshaling falconers, scribes, and the like as rhetorical tools for defining notions of intellectual property that as yet have no legal codification. But when the pamphlet disrupts the system of signs that should help distinguish between self-seeking rogue and authentic "scholar," the professional author emerges as a challenge to this binary. The challenge for readers, then, is to regard the cony-catching author not as one of the "pure," but as a writer whose motive makes the rogue look less like the author's shadowy other, and more like the author's shadow self.

NOTES

1. This point is made by Alexandra Halasz with respect to a conundrum she sees operating in the texts of several early modern English professionals. If writers are not to be totally subject to the market, then they must achieve a sort of "mastery" over it. The failure of this mastery, Halasz writes, "goes without saying" (117).

2. For more on rogue literature with respect to nationalist discourses, see Brooke A. Stafford's essay in this volume.

3. The "draper's shop" appears elsewhere in early-seventeenth-century literature as a sign of the mercantile character. For example, John Taylor "The Water Poet" employed this image to describe the difference between the waterman's work and that of the merchant:

> If a waterman would be false in his trade, I muse what falsehood he could use, he hath no false weights or measures to curtail a man's passage, but he will land a man for his money, and not bate him an inch of the place he is appointed: His shop is not dark like a woollen draper's on purpose, because the buyer shall not see the coarseness of the cloth, or the falseness of the color: no, his work and ware is seen and known, and he utters it with the sweat of his brows. (Qtd. in Humpherus 1:186)

In a legitimating move similar to Dekker's, Taylor uses the transparency of the waterman's work as a metaphor for his own "honest" participation in the literary market.

4. *The Bellman of London* also contains Latinate rogues who, like the devils that I discuss in the next section, are practiced in reading and writing. The case of the "jackman" prefigures the broader consideration of abusive writing practices and mimicry of "true" learning that we find one year later in *Lantern:*

> And because no common wealth can stand without some *Learning* in it, Therefore are there some in this *Schoole* of *Beggers,* that practice writing and *Reading,* and those are called *Jackmen:* yea the *Jackman* is so cunning sometimes that he can speake Latine: which learning of his, lifts him up to advancement, for by that means he becomes *Clarke* of their *Hall,* and his office is to make counterfet licences, which are called *Gybes,* to which hee puts seales, and those are termed *Jarkes.* (103–4)

5. Kinney explains the significance of the black dog in n. 31, 307.

6. Ward writes of the widespread confusion surrounding the relationship between professional identity and personal character in late-sixteenth- and early-seventeenth-century London. According to Ward, the period witnesses an erosion of professional identity as a reliable mark of a person's character and his or her approach to market relations (47).

7. See Woodmansee 425–28; Rose; Chartier 24–59; and Loewenstein 103–23.

WORKS CITED

Beier, A. L. *Masterless Men: The Vagrancy Problem in England, 1560–1640*. London: Methuen, 1985.

Chartier, Roger. *The Order of Books*. Trans. Lydia G. Cochrane. Stanford: Stanford UP, 1994.

Dekker, Thomas. *The Belman of London*. 1607. *The Non-dramatic Works of Thomas Dekker*. Ed. Alexander B. Grosart. 4 vols. Vol. 3. London: Hazell, Watson, and Viney, 1885.

———. *Lantern and Candlelight*. 1608. Kinney. 207–60.

———. *The Second Part of the Honest Whore*. 1630. Ed. Nick de Somogyi. London: Nick Hern for Globe Education, 1998.

Eisenstein, Elizabeth. *The Printing Press as an Agent of Change: Communications and Cultural Transformations in Early Modern Europe*. 2 vols. Cambridge: Cambridge UP, 1979.

Foucault, Michel. "What Is an Author?" *The Foucault Reader*. Ed. Paul Rabinow. New York: Pantheon, 1984. 101–20.

Fumerton, Patricia. "London's Vagrant Economy: Making Space for 'Low' Subjectivity." *Material London, ca. 1600*. Ed. Lena Cowen Orlin. Philadelphia: U of Pennsylvania P, 2000. 206–25.

Halasz, Alexandra. *The Marketplace of Print: Pamphlets and the Public Sphere in Early Modern England*. Cambridge: Cambridge UP, 1997.

Hanson, Elizabeth. *Discovering the Subject in Renaissance England*. Cambridge: Cambridge UP, 1998.

Humpherus, Henry. *History of the Origin and Progress the Company of Watermen and Lightermen of the River Thames*. 3 vols. London: S. Prentice, 1874–86. Reprint, Sudbury, Suffolk: Lavenham, 1999.

Hunt, Mary Leland. *Thomas Dekker: A Study*. New York: Columbia UP, 1911.

Johns, Adrian. *The Nature of the Book: Print and Knowledge in the Making*. Chicago: U of Chicago P, 1998.

Kinney, Arthur, ed. *Rogues, Vagabonds, and Sturdy Beggars*. Amherst: U of Massachusetts P, 1990.

Leishman, J. B., ed. *The Three Parnassus Plays*. London: Nicholson and Watson, 1949.

Loewenstein, Joseph. "Wither and Professional Work." *Print, Manuscript, and Performance: The Changing Relations of the Media in Early Modern England*. Ed. Arthur F. Marotti and Michael D. Bristol. Columbus: Ohio State UP, 2002. 103–23.

Riggs, David. *Ben Jonson: A Life*. Cambridge: Harvard UP, 1989.

Rose, Mark. "The Author as Proprietor: *Donaldson v. Becket* and the Genealogy of Modern Authorship." *Representations* 23 (1988): 51–85.

Siskin, Clifford. *The Work of Writing: Literature and Social Change in Britain*. Baltimore: Johns Hopkins UP, 1998.

Ward, Joseph P. *Metropolitan Communities: Trade Guilds, Identity, and Change in Early Modern London*. Stanford: Stanford UP, 1997.

Woodbridge, Linda. *Vagrancy, Homelessness, and English Renaissance Literature*. Urbana: U of Illinois P, 2001.

Woodmansee, Martha. "The Genius and the Copyright: Economic and Legal Conditions of the Emergence of the 'Author.'" *Eighteenth-Century Studies* 17:4 (1984): 425–48.

BROOKE A. STAFFORD

Englishing the Rogue,
"Translating" the Irish

Fantasies of Incorporation and Early Modern English National Identity

Early modern texts describing the incorporation of imagined rogues and actual Irish subjects, particularly canting dictionaries and Spenser's *A View of
the Present State of Ireland* (1596), display the anxieties of self-imagining for
the early modern English nation. Considered in terms of one another, the fantasies of incorporation described in these texts reveal the instability of the linguistic metaphors used to imagine the English nation. The rogue and Irish
communities have often been examined individually in relationship to English
encounters with external others, particularly in the New World. Yet scholars
have rightly critiqued the notion that early modern English identity was imagined solely in opposition to external others, arguing instead that both lower-
class subjects such as rogues, and the Irish, were "othered" as well.[1] Examining the treatment of these two communities together demonstrates the threat
internal others posed to the imagined English national identity—a threat
made all the more pressing by their similarity to, yet striking difference from,
the imagined English ideal. Both communities are vilified throughout the
period for their mobility, their language, and their customs, and both are dealt
with in similar ways in the texts I examine here. My focus is on the fantasy of
linguistic and cultural incorporation articulated in canting dictionaries—lists
of words translated out of the rogues' language, called cant, into English—
included in many cony-catching pamphlets from the mid-sixteenth century
through the early seventeenth century, and in Spenser's sustained metaphorics

of cultural translation in the colonialist treatise *A View of the Present State of Ireland*.² I read these dictionaries in the context of Spenser's treatise on the Irish crisis because the anxieties both communities raise about English national identity—and the strategies employed to deal with them—are uncannily alike. These texts are presented as instructional manuals, explaining ways in which to apprehend the other and then domesticate him through language; Spenser's culturally capacious sense of "translation" helps us to better understand what is at stake in the "Englishing" of canting dictionaries.

The canting dictionaries and Spenser's treatise are quite different in purpose. The canting dictionaries deal, often playfully, with a community of rogues whose historicity is highly debated, feeding a commercial market of readers seeking entertainment, while Spenser's treatise presents what he sees as a reasonable solution for the very real problem of how to deal with the Irish. However, the canting dictionaries are not wholly innocent. They articulate a fantasy of incorporation that strikingly resembles the fantasy that Spenser entreats his readers to make into a reality. The fantasy of "Englishing" the nation of rogues, who stand in synecdochically for the vagrants who posed a real and pressing problem for the English nation, is analogous to the fantasy of "translation" that Spenser expounds in *A View*. Similarly, the potential these processes have for reversing themselves is also analogous; neither process works in the ways their authors imagine it will. Rather, they are fantasies of wholeness that unwittingly highlight the fractures in the imagined English nation.

English—as a language and as an identity—is the end result of domination and incorporation. Yet the linguistic metaphors used in canting dictionaries and in *A View* prove to be unstable ones since neither Englishing nor translation is a unidirectional process, a fact made apparent by the enduring appeal both the rogues and the Irish hold for the English. Rogues and Irish are threatening because they call English identity into question, exercising a stronger pull on those who identify as English than vice versa. While rogues and Irish resist transformation, many English subjects choose to translate themselves into members of these "other" communities. This is the case with the Roaring Boys in England and the Old English in Ireland; these communities suggest how linguistic metaphors for processes of incorporation may well reverse themselves. Ultimately, the canting dictionaries and Spenser's treatise concerning the Irish indicate the English concern with those communities that remain ideologically—and linguistically—outside the bounds of an imagined Englishness even while they exist within the geographical bounds of the imagined English nation. Despite their interest in containment, these texts unwittingly demonstrate that "Englishing" and translation open a passageway between communities, enabling individuals to move in either direction and evade the control of the initial translator.

Dealing with "Internal Others"

Rogue literature flourished throughout the mid-sixteenth century and into the early seventeenth century, even as vagrancy became an increasing target of legislation; "market-oriented rogue literature was at the very least convenient to those whose ends were served by scapegoating vagrants" (Woodbridge 12). Rogues stand synecdochically for lower-class figures such as vagrants who were a major cause of concern and even fear for the English who struggled to deal with issues of poverty as they also worked to create a prosperous and whole national identity.[3] Indeed, rogue literature represented vagrants as "internal barbarians, for they were nomadic like other barbarians and spoke a barbarous tongue, cant" (160). The rogues, and the vagrants they represent, are clearly "othered" even in early pamphlets like Thomas Harman's *A Caveat for Common Cursitors* (1566). Widely recognized as one of the most influential cony-catching pamphlets, Harman's pamphlet sets out the key elements of the genre and is often plagiarized in later pamphlets. Harman's and other cony-catching pamphlets focus on exposing the rogue as an internal other; rogues are English, yet they remain outside of acceptable English community. Some of the pamphlets even go so far as to represent rogues as a nation that exists within the English nation. Dekker notes in his *Lantern and Candlelight* (1608) that "our country [England] breeds no wolves nor serpents, yet these [rogues] engender here and are either serpents or wolves, or worse than both" (177). The rogue community is distinct from the English nation, yet is native to it. Indeed, those born into the "nation of rogues" are referred to by Harman as "wild rogues" (Judges 78), recalling the term "wilde Irish" used to refer to natives of Ireland, another nation of internal others that disrupts and threatens the imagined English national identity. Further, Dekker calls rogues "savages, yet living in an island very temperate, fruitfull, full of a noble nation and rarely governed" (189). The English people are set apart from the rogues— the English are a "noble nation," while the rogues are "savages" who organize themselves into "tribes" (189). The rogues are nationlike in that they are represented as separate from the English and as having their own order, their own culture, and, as will be discussed in depth, their own language.

Despite many authors' insistence that rogues are distinct from the English nation, the rogue is threatening since he or she may look like a gentleman, a certified beggar, or any number of other personae; the rogue's identity can change quickly and he or she can move between official English culture and rogue culture, speaking English and cant fluently. Authors of rogue literature claim that their pamphlets will allow the reader to recognize, and ostensibly outsmart, rogues when they see them; however, they also reveal the rogue as a not-quite-other who gives rise to anxieties about English identity. Indeed, "some of the finest moments of rogue literature efface the line between rogue life and respectable life, exposing the Othering process that projected the sins of the respectable onto the poor" (Woodbridge 239). Canting dictionaries in particular invite the reader to enter into the community of the rogue, at times even encouraging the effacement of the boundary between the acceptable English community and the rogue community. With these canting dictionaries, the reader has the opportunity to put the textual blurring of boundaries into action by translating himself into a rogue. The synecdochic relationship between the rogues represented in cony-catching pamphlets and real vagrants gives a tangible focus to the fantasy of incorporation the authors of the pamphlets describe, but it also makes the potential for crossing between communities a real threat to the imagined English identity.

At about the same time that cony-catching pamphlets flourished, England's dealings with another internal other—the Irish—intensified. Though England's attempts to subdue and incorporate Ireland began in the twelfth century with Henry II's invasion of Ireland, the effort to make Ireland part of the English nation in more than name was renewed with private colonization ventures by the "New English" in the 1570s. As Bradshaw, Hadfield, and Maley point out in *Representing Ireland*, "Ireland was the site both of English identity formation, and of English identity crises" (8). England's colonial project in Ireland attempted to define Englishness in opposition to Irish otherness. However, what the English find in Ireland is a community of "not-quite-other" people. The likeness between English and Irish is represented by the Old English, a community of earlier English colonizers who have become Irish in name and custom. These English families who take Irish names, speak Irish, and intermarry with the Irish call firm notions of Englishness and of Irish otherness into question. Useful here is Andrew Murphy's idea of proximity: he notes that the issue of proximity is important when considering English-Irish relations since it retains a "sense of that which is 'approximate'—a semblance which is simultaneously similar, yet different" (*Reviewing* 18–19).[4] The Old English, who have become Irish, expose the dangers of this proximity for English imaginings of a national identity. The Irish maintain a position of "transgressive liminality" that disrupts "not only English conceptions of Irish identity, but also, indeed, . . . English notions of their own national identity" (Murphy *Reviewing* 36). It is the transgressive liminality of the Irish, and the anxieties it raises for imaginers of the English nation, that is important here as it resembles that of the rogue community living in England.

Much criticism of rogue literature has appeared over the past several decades, and many critics employ one of two strategies in examining this body of work (Dionne). Some critics read cony-catching pamphlets as "biographical testimonies, or literary recordings of the invisible network of criminals that haunted Shakespeare's England" (Dionne 30) while others read it "from an empirical perspective" (31). Dionne and several other critics of rogue literature challenge both of these approaches and attempt to read these works "dialectically, as both fact and fiction" (33). Recently, rogue literature has been examined in order to shed light on topics as various as the invention of London, the development of the commercial print marketplace, the "Othering" of vagrants in early modern England, and early modern subjectivity.[5] The canting dictionaries included in many cony-catching pamphlets receive some attention from critics, but they are rarely the focal point for critical discussions of rogue literature.[6] Instead, they tend to offer a point of departure for a discussion either of the historicity of canting or of the ways in which cant worked to create a desirable but feared rogue community.

This essay furthers recent work by reading rogue literature, and specifically the canting dictionaries included in Harman, Dekker, and Rid's pamphlets, in the context of the Irish crisis. I start from the English project of imagining a cohesive national identity and examine the ways in which rogues and Irish exist both inside and outside this imagined community. I argue that these communities of "not-quite-others" pose a tangible threat to English identity, even as they are the focal point for English strategies of domination, colonization, and assimilation. The specific strategy that I investigate here is the process of "Englishing" as a specific kind of cultural translation.[7] The implications of "Englishing" become clearer when considered in the context of the sense of translation articulated in *A View of the Present State of Ireland*. Spenser uses "translation" throughout his text as a metaphor for changing not only text, but also people, into English. Similarly, "Englishing" is not only about making a "foreign" text legible to an Englishman, it is about exposing a culture and making it knowable to the larger English community with the intent of transforming that culture, in this case, the rogues as well as the vagrants they synecdochically represent. However, both Englishing and translation not only transform communities into English textually, they also enable English readers to "un-English" or culturally translate themselves into something else—here, a member of the rogue or Irish communities. In this case, we see Bhabha's concept of mimicry working in reverse—the official culture mimics the Other—highlighting the idea that the "*double* vision" of mimicry disrupts the authority of colonial discourse and, here, undermines it (Bhabha 88). Thus, I argue that the strategies of Englishing and translation are more than textual strategies. When these fantasies of incorporation do not work as their authors intend them to, the English resort to violent force, whether in the form of punishments for rogues and vagrants or in the form of garrisons and starvation as proposed by Spenser at the end of his treatise. Fantasies of incorporation have tangible, and often violent, effects on the communities to which they are applied and intimate that the problems of national identity we see in later colonial texts are present even in these early modern texts.

In the rogue literature, as in Spenser's treatise, the textualization of rogues and Irish, respectively, takes a first step toward incorporating these groups into the English nation. Ultimately, the strategies of Englishing and translation aim toward the destruction of the rogues and Irish; once they are incorporated into the English nation, they no longer exist. However, just as once a text has been translated out of one language into another, it becomes possible to move between the versions of the text, so also does a looseness exist in textual projects of translating cultures. Even as cony-catching pamphlets proclaim to expose the rogue community in an effort to "heal" the English nation, these pamphlets enable readers to imitate rogues. Thomas Dekker, in his *Lantern and Candlelight* (1608) and *O per se O* (1612) in particular, exposes the possibility that Englishing can be bidirectional, opening the space for readers to English a canting song and even to compose their own canting songs. Similarly, Spenser's translation project intends to make the Irish knowable to the English people and to shape them into the characters that he, as a member of the New English community in Ireland, wants them to be. However, Spenser's project of translating the Irish is hardly unidirectional; the "degeneration" of the Old English and the refusal of the Irish to allow themselves to be translated reveal the problems of colonial ventures as well as the "looseness" that occurs in any project of translation. Herein lies the problem with "Englishing" and translation—there are no guarantees of unidirectionality. The fact that something can be "Englished" or translated implies that it can also be "un-Englished," or translated into another language.

"Sweetmeats" to "Heal the Nation": Fantasies of Incorporation Undermined by Pleasure

Authors of cony-catching pamphlets present themselves as servants of their nation, performing a necessary function for the benefit of the English people as a whole. They claim to expose rogues in order to correct them; they show the reader what to look for so that when he sees a rogue, he will not be duped. The authors imply that a cautious nation will eventually run rogues out of business by resisting their tricks and reporting rogues to the authorities when possible. However, though the authors proclaim honorable intentions, they are also "always implicated in the discoverable art of cozenage" (Hanson 96); therefore, authors present their reliability and goals throughout the pamphlets in order to justify their knowledge and experience of rogue culture. Authors of rogue literature must prove their allegiance to official English culture so as not to be accused of "falling prey" to the culture they set out to correct, as the Old English did when setting out to colonize Ireland.

Harman, in his *Caveat*, emphasizes the corrective function of his text; he writes "for the utility and profit of his natural country" (Judges 61)—England—implying that the rogues who are his subject matter are "unnatural" and must be made natural once again. He elaborates his intentions, claiming that "as I trust I have deserved no rebuke for my goodwill, even so I desire no praise for my pain, cost, and travail. But faithfully for the profit and benefit of my country I have done it, that the whole body and realm may see and understand their [rogues'] lewd life and pernicious practices, that all may speedily help to amend all that is amiss. Amen say all with me" (67). Harman sets out a utilitarian and moralistic purpose for his project and promises that it will bring England "profit and benefit" (67); his is not only a corrective project, but also a profitable one that he believes all will join in with him. Further, Harman indicates that to recognize a rogue is to be able to understand a rogue and thus, to be able to correct what is wrong with the body of the nation by stopping rogues from deceiving charitable English men and women. The distinction between a rogue and an Englishman is, Harman suggests, clear.

However, though Harman concludes his pamphlet on a similar moralizing note, his final words blur the distinction he sets out to make between rogues and his readers. The pamphlet ends with a long poem, the last stanza of which reads:

> Thus I conclude my beggars' book,
> That all estates most plainly may see,
> As in a glass well polished to look,
> Their double demeanor in each degree;
> Their lives, their language, their names as they be,
> That with this warning their minds may be warned
> To amend their misdeeds, and so live unharmed.

(Judges 118)

This stanza maintains Harman's focus on correcting "misdeeds" through recognition, but interestingly, the pronouns in the stanza are unfixed, revealing the uncontrollable state of rogue culture, even when it is ostensibly presented for corrective purposes. Initially, "their" seems to refer to the second line's "all estates"—the readers. However, in line 4, "their" seems to refer to both the readers and the rogues since in line 5, "their" refers to the lives, language, and names of rogues that have just been described in Harman's pamphlet. The line between the reader and the rogue becomes blurred, and, finally, the two categories merge in the last two lines, as it seems that both the readers and rogues are encouraged to look carefully at themselves and correct their behavior in order to avoid punishment. Harman's fantasy of incorporation does not simply make the rogues part of the English nation; rather, the English reader becomes incorporated into a criminal community whose behavior needs correction. As the reader and rogue become one, so Harman's careful attempts to present rogue material in the name of morality and social improvement escape his control and the danger of the material—"Englished" though most of it may be—reveals itself: the reader and the rogue are not always distinguishable, especially not after the reader has had the opportunity to learn "roguish ways" by reading the pamphlet.

The danger of losing the distinction between the reader and the rogue becomes even more apparent in Dekker's *Lantern and Candlelight* and *O Per Se O*. Though Dekker follows the expectations of the genre by spending a considerable amount of time in his dedicatory epistles to *Lantern and Candlelight* assuring his readers that his intent is to help improve the English nation, he later openly admits that the material he presents is pleasurable and encourages his readers to enjoy it.[8] He starts by addressing the fears that some may have about the effect of the pamphlet on its readers, claiming that "this lancing of the pestilent sores of a kingdom so openly" (Dekker 177) will not infect those who might never have thought of such things.[9] Rather, he promises that this "strong physic" will "restore those parts to perfect strength which by disorder have been diseased" (177). The reader, according to these statements, will not learn to become a rogue by reading this pamphlet; instead, he will become a physician to an ill nation, and he will learn how to tame the monstrous rogues he reads about (177). While these statements partially allay the social fear that good men and women will be corrupted by cony-catching pamphlets, Dekker refuses to completely contain the anxieties the pamphlet evokes. His pamphlets merely "masquerade as practical advice manuals and non-fictional documentaries" (Manley 362); their emphasis is actually on celebrating and enjoying the rogue culture. As Dekker points out the educational and correctional qualities of his pamphlet, he likewise points out the pleasure and delight reading it can bring to the reader. Dekker tells his readers that looking at the activities of the rogues "afar off may delight you, and to know their qualities if ever you should come near them may save you from much danger" (177). The delight provided by the pamphlet, presented as excess by Dekker, prevents the subversiveness of the material from being contained by claims that the pamphlet contributes to the maintenance of social order.[10]

Dekker plays with the anxieties surrounding rogue literature throughout his dedicatory epistles, assuring his fearful or skeptical readers that the pamphlet will allow them to heal the wounds of the nation (178). He tells his audience that he prescribes the poisons of the nation to them "to the end that by knowing the secret mischiefs, abuses, villainies and treacheries of the world, thou mayest arm thyself against them or guard thy friend by advice from them" (183). But again, Dekker does not contain the threat of his pamphlet completely. He ends his final dedicatory epistle to the reader with the instructions, "Read and laugh; read and learn; read and loathe. Laugh at the knavery; learn out the mystery; loathe the base villainy" (183). In these final instructions, Dekker blurs the distinction between the criminal and the upstanding citizen. We are to laugh at knavery and loathe villainy, but how do we distinguish them? When does knavery become villainy, and why is it permissible to laugh at knavery? This distinction is left up to the individual reader. Dekker also instructs the reader to learn the mystery—but why? For the delight of figuring it out? To protect himself and others against it? To be able to replicate it? These questions also remain unanswered. As Paula Blank suggests, the authors of cony-catching pamphlets "pose as literary crimebusters, offering their texts in the service of the State. But this is just another cony-catching ploy" (56). Dekker undermines the idea that the pamphlet intends to stop rogues and reinstate the social order each time he reiterates the pleasure the reader should take in reading and learning about the rogues' activities.

Lantern and Candlelight and *O per se O* are framed with emphases on pleasure. Dekker introduces the idea that his pamphlet may delight the reader in the dedicatory epistles we have looked at and reinforces it when he closes *O Per Se O* with canting songs, some of which are "Englished" for the reader. He tells his reader that "to shut up this feast merrily, as sweetmeats are best last, your last dish which I set before you to digest the hardness of the rest is a canting song, not feigned or composed as those of the Bellman's were out of his own brain, but by the canters themselves and sung at their meetings" (Dekker 300). This final statement reinforces the idea that readers might be attracted to and corrupted by the information in the pamphlet in several ways. First, it presents "authentic" canting as a "sweetmeat." These songs, written in a "language allegedly devised by a criminal underworld of outlaws and thieves"

(Blank 18) for the sole purpose of undermining English law and social order, also provide pleasure and are supposed to aid in the digestion of what has come before. Though cant is supposed to enable rogues to devise their plots without being understood by outsiders, here the songs are not only "attractive," but they also help to make the previous tales about roguish activities part of the reader. In short, the "other" becomes palatable, if not downright pleasurably edible. Second, the fact that the examples of canting songs in *Lantern and Candlelight* are revealed to have been composed by the bellman (the character who guides readers through the world of the rogues) himself shows that the study of rogue culture, even for "good," can make one proficient in the language and able to imitate the song and speech of rogues convincingly. If language and identity are closely linked, then the bellman's ability and willingness to invent his own canting songs suggests that learning the language makes one at least partially "roguish." Finally, by suggesting that these final songs are more appealing *because* they are "authentic," Dekker implies that rogue culture and its products are something to take pleasure in and that they are worth seeking out and experiencing. So, in the end, the danger of the pamphlet is not contained at all; rather, Dekker playfully presents rogue culture as appealing and something that should be sought out and enjoyed.

Dekker's emphasis on pleasure, and his open invitation to his readers into the world of the rogue, was clearly perceived as threatening by other authors of cony-catching pamphlets such as Samuel Rid who responds directly to Dekker, referencing the "Bellman's" pamphlet in the title of his pamphlet, *Martin Markall Beadle of Bridewell: His Defence and Answers to the Bellman of London* (1610). Rid positions himself as an author who does not enjoy his task but rather undertakes it because it is his duty. He immediately presents his work as "folly," asking that when the readers confirm his own opinion of his work that they "reprehend neither the work nor workmaster, but rather themselves, in that they would spend their time so foolishly, being warned of so foolish and idle a subject" (Judges 385). Rhetorically, Rid distances himself from his work, though clearly he finds it worthwhile or profitable enough to justify spending his own time on such a project. He attempts to reconcile this apparent contradiction by claiming that he does this work out of necessity in order to correct mistakes made by Dekker. Whether or not this motivation can be trusted, it appears boldly when Rid "runs over" Dekker's "Canter's Dictionary" (410), as will be discussed later. Further, Rid counters Dekker's emphasis on pleasure by encouraging the reader to disdain the canting language and its speakers as he himself professes to do. Rid begrudges having written all that he has, insisting that "the Bellman through his pitiful ambition hath caused me to write what I would not" (441), perhaps in order to uphold his earlier statement that this work is "folly," or perhaps in order to rescue his own reputation after having revealed the extent of his knowledge about cant. In either case, the final rhyme and the dialogue between "two maunders born and bred up rogues in their native language" (410) that Rid includes in the dictionary portion of his pamphlet are not meant (at least explicitly) to bring pleasure to the reader. Rather, Rid maintains that his project is to be viewed as a corrective one that takes the pleasure out of Dekker's text by discounting it as a mere copy and a presentation of patently false information.

Englishing as Linguistic and Cultural Incorporation

The term *to English* implies not only a desire to make the unknown known, but also a desire to transform that which is to be Englished—in this case, cant and rogue culture. Bryan Reynolds claims that "[o]fficial culture sought to safeguard its power by recording, co-opting, and commodifying cant in legal documents and commercial literature" (68). This is certainly the project that the authors of cony-catching pamphlets claim to be a part of. However, the Englishing process, despite the firm implication of unidirectionality inherent in its name, proves to be unstable, a process that can be used to transform rogues into English, perhaps, but also one that the English can use to transform themselves into rogues. Canting provided entrance into the world of the rogue: "Essentially, any proficient speaker of cant, regardless of whether he or she had ever perpetrated a crime, was a verifiable member of criminal culture" (Reynolds 89). Thus, making knowledge of cant widely available opened the door for English readers who might choose to "slum." Interestingly, the verb *to English* does not appear in the earliest canting dictionaries. Early pamphlets such as John Awdeley's *The Fraternity of Vagabonds* might be read as consisting of nothing more than a canting dictionary of sorts (1561).[11] Awdeley's pamphlet promises to list the "proper names and qualities" (53) of rogues and vagabonds and proceeds to do just that; the pamphlet functions as a sort of encyclopedia of rogue types, listing the names each type goes by and the particular behavior by which they can be identified. The pamphlet exposes the reader to some cant, but it is never identified as such; the notion that the rogues have their own language is merely implied when the author includes such information as the fact that certain rogues called "whip-jacks" carry a "counterfeit licence (which they call a gybe, and the seals they call jarks)" (53). Never are these words referred to as part of a legitimate language that a reader might learn to speak fluently. Rather, these words are presented as mere slang, denying them any larger sense of authority as a language, keeping the rogues firmly placed as internal others.

It is in Thomas Harman's *A Caveat or Warening for Common Cursetors Vulgarely Called Vagabones* that the first canting dictionary appears as a subsection of a larger cony-catching pamphlet. Though Harman follows Awdeley's encyclopedic pattern, listing types of rogues and then explaining their particular behavior, he expands this format by including accounts of specific instances where these tricks were performed, a list of the proper names (first name and surname where possible) of a large number of rogues divided by "rank," and finally, a list of words from "their pelting speech" (Judges 113), with the English equivalents provided alongside them. Notably, in his list of rogues, Harman takes care to indicate which are Irish, and he concludes the list with the caution that "there is above an hundred of Irishmen and women that wander about to beg for their living, that hath come over within these two years" (113). Harman thereby links the Irish crisis and the problem of the rogues: an English rogue is bad enough, an Irish rogue is even worse. The Irish and the rogues—and especially Irish rogues—are vilified together. Both communities are perceived and represented as troubling and persistent problems that plague the English nation.

Harman begins his dictionary with a brief description of the canting language; he tells the readers that he sets before them "the lewd, lousy language of these loitering lusks and lazy lorels, wherewith they buy and sell the common people as they pass through the country; which language they term pedlar's French, a unknown tongue only but to these bold beastly, bawdy beggars and vain vagabonds, being half mingled with English when it is familiarly talked" (113–14). Harman, unlike Awdeley, defines the speech as a language in its own right, and further, he identifies it as a kind of foreign language— "pedlar's French." Additionally, Harman links the language to currency; with this language, rogues can "buy and sell" English people. Alexandra Halasz argues that the world of rogue literature is "an allegorization of the structural presence of capital. Cony-catching, whether great or small, figures (control of) circulation as a form of production, a means of creating wealth" (75). This dynamic is in evidence here; the canting language serves as currency within the rogue community, and now, as a commodity in its own right—a selling point for Harman's pamphlet. Thus begins a process of commodification that continues to intensify throughout the period and which, as we will see, emerges most clearly in the phenomenon of the roaring boys. Harman further exerts control over his list of words by organizing it only by part of speech. Although this organization lends some credence to peddler's French, or cant, as a language by acknowledging that it does have a grammar—one that, significantly, can be "half mingled" with English much as the rogue community intermingles with English society—it also makes the dictionary difficult to use. The dictionary is informational and enables the reader to recognize cant, but it does not encourage the reader himself to gain fluency in the language.

At the end of his dictionary, Harman provides the reader with a short dialogue between an "upright-man" (the second in rank in rogue society, according to Harman) and a rogue, complete with an interlinear translation into English that Elizabeth Hanson claims causes the rogues' discourse to be "rendered sinister and remote, something that we overhear by literally reading between the lines" (106). However, this interlinear translation also creates a closeness between cant and English and renders the rogues as Englishmen. Harman controls the threat of this closeness and its potential to turn the English reader into a rogue by keeping the reader from undertaking his own translation project; the reader has no reason to perform his own translation of the dialogue since it is already provided for him. Harman further indicates that the reader need not attempt to translate the dialogue on his own by claiming that the language is transparent; it requires no study to master it. In fact, despite the fact that the dictionary and dialogue are brief, Harman tells the reader, "By this little, ye may wholly and fully understand their untoward talk and pelting speech, mingled without measure" (Judges 117). He describes the language as limited and primitive, a language so easy to understand that all one needs to know about it can be contained in a few short pages. Yet, as soon as Harman makes this statement, he notes that "they [rogues] have begun of late to devise some new terms for certain things, so will they in time alter this, and devise as evil or worse" (117). The threat of change and an escape back into the un-knowable, the uncontainable, is imminent, even though for the present moment the language is "known and spread abroad" (117).

As a hint of what is to come, and perhaps as a kind of preemptive strike against the looming changes, Harman includes a bit of speech that he does not English since he "learned [it] of a shameless doxy" (117). This is the first and only time that Harman uses the term *to English* in his pamphlet. Notably, he only uses it when he cannot or will not make the cant into English and includes words that are not listed in his dictionary. This bit of cant resists "Englishing" but also serves as an enticement to readers to learn more of the language; the desire to make the unknown known is whetted by Harman's pamphlet and this last piece of cant invites the reader to undertake his own investigation into the language in an effort to know what it means, but leaves him without the tools to do so. Thus, though the danger of encouraging a reader to enter into the world of the rogue without a guide is there, Harman attempts to control that danger by not providing the reader with the necessary knowledge to embark on that journey.

Thomas Dekker's "Canter's Dictionary" in *Lantern and Candlelight* is often discounted since it is almost entirely plagiarized from Harman's text; however, Dekker makes some significant changes to the dictionary and presents it in an entirely different manner than does Harman.[12] Dekker includes in his pamphlet, *Lantern and Candlelight*, a history of the canting language, giving it legitimacy as a language rather than treating it as simple jargon or slang. Additionally, he organizes the dictionary alphabetically in the manner of the *Table Alphabeticall* printed in 1604. Dekker thus makes his dictionary usable and, further, encourages his reader to use it. These changes set his dictionary apart from Harman's despite the fact that the words contained in the dictionary originally appear in Harman's pamphlet.[13] In Dekker's *Lantern and Candlelight,* language and the process of "Englishing" play a central role in the imagining of a national identity and also threaten that identity. Dekker opens his pamphlet with a history of language and its intimate connection to nation. He looks back to times before the Tower of Babel when all people spoke one language and claims that the confusion of tongues at Babel was the basis for nation formation.[14] He says that people ran about after their tongues were confused and, "hearing a man speak like themselves, followed only him, so that they who when the work began were all countreymen, before a quarter of it was finished fled from one another as from enemies and strangers. And in this manner did men at the first make up nations" (Dekker 189). By this account, nations formed out of necessity and are rooted in linguistic identity above all else. Thus, it is not surprising that the canting language functions as a primary marker for the nation of rogues that Dekker describes in this pamphlet. This language unifies them and allows them to "freely utter their minds one to another, yet avoid danger" when they are plotting crimes (190).

So central is the canting language to the nation of rogues that Dekker describes in his pamphlet, that in addition to a brief grammar of the language and a dictionary of select terms, he provides the reader with some translation exercises. Dekker purposely leaves some canting "un-Englished" as lessons "to be construed by him that is desirous to try his skill in the language, which he may do by help of the following dictionary" (192). He provides resources for the reader's entertainment, but also in order to introduce the reader into the culture of the rogues. The dictionary serves as a "little mint where [the reader] may coin words for [his] pleasure" (195). This image is one of agency; the dictionary provides the reader not only with currency for his journey into the underworld, but also with the ability to create more of that currency at his will. The ability to "coin" words is the ability to create riches—whether those riches reside solely in the pleasure the reader will gain by entering into the world of the rogue or in actual goods that he will gain as a result of roguish trickery remains unclear. With this mint, Dekker provides the reader with a passport into the nation of the rogue and then, at the end of *O Per Se O*, he guides the reader on the beginning of his journey with some canting songs "Thus, for Satisfaction of the Readers, Englished" (302).

However, the Englishing of these songs is not complete; Dekker does not translate the final song. He follows this untranslated song with the statement, "Enough of this, and he that desires more pieces of such pedlary ware may out of this little pack fit himself with any colours. *Vale!*" (308). This final statement indicates that, after reading the pamphlet, the reader has the tools to "English" the canting song for himself and, more significantly, that the reader can fashion his own canting songs if he so desires. The reader has the ability to enter the nation of rogues—or at least to impersonate the rogues he has read about—by using what pieces of the canting language he has learned in the course of the pamphlet. Additionally, the reader may fashion "any colours" he likes; he can raise whatever flag is most appropriate and advantageous to his situation. His identity becomes unfixed. The looseness of "Englishing" becomes apparent and the distinctions between the rogue and the upstanding English citizen disappear, because as soon as any English citizen can cant, it becomes impossible to determine who is and is not a rogue. Ironically, the purpose of Englishing a text for entertainment and education, for defining English national identity in contrast to the nation of rogues, ends up blurring the very boundaries it set out to define.

Samuel Rid also includes a canting dictionary in his pamphlet. Rid introduces his dictionary as an effort "not only to show [Dekker's] error in some places in setting down old words, used forty years ago before he was born, for words that are used in these days" but also to expand "his dictionary (or Master Harman's) with such words as I think he never heard of, and yet in use too" (406). Rid's task is a corrective and an additive one; he demonstrates his greater knowledge and authority by issuing a new and improved canting dictionary. Further, he promises the "true Englishing" (407) of the words Dekker has incorrectly Englished as well as additional words not previously included in any canting dictionary. Rid demonstrates his concern with the looseness of Dekker's dictionary; his reader, unlike Dekker's, is not given permission to "coin words for [his] pleasure" (Dekker 195). Instead, Rid attempts to constrain and control the Englishing process, limiting its practice to those who are truly expert and who are committed to using it only to make cant into

English and to do so precisely. He takes special care to clear up any confusion produced in Dekker's dictionary, noting for instance that *smeller,* not *smelling-cheat* means "garden"; a *smelling-cheat* is a "nosegay" (409). Interestingly, he does not address the fact that *smelling-cheat* is defined by Harman and Dekker as both "garden" and "nose." Rid makes no mention of the prior Englishing of *smelling-cheat* as "nose," suggesting that even his effort to give the "true Englishing" of cant fails to be definitive and cannot fully contain the language and the possibilities of translation.

The Sobering Reality of the Irish Crisis

Though fantasies of incorporation present an opportunity for entertainment in rogue literature, similar fantasies of incorporation through linguistic and cultural transformation are posed as real solutions to the Irish crisis by Spenser in *A View.* Neither pleasure nor justification are concerns for Spenser as he presents his text to his reader; Spenser does not face an audience that requires him to justify his treatise since, on the surface, it seems to reinforce the English social order. *A View* can be seen as a "synthesis of the opinions of the New English in Ireland during these decades [at the end of the sixteenth century]" (Canny 169). Spenser presents his dialogue as one that exposes the corruption that has already occurred in the form of the Old English community's "degeneration" into Irish. Spencer claims that nothing in his text has the power to corrupt; rather, he exposes "corruption" both to propose solutions to the Irish problem as well as to suggest methods for preventing the further degeneration of English people. The dialogue opens with Irenius's (the speaker in *A View* whose ideas are often identified with Spenser) expression of the fear that although many plans have been made for the "reformation" of Ireland,

> no purposes whatsoever which are meant for her good, will prosper or take good effect, which, whether it proceed from the very genius of the soyle, or the influence of the starres, or that Almighty God hath not yet appointed the time of her reformation, or that hee reserveth her in this unquiet state still for some secret scourge, which shall by her come into England, it is hard to be unknowne, but yet much to be feared. (11)

He sees Ireland as a corrupted place that has the potential to ruin England if it is not corrected as quickly as possible. Spenser sets out on what he sees as a sincere educational and reformative project in this dialogue.[15] He focuses on the "degenerated" Old English as the greatest threat to England and English national identity since they have *chosen* to become Irish, despite their full knowledge and experience of English identity and customs. Though Spenser's *A View* sets out the potentially corrupting "evils, which seeme . . . most hurt-full to the common-weale of that land" (13), it does so with the intent of rein-forcing English social order by devising a plan for making Ireland English. The Irish are consistently referred to in negative terms throughout *A View* and never is the reader invited to take pleasure in the Irish culture being dis-cussed. Irish words are rarely reproduced in the text and Irish customs are described in detail only in order to emphasize their difference from English customs and thus, their "barbarity." Spenser makes it clear that he describes these "evils" for the reader only so that the reader might join in his proposed plan to finally colonize the Irish.

Spenser's vision of colonization as translation causes the "Renaissance ideal of linguistic community [to be] exposed as a project of 'translation' by which one culture, one 'people,' is transformed into another" (Blank 148). Linguistic community is not "natural"; rather, it is carefully constructed through a transformative translation project. Language, in Spenser's text, is at once the most powerful tool of colonization, "for it hath ever beene the use of the conqueror, to despise the language of the conquered, and to force him by all meanes to learne his" (70), and also a powerful threat to the project of col-onization. Spenser refers to the special relationship between language and empire and seeks to clarify it by claiming that it is the language of the con-queror—or translator—that is supposed to be dominant. However, he acknowledges that this is not always the case. Indeed, Irenius explains that he finds "fault with the abuse of language, that is, for the speaking of Irish among the English, which it is unnaturall that any people should love another's lan-guage more than their owne, so it is very inconvenient, and the cause of many other evils" (Spenser 70). Here Irenius refers to the community of Old En-glish, English colonizers sent to conquer Ireland long before who have instead chosen to assimilate to Irish culture. Language, by Irenius's account, lies at the root of the evils attributed to the Old English, including the failure of En-gland's attempts to fully colonize Ireland.

Irenius persists in his belief that it is language (in combination with force) that will finally translate the Irish, and the degenerated Old English, into En-glish, despite the fact that language allows, and encourages, English settlers to "become Irish." Though by this time legal language has technically accom-plished the translation of the Irish into English subjects, the language of this legal translation does not accomplish the cultural translation it aims for. Nev-ertheless, Irenius claims that language will indeed be the basis for the success-ful translation of those Irish people who survive the imposition of the English garrisons. He claims that the only way to anglicize the Irish successfully is to bring about a "union of manners, and conformity of mindes, to bring them to be one people" (144). This can only be accomplished by a combination of physical and linguistic translation; the first step will be "translating of them and scattering them amongst the English" (145) so they can then have "dayly conversation" (145) (presumably in English) and also be less dangerous in their physical division. Each Irishman must also take an anglicized name that represents "his trade and facultie, or of some quality of his body or minde, or of the place where he dwelt, so as every one should be distinguished from the other, or from the most part, wherby they shall not onely not depend upon the head of their sept, as they now do, but also in time learne quite to forget his Irish nation" (147–48). Through this new system of naming, the man is identified with his trade, making his ability to labor and produce more important than his familial heritage. A descriptive English name, according to Spenser, has the ability to change social dynamics. The Irishman will identify with his trade, and his fellow tradesmen, rather than his clan. Spenser attempts to make a reality out of a fantasy similar to that described in rogue literature with its emphasis on productivity, which encourages "idle rogues" to become productive members of English society. Once again, Spenser links language and identity—an anglicized name will help make a productive Englishman out of an "idle" Irishman and, eventually, will help make an English nation out of Ireland.

However, it is not only changing the language of names that Spenser focuses on; he also draws the readers' attention to changing the language of education. Irenius proposes that an English method of schooling, in English, will produce anglicized Irish children who will then pass their Englishness on to other generations. Irenius claims that "all the sonnes of lords, gentlemen, and such others as are able to bring them up in learning, should be trayned up therein from their child-hoods" (150). Translation through education focuses on the Irish upper class and begins in childhood. As a result of this English education, "they will in short space grow up to that civill conversation, that both the children will loath their former rudenesse in which they were bred, and also their parents will even by the ensample of their young children perceive the foulenesse of their own behaviour, compared to theirs: For learning hath that wonderfull power in its selfe, that it can soften and temper the most sterne and savage nature" (151). Not only are the Irish portrayed as savages here, the English language, as taught by a male schoolmaster in an institutional rather than domestic setting, has the power to civilize the Irish, eradicating the culture they were born and raised in. Irenius claims that teaching children to speak and think in English in school has the power to undo their "mother-tongue," and that of their parents. The work that Spenser attributes elsewhere to the mother is undone by an institutional father figure.

Solving the problem of the Irish mother tongue through schooling does not sufficiently diffuse the threat Spenser discusses earlier in his treatise when Irenius states that the "chiefe cause of bringing in the Irish language, amongst them, was specially their fostering, and marrying with the Irish, the which are two most dangerous infections" (71). By assigning the responsibility for degeneration to language, Spenser intimately links language and cultural or national identity. Significantly, language, gender, and nation become tied together in Spenser's conception of how cultural translation occurs. Spenser claims that it is dangerous for a child to learn Irish as his or her first language since "the speach being Irish, the heart must needs bee Irish: for out of the abundance of the heart, the tongue speaketh" (71). He maintains that the child a woman nurses "must of necessity learne his first speach of her" and this language, his mother tongue, "is ever after most pleasing unto him" (71). In this version of how language and identity intersect, it does not matter if the child later learns English; according to Spenser, his first language will always be his most beloved. The struggle to control language and identity is gendered; though the mother has a lasting influence on the child, her influence is, according to Spenser, a degenerate one.

The threat of the Irish mother tongue and its refusal to be conquered exposes itself in the community of the Old English who resist the reform urged upon them by the New English colonizers. The knowing decision made on the part of the Old English in becoming Irish inverts the process of translation that Spenser sets forth as the solution to the Irish problem. The Old English community is one that realizes the English fear that internal others are in fact "contagious." By choosing to become part of a group that threatens English identity, the Old English suggest that national and cultural identities are chosen, not innate, and that other identities may be more desirable than the English. Throughout Spenser's text runs a tension between the process of translation he envisions and that which he encounters. His ideal translation works only to make Irish English; however, he repeatedly confronts the reality that it can also make English Irish. Translation is an unstable, uncontrollable process that can move in both directions. When this fantasy breaks down, it has real implications for the Irish. Indeed, the methods Spenser proposes to enforce the cultural translation of the Irish involve violence and raise the "troubling possibility that one may not be able to distinguish the problem from the solution with any degree of confidence" (Hadfield xix), causing Spenser to undermine his purpose despite himself.

The Appeal of "Degeneration": Roaring Boys, Roaring Girls, and the Old English

The anxieties addressed by authors of rogue literature as they introduce their texts and the persistent problem of the "degenerate" Old English in *A View* suggest that both the rogue culture and the Irish culture held a certain appeal for Renaissance English subjects. Roaring boys and the Old English each represent groups of people who *chose* to become a part of communities that highlighted ruptures in the imagined English national identity. "Conversion" into each group takes place largely through language, despite the fact that cant "was culturally devalued by its association with the poor and the dispossessed" (Blank 67) and that Irish was legislated against both in the Statutes of Kilkenny (1366), which, among other things, "ruled that the king's subjects speak only English" (Hadfield 22), and in later acts. English subjects were drawn to these communities, despite the threat they posed to English national identity—and perhaps because of it.[16]

We can recognize the threat the appeal of rogue culture, and especially of canting, poses to English national identity in the phenomenon of "roaring boys," young men who were "noisy and riotous . . . [and] who terrorised decent people in the streets of London" (Spearing xiv). Portrayals of roaring boys (or girls) in plays like *The Alchemist* and *The Roaring Girl* depict these characters as young people who are interested in the criminal class and find it fashionable to smoke, swagger, and cant. The portrayal of these characters in drama indicates the "social climbing of popular rogue literature, the 'raising' of the Renaissance underworld and its language" (Blank 58). In fact, in *The Roaring Girl* (1611), written by Dekker and Middleton, the title character, Moll, "gladly and openly reveals the secrets of the canting language to an upper-class public, whose natural distaste for the language quickly gives way to delight" (59). This play serves as an ideal example of the dynamics under consideration here for many reasons, not the least of which is that, as James Knowles notes, the play "recycles Dekker's own prose tracts . . . which in turn draw on Thomas Harman's *Caveat for Common Cursitors*" and uses "canting terms familiar to many of the audience" (Knowles xix). Dekker includes the audience who watches his play in the experience of the rogue world much as he encourages his readers to enter into the rogue world and take pleasure in it in his pamphlets. Indeed, as in his pamphlets, the play places a great emphasis on the pleasure to be had both by the rogue and the Englishman within the world of the rogue community.

Most of the canting in *The Roaring Girl* takes place in a scene between Moll and some of her roguish acquaintances, Trapdoor and Tearcat.[17] Significantly, their canting amuses and entertains the upper class men Moll is with. They clamor at Moll, asking her to "teach me what 'niggling' is, I'd fain be niggling" (5.1.207) and praising her for her talents, exclaiming, "This is excellent. One fit more, good Moll" (5.10.212). Indeed, Moll takes the gentlemen, and the audience, on a tour of the "London underworld," fascinating them with her knowledge and her skills. And yet, though she is disdained and feared by those like Sir Alexander Wengrave who see in her a threat to their own social status, Moll gains credibility and admiration from these young gentlemen who are impressed by her knowledge of the fashionable canting language and the alluring world of petty thieves. Moll's knowledge serves her well in this scene, and in the play more generally, enabling her to move between worlds while she "simultaneously maintains her criminal solidarity with Trapdoor and Tearcat (by not revealing all that transpired between them) and her apparent solidarity with the members of the gentry (by translating for them)" (Reynolds 71). In the canting scene, Moll speaks fluently in cant with cutpurses and then teaches the gentlemen about what she herself has learned through asking, not through experience. Moll confirms that one may enter into the world of the rogue without actually being a rogue; she even promises the gentlemen that if they see a rogue, "so he be in his art a scholar, question him, / Tempt him with gold to open the large book / Of his close villainies, and you yourself shall cant / Better than poor Moll can" (5.1.323–26). The rogue, she indicates, can be bought; his life is a commodity. The world of the rogue can be, as Dekker also suggests in his pamphlets, textualized, Englished, and then used to un-English a common citizen; understanding the rogue culture can open the door to being part of it—even if only temporarily.[18] Indeed, Moll's explanations of the rogue world win her praise from all who respond to her with comments such as "A brave mind, Moll, i'faith" (5.1.350). The delight canting brings to the upper-class characters in the play brings us back to *Lantern and Candlelight* and Dekker's insistence on the delight there is in reading his pamphlet and learning the ways of rogues. The boundaries are blurred when the upper or middle class delights in and imitates the criminal underclass, especially when this underclass threatens their very identity.

The rogues begin this blurring of identities when they successfully imitate gentlemen in order to perform their tricks, many of which depend upon their ability to convince gentlemen that they too are members of the upper class. They count on the fact that the gentlemen they wish to trick will believe their stories solely on the basis that they "carr[y] the shape of an honest man in show and of a gentleman in [their] apparel" (Dekker 247). And, of course, the rogue as gentleman only speaks "proper" English. The greater threat is posed when, rather than reacting to these impersonations by supporting the legislated boundaries between classes, members of the upper class respond by imitating the rogues themselves; those who are supposed to be enforcing Englishness "defect" and glamorize the very community that ostensibly threatens a stable sense of English identity.

Similarly, the community of the Old English represents the appeal of the Irish culture for English colonizers. The Old English expose the problems encountered in attempting to translate people by force. This community of Englishmen who have chosen to become Irish counteract any successful translations of the Irish into English. While the process of colonial translation was successful in some cases—the "wilde Irish, which, being very wilde at the first, are now become more civill"—the Old English, "from civillity, are growne to be wilde and meere Irish" (Spenser 143). The Old English, who choose to become Irish, reveal the "looseness" of the colonial project of translating people. They were sent to Ireland to translate the Irish into English, but instead, they translate themselves and become "almost meere Irish, yea, and more malitious to the English than the Irish themselves" (54). Some of the Old English outside the English Pale go so far as to discard "their English names, and put on Irish that they might bee altogether Irish" (68). Indeed, because of the instability of the project of cultural and racial translation in Ireland, the preoccupation of Englishmen "was not so much with the 'Anglicization' of the Irish as with the 'Gaelicization' of the English" (Blank 145). The Old English reveal the flaws in the English colonial project and enhance already present anxieties about the Irish and their "contagious" culture. The violence that Spenser proposes to enact on the Irish when translation does not work exposes the instability and danger of fantasies of incorporation.

Both Dekker's pamphlet and Spenser's treatise reveal the impossibility of establishing a permanent linguistic identity. Stability cannot be assured, as is especially clear in the case of the Old English. Whether intentionally or not, the texts examined here reveal that the project of linguistic unity and of "cultural recreation . . . according to which, by translating foreign languages into English, the early modern world would be 'reborn' as the British Empire" (Blank 127) is not a straightforward one. There are no guarantees in such a project and, as the appeal of the rogue culture and the Irish culture show us, the threat of "degeneration" always persists. These texts remind us that linguistic and cultural threats to English national identity exist both within and without the bounds of England itself. The persistence and the appeal of subversive linguistic communities reveal the fault lines in what is imagined to be a solid English national identity rooted in language and in difference from the "other." In the end, the metaphors of "Englishing" and "translation" enable bidirectional movement; they are fantasies of incorporation that, when they fail, lead to realities of violence.

NOTES

1. Linda Woodbridge notes that the peoples encountered by the English overseas were often likened to English vagrants (59). See Canny; and Murphy, "Reviewing the Paradigm" and *Irish Sea*, for more on the relationship between the colonization of Ireland and North America.

2. See Linda Woodbridge's introduction to her *Vagrancy, Homelessness, and English Renaissance Literature* for a succinct history of the genre of rogue literature.

3. Linda Bradley Salamon's "Vagabond Veterans" in this volume also addresses the problems of dealing with the displaced in sixteenth-century England—specifically, unemployed soldiers—whose identities are often slippery and who are sometimes viewed with a "sneaking admiration."

4. Murphy's concept of proximity draws on Bhabha's idea of mimicry in which the Other is "a subject of a difference that is almost the same, but not quite" (Bhabha 86). Bhabha's ideas on mimicry are especially significant here since the dynamics between the official culture of England and the "nation" of rogues as well as the Irish prefigure the dynamics of later colonial discourse Bhabha addresses in "Of Mimicry and Man."

5. See Manley; Halasz; Woodbridge; and Hanson for more on these topics respectively.

6. See McMullan; and Beier for two sociohistorical approaches to cant.

7. See Parker, "Conveyers," and "*Merry Wives*" for more on the implications of *convey* and *translate*. See Blank; and Johnson-Haddad for more on "Englishing."

8. As Laurie Ellinghausen points out in this volume, "To read *Lantern and Candlelight* is to be entertained by the stories that unfold."

9. The discourse of disease and infection occurs throughout both Dekker's and Spenser's texts. A complete discussion of this discourse is outside the bounds of this chapter. However, it provides another potent metaphor for circulation and transmission that also indicates the status of these "proximate" communities. They, like a disease or infection, are internal to the English body, but they are also harmful to that body. This discourse implies that these communities work from within the body of the English nation in order to harm or even destroy that body. Additionally, it highlights the fear that these communities were contagious—a fear that we will later see is not entirely unfounded. Both the rogues and the Irish held an extended appeal for the larger English community.

10. William West notes that one result of the work of cant is "the production of delight." (233).

11. With the exception of Dekker's *Lantern and Candlelight*, references to all pamphlets can be found in Judges's *The Elizabethan Underworld*.

12. Judges discounts Dekker's dictionary and excises it from his edition of the pamphlet, claiming that it is "only a copy with a few not very intelligent modifications, of the list of words given by Harman in his *Caveat*" (515 n. 13). However, as I will argue,

Dekker's changes are indeed significant. For this reason, I have not used Judges's edition of Dekker's pamphlet and instead refer to E. D. Pendry's 1968 edition that includes both "The Bellman's Second Night Walk" and "O Per Se O" under the title *Lantern and Candlelight*.

13. See Reynolds 76–77 for more on the significance of Dekker's technical approach to cant in his pamphlet.

14. See Ellinghausen's "Black Acts" in this volume for another reading of this episode in Dekker that focuses on it as a demonstration of the "deleterious cultural effects of the loss of a common language."

15. For other ways to read Spenser's project and his experience in Ireland, see Hadfield.

16. Tina Kuhlisch in this volume also notes that sixteenth-century rogues "were criminals but attractive and socially significant ones" and explores how this dynamic develops later in *Moll Flanders*.

17. See West for an extended discussion of the work of cant in *The Roaring Girl*.

18. West makes a similar observation: despite that fact that, on stage, many representations of cant indicated that it worked "by hiding, tricking, covering, and [having] no other power" (239) and that the "movement between languages, and thus between classes, proceeds resolutely in a single direction" (240), these "axioms of transparency and secrecy" (241) are challenged in plays such as *The Jovial Crew*. In these plays, as in the canting dictionaries I examine, "Cant at least has the potential to master its users" (241) whether or not they are rogues.

WORKS CITED

Beier, Lee. "Anti-language or Jargon? Canting in the English Underworld in the Sixteenth and Seventeenth Centuries." *Languages and Jargons*. Ed. Peter Burke and Roy Porter. Cambridge: Polity P, 1995. 64–101.

Bhabha, Homi. *The Location of Culture*. London: Routledge, 1994.

Blank, Paula. *Broken English: Dialects and the Politics of Language in Renaissance Writings*. London: Routledge, 1996.

Bradshaw, Brendan, Andrew Hadfield, and Willy Maley, eds. *Representing Ireland: Literature and the Origins of Conflict, 1534–1660*. Cambridge: Cambridge UP, 1993.

Canny, Nicholas. "Identity Formation in Ireland: The Emergence of the Anglo-Irish." *Colonial Identity in the Atlantic World, 1500–1800*. Ed. Anthony Pagden and Nicholas Canny. Princeton: Princeton UP, 1987. 159–212.

Dekker, Thomas. *English Villainies Discovered by Lantern and Candlelight*. 1611. Ed. E. D. Pendry. Cambridge: Harvard UP, 1968.

Dionne, Craig. "Playing the 'Cony': Anonymity in Underworld Literature." *Genre* 30.1–2 (1997): 29–49.

Ellinghausen, Laurie. "Black Acts: Textual Labor and Commercial Deceit in Dekker's *Lantern and Candle-light*."

Hadfield, Andrew. *Spenser's Irish Experience*. Oxford: Clarendon P, 1997.

Halasz, Alexandra. *The Marketplace of Print*. Cambridge: Cambridge UP, 1997.

Hanson, Elizabeth. *Discovering the Subject*. Cambridge: Cambridge UP, 1998.

Johnson-Haddad, Miranda. "Englishing Ariosto: *Orlando Furioso* at the Court of Elizabeth I." *Comparative Literature Studies* 31.4 (1994): 323–50.

Judges, A. V., ed. *The Elizabethan Underworld*. 2nd ed. London: Routledge, 1964.

Knowles, James, ed. *The Roaring Girl and Other City Comedies*. Oxford: Oxford UP, 2001.

Manley, Lawrence. *Literature and Culture in Early Modern London*. Cambridge: Cambridge UP, 1995.

McMullan, John. *The Canting Crew*. New Brunswick, N.J.: Rutgers UP, 1984.

Middleton, Thomas, and Thomas Dekker. *The Roaring Girl*. 1611. *The Roaring Girl and Other City Plays*. Ed. James Knowles. Oxford: Oxford UP, 2001.

Murphy, Andrew. *But the Irish Sea betwixt Us*. Lexington: UP of Kentucky, 1999.

———. "Reviewing the Paradigm: A New Look at Early-Modern Ireland." *Eire-Ireland* 31.3–4 (1996): 13–40.

Parker, Patricia. "Conveyers Are You All." *Shakespeare from the Margins*. Chicago: U of Chicago P, 1996. 149–84.

———. "The *Merry Wives of Windsor* and Shakespearean Translation." *MLQ* 52.3 (1991): 225–61.

Reynolds, Bryan. *Becoming Criminal: Transversal Performance and Cultural Dissidence in Early Modern England*. Baltimore: Johns Hopkins UP, 2002.

Spearing, Elizabeth, and Janet Todd eds. *Counterfeit Ladies*. New York: New York UP, 1994.

Spenser, Edmund. *A View of the Present State of Ireland*. Ed. Andrew Hadfield and Willy Maley. Oxford: Blackwell Publishers, 1997.

West, William N. "Talking the Talk: Cant on the Jacobean Stage." *English Literary Renaissance* 33.2 (2003): 228–51.

Woodbridge, Linda. *Vagrancy, Homelessness, and English Renaissance Literature*. Urbana: U of Illinois P, 2001.

The Ambivalent Rogue

Moll Flanders as Modern Pícara

When Daniel Defoe introduced readers to Moll Flanders during the early eighteenth century, he entered an ongoing debate about the social construction of rogues, criminals, and economic practices. Like the sixteenth- and seventeenth-century rogues and vagrants treated elsewhere in this volume, his heroine demonstrates the ideology of the self-fashioned gentle(wo)man whose social and economic ambitions were still, in the eighteenth century, regarded as inimical to the traditional makeup of society. In the figure of the independent itinerant opportunist, Defoe depicts forms of social life that oppose traditional forms like the family and the local established businessman and—while they prove better adapted to capitalist demands—arouse fear of new market processes.[1] Unlike the criminals of Tyburn biographies and cony-catching pamphlets, however, Moll is a rather unspectacular antihero who enjoys her later years in quiet anonymity. As a picaro, this rogue type not only warns readers against common tricks by presenting them with entertaining anecdotes, but the picaresque novel wherever it appears, whether in Spain or England, also expresses unresolved issues in contemporary social discourse.[2] Rogue literature does so, too, more or less consciously, as several authors in this collection argue. The picaresque, however, correlates generic form with content very effectively to that end, as I will show. Typically the authorial attitude toward society oscillates between approval and disapproval of the status quo. A certain double structure typical of the genre expresses the ambivalence.[3] Perhaps more so than other forms of rogue literature, *Moll Flanders* is a thoroughly double-voiced and double-structured work. Defoe exploits the generic features of the picaresque, in form as well as content, to express social criticism. His ambivalence about the demand for unrelenting, impersonal, and often morally questionable economic ambition found an apt form in the ambiguity of the picaresque genre.[4] In the following pages I would like first to explore his employment and adaptation of picaresque characteristics in *Moll Flanders* for his critique of capitalist practice; and second to consider its discursive structures on a somewhat more speculative level in relation to the picaresque double structure of both form and function. Though picaresque on the dynamic view, Defoe's novel differs quite a bit from Spanish picaresque novels—and also from its English roguish forebears—in being conditioned by the contemporary circumstances of eighteenth-century England.[5] Moll's origin, the initiation incident with the older brother, and other themes and motifs belong clearly to the Spanish picaresque tradition.[6] The heroine's character development and her character traits of *homo economicus*, on the other hand, are expressions of a new English middle-class attitude. Economic thought of the early eighteenth century in England, that is, the formal economic individualism described in Ian Watt's *The Rise of the Novel*, modifies several characteristics of the picaresque on such scores as individualism, the pursuit of wealth, and morality. Thus, the rogue is presented in retrospect as a middle-class public-minded citizen who demands respect for her efforts, rather than the criminal hero of many earlier English rogue stories who has gained fame through his unlawful and frequently spectacular feats.[7]

In fact, the new economic attitude as naturalized by Moll, or rather its implications for morality, is largely what Defoe seeks to criticize via the picaresque genre, not so much roguery as such. On the one hand, he seems to support the economic order in which the pursuit of wealth is the principal motive of all actions, and Moll is to be sure financially successful at the novel's end. Although a criminal during part of her life, her activities command admiration as economic endeavors, as both she and the editor emphasize, and she is decriminalized in retrospect. On the other hand, Defoe appears to fear the implications for morality and traditional values, and Moll is repeatedly punished for her vicious life and repents. The picaresque format lent itself to the expression of those anxieties. The picaro's narrative is an example of his "wrong" behavior. An outcast cuckold at the end, for example, Lazarillo's deviant behavior was punished; his narrative hence reaffirmed the values of the dominant class. So does Moll's, in a way. On the other hand, just like earlier picaros, Moll works for various "masters" and moves in different social classes and travels through the country, placing her in different vantage points from which to criticize society. In *Moll Flanders*, as in other picaresque novels, the framing as autobiography and resulting distances in narrative situation contribute to the effect of ambiguity. A repentant narrator relates her former roguish actions. They divert the reader, contrary to the intention stated in the prologue—to show how every evil leads to more evil.

Rogue as Ambivalent Character

Similarities in the sociohistorical developments of eighteenth-century England and of baroque Spain made possible the use of the genre. In Golden Age Spain, society was no longer conceived as fixed and immutable, giving new importance to the individual's responsibility in creating one's own fate. Yet, traditional concepts, especially "purity of blood," excluded some from the possibility of social advancement. In England at the tail end of the long early modern period, the position of the individual had also changed due to an empiricist emphasis upon the individual. A new credit economy challenged the ideal of property-based autonomy of the individual. While the new economy facilitated upward mobility, the established classes exhibited a negative attitude toward upstarts, and economic ambition could come into conflict with established values. The picaro was attractive and threatening in Spain as an example of an individual free from the strict conventions of a complex social order[8]—above all the exclusive concept of honor—and in England as one who overcomes economic class boundaries.

A similarly uneasy attitude toward rogues had prevailed in England since the end of the sixteenth century. They were criminals but attractive and socially significant ones.[9] As Craig Dionne, among others, points out, literature long before Defoe dealt with the phenomenon that these marginalized individuals embodied in many ways novel ideas that were already accepted among large sectors of society. Around 1600 the frequent change of position of vagrants and laboring men was an economic exigency, as Patricia Fumerton shows in this volume, yet it was viewed suspiciously by the upper classes. She argues, for instance, that the actual necessity to take advantage of every new situation and to be thus business-savvy was fictionalized as a series of gratuitous roguish feats in Harman's *A Caveat or Warening for Common Cursetors Vulgarely Called Vagabones* (1566). In Defoe's eighteenth-century novel, on the other hand, the heroine's mind for economic matters itself is stressed. Rogue literature voiced ambivalent sentiments about the underworld as a guildlike ideal organization on the one hand, and as a symbolic Other through which the entrepreneurial middle class constructed its identity on the other. Cony-catching pamphlets, criminal biographies, tracts about beggars, and other new urban literary forms reflected this unsettling consciousness.[10] They often employed formal elements that can also be seen in picaresque novels.[11]

Yet the author's deep ambivalence about the enterprising social deviants was generally not a function of the generic form as in the picaresque with its pervasive formal double structure. William Carroll notes, for instance, that the story of the fraudulent beggar Genings, in Thomas Harman's pamphlet, above all delights in his ruses and contains mere alibi for moral commentary. The Genings episode lacks, however, such constitutive elements of the picaresque as the pseudoautobiographical conceit or the dubious repentance with its moral charge. Other fictionalized accounts of the exploits of condemned criminals celebrated the rogue as martyr in a succession of episodes that did not stress the inexorable path to destruction—like in the picaresque yet contrary to official biographies. Lawrence Manley detects a strategy of diversion and moralizing similar to that in the picaresque novel in Greene's sixteenth-century pamphlets but points to the failure of contemporaries to read them seriously and as a multivoiced form. While similar sentiments about marginalized individuals in early capitalism existed and were implied in earlier and contemporary native literary forms, the picaresque novel was therefore better suited to Defoe's aim through its formal generic two-sidedness.

Moll as Pícara

As is true for other rogues,[12] the reader cannot be sure about Moll's role in the narrative—as moral instance or as rogue. Her present position at the time of narrating, what Spanish critics call the picaro's *caso,* or case, forms a rationale for the narration of her adventures. While in criminals' lives the narrator's experience is described not from his or her perspective but from the outside, the picaro's account is subjective and therefore creates psychological paradoxes. As in Lazarillo, the fact that Moll feels the need to explain her situation at once exculpates her actions yet shows that back in England she is "not so extraordinary a penitent as she was at first," as the editor intimates (6).[13] For instance, she "give[s] the parents a just reproof for their negligence in leaving the poor little lamb to come home by itself" (213). Moreover, she presents her thefts and other bad deeds not only as bad examples for the reader, but also presents the "good side" of these actions, actions to be imitated by her readers. With the right economic mind-set she seized favorable occasions.[14] Moll, the apparently repentant sinner, does not only remain blind to her own inconsistencies even when relating her life retrospectively, but she believes in the values she superficially condemns.

On a deeper level, Defoe's ambivalence of opinion carries over to the language employed and even to narrative method, and the picaresque shared in that ambivalence.[15] While there are two discourses present in both, the heroine's preference at times for one of each pair functions as a guide to her social attitude. In each case, the discursive strategies correspond broadly to distinctive ideologies: the literal rather than the figurative use of language, and the concept of individualized narratives rather than a master narrative, to progressive ideology rather than traditional ideology. Moll's show of traditional ideology can be compared to the Englishing of rogue's cant in order to domesticate outsiders, which Brooke Stafford describes in this collection. Moll's use of economic terms, however, demonstrates her membership in the modern world of business as it was desirable to the modern economic man. Hence, on this deeper level of discourse, the picaresque also comments variously on the social acceptability of the rogue.

One typical characteristic of the picaresque novel—as well as of some English rogue stories—is Moll's origin as a *pícara*, her birth in prison as the daughter of a convicted felon, and hence a trajectory already marked out for her in the lowest strata of society. Moll differs from other picaros and her native predecessors, however, in that the promise of such a future affects her deeply quite early in her life, and she rejects this publicly imposed identity. From the beginning, she does not believe that she is naturally poor but considers herself entitled to a more affluent life. Her Spanish predecessors, on the other hand, are basically content with their lot and try to change it not as a psychological imperative in order to realize their true character but merely as an exercise of ingenuity. As long as they do not have to fear going hungry, which is their greatest concern, they are content with their position, adapt to every situation that offers, and make the best of it for the moment. Her English predecessors' situation is presented similarly in early modern pamphlets. Yet in contrast to both picaros and rogues, the eighteenth-century character cannot simply make herself comfortable in whatever circumstances she happens into. While the Spanish picaros acquire a new identity with each disguise and enjoy taking on different roles, Moll does not do so. She defines her identity through her social position, which results from the material effects of her economic activities. An occupation for her is hence more than simply a temporary bread-winning enterprise. It is a determinant of her self-consciousness. Moll pretends to be a rich widow; at other times she disguises herself as a man, as a beggar, and so on. Ultimately though, her projects fail so that at one point she states, "It was impossible to be so nimble, so ready, so dexterous at these things in a dress so contrary to nature" (235). So Moll disguises herself, and yet she remains the Moll she takes herself to be, never taking on an identity different from the one she wants to assert.[16]

Believing in her stable identity, Moll works to acquire the corresponding social status. Earlier English rogues were more clearly deviant and outside society than she is. They lived in their separate organized underworld; they did not have a banker-friend like Moll, and they usually did not affect virtue in their ruses other than outdated gallantry and gentlemanly honor. And while they conventionally repented in the prison ordinary's biographies, criminals were hanged in the end. Moll's position on the margin of the respectable world, regarding her fortune as well as her values, is less clearly determined, and it offers opportunity for development. She has a greater chance of changing her situation against contrary circumstances than other picaros have against fate. Her skills carry her farther in a society that acknowledges the individual possibility of improving one's lot; farther than do the Spanish picaro's talents in a more static society that has only just recently "discovered" free will; and farther than do the rogue's in early modern England, which inevitably tried to define his place outside legitimate society. Moll's skills are, moreover, actually skills she has to learn and practice, whereas the older picaro's and rogue's "skills" are not much more than ingenuity and daring sharpened through penury. Since Moll has more opportunity of willed and lasting influence on her life, her problems seem more consequential, and her actions tend to evoke more sympathy and identification in the reader. The consequences are perhaps described in a more psychological way in Moll Flanders. Whereas the Spanish picaros seem immune to pain and death and leap up after each blow like toy tumbling figures, Defoe's heroine stresses the impact of her failures on her mood and on her behavior, as when she falls seriously ill under the pressure of the two brothers' advances and their mother's distrust.[17] Her problems are more internalized than the picaros'.[18] In the affair with the husband-brother, for instance, laws or conventions are not what would stand in the way of such a union so much as the *pícara*'s own abhorrence and physical repulsion. Many readers could thus sympathize with her. They would acknowledge Moll's good moral and ethical intentions and would understand her hardships on the way up the social ladder. In the eyes of other readers, the fact that Moll chooses to rise through immoral means despite her avowed knowledge of the wrongs could have made her the agent of her own sufferings. Those readers might well have read the discourse not as criticism of the traditional norms—the barriers upstarts faced and consequential deviant behavior that resulted from them—but rather as diversion, as the necessarily futile attempts of an undeserving low-class character at rising in hierarchic society (see Cruz).

Like the Spanish picaro, Moll is also wakened to being a *pícara*, to a life of distrust. She has one decisive experience—the older son's rejection after seducing her—through which she realizes that she has to be a *pícara* from that point on. Yet while the protagonists of the earlier picaresque novels are suddenly and irrevocably converted into picaros through the initiation incident, in Moll's case this incident triggers a gradual hardening process, in which her actions become more morally and ethically questionable than before.[19] In Bath, only her candid admission that she is looking for financial provision instead of true love is objectionable. Then she allows her friend to disperse false information about her possessions, information that is aimed at deceiving others. In the second part of her life, her actions are more immoral, for she works as a prostitute and a thief. Unlike the traditional picaresque narratives, in Defoe's novel Moll's own development is central to its structure.[20] Her experiences determine her future actions, which also depend directly on the material outcome of previous incidents. For example, because she is still married to the gentleman-tradesman, she cannot yet remarry and therefore has to invent another scheme. Likewise, the *pícara*'s social conversion in the end is only possible through her previous actions, and that conversion facilitates her moral reform. In that sense, there is only one possible causal and temporal order leading up to the ending, which cannot be changed, according to the narrator at least. In earlier picaresque novels, the case lent unity to a narrative consisting of episodes that were not interlocked more than rudimentarily (see Rico). They were separate units following a biographical order but not a causal relation, therefore not leading to any climax in the narration. Moll's *caso*, on the other hand, is more consciously presented as the temporary endpoint of a process and a matter of her personal development in keeping with the image of a more independent individual, and hence the novelistic conventions, of the eighteenth century.[21]

Contemporary thought also appropriated the picaresque feature of the solitariness of the picaro, and, like her baroque relatives, Moll remains a solitary character throughout her life, frequently "being perfectly alone" and "friendless" (174).[22] Yet her solitude is due to economic individualism, a motive that did not figure in the Spanish picaresque novels. While the Spanish picaro is alone as a function of being an outsider, Moll is alone as a function of her being an insider. As economic woman of the eighteenth century, Moll has to be active and self-reliant. She pursues her own economic self-interest, so single-mindedly that any parental responsibility—or indeed any obligations either of "wedlock or mistress-ship in the world" (138)—would get in her way.[23] Moll fears being left alone and turned loose on the streets not because she would miss a friend or because she dislikes loneliness, but because she needs others to do business with her. Therefore, she "had taken care all this while to preserve a correspondence with [her] honest friend at the bank . . . though [she] had not spent [her] money so fast as to want any from him" (175). Although some recurring figures appear various times in the novel or over an extended period, Moll never establishes true relationships with the many people she meets. Instead, she is suspicious of everybody. For example, the fact that on their first try Moll does not tell her Lancashire husband her name or how much money she possesses saves her when they find out about their respective situations. This careful behavior and the fact that she hardly ever tries to reestablish relationships after a move to another place are realistic traits of a criminal. So are the character traits of being self-centered and shutting off all feelings. They are, at the same time, essential to business success. For example, Moll seems hard-hearted toward her children, only mentioning them by the by, and disposing of them when they are materially disadvantageous (136). Yet acting in this way, she becomes independent and can pursue her goals without having any of the burdens of human responsibility. She can move to the hubs of (her) trade and appear as a virgin, for instance. As a character imbued with the spirit of personal success and competition in an unstable hierarchy, Moll the businesswoman has a functional view of the people she meets and is always the beneficiary of a relationship.[24]

Other formal features of the picaresque exist in Defoe's novel under a new ideological perspective. *Moll Flanders* reflects its continental ancestry in that the *pícara* often does not determine beforehand where she is going to stay and what she is going to do, but lets chance, or "the diligent devil," direct her and "prompt [her] to go out and take a walk, that is to say, to see if anything would offer in the old way" (217). This also in part determines the episodic structure of the novel. Some of her actions, however, are planned. She moves to places, to another part of town (72), or Bath (115), where she can attract men, with the aim of improving her financial situation. When she leaves for America with the Lancashire husband, she takes well-considered provisions to facilitate a new start there. Even in her unplanned activities, Moll actually works toward the future. For, unlike Guzmán, Pablos, and others, who do not have to take care of their belongings and are not concerned with more than their current position and alleviating immediate hunger, Moll plans for eventualities: she saves money.[25] Moll thus actively attempts to shape her fate, to rise in society through planned activities. Her eighteenth-century economic attitude determines one of her most important motives, that is, her methodical pursuit of wealth, a feature not present in the Spanish picaresque novels or English rogue literature before Defoe. It determines her actions from the very beginning, when she decides to earn money through independent work in order to rise socially through her own merit. Begging is not an option for her, not because it is dishonorable as in siglo de oro Spain but because laziness in early-eighteenth-century England runs counter to active entrepreneurship. Moll's preference for hard work suggests that she shares her contemporaries' values.

The heroine's character traits are common middle-class and are desirable in the eighteenth century. They lead to success. As Watt argues, they are not considered bad, and the ambitious, restless, and self-centered Moll is, in fact, the perfect economic woman.[26] Actions like counting her money, calling her thievery a "trade" (227), planning her enterprises in Virginia, and so on, are all expressions of period ideology, as are her desires for economic security, a husband, and being a respected "gentlewoman."[27] Her reformation prompted through material success is in keeping with economic individualism in eighteenth-century England.[28] In Spain during the *siglo de oro,* economic gain as the sole motive of an action was viewed negatively. Penitence in Defoe's time, however, does not necessarily have to be supported by religious action but by perseverance and diligence in economic matters. And the character Moll does take her "trade" seriously; she conducts it with skill and prudence. It is not a crime to her. Therefore, she is not punished for her life of vice. Under this view it is not really vicious at all but the natural result of a praiseworthy acceptance of common values.[29] Only when she does not stop stealing after having accumulated enough money to live comfortably is she sent to prison, yet the punishment is commuted. She is transported to Virginia and is financially very successful there, which allows her to lead an outwardly virtuous life and quit her former criminal life. So, in fact, all in all her life is a success story, contrary to the picaro's and the rogue's. She is rewarded for her behavior and character traits that correspond to the exigencies of economic individualism.[30]

Yet Moll's actions are morally ambiguous.[31] They are not always right by the standards of human interaction respectful of each other's needs, even though they might be legal. She transgresses social conventions and is ruthless and selfish in her pursuit of wealth.[32] In this respect, my analysis revises Watt's old thesis that Moll is the perfect economic woman. The author of Moll Flanders had doubts about the social wholesomeness of economic individualism. One aspect especially is questionable regarding its moral charge, although in Defoe's society it was gradually accepted as a "normal" attitude.[33] It is Moll's notion of "necessity" that distinguishes her from older picaros. She not only wants to have enough food and a place to sleep, like the earlier picaros, but she wants to live "handsomely"—more comparable, in fact, to some English rogues, who wanted to acquire wealth and fame. While Lázaro's and Pablos's vicissitudes are reflected in a lack of food, Moll's fortunes are reflected in the amount of money she has, and she "cast[s] up [her] accounts" (138) after each episode. Moll purposefully enriches herself, and for that objective she cheats, steals, and takes advantage of others. Her sinful behavior is therefore not justified by the prospect of starvation like Lazarillo's and Pablos's. Rather, it is an expression of the corrupted value system of her society, which she has accepted as necessary for economic success.[34] Since Moll's actions were justified within her value system, her repentance can only be superficial, and she does not really have a case to explain, whereas the Spanish picaros are radically alienated from society and do not accept its ways or morality,[35] and English con men do the opposite, namely to exploit its ways consciously for their deviant purposes (see Dionne 45). One is not sure whether the approach Defoe seemingly offers to cope with the problems of society—to accept the system—is sincere, or whether he employed the picaresque convention of the *caso* intentionally to raise questions about his contemporaries' morality.[36]

In the narrative situation Defoe follows his native and Spanish predecessors, seemingly intending to *prodesse et delectare*—to delight, that is, in the virtue presented. Yet in rogue pamphlets by Greene, Dekker, and others this object was quite uncertain, for they entertained through the tricks presented much more than through serious moral notes. The ironic discourse of *Moll Flanders*, in any case, allows a double reading. As Anne Cruz notes, the picaresque reasserts aristocratic values at the same time that it criticizes them. Likewise, *Moll Flanders* supports the prevalent contemporary economy while criticizing it, questioning its morals and pointing to the danger of corroding values. Moll's behavior does not conform to society's standards in that she is guilty of moral and ethical transgressions; her "trade" is fortune-hunting, she makes her way through telling lies, and she is a thief and a prostitute. Therefore, the "blows of fate"—two of her husbands turn out to be her brother and a poor criminal, and another dies; she has to go to prison and is transported—are consequences of her violation of basic moral values. She is punished for it. However, she needs to behave the way she does if she wants to rise, and her character traits are desirable ones in the early-eighteenth-century economy. Her success, therefore, reaffirms the prevalent economic attitude, which often contradicts traditional values. Daniel Defoe chose the picaresque genre to express the ambivalent attitude of his contemporaries toward the recent and not yet completed development of economic individualism. Moll's fate—in the end she is wealthy, although the means of obtaining that goal are questionable—as well as the way her adventures are related—retrospectively, as pseudoautobiography, and with diverting pranks and admonishing comments—confirm this ambivalence.

Disjunctions of Appearance: Class as Sign

The manner of relation coincides with epistemic developments at the origin of the picaresque genre in Renaissance Spain and of English rogue literature two centuries before Defoe. These literary forms reflect the problematic relation between signifier and signified that lies at the heart of the transition from the classical age. For Harman the most alarming effect of the vagrant's acts was his disguising, instantiating, thus, "a vagrancy of the signifier—or the surface appearances of social being—from its ground in the signified—the 'natural' hierarchical ordering of rank and status" (Taylor 5). Similar fears are articulated in the picaresque, including Defoe's. Moreover, from its beginnings the picaresque genre reflected the moral need of a literal-minded hero to explain his worldly ambition to an audience better prepared to understand ambition in figurative and otherworldly terms. A residual allegory jostled for meaning alongside a new realism based in materialism—in Spain as well as in England. Retrospectively, the picaro produced a coherent narrative, often with religious explanations, from his individual life. His descriptions of everyday, particular incidents within the broader frame of the allegory of repentant sinner testified to insecurities about the nature of narrative. This mixture of discourses facilitated ambivalence of statement in the picaresque. Defoe developed the germinal two-sidedness in the epistemic and linguistic bases of the genre in order to explore his era's moral dilemma. He equates traditional ideology—that is, criticism of upstarts in general—with the older discourse, and progressive ideology—that is, their praise—with the more recent discourse.[37]

During the Restoration, language, like knowledge, lost its immediacy, and its function of mediate representation was acknowledged.[38] In the earlier "Adamic" view of language, the relation between signifier and signified had been natural and the linguistic sign unitary. Words had named things safely (see Aarsleff). In the second half of the seventeenth century, the binary structure of the sign was acknowledged and the referential nature of language doubted. Despite its widely assumed natural, somatic origin, language was at once regarded as rhetorical, words being selected and combined in social agreement.[39] It was commonly accepted that language was essentially figural, symbolic of the displacement necessary to knowledge. Words were the arbitrary signs of conceptions or ideas and not of the things themselves. As such they could misrepresent and call forth different conceptions in different speech communities.[40] With the shift of emphasis from the things themselves to the ideas of things in epistemology; and from words as natural signs of things to relations entirely in people's minds in linguistics, the agency of definition shifted from God to individuals in society. Questions of the authority of definition and of the stability of meaning arose.[41] Defoe's novel reflects this change.

Throughout the entire relation of her life, with the exception of the moralizing comments, the narrator exhibits uneasiness about the use of figurative language and prefers clear denotations. Often, she clarifies something just related "in plain English" or repeats it "in other words."[42] Referential language, or "plainness" in general, is clearly related to honesty. When this connection is most emphasized, as in the young *pícara*'s interview with her employer, it is at the same time most questionable. Since there is reason to doubt the character's honesty and to regard her naïveté as part of her scheming, these instances demonstrate the period's uncertainty about the possibility of stable relations between signifier and signified—and also how the heroine takes advantage of that situation. She herself employs metaphors and transfers terms from one semantic field to another, for instance, when she employs Protestant vocabulary to denote her midwife's "other calling" as the proprietor of a brothel, or when she employs business terms to denote her unlawful activities (176). Appropriating economic and professional language for her actions, she insists on being an insider, contrary to earlier English rogues, who distinguished themselves from society by way of their special criminals' cant. Moll's own use of language is not as "plain" and honest as she would like the reader to believe. Nevertheless, we do not meet with a purposeful disguise of immoral behavior. The character Moll may sincerely believe that her exploits are a profession or a "trade" and that they are pardonable from an economic perspective. Defoe himself expresses a similar view in *The Complete English Tradesman*, admitting that some business practices are not entirely honest and morally correct but asserting that they are nevertheless acceptable if they are good for the nation (see Andersen 23). Moll the repentant, however, is supposed to know that thieves' activity is not the right kind of trade, and that their "purchase" therefore can only be called so in a figurative twist. After all, her immoral participation in the "trade" is what she is repenting at the time of narration. It is also the editor's explicit goal to teach his readers that vice, that is, criminal actions like Moll's, may not be condoned. Hence, the linguistic uncertainty expresses an ambivalence about social values, and Defoe's novel exhibits also on that count the double-sidedness typical of the picaresque.

As do other picaresque and rogue novels, Defoe's novel problematizes the disjunction of appearance and meaning in the concept of the gentleman. In Defoe's England, traditional notions according to which external markers naturally signified an inner value were juxtaposed with new concepts in which this "natural" relation no longer existed. Extrinsic signifiers, for example wealth, had signified an inward virtue the presence of which had justified the stratification of society. The correspondence of extrinsic signifiers to intrinsic values, however, began to dissolve due to demographic and other developments.[43] Progressive ideology therefore distinguished (internal) virtue and, independent from it, (external) aristocratic rank, repudiating the automatic aristocratic signification of internals by externals. It substituted success in business for noble honor, that is, it defined nobility economically.[44] In a climate of increasing social mobility, it became possible for members of the gentry and the bourgeois "middle class," whose values were openly derived from profit making, to obtain status symbols of the noblility, since these were no longer dependent on honor but on the result of application to business or money.[45] The substitution of a socioeconomic concept of nobility for the "honorific" concept, however, proved illusory, for the latter was equally prone to being drained of real value. All too often the "new men" forsook all moral and religious virtues on their ascent. While Defoe proposes supersession of aristocratic values in *Moll Flanders*, at the same time he illustrates the corruption of upstarts intent only on preserving the *appearance* of nobility through status symbols and transforms the progressive term *industry* into a synonym for opportunistic behavior and ruthless pursuit of profit.[46]

Moll the reformed narrator appears to think noble virtues innate and hence aristocratic rank an expression of inner value, apparent through external markers. Her Lancashire husband would be a natural gentleman, except that his example—like those of the gentleman-tradesman and the banker—illustrates that noble values and status symbols are not automatically connected, and that instead, ample financial means are necessary to be able to display nobility. He who lacks money cannot appear as a gentleman, and Moll only calls her prospective husband "gentleman" in connection with money. Otherwise he is simply her "man" (85) or "fellow" (86).

In contrast, a fortune and thus the appearance of nobility can exist without noble virtue. In the case of the older brother in Moll's teenage years, the discordance between intrinsic and extrinsic is most obvious. He is unquestionably corrupt yet has a "wig, hat, and sword" and will inherit an estate (29). Money becomes proof of his noble honor. Such is the case when Moll is charged with trying to steal plate. The money she can show convinces Mr. Alderman that she has been wrongly accused. And in the image of herself the virtues she claims for herself do not matter: "All these would not do without the dross, which was now become more valuable than virtue itself" (82–83). Even in progressive ideology, wealth—formerly a marker of virtue—overrides the existence of the virtue itself. Substituting business acumen for the intrinsic virtue of noble blood would correspond to progressive ideology and would accord with the tenets of Protestant religion. Yet Moll develops an exaggerated—rogue's—desire for gain that disregards morals, as we have seen. Her status in the end therefore does not reflect the inner merit of honest economic abilities or noble honor. She has to "make [her husband] appear, as he really was, a very fine gentleman," buying him the status symbols of a gentleman (347). He is not the only one to be made into the "gentle" status. Moll herself, the reader realizes, is also a gentlewoman by appearance rather than by nature. The ambivalence of the text lies in the disjunction between Moll, who accepts that internal and external do not form a natural, automatic entity, and the moralist narrator, who insists on the natural correspondence. Moll presents herself retrospectively as naturally noble and entitled to an estate in her providential interpretation of her own life, and naturalizes the substitution of business acumen for virtue in order to justify her actions.

As if these social inconsistencies based on questions of signification were not enough, Defoe introduces an additional twist. In the last consequence, the signified itself, money, becomes uncertain in his novel.[47] Replacing inner value with money makes what people are worth an imaginary value that can vary. Moll can pretend to be worth more than she is (or has) in reality. Alternatively, a woman "can be rendered low-prized" if she is too easy to get, true to the law of offer and demand in the market (74). The "gentleman" on whom the heroine helps her friend take revenge meets with closed doors once rumors have shrunk his reputed income. How wealthy he is in absolute terms does not matter here. Appearance replaces substance with regard to female chastity, too. Women have "to preserve the character of their virtue, even when perhaps they may have sacrificed the thing itself" (151).[48] In many cases, the signified retreats, and a slippage of meaning occurs.

On the level of narrative, Defoe's picaresque novel illustrates a similar evolution in the relation of signifier to signified. In the epistemology of British empiricism, a master narrative encountered particular individualized narratives. In the former discourse, spiritual truth preexisted empirically attainable signs in an individual narrative.[49] The Puritans' "plain" language instrumentalized common phenomena and objects in order to tease out spiritual meaning. That is, they extended typological thought into the realm of the quotidian, and the immediate objective reality was taken to illustrate spiritual truth. Spiritual autobiographies, for instance, depicted individual lives, the selected events illustrating an overarching pattern. These events, *figurae*, were repetitive, known beforehand, and carried symbolical meaning. Disconnected from the web of meaning, however, *figurae* could be reclassified as traces and carry their own meaning. In empiricism, then, concrete everyday circum-

stances and incidents formed unique individual histories of worldly orienta-
tion. Referential narrative overrode the master narrative. The former—previously the signifier of the master narrative—became more important and self-
sufficient. In Defoe's novel, the unique history of the particular life of one
individual, in fact, illustrates the contrary to what the exemplary tale of the
repentant-sinner type teaches.

In *Moll Flanders*, as in other picaresque novels, the two discourses are present. In referential language, the *pícara* gives "an account of all her vicious
practices, and even [descends] to the particular occasions and circumstances by
which she first became wicked," whereas the general pattern and overarching
spiritual truth that is to be affirmed, as well as the Devil's machinations, is
often cast in figurative language. "Now I seemed landed in a safe harbour,"
Moll recapitulates, "after the stormy voyage of life past was at an end, and I
began to be thankful for my deliverance" (206). In the second part of her life,
the contrast between the two discourses is especially pronounced. Descriptions in exact detail of her booty in measured weight, color, and quality, for
example, are followed by moral reflections in figurative language about the
Devil's prompting.

To the repentant Moll, God's will is shown through palpable, immediate
signs, such as a reprieve or money. The relation of such incidents as *figurae*
reaffirms the predetermined order. Moll creates a causal, ordered relation
between the stations of her life, from birth to the present of narrating, in
which the individual points function to explain the whole. Throughout the
entire novel, she will first tell the individual incidents, considering their impact
on her immediate situation, and then integrate them into the overarching narrative, drawing moralizing general conclusions from the incidents. The individual actions lose their singular quality; they are no longer definitive, referential, self-sufficient incidents. The signifier, that is, does not point to the
signified—the description of the crime to the crime itself: the delight in it, the
pride of it, the profit from it—as in the referential, literal language of empiricism. These are, in fact, presumably the parts that had to be cut. But through
the signified the signifier, the particular incident, points to another signified,
namely the moral of it all, the narrative of a converted sinner.

The character Moll, on the other hand, always considers her temporary situation and her current circumstances. When she rids herself of a child, she
muses, "and thus my great care was over, after a manner, which . . . was the
most convenient for me, *as my affairs then stood*, of any that could be thought
of *at the time*" (194; emphasis added). Her goals, as well as her means, are
never guided by moral or spiritual considerations at the narrated time but by

her material circumstances, as when she moves into the banker's house, commenting on the "house well furnished, and a husband in very good circumstances," and only afterward "consider[ing] the real value" of that life.

While Moll blames the outcomes of her exploits on her or other people's skill, attention, caution, and so on, and considers the incidents as disconnected episodes in no particular order, in retrospective, the narrator adduces "fate," "hap," "fortune," or "providence" as the ordering force of her life (8, 288, 300–301). Hence, what at the time of experience is a result of her landlady's connections and Moll's financial means, afterward becomes providential and Moll is "wonderfully pleased and satisfied with what [she] had met with" (183). In similar fashion she presents her downfall as the inevitable consequence of her vicious life, integrating it into the fixed order and disclaiming individual responsibility. At the same time, she vindicates her success with her genteel nature, which she demonstrates at age three with the gypsies and also living with the noble family, where she learns with the daughters of the house, her natural predisposition to genteel education facilitating spontaneous learning. She is handsomer, better shaped, and sings better, and these qualities and abilities "were all the gifts of nature" (19). With hindsight, she feels entitled to a higher social standing because of her inward nobility, which should overcome doubts regarding immoral behavior.

Moll's wavering between discourses illustrates the conflict between the "self-made man" and traditional hierarchy. Moll, the narrator, reinterprets as *figurae* and determined by a higher force what Moll, the character, treats as traces and determined through her efforts in this world. These two voices employ figurative and literal language respectively. However, the two discourses are not as clearly divided as the editor would wish, and it is especially doubtful whether the figural really dominates the literal in the end. The individual narrative does not automatically testify to a higher, preexistent truth. Instead, it depends on the selection and interpretation of the incidents. The editor therefore feels the need to establish the rules for reading beforehand. Every bad thing is punished, every good thing praised, he announces. He generalizes from Moll's example, persuading the reader that the particular can be made into a type, as in Puritan casuistry. Yet he knows that some parts of the narrative have a religious message and "real beauty," while others are of doubtful value. They do not fit into the preconceived fable, and the sinner-character's plain story therefore needs reworking, or "dressing up," to "atone for all the lively description she gives of her folly and wickedness" (3). This reworking is a function of Moll's self-justification and expresses doubt about the admissibility of ill-gained wealth as valid evidence of inner virtue. For all her rhetoric, Moll's individual life does not prove the master narrative, for the attainable signs—the empirically supported incidents in particular time and place—illustrate that dishonest behavior pays, while the figural professes to show that only inner virtue and moral behavior lead to success.

The interwoven yet contradictory discourses in the novel reflect an ambivalent attitude toward morality in business, in line with other picaresque novels that express their divided sentiments on social issues through a double discourse. Under changing social and economic conditions, what was virtuous and what should be condemned,[50] and who deserved social status, was not entirely clear. The entrepreneurial middle class had its own, not yet clearly defined, values, as Defoe was painfully aware. In the case of *Moll Flanders,* the middle class also has its own language, which is literal in immediate, referential narrative, whereas traditional aristocratic notions are related to figurative language and a master narrative. The dynamic picaresque genre allows the adoption of eighteenth-century dimensions, especially contemporary ideas of individual, economic ambition, and the social order in general. A picaresque novel, *Moll Flanders* turns out to be not merely a sensationalist story of a dexterous rogue, geared toward the entertainment-hungry masses. Nor is it a serious volume of Puritan casuistry. It is a much more complex narrative in which the picaro is representative of a whole generation of self-made men who even in late modern England still have to defend their unstable social position and to delimit their practices against those of social deviants.

NOTES

1. In this collection see Brooke A. Stafford, Karen Helfand Bix, and Patricia Fumerton, who discuss parallels between early modern commercial practices and the cony's and vagrant's outlaw activities.

2. Daniel Eisenberg has asked whether the picaresque even exists. Those answering in the affirmative have developed various definitions of the term. At the one end of the spectrum are critics who tend to restrict the historical and national range of the genre to *siglo de oro* Spain. See, for instance, Alter; Rico; Dunn; and Lázaro Carreter for a narrow view of the genre. At the other extreme are those who seek to offer a comprehensive list of characteristics as a universal category. Parker and Blackburn offer a slightly wider notion of the picaresque. Guillén and Wicks treat the picaresque as a very broad category. In general, I would regard the picaresque as a dynamic genre, that is, a "theoretical genre" that incorporates the "historical genre," to use Tzvetan Todorov's terms. While the picaresque adapts to new circumstances, it can only be theorized historically. The features of a genre do not constitute an absolute norm but always fluctuate around an imagined one. They change over time, accommodating new cultural and social developments. On the dynamic view, authors who perceive their sociocultural background as similar to that of the historical Spanish genre of the picaresque could use its conventions for their own

purposes, while working within their own national literary conventions, of course. Novels from various periods and nationalities can hence agree in enough aspects to be considered representative of the picaresque as a dynamic genre, including *Moll Flanders*. Turner Gutiérrez develops a similar concept of genre as "modal mixture."

3. The most common description of the picaresque today as a work that criticizes the dominant social order through the representation of a marginalized figure is limited in that it does not adequately account for the genre's complexities of form and content. Picaresque novels do *not* use a double structure merely to mask their criticism for fear of repression or censure.

4. Gladfelder holds that "Defoe meant every word of [his writings] literally," even where he argued for contrary positions, as in *The Great Law of Subordination Consider'd* and *Street Robberies Consider'd* (119).

5. Apart from these differences, Robert Greene's "The Conversion of an English Courtesan" in *The Thirde and Last Part of Conny-Catching* (1592) is in many ways a blueprint for Defoe's novel. Its *Guzmán*-style lengthy exhortations are more clearly distinguished from the accounts of vicious behavior, for example in the uncle's "watch-word," and the heroine stresses her good upbringing by wealthy parents. In comparison, Defoe introduced elements of both picaresque and rogue literature to his rendering of the material.

6. Generally, the picaro is poor and suffers from his low social status. He tries to improve his situation, not accepting his assigned state. There is an external rhythm to the narration of the picaro, namely that he is confronted with an incident, appears to triumph and yet does not, and then has to rise again. No matter how ingenious the hero is, his situation is always worse than before, and in the end he fails. Typically the picaro feels excluded from society, and while he wants to be included, he is never accepted; he remains outside, even though he may temporarily appear to be an insider, adopting the ostentation of status symbols typical of his society. As a solitary, he has neither stable relationships nor true affections for others. In fact, ruthless competition often forces him to fend for himself violently and aggressively against other rogues. Certain recurring themes are treated in the picaresque novel, such as the liberty of the picaro and the opportunities of the city, his constant preoccupation with hunger, his lack of principles, and his complacence about not having traditional honor. Typical motifs are the picaro's unusual birth (in a river, of unknown parents, and so on), the trap that wakens the picaro to his trickster attitude, his transition from childhood to maturity, his changing roles and identities, his expulsion from home, and his travels.

7. The latter is the case in Thomas Dangerfield's *Don Tomazo, or the Juvenile Rambles of Thomas Dangerfield*. For a discussion of this seventeenth-century work, which announces itself to be written in the vein of the Spanish picaresque, see Colahan.

8. Cruz examines the Spanish *siglo de oro* picaresque novel as one form of contemporary discourse among many, literary as well as nonliterary; each illuminates in some way the perception and function of the poor in the Spanish society of that time. Her application of Derrida's concept of *pharmakos* has been an invaluable inspiration to this chapter. Carroll takes a similar approach to English texts of that period. His description of the general sentiment toward beggars as fraudulent parasites on the one hand and as necessary agents for the spiritual well-being of the rich resembles that of Cruz. Dionne likewise affirms the vagabonds' and sturdy beggars' function as scapegoats for tradesmen who felt

under pressure to legitimize their own novel activities. Manley illumines the literary strategies of the pamphleteers and playwrights who were themselves "victim-participants," secular moralists outside the official institutions of church and city. One strategy was the ironized representation of an informer-reporter of the vices, a double perspective that grew out of the "earlier alliance between the moralizing observer and political authority" (315).

9. In fact, Carroll calls the peddlers and tinkers "prototypes of early capitalist entrepreneurs" (162).

10. The literary forms, which disseminated the views of the innovative merchant class, developed mainly in London as the city expanded and its institutions were perceived as no longer morally adequate to the novel urban conditions. Deviating from authoritative norms of discourse, pioneering professional writers in the burgeoning literary marketplace transformed outmoded conventions and morals into working structures adapted to the contemporary society. See Manley.

11. Turner Gutiérrez finds features of the picaresque in criminal biographies, jestbooks, and so on, but they do not have the function they have in the picaresque. When Spanish picaresque novels were translated and adapted to the English tradition, these English versions were mere trivializations adopting those aspects of form or content that corresponded to already existing conventions.

12. Ellinghausen in this collection argues this point using the example of Pamersiel.

13. My page references are to Daniel Defoe, *The Fortunes and Misfortunes of the Famous Moll Flanders* (London: Penguin, 1994).

14. Contrary to Moll, her brother husband tries to commit suicide and the banker husband gets sick after a failed business deal. They do not have her economic (and criminal) energy. Only her two closest acquaintances resemble Moll: the governess who "stood upon her legs" (216) and the Lancashire husband who knows he "must try again; a man ought to think like a man. To be discouraged is to yield to the misfortune" (164). Only their stories, of all, would merit relating, Moll maintains.

15. Defoe draws the connection between morals and language in *Complete English Tradesman*, 165.

16. Gladfelder takes an opposite stance on the issue of Moll's identity. He considers the autobiography "a strategy of evasion, a way of assaying and multiplying identities" (130).

17. Watt points out that to Moll "everything happens and nothing leaves scars" (148).

18. See Starr for a discussion of Moll's internal struggles.

19. To Alter, the picaro is incorruptible. If he does develop a mean character, crossing the boundary from misdemeanor to crime without qualms, he is no longer a picaro. Waley also holds that Lazarillo is not morally bad. Grass's analysis, on the other hand, finds ample moral judgment in *Buscón*, *Guzmán*, and *Lazarillo*.

20. According to Parker, Loretelli, and Backscheider, a *process* of hardening forms the basic pattern of Moll's spiritual development.

21. Whether that is positive or negative is the question here, whereas in criminal biographies their deaths conclusively prevented a permanent success.

22. Unlike that of the picaro, the literary depiction of English rogues commonly stressed their organization in bands. See Dionne.

23. Contrary to Moll, Defoe considers family of great importance to a tradesman: "That tradesman who does not delight in his family, will never long delight in his business; for, as one great end of an honest tradesman's diligence is the support of his family, so the very sight of, and above all, his tender and affectionate care for his wife and children, is the spur of his diligence" (*Complete English Tradesman*, 91).

24. See Watt for an analysis of economic man's character traits.

25. Lázaro saves money once, but spends it soon. Alter calls Lazarillo's pursuit of wealth "economic adventurism," while Moll's endeavors are to him "rational" in Max Weber's sense (46–48).

26. The irony readers today observe in the novel's message is therefore unintended, according to Watt, although on the sentence level he does point to instances of intended irony. See also Weimann; and Alter 48.

27. "The social setting of *Moll Flanders* is a classic instance of one of Marx's 'periods of transformation,' in which 'the material forms of production in society come in conflict with the existing property relations of production,' and the heroine, with her bourgeois enterprise on the one hand and her desire for a genteel spouse on the other, embodies historically conflicting classes." Hence, "she is as much a catalyst for her author's ambivalence about his class as are the characters of Balzac and Tolstoy" (Chaber 181–201).

28. Moll repents her crimes but not her economic desires and pursuit of status. "There is no reason," Gladfelder affirms, "to question the authenticity of Moll's Newgate conversion." Yet it is a conversion different from those in criminal lives: "She is not cripplingly repentant"—or hanged (126).

29. Whether it matters that Moll is a female picaro, especially with regard to the economic order, remains to be examined. For an admirable analysis of her position and Defoe's apparent critique of the patriarchal social structure, see Pollak. Turning the systems of exchange (economic, linguistic, and sexual) to her own advantage, Moll creates herself and redefines her position as woman in a patriarchal society. In the sense that Moll does not participate in honest economic ventures, she remains an outsider, like the other picaros, I would argue. Her *homo economicus* character traits surface only in criminal or morally questionable activities, while most men around her are honest bankers, merchants, and planters. Contrary to the men, she does not trade in money or agricultural goods but in her own body, especially in the second part of the novel when she works as a prostitute. When she does try to invest money as her male contemporaries do, she finds that as a woman she is economically dependent and needs a "friend to commit the management of [the money] to" (142).

30. While Defoe's picaro thus reaffirms the possibility of social rise based on economic merit, "the true crime of the vagabond," according to Dionne, "was to remind everyone of the ephemeral nature of the social order, his presence an unpleasant symbol to these newly 'stalled' men in the legitimate corridors of power that their own identity was also a sham" (47).

31. On Defoe's attitude toward trade and morality, see Andersen. Spadaccini demonstrates in *Moll Flanders* what Andersen shows in Defoe's nonfictional writings, that to Defoe economic purposes justify behavior that in other circumstances would be regarded as morally wrong. Novak, "Problem," discusses Defoe's condoning crime in the case of

necessity while not defining the term clearly. In chapter 4 of *Economics and the Fiction of Daniel Defoe,* Novak finds differences in Defoe's concept of poverty compared with his contemporaries'. Upbringing and gender palliate his heroes' guilt. Novak denies a conflict of ideals in Defoe between Puritan morality and commercial spirit. To Novak, it is very clear that Defoe championed the latter.

32. Parker claims that Moll leads a perfectly virtuous life at first.

33. Preservers of traditional ways had reason to feel threatened by such Otherness as Moll's, which was becoming accepted, in a process similar to that in the seventeenth century regarding rogues and Irish, as described by Stafford in this volume.

34. See also Bjornson 13. In his *Complete English Tradesman* Defoe does not apply the same standards to "an honest man" and to "a tradesman": "There are some latitudes, like poetical licences in other cases, which a tradesman is and must be allowed, . . . which cannot be allowed in other cases to any men" (159).

35. Alter expresses a contrary opinion (40).

36. Bjornson establishes this opposition as the central dilemma of the picaresque: "they [the picaros] are invariably confronted by a choice between social conformity (which is necessary for survival) and adherence to what they have learned to consider true or virtuous" (11).

37. Regarding the structures that determine thought and hence narrative discourse, Michel Foucault taught that representation replaced resemblance in the classical age. His system has been translated and applied to narrative and language, among others, by McKeon; Zimmermann; Kroll; and Cohen. Zimmermann examines the epistemological transformations in narrative discourses. Regarding the delimitation of the concepts of history and fiction, he distinguishes in the early eighteenth century the dominant analytico-referential discourse from a residual figural discourse. McKeon makes a similar distinction between the earlier discourse of romance, idealism, and the later, literal one, empiricism. He examines not only the novel's position with respect to epistemological changes concerning attitudes toward narrative, but also how it represents the relation between internal morals and external status in social categories, and thus McKeon distinguishes aristocratic and progressive ideologies. Kroll notes a Foucauldian shift in the concepts of language and knowledge that occurred between 1640 and 1660. Yet he rejects other scholars' theories of "plain style" as a particularly eighteenth-century argument. Cohen likewise examines linguistic theories. He describes the development toward a syntactical and logical view of the relationship between language and knowledge.

38. Ayers summarizes Locke's argument against "innate notions" of things and for the sign as mediator, as well as similar proposals by Glanvill (19–46).

39. Kroll traces the ideas seventeenth-century linguists like Wilkins and Bulwer developed about the origin of words.

40. As an example of an order of "*Spanish*" (that is, Spanish cloth) in a chapter on "The Trading Style" in his *Complete English Tradesman* demonstrates, Defoe was aware that one term could have various meanings and that misunderstandings could occur. He also knew of the different registers, for sailors and parsons, for instance (25).

41. The "cheat of words," as it was commonly called, dismayed many philosophers in the late seventeenth century, as Aarsleff explains. They worked to reinstitute a precise correlation of words and notions in new languages (24).

42. In *The Complete English Tradesman*, Defoe rejects "dark and ambiguous speakings" and "obscure" language.

43. See McKeon, who discusses the absorption of "others" into the aristocracy. Defoe mocks the "mixtures" in the blood of the nobility in *The True-Born Englishman: A Satyr* (1700).

44. Defoe, *Complete English Tradesman*, distinguishes between tradesmen and gentlemen. The former can take on gentlemen's markers, namely "long wigs and swords," and become gentry through their wealth (43, 78).

45. On the terms *gentry* and *middle class*, see McKeon 155.

46. Maravall discusses the usage of the word *industria* in the Spanish baroque picaresque novels. As Carroll holds, when the sixteenth- and early-seventeenth-centuries English beggars disguised themselves as "the middling sort," "a general crisis of the sign" became visible. "The nature of representation itself thus [came] under interrogation, and the arbitrariness of the sign [was] exposed" (46).

47. Credit does not have to correspond to "real" stock, as Defoe is aware (*Complete English Tradesman*, 48).

48. Defoe draws the same connection in *Complete English Tradesman:* "A tradesman's credit and a virgin's virtue ought to be equally sacred from the tongues of men" (133).

49. For a description of scriptural exegesis in empiricism, see McKeon 77.

50. Certain behavior that "may be a Vice in Morals, may at the same time be a Vertue in Trade," states Defoe (qtd. in Andersen 26).

WORKS CITED

Aarsleff, Hans. *From Locke to Saussure: Essays on the Study of Language and Intellectual History*. Minneapolis: U of Minnesota P, 1982.

Alter, Robert. *Rogue's Progress: Studies in the Picaresque Novel*. Cambridge: Harvard UP, 1964.

Andersen, Hans H. "The Paradox of Trade and Morality in Defoe." *Modern Philology* 39 (1941): 32–46.

Ayers, Michael R. "The Foundations of Knowledge and the Logic of Substance: The Structure of Locke's General Philosophy." *The Empiricists: Critical Essays on Locke, Berkeley, and Hume*. Ed. Margaret Atherton. Lanham, Md.: Rowman and Littlefield, 1999.

Backscheider, Paula. *Moll Flanders*. Boston: Twayne, 1990.

Bjornson, Richard. *The Picaresque Hero*. Madison: U of Wisconsin P, 1977.

Blackburn, Alexander. *The Myth of the Picaro: Continuity and Transformation of the Picaresque Novel, 1554–1954*. Chapel Hill: U of North Carolina P, 1979.

Carroll, William C. *Fat King, Lean Beggar: Representations of Poverty in the Age of Shakespeare*. Ithaca: Cornell UP, 1996.

Chaber, Lois A. "Matriarchal Mirror: Women and Capital in *Moll Flanders*." *Critical Essays on Daniel Defoe*. Ed. Roger D. Lund. London: Prentice-Hall, 1997.

Cohen, Murray. *Sensible Words: Linguistic Practice in England, 1640–1785*. Baltimore: Johns Hopkins UP, 1977.

Colahan, Clark. "Dangerfield's Picaresque *Don Tomaʒo:* English Novelists as Spanish (Anti)heroes." *Neohelicon* 25.2 (1998): 311–28.

Cruz, Anne. *Discourses of Poverty: Social Reform and the Picaresque Novel in Early Modern Spain.* Toronto: U of Toronto P, 1999.

Dangerfield, Thomas. *Don Tomaʒo, or the Juvenile Rambles of Thomas Dangerfield.* 1680. Ann Arbor, Mich.: Xerox microform systems, 1976.

Defoe, Daniel. *The Fortunes and Misfortunes of the Famous Moll Flanders.* London: Penguin, 1994.

———. *The Complete English Tradesman.* 1701. Gloucester: Sutton, 1987.

Dionne, Craig. "Playing the Cony: Anonymity in Underworld Literature." *Genre* 30.1 (1997): 29–50.

Dunn, Peter. *Spanish Picaresque Fiction: A New Literary History.* Ithaca: Cornell UP, 1993.

Eisenberg, Daniel. "Does the Picaresque Novel Exist?" *Kentucky Romance Quarterly* 26 (1979): 203–19.

Gladfelder, Hal. *Criminality and Narrative in Eighteenth-Century England.* Baltimore: Johns Hopkins UP, 2001.

Grass, Roland. "Morality in the Picaresque Novel." *Hispania* 42 (1959): 192–98.

Greene, Robert. *The Thirde and Last Part of Conny-Catching.* 1592. Reprint, London: John Lane, Bodley Head, 1923.

Guillén, Claudio. *Literature as System.* Princeton: Princeton UP, 1971.

Kroll, Richard H. F. *The Material Word: Literate Culture in the Restoration and Early Eighteenth Century.* Baltimore: Johns Hopkins UP, 1991.

Lázaro Carreter, Fernando. *"Laʒarillo de Tormes" en la Picaresca.* Barcelona: Ariel, 1972.

Loretelli, Rosamaria. *Da Picaro a Picaro: Le Transformaʒioni di un Genero Letterario dalla Spagna all'Inghilterra.* Rome: Bulzoni, 1984.

Manley, Lawrence. *Literature and Culture in Early Modern London.* Cambridge: Cambridge UP, 1995.

Maravall, José Antonio. *La literatura picaresca desde la istoria social (siglos XVI y XVII).* Madrid: Taurus, 1986.

McKeon, Michael. *The Origins of the English Novel, 1600–1740.* Baltimore: Johns Hopkins UP, 1987.

Novak, Maximilian. "The Problem of Necessity in Defoe's Fiction." *Philological Quarterly* 40 (1961): 513–24.

Novak, Maximilian. *Economics and the Fiction of Daniel Defoe.* Berkeley and Los Angeles: U of California P, 1962.

Parker, Alexander. *Literature and the Delinquent: The Picaresque Novel in Spain and Europe, 1599–1753.* Edinburgh: Edinburgh UP, 1967.

Pollak, Ellen. *"Moll Flanders,* Incest, and the Structure of Exchange." *Critical Essays on Daniel Defoe.* Ed. Roger D. Lund. London: Prentice-Hall, 1997.

Rico, Francisco. *La Novela Picaresca y el Punto de Vista.* Barcelona: Seix Barral, 1969.

Spadaccini, Nicholas. "Daniel Defoe and the Spanish Picaresque Tradition: The Case of *Moll Flanders.*" *Ideologies and Literature* 2.6 (1978): 10–26.

Starr, G. A. *Defoe and Casuistry.* Princeton: Princeton UP, 1971.

Taylor, Barry. *Vagrant Writing: Social and Semiotic Disorders in the English Renaissance.* New York: Harvester Wheatsheaf, 1991.

Todorov, Tzvetan. *Genres in Discourse*. Trans. Catherine Porter. Cambridge: Cambridge UP, 1990.

Turner Gutiérrez, Ellen. *The Reception of the Picaresque in the French, English, and German Traditions*. New York: Peter Lang, 1995.

Waley, Pamela. "*Lazarillo*'s Cast of Thousands, or the Ethics of Poverty." *Modern Language Review* 83.3 (1988): 591–601.

Watt, Ian. *The Rise of the Novel: Studies in Defoe, Richardson, and Fielding*. Berkeley and Los Angeles: U of California P, 1960.

Weimann, Robert. *Daniel Defoe: Eine Einführung in das Romanwerk*. Halle: Verlag Sprache und Literatur, 1962.

Wicks, Ulrich. *Picaresque Narrative, Picaresque Fictions: A Theory and Research Guide*. New York: Greenwood P, 1989.

Zimmermann, Everett. *The Boundaries of Fiction*. Ithaca: Cornell UP, 1996.

Afterword

(Re)presenting the Early Modern Rogue

> The variety of historical evidence is nearly infinite. Everything that man
> says or writes, everything that he makes, everything he touches can and
> ought to teach us about him.
>
> —MARC BLOCH

In late September 2002 the Irish Travelers in North Augusta, South Carolina,
halted their pickup trucks in the middle of the road to acknowledge that a fellow member of their autarky, Madelyne Gorman Toogood, had been seen on
a surveillance video in Indiana beating her four-year-old daughter. For a brief
moment she had exposed their community of gypsies, which depends on
anonymity and secrecy, fostered by a tradition in the United States that is at
least 150 years old. That was the time when the first Irish Travelers, self-
employed as tinkers, originally came to America to escape the Irish potato
famine. They began their life in the New World as horse traders; today
between twenty thousand and one hundred thousand English, Scottish, and
Irish Travelers (their actual population is not publicly known) live as roaming
laborers. Not unlike their Tudor predecessors, they roam the nation for six
months of the year painting houses and return to their own autonomous universe in South Carolina for the winter months. Like the vagabonds described
by Thomas Harman or Robert Greene, the Irish Travelers are known by their
nicknames—Mikey's Boy, One-Eyed Pete, Curly Joe; and, like their counterparts in the Tudor and early Stuart rogue literature, they arrange their children's marriages, speak their own "canting tongue," a strange Gaelic-English
dialect in which *Misli shayjo* means "Go away, the police are here!" and are
accused by outsiders as con artists who cheat the elderly by overcharging them
or by performing faulty work. In 2001, six Irish Traveler *yonks*—their canting

word for thieves—pleaded guilty in North Augusta for using forged documents to purchase cars. More customarily, though, as Harman and Greene note of their ancestors, they patrol their own bands, establish their own rules, and punish those who break them. As one of them remarked to the press, "We don't put our old folks in rest homes. We don't have as many divorces. And when a woman gets raped or a bank gets robbed, law enforcement doesn't come to Murphy Village" (Ripley 10).

The lives of America's Irish Travelers have their resonances in the practices of Tudor and early Stuart vagabonds and the "Articles of their Fraternities"—ten in number, like the Ten Commandments—that Thomas Dekker records in *O Per Se O* in 1612:

1. Thou shalt my true Brother be, keeping thy faith to thy other Brothers (as to my selfe) if any such thou have.
2. Thou shalt keepe my counsell, and all other my brothers, being knowne to thee.
3. Thou shalt take part with mee, and all other my brothers in all matters.
4. Thou shalt not heare me ill spoken of without reuenge to thy power.
5. Thou shalt see mee want nothing, to which thou canst help mee.
6. Thou shalt giue mee part of all thy *winnings* whatsoeuer.
7. Thou shalt not but keepe true pointments, with mee for meetings, be it by day or night, at what place soeuer.
8. Thou shalt teach no Housholder to *Cant*, neyther confesse any thing to them, be it neuer so true, but deny the same with oathes.
9. Thou shalt doe no hurt to any *Mawnder*, but with thine owne hands: and thou shalt forbeare none that disclose these secrets.
10. Thou shalt take Cloathes, Hennes, Geese, Pigs, Bacon, and such like, for thy *Winnings*, where-euer thou canst haue them.

(Sigs. N2v–N3)

Their rules, like the practices of the Irish Travelers, are designed to keep them together, sharing with one another, and to keep them apart, independent of those constituting the larger society. Membership in the Irish Traveler communities, as in Dekker's fraternities of vagabonds, is clearly delineated and clearly defined, underwritten and confirmed by social and linguistic practices.

And, like the Travelers of today, the identification and numbers of their Tudor predecessors were largely unknown, even when the government set out to learn about them. In 1569, for instance, the queen's Privy Council ordered a series of "privy watches or searches" for vagabonds throughout England, instituting a series of investigations performed, irregularly and unevenly from parish to parish and town to town, over the next four years. By law each constable was ordered to apprehend all vagabonds and masterless men and to send them home or where they had last lived for a two-year period, and to return certificates with their names to the council. A document preserved in the British Museum notes that in 1569 such watches and searches apprehended some thirteen thousand petty criminals. In 1596, Edward Hext, a justice of the peace in Somersetshire, reported to the queen's lord treasurer frequent thefts occurring in his district and mourned those criminals who, unlike Madelyne Gorman Toogood, had escaped. This despite the record of achievement that he appended:

> In all, executed this year, 1596, forty. So it appeareth, that besides those that be executed, and those that be burnt in the hand, 35. Whipped for felony, 37. Felonies acquitted by the grand jury, 67. Felonies acquitted by the petty jury, 45. That be cast men, and reprieved to the gaol, they are set at liberty this year of men committed, or bound over for felonies, 183. The greatest part whereof must of necessity live by spoil. (Kinney 15)

In the same year, justices of the peace in Middlesex were asked to suppress

> a great nomber of dissolute, loose and insolent people harboured and maintained in such and like noysom and disorderly howses, as namely poor cottages and habitacions of beggars and people without trade, stables, ins, alehowses, taverns, garden howses converted to dwellings, ordinaries, dicyng howses, bowling allies and brothell howses. The most part of which pestering those parts of the citty with disorder and uncleannes are either apt to breed contagion and sicknes, or otherwize serve for the resort and refuge of masterles men and other idle and evill dispozed persons, and they are the cause of cozenages, thefts, and other dishonest conversacion and may also be used to cover dangerous practizes. (Kinney 15)

Historians now estimate that by the end of the sixteenth century in England more than eight hundred persons were executed annually; at one assizes alone, held in Exeter in 1598, 134 prisoners were indicted, 17 to the gallows.

Such statistics suggest far more knowledge about Tudor rogues, vagabonds, and sturdy beggars against which the Elizabethans issued a series of legislative acts and regulations than we have at hand about the Irish Travelers of our very own day. Yet how certain can we be about the historical record four centuries ago if we cannot even penetrate the secret communities around us? Marc Bloch urges us to such an investigation, yet with all the documents that have been uncovered about the period, historians still can only guess the annual crime statistics around 1600.

The philosopher Karl Popper has addressed just such a concern directly in *Conjectures and Refutations*. There he critiques Francis Bacon's early modern method of induction before noting that, whenever we attempt to establish the truth or facticity of any observation, we are forced to question our sources and their reliability and validity with a set of questions that are never-ending, that form a sequence of "infinite regress." The example he provides is a newspaper statement that seems innocent and innocuous enough: "The Prime Minister has decided to return to London several days ahead of schedule." How, he asks, do we ascertain the truth of such a statement? You can reply that you read it in the *Times*, but that only leads him to ask, *was* it the *Times*? And, if so, did it report the matter correctly? Suppose you ask the editor of the *Times*, who might reply that one of the reporters took a call from the prime minister's office. You could talk to the reporter to see if this is so, but even then you could remain at least partly unconvinced.

> There is a simple reason why this tedious sequence of questions never comes to a satisfactory conclusion. It is this. Every witness must always make ample use, in his report, of his knowledge of persons, things, linguistic usages, social conventions, and so on. He cannot rely merely upon his eyes or ears, especially if his report is to be of use in justifying any assertion worth justifying. But this fact must of course always raise new questions as to the sources of those elements of his knowledge which are not immediately observational. This is why the program of tracing back all knowledge to its ultimate source in observation is logically impossible to carry through: it leads to an infinite regress. (Qtd. Windschuttle 219)

These questions are raised about a present-day event, such as we might raise about the Irish Travelers, with even more difficulty than the example of the prime minister provides. The past, says Popper—the common subject of the essays in the present collection—is even more difficult. Here we are limited to that which is still extant in documents or other evidence. The evidence will always be partial. The documents we have may be biased, partial, contingent. They may reconstruct events imperfectly, blindly, innocently. Even eyewitnesses to events, as lawyers would tell us, can be a source of doubt. They are limited to their own perspectives on events and, perhaps, their own interpretations as well. Such fundamental skepticism calls into question the very texts, the very evidence, used again and again in the essays here; it is not something we can easily dodge nor wish to lay to rest. Yet I think the authors in this book have confronted such matters, as I wish to show. First, though, we can put this collection into a fuller perspective of our own by looking at responses to evidence of rogues others have made elsewhere.

Speculations and Microhistory

> Where calculation is impossible we are obliged to employ speculation.
> —MARC BLOCH

Tudor writers acknowledging the sharp and steady increase in poverty, vagabondage, and crime and further speculating on their possible connection tried to answer some of the questions Karl Popper's historian would ask. Coming from an earlier age that had chronicled the world, as well as England, as the working out of God's divine order, reminded or strengthened by the reformists' understanding of the individual's choice of virtue or vice and its consequent rewards and punishments, some of the Tudor authors—such as Thomas Dekker especially, but Greene and Harman more implicitly—saw the increased number of rogues, vagabonds, and sturdy beggars as a sign of man's fallen nature generally and wrongful choices in life individually. There were other speculations. In 1536 Richard Maryson had this to say:

> How much ground is lost in England? How much corn might we carry into other countries if we would use the commodities of our realm? How many heaths be there that would bear other fruits than shrubs, brakes, broom, and fern if they were well handled? How many cities are decayed, how many towns that are now hamlets, quite down that would stand if the third part of England did not live idly? Towns would up again if crafts were set up. There are few nations, but many be idle. Yet I think there is not two of the greatest nations in Christendom that hath half so many that live without crafts as little England hath. (Qtd. Berkowitz 136–37)

The lack of skill and sloth was for Maryson a threatening combination. For Alexander Strange, vicar of Layston, Hertfordshire, writing in 1636, the problem was one of covetousness, "the roote of all evil." The covetousness he had in mind was practiced by those who profited by providing cottages to "the visible hurt and prejudice of that little commonwealth wherof yourselves are the principall members." He wanted those persons fined, the cottages pulled down, and charitable relief directed instead to "auntient poor . . . such as have been a good tyme dwellers": he was not concerned with the dispossession and loss of the poor but by its consequences for the poor rate in his parish. For him, covetousness was a rogue's trick (Wrightson 220).

Historians of our own time, looking at the situation from a greater distance and armed with a sense of the *longue durée,* cite other causes for the rise in roguery, vagabonds, and sturdy beggars. Soldiers returning from Drake's failed expedition against Portugal in 1589 is one factor, when London's streets were closed off from the unemployed and indigent, and customary peace and order were not restored for six months; disbanded soldiers, also out of work and out of pocket after the wars in the Low Countries (or, earlier, for Calais), were another. The Reformation had not only given the English a renewed sense of piety but presented Tudor society with itinerant friars and pardoners who were also suddenly unemployed and finding themselves without other requisite skills. Small landholders were evicted from their generations-old livelihood as arable land was enclosed for pasturage; peasant and tenant farmers were also deprived of land and work. Necessarily turning to vocations of begging or vagabondage or even to theft, such families necessarily taught their children the habits of their trade. According to Gāmini Salgādo, "They served a variety of purposes, including wriggling through small openings to pilfer, distracting attention while the parents went about their nefarious business, and looking suitably pathetic in order to soften the hearts of the villagers" (117). What both these early modern and such contemporary writers as Salgādo share is an attempt to locate the cause of the increasing presence of rogues, vagabonds, and sturdy beggars so that, having explained their increased presence in Tudor and early Stuart society, they can accept the validity of such a presence and so interpret it.

Postmodernist historians follow suit: by looking at life from below and through the practice of microhistory, they find their own enabling justification. Thus we are told of Thomas Bouling, a shepherd who was given a basic retainer of seven pounds, ten shillings a year, which he augmented through the spring and summer by odd jobs such as carting, hedging, threshing, and harvesting, bringing his annual income to ten pounds, five shillings, two pence, with his wife adding another nineteen shillings, six pence a year weeding, haymaking, and harvesting. We hear of John George, a hedger and ditcher, who also worked often as a thresher, but there was a long gap between early July and mid-September when he found only one day's work building a haystack. There was Margaret Knowsley of Nantwich, Cheshire, a laborer's wife who, pregnant in 1626, supported three young children and a baby by working as a domestic for the parish minister, cleaning, laundering, gardening, and fetching fuel and water—but who also took on seasonal agricultural work and occasional knitting. Henry Savery of Stow Bardolph, Norfolk, went to London in 1629 to become a seaman, returned home to work as a day laborer, left with seven shillings for Suffolk, then London, and then Yorkshire, before he was taken in due course as a vagrant. In 1568 a man reported to the magistrates in Montgomeryshire that he "dwells nowhere nor has no abiding but there as he may have work"; in 1574, a woman in Cheshire confessed that "she has used the art of begging from her cradle." For such persons, life was always pragmatic, expedient, makeshift according to their testimony. Such decidedly discrete examples do not always cohere easily nor especially well, but they do provide groundwork for the possibility, if not the assured specu-lation, that the rogue pamphlets of Harman, Greene, and Dekker are based in the realm of a certain facticity. Rather than attempting to reveal an efficient cause for the truth of the observations in the rogue books, they work by way of what Theodore Zeldin identified in 1976 as a pointillist method, which composes a conditional picture by connected discrete dots, allowing a reader to make similar links for himself that might guarantee the fundamental verac-ity of rogue literature.

Still a third way to give credence to rogue books as sufficiently reliable accounts is that of a "master narrative," which Hayden White has identified as a method practiced by many historians. The master narrative discloses explicit or implicit alliances among researched discoveries that allow a large number of observations in early modern rogue texts to make sense. Such alliances heighten probability. They also convey history in a form most accustomed to the broadest range of readers. One master narrative, or pattern, or frame, is that of the guild. This is what Salgãdo practices when he writes,

> Whatever may have been the case with petty criminals on the road, it is clear that the London underworld was highly organized—far more efficiently organized indeed, than the forces of law and order. Division of labour, demarcation of area, prompt disposal of goods and the systematic training of recruits were as much a part of the underworld as they were of the wealthiest and most respectable livery guild. (33)

Building on the interviews conducted by Thomas Harman and the canting terms he appends to his work as well as on the parallel metaphor of "frater-nity" employed by John Awdeley, Salgãdo constructs his study *The Eliza-bethan Underworld* by establishing a hierarchical government and society that maintains order and functions to apprentice young men and women to the established practices of the various trades of rogues. Such a microcosm, or lit-tle world within the larger Tudor and Stuart one, insures its own operation, regulation, and security by aping the philosophical framework of the larger society and applying its principles and practices: as the guild system and the servant's livery maintain the economy of business and court life, so rogues and vagabonds maintain their own existence. As evidence for this theory, and to suggest that the accounts of someone like Robert Greene have a basis in lived experience, Salgãdo cites

> Laurence Pickering, whom Greene calls the King of Cutpurses and brother-in-law to no less a personage than Bull the Tyburn hangman, organized weekly meetings of the thieving fraternity at his house in Kent Street where, amidst the general merrymaking, serious items of news were exchanged regarding like "prospects" as well as the activities of law-enforcing bodies. The underworld also had its own special quarters in London where a criminal on the run could find refuge from the hue and cry. One such district was Alsatia, the area between Whitefriars and Carmelite Street, with the Thames as its southern boundary and Fleet Street to the north. Another was Southwark, noted . . . for its stews, as well as other "safe" southern suburbs such as Newington Butts. The brick kilns of Islington and the Savoy were well-known underworld haunts, as were Whitefriars, Whetstone Park, Ram Alley and St Martins; yet others went by such names as the Bermudas, Damnation Alley and Devil's Gap. (7)

The diagrammatic and geographic description that Salgãdo draws is so compatible with passages from extant documents—particularly repeated bits of evidence—that the schema is extended to political and social as well as economic relationships, and the whole fosters the kind of narrative that, once composed, makes sense of what might otherwise remain fragmented or, in odd instances, stubbornly mysterious.

Documents other than rogue literature support Salgãdo's speculations and others' in concert with him. On July 7, 1585, for instance, William Fleetwood, the recorder of London, wrote to Lord Burghley, lord treasurer and a member of the queen's Privy Council, that training practices among rogues further resembled Elizabethan schoolrooms.

> One Wotton, a gentilman borne, and sometyme a marchaunt man of good credyte who fallinge by tyme into decaye, kepte an Alehowse att Smarts Keye, neere Byllingesgate, and after, for some mysdemeanor beinge put down . . . in the same Howse he procured all the Cuttpurses abowt this Cittie to repaire to his said howse. There was a schole howse sett upp to learne young boyes to cutt purses. There were hung up two devises, the one was a pockett, the other was a purse. The pocket had in yt certen cownters, and

was hunge abowte with hawkes bells, and over the toppe did hannge a litle sacring bell; and he that could take owt a cownter without any noyse, was allowed to be a *publique Foyster:* and he that could take a peece of sylver owt of the purse without the noyse of any of the bells, he was adjudged a *judiciall Nypper.* Nota, that a Foister is a Pick-pockett, and a Nypper is termed a Pickpurse, or a Cutpurse.

Fleetwood found in Wotton's establishment, he tells the Elizabethan government, "a table" on which is written poetry in cant: "Si spie, si non spie, Foyste, nyppe, lyfte, shave and spare not," and then translates the terms by such canting vocabulary as Harman had already published: "*Foyste* is to cutt a pockett, *nyppe* is to cutt a purse, *lyft* is to robbe a shoppe or a gentilmans chamber, *shave* is to fylche a clooke, a sword, a sylver sponne or suche like" (Reynolds 81). Thus cant was both a spoken *and* a written language if we are to believe Fleetwood; and there is no obvious reason to doubt the fact that he wrote Burghley even if we are not now entirely clear about his motive for doing so. The ease by which the framework of the underworld accommodates such a document helps to support the master narrative by which Salgãdo, along with many others, can establish and maintain an account of roguery in early modern England congruent with the rogue pamphlets that are cited so often in this collection. Such accommodations, the master narrative, causes advanced for the rise in criminality, and microhistories all work to affirm the rogue literature that is the subject of this book. All these rationales—for that is what they are—rest on those very documents that Karl Popper, for one, saw reason to doubt. Granted that they help us to gain perspective on rogue literature, are they reliable enough to use for investigation, analysis, evidence, and interpretation? Do they confirm the authenticity of the content? Should they be taken either as stenographic report or entertaining jestbook? To answer these questions we need to inquire whether an authentic document—one clearly written and published in the early modern period—is authentic in what it has to say.

History and Textuality

Texts both mirror and generate social realities which they may sustain, resist, contest, or seek to transform, depending on the case at hand.
— GABRIELLE M. SPIEGEL

The distinguished historian Arnaldo Momigliano has described the foundation of modern historical scholarship this way:

The whole modern method of historical research is founded on the distinction between original and derivative authorities. By original authorities we mean statements by eye witnesses, or documents and other material remains that are contemporary with the event they attest. By derivative authorities we mean historians and chroniclers who relate and discuss events which they have not witnessed, but which they have heard of or inferred directly or indirectly from original authorities. (Qtd. Evans 93)

Such a distinction has been a commonplace principle with historians since at least the nineteenth century. Yet with this distinction in mind, what do we make of the following passage from Dekker's *O Per Se O?*

For my better painting forth these Monsters, I once tooke one of them into my seruice (being a sturdy big-limde young fellow) of him I desired some knowledge in their gibrish, but hee swore hee could not *Cant,* yet his Roague-ship seeing himselfe vsed kindly by mee, would now and then shoote out a word of *Canting,* and being thereupon asked why with oathes hee denyed it before, hee told mee, that they are sworne neuer to disclose their skill in *Canting* to any Housholder, for if they doe, the other *Mawnder-ers* or Roagues, *Mill* them (kill them,) yet hee for his part (hee said) was neuer sworne, because hee was a *Clapperdogeon,* that is to say, a Begger-borne. This *Clapperdogeon* staid with mee so long as hee durst, and then *binged a waste in a darkmans,* stole away from mee in the night time. (Sig. L2v)

What can we possibly make out of this passage? Is it, first of all, a primary document—written of the time in the time by someone's personal experience—or a secondary document recording the mediated conversation with a rogue in which the only matter known is what the rogue himself chooses to reveal? Or is it in some liminal space in between? For us, moreover, the "facts" here are twice mediated, since the whole account, in which it is revealed to Dekker (though he seems not to suspect it) only what the rogue wishes to reveal, and there is some evidence not to trust him since he breaks the contract of silence with his own fraternity; and mediated once again by Dekker whose admiration of the "sturdy big-limde young fellow" and whose pleasure at being given the knowledge of an insider, colors his account. Should we, then, give particular value to this passage since it relies on direct observation and experience or should we hold it at arm's length for virtually the same reasons?

One answer may lie in a principle put forth by Sir Herbert Butterfield in his well-known work *The Whig Interpretation of History:* "all history perpetually requires to be corrected by more history" (131). This is a good deal safer, at least, then Geoffrey Elton's definition of a historical fact as something in the past that has left its traces in a document of its time and that can be relied upon if read "in the context of the day that produced it. . . . The present must be kept out of the past if the search for the truth of that past is to move towards such success as in the circumstances is possible" (65). Although Elton hedges at the end, he nevertheless believes that contextualized documents are largely reliable because historians can sweep documents clean of ideological debris that might cloud judgment at a later time but which would not have hindered the document's first audiences. With Elton, we can contextualize Dekker's report of hosting a rogue and learning some secret canting terms from him, but I think his principle ignores the larger and more important question of what Dekker may actually (consciously or not) be saying. We are much better off, and still in compliance with Butterfield, if we follow the counsel of two American historians, Ellen Somekawa, and Elizabeth A. Smith.

Documents cannot be viewed as simple manifestations of a creator's intentions; the social institutions and material practices which were involved in their production played a significant part in shaping what was said and how it was said. The historian's meticulous reading of the evidence may therefore have little in common with what the author intended to say or what the contemporary reader understood to be said, whether that was what the author had in mind or not. (It was, after all, what the society permitted.) (150)

Somekawa and Smith may, in turn, be drawing on the great nineteenth-century German historian Leopold von Ranke, who insisted on establishing in detail the provenance of any primary document, inquiring into the motives of the author, the circumstances under which the work was written, and its relationship to other works of the same time on the same subject. Through such exercises, von Ranke sought *wie es eigentlich gewesen,* or "how it essentially was," by which he meant how it could have been (and then would have been) construed in its own time. On the one hand, Ranke sought to get into the discrete consciousness of a past period of history; on the other, he wanted to eliminate later knowledge of history that might recontextualize the earlier work, such as the sense of progress. To prevent that, Ranke proposed what many writers in this book do: he applied to the study of historical documents the same philological skills that literary textual scholars apply in order to understand more sharply the characteristics and significances of a primary document of the past, and to cleanse the text of later interpolations.

In some ways, Ranke's influence has been filtered down to us in the view expressed by Lawrence Stone. Although he pays homage there to E. H. Carr, who proposed in 1961 that we should read the background of those we read, Stone, refers back to those days "forty or fifty years ago" when he was taught "that documents—we did not call them texts in those days—were written by fallible human beings who made mistakes, asserted false claims, and had their own ideological agenda which guided their compilation [and] should therefore be scrutinized with care, taking into account authorial intent, the nature of the document, and the context in which it was written" (189–90). Moreover, Stone's emphasis on written texts reminds us that we have lost signifiers that were not written in texts, such as voice and gesture, and that we have lost some of the written texts as well. Recently John Vincent has reminded us, too, that written texts are made by and addressed to the literate of the society, which further restricts their applicability (qtd. Evans 164). Finally, not all documents are equal in their reliability even when they are official: we all know literary scholars who, like the historian A. F. Pollard, have based their historical understanding on the Calendar of State Papers, which is selective, occasionally erratic, and always taking a particular position that may only seem objective but is not so (Evans 22). All of these textual liabilities and methodological precautions are now recognizable, fortunately for the authors of this book and for us, however, because of the "linguistic turn" of postmodernism that has taught us how to convert documents into discourses, in effect making the documents potentially richer while enfolding into our practiced reading of them the questions Popper advocated. As Richard J. Evans puts it, "Few historians [and we can add literary scholars] would now defend the hard-line concept of historical objectivity espoused by Elton. The prevalence of historical controversy, endemic in the profession for decades, has long since disabused historians of the idea that the truth lies buried in the documents, and that once the historian has unearthed it, no one ever need perform the same operation again" (3). Rather like the early modern rogue whose changes of costume and forged papers allowed him to take on differing identities, we can attempt to uncover the potential multiplicity of discourses in a single document, extending and varying the responses of early modern readers even if we can no longer ascertain with certainty the (ever singular?) motive of the author.

There is perhaps a simple illustration in "The Bel-mans Cry" that Dekker includes in *O Per Se O:*

Men and Children, Maides and Wiues,
'Tis not late to mend your lives,
Locke your doores, lye warme in Bed,

Much losse is in a Maiden-head:
Midnight feastings are great wasters,
Servants ryots undoe masters:
When you heare this ringing Bell,
Thinke it is your latest Knell,
When I cry, Maide in your Smocke,
Doe not take it for a mocke:
Well I meane, if well 'tis taken,
I would have you still awaken:
Foure a clocke, this Cock is crowing;
I must to my home be going,
When all other men doe rise,
Then must I shut up mine eyes.

"The Bel-mans Cry" is pretty likely not an authentic bellman's cry. The admonitory tone would lose force if it were repeated. So this is not a poem of record but a poem of commentary. Functioning this way, is the poem meant to warn readers (if not the town's inhabitants) and to remind them of the customary dangers of the night? Is it meant to delineate the bellman's sense of potential danger, or his own self-description, or a portrait of early Stuart village life? Or, somewhat more grandly, is it meant to be a work of poetry, transforming the commonplace possibilities of night into a mnemonic, or entertaining, or accomplished work of art? It could, of course, be more than one of these, or all of these, which is the point: the document can rarely if ever be held to a single intention, functioning in a singular way.

In a similar passage of greater length in *The Dead Tearme,* Dekker speaks in the ventriloquized voice of St. Paul's.

What whispering is there in *Terme* times, how by some slight to cheat the poore country Clients of his full purse that is stucke under his girdle? What plots are layde to furnish young gallants with readie money (which is shared afterwards at a Tavern) therby to disfurnish him of his patrimony? What buying up of oaths, out of the hands of knights of the Post, who for a few shillings doe daily sell their soules? What layinge of heads is there together and sifting of the brains, still and anon, as it growes towardes eleven of the clocke, (even amongst those that wear gilt Rapiers by their sides) where for that noone they may shift from Duke *Humfrey,* and bee furnished with a Dinner at some meaner mans Table? What damnable bargaines of unmercifull Brokery, and of unmeasureable Usury are there clapt up? What swearing is there: yea, what swaggering, what facing and out-facing? What shuffling, what shouldering, what Justling, what leering, what byting of

Thumbs to beget quarrels, what holding uppe of fingers to remember drunken meetings, what braving with Feathers, what bearding with Mustaschoes, what casting open of cloakes to publish new clothes, what muffling in cloaks to hyde broken Elbows, so that when I heare such trampling up and downe, such spetting, such halking, and such humming (every mans lippe making a noise, yet not a word to be understoode), I verily beleeve that I am the Tower of *Babell* newly to be builded up, but presentlie despaire of ever beeing finished, because there is in me such a confusion of languages.

For at one time, in one and the same ranke, yea, foote by foote, and elbow by elbow, shall you see walking, the Knight, the Gull, the Gallant, the upstart, the Gentleman, the Clowne, the Captaine, the Apple-squire, the lawyer, the Usurer, the Cittizen, the Bankerout, the Scholler, the Begger, the Doctor, the Ideot, the Ruffian, the Cheater, the Puritan, the Cutthroat, the Hye-men, the Low-men, the True-man, and the Thiefe: of all trades and professions some, of all Countryes some; And thus dooth my middle *Isle* shew like the *Mediterranean Sea,* in which as well the Merchant hoysts up sayles to purchace wealth honestly, as the *Rover* to light upon prize unjustly. Thus am I like a common Mart where all Commodities (both the good and the bad) are to be bought and solde. Thus whitest devotion kneeles at her prayers, doth prophanation walke under her nose in contempt of *Religion.* But my lamentations are scattered with the winds, my sighes are lost in the Ayre, and I my selfe not thought worthy to stand high in the love of those that are borne and nourished by mee.

The sheer density of this passage would belie the single dominant discourse that a follower of Michel Foucault might put upon it; rather, the confusion that seems so thematic to this excerpt not only underscores the kind of social, professional, and economic cross-cutting (and perhaps cross-dressing) that is alive in the scene depicted here, but holds as in amber the subjectivity, transparency, pride, miscalculation, and opportunism that through its sheer vitality both celebrates and endangers those who step into London's great cathedral during weekdays. Just as the sanctuary doubled during the week as a market, so lawyers searching for clients prey upon men and women much as the criminals they are meant to condemn do. Just as courtiers strut, so they closely imitate foists. Sporting fencers can be misidentified as discharged soldiers, crooks as clients, merchants as usurers, citizens as clowns (that is, foolish men perhaps straying from Bedlam), professionals as Puritans (who are themselves a kind of professional), high man as low, true man as thief. The very alliteration of this last gives us pause, and disjoins us from the otherwise seductive pull of the vigor of the presentation. The alliteration may suggest the self-consciousness of the writer, adding to the art but detracting from its fidelity to sheer fact. The "damnable bargaines of unmercifull Brokery," on the other hand, may be a deliberate forewarning of the quotation's final concern: the profanation of the sacred as this cross-section of London society and country visitors blasphemes in their secular celebrations of life and their denial of the alternative opportunity to search for eternal life. In such an atmosphere, devotion kneeling at her prayers has no chance to be heard and serves no purpose to her fellow man, while this ventriloquized St. Paul's despairs that "my lamentations are scattered with the winds." Yet that sorrow, that lamentation, when combined with the rueful self-presentation as the Tower of Babel "newly to be builded up," both source and scene of departure from God, may suggest why, for Dekker, this excerpt belongs to the *dead* term. Its sheer energy seems at once accomplished and futile, productive and moribund. Yet this primary document of the time, mediated through the prosopopoeia of the church it envisions, is not merely a document recording the London life under James I. Nor is it simply the messiness of history. Rather, it is what postmodernists label the "new pluralism," its meanings forever in flux, in slippage, equivocating without end.

Mediating Fact and Fiction

In 1837, Michelet explained to Sainte-Beuve: "If I had introduced only political history into my narrative, if I had taken no account of the diverse elements of history (religion, law, geography, literature, art, etc.), my procedure would have been quite different. *But a great vital movement was needed, because all these diverse elements gravitated together in the unity of the story.*" A generation later, Fustel de Coulanges, in his turn, announced to his listeners in the Sorbonne: "Supposing a hundred specialists had divided the past of France according to lot, do you think that, in the end, they would have written the history of France? I very much doubt it. At the very least, they should miss the linkage of facts: now, *this linkage is itself a historical truth.*" The contrast of the images is significant. Michelet thought and felt in terms of the organic; Fustel, son of an age for which the Newtonian universe seemed to furnish the ultimate scientific pattern, took his metaphors from space. Their fundamental agreement is all the more impressive. These two great historians were too great to overlook the fact that a civilization, like a person, is no mechanically arranged game of solitaire; the knowledge of fragments, studied by turns, each for its own sake, will never produce the knowledge of the whole; it will not even produce that of the fragments themselves.

—MARC BLOCH

Reading historical documents such as the rogue literature that is the subject of this book is both a matter of construction—of seeing how it forges linkages with other documents as discourses in the same time period, as a kind of Derridean supplement—and a matter of deconstruction, of exposing, in what appears a singular document, various, often competing, discourses. Reading rogue literature against the grain of other documents, the social historian J. A. Sharpe asserts that we need to distinguish "between what was actually happening, and what contemporaries thought was happening."

> The first impression to strike anyone turning from the statutes and the rogue literature to court archives . . . is that the vagrant emerges as a much tamer phenomenon from the second than from the first. The large bands of vagrants, generally speaking, are absent; there is little evidence of a "fraternity of vagabonds"; and the justices examining vagabonds seem not to have been in any way concerned about such matters. Most of those apprehended do not seem to have been the professional rogues legislated against in Parliament, but were usually unremarkable representatives of the lower, and hence more vulnerable, strata of society. (142–43)

Prevalent mobility complicates the picture, Sharpe contends, since those on the road might be migrant workers, harvesters, women pregnant and dismissed from work, those whose terms of service had ended, those in search of their first jobs or apprenticeships. Sharpe cites Henry Bristow, taken in Southampton in 1641, who was found with a map of England and who told those who apprehended him that "he bought it at the Exchange in London being desirous to travel to see the country"; "John Bodle, examined by the authorities of the same town in December 1639, informed them that he was 'by profession a bricklayer, and that hee doth not use to worke at his profession In the winter time'" (Sharpe 142). Deconstructing the generalities of rogue books (whose tales construct a different generalization) suggests that other documents can provide a counterreality. Sharpe's method of investigation is through microhistories.

> Vagabonds examined by the town authorities at Warwick, for example, were almost always far less threatening than their counterparts in the popular literature of the period. Most of them claimed to be wandering in search of employment. A girl from Cheltenham claimed that she was going in search of service in the north country; a man from Henley-on-Thames declared that "he hath no trade to live by but onely a labourer an is come into the country to seek woork, but can fynd none"; another man explained

that "he had bene that time in divers places to seek work of his occupacion being a silk wever an now was determyned to goo towards London." Others had hard luck stories to tell. William Wilson told how he had once kept an inn at Southwark, but "being fallen in debt was fayne to come from there," while John Weaver of Stratford-upon-Avon claimed that "he hath bene an occupeier of small wares, and was robbed of them & so forced to go abrode." For such people, begging must have been the obvious alternative when there was no work to be had. (143)

Sharpe does find rings of highwaymen and horse-thieves in the country and of prostitutes in London. "Highwaymen, horse-thieves and the hardened 'professional' vagrant rogue were often known to each other over surprisingly wide geographical distances, and seem to have been able to pick up local contacts fairly rapidly when they moved into a new area. . . . But . . . organized crime outside London was rarely very sophisticated or permanent" (171). Penry Williams concurs: "The huge and threatening bands of sturdy beggars were largely mythical" (217). Inside London, Sharpe turns to the personal history of Margaret Ferneseed,

> who was burnt for murdering her husband. Although she claimed to be innocent of the killing to the last, she confessed to having been a whore since puberty and to having run a brothel. Her recruiting methods were well planned. She kept close contact with carriers, so that she could "make spoile of yong maidens who were sent out of the countrie by their friends, here with hope to advance themselves." These girls were debauched, and put on the streets, each of them being compelled to give "ten shillings a week out of their gettings" to Ferneseed. She also made use of discontented wives. She would note "any breach or discontent" between likely women and their husbands, and would then persuade them that "they were not beloved of their husbands," or that "their husbands maintained them not sufficiently to expresse their beauty, and according to their owne deserts." Once these women had prostituted themselves, Ferneseed ensured their continued service by a simple form of blackmail, threatening to expose them to their husbands if they refused to continue to accommodate her customers. (Sharpe 165–66)

Reconfiguring rogue literature in the light of such individual court records, Sharpe concludes that "Much of the appeal of the rogue literature, and of later popular works on crime, lay in its entertainment value. From the start, the tricks and exploits described in the rogue pamphlets are recounted with evident relish and panache, and reading them can still be an enjoyable experience.

On the other hand, behind the relish there lurks the conviction that the underworld is dangerous: it may in many ways be presented as a mirror image of straight society, but (and possibly because it is such a mirror image) it threatens it. Could it be that descriptions of the 'Elizabethan underworld,' or of gangs, tell us more about the fears of society, and ultimately of the government, than they do of reality? Many of the ideas that crystallized in the rogue pamphlets as the genre developed were commonplaces of governmental thinking, enshrined in numerous statutes and proclamations: above all, the danger of idleness, and the need to preserve order" (235). He goes on to suggest further that the underworld described in the rogue literature not only made the known crimes more comprehensible to readers of the early modern period, but helped to relieve such fears by seeming to contain them through explanation and exposure. Thus the documents turned into discourses at first deconstruct a master narrative and then explain why such an implied master narrative came into being. Consequently, our job is to deconstruct that master narrative once more in order to understand its creation, power, and function.

The sheer popularity of rogue literature in early modern England attests to its power and endurance, but it is the endurance of narrative—anecdote, report, tale—that *mediates between* fact and fiction: the literature of roguery would lose its power—and any hope for authority—if it were *not* grounded in facticity. Thus the radical historian Raphael Samuel observes that "the deconstructive turn in contemporary thought" permits us, as it did not seem to permit many of our predecessors, to re-view history "not as a record of the past, more or less faithful to the facts," as Sharpe's court records seem to do, although based on personal testimony, but, rather, "as an invention, or fiction, of historians themselves" who understand, as the pamphleteers did, the mediating power of language (220–21). Bryan Reynolds makes a similar point: "all historiography is necessarily both actual and imaginary," perhaps because writers then and readers now know that with the multiplicity of possibilities and the messiness of history no complete record would be comprehensible, even if it could ever be attainable. Rather, Reynolds comments, "The literary representation of criminal culture is itself a differential space where the actual and the imaginary collide and coalesce" (214). Documents, Dominick LaCapra remarks, "are texts that supplement or rework 'reality' and not mere sources that divulge facts about 'reality'" (11). They can hope at best to represent, to re-present, the world they convey; they cannot actually re-create or duplicate it, and they do so by means of what Jonathan Gil Harris has labeled "the double helix of matter and form," substance and genre (50).

In a new book entitled *The Landscape of History: How Historians Map the*

Past (2002), John Lewis Gaddis finds help in reconsidering the scientific method.

The best introduction I know to the scientific method, John Ziman's *Reliable Knowledge: An Exploration of the Grounds for Belief in Science*, points out that scientific insights often arise from such realizations as "that the behavior of an electron in an atom is 'like' the vibration of air in a spherical container, or that the random configuration of the long chain of atoms in a polymer molecule is 'like' the motion of a drunkard across a village green." "Reality is still to be embraced and reported without flinching," the sociologist Edward O. Wilson has added. "But it is also best delivered the same way it was discovered, retaining a comparable vividness and play of the emotions." It's here, I think, that science, history, and art have something in common: they all depend on metaphor, on the recognition of patterns, on the realization that something is "like" something else. (2)

So too Richard J. Evans: "History is as much about the obviously other as it is about the seemingly familiar. It is about bridging a series of gaps, in time, culture and experience, through the use of a disciplined historical imagination" (214). That is precisely the sense of rogue literature shared by contributors to this volume. Thus Craig Dionne posits a connection between bartering and capital investment and the schemes of rogues, noting that images of rogues closely united and ignoring legal and economic regulations served as metaphoric models for merchants. Linda Woodbridge sees Wenceslaus Hollar's engraving of the Royal Exchange mediating between two Dutch merchants and a woman balladeer. Patricia Fumerton finds a mediating principle in the double life of Nicholas Jennings, as later Lee Beier also does, while using Jennings's situation to comment on itinerant laborers, day jobbers, nomadic workers, and the authentically destitute. For Lee Salamon, Victor Turner's sense of liminality functions as Ziman's simile and Reynolds' mediation and LaCapra's supplement do, finding a jointure alongside, or partially within, the rogue books but not, finally, the substance of them. For others—Brooke Strafford, Adam Hansen—the liminal status of the rogue books is seen as the blurring of normalized boundaries. As a result, Martine van Elk notes, "Rogue literature of the early modern period is notoriously ambiguous in its presentation," although for her the terms that must be mediated are the entertaining subject matter and the stern moral voice that recounts it. Formulating linkages, as the essays here do, at once re-creates, represents, and refashions the rogue literature itself; seeing the rogue pamphleteers deliberately making metaphor out of reality and holding onto both through comparison is what finally conveys impression and meaning to rogue literature. And, as these contributors also demonstrate, meaning rests, too, on reception, through readers' active engagements.

Whether or not the secret activities of the Irish Travelers will ever realize such attention is doubtful: they are too secretive, too locked away to permit observers and readers from making linkages that will turn their lives into reflectors that mediate our own. We may also be too close to them in time as well as too far from them in space. The "outing" of Madelyne Gorman Toogood as a mediating force may be a singular event. If it is, the Irish Travelers will likely retain the obscurity they seek. But if her arrest in Indiana, when a surveillance video from the dominant society invaded the activity of her private one, becomes a matter of concern, we can know how to understand even the puzzling subsets in our own present-day society.

WORKS CITED

Berkowitz, D. S., ed. *Humanist Scholarship and Public Order*. Washington, D.C.: Folger Books, 1983.

Bloch, Marc. *The Historian's Craft*. New York: Vintage, 1953.

Butterfield, H. *The Whig Interpretation of History*. New York: Charles Scribner's Sons, 1951.

Elton, G. R. *Return to Essentials: Some Reflections on the Present State of Historical Study*. Cambridge: Cambridge UP, 1991.

Evans, Richard J. *In Defence of History*. London: Granta, 1997.

Gaddis, John Lewis. *The Landscape of History: How Historians Map the Past*. Oxford: Oxford UP, 2002.

Harris, Jonathan Gil. "Atomic Shakespeare." *Shakespeare Studies* 30 (2002): 47–51.

Kinney, Arthur F. *Rogues, Vagabonds, and Sturdy Beggars*. 2d ed. Amherst: U of Massachusetts P, 1990.

LaCapra, Dominick. *History and Criticism*. Ithaca: Cornell UP, 1987.

Popper, Karl. *Conjectures and Refutations: The Growth of Scientific Knowledge*. 2d ed. New York: Basic Books, 1965.

Ripley, Amanda. "Unwelcome Exposure." *Time*, October 7, 2002, 10.

Reynolds, Bryan. *Becoming Criminal: Transversal Performance and Cultural Dissonance in Early Modern England*. Baltimore: Johns Hopkins UP, 2002.

Salgãdo, Gãmini. *The Elizabethan Underworld*. 1977. Reprint, Phoenix Mill: Alan Sutton, 1992.

Samuel, Raphael. "Reading the Signs II." *History Workshop Journal* 33 (1992): 220–51.

Sharpe, J. A. *Crime in Early Modern England, 1550–1750*, 2d ed. London: Longman, 1999.

Somekawa, Ellen, and Elizabeth A. Smith. "Theorizing the Writing of History; or, 'I

Can't Think Why It Should Be So Dull, for a Great Deal of It Must Be Invention.'" *Journal of Social History* 22 (1988): 149–61.

Stone, Lawrence. "History and Post-modernism II." *Past and Present* 135 (May 1992): 189–94.

Vincent, John. *An Intelligent Person's Guide to History*. London: Duckworth, 1995.

Williams, Penry. *The Later Tudors: England, 1547–1603*. Oxford: Clarendon P, 1998.

Windschuttle, Keith. *The Killing of History: How Literary Critics and Social Theorists Are Murdering Our Past*. San Francisco: Encounter Books, 2000.

Wrightson, Keith. *Earthly Necessities: Economic Lives in Early Modern Britain, 1470–1750*. London: Penguin, 2002.

Contributors

A. L. BEIER is Professor of History at Illinois State University and also taught history at Lancaster University from 1967 to 1990. He is the author of *Masterless Men: The Vagrancy Problem in England, 1560–1640* (1985); his recent research concerns Henry Mayhew and the question of the "dangerous class" in mid-nineteenth-century England.

KAREN HELFAND BIX is a doctoral candidate at the University of Maryland, College Park. She is currently completing a dissertation that examines early modern English economic discourses. She has presented papers about rogue literature at meetings of the Modern Language Association (2001) and the Northeast Modern Language Association (2000).

CRAIG DIONNE is Associate Professor of English at Eastern Michigan University, where he teaches Shakespeare, early modern English literature, and literary criticism. He is coeditor of *Disciplining English: Alternate Histories, Critical Perspectives* (SUNY Press 2002) and has published essays on Shakespeare and English Renaissance literature.

LAURIE ELLINGHAUSEN is Assistant Professor of English at University of Missouri, Kansas City. Her current research investigates representations of writing as labor by nonaristocratic authors in the late sixteenth and early seventeenth centuries. Her forthcoming work includes articles in *Studies in English Literature, 1500–1900* and the *Ben Jonson Journal*.

PATRICIA FUMERTON is Professor of English and Director of the Early Modern Center at the University of California, Santa Barbara. She is author of *Cultural Aesthetics: Renaissance Literature and the Practice of Social Ornament* (University of Chicago Press, 1991) and coeditor of *Renaissance Culture and the Everyday* (University of Pennsylvania Press, 1999). She is currently completing a book on early modern vagrancy and lower-order mobility as well as working on a study of blackletter broadside ballads of the period.

ADAM HANSEN taught at the University of Lodz (Poland) and is currently based at the University of York, where he is researching representations of rogues, vagrants, and vagabonds in English prose from the Renaissance to the nineteenth century, with particular emphasis on the works of Daniel Defoe, William Godwin, and Charles Dickens. At present he is preparing articles for publication on these authors from work undertaken as part of his doctoral thesis.

ARTHUR F. KINNEY is Thomas W. Copeland Professor of Literary History and Director of the Massachusetts Center for Renaissance Studies at the University of Massachusetts, Amherst, and founding editor of the journal *English Literary Renaissance* and the book series Massachusetts Studies in Early Modern Culture. He is the editor of *Rogues, Vagabonds, and Sturdy Beggars*, first published in 1974 for the Imprint Society (second edition, 1991, 1994). He is also the editor of *Elizabethan Backgrounds, Titled Elizabethans, Tudor Encyclopedia, Renaissance Drama, A Companion to Renaissance Drama*, and the *Cambridge Companion to English Literature, 1500–1600*. His most recent books are *"Lies Like Truth": Shakespeare, Macbeth, and the Cultural Moment* (2001) and *Shakespeare by Stages* (2003).

TINA KUHLISCH is a doctoral candidate at the University of Nevada, Las Vegas. She was educated at the Complutense University, Madrid, and Humboldt University, Berlin, where she received her master's degree (Staatsexamen) in English and Spanish literature and linguistics. She taught English and Spanish at a Berlin gymnasium and also at the University of Nevada, Las Vegas. Her research interests are English and Spanish picaresque narratives in their sociocultural and epistemic conditions, and literature instruction in undergraduate classrooms, an interest she pursues as contributor to the World Literature hypermedia project of UNLV's Department of English.

STEVE MENTZ is Assistant Professor of English at St. John's University. He has published articles on Shakespeare, Sir Philip Sidney, Robert Greene, and Thomas Nashe, and has articles forthcoming on John Lyly and George Gascoigne. He is currently finishing a book on prose fiction and the book market in Elizabethan England. His interest in rogues arises from their intimate connections with the conditions of early modern authorship and publication, the changing nature of the book market, and the growing self-consciousness of urban culture.

BRYAN REYNOLDS is Associate Professor and Head of Doctoral Studies in Drama at the University of California, Irvine. He is the author of *Becoming Criminal: Transversal Performance and Cultural Dissidence in Early Modern*

England (Johns Hopkins UP, 2002) and *Performing Transversally: Reimagining Shakespeare and the Critical Future* (St. Martin's/Palgrave, 2003). He is also coeditor with Donald Hedrick of *Shakespeare without Class: Misappropriations of Cultural Capital* (St. Martins/Palgrave, 2000), and has published articles on the work of Shakespeare, Cixous, Certeau, Dekker, Deleuze, Foucault, Guattari, Rousseau, Middleton, Polanski, and Robert Wilson. He is also a playwright, a director of theater, and a screenwriter.

LINDA BRADLEY SALAMON is Professor of English and Human Sciences at George Washington University, where she previously served as Dean of Arts and Sciences. Her monograph "The Art of Nicholas Hilliard" appears in *Nicholas Hilliard's Arte of Limning* (1983), coedited with Arthur Kinney; her "Theory *avant la letter*" appears in *After Poststructuralism: Writing the Histories of Theory* (University of Toronto Press, 2002), edited by Tilottama Rajan and Michael J. O'Driscoll. Her articles consider filming *Richard III*, intertextuality in Elyot, Ascham, and Gascoigne, and early modern resonances in T. S. Eliot. Her current projects include early Tudor "orientalizing," pedagogy in Shakespeare, the life cycle of the sundial, and self-improvement texts among early books.

JANNA SEGAL is an Associate Instructor and doctoral student in the University of California, Irvine/University of California, San Diego joint Ph.D. program in Drama and Theatre. She completed her B.A. in theater at the University of California at Santa Cruz, and her M.A. in Theatre Literature, History, Criticism, and Theory at California State University, Northridge. In addition to her work with Bryan Reynolds on Moll Cutpurse and *The Roaring Girl* in this collection, Segal and Reynolds have coauthored essays on *Othello* and Dario Fo's *Elizabetta*, both of which can be found in Reynolds' *Performing Transversally: Reimagining Shakespeare and the Critical Future* (St. Martins/Palgrave, 2003).

BROOKE A. STAFFORD is a Ph.D. candidate in English and codirector of the Educational Opportunity Program writing courses at the University of Washington. Her dissertation explores displacement and identity in sixteenth- and seventeenth-century representations of adventurers, captives, slaves, merchants, and pirates.

MARTINE VAN ELK is an Assistant Professor at California State University, Long Beach. She has a number of publications out and forthcoming, including essays on Shakespeare in *Philological Quarterly* and *Studies in English Literature*. She is currently working on a book-length study of identification and misidentification in Shakespeare and early modern culture, tentatively entitled *Deciphering the Other.*

L I N D A W O O D B R I D G E is Distinguished Professor of English at Pennsylvania State University. Her books include *Vagrancy, Homelessness, and English Renaissance Literature,* 2001; *The Scythe of Saturn: Shakespeare and Magical Thinking,* 1994; and *Women and the English Renaissance: Literature and the Nature of Womankind, 1540–1620,* 1984.

Index

Aarsleff, Hans, 347, 357n. 41
able-bodied poor, unemployed, 45–49;
    contempt for, 17; employments of,
    194–200, 366–67, 376–77; policing of,
    111–12; sexuality of, 46–48; slavery
    proposed as punishment, 112; as sturdy
    beggars, 42
the Abraham Man (counterfeit crank),
    129, 197–98
An Act for Punishment of Rogues,
    Vagabonds and Sturdy Beggars
    (*Statutes of the Realm*, 39 Elizabeth c.
    4), 207n. 14
Act for the Punishment of Vagabonds
    (1572), 44–45, 150, 196, 203
Addison, William, 145–46
The Adventures of Master F.J. (Gascoigne),
    250
Aesop's fables, 256n. 20
Aethiopian History (Heliodorus), 241
Agnew, Jean-Christophe, 125, 185, 190n.
    2; as economic historian, 13; quoted,
    191n. 8, 201, 230; referenced, 178–80,
    182–83, 203
agrarian ethics, demise of, 23
The Alchemist (Jonson), 190n. 6; roaring
    boys, roaring girls in, 331
Alderman, Mr. *(Moll Flanders)*, 349
All about My Mother (film), 66
alliteration, 226, 374–75
Alonso, King *(The Tempest)*, 74
Alter, Robert, 353n. 2, 355n. 19, 356nn.
    25–26, 357n. 35
Althusser, Louis, 12, 38, 63, 88n. 2, 105,
    112, 115n. 13, 254, 257n. 30

Althusserian dialectical materialism, 11
Alyn, John (tailor), 132
ambiguity, and rogues, 8–9
ambition, cony-catching pamphlets on,
    171–90
*Ambition and Privilege: The Social Tropes
    of Elizabethan Courtesy Theory*
    (Whigham), 55
ambivalence: Balzac and class ambivalence
    toward his characters, 356n. 27; in
    Bridewell Court Books, 121; certain
    behavior as vice or virtue, 358n. 50;
    class ambivalence, 356n. 27; in
    cony-catching pamphlets, 171–90, 231;
    Moll Flanders, ambivalence of Defoe
    toward, 257n. 28; Moll Flanders as
    ambivalent rogue, 26–27, 337–60;
    moral ambivalence, 17; Tolstoy, class
    ambivalence toward his characters,
    356n. 27; vagrancy, ambivalence
    toward, 121
Amends for Ladies (Fields), 20, 91n. 25
The Anatomie of Abuses (Stubbes), 58n. 14
Andersen, Hans H., 348, 356n. 31, 358n. 50
*Annales, or, a Generall Chronicle of En-
    gland* (Stow), 153
antihero, trickster as, 12
Antonio *(The Tempest)*, 74
Appleby, Joyce, 174, 177
apprentices, 17, 194–95, 205, 367. *See also*
    servant-master conflicts
Archer, Ian W., 116n. 17, 123–24, 137n. 11,
    205nn. 4, 8, 206n. 9, 232n. 8
archivalism, traditional, 11
Arden of Feversham (anon.), 146

aristocracy, absorption into, 358n. 43
Arlington National Cemetery, 261
Armstrong, Clement, 156–57
The Army of Flanders and the Spanish Road, 1567–1659 (Parker), 270–73, 276, 289n. 22, 290n. 33
Arnold, Thomas, 288n. 16
Artful Dodger *(Oliver Twist)*, 8
"Articles of their Fraternities" (Dekker), 362
artists, 16
The Art of Juggling or Legerdemain (Rid), 206n. 14, 218, 228, 233n. 13
Art of Living in London (Peacham), 35, 56
Art of War (Machiavelli), 270
Ascham, Roger, 288n. 17
Ashton, Robert, 233n. 11
assimilation, 316
As You Like It (Shakespeare), 66, 154
Augustine, 214
Austin, J. L., 65
authors: corrective function of, 317–18; falconers and, 25–26; legitimacy of, 294–96; motives of, ascertaining, 372–73; professional authors, 294–300, 305; relationship to readers, 307–9
Autolycus *(Odyssey)*, 241
Autolycus *(The Winter's Tale)*, 13, 15
Awdeley, John, 33, 267–69, 287n. 10; on the Courtesy Man, 268; Dekker plagiarizing from, 294; "fraternity" metaphor of, 367; referenced, 128–29, 216, 266; on the Ruffler, 266; on the Upright Man, 267–68. See also *The Fraternity of Vagabonds*
Aydelotte, Frank, 14, 203, 205n. 1, 206n. 14
Ayers, Michael R., 357n. 38

Babylon, 218
Backscheider, Paula, 355n. 20
Bacon, Francis, 178
Badford, Nell, 122
Baines, Barbara J., 167n. 2
Bakhtin, Mikhail, 59n. 15, 233n. 14, 234n. 30
Baldo, Jonathan, 290n. 36
ballads, 204; rogues, molls depicted in,

1–2; *Turner's Dish of Lentten Stuffe, or a Galymaufery,* 204
ballad-sellers, 150–51
Balzac, Honoré de, 356n. 27
Bankes, John (vagrant), 126–27
Barbary Company, 167n. 4
Bardolph *(Henry V)*, 280–83, 286
Barker, W. W., 253
the Barnard's law (card trick), 51–52, 130, 176, 190n. 7, 241
barter, and rogue economy, 7
Baston, Jane, 79, 93nn. 30, 32, 94n. 36
Bates *(Henry V)*, 284
Baumgartner, Paul R., 234n. 26
Beckett, Samuel, 308
Becoming Criminal: Transversal Performance and Cultural Dissidence in Early Modern England (Reynolds), 8–9, 15–16, 39, 73, 89nn. 3, 10, 12, 93n. 32, 135n. 2, 190n. 5, 233n. 17
beggars: disguised as the "middling sort," 358n. 46; fetishization of, 135n. 2; rogues as, 197–98; veteran soldiers as, 267
Beier, A. L., 21–22, 42–43, 121, 196, 218, 222, 264; on cant, 334n. 6; on double life of Jennings, 379; on existence of criminal underground, 295; on Harman, 126; *Masterless Men: The Vagrancy Problem in England, 1560–1640*, 36, 99, 116n. 17, 116n. 26, 116n. 31, 121, 136n. 3, 196, 206n. 9, 218, 232n. 7, 233n. 17; on mediation, 379; referenced, 45, 57n. 5, 115n. 7, 116nn. 17, 22, 26, 28, 31, 136nn. 3–4, 8, 137n. 11, 200, 205n. 4, 206n. 9, 232n. 7, 233n. 17, 234n. 24, 246, 256n. 19
Beldam, Richard (laborer), 195
bellman *(Lantern and Candlelight)*, 302–7, 320–22
The Bellman of London (Dekker), 22–23, 48–49, 171, 220–21; latinate rogues in, 309n. 4; Rid on, 321–22
"The Bellman's Second Night Walk" (Dekker), 334n. 12
"The Bel-man's Cry" (Dekker), 372–73
Ben-Amos, Ilans Krausman, 195, 205n. 5
Berkowitz, D. S., 365
Berlin, Normand, 205n. 1, 234n. 26

Bertrande (wife of Martin Guerre), 277–79
Bertrande de Rols *(Henry V)*, 285
Bess of Hardwick, aka Elizabeth, countess of Shrewsbury, 104
Best, Alexander (master), 132
Bhabha, Homi, 316–17, 334n. 4
Bindoff, S. T., 116n. 30
bin Laden, Osama, 73
Bisson, Douglas, 155, 164–65, 168n. 14
Bjornson, Richard, 357nn. 34, 36
Black, Jeremy, 270, 287n. 13, 288n. 16
The Black Book's Messenger (Greene), 221–24; Dekker plagiarizing from, 294
Blackburn, Alexander, 353n. 2
The Black Dog of Newgate (Hutton), 176, 224, 233n. 10, 304
Blank, Paula, 320, 328, 331, 333, 334n. 7
Bledstein, Burton, 8
Bloch, Marc, 361, 364–65, 375
Blount, Nicholas. *See* Jennings, Nicholas, aka Blunt
Blunt. *See* Jennings, Nicholas, aka Blunt
Bodle, John (vagrant), 376
body, political technology of, 21
Bonahue, Edward T., Jr., 162, 167n. 2
books, rogues, and emerging book market, 13
Bosom Buddies (television show), 66
Boughton family, 106
Bouling, Thomas (shepherd), 366
Boulogne, 220
Boulton, Jeremy, 195–96
Bowes, Sir Martin, 108–9, 111, 113
Boynton, Lindsay, 28n. 20, 274, 288n. 17
Boys Don't Cry (film), 66
Bradshaw, Brendan, 315
Braudel, Fernand, 232n. 5
Breight, Curtis, 272, 274, 279–86
Brenner, Robert, 58n. 9
Bridewell Court Books, 121, 124, 127, 129, 134; ambivalence in, 121; deviance in, 21, 121; form, contents of, 124; identification in, 126–27; as narrative, 124; parallelism with rogue literature, 120; servant-master conflicts in, 123–24; sexual transgressions in, 123; as spectrum of socially condemned behavior, 121
Bridewell Court of Governors, 21, 122–23,

126–27, 130, 133, 136n. 9, 137n. 12; and elimination of sturdy beggars, 123; minutes of, 21; on vagrants, 21
Bridewell Hospital: cony threatened with, 6; creation of, 113; founding of, 111, 123; Jennings/Blunt at, 109–10; punishment at, 21
Bridget *(The Life and Death of Mrs. Mary Frith)*, 84–85
Bristol, Michael, 59n. 15
Bristow, Henry (vagrant), 376
Brome, Richard, 91n. 25
Browne, Ned *(The Black Book's Messenger)*, 178–79, 181, 221
Brunning, Alizon, 180
Bull (the Tyburn hangman), 368
Bulwer, John (linguist), 357n. 39
Burbie, Cuthbert (publisher), 247
Burford, E. J., 233n. 11
Burghley, Lord (Lord Treasurer), 368–69
Burke, Peter, 216, 231, 233n. 17
Burnett, Mark Thornton, 188
Burt, Richard, 91n. 20
Buscón (picaresque novel), 355n. 19
business owners as rogues, 9
Butler, Judith, 65
Butterfield, Sir Herbert, 370–71

Cage, Nicolas, 9
Cahill, Patricia Ann, 289n. 25
Calendar of State Papers, 372
Callaghan, Dympna, 90n. 14
Cambridge *(Henry V)*, 282
cannibals, 38
Canny, Nicholas, 327, 334n. 1
cant: as antilanguage, 233n. 17; canting, 136n. 4; canting dictionaries, 26, 99, 226, 312–13, 315–16, 322–27; canting songs, 320, 326; discourses on, 16; Englishing of, 226, 322–27; existence of, 233n. 17; of the Irish Travelers, 361–62; lexicons of, 2; as mastering its users, 335n. 18; as "Pedlars' French," 150, 227; in plays, 335n. 18; in *The Roaring Girl*, 331–33, 335n. 17; in rogue pamphlets, 2; at school for cutpurses, 369; as spoken language, 369; and Tower of Babel, 296–97, 299; translation and, 225–30, 370–71; as written language, 369

The Canting Crew: London's Criminal Underworld (McMullan), 36–37

capitalism, 14–15; American capitalism, 9; cony-catching pamphlets on, 171–90; in early modern London, 40–43; game of, 8; in *Moll Flanders*, 26–27; peddlers, tinkers as capitalist entrepreneurs, 354n. 9; rogue capitalism, 9; rogue literature and, 323; rogues and, 8; surplus labor and, 195. *See also* commerce

Capp, Bernard, 104

Caravaggio, 18–19, 28n. 3

Caravaggio: A Life (Langdon), 28n. 3

The Cardsharps (Caravaggio), 18–19, 28n. 3

Carleton, Sir Dudley, 91n. 25

Carr, E. H., 372

Carreter, Lázaro, 353n. 2

Carroll, William C., 105, 121, 136n. 5, 137n. 12, 177, 200–201; beggars, on sentiment toward, 354n. 8; on beggars disguised as the "middling sort," 358n. 46; on *A Caveat or Warening for Common Cursetors Vulgarely Called Vagabones*, 339–40; *Fat King, Lean Beggar: Representations of Poverty in the Age of Shakespeare*, 121, 135n. 2; peddlers, tinkers as capitalist entrepreneurs, 354n. 9; quoted, 175, 190n. 3, 201–2; referenced, 98–101, 103, 115nn. 1, 3, 116nn. 17, 24, 127, 137n. 13, 205n. 1; as Shakespeare scholar, 13

Cascoigne, George (gentleman veteran), 268

Case, Sue-Ellen, 92n. 27

"The Case of Nicholas Jennings Alias Blunt before London's Court of Aldermen, 13 January, 9 Elizabeth I" (1567), 114–15

Castiglione, Baldassare, 55

Catch Me If You Can (film), 9

caterpillars of the commonwealth, 1, 42, 175

cathedrals, as marketplaces, 22

Catherine *(Henry V)*, 285

A Caveat or Warening for Common Cursetors Vulgarely Called Vagabones (Harman), 7, 14, 21, 23, 33, 45–48, 51, 98–115, 150, 193, 226, 234n. 22, 244,

266, 295; Blunt's story in, 109–10; business savvy in, 339; canting dictionary in, 323–24; corrective function of, 318; Dekker plagiarizing from, 294; Freudian interpretation of, 99–105, 113; jestbook tradition and, 16; names, list of, 126; new historicism on, 98–115; as noncanonical, 98; plagiarized by others, 98, 294; printings, number of, 33; publishing history of, 27n. 1, 98; traditional historical methods and, 112–13

Cecil, Sir William, 112

Certain Discourses Military (Smythe), 272, 288n. 17

Certeau, Michel de, 286n. 1, 287n. 7

Cervantes, Miguel de, 28n. 21, 272

Chaber, Lois A., 356n. 27

Chamberlain, John, 77, 91n. 25, 93n. 30

Chandler, F. W., 14

chapman, 163–64

charivari, 102–3, 289n. 29

Charles VI *(Henry V)*, 282, 285

Chartier, Roger, 241, 307–8, 309n. 7

A Chaste Maid in Cheapside (Middleton), 147

"cheat of words," 357n. 41

Cheney, Patrick, 92n. 28, 93n. 31, 94n. 36

Chester, Sir William, 148

children, uses of, 366

Christianity: on sex, marriage, 101; and social order, 184

Christ's Tears over Jerusalem (Nashe), 218–20

Chronicles (Holinshed), 98

Ciapelletto *(The Decameron)*, 241

Cicero, 253

city. *See specific topics;* London

city comedy, 240

city handbooks, 39–40

The City Staged (Leinwand), 178, 186

civil wars, 103

Clark, Andrew, 205n. 5

Clark, Peter, 116n. 28, 216, 232n. 4

Clark, Sandra, 231

class: Balzac, characters of, class ambivalence of, 356n. 27; identity and underworld counterpart, 5; lower classes, 177, 189 *(see also* lower orders, classes); *Political Power and Social Classes*

(Poulantzas), 89n. 4; poor classes, 17; and problem of identity, 21; rogues, social classes of, 33–35; rogues and, 1; *Shakespeare without Class* (Hedrick and Reynolds), 89n. 13; and social differentiation, 177–78; social identity and, 62–65; Tolstoy, characters of, class ambivalence of, 356n. 27; transient classes, 17. *See also* middle class

Claudius *(Hamlet)*, 154

Clooney, George, 9

Cloten *(Cymbeline)*, 101

clothing: in Caravaggio's *The Card Sharps*, 28n. 3; false seeming and, 54–56; as identity counterfeiting, 133; of Jennings/Blunt, 109–10; of Pamersiel, 302; rogues and, 203; vagabonds and, 221

clowns, 15

clowns *(Dr. Faustus)*, 15

cobblers, 150–51

Cockburn, J. S., 116n. 17

Cockes, John (Richard Kelley as), 133

Codde, Richard (counterfeiter), 128

Cohen, Murray, 357n. 37

Colahan, Clark, 354n. 7

Cold War, 89n. 6

Colie, Rosalie, 253

Collett, William (vagrant), 126

colonialism: colonization of Ireland, North America, relation between, 334n. 1; "Englishing" and, 313, 315, 317, 333; Englishing as cultural translation, linguistic incorporation, 322–27; English strategy of, 316; of Ireland, Spenser on, 327–30 *(see also specific topics);* Ireland and, 26; mimicry as disruptive of, 316–17, 333; the New English and, 315, 317; Old English and, 318; and the Old English in Ireland, 313, 315, 317, 333; rogue practices of, 10; and Spanish conquest of New World, 10; translation and, 313, 315, 317, 328, 333

Colyns, Roger (tapster), 131

Comensoli, Viviana, 79, 93nn. 31–32, 94n. 36

commerce: attitudes about, 23; as cony-catching, 220; and cony-catching pamphlets, 53, 171–90; evolution of, 144–51; and international trade, 147, 152, 155–56, 164–66, 168n. 14; middlemen and, 156–57; retail shops and, 156–57; rogue pamphlets and, 40–42; rogues as threat to, 7; spectrum of, 143–44; stalls, sheds, permanent shops, 146–48; traditional producer/seller patterns, 156; travail, value of, in, 180; valorization of, effect of, 174. *See also* capitalism

commonwealth, 111, 171–72, 221

compassion, of Reformation, 17

competitiveness, cony-catching pamphlets on, 171–90

complaint literature, 42–43, 52, 184

The Complete English Tradesman (Defoe), 348, 355n. 15; on credit, 358n. 47; family, on importance to tradesman, 356n. 23; and the meanings, use of words, 358n. 42; standards, latitude in, 357n. 34; tradesmen, gentlemen, on differences between, 358n. 44; "The Trading Style," 357n. 40

A Complete History of the Lives and Robberies of the Most Notorious Highwaymen, Shoplifts, and Cheats of Both Sexes (Smith), 91n. 25

complicity, rogue pamphlets and, 19

conduct books, rogue pamphlets as, 19

con games: crossbite, crossbiting law, 6–7; depiction of, 2

conies: as accomplice, 7; arming self with literacy, 10; conning others, 222–23; as greedy, arrogant, morally corrupt, 180–81; and market relations, 24–25

Conjectures and Refutations: The Growth of Scientific Knowledge (Popper), 364

"Considerations delivered to the Parliament" (anon.), 112

The Consistory of London Correction Book, 66, 89n. 7, 91n. 25

"The Conversion of an English Courtesan" (Greene), 247, 249–52, 354n. 5

Cony-Catcher, Cuthbert *(The Defence of Cony-Catching)*, 189, 246–48; Greene as, 2, 134, 220, 247; quoted, 1

cony-catchers, 171–92; alchemical capacities of, 181; analogies between outlaw and respectable cony-catchers, 172; as

cony-catchers (*continued*)
businessmen, 182; as energetic, exuberant, 175; fellowship of, scope and effect of, 183–89; financial talents of, 176; as industrious commercial marketplace laborers, 171–90, 224–25; as laborers, 175–76; legal-if-suspect commercial practices of, 177–78; magic, occult practices of, 181, 191n. 8; and market relations, 24–25; merchants as, 220; mobility and, 183–84; as possessing qualities of merchants, 176–77; as rogues, 1; self-display of, 12; self-interest and, 184–85
Cony-Catchery and Bawdy Baskets (Salgādo), 15
cony-catching: alliance, collusion, cooperation in, 185–87; commerce as, 220; as subversive, retributive, 186; as trade, art, 178–80
cony-catching pamphlets: ambiguity in, 225; ambivalence in, 171–90, 231; canon of, 14; containment/subversion model and, 234n. 26; corrective function of, 317–18; double tone of, 171; general contents of, 2; jestbook tradition and, 16; laughter-inducing, 223–25; as magic books, 246–52; as new tactics in urban life, 245–46; as prose romances, 240–42; radicalism of, 189–90; readers protected by, 247; as realistic observation, 16; scholarly approaches to, 11–19; subversive power of, 190. *See also* rogue pamphlets
Cooke (vagrant), 126
Cooper, Cynthia, 9
Copland, Robert: *Highway to the Spital-house*, 14, 52, 184, 221, 228, 240; referenced, 52, 233n. 19, 240
Coras, Jean de (magistrate), 275, 277–78, 289n. 28, 290n. 30
corporal punishment. *See* punishment
corporate hegemony, 40–42
Corum, Richard, 290n. 34
coterie culture, 2
Cottaar, Annemarie, 232n. 6
Coulanges, Fustel de (historian), 375
Counterfeit Crank, 23
counterfeiting: as being deserving poor,

128–29; of identity, 122, 125–30, 133–35; of licenses, passports, other documents, 127–28, 131, 218
Counterfeit Ladies: The Life and Death of Mal Cutpurse, The Case of Mary Carleton (Todd and Spearing), 89n. 7, 93n. 30
The Counter's Commonwealth (Fennor), 184, 191n. 8, 215, 218
The Couriers Academie (Romei), 54–55
Court *(Henry V)*, 284
The Court Beggar (Brome), 91n. 25
Courtney, Wilmot (counterfeit), 131
Court of Aldermen, London, 109–10, 148, 154–55
court records, rogues, molls depicted in, 2. *See also* Bridewell Court Books
craftsmen, 22
Cranes (vagrant), 126
credit and credit culture, 155, 174, 184, 191n. 9, 358n. 47; Defoe on, 358nn. 47–48; rogues and, 184
Cressida *(Troilus and Cressida)*, 101
Crime in Early Modern England, 1550–1750 (Sharpe), 121
crime in London, 216–17
crime statistics, 364
crime writing: Foucauldian theoretical mode of reading, 16; as precursors to novels, 16; scope of, 16
criminal biographies: as crime writing, 16; and Mary Frith/Moll Cutpurse, 20; Tyburn biographies, 337
criminal culture: interpretation of, 35–40. *See also specific topics*
Criminality and Narrative in Eighteenth-Century England (Gladfelder), 16, 39
criminals, 16; fetishization of, 135n. 2; historical populations of, 16
criminal underworld. *See* urban underworld
crossbiters, crossbite, crossbiting law, 6–7
cross-dressing, 65–67, 133; in film, 66; in television shows, 66
Cruikshank, C. G., 28n. 20, 274, 288n. 18, 289nn. 23–24
Cruz, Anne, 342, 354n. 8
The Crying Game (film), 66

cultural incorporation: and birth of British Empire, 333; Englishing as, 322–27
cultural landscape, rogues and, 17
cultural materialists, 12
cultural nonconformists, 16
cultural phenomena, 16
culture of self-display, 7
Cuming, Matthew (Scottish peddler), 152
Cunnington, B. H., 116n. 31
Curtis, T. C., 234n. 26
The Customers Reply . . . an answer to a confused treatise of public commerce, . . . in favor of the private society of Merchants Adventurers (Milles), 164
Cutpurse, Moll. *See* Moll Cutpurse
cutpurses, 126–27, 133, 179, 368–69; school for, 368–69

Dangerfield, Thomas, 354n. 7
Dauphin *(Henry V)*, 285
Davis, Geena, 3–5
Davis, Lloyd, 90n. 14
Davis, Natalie Zemon: on charivari, 289n. 29; referenced, 101, 289n. 28, 290n. 30; *The Return of Martin Guerre*, 275–78, 289nn. 28–29, 290n. 30
Day, John, 91n. 25
day laborers, displaced, 17
The Dead Tearme (Dekker), 373–75
Deane, Thomas (haberdasher), 143, 147, 152, 156–57
The Decameron (Boccaccio), 241
The Defence of Cony-Catching (Greene), 134, 189–90, 220–21, 231, 246–48, 256n. 21; as purported attack on Greene, 2; quoted, 240; as romance, 247; urban life, as critique on, 2
Defoe, Daniel, 26–27, 264, 269; on certain behavior as vice or virtue, 358n. 50; on credit, 358nn. 47–48; crime writing as precursors to novels of, 16; economic purposes, behavior for justified, 356n. 31; family, on importance to tradesman, 356n. 23; *The Fortunes and Misfortunes of the Famous Moll Flanders* (see *Moll Flanders*); *The Great Law of Subordination Consider'd*, 354n. 4; on the meanings, use of words, 357n. 40, 358n. 42; on morality, 356n. 31; morals and language, on connection between, 355n. 15; referenced, 257n. 28; *Street Robberies Consider'd*, 354n. 4; on trade, 356n. 31; tradesmen, gentlemen, on differences between, 358n. 44; *The True-Born Englishman. A Satyr*, 358n. 43. See also *The Complete English Tradesman; Moll Flanders*

degeneration, 333
de Grazia, Margreta, 81–82
Dekker, Thomas, 14, 23–26, 48–49, 231; "The Bellman's Second Night Walk," 334n. 12; cant, technical approach to, 335n. 13; canting dictionaries of, 316, 334n. 12; *The Dead Tearme*, 373–75; disease, infection, discourse on, 334n. 9; on educational, corrective function of pamphlets, 319–20; on Englishing as bidirectional, 317; as entertainer, not moralizer, 346; facticity of, 367; *If It Be Not Good, the Devil Is in It*, 91n. 25; on improving the English nation, 319–20; *The Magnificent Entertainment: Given to King James*, 299–300; on man's fallen nature, wrongful choices, 365; others, othering by, 314; as plagiarist, 98, 115n. 1, 294, 331; *The Plague Pamphlets*, 214; on pleasures of his pamphlets, 320–21, 332; quoted, 48–49, 214, 220–21, 224, 226, 229–30; as reader of pamphlets, 256n. 12; referenced, 93n. 30, 148, 180–81, 204, 220, 233n. 20; as rogue, 11; on the rogue who stayed with him, 370; *The Second Part of the Honest Whore*, 297–98, 300; *The Seven Deadly Sinnes of London*, 214; *Table Alphabeticall*, 325; Twyning on, 234n. 26; what he might actually be saying, 371; *The Witch of Edmonton*, 91n. 25. See also *The Bellman of London; Lantern and Candlelight; O Per Se O; The Roaring Girl*
Deleuze, Gilles, 57n. 7, 73–74
Deleuze and Guattari: New Mappings in Politics, Philosophy, and Culture (Kaufman and Heller), 90n. 16
Deleuzian poststructuralism, 11
Deloney, Thomas, 41
democratic social relations, 171–90
Dent, Arthur, 252, 257n. 27

Derrida, Jacques: concept of *pharmakos*, 354n. 8; referenced, 70, 89n. 9; theory of *différance*, 70, 75–76
Derridean supplement, 376
Description of England (Harrison), 33, 98
Desdemona *(Othello)*, 74
deviance: complicity with, 39; Frith, Mary, and, 67; Harman's works and, 111; lewdness as criminal deviance, 124–25; linking vagrancy to crimes of, 121–22; rogue literature and, 120–21
deviants: Bridewell Court of Governors on, 21; rogues as, 2
Devil, the *(Lantern and Candlelight)*, 302–5
Devil, the *(Moll Flanders)*, 351
devils, and print culture, 303–4
de Vries, Jan, 215
dialectical materialism, Althusserian, 11
DiCaprio, Leonardo, 9
Dickens, Charles, *Oliver Twist*, 8
différance, theory of, 70
Dionne, Craig, 20, 93n. 29, 121, 136n. 6, 190n. 7, 206n. 11, 243, 256nn. 11, 16, 264, 316; beggars, on sentiment toward, 354n. 8; referenced, 81–82, 115n. 3, 115n. 9, 116n. 27, 130, 136n. 5, 256nn. 11, 13, 339, 346; on rogue literature as both fact and fiction, 316; on rogues as metaphoric models for merchants, 379; on rogues in bands, 355n. 22; vagabonds, on true crime of, 356n. 30
Directions for Speech and Style (Hoskyns), 54
disability, representation of, 290n. 31
Di Scipio, Giuseppe C., 28n. 19
Discipline and Punish: The Birth of the Prison (Foucault), 58n. 11
Discourse on the Commonweal of this Realm of England (Smith), 165
disease, 221; in Dekker's works, 334n. 9; in Spenser's works, 334n. 9; venereal disease in London, 216
disenfranchisement, 14–15
disguise, rogues and, 19
displaced day laborers, 17
displaced people, 45–49; in London, 215; as rogues, 1
dispossessed populations, 14–15, 17, 366;

jestbook tradition and, 39
A Disputation between a He Cony-Catcher and a She Cony-Catcher (Greene), 132–33, 179, 217, 223–24, 226, 233n. 9, 247, 252, 255n. 6
dissembling: and cony-catching, 240; as criminal category, 59n. 17; false seeming and, 54–56; necessity of, in city, 2; rogues and, 19; vagrants and, 128
Dixon, Deborah, 290n. 31
Doctor Story *(Lantern and Candlelight)*, 302–4
documents: authenticity and veracity of, 36–37, 369–73, 375–78; of Calendar of State Papers, 372; as evidence, 364, 368; linkages with other documents, reading as creating, 376; provenance of, establishing, 371; reading as construction, deconstruction, 376; reliability of, 372; rogues, molls depicted in, 1–2; as supplementing, reworking reality, 378
Dolan, Frances E., 99
Doll (Jonson), 15
Dollimore, Jonathan: as cultural materialist, 12; quoted, 222; *Radical Tragedy: Religion, Ideology, and Power in the Drama of Shakespeare and His Contemporaries*, 94n. 35; referenced, 79, 93n. 32, 94nn. 35–36, 290n. 34; *Sexual Dissonance*, 93n. 32
Doll Tearsheet *(II Henry IV)*, 2
domestic handbooks, 39–40; rogue manuals as, 45–49
domination, 316
Don Quixote (Cervantes), 28n. 21, 244
Don Quixote *(Don Quixote)*, 28n. 21, 244
Don Tomazo, or the Juvenile Ramblings of Thomas Dangerfield (Dangerfield), 354n. 7
double-crosses, 4
double identity, 4
Downame, John, 156, 162
doxies: as rogues, 1; sexuality of, 13
Drake, Sir Francis, 287n. 4, 366
Dramas, Fields, and Metaphors: Symbolic Action in Human Society (Turner), 287n. 6
Dressed to Kill (film), 66

Dr. Faustus (Marlowe), 15, 143
Dubrow, Heather, 205n. 1
Ducklyn, Henry (laborer), 195
Duke Senior *(As You Like It)*, 154
Dunn, Diana E. S., 288n. 16
Dunn, Peter, 353n. 2
duplicity, 50
Durant, David N. , 115n. 11

Earle, John, 225
East India Company, 167n. 4
Eastland Company, 167n. 4
Ebel, Julia G., 233n. 21
Ebert, Teresa, 65
economic changes, 43; cony-catching
    pamphlets on, 171–90; rogues and, 1;
    and social differentiation, 177–78;
    vagrant economy and, 23, 194–97
economic history, 13
economic individualism, 2
economic literature, early modern, 22
Economics and the Fiction of Daniel Defoe
    (Novack), 356n. 31
economy of rogues, 7–8
Edgar *(King Lear)*, 13
Edward, king of England *(If You Know
    Not Me, 2)*, 160
Edward IV, king of England, 168n. 14
Edward IV (Heywood), 167n. 9
Edward VI, king of England, 108
Egmond, Florike, 232nn. 7–8, 233n. 14
Eisenberg, Daniel, 353n. 2
Eisenstein, Elizabeth L., 226, 256n. 18,
    307–8
Eliot, T. S., 77–78, 82
Elizabeth, countess of Shrewsbury, aka
    Bess of Hardwick, 104
Elizabethan Poor Laws, 246
Elizabethan Rogues and Vagabonds (Ayde-
    lotte), 14
The Elizabethan Underworld (Judges), 14,
    33, 35, 334n. 11
The Elizabethan Underworld (Salgãdo), 15,
    35, 225, 367–68
Elizabeth I, queen of England, 168n. 14;
    1572 Act of, for the Punishment of
    Vagabonds, 44–45, 150; language abili-
    ties, 158; quoted, 44; renaming of the
    Royal Exchange by, 166

Elizabeth I, queen of England *(If You
    Know Not Me, 2)*, 165–66
Ellinghausen, Laurie, 25–26, 264, 301; on
    disease, infection in work of Dekker,
    Spenser, 334n. 9; on reading *Lantern
    and Candlelight*, 334n. 8; referenced,
    335n. 14, 355n. 12; on Tower of Babel
    episode in Dekker, 335n. 14
Elton, Geoffrey, 371–72
Emilia *(Othello)*, 2
empirical methodologies, scholarship, 11,
    13; and rogue studies, 13; scriptural exe-
    gesis in empiricism, 358n. 49
employment: multiple, serial, and itinerant
    employment, 194, 366, 376–77; vagrant
    economy and, 194–97; of vagrant
    laborers, 194–97
enclosure movement, 15, 43, 366
The English Alehouse: A Social History
    (Clark), 216
English culture, 313–15
Englishing, 334n. 7; as bidirectional, 317;
    and birth of British Empire, 333; of
    cant, 226; cant dictionaries and, 323–27;
    as cultural translation, 312–13, 316,
    322–27; as incorporation into English
    nation, 319; of the Irish, 316–17,
    322–30; as language standardization,
    226–27; as linguistic, cultural incorpo-
    ration, 322–27; Statutes of Kilkenny
    and, 331; undermined by imitating the
    rogue, 332–33; and un-Englishing, 316,
    332
English people: defining Englishness, 313,
    315–17; improving the English nation,
    319–20; incorporation into English
    nation, 319. *See also specific topics*
The English Poor Law, 1531–1782 (Slack),
    206n. 9
The English Rogue (Head), 98
English Travelers, 361
environment, pastoral to urban, 14
equality, 171–90
Erasmus, 28n. 19
Erikson, Erik H., 101, 115n. 8
Essays (Montaigne), 279
Eurykleia *(Odyssey)*, 277
Evans, Elizabeth (gentlewoman), 134–35
Evans, Richard J., 370, 372, 379

evidence: documents as, 364, 368; establishing truth, facticity of, 364–65; of pervasiveness of rogues, 2

exchange: changes in, effect of, 22; cony-catching pamphlets on, 171–90; identity counterfeiting as, 122; and problem of identity, 21

exchanges, as marketplaces, 22. *See also* Royal Exchange

execution, 363

The Execution of Neschech and the Confining of His Kinsman Tarbith, or a Short Discourse Showing the Difference betwixt Damned Usury and That Which Is Lawful (anon.), 155

experience, private, 11

facticity: determination of, 364–65; of documents, 369–73; fact-or-fiction split in rogue studies, 11; and Mary Frith/Moll Cutpurse, 20; mediation between fact and fiction, 375–79; of rogue pamphlets, 245, 367, 378; rogues as both fact and fiction, 11

fairs, 145; as marketplaces, 22; shunning of, 22; and traditional producer/seller patterns, 156

falconers, 294–96, 300–301; as manipulators of print culture, 25–26

false seeming, 54–56

Falstaff *(I Henry IV)*, as rogue, 2, 15, 25, 36, 105, 280

Fat King, Lean Beggar: Representations of Poverty in the Age of Shakespeare (Carroll), 121, 135n. 2

Faustus, Dr. *(Dr. Faustus)*, 143

faux journalism, 15

female cony-catchers, 13

feminist politics, 20, 68, 93n. 32

feminists, 65

Fennor, William: *The Counter's Commonwealth*, 184, 191n. 8, 215, 218; referenced, 191n. 8, 215, 220, 229, 233nn. 10, 13–14

Ferneseed, Margaret (prostitute, pimp), 377

fiction: fact-or-fiction split in rogue studies, 11; history as invention or fiction of historians, 378; and Mary Frith/Moll Cutpurse, 20; mediation between fact and fiction, 375–79; pamphlets as works of, 306; rogue pamphlets as fact and fiction, 38; rogues as both fact and fiction, 11

Fideler, Paul A., 99, 115n. 6

Fielding, James, 16

Fields, Nathaniel, 20, 91n. 25

films: cross-dressing in, 66; rogues in, 3–5, 7, 9

Finlay, Roger, 200, 215

Fissell, Mark, 288n. 17

Fitzpatrick, Joseph, 91nn. 21–22

Flanders, Moll. *See* Moll Flanders

Fleetwood, William (recorder of London), 368–69

Flesh and Stone (Sennet), 213

Flodd, Richard (counterfeit crank), 129

Florio, John, 10, 27n. 2

Fontaine, Laurence, 145, 150–52, 163, 232n. 6

Ford, John, 91n. 25

Forman, Valerie, 79–80, 93nn. 31–32

The Fortunes and Misfortunes of the Famous Moll Flanders (Defoe). See *Moll Flanders*

Fortune Theatre, 78, 91n. 25, 93n. 30

Foucauldian new historicism, 11, 105, 113–14

Foucauldian scholars, 21

Foucauldian theoretical mode of reading, 16

Foucault, Michel, 58n. 11, 70–71, 105, 114; on authors, 296; *Discipline and Punish: The Birth of the Prison*, 58n. 11; followers of, 374; influence on new historicists, 12; quoted, 58n. 11; referenced, 67, 99–100, 105, 112; referencing Beckett, 308; on representation replacing resemblance, 357n. 37

Fourquevaux, Raymond de Beccarie de Pavie, Baron de: *Instructions for the Warres . . . Discoursing the Method of Militarie Discipline*, 273–74, 288nn. 14–15, 289n. 22; referenced, 28n. 19, 273–74, 288n. 18

France, veteran soldiers of, 273–74

François I, king of France, 277

fraternities of rogues, 2, 48–49

The Fraternity of Vagabonds (Awdeley), 7,

14, 25, 33, 45, 127, 131, 266; canting dictionary in, 322; Dekker plagiarizing from, 294

Frederick *(As You Like It)*, 154

freemen, 176

Freud, Sigmund: as controversial icon, 73; Laclau/Mouffeian borrowing from, 70; referenced, 99, 101, 104–5, 112; theories used by new historicists to reinterpret texts, 99

Freudian interpretation, 99–105, 113

friars, itinerant, 366

friendship, counterfeit, 50

Frith, Mary, 11, 20; cross-dressing of, 66–67; dual historical persona of, 74–75; as fictional Moll Cutpurse, 67; interpretive readings of, 81–84; and *The Life and Death of Mrs. Mary Frith*, 20, 77; "Marlowespace" and, 86–88; "Mary/Mollspace," 68; as portrayed in *The Roaring Girl*, 62, 331–33; re-created in "Mary/Marlowespace," 85–88; reinvention of, 84–85; revaluing, reimagining of, 77–81; sexuality of, 68; sociosexual identity of, 85; transversal identity of, 74–75

Frye, Northrop, 17

Fumerton, Patricia, 23–24, 187, 216, 228, 264; on double life of Jennings, 379; on existence of criminal underground, 295; on mediation, 379; on parallels between commercial practices, outlaw activities, 353n. 1; referenced, 167n. 5, 205n. 2, 234n. 25, 256n. 13, 339

Furnivall, Frederick J., 14

"Furor Poeticus" *(Parnassus* plays), 299

Gaby, Rosemary, 205n. 1

Gaddis, John Lewis, 378–79

Galford, Ellen, 84–85

gallows writing, 16

Gandhi, Mahatma, 101

Garber, Marjorie, 65, 79–81, 93n. 32, 94n. 36

Gascoigne, George, 243, 249–50, 256n. 24

Gazophylacium, city of *(Martin Markall)*, 217, 226, 233n. 19

gender: Mary Frith/Moll Cutpurse and, 68; social identity and, 62–65

Geneva School, 75–76

Genings, Nicolas. *See* Jennings, Nicholas, aka Blunt

gentlemen tradesmen, 358n. 44

gentry, tradesmen, on differences between, 358n. 44

George, John (hedger, ditcher), 366

Germans, Venetian ghettoization of, 213

Gesta Henrici Quinti, 280

Getley, Thomas (baker), 127

ghettos, 213–14

Gibbons, Brian, 159

Gilds and Companies of London (Unwin), 58n. 9

Gladfelder, Hal, 16, 39; on complex identification with the rogue, 19; *Criminality and Narrative in Eighteenth-Century England*, 16, 39; groundbreaking work of, 17; on literalness of Defoe, 354n. 4; on Moll Flanders, 355n. 16, 356n. 28; referenced, 116n. 27

Glanvill, Joseph, 357n. 38

Gmelch, Sharon, 232n. 6

Goldberg, Jonathan, 12, 90n. 14

Goneril *(King Lear)*, 287n. 4

Goodey, Brian R., 214

gossips, 102

Gould, J. D., 107

Gowing, Laura, 103, 215, 233n. 12

Grafton, Anthony, 255n. 7

Grant, Alexander, 116n. 32

Grass, Roland, 355n. 19

Grassby, Richard, 176

Gray, Christopher, 230

The Great Law of Subordination Consider'd (Defoe), 354n. 4

Greeks, Venetian ghettoization of, 213

Greenblatt, Stephen J., 37–38, 105–8, 193, 234n. 26, 244–46, 256n. 15, 289n. 29, 290n. 34; *Learning to Curse: Essays in Early Modern Culture*, 226, 265–66, 287n. 3; as new historicist, 12, 37; quoted, 16, 37–38, 108, 226–27, 265–66; referenced, 98, 115nn. 1, 12, 205n. 1, 234n. 26, 244, 256n. 19, 287n. 3; *Shakespearean Negotiations: The Circulation of Social Energy in Renaissance England*, 227, 234n. 26

Greene, Robert, 14, 23–25, 33, 36, 45, 48, 51–52, 217, 222–24, 226, 269, 287n. 12, 368; as author, 345; career of, 253–54; *A Caveat or Warening for Common Curse-tors Vulgarely Called Vagabones*, 295; "The Conversion of an English Cour-tesan," 240, 247, 249–52, 354n. 5; on counterfeiting, 125; as Cuthbert Cony-Catcher, 2, 134, 247; Dekker pla-giarizing from, 294; diversion, moraliz-ing in pamphlets, 340; as entertainer, not moralizer, 346; as fiction writer, 241; *Greenes Groatsworth of Wit*, 245; *Greenes Never Too Late*, 245; on Gresham, 148–49; "imagined reader" of, 243; as "King of the Paper Stage," 243; lived experience of, 368; on man's fallen nature, wrongful choices, 365; *Menaphon*, 242; "Of the Subtlety of a Curber in Cosening a Maid," 137n. 24; *Pandosto*, 242; as plagiarist, 7; as prodi-gal writer, 249; prose romance of, 253–54, 255n. 3; quoted, 45, 48, 51–52, 220–22, 225–26, 230; readers of, 243–47, 252–53; referenced, 137n. 24, 138n. 34, 204, 221, 233nn. 9, 14, 20, 234n. 23; *The Repentance of Robert Greene, Master of Arts*, 230; rereading of pamphlets of, 242–47; as rogue, 7, 11; *The Royal Exchange*, 148–49; *The Sec-ond Part of Cony-Catching*, 130, 217, 222–25, 233n. 14, 255n. 5; self-help mes-sage of, 243; "A Tale of a Nip," 188–89; *The Third and Last Part of Cony-Catch-ing*, 222–24, 255n. 5, 354n. 5; Twyning on, 234n. 26; use of materials from Har-man, Walker, 240; works as prose romances, 240–42. See also *The Black Book's Messenger; The Defence of Cony-Catching; A Disputation between a He Cony-Catcher and a She Cony-Catcher; A Notable Discovery of Cosenage*
Greenes Groatsworth of Wit (Greene), 245
Greenes Never Too Late (Greene), 245
Gresham, John *(If You Know Not Me, 2)*, 160–61, 163, 167n. 10
Gresham, Sir Thomas, 148, 157, 165, 168n. 14

Gresham, Thomas *(If You Know Not Me, 2)*, 143, 153–54, 157–64, 165, 167n. 10
Greville, Fulke (gentleman veteran), 268
Grey *(Henry V)*, 282
Griffiths, Paul, 205n. 4, 215–16, 232n. 8
Grocers (livery company), 146–47
The Groundworke of Conny-Catching, 206n. 12
Gruber von Arni, Eric, 272, 275, 289n. 25
Guattari, Félix, 57n. 7, 73–74, 136n. 6
Guerre, Martin, 286, 289n. 25; granted position, 289n. 29; narrative of, 264; as veteran soldier, 275–79; wounding of, 289n. 28
guildhalls, 22
guilds, 22, 367
Guillén, Claudio, 353n. 2
Gullman, Frances, 3
Guzman de Alfarache, 344, 355n. 19
gypsies, 207n. 14; arrival of, effect of, 15; connection with rogues, 135n. 2; ease of detection of, 204; fetishization of, 135n. 2; gypsy personae and, 16, 135n. 2; pre-tend gypsies as rogues, 207n. 14. *See also* Irish Travelers

Hadfield, Andrew, 315, 330–31, 335n. 15
Hal *(Henry IV* plays), 256n. 15
Halasz, Alexandra, 13, 233n. 16, 309n. 1, 323, 334n. 5
Hale, F. M., 234n. 26
Hale, J. R., 28n. 19, 270, 272, 288n. 16, 289n. 28
Hall, Bert S., 272, 288n. 15, 289n. 22
Hall, Kim F., 99
Halpern, Richard, 42–43, 54, 255n. 9
Hamlet *(Hamlet)*, 2
Hamlet (Shakespeare), 2, 154
Hamlin, William, 27n. 2
Hanawalt, Barbara A., 103
Hanse, Hanseatic League (Germanic trad-ing league), 168n. 14
Hansen, Adam, 24; on liminal status of rogue books, 379; referenced, 242–43, 255n. 10, 256n. 16
Hanson, Elizabeth, 175, 190n. 4, 193; on authors implicated in cozenage, 318; on cony-catching pamphlets, 305; on exis-tence of criminal underground, 295; ref-

erenced, 183, 205n. 1, 334n. 5; on
rogues' discourse, 324
Hapsburg forces, 271
Harkness, Deborah, 206n. 10
Harlin, Renny, 3
Harman, Thomas, 12, 16, 17, 23, 33,
45–48, 57n. 8, 98–119, 226–27, 231,
234n. 22, 244–46, 266–69, 287nn. 10,
12; on alarming effect of vagrant's acts,
347; canting dictionaries of, 316, 369; as
coiner of word *rogue*, 1–2; on corrective
function of pamphlets, 318–19; on
counterfeiting, 125; Dekker plagiarizing
from, 294; facticity of, 367; Foucauldian
scholars on, 21; Freudian interpretation
of, 99–105, 113; on the "Jarkman,"
290n. 30; and Jennings/Blunt, 109–10;
lifting from *A Manifest Detection of
Dice-Play* (Walker), 33; Marxist/Fou-
cauldian interpretation of, 105, 113–14;
others, othering by, 314; on peddlers,
150; post-Marxist scholars on, 21; purpose of his works, 108–12; quoted, 221,
225; referenced, 16, 58n. 14, 222–23,
228, 266, 287n. 8; on the Ruffler,
266–67; sexuality, attitudes toward,
99–101, 104–5, 113; social origins of, 21,
105–8, 113 (*see also* punishment); on tinkers, 150; trickster as Machiavellian
antihero, 12; on the Upright Man, 268;
women, attitudes toward, 99–100. See
also *A Caveat or Warening for Common
Cursetors Vulgarely Called Vagabones*
Harris, Jonathan Gil, 378
Harrison, William, 33–34, 42–43, 98,
115n. 2
Hasted, Edward, 116n. 16
Hawes, Stephen, 262
Hawkesworthe, Nicholas (apprentice), 132
Hawkins, Sherman, 290n. 34
Head, Richard, 98
Hecuba *(Hamlet)*, 2
Hedrick, Donald, 68–69, 73, 89nn. 11, 13,
91n. 22
*Hegemony and Socialistic Strategy:
Towards a Radical Democratic Politics*
(Laclau and Mouffe), 64, 89n. 6
Helfand Bix, Karen, 22–23, 206n. 11; on
parallels between commercial practices,

outlaw activities, 353n. 1; referenced,
167n. 8, 242, 257n. 26
Helgerson, Richard, 228, 249, 257n. 29
Heliodorus, 255n. 6
hell, 302–3
Heller, Herbert Jack, 79, 93n. 32, 94n. 36
Heller, Kevin Jon, 90n. 16
Hell's Angels, 110
Henry II, king of England, 315
Henry III, king of England, 304
Henry IV plays (Shakespeare), 2, 105,
191n. 9, 256n. 15, 288n. 18
Henry V, called "Harry" *(Henry V)*,
280–86, 290n. 34
Henry V, king of England, 264
Henry V (Shakespeare), 25, 264, 279–86,
290nn. 33–36; military justice in, 288n. 18
Henry VII, king of England, 106, 288n. 17
Henry VIII, king of England, 114, 155,
266, 270–71, 287n. 5, 288n. 17
Herodotus, 269
Hext, Edward (justice of the peace),
203–4, 206n. 14, 363
Heywood, Thomas: on economics, 165;
Edward IV, 167n. 9; *If You Know Not
Me, You Know Nobody, Part 1*, 167n. 9;
*If You Know Not Me, You Know
Nobody, Part 2*, 22, 143–44, 151, 153–54,
157–64, 165, 167nn. 3, 9, 167n. 11
Highway to the Spital-house (Copland), 14,
52, 184, 221, 240
Hill, Christopher, 221
Hill, Jane, 91n. 24
Hill Knight, Sir Roland, 132
Hindle, Steve, 196–97
historical objectivity, 372
historical records, rogues, molls depicted
in, 1–2. *See also* documents
historical revealing, 12
history: authenticity and veracity of, 9;
and definition of historical fact, 371; and
documents, authenticity and veracity
of, 369–73, 375–77; as invention or
fiction of historians, 378
History of Great Britain (Speed), 262
history-of-the-book scholars, 13
*A History of Vagrants and Vagrancy and
Beggars and Begging* (Ribton-Turner),
14

Hobson *(If You Know Not Me, 2)*, 144, 159–60, 162, 167n. 10, 168nn. 12–13
Hobson's apprentices *(If You Know Not Me, 2)*, 160–61
Holderness, Graham, 12
Holinshed, Raphael, 98
Hollar, Wenceslaus (engraver), 149, 379
Holmes, Martin, 145–46
homeless populations, 45–49; historical populations of, 16; reshaped as rogues, 7; rogue pamphlets and, 16; sources of, 184
Homer, 241
honesty, 171–90
Hooker, Richard, 262
Hopkins, D. J., 91n. 22
Hoskins, W. G., 107
Hoskyns, John, 54
Housely, Norman, 28n. 19
housing, 215–16
Howard, Jean E., 79, 81–82, 93nn. 30, 32, 94n. 36, 115n. 4, 232n. 2, 256n. 14, 290n. 34
Howard, Lord Admiral, 272
Howard, Michael, 287n. 13
Howard, Sir William, 134
Hufton, Olwen, 232n. 6
Humpherus, Henry, 309n. 3
Hunt, Mary Leland, 300
Hurtsfield, Joel, 116n. 18
husband-beating, 102, 104
Husserlian focus, 75–76
Hutson, Lorna, 167n. 7, 255n. 7
Hutton, Luke: *The Black Dog of Newgate*, 176, 224, 233n. 10, 304; *Lamentation*, 218
Hythlodaye, Raphael *(Utopia)*, 262–63, 265, 286n. 2

Iago *(Othello)*, 2, 8, 74
identitarian critical theory, 65
identity: blurring of, by rogues, 33, 332; counterfeiting of, 122, 125–30, 133–35; cross-dressing and, 65–67; defining of, in urban space, 18; as differences between classes, 21; double identity of rogues, 4; early modern subjectivity and, 16; English identity in opposition to external others, 312; as exchange and

negotiation, 21; feminism and, 65; gypsy personae and, 135n. 2; identification of, 126; identitarian critical theory and, 65; language and, 329–30; linguistic identity, 333; as Londoner, 216; of middle class, 5; modes of, 16; offenders, fixing of, 122, 124–26, 129–30, 133–35; rogues and, 5; self-constructed, 122; social identity, 62–65; transversal identity, 16; vagrancy as open identity, 216; of vagrant poor, 203–4. *See also* national identity
If It Be Not Good, the Devil Is In It (Dekker), 91n. 25
If You Know Not Me, You Know Nobody, Part 1 (Heywood), 167n. 9
If You Know Not Me, You Know Nobody, Part 2 (Heywood), 22, 143–44, 151, 153–54, 157–64, 165, 167nn. 3, 9, 168n. 11
The Image of America in Montaigne, Spenser, and Shakespeare: Renaissance Ethnography and Literary Reflection (Hamlin), 27n. 2
Imray, Jean, 147, 154
inclusive social relations, 171–90
individualist ethics, 171–90
Industrial Organization in the Sixteenth and Seventeenth Centuries (Unwin), 58n. 9
infection, idleness as, 45
Ingenioso *(Parnassus* plays), 299
Ingram, Martin, 103, 115nn. 9–10
Ingram, William, 167n. 7
in-law world, crime writing and, 16
Innes, Joanna, 123–24
Instructions for the Warres . . . Discoursing the Method of Militarie Discipline (Fourquevaux), 273–74, 288n. 14, 289n. 22
insubordination, 121–22, 131–32
insurance underwriting, 167n. 6
internal aliens, 26, 215, 221, 330
international trade, 147, 152, 155–56, 164–66, 168n. 14
Interregnum, 103
Intriligator, James, 91n. 22
Ireland: colonialism and, 26; colonization of Ireland, North America, relation between, 334n. 1; English garrisons in,

317; invaded by Henry II, 315; and the
Irish Crisis, 327–30; and the New English, 315, 317; Old English in, 313, 315,
317, 333; Spenser on, 327–30, 333. *See
also* Irish in Ireland
Irenius *(A View of the Present State of Ireland)*, 327–30
Irish in Ireland, 312–15; cultural translation of, 333; Englishing as cultural, linguistic incorporation, 312–13, 327–30;
Englishing of, 26, 316–17, 322–30;
incorporation into England as extinction, 317; incorporation into English
nation, 317; as internal aliens, 26, 315;
and the Irish Crisis, 316, 327–30; language legislated against, Statutes of
Kilkenny, 331; likeness between English and Irish, 315; as others, othering,
313; racial translation of, 333; Spenser
on, 312–14, 327–30, 333; starvation of,
317; transgressive liminality of, 315–16;
translation of, into English, 315, 317,
322–30, 333; violence against, 317, 330,
333–34; the "wilde Irish," 314. *See also*
Irish Travelers
Irish Travelers, 361–64, 380
itinerant friars, 366
itinerant laborers: ballads, songs as voices
of, 204; by-employments of, 194–95;
multiple, serial, itinerant employment
of, 194, 366–67, 376–77; vagrant economy and, 194–97; as vagrants
itinerant merchants: classified as rogues,
vagabonds, effect, 150–51; disdain for,
149
itinerant pardoners, 366
itinerant players, 194
itinerant populations: by-employments of,
194–95, 366–67, 376–77; historical populations of, 16; invisibility of, 204; multiple, serial, itinerant employment of,
194, 366–67, 376–77; rogue pamphlets
and, 16; vagrant economy and, 194–97
itinerant tradesmen: classified as rogues,
vagabonds, effect, 150–51; stigmatized
as rogues, 144

the "Jackman," 309n. 4
Jack of Newbury (Deloney), 41

Jackson, Samuel L., 3–5
Jacobs, Deborah, 79–80, 82–83, 93n. 32,
94n. 36
James I, king of England, 375
Jameson, Fredric, 59n. 16, 64–65, 67, 242,
254, 257n. 31
Jankowski, Theodora A., 162, 167nn. 2,
9–10, 205n. 1
Jardine, Lisa, 255n. 7
the "Jarkman," 290n. 30
Jennings, Nicholas, aka Blunt, 11, 109–10,
113–15, 193, 200–203; case of, 114–15,
200–203; delights in his ruses, 340;
double life of, as mediating principle,
379; multiple roles, identities of, 193–94
Jerusalem, 218–20
jestbook tradition, 16–17, 256n. 120, 369
jesting, Tudor, 17
Jesus of Nazareth, 73
Jews, 38, 213–14
Johns, Adrian, 256n. 18, 308
Johnson, Richard, 214, 217, 220, 223,
233n. 13
Johnson-Haddad, Miranda, 334n. 7
Jones, Norman, 167n. 7
Jones, W. R. D., 116n. 29
Jonson, Ben, 15, 159, 228, 234n. 25; *The
Alchemist*, 190n. 6, 331; as pageant col-
laborator with Dekker, 300; referenced,
190n. 6, 232n. 1; on Shakespeare, 296
Jordan, John Clark, 255n. 8, 257n. 29
journalism, faux, 15
The Jovial Crew, 335n. 18
Judges, A. V., 40–41, 99; on capitalism,
14–15; on Dekker's cant dictionary,
334n. 12; *The Elizabethan Underworld*,
14, 33, 35, 334n. 11; quoted, 33, 41, 45;
referenced, 115nn. 2, 5, 205n. 1, 314; on
rogue literature, 14–15
Jung, Carl, 100–101
Jütte, Robert, 215, 228

Kate *(The Taming of the Shrew)*, 101
Kaufman, Eleanor, 90n. 16
Kelley, Richard (smith), 133
Kelly, Thomas J., 287n. 4
Kermode, Lloyd Edward, 79, 81, 93n. 32,
94n. 36, 103
Kezar, Dennis, 290n. 35

King Lear (Shakespeare), 13, 101, 154, 162, 193, 287n. 4

Kinney, Arthur F., 19, 27, 186, 266, 287nn. 4, 9; on the black dog, 309n. 5; quoted, 36, 43–45, 363; referenced, 115nn. 1–2, 4, 206nn. 12, 14, 267–69, 272, 287n. 5, 290n. 30; *Rogues, Vagabonds, and Sturdy Beggars: A New Gallery of Tudor and Early Stuart Rogue Literature*, 15, 27, 36, 266

Kirkus, A. Mary, 107

Knapp, Jeffrey, 183, 205n. 1

Knowles, James, 331

Knowsley, Margaret (laborer's wife), 366–67

Koch, Mark, 116n. 28

Komunyakaa, Yusef, 286n. 1

Krantz, Susan E., 79, 93n. 32, 94n. 36

Kroll, Richard H. F., 357nn. 37, 39

Kuhlisch, Tina, 26–27, 264; referenced, 257n. 28; on rogues as attractive criminals, 335n. 16

Kyteley, Raffe (rogue), 198

laborers: by-employments of, 194–95, 366–67, 376–77; displaced day laborers, 17; itinerant laborers, as vagrants, 194, 366–67, 376–77; poor laborers, invisibility of, 204; as resource, 177; as sturdy beggars, 42; vagrant economy and, 23, 194–97; vagrant laborers, 23; and value of toil, 180

Lacan, Jacques, 67, 70, 89nn. 5–6, 8, 254, 257n. 30

Lacanian imaginary, 257n. 30

Lacanian psychoanalysis, 70

LaCapra, Dominick, 378–79

Laclau, Ernesto, 64–65, 70–72, 89nn. 5–6, 9, 90n. 17

Laclau and Mouffe: The Radical Democratic Imaginary (Smith), 65

Lake, Peter, 234n. 28

Lamentation (Hutton), 218

The Landscape of History: How Historians Map the Past (Gaddis), 378–79

Lane, Robert, 290n. 32

Langdon, Helen, 28n. 3

language: abusers of, 303; and birth of British Empire, 333; cant as written language, 369; and the "cheat of words," 357n. 41; common language, loss of, 335n. 14; Englishing as linguistic, cultural incorporation, 322–27; false seeming and, 54–56; hell and, 302; and identity, 329–30; Irish, legislated against, Statutes of Kilkenny, 331; the Irish Crisis and, 327–30; Latin, 297–300; linguistic identity, 333; as linguistic mission, 226–27; and the meanings, use of words, 357n. 40, 358n. 42; meanings and misunderstandings of, 357n. 40; and national identity, 26; the new language of urban world, 25; Pedlars' French, 45, 150, 227; Protestantism, Christocentric language of, 111; of rogues, 8, 9; rogues and, 1; secret languages of rogues, 8; self-fashioned gentlemen and, 1; translation and, 225–30

Lantern and Candlelight (Dekker), 22–23, 25–26, 98, 171, 180–81, 214, 220, 224, 228–30, 233n. 20, 294–309, 314, 319; canting dictionary in, 325–26; educational, corrective function of, 319–20; reading of, as entertainment, 334n. 8

Latin, 297–300

Lawrence *(A Disputation between a He Cony-Catcher and a She Cony-Catcher)*, 179

Laws of Ecclesiastical Polity (Hooker), 262

lawyers, 302–3, 374

Laxton *(The Roaring Girl)*, 67

Lazarillo (a *picaro*), 338, 340, 346, 355n. 19

Lear, King *(King Lear)*, 162

Learning to Curse: Essays in Early Modern Culture (Greenblatt), 226, 265–66, 287n. 3

legal documents, counterfeiting of, 127–28

legal records, as evidence of vagrants, 121. *See also* Bridewell Court Books

Leinwand, Theodore B., 167n. 8, 178–80, 186, 190n. 6

Leishman, J. B., 299

Leith, Dick, 233n. 21, 234n. 23

Leonard, Elmore, 9

Levant Company, 167n. 4

Levin, Richard, 76

Levine, David, 205n. 8

Levine, Nina, 191n. 9

lewdness, 124–25, 135
The Life and Death of Mrs. Mary Frith, Commonly Called Mal Cutpurse (anon.), 20, 77, 84–85, 91n. 25, 92n. 26
linguistic incorporation: and birth of British Empire, 333; Englishing as, 322–27
linguistic prowess, 1
literacy: cony arming self with, 10; criminal literacy, 307–9; as stratagem against rogues, 10; underworld literacy, 3
literary documents, rogues, molls depicted in, 2. *See also* documents
literary historians, 35–36, 38
literary representing, 12
literary studies, and rogue studies, 13
literature: canonical works, 13; of city comedy, 240; of settlement, 240; of urban pamphlets, 240; of verse satire, 240
Literature of Roguery (Chandler), 14
Loach, Jennifer, 116n. 29
Locke, John, 357n. 38
Lodge, Thomas, 241, 243
Lohman, Alison, 9
London: cultural geography of, 24; displaced persons in, 215; idea of "urban condom" and, 217; internal aliens in, 215, 221; as Jerusalem and Babylon, 218; as largest shared experience in Britain, 243; lawful London and criminal underworld, 15; rogues in, 213–31; social dislocation and, 18; sociogeography of, 215–16, 225; as Tower of Babel, 225; urban life and environment of, 214–17; wealth in, 217. *See also specific topics;* urban life; urban underworld
London Dispossessed: Social and Semiotic Disorders in the English Renaissance (Twyning), 234n. 26
The Long Kiss Goodbye (film), 3–6
Look on Me London (Johnson), 217
Loretelli, Rosamaria, 355n. 20
Lowenstein, Joseph, 309n. 7
lower orders, classes, 177–78, 189; ballads, songs as ownable text, 204; employments of, 194–97, 366–67, 376–77. *See also* poor populations
Lucassen, Leo, 232n. 6

Lupton, Donald, 149–50
Luther, Martin, 101
Lyly, John, 243, 249

Macbeth *(Macbeth)*, 74
Macbeth (Shakespeare), 91n. 21
Macdonald, Virginia, 255n. 2, 256n. 2,
Machiavelli, Niccolò, 28n. 19, 270, 288n. 18
Madde Pranckes of Mery Mall of the Banckside, with Her Walks in Mans Apparel, and to What Purpose (Day), 91n. 25
Madonna (entertainer), 77, 80
A Mad World, My Masters (Middleton), 1, 3
magic, 103
magic books, 246–52
The Magnificent Entertainment: Given to King James (Dekker), 299–300
Maley, Willy, 315
A Manifest Detection of Dice-Play (Walker), 7, 14, 33, 49–51, 53, 134, 191n. 10, 220, 240
Manley, Lawrence, 190n. 7; on diversion, moralizing in Greene's pamphlets, 340; pamphleteers, on literary strategies of, 354n. 8; playwrights, on literary strategies of, 354n. 8; quoted, 319; referenced, 173, 181, 186–88, 221, 232n. 8, 233n. 19, 240, 243, 255nn. 1, 9–10, 256n. 25, 334n. 5, 354n. 10
Mao Tse-Tung, 73
Maravall, José Antonio, 358n. 46
Margolies, David, 231
market culture: double tone of, 171; literature on, 173–74
marketplace: changes in, effect of, 22; circulation, anonymity of, 13; cony-catching pamphlets on, 171–90; social miming and, 52
Marlowe, Christopher, 77; *Dr. Faustus*, 15, 143; "Marlowespace" and, 86–88; re-created in "Mary/Marlowespace," 85–88; sexuality of, 68
marriage, 101
Marston, John, 232n. 1
Martin, Dean, 9
Martindale, Kathleen, 65
Martin Guerre. *See* Guerre, Martin

Martin Markall Beadle of Bridewell: His Defence and Answers to the Bellman of London (Rid), 217, 226, 233n. 19, 321–22, 326–27

Marx, Karl, 50, 73, 99–100, 105, 112, 356n. 27

Marxism, 21, 89n. 5, 105, 113–14, 115n. 13

Mary I, queen of England, 107, 122

Mary I, queen of England *(If You Know Not Me, 2)*, 160

Maryson, Richard, 365

masterless men: as growing group, 21; as resource, 177; as rogues, 1; veteran soldiers as, 265

Masterless Men: The Vagrancy Problem in England, 1560–1640 (Beier), 36, 99, 116nn. 17, 26, 31, 121, 136n. 3, 196, 206n. 9, 218, 232n. 7, 233n. 17

Matchstick Men (film), 9

materialists, cultural, 12

Material London (Orlin), 214–15

Matthew 25:35–36, 289n. 25

Maus, Katherine Eisaman, 12, 78, 80, 280

Mayhew, Henry, 110

McCallum, Pamela, 65

McClure, Millar, 257n. 27

McDonald, Marcia A., 205n. 1

McKeon, Michael, 357n. 37, 358nn. 43, 49

McMullan, John L, 36–37, 205n. 1, 216, 233nn. 9, 11, 334n. 6

McPeek, James A. S., 205n. 1, 206n. 14

McRae, Andrew, 43, 177, 179–80

men, cross-dressing and, 65–67. *See also specific topics*

Menand, Louis, 286n. 1

Menaphon (Greene), 242

mendicant friars, 287n. 2

Mentz, Steve, 58n. 13, 115n. 3, 233n. 15, 234n. 26, 255n. 6, 256n. 24

mercantile tracts: rogue pamphlets as, 40–42; rogues in, 2

mercantile trading companies, 40–41

Mercers (livery company), 146–47

Merchant Adventurers (export consortium), 147, 152, 155–56, 164, 168n. 14

merchants: as cony-catchers, 220; cony-catching pamphlets on, 171–90; qualities of, 176–77; as rogues, 9, 220; rogues as metaphoric models for, 379;

valorization of, effect of, 174; and value of toil, 180

Merrett, Kathryn Chase, 149

Michelet, Jules, 375

microhistory, 366, 376

middle class, 358n. 45; identification of, with outlaw heroes, 16; identity and underworld counterpart, 5; identity of, 5; as rogues, 8

Middleton, Thomas: *A Chaste Maid in Cheapside*, 147; referenced, 93n. 30, 232n. 1. See also *The Roaring Girl*

migrant vagabonds, 42

Mikalachki, Jodi, 79, 93n. 32, 94n. 36, 100, 103, 203, 206n. 13

military records, 2

Miller, Edwin Haviland, 216

Miller, Jo E., 79, 93n. 32, 94n. 36

Milles, Thomas, 156, 164

mimicry, 316–17

Mirren, Helen, 92n. 27

mirrors, rogues as, 15, 206n. 10, 378

Mitchell, David T., 290n. 31

mobility: as alternate ways home, 243; cony-catchers and, 183–84; culture of, in street literature, 204; of rogues, 125; rogues and, 1; of vagrants, 125, 194

Moll Cutpurse. *See* Frith, Mary

Moll Cutpurse: Her True History (Galford), 84

Moll Flanders (Defoe), 26–27, 247, 337–60; capitalism in, 26–27; Greene's work as model for, 354n. 5; and patriarchal society, 356n. 29; and possibility of social rise, 356n. 30; on rogues as attractive criminals, 335n. 16; social setting of, 356n. 27

Moll Flanders *(Moll Flanders)*, 26–27, 252, 269, 337–60; ambivalence of Defoe toward, 257n. 28; banker husband of, 355n. 14; brother husband of, 355n. 14; as *femina oeconomica*, 264; hardening of, 355n. 20; as *homo economicus*, 338, 356n. 29; identity of, 355n. 16; Lancashire husband of, 355n. 14; Newgate conversion of, 356n. 28; as not-quite-picaro, 264; otherness of, 357n. 33; as picara, 340–46, 356n. 29; repentance of, 356n. 28

molls: as rogues, 1; sexuality of, 13, 101–4.
  See also specific topics; rogues
Momigliano, Arnaldo, 369–70
monasteries: closure of, 15; pensions, secular endowments for the religious, 14–15;
  as soldiers' homes, 274–75
moneylenders, 153–55
Montaigne, Michel de, 10, 27n. 2; disability, representation of, 290n. 31; *Essays*,
  279; on Martin Guerre, 275–79, 286,
  289n. 26; "Of Cannibals," 289n. 26;
  "Of Cripples," 275, 279
Montrose, Louis, 12, 115n. 4, 263, 287n. 3
moral ambivalence, 17
More, Thomas, 25, 214, 262–63, 286n. 2,
  288n. 19
Morton, Cardinal John *(Utopia)*, 262
morts, sexuality of, 13
Mouffe, Chantal, 64–65, 70–72, 89nn. 5–6,
  9, 90n. 17
Muldrew, Craig, 155, 184, 191n. 9
Mulholland, Paul A., 79–80, 91n. 25, 92nn.
  27–28, 93n. 32
Murphy, Andrew, 315, 334nn. 1, 4
Muscovy Company, 167n. 4
myth: of the historical rogue, 15–16; of
  rogues, 3, 10

Nakayama, Randall S., 79, 93nn. 30, 32
Nan *(A Disputation between a He
  Cony-Catcher and a She Cony-Catcher)*,
  217, 249, 256n. 21
Nashe, Thomas, 24, 255n. 6; *Christ's Tears
  over Jerusalem*, 218–20; Ingenio of *Parnassus* plays modeled on, 299; *Pierce
  Penniless*, 227; as reader of pamphlets,
  256n. 12
national identity, 312; language and, 26;
  nation-making processes and, 26; Old
  English in Ireland, effect on, 315;
  rogues and, 19
negotiation, and problem of identity, 21
Nell *(Henry V)*, 284
Newberry (or Newborowe), Mall, 122–23,
  135
New English, 315
Newgate prison, 124
new historicism, 11–12, 37, 42, 98–115
Newman, Paul, 9

New World, Spanish conquest of, 10
Nim *(Henry V)*, 280–81, 283
nomadic labor pool, 105, 194
nonconformists, 16
Norwich Census of the Poor (Pound),
  206n. 9
*A Notable Discovery of Cosenage, Now
  Daily Practiced by Sundry Lewd Persons*
  (Greene), 5–7, 22–23, 33, 45, 51–52,
  125, 138n. 34, 171, 217, 220, 222–23,
  225–26, 228, 233nn. 14, 20, 234n. 23,
  242, 252, 255n. 5, 269; con games
  depicted in, 5–7; Dekker plagiarizing
  from, 294; quoted, 40, 45
Novack, Maximilian, 356n. 31
novella, Boccaccian, 241, 256n. 20
novels: crime writing as precursors, 16;
  rogue pamphlets as birth of, 15; rogues,
  molls depicted in, 8
Nugent, Teresa Lanpher, 167n. 7

objectivity, historical, 372
observation, realistic, 16
Ocean's Eleven (film), 9
O'Connor, Marion F., 256n. 14
Odysseus *(Odyssey)*, 241
Odyssey (Homer), 241
"Of Cannibals" (Montaigne), 289n. 26
"Of Cripples" (Montaigne), 275, 279
"Of the Subtlety of a Curber in Cosening
  a Maid" (Greene), 137n. 24
Old English in Ireland, 313, 315, 317, 333;
  colonialism and, 318; degeneration of,
  317; Spenser on, 327–30, 333
Oliver Twist (Dickens), 8
O Per Se O (Dekker), 226, 229–30, 319,
  334n. 12; "Articles of their Fraterni-
  ties," 362; "The Bel-man's Cry,"
  372–73; educational, corrective function of, 319–20; Englished cant songs
  in, 326; quoted, 370
opportunism, 171–90
*Orders Appointed to be executed in the Cittie
  of London, for setting roges and idle persons to worke, and for releefe of the poore*,
  205n. 7
Orgel, Stephen, 12, 79, 81, 94n. 36
The Origins of War in Early Modern Europe
  (Black), 287n. 13

Orlin, Lena Cowen, 214–15, 232n. 3, 255n. 9
Ornstein, Robert, 290n. 34
Othello *(Othello)*, 74
Othello (Shakespeare), 2, 8, 91n. 21
others, othering, 312–16; absorption into aristocracy, 358n. 43; acceptance of, 357n. 33; English identity in opposition to, 312; excrementalizing of, 233n. 14; history on, 379; Irish as, 313; of Moll Flanders, 357n. 33; rogue literature as, 264; rogues as, 313
outlaw worlds. *See specific topics*
outward shows, science of, 12, 123

Pablos (a *picaro*), 344–46
Pamersiel (devil's footman, *Lantern and Candlelight*), 302–7
pamphlets: rogues, molls depicted in, 1–2. *See also specific types, topics*
Pandosto (Greene), 242
Pansette. *See* Tilh, Arnaud du, called "Pansette"
paranoia, public, 11
pardoners, itinerant, 366
Park, Robert, 215
Parker, Alexander, 353n. 2, 355n. 20, 357n. 32
Parker, Geoffrey, 270–73, 276, 288n. 16, 289n. 22, 290n. 33
Parker, Patricia, 334n. 7
Parliament, 113–14
Parliament's New Model Army, 289n. 25
passports, counterfeiting of, 127–28
Paster, Gail Kern, 214
Pastime of Pleasure (Hawes), 262
Patient Griselda *(The Decameron)*, 241
Patterson, Annabel, 190n. 1, 290n. 34
the Pawn at Royal Exchange, 143; architecture of, 148; origin of name, 167n. 1; patriotism and, 157; peddlers in, 149–50; shady practices at, 149–50, 154
Peacham, Henry, 35, 56
Pearl, Valerie, 215
peddlers: as capitalist entrepreneurs, 354n. 9; classified as rogues, vagabonds, 150–51, 198–99; demonized as vagabonds, 22; exclusion, banishment of, 22; at fairs, 144–45; in *If You Know*

Not Me, 2, 158–63; international networks of, 151–52, 195; at markets, 145–46; as middlemen, 156; in the Royal Exchange and Pawn, 149–50; as scapegoats, 157, 163; stigmatized as rogues, 144; and traditional producer/seller patterns, 156
Pedlars' French, 45, 150, 227
Pendry, E. D., 334n. 12
Penelope *(Odyssey)*, 241
penitence, 249
Pepperers, Grocers as previously, 147
Performing Transversally: Reimagining Shakespeare and the Critical Future (Reynolds), 89nn. 3, 12–13
Pewter, Edward (counterfeit dummerer, blind man), 129–30
Phelips, Jane (deceiver), 129–30
philosophers, 16
picaresque genre: the dilemma of, 357n. 36; in *Moll Flanders*, 26–27
picaro, incorruptibility of, 355n. 19
Pickering, Laurence (King of Cutpurses), 368
Pierce Penniless (Nashe), 227
Pipe Rolls, 107
Pistol *(Henry V)*, 280–85, 290nn. 33, 35
Pitt, Brad, 9
The Plague Pamphlets (Dekker), 214
plagues, 111
Plato, 253
plays: rogue pamphlets in relation to, 35–36; rogues, molls depicted in, 1–2, 8; shopping in Jacobean city comedies, 143, 148
playwrights, literary strategies, 354n. 8
pleasure, Dekker on, 320–21, 332
poems, rogues, molls in, 1–2
points de capiton (Lacan), 67, 89n. 8
political nonconformists, 16
Political Power and Social Classes (Poulantzas), 89n. 4
political reforms, 17
The Political Unconscious: Narrative as a Socially Symbolic Act (Jameson), 64–65
politics of privilege, 1
Pollack, Ellen, 356n. 29
Pollard, A. F., 372
polyvalence of rogues, 17–18, 27

poor classes, 17. *See also* lower orders, classes

Poor Laws: Elizabethan, 246; rogues, molls depicted in, 1; social histories of, 14; studies on, 13–14; Tudor, 1, 44

poor populations: by-employments of, 194–95, 366–67, 376–77; as a class, 17; dehumanization of, 246; as the deserving poor, 173; effects of enclosure on, 15, 43; and housing, 215–16; invisibility of, 204; jestbook tradition and, 39; lack of compassion for, 15; and the legal poor, 45; multiple, serial, itinerant employment of, 194, 366–67, 376–77; nonworking poor, 15; poor householders and, 196–97; as scapegoats, 174; vagrant economy and, 194–97; as vagrants, 43–45 (*see also* vagrant poor)

poor tax, 44, 196

Poor Tom *(King Lear)*, 162

Popper, Karl, 364–65, 369, 372

Popular Culture in Early Modern Europe (Burke), 216, 231

Pories, Kathleen, 203, 206n. 13

Porter, Roy, 233n. 17

Portis Latro (friend of Seneca), 290n. 30

post-Marxist scholars, 21

postmodernist historians, 366

poststructuralism, Deleuzian, 11

Poulantzas, Nicos, 88n. 2, 89n. 4

Pound, John F., 115n. 5, 206n. 9

poverty, 14–15; as factor of crime, 223; poor householders and, 196–97; rogues in relation to, 15; social histories of, 14; sources of, 189; studies on, 13–14; of veteran soldiers, 263

Poverty and Policy in Tudor and Stuart England (Slack), 232n. 8, 233n. 17

Poverty in Early-Stuart Salisbury (Slack), 206n. 9

The Poverty of Theory and Other Essays (Thompson), 115n. 13

power, dynamics of, 12

Power, Eileen E., 116n. 30

Power, M. J., 216, 232n. 8

Prestwich, Michael, 28n. 19, 280, 288n. 16

Price, George R., 234n. 26

priggers, 198

Prince of Wales *(Henry IV)*, 105

print culture, 256n. 18; circulation, anonymity of, 13; compared to scribal culture, 307; controversies of, 303–4; devils and, 303–4; falconers and, 294–96; falconers as manipulators of, 25–26; popular print culture, 23; and social order, 245

print industry: and cant, 226; and history of the book scholarship, 13; of London, 41–42; rogue pamphlets and, 8, 306–7; rogues, molls depicted in, 8

Privy Council, 362–63, 368

Prodigal Son (Bible), 249

profit motive, 23

prose romance, 240

Prospero *(The Tempest)*, 74

prostitutes, 223, 246–47, 249, 251

prostitution, 130–31, 216; of women vagrant laborers, 199

Protestantism, Christocentric language of, 111

protest literature, 17

"Proud Mary," 80, 94n. 34

Pruvost, René, 257n. 29

punishment, 108; at Bridewell, 21; corporal *(see specific topics);* execution as, 363; hanging proposed as punishment for vagrancy, 112; of Jennings/Blunt, 109–10; medieval punishments, 21; offenders, fixing of identity, 122, 124–26, 129–30, 133–35; penal technologies and, 21; and political technology of the body, 21; punishable crimes, 44–45; range of, 124; of rogues, vagabonds, 44–45; of sexual transgressions, 123; slavery proposed as, 112; statistics of, 363

Puritans, 180, 374

purpose-built rooms, 147–48

Puzo, Mario, 9

queer politics, 20, 68, 85, 93n. 32

Quickly, Mistress, 36

Rabelais and His World (Bakhtin), 59n. 15, 233n. 14

Rackin, Phyllis, 290n. 34

Radical Tragedy: Religion, Ideology, and Power in the Drama of Shakespeare and His Contemporaries (Dollimore), 94n. 35

Ranke, Leopold von, 371–72
Rappaport, Steve, 205n. 4, 215, 232n. 8
readers: active engagement of, 380; complicity of, 39; constructing social imaginary of, 17–18; of Greene, 243–47, 252–53; historical transition and, 41; imitation rogues, 317; protected by cony-catching pamphlets, 247; relationship to authors, 307–9; sophistication of, 17. *See also* urban readers
reading: as construction, deconstruction, 376; as entertainment, 334n. 8
reality, 379
The Records of the Commissioners of Sewers in the Parts of Holland (ed. Kirkus), 107
Redford, Robert, 9
Reformation compassion, 17
Reformation England. *See specific topics*
Regan *(King Lear)*, 287n. 4
Reliable Knowledge: An Exploration of the Grounds for Belief in Science (Ziman), 379
religion, 111, 374
religious pensions, secular endowments for, 14–15
Relihan, Constance L., 234n. 29
Renaissance criticism, 12, 14
repentance, 230
The Repentance of Robert Greene Master of Arts (Greene), 230
representation: crime writing and, 16; cultural representation, 12; literary representing, 12; literary scholars on, 13–14; poststructural theories of, 12; as replacing resemblance, 357n. 37; theater and the rogue, 37; theories of, 12–14
Representing Ireland: Literature and the Origins of Conflict (ed. Bradshaw, Hadfield, and Maley), 315
resemblance, representation replacing, 357n. 37
retailers, evolution of, 144–51
The Return of Martin Guerre (film, Vigne), 275–78, 289n. 26
The Return of Martin Guerre (novel, Davis), 275–78, 289nn. 28–29, 290n. 30
revealing, historical, 12
Reynolds, Bryan, 8–9, 15–16, 20–21, 39, 54, 57n. 7, 90nn. 14–16, 105–6, 116n. 14,

121, 135n. 2, 136nn. 5–6, 137n. 18, 233n. 17; on acts of subversion, 19; and Althusserian philosophy, 105; *Becoming Criminal: Transversal Performance and Cultural Dissidence in Early Modern England*, 8–9, 15–16, 39, 73, 89nn. 3, 10, 12, 93n. 32, 135n. 2, 190n. 5, 233n. 17; on cant, canting, 322, 335n. 13; on *A Caveat or Warening for Common Cursetors Vulgarely Called Vagabones*, 100; groundbreaking work of, 17; on historiography as actual, imaginary, 378; on Moll Cutpurse in *The Roaring Girl*, 332; *Performing Transversally: Reimagining Shakespeare and the Critical Future*, 89nn. 3, 12–13; quoted, 16, 54, 69, 369; referenced, 63, 68–69, 79, 88n. 1, 89nn. 3, 10, 12, 91nn. 21–23, 93n. 32, 94n. 34, 115nn. 1, 13, 116n. 17, 127, 136n. 4, 186–87, 190n. 5, 205n. 1, 206n. 14, 233n. 17, 335n. 13; on "Shakespace," 68–69, 73, 89nn. 11, 13; *Shakespeare without Class*, 89n. 13
rhetorical methodologies, scholarship, 11
Ribton-Turner, Charles, J., 14, 44
Rich, Barnabe (captain, military theorist), 243, 271–72
Richard II (Shakespeare), 167n. 1, 288n. 18
Richard III, king of England, 113, 116n. 32
Rico, Francisco, 343, 353n. 2
Rid, Samuel: *The Art of Juggling or Legerdemain*, 206n. 14, 218, 228, 233n. 13; canting dictionaries of, 316; on duty, corrective aspects of his task, 321–22; Englishing by, 326–27; *Martin Markall Beadle of Bridewell: His Defence and Answers to the Bellman of London*, 217, 226, 233n. 19, 321–22
"ridings," women and, 103
The Rise of the Novel: Studies in Defoe, Richardson, and Fielding (Watt), 338
The Ritual Process: Structure and Anti-structure (Turner), 287nn. 6–7
Roaring Boys, 313, 331
The Roaring Girl (Middleton and Dekker), 20, 62, 66–68, 73–75, 77–80, 82, 84, 86, 89n. 7, 91n. 25, 92n. 28, 93nn. 29, 32; cant in, 335n. 17; canting language in, 331–33; feminist/queer readings of,

93n. 32; iconic status of, 69; interpretive readings of, 81–84; "Marlowespace" and, 86–88; Moll Cutpurse, portrayal of, 331–33; re-created in "Mary/Marlowespace," 85–88; revaluing, reimagining of, 77–81; revivals of, 92n. 27; roaring girls in, 331–32; transversality in, 74–75

roaring girls, 331–32

Roberts, Michael, 270

Robin, Gerald D., 233n. 10

Rogers, Sir Edward, 106

rogue: origin of word, 1–2; use of word in modern culture, 8. *See also specific topics*

rogue capitalism, 9

rogue culture: Englishing and, 26; as opposed to English culture, 318; organization of, 367; scope of, 33–35; self-display in, 7; taking pleasure in, 320–21 *(see also specific topics)*

rogue literature: as actual, imaginary, 378; ambiguity of, 379–80; ambiguous appeal of, 27; as both fact and fiction, 11, 316; capitalism and, 323; court records and, 376–77; creating linkages with other documents, 376; deconstruction of, 376–77; and deviance, 21, 120–21; as emerging genre, 37; history of genre, 334n. 2; interpreting, methodologies for, 35–40; liminal status of, 379; literary studies of, 13; and loss of texts, 372; mediation between fact and fiction, 375–79; as noncanonical, 33; as othering, 264; parallelism with Bridewell Court Books, 120; picaresque genre and, 26–27; rogue pamphlets as fact and fiction, 38; rogues as both fact and fiction, 11; as tabloids, 246; veracity of, 369–73, 375–77

rogue manuals, 16; as guides, 53; as informing the urban reader, 3, 5

rogue nations, 10

rogue pamphleteers: ambiguity of, 379–80; conservatism of, 230; as delighting in their subject, 223; literary strategies of, 354n. 8

rogue pamphlets: authenticity and veracity of, 35–40; as birth of novel in England, 15; as both fact and fiction, 11, 316;

comic side of, 17; complicity and strategy in, 3; conservatism of, 230; corrective function of, 318–20; as critique of urban life, 2; as domestic handbooks, 39–40; as entertainment, 39, 306–7, 377; evolution of, 240; as fact and fiction, 38; facticity of, 367, 378; as factual histories, 245; influence on social, political reforms, 17; interpreting, methodologies for, 35–40; jestbook tradition and, 16–17, 369; and mainstream literary studies, 14; mediation between fact and fiction, 375–79; plays, relationship to, 35–36; as protest literature, 17; reading, interpretation of, 35–40; rereading of, 242–47; rogue pamphlets as fact and fiction, 38; rogues as both fact and fiction, 11; *Rogues, Vagabonds, and Sturdy Beggars* as definitive collection of, 27; scope of, 2; shift from pastoral to urban, 14; as social complaints, 16; as sociological documents, 16–17; subversive influence of, 17; as transhistorical, 37; as urban conduct books, 19; and urban space, 8, 34. *See also* cony-catching pamphlets

roguery, the fall into, 191n. 10

rogues: ambiguous feelings toward, 8–9; as attractive criminals, 335n. 16; in bands, 355n. 22; as beggars, 197–98; as both fact and fiction, 11; capitalism and, 8; in *The Cardsharps*, by Caravaggio, 18, 19; commonalities with self-fashioned gentleman, 1; as cony-catchers, 173; counterfeiting and, 125–30; criminal literacy of, 307–9; cultural hybridity of, 27; cultural meanings of, 10; as deviants, 2; and disguise, 19; dissembling and, 19; double identity of, 4–5; employments of, 194–200, 336, 367, 376–77; as enforced soldiers, 271–72; evidence of, 2; as excremental, 221; as fact and fiction, 11; and the fall into roguery, 191n. 10; as false seemers, 7; in film, 3–5, 7, 9; fraternities of, 2, 48–49; gypsies, connection with, 135n. 2; as honest laborers, 199–200; identification with, 19; as internal aliens, 26, 314–15; invisibility of, 204; Latin, use of,

rogues (*continued*)
297–302; legal-if-suspect commercial practices of, 177–78; in London, 213–31; as metaphoric models for merchants, 379; as mirror for Renaissance culture, 15, 206n. 10, 378; in modern, contemporary contexts, 3–5, 7, 9; myth of, 3, 10, 15–16; as others, othering, 313; as outcasts, 2; pervasiveness of, 1–2; polyvalence of, 17–18; in popular culture, 8–9; pretending to be pretend gypsies, 207n. 14; pretensions of legitimacy, 179; as scapegoats, 174; secret languages of, 8; sexuality of, 13, 101–4; as shirking work, 175; social classes of, 33–35; as social deviants, 2; social history of, 13–14; speculations on, 365; as stand-ins for vagrant poor, 13; supposed network of, 7; training practices of, 368–69; as tricksters, 2, 16–17; typologies of, 25–27; upward mobility of, 125; as urban doppelgängers, 19; and vagrant economy, 197–98; vagrants as, 1–2; writing about, use of alliteration in, 226, 374–75. *See also specific topics; molls*
The Rogues and Vagabonds of Shakespeare's Youth (Viles and Furnivall), 14
rogue studies: canon-margins and, 15–16; city-country and, 15–16; convergence within, 15–16; empirical modes of, 11; fact-or-fiction split in, 11; history-theory and, 15–16; literary criticism/cultural studies and, 15–16; political inflection of, 14; rhetorical modes of, 11; rival schools of, 11–19
Rogues, Vagabonds, and Sturdy Beggars: A New Gallery of Tudor and Early Stuart Rogue Literature (ed. Kinney), 15, 27, 36, 266
"Rolling Thunder" (veteran bikers), 261–62, 267
romance: ancestry of, 256n. 120; Elizabethan, wandering-recovery pattern of, 241–42; Greene's works as, 240–42; prose romance, 240–42
Roman ghetto, 214
Rome, Italy, 18
Romei, Annibale, Count, 54–55
Romeo and Juliet (Shakespeare), 69, 90n. 14

Rose, Mark, 309n. 7
Rose, Mary Beth, 77, 79, 81–82, 92n. 28, 93nn. 31–32, 94n. 36
Rowland, John *(If You Know Not Me, 2)*. *See* Tawnycoat, aka John Rowland
Rowley, Coleen, 9
Rowley, William, 91n. 25
Royal Exchange: commercial activities at, 167n. 6; cony-catchers at, 180–81; engraving of, as mediation, 379; exclusion, banishment from, 22; in *If You Know Not Me, 2*, 158–63; importance of, 148–49, 154–55, 157; insurance underwriting at, 167n. 6; patriotism and, 157; peddlers in, 149–50; roofless, purpose, effect, 153–55; sponsored by Merchant Adventurers, 147. *See also* the Pawn at Royal Exchange
The Royal Exchange (Greene), 148–49
Royal Shakespeare Company, 92n. 27
rural migrants, 2
Rustici, Craig, 79–80, 93n. 31, 94n. 36

Sacks, David Harris, 193, 205n. 3, 215
Sainte-Beuve, Charles-Augustin (historian), 375
Salamon, Linda Bradley, 25; and displaced persons, 334n. 3; referenced, 256n. 16; on Turner, 379
Salgãdo, Gãmini: children, on uses of, 366; *Cony-Catchery and Bawdy Baskets*, 15; *The Elizabethan Underworld*, 15, 35, 225, 367–68; on organization of London underworld, 367–69; quoted, 35–36, 225, 228; referenced, 115n. 2, 172, 177–78, 189, 205n. 1, 206n. 14
Samuel, Raphael, 378
Saunders, Ann, 143, 147–48, 157, 189
Savery, Henry (seaman), 367
Savoyards (peddling network), 150
scapegoats, 157, 163, 174, 314
schizoids, 16
scholars, 294–95, 300–301, 306
Schwab, Gabrielle, 65
Schwoerer, Lois G., 289n. 23
scientific method, 378–79
scolds, 103–4
Scott, William, 177–78, 187–88
Scottish Travelers, 361
scribal culture, 307

Scrope *(Henry V)*, 282

The Second Part of Cony-Catching (Greene), 130, 217, 222–25, 233n. 14, 255n. 5

The Second Part of the Honest Whore (Dekker), 297–98, 300

Segal, Janna, 20, 90n. 14, 94n. 34

self-display, 7; of cony-catcher, 12; false seeming and, 54–56; in rogue culture, 7; of rogues, 53

self-fashioned gentleman: commonalities with rogues, 1; as exemplar, 1; false seeming and, 54–56; rogue pamphlets and, 31

self-interest, 184, 222; commerce, trade, and, 23

self-invention, 2

self-presentation, 131

Sennet, Richard, 213, 217

Sermon of Repentance (Dent), 257n. 27

servant-master conflicts, 123–24, 131–33

servants, 194–95

settlement literature, 240

The Seven Deadly Sinnes of London (Dekker), 214

Sexual Dissonance (Dollimore), 93n. 32

sexuality: of able-bodied unemployed, 46–48; Christianity on, 101; of Frith, Mary, 68; Harman's attitudes toward, 99–105, 113; linking vagrancy to crimes of, 121–22; of Marlowe, 68; and Mary Frith/Moll Cutpurse, 20; of Moll Cutpurse, 68; of rogues, molls, 13, 46–48, 101–4; sexual transgressions in Bridewell Court Books, 123; social identity and, 62–65; of soldiers, 264; of veteran soldiers, 25, 269

"Shakespace," 68–69, 73, 89nn. 11, 13

Shakespeare, William, 37–38, 68–70, 73–74, 81; *As You Like It*, 66, 154; on castle garrisons, 288n. 18; cross-dressing in plays of, 66; deceit, hypocrisy in, 154; England of, 35; *Hamlet*, 2, 154; *Henry IV* plays, 2, 105, 191n. 9, 256n. 15, 288n. 18; *Henry V*, 25, 264, 279–86, 290nn. 33–36; Jonson on, 296; *King Lear*, 13, 101, 154, 162, 193, 287n. 4; *Macbeth*, 91n. 21; *Othello*, 2, 8, 91n. 21; poverty, roguery in plays, 13; as reader of pamphlets, 256n. 12; *Richard II*, 167n. 1, 288n. 18; *rogue* as used by, 2; romances of, 241; *Romeo and Juliet*, 69, 90n. 14; "Shakespace" and, 68–69; *The Taming of the Shrew*, 13, 101; *The Tempest*, 91n. 21; *Troilus and Cressida*, 101; *Twelfth Night*, 66; vagabondage in works of, 98–99; *The Winter's Tale*, 13, 15

Shakespearean Negotiations: The Circulation of Social Energy in Renaissance England (Greenblatt), 227, 234n. 26

Shakespeare in Love (film), 66

Shakespeare without Class (Hedrick and Reynolds), 89n. 13

shape-shifting, 305–6

Sharpe, J. A., 121, 232n. 8, 234n. 26, 376–78

Sharpe, Leonard (constable), 137n. 12

Shaw, Phillip, 234n. 27

Shenandoah Shakespeare Company, 93n. 29

shopkeepers valorized, 22

shopping: evolution of, 144–51; in Jacobean city comedies, 143, 148

Sidney, Philip, 241, 262, 268

signifying: lost signifiers, 372; rogues and, 2

Silence of the Lambs (film), 66

Sinatra, Frank, 9

Sinfield, Alan, 12, 233n. 18, 290n. 34

Siskin, Clifford, 301

Slack, Paul, 57n. 5, 99, 108, 137nn. 11, 13, 174, 206n. 9, 232n. 8, 233n. 17

Sly, Christopher *(The Taming of the Shrew)*, 13

Smith, A. Hassel, 195–96

Smith, Alexander, 91n. 25

Smith, Anna Marie, 65

Smith, Elizabeth A., 371

Smith, Henry, 252

Smith, Paul, 67

Smith, Sir Thomas, 165

Smythe, Sir John, 272, 274, 288n. 17

social changes: cony-catching pamphlets on, 171–90; rogues and, 1

social deviation, 21

social differentiation, 177–78

social dislocation, 18

social exchange, 12

social historians, 36–37, 99

social history, 13–14

A Social History of English (Leith), 233n. 21

social honesty, 171–90

social identity, 62–65

social miming, 52

social nonconformists, 16

social order: Christian notions and, 184; cony-catching pamphlets on, 171–90; and market-based exchange, 135; print culture and, 245; undermined by canting song, 320–21; urban dangers as formulaic, part of new stable order, 241–42; violations of, 134

social reforms, 17

social rising, 356n. 30

society, Laclau and Mouffe on, 70–72. *See also specific topics*

sociogeography, 215–16, 225

sociopaths, 16

sociopolitical critical theory, 65

soldiers: compensation of, 271, 273, 287n. 11; disbanded soldiers, 270; disbanded soldiers of Drake as threat to London, 287n. 4, 366; disbanding of, 15; ex-soldiers (*see* veteran soldiers); in *Henry V*, 275, 279–86; life after war, 265–68; life during war, 271–75; as mercenaries, 288n. 19; numbers of, 270–71; as powerful male bodies, 264–65; rogues as enforced soldiers, 271–72; rogues living life of, 175; sexuality of, 264; vagabond soldiers of Rome, 18; vagabond veterans (*see* veteran soldiers); vagrants in soldiers' clothing, 221; and Vietnam Memorial, 261–62

Solomon, Julie Robin, 174, 176–78

Solomon, King (*A Notable Discovery of Cosenage*), 228

Somekawa, Ellen, 371

songs: canting songs, 320; canting songs Englished in *O Per Se O*, 326; as ownable text, 204; *Turner's Dish of Lentten Stuffe, or a Galymaufery* (ballad), 204

sonneteer ("The Conversion of the English Courtesan"), 250

sottoportegho (Venetian ghetto), 213–14

Spadaccini, Nicholas, 356n. 31

Spain: *siglo de oro* Spain, 26–27; veteran soldiers of, 273

Spanish Armada (*If You Know Not Me, 2*), 166

Spearing, Elizabeth, 79, 81, 89n. 7, 92n. 26, 93nn. 30, 32, 331

Speed, John, *A History of Great Britain*, 262

Speigel, Gabrielle M., 108, 369

Spencer, Janet M., 290nn. 34–35

Spenser, Edmund: advocating violence against the Irish, 317, 333; disease, infection, discourse on, 334n. 9; experience in Ireland, 335n. 15; the Irish crisis and, 327–30; as New English, 315, 317; referenced, 92n. 28; romances of, 241; use of "translation," 316; *A View of the Present State of Ireland*, 26, 31, 312, 316

Spickerenell, Thomas (vagrant), 195

Spierenburg, Pieter, 116n. 22

Spraggs, Gillian Mary, 217

Sprinker, Michael, 257n. 30

Spufford, Margaret, 205n. 6

sacredness of profaned, 375

Stabile, Carol, 65

Stafford, Brooke A., 26, 264, 272; on liminal status of rogue books, 379; on parallels between commercial practices, outlaw activities, 353n. 1; referenced, 309n. 2, 341, 357n. 33

Staniland, Kay, 143, 147, 152, 156–57

Staplers (export company), 147, 155

Starr, G. A., 355n. 18

State, Power, and Socialism (Poulantzas), 88n. 2

Stationer's Register, 91n. 25

Statute of Artificers, 164

Statutes of Kilkenny, 331

Statutes of the Realm, 206n. 9; 39 Elizabeth c. 4, 207n. 14; 1 James c. 7, 207n. 14

Steele, John (counterfeit), 128

Stevenson, Laura Caroline, 41, 58n. 9

Stewkeley (*If You Know Not Me, 2*), 159

Steyre, Sybbell (counterfeit), 131

Stiles, Giles (counterfeit), 128–29

The Sting (film), 9

St. John of Jerusalem (military order), 289n. 29

Stoller, Robert J., 290n. 31

Stone, Lawrence, 193, 372

Stourton, Lord, 198

Stow, John, 145–46, 154

St. Paul's Cathedral, 52; cony-catchers at, 180–81, 187; as multiple-use venue, 216, 374
Strange, Alexander (vicar), 365–66
street literature, 204
Street Robberies Consider'd (Defoe), 354n. 4
Stubbes, Philip, 58n. 14
sturdy beggars: Bridewell and, 124; elimination of, 123; punishment of, 44; rogues as, 197–98; as shirking work, 175
Styles, Jane, 91n. 24
subaltern groups, histories of, 13
subjectivity, early modern, 16
subjunctive space, 20
Subtle *(The Alchemist)*, 15
suburban areas, 217–18
subversion-containment dialectic, 12, 15
Sullivan, Ceri, 184
Sullivan, Garret A., Jr., 205n. 1
A Survey of London (Stow), 145–46
Sutcliffe, Matthew (military theorist), 274
Sycorax *(The Tempest)*, 74

Table Alphabeticall (Dekker), 325
tabloids, 246
the taker-up, 50–52
"A Tale of a Nip" (Greene), 188–89
Tamburlaine *(Tamburlaine)*, 143, 158
Tamburlaine (Marlowe), 290n. 34
The Taming of the Shrew (Shakespeare), 13, 101
Taunton, Nina, 283–84, 288n. 18, 290n. 34
Tawney, R. H., 116n. 30
Tawnycoat, aka John Rowland *(If You Know Not Me, 2)*, 144, 151, 161–63, 165, 168n. 11
Taylor, Barry, 221, 233n. 21, 234n. 22, 347
Taylor, Gary, 290n. 36
Taylor, John, 20, 309n. 3
Taylor, Rogan, 115n. 8
Tearcat *(The Roaring Girl)*, 331–32
television shows, cross-dressing in, 66
The Tempest (Shakespeare), 91n. 21
textuality, theories of, 13–14
Thames River, 107
theater: equating with criminality, 45; itinerant players, 194; nomadic space of, 16; rogue pamphlets in relation to, 35–36; suburban, nomadic space of, 16
Theatre, Finance, and Society in Early

Modern England (Leinwand), 179–80, 190n. 6
theoretical formulations: and Mary Frith/Moll Cutpurse, 20; and rogue studies, 13
The Third and Last Part of Cony-Catching (Greene), 179, 222–24, 255n. 5, 354n. 5
Thirsk, Joan, 195, 205nn. 7–8
Thomas, Phillip V., 232n. 8
Thompson, Ayanna, 91n. 21
Thompson, E. P., 115n. 13
Thompson, Hunter S., 110
Tilh, Arnaud du, called "Pansette," 276–79, 286, 290n. 30
tinkers: as capitalist entrepreneurs, 354n. 9; classified as rogues, vagabonds, effect, 150–51
Tittler, Robert, 116n. 29
Todd, Janet, 79, 81, 89n. 7, 92n. 26, 93nn. 30, 32
Todman, Thomas (counterfeit crank), 129
Todorov, Tzvetan, 353n. 2
toleration, 171–90
Tolstoy, Leo, 356n. 27
Toogood, Madelyne Gorman (Irish Traveler), 361, 363, 380
Tootsie (film), 66
Torfing, Jacob, 90n. 17
torture, 44
Tower of Babel, 296–97, 299, 303, 374–75; London as, 225
The Town Crier (broadside), 204
Toxophilus (Ascham), 288n. 17
trade: attitudes about, 23; evolution of, 144–51; as legitimate civic practice, 22
tradesmen: changes in marketplace, effect on, 22; subsistence, policing of, 22; tradesmen, gentlemen, on differences between, 358n. 44. *See also* itinerant tradesmen
"The Trading Style" (Defoe), 357n. 40
transient classes, 17
transient poor, 43–45
translation: and birth of British Empire, 333; of cant, 225–30; Englishing as cultural translation, 316; the Irish Crisis and, 327–30, 333; as un-Englishing, 316
transversal identity, 16, 74–75
transversal territory, 72–75

transversal theory, 88n. 1
Trapdoor (The Roaring Girl), 331–32
Traubridge, John (gentleman), 131
travail, value of, 180
travelers. See Irish Travelers
trial reports, 16
tricksters, 16–17; generally (see rogues); of
    jestbook, 17; as Machiavellian antihero,
    12; protocols of, 2; as sirens, 130
Triumph of Love (film), 66
Troilus and Cressida (Shakespeare), 101
The True-Born Englishman: A Satyr
    (Defoe), 358n. 43
Tudor era, social reform of, 17. See also
    specific topics
Tudor Poor Laws, 1, 44
Turks, Venetian ghettoization of, 213
Turner, Victor, 265, 287nn. 6–7, 379
Turner Gutiérrez, Ellen, 353n. 2, 355n. 11
Turner's Dish of Lentten Stuffe, or a Galy-
    maufery (ballad), 204
Tuvill, Daniel, 176–77
Twelfth Night (Shakespeare), 66
Twyning, John A., 38–39, 44, 215, 219,
    231, 234n. 26, 255n. 9
Tyburn biographies, 337

Ulysses (Odyssey), 277
underworld literature. See cony-catching
    pamphlets; rogue pamphlets
Ungerer, Gustav, 79–80, 91n. 24, 92n. 26,
    93nn. 30, 32
Unwin, George, 58n. 9
the Upright Man: veteran soldiers as,
    267–68; as vigorous worker, 199–200
urban citizens, 24–25
urban con artists, rogues as, 2
urban culture, rogue pamphlets and,
    39–40. See also specific topics
urban environment: changing, effect of,
    24; organization of, 213–17; shift from
    pastoral to, 14
urban life: cony-catching pamphlets as
    new tactics in, 245–46; cony-catching
    pamphlets on, 171–90; dangers as for-
    mulaic, part of new stable order,
    241–42; in London, 214–17; mobility,
    effect on, 183–84; rogue pamphlets as
    critique of, 2
urban pamphlets, 240

urban readers: as apprentices to under-
    world mysteries, 18, 19; awareness of, 3;
    complicity, rogue pamphlets and, 19;
    informed by rogue manuals, 3, 5; and
    the new language of urban world, 25
urban space: defining identity in, 18;
    organization of, 213–17; rogue pam-
    phlets and, 34; as shaped by rogue
    pamphlets, 8
urban underworld: cony-catching pam-
    phlets and, 2; glamorization of, 183; as
    imaginary, 7, 33; as indicator of
    changes, 2; literacy in, 3; as mirror of
    in-law society, 15, 206n. 10, 378; orga-
    nization of, 367–69; post-Deleuzian
    reading of, 16; readers as apprentices to
    underworld mysteries, 18, 19; social
    classes of, 33–35
usury, 155–56, 167n. 7, 184, 373
Utopia (More), 25, 214, 262–63

vagabond crisis, 24, 217, 266
vagabonds: and 1572 Act for the Punish-
    ment of Vagabonds, 44–45, 150; cloth-
    ing of, 221; demonized as rogues, 33;
    effects of enclosure on, 15, 43; migrant
    vagabonds, 42; as parasites, 43; peddlers
    demonized as, 22; reshaped as rogues,
    7; sexuality of, 46–48; as shirking work,
    175; social classes of, 33–35; statistics
    on, 99; vagabond crisis and, 24, 217,
    266. See also soldiers
vagrancy: ambivalence toward, 121; as
    crime, 21; and deviancy, 21–22; hang-
    ing proposed as punishment for, 112;
    linked to crimes of sexuality, insubordi-
    nation, 121–22; as open identity, 216;
    slavery proposed as punishment for,
    112; sources of, 189
Vagrancy, Homelessness, and English
    Renaissance Literature (Woodbridge),
    15–17, 39, 89n. 10, 121, 135n. 1, 233n. 14,
    334n. 2
vagrant economy, 194–98
vagrant poor: ballads, songs as voices of,
    204; by-employments of, 194–95,
    366–67, 376–77; histories of, 13; invisi-
    bility of, 204; lives of, 110; multiple,
    serial, itinerant employment of, 194,
    366–67, 376–77; as resource, 177;

rogues disguised as, effect, 203–4; vagrant economy and, 194–97

vagrants: ballads, songs as voices of, 204; Bridewell Court of Governors on, 21; counterfeiting being deserving poor, 128–29, 203; crafty vagrants, 23; disguise and, 23; downward mobility of, 125; as enforced soldiers, 271–72; fetishization of, 135n. 2; identification of, 99, 126; legal records on, 121; legal vagrants, 194; in London, 216; policing of, 21; as rogues (*see* rogues); roundups of, 112; as scapegoats, 174, 314; sexuality of, 46–48; statistics on, 99; in theatrical works, 193; vagrant economy and, 194–97; violence against, 317

van Elk, Martine, 21–22, 59n. 17; on ambiguity of rogue literature, 379–80; referenced, 59n. 17, 256nn. 13, 16

venereal disease in London, 216

verse satire, 240

Vespucci, Amerigo, 262

Vested Interests: Cross-Dressing and Cultural Anxiety (Garber), 65

veteran soldiers, 261–86; as able-bodied unemployed, 17; as beggars, 267; compensation of, 271, 274, 287n. 11; as counterfeit veterans, 265–66; as disbanded soldiers, 270; discharged veterans, 17, 270; and displaced persons, 334n. 3; as ex-soldiers, 262, 273; gentleman veterans, 262, 268; as killers, 269; life after war, 265–71; as long-term soldiers, 262; Martin Guerre as, 264, 275–79; as masterless men, 265; as mercenaries, 288n. 19; monasteries as soldiers' homes, 274–75; poverty of, 263; as rogues, 25, 265; in rogue texts, 263–64; of "Rolling Thunder," 261–62, 267; as Rufflers, 266–67; sexuality of, 25, 269, 290n. 31; as Upright Men, 267–68; in *Utopia*, 262–63; as vagabonds, 25, 264; *veteran* defined, 262; war wounds of, 266

Vickers, Brian, 76

Victor/Victoria (film), 66

Vietnam Memorial, 261–62

A View of the Present State of Ireland (Spenser), 26, 312–13, 316; the Irish crisis and, 327–30

Viles, Edward, 14

Vincent, John, 372

violence against the Irish, 317, 330, 333–34. *See also* punishment

Virginia Company, 167n. 4

Virgin Mary, 77, 80, 83

vocational literature, 180, 182

Volpone (Jonson) 159

von Ranke, Leopold, 113

Wales, Tim, 206n. 10

Waley, Pamela, 355n. 19

Walker, Garthine, 103

Walker, Gilbert, 33, 49–51, 53, 138n. 34, 217; *A Manifest Detection of Dice-Play*, 7, 14, 33, 49–51, 53, 134, 191n. 10, 220, 240; referenced, 181, 220, 240

walking morts, 102, 269

war, 266–67; American Civil War, 261; civil wars, 103; Cold War, 89n. 6; constancy of, 269; large-scale conflicts and England, 111; length of, 270–71; locations of, 269, 271; and Machiavelli's *Art of War*, 270; and military medicine, 289n. 25; military practices during, 270–71, 288n. 18, 290n. 34; pleasures of performing, 290n. 35; as "seasonal form of hunting," 287n. 13; vagabond veterans of, 261–86

War and Society, 1450–1620 (Hale), 28n. 19, 272, 289n. 28

Ward, Joseph P., 216, 309n. 6

"The Water Cormorant" (Taylor), 20

"The Water Poet" (Taylor), 309n. 3

Watkins, Sherron, 9

Watt, Ian, 338, 345, 355n. 17, 356nn. 24, 26

Weaver, John (vagrant), 377

Webb, Henry J., 290n. 34

Webb, John, 206n. 9

Weber, Max, 42, 356n. 25

Webster, John, 148

Weimann, Robert, 356n. 26

Wells, Susan, 232nn. 1, 4

Wengrave, Sir Alexander *(The Roaring Girl)*, 332

West, William, 79–80, 93n. 32, 334n. 10, 335nn. 17–18

Wheatley, Elizabeth (counterfeit), 131

Wheeler, John, 147, 155

Whigham, Frank, 55

The Whig Interpretation of History (Butterfield), 370–71

Whigs and Hunters: The Origin of the Black Act (Thompson), 115n. 13

White, Hayden, 367

Whitefriars, London, 109–10

Wicks, Ulrich, 353n. 2

Wife of Bath (Chaucer), 101

Wilkins, John (linguist), 357n. 39

Willems, Wim, 232n. 6

Williams *(Henry V)*, 284, 290n. 35

Williams, Penry, 377

Williams, Raymond, 75

Willoughby, Sir Henry, 289n. 23

Wilson, Edward O., 379

Wilson, William (vagrant), 377

Wiltonberg, Joy, 41

Windschuttle, Keith, 364

Winkler, John J., 255n. 4

The Winter's Tale (Shakespeare), 13, 15

Wirth, Louis, 215

witchcraft, 103

witches, 38

The Witch of Edmonton (Rowley, Dekker, and Ford), 91n. 25

women: and the able-bodied unemployed, 46; as active agents in world, 103–4; by-employments of, 194–95, 366–67, 376–77; cross-dressing and, 65–67; employments of, 194–97, 366–67, 376–77; female cony-catchers, 13; as gossips, 102, 104; Harman's attitudes toward, 99–102; histories of, 13; and Mary Frith/Moll Cutpurse, 20; masterless, as growing group, 21; multiple, serial, itinerant employment of, 194, 366–67, 376–77; "ridings" and, 103; as scolds, 103–4; sexuality of, 101–3; social identity and, 62–65; as vagrant laborers, 199; as walking morts, 269. *See also specific topics;* prostitutes

Women and the English Renaissance (Woodbridge), 92n. 28

Wood, Ellen Meiksins, 65, 121

Wood, Roger (servant), 132

Woodbridge, Linda, 15–18, 21–22, 39, 57n. 8, 92n. 28, 136n. 4, 172, 180, 183, 193, 195, 246, 263–64, 287n. 4; as

archivalist, 15–16; on dehumanizing rough play, 19; on the English overseas encounters, 334n. 1; groundbreaking work of, 17; on Harman, 57n. 8; on history of rogue literature genre, 334n. 2; on *Lantern and Candlelight*, 296; on mediation, 379; on the Othering process, 315; quoted, 17, 57n. 8, 121, 190n. 1; referenced, 89n. 10, 98–99, 115n. 1, 135n. 1, 174, 200, 203, 205n. 1, 206n. 13, 232n. 6, 233n. 14, 256n. 13, 334n. 5; on scapegoating, 314; *Vagrancy, Homelessness, and English Renaissance Literature*, 15–17, 89n. 10, 121, 135n. 1, 233n. 14, 334n. 2; *Women and the English Renaissance*, 92n. 28

woodcuts, rogues in, 2

Woodmansee, Martha, 309n. 7

words: and the "cheat of words," 357n. 41; meanings and misunderstandings of, 357n. 40

workers. *See* laborers

Worlds within Worlds: Structures of Life in Sixteenth-Century England (Rappaport), 205n. 4

Worley, Edward (servant), 132

Worrall, William (counterfeit dummerer), 129–30

Wotton (gentleman), 368–69

Wrightson, Keith, 125, 205n. 8, 366

writers: authors constructed as rogues, 11; falconers and, 25–26; legitimacy of, 294–96

writing: alliteration and, 226, 374–75; cant as written language, 369; crime writing, 16; jestbook tradition, 16–17; mystification of, 301; rogues and, 300–301

Yentl (film), 66

Youth and Authority: Formative Experiences in England, 1560–1640 (Griffiths), 205n. 4

youths, in nomadic labor pool, 105, 194

Zeldin, Theodore, 367

Ziman, John, 379

Zimmermann, Everett, 357n. 37

Žižek, Slavoj, 70–71